Folly of God

A History of Christian Preaching—Volume 1

Folly of God
The Rise of Christian Preaching

RONALD E. OSBORN

Chalice Press
St. Louis, Missouri

Scripture quotations marked (NRSV) are from the *New Revised Standard Version Bible*, copyright 1989, Division of Christian Education of the National Council of Churches of Christ in the USA. Used by permission.

Those quotations marked RSV are from the *Revised Standard Version of the Bible*, copyright 1952, [2nd edition, 1971] by the Division of Christian Education of the National Council of the Churches of Christ in the United States of America. Used by permission. All rights reserved.

Excerpts from *The Jerusalem Bible*, copyright 1966 by Darton, Longman & Todd, Ltd., and Doubleday, a division of Bantam Doubleday Dell Publishing Group, Inc. Used by permission.

Excerpts from *The New Jerusalem Bible*, copyright 1985 by Darton, Longman & Todd, Ltd., and Doubleday, a division of Bantam Doubleday Dell Publishing Group, Inc. Used by permission.

Those quotations marked REB are from the *Revised English Bible with the Apocrypha*, copyright © Oxford University Press and Cambridge University Press 1989.

Excerpts from the translation designated *Tanakh* is copyrighted by the Jewish Publication Society, 1985.

Cover design: Cecil King, Dreamtek
Art direction: Michael Domínguez
Interior design: Elizabeth Wright
Scripture Index: David P. Polk
Index of Names and Subjects: Robert R. Howard

Visit Chalice Press on the World Wide Web at
www.chalicepress.com

10 9 8 7 6 5 4 3 2 1   99 00 01 02 03 04

Library of Congress Cataloging-in-Publication Data

Osborn, Ronald E.
    A history of Christian preaching/ Ronald E. Osborn.
        p.   cm.
    Includes bibliographical references and index.
    Contents: v.   1. Folly of God.
    ISBN 0-8272-1429-4 (hardcover). — ISBN 0-8272-1428-6 (pbk.)
    1. Preaching — History. I. Title.
BV4207.O83   1997   97-17416
251'.009 — dc21   CIP

Printed in the United States of America

to Nola
and the family she gave me

For since, in the wisdom of God, the world did not know God through wisdom, it pleased God by the folly of preaching, to save those who believe...For God's foolishness is wiser than human wisdom.

1 Corinthians 1:21, 25 (RSV, NRSV, alt.)

Contents

PART TWO. PEOPLE OF THE WORD
Jewish Preaching in Hellenistic Times

PART THREE. PREACHER OF GOOD NEWS
Jesus of Nazareth

Preface

This book tells how seekers and idlers first heard the claims and promises of the Christian faith during the five centuries of its beginning. Here the reader will meet the preachers of this new way as by word and life they drew thousands of hearers to the Christian faith. The substance of this study is not the esoteric abstractions of sophisticates playing intellectual games as professional (or professorial) theologians, but the words of pastors and missionaries and teachers involved in the lives of everyday folk. It recounts their efforts to engage their communities of believers in comprehension of the most profound mysteries of their religion, commitment to the one God they had confessed as supreme over any earthly ruler or spiritual power, and faithfulness to their vocation as followers of Jesus Christ.

Our subject is a foundational element of the church's life and witness, that public proclamation of the faith that we call preaching. "Creeds, sermons, prayers, catechetical literature are examples of primary discourse in Christian faith," a noted theologian has written; "Theology is a secondary form of discourse, having as its purpose reflection upon, appraisal, criticism and defense of these primary words."[1] *Preaching is primary.* Recurrently vital, at times surprisingly attractive, in crucial moments compelling, this open public address by a speaker in direct interaction with listeners commends the gospel and presses the appeal to confess it in word and life.

Speaking to outsiders, especially in a setting that permits freedom to leave or to stay, the skillful preacher attempts to catch the hearers' interest from the start and to sustain it throughout, engaging their problems and concerns, passing on the tradition, guiding understanding, correcting false impressions, answering objections, projecting a vision, undertaking to persuade, imparting grace. Presenting a sermon in church, however, the unwary preacher may fall into a trap: presuming that the listeners have come in fulfillment of religious obligation and even that it is not important to relate the sermon to their questions and interests. From such cavalier disregard spring many of the obvious sins of the pulpit—didacticism, irrelevance, dolefulness, repetitiousness, mediocrity, mindlessness—which induce sleep in Zion. The careless or clumsy cleric may thresh old straw, trim the gospel's demands, cater to prejudice, exploit the moment in the spotlight, indulge in self-promotion, canter furiously on a personal hobbyhorse, or scold, or nag. Such distortions have settled into the collective memory, with the result that the very word *preaching* not uncommonly evokes a negative response: "Don't *preach* at me!" or (even worse) "*Boring!*"

Because preaching is now and again dismissed out of hand on the basis of unfortunate experience, its significance is commonly overlooked. Students of literature may occasionally encounter a preacher of an earlier time, but historians (even members of the guild who deal with religion) tend to lose sight both of preachers and of those who came to hear them. Yet before electronic media, before the printing press, public address was the chief mode of disseminating ideas, the most readily available opportunity for entertainment, the primary means of evoking commitment to the common good, and, in the case of preaching, a personal vehicle for transmitting religious faith and practice. Across Christendom, the sermon or homily became the most frequently heard form of public address.

The deep mines of sermonic literature from centuries past therefore hide veins of rich ore for students, scholars, and preachers today. Here we can trace the reciprocal impact of culture and religion, as historical circumstance has molded the church and its spokespersons have undertaken to reshape society. As for the literary tradition, the discourse of preachers and other orators has been, more than is commonly recognized, a distinctive and sometimes influential element; in the period covered by the latter half of this volume the notable preachers hold a place among the most important literati of the time. As an expression of faith at the grass roots, preaching has significance for the student of popular culture as well as of religion. Again and again through history, certainly in the first five Christian centuries, preaching has proved a potent force in the life of the church. Our study, then, has relevance to the interests of social and intellectual historians, scholars in literature, historians of religion, and spiritual seekers, as well as to the work of preachers and students for the ministry.

Taking a fresh look at the Christian past, we discover that in its earliest centuries the movers and shakers of the church were, to a surprising extent, its outstanding preachers. These were the voices who, despite the opposition of the Caesars and the disdain of the cultural elite, drew the people of the Greco-Roman world to faith in Jesus Christ, the thinkers who hammered out the classical formulations of the new ecumenical faith, the builders of the church who formed a far-flung company of believers into an institution ecumenical in scope, the pioneers of a new ethic and vocation that invited ordinary folk, even slaves, to an unprecedented dignity, a distinctive purity of life, a generous compassion, a quiet humility, and an ethos of service.

Yet while historians of Christianity concentrate on major movements, seminal theologians, and decisive institutional developments, it never dawns on many students of church history that the classic theological works of the patristic era (the "treatises" of Athanasius, Gregory Theologos, Augustine of Hippo, and their colleagues) originated, not in an academic setting, but in the pulpit. Or that the *Sayings* of the anchorites in the desert, destined to provide spiritual guidance to Christians for centuries to come, were first *spoken* by preachers before being jotted down by stenographers, transcribed, assembled, and copied into books. The ironic result is that seminarians preparing to serve as ministers lose sight of *congregations* and *pastors* in generations past; though they earn diplomas certifying them as academically qualified to receive ordination as ministers, they suffer a deprivation of personal examples and role models engaged in the very work into which their ordination will launch them, examples who might have inspired them for a lifetime of Christian ministry in parish and pulpit.

More than a generation ago a noted ecumenist urged a new approach to church history: "What we need is an ecumenical history of the experience of the Christian community from its beginnings till now, in which the old lines of distinction between church history, history of doctrine, symbolics and liturgics are broken down and reformed. We need an historically honest answer to the question 'How has the gospel been received, expressed and transmitted in the succeeding generations of the people of God?'"[2]

With like concern I have long felt the need for a history of Christian preaching that takes seriously for each period its understanding of scripture and its witness to faith borne within the common life; attempts to discern how the cultural tradition and the circumstances of the era combined with the gospel to produce a message characteristic of the times; observes what the preaching reveals of the spirit of the age; and notes, with regard to its rhetorical intent as persuasion, its effect on personal and corporate decisions.[3]

The history I have envisioned enables the reader to "hear" the distinctive voice and particular message of influential preachers and gives attention in a general way to the preaching of a given period. It notes recurring themes in a preacher's sermons, the use of the Bible, and the preacher's relation to the hearers; and it attempts to discover her or his secret of spiritual power. It observes the course of action urged on the hearers, takes into acccount the dimensions of personal faith, religious experience, theological interpretation, and exegesis— and marks the effect on the Christian tradition. Such an ideal study, as a phase of literary history, takes note also of the form and style employed by a preacher; observes the relation of the preaching to contemporary rhetoric, oratorical practice, and literary criticism; assesses effectiveness; and suggests continuing influence.

Such a work, if the dream were to be realized, even in part, might interest historians generally, as well as church historians, and prove useful to students of the literary, rhetorical, and oratorical traditions. Social history is somehow part of all literature, and all literature is part of it. Cultural history, intellectual history, and the history of ideas are inescapably interrelated, and preaching is involved with them all; it can be further argued that a comprehensive survey of literature rightly includes the written legacy of the poet, the orator, and the preacher, all of which began with the *spoken* word.

In scope and method the work envisioned requires, along with a feel for preaching, knowledge of the scriptures and biblical hermeneutics, attention to the classical tradition and the history of literature, and sound historiography. Now, after a lifetime of involvement in the project, a haunting question induces fear and trembling: *Can any one person live long enough to produce such a synthesis?* (Especially one who spent eleven years as an academic dean and has been heavily involved for decades in the work of the church, congregational, regional, general, and ecumenical.) Under no illusion that I have succeeded in the venture envisioned, I nevertheless salute the banner I have trailed for so long.

This study proceeds on the basis of a comprehensive definition of *preaching* as public discourse concerning the gospel, inspired by it, and offering a biblical witness and Christian perspective on psychic or social or theological issues confronting the hearers. Without abandoning the original evangelical or missionary dimension of the term as address to outsiders in the attempt to persuade them to profess Christian faith, it is used here to include also discourse addressed to the believing community, commonly though not necessarily spoken within the context of the liturgy.[4]

A fundamental question, first asked of another work, here demands our attention: "What principle or principles govern the choice of preachers included in an opus...dedicated to great preaching?"[5]

For the period covered by this volume, so far removed from our own time, history itself has in large measure determined the issue. We are limited to those relatively few preachers whose sermons have survived mold and mice and rot and fire and flood, not to mention the ignorance or carelessness of conservators who failed in their responsibility or deliberate destruction by enemies. Yet even the greatly reduced stock of ancient sermons extant presents an overwhelming mass of homiletical literature that few persons have read or could read in its entirety. I make no claim to have done so.

Intervening generations of Christians have guided the selection by their repeated reading of certain preachers across the centuries. The value they placed on particular sermons led to the copying and recopying of manuscripts through the Middle Ages, then, after Gutenberg, to the printing of collections, and since the Renaissance, to the preparation of critical texts (for many documents had become corrupted, confused, and wrongly attributed), and the publication of translations into modern languages. Occasionally in our own time new discoveries have brought long-lost manuscripts to light, such as the library at Nag Hammadi. This study depends on published collections and editions, particularly those in translations accessible to students who work in English; a multitude of editors and translators have helped in the selection.

If the historian's task involves the isolation and analysis of the decisive moments in the enterprise being treated, we have a further principle for selection, which requires us to look for preachers who spoke at critical junctures in the history of preaching, who represented a significant change in its development, or who exerted a noteworthy influence on the course of the art. Sermons preached at turning points in the church's life require attention, as do sermons representative of notable preachers or movements.

In order to be properly understood, any human endeavor, especially any art, must be experienced at its best; millions around the world who rarely go to a track meet watch the Olympic Games. Without benefit of scoring by an official panel of judges, selections for this study reflect the judgment, prejudices, and limitations of its author—

who has, however, taken into account the opinions of generations of Christian scholars.

Readers searching among the preachers for women who proclaimed the gospel will be disappointed at the rarity of their appearance and the scarcity of sermons by them. The condition arises from the way things were, not from any desire of this historian to minimize or conceal. Christianity emerged in a world of patriarchy, and though Jesus himself ignored prevailing structures of male dominance, the church did not succeed for long in breaking free of old restrictions. In general, women emerged as preachers in those Christian movements that found freedom in the Spirit, movements that the hierarchy tended to suppress by excommunication and the destruction of manuscripts. A few pieces by women have come to light in our time (as at Nag Hammadi), and a new generation of historians is diligently searching for information about women long forgotten.[6] Where such information has become available, this book presents the work of preaching women.

In this study we meet some of the most engaging, impressive, and influential personalities in Christian history, speakers who presented the gospel so convincingly, so persuasively, so inspiringly, that their words have been cherished and preserved from that day to this. Some of these preachers are quoted generously; others only in passing, for the sake of a representative utterance; some are barely listed. Jesus rates three chapters, many a notable preacher scarcely a page. All who are mentioned make up but a tiny fraction of the thousands of preachers who lived and contended and pleaded and touched the lives of their hearers—and now are long forgotten. It would be an endless task to list them all, as Quintilian observed of orators some nineteen centuries ago.[7] Our purpose is to discern what was happening in and to preaching as an enterprise, as demonstrated through the work of notable practitioners, to recount major developments, and to analyze trends as exemplified by representative voices.

In surveying the course of preaching during the first three centuries of the church's life this book falls into five parts, the first two setting forth the cultural context of the first Christian proclamation, the others advancing chronologically. Since each part employs a topical scheme, some notable preachers appear in more than one discussion. The book is not intended as a biographical encyclopedia, but essential personal information places the preacher's life and work within the historical setting. As to style, the intent has been to write in the direct manner of good preaching, keeping the discussion accessible, vivid, and relevant, and offering clear examples of technical aspects of rhetoric.

My vast indebtedness to other scholars is made clear in the notes and bibliography. My basic procedure has involved sampling, reading, and studying published sermons, then building up an account of the preaching, with the aid of standard histories, biographies, and reference works. With rare exceptions, the dates are those used in *The Westminster Dictionary of Church History*. As a matter of principle I have avoided reproducing in blocks passages from historians and other scholars, although I have quoted here and there a sentence or two that states a point with particular felicity. Otherwise, when it comes to quotations, I want the reader to "hear" the preachers.

In an effort toward inclusive language I have made appropriate corrections in earlier translations that intended "man" and "he" to embrace both genders, except where it is evident that the preacher clearly meant to designate males and not people generally. When a preacher has chosen to use paternal or other male imagery for God, I have allowed it to stand, in the interest of historical fidelity, choosing not to interject "[*sic*]" or other such commentary into the text. My policy has been to present what the preachers said, without interposing a hermeneutic of suspicion or attempt at deconstruction.

Normally when writing of a character later beatified I have not used the title *Saint* as part of the name, but have referred to the person as Christian contemporaries would have done. I have generally followed the same practice with regard to other honorific designations posthumously awarded.

Titles of sermons are placed in quotation marks, except those which common practice cites as independent works, in which case italics are used. In a précis of a sermon with brief excerpts, the present tense is intended to suggest the process of listening to the speaker. The "historical present" is not otherwise used for vividness in narration.

Under no compulsion to critique or defend every action described or every argument quoted (although the student may profit from doing so), I have, however, offered some rhetorical or homiletical criticism and occasional historical appraisal. Since one cannot write responsibly regarding a work of literature without an element of judgment, criticism is always at least implicit.

Yet it is important to engage each culture and period seriously on its own terms and to assess its significance for the preaching that came afterward.[8] When expounding a sermon I am interested in the work itself as a mirror of its time, in influences on the preacher's thinking and mode of expression, and in the impact on later generations. I share the interest of the literary critic in the distinctiveness of a particular sermon and its artistic worth, seeking to discern its importance for its own day and its value for ours, considerations not mutually exclusive. (In literary criticism I am an amateur, though not unacquainted with the history of rhetoric.)

Attempting to spell out all these concerns mechanically with every sermon under consideration would be a tedious and interminable task, but keeping them in mind, I have made one or another explicit as the situation demands. My primary effort, however, is not so much to pass judgment on the preachers as to present them, believing that their work has been a significant influence in the life of the church.

My understanding of what preaching ought to be is implicit throughout. Theologically I am a Christian of the twentieth century, a Protestant imbued with the tradition of the Enlightenment, but not untouched by the heritage of revivalism, influenced by the evangelical liberalism prevalent in my youth, and subsequently by neoorthodoxy and process thought. My most serious theological engagements took place in the ecclesiological discussions of the Faith and Order enterprise of the World Council of Churches, the Consultation on Church Union, and the Commission on Restructure for the Christian Church (Disciples of Christ).

At the end of each major section of this volume I offer an assessment of the achievement of the culture or period in the field of preaching (or oratory) and suggest its importance for the preaching that came afterward.

As to mechanics, the initial note for each chapter and for some sections refers the reader to collections of sermons and to major studies for supplemental reading. The rubric "Additional works consulted" gives credit to titles that provided general information during the writing and which are not otherwise indicated in the notes for that bloc of material. The notes give the full title of a work in its first citation in a chapter; thereafter a short title replaces the now archaic *op. cit.* In transliteration, *e* represents the Greek *epsilon* and *é* represents *éta.*

In some respects this study undertakes an impossible task, for the historian cannot bring to life the preachers of long ago, much less the crowds who thronged to hear them or the times in which they spoke. Our ears miss the distinctive quality of voice, the characteristic accent, the solemnity, the urgency, the calm assurance; our eyes cannot see the preacher's form, imposing or diminutive, the peculiar gestures, the flash of the eyes. We scarcely feel the restlessness or listlessness or excitement of the congregation. "Reading sermons," Phillips Brooks suggested, "is like listening to an echo."[9]

Yet by reading selections with the openness we accord a minister we are eager to hear, we can engage the mind and spirit of the preacher, noting the relevance to the particular hearers, reflecting on the meaning for them, trying to understand why people preserved *this* sermon generation after generation, and pondering what it says to us. As with any history, we can trace ideals and movements and developments and results. And if we are called to this ministry we can learn from its great exemplars who conveyed the power of the living word.

To grasp the history of any art we must encounter the work of its most influential practitioners. If it is music, we listen to performances. If painting or sculpture, we contemplate pictures or statues—ideally the originals, but, for most of us, reproductions. If it is architecture, we gaze on imposing buildings, walk through them, and linger within. With music the engagement is auditory; with the plastic arts, visual; with architecture, kinesthetic. But with all three it is also emotional and intellectual.[10] So it must be with preaching; without snatches from sermons, any history of it would be merely external—and dull!

To give the impression of *hearing* the preachers, their words are presented to the eye in the way they come to the ear, a phrase or a few words at a time. The reader is urged not to skim over these selections (as one may be inclined to do with block quotations), but rather to linger over them as over poetry, attempting in imagination to *hear* the voice of the preacher. Passages quoted are necessarily brief, chosen to give a feel for the sources and to invite to them.

The world does not stand still. The spirit of one time yields to quite a different spirit in another. My generation of seminarians thrilled to the sermons of Phillips Brooks, who had flourished fifty years earlier; but a century after his heyday, few of my students were drawn to his preaching. Even so, it is important to discover why he was heard so eagerly in his time, as it is in the case of every preacher who won a significant hearing.

While all who respond to any art can be instructed and even uplifted by coming to know its history, that process conveys special meaning to one who would practice it. In his memoirs the sculptor Alexander Phimister Proctor tells of visiting Olympus and his excitement at seeing Praxiteles' statue of Hermes. "The Greeks, to my mind, reached the pinnacle of sculptured art." In the absence of the guard, the young enthusiast mounted a table so that he could run his hands over all the contours of the figure. "Face to face the glorious creation was almost more than I could bear...Feeling the marvelous modeling gave me a joy greater than my eyes had given me."[11] Perhaps some reader of a sermon from the long past may contemplate with the same thorough eagerness the work of one or another of the master preachers treated in this book.

Abbreviations

AHR	*American Historical Review*
ANF	The Ante-Nicene Fathers
ApF	*The Apostolic Fathers*
DP	*The Dialogues of Plato*
EH	Eusebius, *Ecclesiastical History*
FC	The Fathers of the Church
IB	*The Interpreter's Bible*
IDB	*The Interpreter's Dictionary of the Bible*
IDB-S	*The Interpreter's Dictionary of the Bible, Supplementary Volume*
JBL	*Journal of Biblical Literature*
JBR	*Journal of Bible and Religion*
JS	Jesus Seminar
LCC	Library of Christian Classics
LCL	Loeb Classical Library
ML	Modern Library
NH	*The Nag Hammadi Library in English*
PA	Pirqe Abot
PMLA	*Publications of the Modern Language Association of America*
SBL	Society of Biblical Literature
WDCH	*The Westminster Dictionary of Church History*

Acknowledgments

Once, in his own pulpit, I listened to Ernest Fremont Tittle. At church conventions through the years I heard Eugene Carson Blake, George A. Buttrick, Anthony Campolo, James W. Clarke, James Forbes, Georgia Harkness, Leontine Kelley, Benjamin Mays, Martin Luther King, Jr., J. Lesslie Newbigin, Paul E. Scherer, Joseph Sittler, Marjorie Suchocki, Desmond Tutu, Henry Pitney Van Dusen, W. A. Visser 't Hooft, Pauline Webb, Andrew Young, and other notable pulpiteers from the wider church, as well as impressive voices from my particular household of faith, including Kathleen Bailey Austin, Spencer P. Austin, Jesse M. Bader, William G. Baker, Charles H. Bayer, George G. Beazley, Jr., William Barnett Blakemore, Eugene Wayne Brice, Lin D. Cartwright, K. David Cole, Fred Craddock, Frank Elon Davison, A. Dale Fiers, Warren Grafton, Perry Epler Gresham, Cynthia Hale, Kenneth E. Henry, William Jackson Jarman, Joseph R. Jeter, Jr., Edgar DeWitt Jones, Michael Kinnamon, Raphael H. Miller, Charles Clayton Morrison, S. S. Myers, C. William Nichols, Roger T. Nooe, Kelly O'Neal, John Paul Pack, Florence Sly, Virgil A. Sly, William Martin Smith, Roy C. Snodgrass, Rhodes Thompson, Mae Yoho Ward, Rosa Page Welch, and Mossie Wyker. All of these preached sermons which ranged from better than good to superb and in so doing exalted the work of preaching.

Meanwhile, at the University of Oregon it was my privilege to study ancient and medieval history with Quirinus Breen, read medieval Latin (mostly sermons) with Edna Landros, plunge into medieval and Renaissance literature with Chandler Beall and Hardin Craig, and explore the history of rhetoric with Robert D. Clark.

In my years as a professor of church history my life was enriched by colleagues who had great gifts for preaching, among them Ward A. Rice, Roger Carstensen, Frederick D. Kershner, Abram E. Cory, Orman L. Shelton, Cyrus M. Yocum, Beauford A. Norris, Joseph Martin Smith, Winifred Watson Smith, Henry K. Shaw, Ray W. Wallace, James Armstrong, Robert S. Paul, Cynthia Wedel, Theodore Wedel, Jacob S. Quiambao, Daniel Arichea, Thomas F. Trotter, Joseph C.

Hough, Jr., K. Morgan Edwards, and Henry Kuizinga. (I dare not begin listing my students.)

In youth, long before thoughts of undertaking such a book as this had entered my mind, I was already a preacher, having delivered my first sermon on the Sunday prior to departure for college, and serving student pastorates from my sophomore year on. After seminary came a rewarding ministry with a challenging and supportive congregation, First Christian Church in Jonesboro, Arkansas. On entering into a lifelong editorial and educational ministry I preached at least once, usually twice, almost every Sunday for the next fifteen years, and for thirty years after that kept a busy schedule preaching at religious gatherings, local, regional, and national, and at colleges and seminaries in this country and occasionally abroad. This study deals with a task that has commanded my attention for sixty years and with the gospel that can be faithfully proclaimed only when it has been heard in the preacher's mind and heart.

Loving the preachers here discussed, I respond to their work much as historians of art or literature do to the creations of which they write. Personal involvement has sensitized me to the dynamics of preaching and the achievement represented in a sermon that accomplishes its purpose, yet it has not left me blind to the perils and shortcomings of the venture. To write a truly critical history of an art, one must love it.

Throughout the time I have been at work on this project, encouraging conversations with Ron Allen, Charles B. Ashanin, David Buttrick, Jay R. Calhoun, Fred Craddock, Jane Dempsey Douglass, J. Gerald Janzen, Rodney L. Parrott, Calvin L. Porter, David C. Pellett, Eric Titus, Mary Donovan Turner, Keith Watkins, Clark M. Williamson, Donald R. Wismar, and especially Joseph R. Jeter and David P. Polk have provided helpful counsel at various stages.

Dialog with my students in the history of preaching at Christian Theological Seminary and the School of Theology at Claremont has had a large part in shaping the project. My research assistants have borne much of the burden of "donkey work" involved in a study of this kind: Daniel E. H. Bryant, Robert Coalson, Claudia Ewing (Grant), Joseph R. Jeter, Jr., Geoffrey H. Moran, Nancy Olson, Donald R. Sarton, Ernest Schmid, and Martha Ann Williams. The librarians of Butler University, Christian Theological Seminary, Claremont Graduate School, Northwest Christian College, the School of Theology at Claremont, and the University of Oregon have been unfailingly helpful. Prudence Dyer, Steven N. Goetz, Ronald W. Graham, Ed Irvin,

Joseph R. Jeter, Jr., George M. Knox, Naomi E. Osborn, Rod Parrott, Dale Waddell, and Gary Wilson have read and commented helpfully on earlier drafts, and Nola L. Osborn has prevented many an error in the final manuscript.

To all these who have taught me to love the work of preaching, who have guided me in learning the historian's craft, and especially to these who have helped as indicated in the development of this study, my heartfelt gratitude.

> At this point therefore let us begin our narrative,
> without adding any more to what has already been said;
> for it would be foolish to lengthen the preface
> while cutting short the history itself. [2 Macc. 2:32]

One generation shall laud your works to another,
and shall declare your mighty acts.
On the glorious splendor of your majesty,
and on your wondrous works, I will meditate.
The might of your awesome deeds shall be proclaimed,
and I will declare your greatness.
They shall celebrate the fame of your abundant goodness,
and shall sing aloud of your righteousness.

Psalm 145: 4–7 (RSV)

PART ONE

Context of Oratory

The Greco-Roman Setting of Early Christian Preaching

INTRODUCTION TO PART ONE

The Origin of Christian Preaching in a Rhetorical Culture

CHAPTERS

1. A Tradition of Eloquence

2. Philosophers, Mystagogues, and Moralists

3. Rhetoric and Humane Education

CONCLUSION TO PART ONE

The Significance of Hellenistic Oratory for
Christian Preaching

The Origin of Christian Preaching in a Rhetorical Culture

In the days of Augustus Caesar (27 B.C.E. − 14 C.E.) a colorful crowd of orators thronged the highway to public acclaim. The merely ambitious took to the route of declamation as the open road to fame; and they had their reward, if only for a moment. So when Herod Agrippa, the Roman puppet-king of Judea, "attired in his royal robes and seated on the rostrum, addressed the populace" in Caesarea, they shouted their empty praises:

> It is a god speaking, not a man! [Acts 12:22 REB]

Even so, serious intellectuals, aesthetes, moralists, and religionists also chose the way of the orator in quest of influence and popular esteem. Teachers of rhetoric, the art of public address, dominated the field of education, the most successful among them enjoying both fame and wealth. When an ambitious father asked the philosopher Antisthenes, first of the Cynics, whom to engage as teacher for his son, he was told:

> If you want him to live together with the gods, a philosopher;
> if, however, with men, a rhetorician.[1]

Under the reign of Tiberius Caesar (14–37) a new company of speakers appeared in the East proclaiming yet another new faith. These were the preachers of the Christian gospel.

For centuries to come the classical art of public speaking, called rhetoric, would influence the preaching of their successors, both in substance and in style. More thoroughly than any other aspect of the church's life—indeed, as fully as any other aspect of Western culture—

the Christian pulpit has perpetuated to the present moment undeniable marks of our secular heritage from the Greeks and the Romans. The appropriation did not occur all at once nor without anxiety among the preachers. But insofar as the sermon necessarily has form as well as content, our consideration of Christian preaching requires attention to Hellenistic oratory and rhetoric. Without a knowledge of the ancient orators and their art, neither the mind nor the mode of the preachers, neither the expectations nor the response of the hearers, can be fully understood, even if their sermons were to be studied word for word.

Part One of this study presents the classical tradition of oratory as background and context for the first preaching of Christian faith. Chapter 1 sketches this tradition by suggesting the rhetorical character of the culture and by presenting the exemplary orators to whom generation after generation looked as models. The second chapter discusses the remarkably vital "preaching" that flourished in pagan circles at the time of Christianity's rise. The third describes the development of rhetoric, which profoundly influenced the course of western education and the form of the Christian sermon. The conclusion to Part One assesses the significance of Hellenistic oratory and rhetoric for the history of Christian preaching.

CHAPTER 1

A Tradition of Eloquence

A RHETORICAL CULTURE[1]

Throughout the world in which the gospel was to be preached, people spent their leisure listening to the human voice, reveling in words. Before computers, television, radio, cinema, or printing press, people depended on songs, dance, games, and speeches for entertainment and information.

The Bards. Homer[2]

In its beginnings "literature" was oral, taking its rise with the singing of bards who celebrated in song the mighty deeds of ancient heroes and gods. The Greeks of classical times accorded first place among poets to Homer, a bard reputedly blind, presumed to have sung in the eighth century B.C.E.

Inspired by the artist's mysterious gift (was it not conferred by the Muse, daughter of the supreme god?), calling up memories of stories they had heard from famous tellers of tales and had themselves told again and again, drawing on a stock of recurring themes and well-loved formulas, paced by the strumming of the lyre in sustaining fidelity to the rhythmic demands of hexameter—the bards composed their haunting songs anew at each performance, recounting in freshly minted verse the rivalries and exploits of the heroic age. Reliance on improvisation rather than memorization imparted uniqueness to each presentation; the *poet* was literally a *maker.*[3] Homer's work survives, performances of *The Iliad* and *The Odyssey* having been committed to writing while the unrecorded songs of other bards vanished on the trembling air.

Repeatedly Homer notes the power of forceful *speakers* to direct the thinking of a popular assembly, to stir emotion, and to move to action[4] —even as he relies on the medium of song to narrate his tales. Early in *The Iliad* he describes the effect of a speech by Agamemnon in which that king, employing a ruse agreed upon by the leaders in council, urges the Achaians to suspend their nine-year siege of Troy and launch their ships for the homeward voyage:

> "Our work drags on as always, hopeless—
> the labor of war that brought us here to Troy.
> So come, follow my orders. All obey me now.
> Cut and run! Sail home to the fatherland we love!
> We'll never take the broad streets of Troy."
> ...And the whole assembly surged like big waves at sea,
> the Icarian Sea when East and South Winds drive it on,
> blasting down in force from the clouds of Father Zeus,
> or when the West Wind shakes the deep standing grain
> with hurricane gusts that flatten down the stalks—
> so the massed assembly of troops was shaken now.
> They cried in alarm and charged toward the ships
> and the dust went whirling up from under rushing feet
> as the men jostled back and forth, shouting orders—
> "Grapple the ships! Drag them down to the bright sea!"[5]

The spell of the bards lingered for generations to come. The poets were the earliest educators of *Hellas* (Greece), inspired by the Muses, with a divine mission to speak "the truth."[6] The melding of ethics with aesthetics in the speeches Homer composed for his heroes imbued the culture with an ennobling grandeur of spirit, the haunting ideal of *areté*, or excellence.[7] Long after the bards had passed from the scene recitations of Homer's works by skillful readers enchanted crowds of listeners. In the words of Pindar, supreme poet of the fifth century B.C.E.:

> The word lives longer than deeds.[8]

The Fabulists.[9] *Aesop*

Another kind of storyteller gained a wide popular hearing, not with epic accounts of gods and heroes larger than life, but with *fables,* simple tales wryly exposing the foibles of ordinary mortals, in high station or low. Commonly the fabulist casts an ape, a crow, an eagle, a fox, a mouse, as the leading character, evoking smiles or even laughter at ridiculous behavior that the hearer quickly realizes is not that of an animal at all, but of a pompous or foolish neighbor—or (suddenly in mid-guffaw) one's own self. This moral sermonizing is not unlike that of the wisdom literature of the East, salting shrewdness of observation with sarcasm, satire, and surprise.

Such stories gained a hearing for the poets Hesiod (eighth century) and Archilochus (seventh century). The historian Herodotus attributed many of the well-known fables to Aesop, a slave in sixth-century Samos, whose wit overcame the burden of physical deformity and who eventually received his freedom.[10] Moralists and preachers have retold for centuries the tale of "The Fox and the Crow" as a warning against vanity:

A coal-black crow once stole a piece of meat.
She flew to a tree and held the meat in her beak.
A fox, who saw her, wanted the meat for himself.
so he looked up into the tree and said,
"How beautiful you are, my friend.
Your feathers are fairer than the dove's.
Is your voice as sweet as your form is beautiful?
If so, you must be the queen of birds."
The crow was so happy in his praise
that she opened her mouth
to show how she could sing.
Down fell the piece of meat.
The fox seized upon it and ran away.[11]

Despite the linking of Aesop's name with this type of sermon-story through the generations, little is known of him with certainty, not even which (if any) of the fables are actually his; the tales were told and retold, worked over by various authors, ancient and modern, and augmented by new yarns. If Aesop really existed, he may never have heard some of the stories which go by his name. But simple folk and intellectuals alike have loved the fables ever since.

The Dramatists[12]

The most sublime form of artistic entertainment offered in classical Greece was the tragic drama. In their spacious, open amphitheaters, Athenians, Ephesians, and other city-dwellers watched and listened as players reenacted the ancient stories of heroic women and men locked in agonizing struggle with the decrees of the gods. The most gifted poets of a brilliant age—Aeschylus (525–456 B.C.E.),

Sophocles (496–406 B.C.E.), and Euripides (484–406)—poured their genius into scripts whose power has haunted hearts and minds ever since. For the most part, people did not read these words; they *heard* them.

In memorable and moving lines the tragedians dealt with the most profound questions of life, inquiries into justice and duty, love and hate, faith and doubt, freedom and fate. With eloquent words and sweeping gestures the actors delivered stirring speeches that searched urgent issues of ethics and politics, philosophy and theology. In a lighter vein the writers of comedy, most notably Aristophanes (ca. 450–388) and Menander (342–292), held up to view problematic aspects of human relationships and commented sarcastically on current events.

An integral part of Greek tragedy was the Chorus. Stationed in the *orchestra* between the audience and the stage (*skéné*), this group chanted lines which elaborated, intensified, or offered sermonic commentary on words just spoken by the actors. Such a passage occurs in *Oedipus the King* by Sophocles:

> But if any man walks haughtily in deed or word,
> with no fear of Justice, no reverence for the images of gods,
> may an evil doom seize him for his ill-starred pride,
> if he will not win his vantage fairly, nor keep him from unholy deeds,
> but must lay profaning hands on sanctities.
> Where such things are, what mortal shall boast any more
> that he can ward off the arrows of the gods from his life?
> Nay, if such deeds are in honour,
> wherefore should we join in the sacred dance?[13]

Anyone concerned with the rise of Christian preaching does well to note that, though relatively few people in the ancient world *read* treatises inquiring into matters most deeply troubling to the thoughtful mind or the sensitive soul, they were familiar with such discussions, often profound; *they heard them*—and freely discussed what they heard.

Throughout the ancient world people continued to acquire information primarily by hearing. When most of the folk could neither read nor write, persons with training for performance *recited* works of literature, and the masses absorbed the culture by watching and listening rather than by poring over books[14]—as, increasingly, the children of our television era do also. Even when reading alone, one ordinarily reads aloud,[15] and the letters of the Christian apostles were written to be *heard* in public rather than for silent perusal. In everyday experience, public speakers were celebrities, and people knew how to listen.

A Common Culture

With the victories of Alexander the Great (356–323 B.C.E.), the language and outlook of classical Greece (*Hellas*) spread through the lands around the eastern shores of the Mediterranean Sea. The young Macedonian conqueror dreamed not only of world dominion but of one people unified by the high culture he had learned from his tutor, Aristotle. Though his empire shattered after his death in Babylon, Hellenism endured, a common universe of discourse dominated by Greek ideals.

When the Romans began in the third century to conquer the lands once held by Alexander (adding to them North Africa, Gaul, Spain, and eventually Britain), they too appropriated that culture. Their generals adorned their triumphs with the most prestigious of trophies— Greek libraries, along with poets and intellectuals taken captive and brought to Rome as domestic slaves to tutor the children of the conquerors. As philhellenism came into vogue, aspiring authors forsook their native Latin to write in Greek, the prestigious language of learning.

In time Rome began to produce a literature in its own tongue. But in the first century of the Caesars, Greek in the "common" *(koiné)* dialect was the language of education and commerce, and Latin the language of government, throughout the far-flung Roman Empire. A common culture flourished in the great Hellenistic cities and in regions like Galilee, an exhilarating universalism having now replaced the old loyalties to *polis* and tribe.

THE PROMINENCE OF ORATORY

It was a culture of oratory, public address being essential to the conduct of public life. Across the *oikoumené*, from Marseilles to Carthage to Alexandria to Antioch to Ephesus to Athens and back to Rome, the design of education was to produce eloquent and persuasive speakers.

Political Oratory

Before the Roman republic gave way to the imperial rule of Caesar Augustus in 27, oratory had long served as a primary means of *political* influence. From time immemorial, when the folk of the oral cultures took counsel together the speaker who could analyze a problem and persuasively present a plausible course of action was looked to as honored guide. The early Babylonian epics, as well as those of the Greeks, depicted the excitement of such meetings, narrating speeches by impressive orators who influenced their decisions.[16]

At the dawn of history tyrants ruled the Greek city-states, but late in the sixth century B.C.E., the citizens overthrew them, establishing the rule of the populace, *démos*, and giving democracy its name. Each city transacted its public business in a large popular assembly (also called *démos*) and a smaller council. At about the same time the Romans expelled their royal house, the Tarquins, placing government in the hands of the Senate. In these bodies of citizens, free males could win influence through effectiveness as public speakers, and the art of political (deliberative) oratory flourished in democracy and republic.[17] The Roman Senate's designation of Octavian as "first citizen" (*princeps*) or dictator, with the title *Augustus*, radically diminished the function of political oratory, reducing it in large part to propaganda for the emperor. But the vision of the masterful speaker guiding the course of the commonwealth by wisdom and eloquence continued to excite the cultural imagination.

Judicial Oratory

A citizen involved in *judicial* proceedings (a not infrequent state of affairs) needed the ability to persuade the judges. In the early days of Greek democracy and the Roman republic a man had to argue his own case before the court; later the rules were changed to permit engaging the services of an advocate. Even then, obvious advantages accrued to the citizen who had mastered the principles of judicial or forensic oratory and acquired some skill in pleading his cause.

Ceremonial Oratory

Many kinds of public occasions featured *ceremonial* oratory. Speakers with reputations for eloquence in politics and law commonly held forth at such gatherings, honoring a fallen hero, celebrating victory in battle, paying tribute to a leading public figure, observing a notable anniversary. A major attraction at the Olympic Games, along with the athletic contests, the carnival booths, the jugglers and other entertainers, was the appearance of famous orators or writers delivering addresses from the porticoes of the temple of Zeus; the Pythian Games also featured contests in music, poetry, and oratory.[18]

Ceremonial speechmaking—the Greek rhetoricians called it *epideictic* oratory—could descend to the kind of bombast which still frequently occupies party conventions and ecclesiastical assemblies. But it could also rise to an elegant level of entertainment, "a game of culture."[19] Its kinship to deliberative oratory is evident in that it *praises* actions which the political speaker *recommends*;[20] when used by a philosopher to extol a virtue or decry a vice, it offered an important tool for ethical exhortation.[21] At its best it could give memorable expression to the ideals of a movement or a society.

Such ceremonial speaking held a large place in the popular life of the ancient world. It helped to shape the form of Christian sermons, especially those commemorating the events celebrated in the liturgical calendar.

THE EXEMPLARY ORATORS—GREEKS[22]

The Orator as Model

Every culture holds before its youth models for emulation. In Greek democracy and Roman republic the model was the effective citizen. It was assumed that the citizen would be a good soldier, serving bravely in war and cultivating those virtues of character and intelligence required for military command. But the schoolmasters professed a primary interest in the arts of public leadership in peacetime, and the model was the successful orator.

Celebrated Greek and Roman speakers received honored attention in the educational curriculum of the classical era, lingered in the common memory at least as names during the Middle Ages, recovered cultural primacy in the Renaissance, and long held their position of eminence in the tradition of Western education wherever the liberal arts were taught. Their speeches, their style of expression, their ideals, their *personae* exercised an abiding influence on the development of Christian preaching.

The Greeks held in highest honor a company of notable speakers, favored by circumstance, who voiced the interests of the Athenian upper class[23] and imparted to the classical tradition of oratory an aristocratic tone sustained for generations in the rhetorical schools. It signified the lifestyle of the rich and famous, and those who aspired to better things sought to make it their own.

Pericles

In his *History of the Peloponnesian War*, Thucydides tells of a memorable oration cherished in antiquity: From a high platform erected to enable as many as possible to hear his voice Pericles (495?–

429 B.C.E.), the chief magistrate of Athens, offered a funeral oration over those who had fallen in battle. While some hold out for his version of the speech as authentic, scholars tend to see it as a fabrication by Thucydides himself, who confesses to composing appropriate orations when texts were lacking, following an accepted custom of that rhetorical age.[24] In any event, Athenians cherished its words from that time forward as the supreme expression of the spirit of their democratic state.

Having presided over the public life of Athens in its most glorious century, Pericles stands as its foremost interpreter, celebrating the ancestors who bequeathed the heritage of freedom to the present generation, the glory of the empire, the victories won in past battles, and especially the city's political institutions.[25]

> We enjoy a form of government
> which does not copy the laws of our neighbors...
> In name, from it not being administered for the benefit of the few,
> but of the many, it is called a democracy;
> but with regard to its laws, all enjoy equality.

Pericles points to his city's enviable lifestyle and its courage in war, but directs his eloquence primarily to the spirit of its people.

> For we study taste with economy,
> and philosophy without effeminacy;
> and employ wealth rather for opportunity of action
> than for boastfulness of talking;
> while poverty is nothing disgraceful for a man to confess,
> but not to escape it by exertion is more disgraceful.
> Again, the same men can attend at the same time
> to domestic as well as to public affairs;
> and others, who are engaged with business,
> can still form a sufficient judgment on political questions.
> For we are the only people that consider the man
> who takes no part in these things,
> not as unofficious, but as useless.

Here the orator strikes a blow for the Athenian conduct of the city's affairs by public debate:

> We do not regard words as any hindrance to deeds,
> but rather [consider it a hindrance]
> not to have been previously instructed by word,
> before undertaking in deed what we have to do.

Devotion to law, civic splendor, and hospitality to those who come from afar to marvel at the common life and achievements of Athens have made it "a school for Greece" and the admiration of generations to come.

The orator closes his encomium with a tribute to the fallen heroes:

> For of illustrious men the whole earth is the sepulchre;
> and not only does the inscription upon columns in their own land
> point it out, but in that also which is not their own
> there dwells with everyone an unwritten memorial of the heart.

He offers consolation to the parents, siblings, and children of the dead, and to their widows with the assurance that

> the love of honor is the only feeling that never grows old.

Pericles' tribute to the honored dead, and to their city as Athenians loved to envision it, has lingered in the minds of subsequent generations as a haunting assertion of the grandeur of the human spirit.

Though critics of a later time who compiled the Canon of Attic Orators did not rank Pericles in their "top ten," the dramatist Eupolis gave him high praise: "Persuasion sat upon his lips, he so charmed all hearers, and alone of all orators he thrilled the souls of those who listened."[26] The Romans looked back to him as "the most eloquent man at Athens" in his time, noting his "peculiar vigour" and observing that he was "accurate, pointed, terse, and wealthier in ideas than in diction."[27] Pericles himself is said to have prized great speaking so highly that he wanted history to include the orations of Antiphon even if the proud naval victory of Athens at Salamis must be passed over.[28] Yet in his speaking he appealed to the minds of the hearers rather than the passions; it was said that he prayed to the gods "that he might never utter a word that was not to the point."[29]

Excluded Eloquence: Aspasia

Women accounted respectable rarely appeared outside the home and, except for religious ceremonies, did not participate in public life. For intellectual companionship and cultured conversation some men distinguished in mind and spirit turned to a scintillating company of women among the *hetairai* ("friends"), the foreign courtesans who had found a place for themselves in the economy of the city. Relying on quickness of intellect and aesthetic sensitivity, some of these women achieved celebrity as well as a degree of honor that set them apart from their less-favored sisters, and they frequently appeared at public events in the company of leading citizens. Accepted in intellectual and cultural circles, they flaunted their disdain for the repressive code of feminine propriety.

Most impressive of these women was the talented Aspasia, from Miletus. Excluded from any possibility of official status among leading Athenians—she was a woman, a foreigner, and a *hetaira*—she could not marry Pericles, despite their mutual and publicly acknowledged love, but she had his esteem, affection, and respect; he took her into his home, and she became the mother of his son. It was said that she composed some of his orations. Socrates acknowledged her ability, presenting in Plato's dialog *Menexenus* a speech he had heard her rehearsing; and an impressive circle of listeners admired her skill in oratory.

A panegyric for the warriors recently fallen in battle, the oration reported by Socrates celebrates the spirit of Athens, resounding with patriotic pride in victories won by its soldiers and sailors:

> The country which brought them up is not like other countries,
> a stepmother to her children, but their own true mother;
> she bore them and nourished them and received them,
> and in her bosom they now repose…
> And when she had nursed them and brought them up to manhood,
> she gave them Gods to be their rulers and teachers…
> They are the Gods who first ordered our lives.[30]

The orator praises the political constitution of the city:

> Our government was an aristocracy—
> a form of government which…is sometimes called democracy,
> but is really an aristocracy or government of the best
> which has the approval of the many.[31]

She insists that its leaders are chosen not for wealth or status, but for wisdom and virtue.

After rehearsing in conventional militaristic tone a record of engagements fought on land and sea, Aspasia concludes dramatically by speaking to the citizens of the present as the voice of all the Athenian warriors fallen in the past:

> Sons…Remember our words, and whatever is your aim
> let virtue be the condition of the fulfilment of your aim…
> All knowledge, when separated from justice and virtue,

is seen to be cunning and not wisdom; wherefore
make this your first and last and constant and all-absorbing aim,
to exceed, if possible, not only us but all your ancestors in virtue;
and know that to excel you in virtue only brings us shame,
but that to be excelled by you is a source of happiness to us.[32]

Such snatches of eloquence suggest an oratory which, delivered in silver, feminine tones, might have enriched the life of Athens and the tradition of classical culture had patriarchy not barred women from participation in civic affairs and excluded their voices from the conduct of public business.

Isocrates

Prevented by physical infirmity, the most celebrated orator in the generation after Pericles did not actually *deliver* his speeches; others spoke them for him, and many of them circulated as tracts. Yet Isocrates (436–338 B.C.E.) succeeded so brilliantly as a teacher of eloquence and for critical occasions wrote pieces so masterful in form and style and so stirring in treatment of the issues that he was universally conceded the title *orator*. On his tomb the Greeks carved a siren.

Like the speeches of the other supreme Athenians—Antiphon (480–411), Isaeos (fourth century), and Demosthenes (384–322)—many of Isocrates's pieces owed their effectiveness to their cogency in handling complex political issues that do not now yield to summarization in a line or two. Most significant is his *Defense regarding the Antidosis,* composed at the age of eighty-two. Justifying his career as a teacher of speakers, he says to the Athenians:

You yourselves are preeminent and superior to the rest of the world,
not in your application to the business of war,
nor because you govern yourselves more excellently
or preserve the law handed down to you by your ancestors
more faithfully than others, but in those qualities
by which human nature rises above the other animals,
and the race of the Hellenes above the barbarians,
namely by the fact that you have been educated
as have no other people in wisdom and in speech.[33]

The old myth that humanity had been raised out of barbarism by the powers of music, and the alternative claim put forward in behalf of philosophy, Isocrates recasts to present the orator as civilizer of the race. The power of Reason, the Logos, operates through the persuasion of human speech, and

The right word is a sure sign of good thinking. [34]

Isocrates commends the orator's vocation, both for its contribution to society and for the rarity of the abilities it requires:

> Those who make it their duty to invent discourses
> [upon questions of the common good]
> should be held in higher esteem
> than those who propose and write down laws,
> inasmuch as they are rarer, have the more difficult task,
> and must have superior qualities of mind.[35]

The educated speaker, moreover, stands in a great tradition of ideas and words. Isocrates "more than any other person inspired in...Western traditional education a predominantly literary tone."[36] Wherever the ideal of the preacher as a woman or man of letters persists, the influence of this orator continues.

Demosthenes

The paragon of Greek orators threw all his mental powers, passion, and persuasiveness into the battle for freedom against the threat of a foreign autocrat. Throughout his public career Demosthenes (384?–322 B.C.E.) gave himself to rallying the citizens of the Greek city-states to make a united stand against the military expansion of Macedon, fueled by the ambition of King Philip.

The eloquent Athenian argues by reciting one example after another, detailing step-by-step the expansion of Philip's power, warning against his method of divide-and-conquer, decrying his protestations of friendship to states he was about to attack, protesting the dithering of the potential victims:

> Yet the Greeks endure to see all this;
> methinks they view it as they would a hailstorm,
> each praying that it may not fall on himself,
> none trying to prevent it.[37]

Scathingly, Demosthenes denounces those Greeks who have allowed the Macedonian to buy their friendship, contrasting current impotence with the heroism of a glorious past:

> There must be some cause, some good reason,
> why the Greeks were so eager for liberty then,
> and now are eager for servitude.

There was something, men of Athens,
something in the hearts of the multitude then,
which there is not now,
which overcame the wealth of Persia
and maintained the freedom of Greece,
and quailed not under any battle by land or sea;

Posing a rhetorical question, "What was this?" the orator answers with a telling diagnosis:

Nothing subtle or clever: simply that whoever took money
from the aspirants for power or the corrupters of Greece
were universally detested:
it was dreadful to be convicted of bribery...
But now all such principles have been sold as in open market,
and those imported in exchange
by which Greece is ruined and diseased. What are they?
Envy where a man gets a bribe; laughter if he confesses it;
mercy to the convicted; hatred of those that denounce the crime;
all the usual attendants of corruption.[38]

Demosthenes here speaks of character, the politician as moralist.

The Greek city-states rallied to field a united resistance against the invader. But when his troops overwhelmed their forces at Chaeronea, Philip is said to have reeled over the battlefield that night, drunk with victory and too much wine, deliriously repeating among the bodies of the fallen,

Demosthenes, Demosthenes, son of the Paeanian deme

—the words with which the Athenian orator had for so long prefaced the decrees calculated to halt his imperialistic advance.[39]

Though democracy went down before Philip and his son Alexander (the Roman republic also would give way three centuries later to the principate of Octavian and the Caesars who succeeded him), Demosthenes' Philippics, as his eloquent speeches in the lost cause are known, hold an honored place in the literature of freedom.

Like Isocrates, Demosthenes is also remembered for a celebrated apology, the carefully detailed and tellingly documented defense of a brilliant lawyer against charges filed by his rival Aeschines. Entitled *On the Crown*, it demonstrates the skill of an unrivaled debater, its carefully composed substance spiced with merciless invective against his opponent.

For centuries schoolchildren have been admonished by the legend of the young orator's persistence in overcoming handicaps—practicing speech with pebbles in his mouth to improve articulation, speaking above the sound of the surf or while climbing uphill to strengthen his voice, rehearsing before a large mirror to work out the most effective gestures, copying masterpieces of prose again and again.[40] More inspiring are the precision of argument and the artistic finish of the orations he delivered in his prime to the citizens gathered in assembly, his stubborn determination to "communicate conviction to the multitude,"[41] his courageous witness against tyranny. His name has stood ever since as the type of Athenian eloquence, of democratic oratory at its best.

THE EXEMPLARY ORATORS—ROMANS [42]

Early Roman Oratory

Celebrating their own tradition of Latin eloquence, the Romans pictured blind Appius Claudius as swaying the Senate in the early days of the republic. Cicero prized a copy of the oration believed to have dissuaded the senators from making peace with Pyrrhus, and Plutarch reproduced it. The readiness of the Romans to accept such legends indicates their high esteem for oratory.

In the second century B.C.E. scores of participants in the vigorous life of the young republic won reputations for eloquence in the Senate and the forum.[43] Two towered over all the others.

Cato the Elder

The very "archetype of an old Roman,"[44] Marcus Portius Cato the Elder (234–139), left copies of more than 150 speeches, judicial and political. Known as Cato the Censor, he dominated republican Rome by character and devotion to the old virtues. Addressing a current crisis, he admonished the Senate:

> Do not suppose that our ancestors, from so small a commencement,
> raised the republic to greatness merely by force of arms...
> There were other things which made them great,
> but which among us have no existence;
> such as industry at home, equitable government abroad,
> and minds impartial in council,
> uninfluenced by any immoral or improper feeling.
> Instead of such virtues, we have luxury and avarice;
> public distress, and private superfluity;
> we extol wealth, and yield to indolence;

no distinction is made between good men and bad;
and ambition usurps the honors due to virtue.
Nor is this wonderful; since you study each his individual interest,
and since at home you are slaves to pleasure,
and here to money or favor; and hence it happens
that an attack is made on the defenseless state.[45]

Blunt, plain-spoken, given to wry irony, Cato relied on force of character for persuasion, willing to stand alone against popular clamor. Plutarch describes him confronting a crowd of demonstrators who demanded free grain:

It is a hard matter, my fellow citizens,
to argue with the belly, since it has no ears.[46]

Livy quotes Cato affirming the traditional authority of the husband and opposing the demands of Roman women for a degree of personal liberty.[47] Reputedly Cato concluded every speech in the Senate, no matter the subject, with the cry:

Besides, I hold that Carthage must be destroyed.[48]

Adopting his policy at last, Rome emerged from the Punic Wars as the dominant power in the western Mediterranean.

Long an antagonist to philhellenism, Cato nevertheless began to study Greek in his old age and came to admire the foreign literature he could now read. But he inspired a tradition of Latin prose with a dignity and power of its own.

Cato lived on in the speeches of patriots and moralists and, after the triumph of Christianity, in the sermons of preachers, who esteemed his rugged integrity and commonly cited him as an example of earnest rectitude.

Scipio Aemilianus

Cato's younger contemporary Scipio Aemilianus (185–129 B.C.E.), the conqueror of Carthage, won fame as soldier, bibliophile, writer, and speaker. One of the most knowledgeable lovers of the art would later list him and Cato among "the Attic Orators of Rome."[49]

The celebrated "Scipionic Circle" included the most glittering names of the age—notables from politics, law, the military, philosophy, poetry, history, and oratory, Greeks as well as Romans. Two members of that circle stand as distinctive exemplars of the republican orator—Cato the rough-hewn old Roman, all flint and ruggedness, displaying no grace except blunt honesty; Scipio the polished embodiment of *humanitas*, with the sheen of urbanity; and both cut from the same quarry.

Orators of the 1st Century B.C.E.

In the last century of the Roman republic, oratory flourished in a climate of political freedom, which promised great prizes, yet was fraught with perils. The list of distinguished speakers is long, and most of the well-known Romans of the time successfully mastered the art; looking back, a later generation recalled "the vigour of Caesar...the gravity of Brutus...and the bitterness of Cassius."[50] Hortensius (114–50 B.C.E.) was master of the Asianic style, flowery, elegant, and aphoristic. Undone in his later years by overreliance on a retentive memory at the expense of careful preparation and by a tendency to rely on fine phrases rather than substance, he nevertheless inspired the youthful Cicero, whose book called *Hortensius* first turned young Augustine of Hippo toward philosophy four centuries later.

Opportunities for women to participate in public life were limited, but in the waning days of the republic Hortensia won fame for her eloquence. The historian Valerius recorded that she "pleaded the cause of the women before the triumvirs with both constancy and felicity."[51] A century later the satirist Juvenal composed the shrillest of screeds against women, mocking every aspect of female behavior. He ridiculed those who insisted on participating actively in legal proceedings:

> Almost no day in court goes by without cases which women
> Prompt, one way or another, plaintiff, defendant, no matter.
> They draw up the briefs themselves, prepare the indictments,
> Ready to draft or dictate all the speeches of counsel.[52]

Obviously they were not wanted.

Cicero

Of all Rome's exemplary orators, Marcus Tullius Cicero (106–43) attained highest eminence. For centuries the name of Tully served as cliché for eloquence in Latin, as that of Demosthenes did in Greek. Though unable to assert commanding leadership in the last, bloody days of the republic which brought him violent death, he was acclaimed as Rome's supreme orator.

Cicero's style impresses contemporary taste as overwrought, but he strove for a middle course between the florid Asianic mode of expression affected by many of his peers and the restrained Attic manner cultivated in opposition to it, which he regarded as dry and colorless. Whenever later generations looked for a model of Latin eloquence—and Latin remained the literary language of Europe for sixteen centuries—Ciceronianism flourished anew.

Cicero devoted all his efforts to the cultivation of his powers as an orator. To him this meant the enlargement of his capacities as a human being, a greater realization of *humanitas*, the fullness of a cultured mind and spirit. Of two older contemporaries whom he greatly admired, Marcus Antonius and Licinius Crassus, he observed that they would remain unsurpassed until "by the assistance of a more complete and extensive knowledge of philosophy, jurisprudence, and history" some succeding orator should attain a higher degree of perfection.[53] That high task Cicero conceived as his mission, and he carried it to fulfilment. He read widely in those fields, as in literature, and commended them to his hearers.

In later life, when military commanders had usurped the functions of republican institutions and the orator was no longer free to exercise his powers in the forum, Cicero turned to philosophy, both for intellectual stimulation and for consolation.[54] In seclusion, though he regarded writing as second best to speaking,[55] he composed essays and dialogs, dealing both with the art of oratory and with issues of living that preachers still find themselves moved to address. In them all, he wrote as orator, the eye of his imagination searching his audience, his mind eager to engage theirs and to persuade.

So he commended friendship:

All that I can do is to urge you
to put friendship before all things human;
for nothing is so conformable to nature
and nothing so adaptable to our fortunes
whether they be favourable or adverse.[56]

Here he made clear his ethical concern:

Let this law be established in friendship:
neither ask dishonourable things, nor do them, if asked.[57]

Even more "pastoral" (to borrow a term applied to Christian ministry) is his piece on old age:

When I reflect on this subject
I find four reasons why old age appears to be unhappy:

first, that it withdraws us from active pursuits;
second, that it makes the body weaker;
third, that it deprives us of almost all physical pleasures;
and fourth, that it is not far removed from death.[58]

To each of these objections, the orator counters with a telling refutation.

Those alleging lack of useful activity in age, he pictures in humorous and unflattering likeness:

[They] would say that the pilot does nothing in the sailing of the ship,
because, while others are climbing the masts,
or running about the gangways, or working at the pumps,
he sits quietly in the stern and simply holds the tiller.

In "reflection, force of character, and judgment," qualities necessary to the well-being of society,

old age is usually not only not poorer, but is even richer.[59]

To the objection of bodily weakness, he counters that the voice of an older speaker frequently gains a "magnificent resonance," which, he claims proudly, he has not lost, adding the observation,

Very often the sedate and mild speaking of an old man
wins itself a hearing.[60]

As to lessening of physical pleasure in age, the orator turns the tables, claiming it as an advantage:

Old age lacks the heavy banquet,
the loaded table, and the oft-filled cup;
therefore it also lacks drunkenness, indigestion,
and loss of sleep.[61]
And the imminence of death?

The same fate befalls the young…When the young die,
I am reminded of a strong flame extinguished by a torrent;
but when old people die it is as if a fire had gone out…
of its own accord, after the fuel had been consumed…
The nearer I approach death
the more I feel like one who is in sight of land at last
and is about to anchor in…home port after a long voyage.[62]

Though Cicero's philosophical writings are not distinguished for intellectual originality, they address existential concerns with ethical sensitivity and calm assurance. Century after century they would turn his readers to thoughtful reflection and to the thinkers he celebrated. Though he loved overmuch the ease and adulation won by his eloquence, manifesting that weakness of character which often accompanies privilege, yet his carefully cultivated mind and spirit would draw generations of admirers to the study of classical literature in quest of the grace and elegance he so engagingly embodied.

Through the centuries readers have pored over Cicero's speeches before the Senate, the courts, or occasional audiences. The dialogues "On Friendship," "On Old Age," and on assorted other topics became literary models. He wrote stirringly on famous orators, on rhetoric, and on the duties of public officials. (See chapter 3.) If Pericles states most memorably the ideals of Athenian democracy, Cicero ranks with the poet Virgil in exemplifying the cultivation of the human spirit; the voice of the orator, as of the poet, had no equal among the Romans. Generations of orators and preachers would look back to Cicero for inspiration and example.[63]

END OF AN ERA

The deliberative institutions in which the exemplary orators had found their public careers collapsed before the ruthless ambitions of generals with armies at their backs. Political structures that once had allowed citizens to debate the issues confronting their city proved inadequate to the governing of empire and to absorbing the rivalries of commanders whose legions had enlarged it by massive conquests. After a century of turmoil, civil war, and unconstitutional rule, the Senate in 28 B.C.E. formally declared Octavian first *(princeps)* among its members and the following year bestowed on him the title Augustus. The new benevolent dictatorship put an end to the vitality of the Senate: Senators still made speeches; Caesar Augustus made decisions.

Without political freedom political oratory subsided, and even judicial eloquence was muted. Cicero lamented the end of free institutions:

> The voice of Hortensius was silenced only by his own death,
> mine by the death of the republic.[64]

The sun had set on the stirring oratory of the republic. As for Cicero and his colleagues, who once had persuaded excited audiences,

> We are left to be the guardians of orphaned eloquence...
> The night, which has fallen upon the commonwealth,
> has overtaken me before my journey was ended.[65]

When Cicero's enemies struck him down in 43 they beheaded the corpse and drove a nail through the tongue. That grisly affront to the eloquence of the man ominously signified the fate of political speech itself. The courts remained open, but the field of popular speaking had drastically shrunk, occupied chiefly now by the oratory of ceremony and display.

Even so, two Romans contemporary with the apostles earned reputations that caused later generations to take note: Domitius Afer and the Gaul, Julius Africanus; admirers recalled the latter's strength and Afer's "mellowness" and wit.[66] The young Quintilian once asked Afer what poet in his opinion most nearly approached Homer; long afterwards he remembered the noted orator's reply:

> Virgil comes second,
> but is nearer first than third.[67]

The orator's art was not ready to die. The habit of listening to speeches would continue for another five centuries, so long as urban life and classical culture endured. Education, designed to produce orators, would not deviate from its rhetorical tradition, even though the end of the republic had drastically altered conditions: Public speakers might no longer deal so readily with matters of political substance.

But in the marketplaces, public squares, and other spots where the people gathered, speakers of another sort, in colorful and varied profusion, were seeking out whatever audiences they could attract and haranguing them about the issues that faced them within their troubled minds and spirits.

CHAPTER 2

Philosophers, Mystagogues, and Moralists[1]

AN AUDIENCE FOR MORAL AND SPIRITUAL DISCOURSE

People stopped in the streets to listen. The wandering speakers were adept entertainers, good for a half hour's free amusement. Some advocated outlandish opinions, furnishing matter for argument through the rest of the day. Not a few held forth simply for the pleasure of addressing an audience or demonstrating rhetorical technique. Listeners who grew tired or bored could always move on, leaving the speaker stranded.

But something deeper than idle entertainment was going on. Political turmoil, public violence, the passing of familiar institutions, societal uncertainty had left people inwardly ill at ease. Their ancestors had found identity in the life of the self-contained city-state, the *polis*, with its familiar political processes, its leaders known by sight, its populace made up of old acquaintances, its problems regarding which one's opinions counted, its religion informed by and inspiring the life of the city.

Now people found themselves nonentities in the vast magnitude of universal empire. On the streets of first-century Rome, Alexandria, and Antioch, the great cities, and even in the provincial towns, crowds of folk from three continents jostled one another. Although they spoke Greek or Latin rather than their mother tongues, their customs, costumes, and cults were curious and discordant. At the very time when an authoritative, impersonal government sought to impose unity on society, the unity of local culture had been shattered. The new official religion of the state with its deified Caesar had little appeal to the hearts of the populace.

The brevity and futility of life evoked recurring sighs in literature. For the meaning people craved and that the strange new world about them no longer provided, they had begun to turn inward. A new individualism was emerging in religion, literature, and philosophy, catching up the thoughtful in a search for personally satisfying answers to life's questions. Such perplexities a new breed of more existentially sensitive orators undertook to address. They offered solutions in a variety of packages.

Intellectuals and Street Preachers

Appealing to the more thoughtful came the philosophers, "lovers of wisdom," esteemed as instructors in issues of morality and truth. Though *philosophy* evokes an image of sedate origins in the grove of Akademe in stately Athens, it was in the time of the Caesars a more rough-and-tumble affair. Philosophers now were not ivory-tower intellectuals writing texts, but "street-corner orators," popularizers, entrepreneurs, working the territory near and far, offering their belief systems as "cures for [the] ills" of the hearers.[2] As a lad, Jesus could hear them in Galilee.

Each major school of thought looked back to a venerated founder, whose ideas the speakers interpreted as guidance for the present. For orators and listeners alike, the presentation could become an earnest, even fateful, engagement.

The Socratic Heritage

The great exemplar was Socrates (ca. 470–399 B.C.E.), whose good-natured, though relentless probing of assumptions taken for granted by his partners in discussion, imparted to philosophy a heritage of high intellectual integrity. His independence of thought, feared by many while he lived, had won for him these five centuries past widespread regard as a hero of the mind.

In the practice of Socrates, given immortality as literature in the dialogues of his disciple Plato (428–348 [or 347]), conversation is serious business. He uses it to question conventional wisdom and the clichés of the sophists, as with his colleagues he probes affirmations that others are ready to take for granted. But he is not playing games; rather, his annoying insistence on examining easy assumptions involves in equal measure a commitment to truth and a concern for his partner in discussion.[3] His readiness to honor women by recognizing their skills and insights and his willingness to learn from Aspasia and

Diotima, not just from men, reveal a mind at liberty to seek for truth, unconfined by the maxims of patriarchy.

Socrates dismisses rhetoric, with its arguments from probability, as worthless diversion from the truth, insisting on dialectic, the art of reasoning, to prove or disprove the validity of every assertion. He refuses to be addressed as teacher or to commit his reflections to writing; to him the relationship uniting companions of the intellectual quest is all-important. And his speech is altogether unpretentious.

> His words...are ridiculous when you first hear them...
> for his talk is of pack-asses and smiths and cobblers and curriers,
> and he is always repeating the same things in the same words,
> so that the ignorant or inexperienced person
> might feel disposed to laugh at him;
> but whoever opens...and sees what is within
> will find that they are the only words which have a meaning in them,
> and also the most divine,
> abounding in fair images of virtue, and of the widest comprehension,
> or rather extending to the whole duty of a good and honourable man.[4]

His apology to those who accused him of corrupting the youth of Athens glorifies what he understands as his divine vocation; from it he will not waver:

> Athenians, I honour and love you;
> but I shall obey God rather than you,
> and while I have life and strength
> I shall never cease from the practice and teaching of philosophy,
> exhorting any whom I meet and saying to him after my manner:
> You, my friend,
> a citizen of the great and mighty and wise city of Athens,—
> are you not ashamed of heaping up
> the greatest amount of money and honour and reputation,
> and caring so little about wisdom and truth
> and the greatest improvement of the soul...?
> And if the person with whom I am arguing says: Yes, but I do care;
> then I do not leave him or let him go at once;
> but I proceed to interrogate and examine and cross-examine him...
> And I shall repeat the same words to every one whom I meet,
> young and old, citizen and alien....
> For know that this is the command of God...

I do nothing but go about persuading you all, old and young alike
not to take thought for your persons or your properties,
but first and chiefly
to care about the greatest improvement of the soul.[5]

In faithfulness to his vocation Socrates goes serenely to his death.

The high-minded, morally searching, spiritually intense conversations of Socrates profoundly influenced the tone of the symposium,
an institution in Greece that provided congenial intellectuals an occasion for discussing issues of philosophy over good wine and a good
meal. In this tradition it may be noted that the earliest name for the
Christian sermon would be *homilia* (homily)—a serious conversation
with like-minded seekers after the true Way, taking place about a
table.[6]

The moral earnestness of Socrates imparts urgency to his protreptic
or hortatory speeches, "the germ out of which grew the diatribe (the
stump-sermon delivered by the travelling Cynic and Stoic preachers
of the Hellenistic age), and in its turn the diatribe influenced the
structure of the Christian sermon."[7]

Socrates' chief importance for the spiritual life of the Greeks and
for Christian preaching arises from the meaning he infused into the
word *psyché* or *soul*.[8] The "ethical or religious overtones" associated
with that word for two and a half millennia derive from his usage, in
contrast with the mechanistic thrust in much contemporary psychology. For Socrates (as represented in Plato's *Phaedrus*), the orator's
essential business is *psychagogy*, i.e., influencing souls—a task in which,
Isocrates would later point out, the poets excel. Socrates' intellectual
labor in seeking the truth through dialog "was, for him, a form of
worship," because he believed "that paideia [instruction] is the true
service of God and that care for the soul is true paideia."

An admiring company of Greek writers, privileged to have been
part of the Socratic circle, "imitated the moral sermons of their master" in works now long lost.[9] But his most famous disciple, Plato, cast
him as hero and mentor of numerous dialogs, establishing a literary
form beloved of pagans and early Christians alike, who reveled in the
high artistry of serious intellectual play and drew inspiration from the
lofty moral tone and spiritual sensitivity of the conversations. Philosophy in this tradition has become "a new religion," the longing of the
human spirit and its ascent toward the perfect Good being described
in imagery borrowed from the mysteries; ultimately God becomes
the "teacher of the whole world" in the knowledge of the Beautiful

and the Good.[10] Accordingly, education in philosophy necessitates *conversion*—a term which the Christian preachers would take over from Plato. As educator, the philosopher is a physician, his concern "the health of the soul."

Thus Socrates and Plato gave to philosophy a strong moral bent and spiritual intent that would continue to characterize leading thinkers throughout the classical era; some of these would embrace the Christian gospel.

In the first century of the empire political resistance against the new autocracy drew inspiration and courage from the teachings of the philosophers. More than one nervous Caesar expelled them from Rome, even executing some—in the train of Socrates, martyrs for the life of the mind. But the primary concern of the philosophers was intellectual integrity rather than political freedom.

PHILOSOPHERS BY SCHOOLS[11]

In the centuries after Socrates several major "denominations" or "schools" of philosophy had emerged. For all their differences among themselves, they affirmed human dignity and, in most cases, ethical responsibility. More than a system of thought, their speakers promulgated a way of life. They promised salvation.

Cynics

Inspired by "the Encourager" or "the Persuader," Antisthenes (ca. 445-ca. 365), friend and disciple of Socrates, the Cynics took a serious and disciplined view of life. Diogenes (412?–323), the best-known exemplar of their way, affirmed human equality and questioned all distinctions of class. Memorably dramatizing a point, he carried a lighted lamp through the city by day in search of an honest man.

A student of nature, Diogenes reflected on ultimate theological questions suggested by the order and apparent purpose of the universe, being described by science, which was then new. To him all of this seemed the work of a supreme Mind. Observing that all living things breathe and that the soul vanishes once breathing stops, he mused:

It seems to me that that which has the power of knowing
is the thing that we call air,
and that it steers all things and controls all things.
For I feel that this is God, and that it extends everywhere
and disposes all things and is contained in all things.
And there is nothing that does not have a share in it.[12]

The street-preacher had begun to struggle with natural theology.

Diogenes' disciple Crates (4th century B.C.E.) gave Antisthenes' doctrine of human equality even greater emphasis than the founder, pushing it in the direction of "something like Christian love."[13]

Cynic preachers, both women and men, took their stand wherever they could find an audience, urging their views on their hearers "less as a reasoned system of beliefs about the universe than as a divine revelation."[14] In a time when old standards were eroding, they advocated a rigorous morality, a principled independence (*autarkeia*) of external circumstance, and a lifestyle of utmost simplicity, limiting themselves each to a single garment, spurning sandals or shoes, sleeping on the ground.[15] Their wandering orators delivered diatribes against the sophisticated impudence of the erotic poets; from the third century on, their sermons provided a staple of philosophical oratory.

As moralists, the Cynics assumed a confrontational stance, cultivating *parrésia* (forthrightness or frankness or unblinking honesty) in their street-corner harangues. In the more sensitive and self-restrained among them, such bluntness admirably blended truth-speaking, courage, and genuine concern for their "patients." But a rougher, unprincipled sort of speaker also affected the dress and unpolished manner of the Cynics, displaying a crude disregard for the niceties of acceptable behavior and engaging with ill-concealed delight in scathing denunciation that "really took the hide off" those whom they attacked.[16] At its best *parrésia* designated the philosopher's freedom of speech exercised boldly and compassionately in the interest of those who paused to listen.

Epicureans

Taking their name and inspiration from Epicurus (ca. 342–270), his disciples honored the way in which he had looked at life with a hard eye, rejecting popular religion with its superstitions, unmasking all the terrors before which mortals quail, emphasizing a rational ethic, spurning the easy hedonism of momentary pleasure.

Epicurus speaks forthrightly, unconventionally, pragmatically:

> The just person is most free from trouble,
> the unjust most full of trouble.[17]

And what is justice?

> Justice never is anything in itself,
> but in the dealings of persons with one another...
> it is a kind of compact not to harm or be harmed.[18]

He scoffs at the suspicious rigorism so common among moralists:

No pleasure is a bad thing in itself:
but the means which produce some pleasures bring with them
disturbances many times greater than the pleasures themselves.[19]

Epicurus draws a distinction between the realism of the pleasure he commends and the unreflective hedonism of those who would cast off all restraints:

It is not possible to live pleasantly
without living prudently and honourably and justly,
nor again to live a life of prudence, honour, and justice
without living pleasantly.
And the person who does not possess the pleasant life
is not living prudently and honourably and justly,
and the person who does not possess the virtuous life,
cannot live pleasantly.[20]

Like their founder, the Epicureans of the first century laid responsibility for human destiny squarely on the individual. The gods, they said, play no part in human affairs. Rather, each person must take charge of one's own life and make wise decisions with a view to the largest degree of pleasure or satisfaction open to one in the circumstances. As the supreme virtue, which requires unremitting intellectual honesty, the Epicureans commended imperturbability (*ataraxy*) in the spirit of their master when he observed:

In a philosophical discussion he who is worsted
gains more in proportion as he learns more.[21]

Less reliant on street-corner speakers than Cynics and Stoics, the Epicureans put up statues of their founder in public places, hoping to attract kindred spirits to their philosophy of materialism and sensationalism. Their most eloquent advocate was the Roman poet Lucretius (ca. 99–55 B.C.E.), who celebrated the liberation of Epicurus from religion:

He longed the Gate
To burst of this low prison of our fate.
By "the living ardour of his mind" he labored to make us see
At last what can, what cannot, come to be.[22]

Stoics

The Stoic tradition began with Zeno (ca. 336–ca. 264), a disciple of Crates "the gentle Cynic." In the face of all life's vicissitudes Zeno cultivated *apatheia*, indifference to one's personal fortune, as the way of deliverance from fear and desire. He affirmed that Right Reason (*orthos logos*) is the same as Zeus; from that concept came the Roman idea of universal law before which all persons are equal. A line from the great Stoic hymn to Zeus by Cleanthes (300?–220?), quoted in the Lukan account of Paul's preaching at Athens (Acts 17:28), sings the high concept of human dignity justifying Stoic individualism.

From thee we spring, with reasoned speech endowed.[23]

In the spirit of Socrates Zeno infused into philosophy "a quite un-Greek passion for righteousness and zeal for conversion."[24] He and his disciple Chrysippus (280–206), who systematized Stoic ideas, established the diatribe as an important form of public discussion among the philosophical élite. Their successors in the Augustan age brought Stoicism to popular audiences, commending the four cardinal virtues of wisdom, courage, self-control, and justice. As a youth in Tarsus, Saul, later called Paul, might hear them (and Cynics also) haranguing in the streets of his city.

The "courageous…idealism"[25] of the tradition inspired Posidonius (135?–51?), counted the leading mind of the century before Christ, to write a universal history, giving intellectual substance to the new ecumenical ideal emerging from the broad reach of Alexander's empire and the enlargement of Roman experience across the world. Pompey and Cicero heard Posidonius lecture, and in his mature philosophical works Cicero advocates the doctrine of universal law. Parallels to Stoic thinking appear in the Wisdom tradition of Hellenistic Judaism and in the thought of the Apostle Paul, though which may have influenced the other is a question yet unsettled. Clearly, however, elements of Stoicism appealed to the nobler minds of the age, including some Christians; the influence of Posidonius reached to Augustine and Jerome.[26]

Even so, the great first-century authority on rhetoric characterized the early Stoics as "shrewd thinkers rather than striking orators, which indeed they never aimed at being…[They] indulged their eloquence comparatively little."[27] Their zeal was for morality and truth, not the dazzling effects of clever speech-making. Later in this chapter we shall consider two well known Stoic orators, Dio[n] of Prusa and Epictetus, as moralists.

Skeptics

In contrast with the moral earnestness of Cynics, Epicureans, and Stoics, a more permissive and speculative type of orator appeared under the banner of the New Academy. In 155 B.C.E. Carneades (214–129) had come to Rome retailing his dogmas that no truth can be known with certainty, that the most one can claim for any assertion is probability. As old as the original Academy of Socrates, the doctrine had enjoyed periods of recurrent vitality, and Cicero was persuaded. Before he advanced to Stoicism, he set forth the skeptical argument in a set of dialogs under the title *Academica*. Offering no salvation, only despair of ever knowing truth, such thinking led to moral nihilism, but it provided occasion for much disputation and appealed to persons chafing under old restraints. Skeptics championed intellectual freedom and forthright rationality, whatever the consequences.

+

Despite the differences among the various schools, the philosophers impressed the people who heard them as free minds with the courage to call into question prevailing assumptions and in most cases to urge people to a nobler way of living. No wonder that the Gospel of Thomas, recounting the question of Jesus to his disciples, "Tell me what I am like," attributes to Matthew the answer, "You are like a wise philosopher."[28]

Psychological and Exegetical Insights

The philosophers of all the schools pursued compelling intellectual interests, some pressing more toward existential, others more toward speculative, concerns. Inevitably their reflection led to questions about traditional religion with its exuberance of myths about gods and goddesses. In undertaking to say what these ancient anthropomorphic tales "really mean," the philosophers moved to psychological insights suggested by symbolic or allegorical interpretation. (We have already seen Zeno identifying Zeus with Right Reason.) They undertook to affirm in terminology more precise—or abstract— than the language of religion the truth they discerned in the myths, and also to warn forthrightly against false perceptions of reality conveyed in the old stories.

They developed an allegorical exegesis of Homer that enabled them to use the epics from the archaic age as guidebooks for right living. Thus *The Odyssey* was read not just as the adventure of an ancient hero, much less as an account to be taken literally, with its one-eyed giant and sailors turned into swine, but as a representation of the human journey through life, a *Pilgrim's Progress* long before Bunyan.

A degree of allegorical interpretation could commend itself to general audiences, but when the critical mode denied old understandings too explicitly, hearers grew uneasy. The speakers faced two types of audience—the mass of plain folk with their practical concerns and a smaller group of intellectuals who found pleasure in sophisticated speculation—and few could satisfy both. So Strabo (63? B.C.E.–C.E. 24?) acknowledged, "Philosophy…is for the few, whereas poetry is more useful to the people at large."[29]

Popular Suspicion of Philosophy

Philosophy lives a precarious existence. When they press the war against poetry by undercutting traditional beliefs too forthrightly, philosophers suffer. Popular prejudice takes up 'sophist' and 'sophistry' as terms of reproach, viewing them with that suspicion which recurrently breaks out among plain folk against professors or intellectuals. The philosophers bring it on themselves. When their enterprise becomes an intellectual game, high seriousness sometimes gives way to an irresponsible playing with great issues. Popular champions of accepted belief then make war upon the skeptical denial that truth may be known and the easy dismissal of moral precepts.

In times of uncertainty some grow uneasy at even cautiously stated reservations concerning the literal truth of the sacred tradition. Many persons of the Augustan age who longed for a word of salvation turned away, not having heard from the philosophers the answer they longed for. But speakers of another kind seemed to offer a more acceptable message. These were the preachers of the the "mysteries," religions which exerted a powerful appeal throughout the Hellenistic world.

MISSIONARY MYSTAGOGUES[30]

Emptiness of the Old Faiths and Appeal of the Mysteries

The disappearance of the city-state had drained the traditional religions of their power. Their public function had been related to the life of the *polis*, and now the *polis* was gone, its political life reduced to trivial decisions, the responsibilities once handled by its institutions of state absorbed into the autocratic and impersonal processes of empire. The imposing shell of the old religions endured; for three centuries after Augustus the Caesars continued to erect dazzling temples to the gods, paying the builders with public funds. But the shell was hollow.

Both Greeks and Romans had worshiped a company of gods and goddesses whose names can be more or less equated (Zeus=Jupiter, Hera=Juno, Ares=Mars, Athene=Minerva, Aphrodite=Venus, etc.). The list of minor deities ran on endlessly, each being related to some human need or activity, so that common folk, whom philosophers regarded as superstitious, had a special god or goddess to invoke with every move they made.[31]

But ordinary folk, though they maintained the form of the traditional observances, now experienced them as irrelevant, feeling the emptiness, even if they had not, like some philosophers, rejected the old faith intellectually. They "believed," but the civic reality in which that old faith had been rooted no longer existed. Unable to articulate the problem, much less think through an explanation, they struggled with uncertainty that may have fueled the popular hostility toward the sophists, for philosophers seemed bent on taking away the little faith they could still muster. That gone, what would be left to cling to?

In that time of spiritual emptiness the mystery religions seemed to give promise of filling the void,[32] offering initiation into the divine life of a god and a promise of immortality. Some of the mysteries had roots in Greece's far past; others were more recent imports from Egypt or Asia. It was not an intellectual problem for polytheists to introduce yet another deity alongside, or in place of, the gods they had previously worshiped; as best we can tell, doctrine and practice were strikingly syncretistic. Thousands responded eagerly to the appeal which the mysteries directed to the individual. These religions offered personal salvation, symbolized by and effected through secret rites, along with the secret teachings; both rite and teaching constituted the "mystery." Ceremonies were attended by women as well as men, religious observance providing the major occasion when respectable Greek women gathered in public.

With colorful processions, flaring torches, dramatic liturgies, fasting and other deprivations, purifications, sacraments, display of holy relics, a sacred "passion play," personal attention to the neophyte from one's own mystagogue or sponsor who imparted the secrets, and the exhilaration of being surrounded by thousands of worshipers, the Eleusinian initiation was colorful, impressive, lengthy, and sometimes trying. Commonly it produced a highly charged emotional experience, bringing both release from tension and a sense of inner assurance.

The Various Mysteries

People generally knew something about the various mysteries, as today they may have impressions, more or less accurate, concerning a number of different denominations. But because the newly popular religions centered in secret ceremonies to which converts were admitted only after swearing fearsome oaths not to divulge them, public information was limited and impressionistic. It still is.

Some of the cults had flourished for centuries, notably the Eleusinian mysteries with the torch-lit procession from Athens to the celebrated shrine fourteen miles away. So famous was Eleusis that in the time of the emperors it had become de rigueur for celebrities to travel there for initiation.

The cult of Dionysus, which lasted for centuries and gained adherents throughout the Mediterranean world, induced ecstasy through intoxication and frenzied dancing, spiritual techniques employed in the archaic past by shamans and, in the case of the dance, by the first prophets of Israel nearly a thousand years before the Caesars.

The reformed Orphic tradition cultivated rationality and sought identification with the god through asceticism rather than frenzy. The initiation alone could not assure deliverance, but had to be followed by a "complete Orphic life" of purity and self-denial. Only thus could one hope that one's "soul, by the intervention of divine grace, would free itself of the original impurity, would escape the Great Circle of Necessity, and the ever-recurring, weary cycle of rebirth, would attain redemption, and become 'God from *human being*.'"[33]

Relatively recent imports to Greece and Italy were the cults of the Great Mother (*Magna Mater*), the Phrygian religion of Cybele and Attis, and the Egyptian mystery of Isis and Osiris, each with its myth of a dying and rising god. "The cult of Isis, unlike any previous cult, was not for the benefit of the state, but to meet the religious and emotional needs of individuals. Isis promised healing, blessing, sympathy, and understanding for her devotees' sorrow and pain, for she herself had lost a son."[34] The ritual of this religion helped worshipers come to terms with the "different world" in which they must now live; it also emphasized the importance of "the marital couple as the central social unit."[35]

Most popular among the Roman legions was Mithraism, a derivative of Persian Zoroastrianism. Coming to Rome with captives taken by Pompey, it sustained a vigorous missionary effort and spread widely.

Instruction and Proclamation

The mysteries were not meant to be preached; though the ceremonies made sufficient public display to awaken general curiosity, officials rigorously enforced the dread vows of secrecy, with threats of dire consequences for those guilty of disclosure. As a result, such proclamation as may have occurred during the celebrations, whether ritual recital or address prepared for a specific occasion, is almost totally unkown to us.

ELEUSINIAN RITUAL. In preparation for the initiation at Eleusis the chief priest of Demeter, known as the *hierophant*, and the official next in rank, the torch-bearer (*dadoukos*), composed a proclamation (*prorrhesis*), which the sacred herald (*hierokérux*), evidently chosen for the power of his voice, read to the awestruck multitude. (In early Christian writings *kérux*=herald is the word for *preacher*.)

The public proclamation preceding initiation warned against making known the sacred secrets or approaching the sacrament without due reverence and fear. The herald may have preached demands something like these:

> Everyone who has clean hands and intelligible speech,
> who is pure from all pollution and whose soul is conscious of no evil
> and who has lived well and justly.[36]

Only such a person was eligible to go forward with the initiation. All others were warned to abstain. The religion involved ethics as well as liturgy.

At Eleusis great importance was attached to the relics (*deiknymena*) disclosed to the initiates and the sacred words (*legomena* or *hieroi logoi*) of the mystery disclosed by the hierophant. One devotee dreamed of following the proceedings with care but not being able to hear the secret sayings; consequently the inititation was ruled invalid.

DIOTIMA'S TEACHING. Of all the spiritually elevated speech of antiquity few passages equal in beauty or influence the instruction given to Socrates by Diotima, prophetess at Mantinea and his mystagogue at his initiation into the mystery. In one of his most memorable passages, Plato recounts the master's presentation of her teaching to his friends.[37]

> All creation or passage of non-being into being is poetry or making,
> and the processes of all art are creative,

and the masters of arts are all poets or makers...
Still...you know that they are not called poets, but have other names;
only that portion of the art which is separated off from the rest,
and is concerned with music and metre, is termed poetry,
and they who possess poetry in this sense of the word are called poets.

Noting her hearer's assent, Diotima makes her point by analogy:

The same holds of love.
For you may say generally that all desire of good and happiness
is only the great and subtle power of love;
but they who are drawn towards the god by any other path
...are not called lovers—
the name of the whole is appropriated to those
whose affection takes one form only—
they alone are said to love, or to be lovers.

The teacher moves on toward the heart of the matter.

... there is nothing which mortals love but the good.

This line of argument leads to a pointed conclusion:

Love may be described generally
as the love of the everlasting possession of the good.

Diotima now shifts from speaking of the good to speaking of
beauty, "whether of body or soul," urging that one who would go
beyond "the lesser mysteries of love"

should begin in youth to visit beautiful forms;
and first, if...guided...aright, to love one such form only

and out of that to "create fair thoughts"; and soon to perceive

that the beauty of one form is akin to the beauty of another;
and then...to recognize that the beauty in every form
is one and the same!

So the spiritual pilgrim

will become a lover of all beautiful forms,

then will consider that

the beauty of the mind is more honourable
than the beauty of the outward form.

The spiritual quest will lead one

> to contemplate and see the beauty of institutions and laws...
> [to] go on to the sciences, that one may see their beauty...
> until on that shore...at last the vision is revealed...
> of a single science, the science of beauty everywhere.

At length the seeker

> who has been instructed thus far in the things of love,
> and who has learned to see the beautiful
> in due order and succession...
> toward the end will suddenly perceive a nature of wondrous beauty...
> a nature which in the first place is everlasting,
> not growing and decaying, or waxing and waning;
> secondly, not fair in one point of view and foul in another...
> but beauty absolute, separate, simple, and everlasting,
> which without diminution and without increase, or any change,
> is imparted to the ever-growing and perishing beauties
> of all other things.
> The one who from these ascending under the influence of true love,
> begins to perceive that beauty, is not far from the end...
> and at last knows what the essence of beauty is.

Diotima's instruction concerning God as ultimate beauty, to be apprehended in the ascent of love, was destined to stand for centuries as foundational text in mysticism—for Neoplatonic philosophers, for Christian ascetics in the tradition of St. Augustine, for the Florentine Platonists of the Renaissance, and for more recent pilgrims of the spiritual journey. Addressed to a single neophyte under personal tutelage, it was not public proclamation. But cast in Plato's deathless prose, it reads almost like a profound and haunting sermon, suggesting what preaching in the mysteries might have been. Few sermons have probed the human spirit with keener insight. In later times it would inspire mystical contemplation and evoke from those who pondered its insights a noble literature of spiritual aspiration and sublime preaching.

DIVINE SELF-PREDICATION. Some of the mysteries went public. In Egypt a traveler from Asia Minor, impressed by an inscription on a stele erected before the temple of Hephaistos in Memphis, copied the words that the goddess Isis was believed to have spoken:

I am Isis, the mistress of every land,
and I was taught by Hermes, and with Hermes I devised letters...
I gave and ordained laws for mortals, that no one is able to change...
I am she that findeth fruit for men...
I am she that is called goddess by women...
I divided the earth from the heaven.
I showed the paths of the stars.
I ordered the course of the sun and the moon...
I brought together woman and man...
I ordained that parents should be loved by children...
I revealed mysteries unto mortals.
I taught them to honor the images of the gods...
I broke down the government of tyrants...
I made the right to be stronger than gold and silver.
I ordained that the true should be thought good.
I devised marriage contracts.
I assigned to the Greeks and barbarians their languages...
With me the right prevails.[38]

The form is that of self-predication, with Isis listing her works, as gods were wont to do. (The list is called her aretalogy.) Did the goddess first speak these words through an inspired prophet? Or were they composed more reflectively by a priest-theologian who prepared a text for the artisan? Whatever the answer, we have here a dazzling sample of preaching, a public proclamation concerning the deity worshiped in the mystery religion of Isis and Osiris.

+

The mysteries also prompted "preaching" of an earthier sort. Their emphasis on a profound sense of the numinous and intense religious experience attracted a colorful crew of charismatic figures who gave the impression of being in direct touch with the divine. Their behavior gave a new lease on life to a powerful strain in the old piety, which since archaic times had venerated the ecstatic, sought the voice of the gods in oracles, and astounded the simple with miracles.

The world of the first Caesars teemed with "seers, astrologers, spiritualists, exorcists," and wonder-workers.[39] Some seem to have been authentic visionaries in a tradition as old as primitive shamanism, bringing healing insight to troubled spirits. Some larded their speech with a portentous philosophical vocabulary, with varying degrees of understanding and illumination. Some were outright quacks, exploiting the credulous, and the charlatans may well have constituted the majority.

Everywhere fakirs and gurus appeared, offering new roads to salvation.[40] Though not bound to service at any local shrine, these new preachers presented themselves as priests—and prophets as well, speaking ecstatically, giving out predictions, dazzling their hearers with miracles. In such a context some "itinerant practitioners"[41] achieved popular repute as "divine persons," i.e., human beings in whom a god was manifestly present. Appolonius of Tyana and Jesus of Nazareth won such acclaim, though there were those who charged that the latter was in league with demons. Less savory were the "mystery mongers" dubbed *Orpheotelestai*, who claimed to know the sacred rituals and formulas of the Orphics, which promised safe passage through the underworld after death; these unscrupulous operators hawked hope of redemption, shamelessly squeezing large sums from the bereaved and the fearful willing to pay for the knowledge. Scandalized by the travesty, true Orphics had nothing to do with them, and thoughtful people generally held them in contempt.

Yet the response of thousands of seekers to the message of the mystagogues measures the intensity of the spiritual hunger of the masses unfed by the lingering cults of the old divinities.

Gnosticism[42]

A remarkably appealing and elaborate compound of notions from various religions, spiced with a pretentious philosophical vocabulary, came to be known as Gnosticism. Emerging at roughly the same time as Christianity, perhaps within some Christian communities, it competed with the church for converts, absorbed important Christian elements, permeated the Christian movement in a number of forms ultimately declared heretical, and persisted for several centuries in an assortment of sects. Tossing up a mixed salad of terms plucked from mysticism and philosophy, but uncontrolled by any rigor of method, it posited a metaphysical dualism of matter and spirit, darkness and light, evil and good, and prescribed for salvation a mode of escape from the prison house of matter into the freedom of pure spirit.

Able and persuasive advocates proclaimed this faith through the lands around the Mediterranean and produced an abundant literature, most of which the Christians destroyed after their victory. The largest extant body of Gnostic writings, the Nag-Hammadi texts, derives from a Christian Gnostic library buried near the close of the fourth century; it will be considered in chapter 16.

The best-known form of early Gnosticism, with preachers at work around the empire, is the religion of the Hermes Trismegistus. (The title *Thrice-Greatest Hermes* designated a divine revealer, identified by some students of the text with the Egyptian god Thoth.) Some writings from this eclectic faith are extant, dated by scholars to the second century or possibly earlier and preserving an older oral tradition.

One of these, "Poimandres," recounts a revelation in which the deity under that name—it means "the knowledge of God"—commissioned the prophet to make known the way of salvation as ascent from the body of fallen human nature so as to enter at last into God. Then, says the prophet,

> I began to preach to mortals the beauty of piety and knowledge:
> "O peoples, earth-born mortals, who have given yourselves up
> to drunkenness and sleep and to ignorance of God,
> be sober, cease your orgies,
> bewitched as you are by irrational sleep."[43]

Appealing to the same hopes and fears that drew many to the mysteries, devotees of Gnosticism preached widely, in public and in private, issuing an urgent call to repentance. Both their activities and their vocabulary show striking parallels with Christianity, though demonstrable influence, especially its direction, remains uncertain.

Impact of the Mysteries

The great number of mystagogues preaching their various faiths throughout the first-century world signals a widespread longing for a form of belief more satisfying than the myths of the traditional religions or the open questions of the philosophers. People shifting away from a mood of skepticism and toward readiness to believe in the survival of the soul after death sought convincing assurance such as the mysteries promised.

Experimenting with various religions, men and women sometimes professed several at the same time. The mysteries offered salvation by initiating converts into a relationship with a friendly god. They upheld a code of virtuous behavior and conveyed a sense of personal worth. In one of his dialogues Cicero has one of his interlocutors declare,

> In the mysteries we learn
> not only to live happily but to die with fairer hope.[44]

Among persons sober by nature and ethically concerned who turned inquiringly to the eastern religions an interest in Judaism emerged. (See Part Two.) The early Christian preachers directly addressed many of the needs that turned people to the mysteries, and they found in the mystagogues their greatest rivals. (Acts 8 presents Simon Magus as the type of this opposition.)

The preachers of the philosophical schools, the mysteries, emergent Gnosticism, missionary Judaism, and Christianity shared an extensive spiritual vocabulary in common and thought in strikingly similar concepts—though the Christians caused scandal by repudiating all gods except one. The fervent preaching of varied messengers of salvation, either philosophical or religious, constituted a noteworthy proportion of the oratory of the first-century world.

POPULAR MORALISTS AS ORATORS[45]

Introduction

Among the considerable number of popular "preachers" leaving a literary legacy sufficient for us to know them as thinkers and advocates is a company of moralists who combined with spiritual sensitivity a commitment to serious reflection and to the virtuous life, determined to carry these concerns to the public rather than while away their time in rarefied discussions with other intellectuals or court the adulation of the masses in empty displays of rhetorical virtuosity.

While some of the popular moralists showed interest in the mysteries, their emphasis fell not on mysticism but on character. If they did not attain the stature of the classic exemplary orators as symbols of the rhetorical tradition, they remarkably foreshadowed the role of the Christian preacher. Their speeches, tracts, and letters make up a significant part of our ethical heritage from antiquity, and the number of hearers who listened respectfully to their pleading in the marketplaces indicates a widespread aspiration for upright living.

Half a century after Augustus Caesar's rise to the principate, there began a series of quiet and unspectacular "conversions" from rhetoric to philosophy. (See "The Socratic Heritage," in chapter 2.) Increasingly frustrated by the hollow ring of that public oratory that exhausted itself in flattery or clever appeals to plausibility in courts of law, some notable and talented speakers transferred their affections from the pursuit of celebrity through eloquence to the quest for wisdom and virtue.

Seneca

First in time was Lucius Annaeus Seneca (4 B.C.E.–65 C.E.), son of a famous teacher of rhetoric. Inspired by the example of Diogenes, Seneca the Younger turned in revulsion from the highly spiced dishes concocted by the ceremonial orators to the meager diet of an ascetic and then to the plain bread of Stoicism. Bitingly, he deplored the prostitution of rhetorical skill:

> Some have presented their beauty for sale,
> some their eloquence for sale.[46]

Seneca raised serious ethical questions about slavery and condemned the murderous gladiatorial games. Despite his exclusively moral interest in literature, he has been faulted for too highflown a style in his philosophical speeches. They nevertheless gained the attention of audiences who would have walked away from lectures in a purely philosophical mode. Cicero had considered the Stoic orators of his time to be dry, "too precise, and not at all adapted to engage the attention of the common people."[47] Seneca's flourish, like his restraint, was deliberate; in his letters he offers pointed comments on the manner of speaking he considers appropriate to the philosopher. Even more important

> is the highest duty and the highest proof of wisdom—
> that deed and word should be in accord.[48]

Appointed tutor to the young Nero and honored with the public title of his "friend," he poured his hopes into an oration "On Mercy" (*De clementia*), presumably prepared for his charge to deliver in the Senate on assuming the principate.[49] Nero disappointed him bitterly, but the accession of Nerva in 96 C.E. began a line of Caesars profoundly committed to Stoic principles.

Philosopher, moralist, tragedian, Seneca the Younger was one of the few pagans whose works early Christians came to honor; the medievals valued a compilation of purported correspondence between him and the apostle Paul, and John Calvin's first literary work was a commentary on the *De clementia*.

Apollonius of Tyana

A celebrated holy man, miracle worker, and preacher of morality who traveled the world in the latter half of the first century, Apollonius of Tyana was a teacher of philosophy instrumental in a Pythagorean revival. He is known through a collection of his epistles and an admonitory biography, which might be characterized as pagan hagiography, published early in the third century. It sets forth various episodes in his career as a wandering teacher, including exchanges with hecklers and the exorcism of a devil from a licentious youth. It paints an idyllic picture of the orator addressing the crowd from the platform of the temple at Olympia, commending "wisdom and courage and temperance, and…all the virtues."[50] Though his discourses resulted in an increase of popular zeal for the worship of the gods, he was refused initiation into the Eleusinian mysteries. But legend gathered about his name.

It is proper for a sage, Apollonius is reported to have said, to converse like a law-giver,

> for it is the duty of the law-giver to deliver to the many
> the instructions of whose truth he has persuaded himself.[51]

Such conversation, he warned, requires restraint:

> Loquacity has many pitfalls, but silence none.[52]

In a letter to a traveling preacher who made appearances in major cities from Syria to Italy, clad like a philosopher and affecting a long white beard, Apollonius excoriated him for profiteering, accusing him of returning home "with a full cargo of silver, of gold, of vases of all sorts, of embroidered raiment, of every other sort of ornament, not to mention overweening pride, and boasting and unhappiness." He reminded the reprobate that Zeno never bought anything but dried fruits.[53]

In his philosophizing Apollonius demonstrated theological insight and a prophetic spirit:

> In no other manner, I believe,
> can one exhibit a fitting respect for the divine being…
> than by refusing to offer any victim at all to God
> whom we termed First, who is One and separate from all,
> to whom we must recognize all the rest as subordinate;
> to Him we must not kindle fire
> or make promise to Him of any sensible object at all.
> For He needs nothing even from beings higher than ourselves.
> Nor is there any plant or animal which earth sends up or nourishes,
> to which some pollution is not incident.
> We should make use in relation to Him solely of the higher speech,
> I mean of that speech which does not issue from the lips;

and from the noblest of beings
we must ask for blessings by the noblest faculty we possess,
and that faculty is intelligence, which needs no organ.[54]

Apollonius left with posterity the impression of a wise man, a man of holiness, healing power, and forthright speech.

+

In the last quarter of the century appeared a quartet of distinguished moralists who used the medium of oratory as the means of extending their influence. All were born between 40 and 50 C.E. and lived to the year 120 or thereabouts.

Though not himself famed as a speaker, Quintilian (40–118?) was the classical world's supreme teacher of the art; his book on the education of the orator, with its concern for the character of the pupil, profoundly influenced the schools of western Europe for centuries. The three other members of this remarkable group of contemporaries were Dio[n] of Prusa (40–120), Plutarch (ca. 45–125), and Epictetus (ca. 50–120).

Dio of Prusa

Enamored of the elaborate rhetoric which went under the name of the Second Sophistic, Dio went in for archaisms and other artificialities of style. His scores of orations—eighty are extant—earned wide acclaim and, for him, the appellation *Chrysostom*, Golden Mouth. His sophistical speeches include showpieces like a lament for Nero, praise of a parrot, and a demonstration that, Homer to the contrary notwithstanding, the Greeks did not capture Troy, legendary home of Rome's founders.

Some of Dio's orations, however, are more serious, dealing with criticism of art and literature; *On Training for Public Speaking,* for example, sets forth a program of reading for the aspiring orator. Enthusiastically he celebrates the art:

For when people are afraid,
what does more to inspire them than the spoken word?
And when they wax insolent and uplifted in spirit,
what more effectively brings them down and chastens them?
What has greater influence
in keeping them from indulging their desires?
Whose admonitions do they endure more meekly than the person's
whose speech delights them?[55]

These speeches derive from the period before his conversion to philosophy under the Stoic teacher Musonius. After the downfall of his patron, Dio spent fourteen years as a wandering philosopher, banished from Rome in 82 C.E., and holding forth wherever he could find an audience. A number of the orations now bear the name of the townsfolk whom he addressed across Asia Minor, including two to the people of Tarsus.

Dio's most impressive speeches dealt with moral themes; they have been called "gems of homiletic literature."[56] Four of these, apparently addressed to Trajan after Dio had returned to Rome, speak from the Cynic-Stoic tradition to extol the ideal of the emperor as servant of the common good.[57]

Dio had a keen eye for the color of daily life, a sure sensitivity to the reaction of his audiences, a sense of drama that made him particularly effective with dialog, a capacity for breaking tension by playful sallies, and a gift for the telling use of humor. His extensive learning provided him with a great store of examples. Though not a profound intellectual, Dio came across as a man of intense moral earnestness dealing with important themes.

Plutarch

The most finished intellectual among the moralistic orators was the Greek essayist Plutarch. With an encyclopedic knowledge of the cultural and literary heritage gained from wide reading and from travel to Athens, Rome, and possibly Alexandria, he counted the leading Romans of his time among his circle of friends.

Yet he chose to live in provincial Chaeronea, holding a municipal office, serving as a priest at Delphi, and addressing his public as a writer. Though most of his pieces come to us in essay form, they are obviously rhetorical, easily convertible to or from speeches.

Plutarch praised Pericles and Cato for nobility of character, hailing the latter as "the Roman Demosthenes."[58] He ranged widely over many themes: childhood, education, advice to a couple about to be married, the virtue of women, condolence to the bereaved, friendship, virtue and vice, kindness to animals, the study of poetry, the art of listening to lectures, public affairs, the civic responsibility of philosophers.[59]

He also took on theological topics (e.g., the delay of divine retribution), defended values in the traditional cult, and challenged various schools of philosophy. In his *Parallel Lives* he helped fix the place of Demosthenes and Cicero as exemplary orators in the western tradition. And in his work on Isis and Osiris he perpetuated the belief of Isocrates and Cicero in the orator as the original civilizer of the race.

> One of the first acts related of Osiris…was to deliver the Egyptians
> from their destitute and brutish manner of living.
> This he did by showing them the fruits of cultivation,
> by giving them laws, and by teaching them to honour the gods.
> Later he traveled over the whole earth,
> civilizing it without the slightest need of arms,
> but most of the peoples he won over to his way
> by the charm of his persuasive discourse,
> combined with song and all manner of music.[60]

Epictetus

Brought to Rome from Phrygia as a slave, Epictetus was granted his freedom. He studied under the Stoic Musonius (who had converted Dio of Prusa) and became himself a philosopher of repute. When Domitian expelled the philosophers from Rome, Epictetus crossed the Adriatic and set up in Nicopolis as a teacher. There he could possibly have heard one of the first evangelists of the Christian faith, when Epaphras evangelized Colossae and its neighboring towns. Considered the most religious of the Stoic philosophers, Epictetus accepted his lameness with equanimity.

His *Discourses* (four books are extant of the eight books of notes taken by a student) have been characterized as "informal homilies on the conduct of life."[61]

Epictetus spoke with high seriousness, a clarity that kept hearers following his argument, and an aphoristic mode of speech that has made him eminently quotable: His reverence for God as understood in the Stoic-Cynic tradition issued in a doctrine of divine providence and belief in a reasonable universe. He proposed a secret of serenity:

> Ask not that events should happen as you will,
> but let your will be that events should happen as they do,
> and you shall have peace…
> When anything happens to you, always turn to yourself and ask
> what faculty you have to deal with it.[62]

He was adept at helping people see through self-deception:

Be not elated at an excellence which is not your own.
If the horse in his pride were to say, "I am handsome,"
we could bear with it.
But when you say with pride, "I have a handsome horse,"
know that the good horse is the ground of your pride.[63]

He also had the gift of keeping things in perspective. To a prospective patron he spoke plainly:

I am richer than you. *I* don't care what Caesar thinks of me.
I flatter no one. This is what I have instead of your silver or gold plate.
You have *silver* vessels, but *earthenware* reasons, principles, appetites...
All your possessions seem small to you, mine seem great to me.
Your desire is insatiate, mine is satisfied.[64]

Epictetus' sense of vocation to declare the truth speaks for all the moralist preachers:

The true Cynic...must know that he is sent as a messenger
from God to mortals concerning things good and evil,
to show them that they have gone astray
and are seeking the true nature of good and evil
where it is not to be found, and take no thought where it really is.
He must realize, in the words of Diogenes when brought before Philip
after the battle of Chaeronea, that he is sent "to reconnoitre."
For indeed the Cynic has to discover
what things are friendly to mortals and what are hostile:
and when he has accurately made his observations
he must return and report the truth,
not driven by fear to point out enemies where there are none,
nor in any other way disturbed or confounded by his impressions.
He must then be able, if chance so offer
to come forward on the tragic stage,
and with a loud voice utter the words of Socrates:
    "O race of mortals, whither are ye hurrying?
    What are you doing, miserable creatures?
    You wander up and down like blind folk:
    you have left the true path and go away on a vain errand,
    you seek peace and happiness elsewhere,
    where it is not to be found, and believe not
    when another shows you the way."[65]

Standing with solitary courage against an unseeing populace, "the classical orator is a fighter in a lonely contest."[66]

CONCLUSION

By the end of the century in which Christianity emerged a strange cultural reversal had occurred: Speechmaking, which had established itself as a central instrument of public life in the free societies of Greece and Rome had now, to a large extent, lost its old deliberative function. Under the Caesars the oratory of state served not to debate political issues for decision by the citizenry, but to celebrate the glory of the emperor. The art of rhetoric still held a place in the schools, and educated citizens had developed skills of speech, but the opportunity to use them called for displays of virtuosity.

Yet the obverse side of the coin showed an unexpected face: The most vital oratory now was coming, not from politicians, but from persons concerned with the inner life, for whom speechmaking was less a matter of personal advancement than of opening a way of salvation. Though some mystagogues and knaves employed trickery to gain wealth and adulation, the philosophers and moralists had not turned to speechmaking for the money.

The language of religion and ethics, for so long a matter of cultic repetition, now infused the most vital public address. The appearance of the Christian preachers would enhance that vitality. So we turn now to consider the development of the art of rhetoric, which the preachers could not and did not ignore.

CHAPTER 3

Rhetoric and Humane Education[1]

ORIGINS OF RHETORIC[2]

After the Greeks in colonial Sicily had overthrown their tyrant and established democracy in 472 B.C.E., the unrest attending social change produced a great amount of litigation. Citizens haled into court looked for instruction in oratory in order to plead their cause. A Sicilian Greek named Corax and his pupil Tisias responded by compiling manuals on rhetoric, the art (*techné*) of persuasion, giving attention to argument and to the ordering of a speech. Thus began the characteristic Greek practice of analyzing in formal treatise the basic principles of a discipline.[3] The study of rhetoric soon came to dominate the tradition of classical education.

MASTERS OF THE DISCIPLINE

Gorgias

In 427 B.C.E. the Sicilian rhetorician Gorgias (485?–380?) arrived in Athens and opened a school, proposing to teach young men how to speak. Aiming to create a prose style marked by the color, vividness, and emotional power of poetry, he promoted the use of those poetic devices with which his teacher, Empedocles of Agrigentum, had adorned public address. These rhetorical ornaments of style became for centuries substantive elements in education. Gorgias recommended parallelism (use of symmetrical clauses), antithesis (parallelism with a negative twist, either grammatical or conceptual), alliteration, assonance (the calculated repetition of a similar sound in a series of words), and an occasional use of rhyme. He laid emphasis on figures of speech, especially metaphor. His contemporary

Thrasymachus also advocated rhythmic prose, "correctness" in language, and the periodic sentence, which builds suspense as it moves through a series of delays to a dramatic climax. He compiled an *Art of Rhetoric*.

The label *sophist* affected by the rhetoricians literally meant *wise person* or *expert*, but the mental gymnastics of some shysters soon gave a pejorative twist to the term. While the "wisdom" peddled by the sophists undertook to furnish the keys to success in pleading cases at law, some who claimed the title gave the impression of lacking in seriousness. (Our slang term *wise guy* expresses a common opinion of them.) In the face of popular prejudice even Socrates and then Isocrates had found it necessary to defend their vocation as intellectuals—like American professors from time to time. Yet despite the critique of the discerning and the dullness of the uncomprehending, the trade flourished.[4]

It is not known if Gorgias wrote a technical manual, but his teaching gained a large following in Athens. "The Greek delight in the sound of words is of the same sort as the Italian delight in arias and coloratura"; speechmaking now became a recognized art form with "virtuoso technique" that attracted knowing and enthusiastic audiences.[5] Wherever hearers and readers prize a finished style of prose, the influence of Gorgias continues.

Aspasia

Soon other teachers had set up shop in Athens, among them the eloquent Aspasia, who, defying the customs of patriarchy, boldly opened a school of rhetoric and philosophy for women. Despite her profession as *hetaira*, many daughters of good families came to listen to her instruction, as did respectable wives accompanied by their husbands, and leading men of the city. When Pericles took her into his home, she made it a gathering place of cultured celebrities who came to talk art and literature and philosophy and science. She had the mind for it, even if the exclusion of women from formal education may have denied opportunity to learn to read and write.[6] But conservative moralists, rival politicians, and comic dramatists attacked her for affront to Athenian propriety, and their assaults broke both the power and the health of Pericles. The guardians of tradition were not ready to admit a foreign woman, no matter how able, to participation in public life. Custom allowed no female rhetorician to attain major influence in classic times.

Aristotle

The immense popularity of rhetoric in Athens and the use of flashy tricks of speech by manipulators of the crowd prompted a negative reaction among the more thoughtful, and in the generation after Gorgias, philosophers tended to hold the art in contempt. But the greatest systematic mind among them, believing that the reaction had swung too far, undertook a series of lectures to give the study a proper place. The *Rhetoric* of Aristotle (384–322 B.C.E.) survives only in the notes of his students.

Aristotle defined rhetoric as "the faculty of observing in any given case the available means of persuasion" (I.2, 24);[7] it is a practical faculty, not a science (I.4, 35). Since it "exists to affect the giving of decisions" (II.1, 90), the particular hearers determine the "end and object" of any speech.

> Political speaking urges us either to do or not to do something...
> Forensic speaking either attacks or defends somebody...
> The ceremonial oratory of display
> either praises or censures somebody....
> The political orator is concerned with the future...
> The party in a case at law is concerned with the past...
> The ceremonial orator is...concerned with the present.   [I.3, 32]

Aristotle would not let the budding speaker forget that every address has a specific purpose, even the ceremonial oration:

> To praise someone is...akin to urging a course of action.

Consequently, whenever you want to praise anyone,

> think what you would urge people to do;
> and when you want to urge the doing of anything,
> think what you would praise a man for having done.   [I.9, 63–64]

The speaker necessarily deals with a particular audience, for a statement is not persuasive unless "there is somebody whom it persuades" (I.2, 27). Unlike the philosopher, however, who in reasoning with one's peers can assume a familiarity with and interest in the processes of dialectic, the orator addresses untrained hearers who reach their decisions less systematically (I.2, 27).

Aristotle consequently devotes major attention to the psychology of audiences. Besides offering a persuasive argument, "the orator must also make his own character look right and put his hearers who are to decide into the right frame of mind" (II.1, 90). He lists three things that, by inspiring "confidence in the orator's own character," induce the hearers "to believe a thing apart from any proof of it: good sense, good moral character, and goodwill" (II.1, 91). The *ethos* of the speaker, that is, the orator's character *as perceived by the audience,* is a crucial element in persuasion (I.2, 25).

Observing how feelings influence decision-making, he analyzes the emotions, considering how each is aroused and how it may serve the orator's purpose by affecting the judgments of the hearers (II.1, 91–92). He deals with various types of character (youth, age, wealth, power, etc.) and the appeal most effective with each.

From the psychology of public speaking, Aristotle moves to the modes of persuasion most effective with hearers. Some of these are nontechnical means—the citation of laws, the appeal to witnesses, and so on (I.14, 83–86). Among the arguments common to all oratory he lists certain "commonplaces" or topics (*topoi*): Possible and Impossible, Questions of Past Fact, Greatness and Smallness, and so forth. The topics give the orator a *place* to take hold of any kind of question (II.18–19, 129–132). These lead to the various "lines of proof and disproof" that one must consider in developing any case (II.22, 141 ff.); he gives an example of "buying the marsh with the salt" or *divarication,* turning an opponent's argument by affirming its opposite:

> The priestess enjoined upon her son not to take to public speaking:
> "For," she said, "if you say what is right, people will hate you;
> if you say what is wrong, the gods will hate you."

The reply might be,

> "On the contrary, you *ought* to take public speaking:
> for if you say what is right, the gods will love you;
> if you say what is wrong, people will love you."   [II.23, 150]

Aristotle presents two general modes of persuasion most adaptable to speaking: the example (illustration, analogy, fable) (II.20, 133–35) and the enthymeme. The latter is the orator's incomplete syllogism, which moves directly from a single premise to conclusion without boring the audience by tedious logical exercise; one form of it is the maxim, a simple conclusion memorably stated (II.21, 135–40). These persuasive procedures of rhetoric differ from the rigorous methods of dialectic, which are designed for logical demonstration (I.1, 19).

The master takes up more briefly those aspects of rhetoric which so largely occupied Gorgias and the conventional teachers, namely style, delivery, and arrangement.

> It is not enough to know *what* we ought to say;
> we must also say it *as* we ought.   [III.1, 164]

A good style must be both clear and appropriate (III.1, 167). The style of effective speech differs from that of literature designed to be read; it dramatizes by greater intensity, it keeps the listener with the speaker by the repetition of words and phrases (III.12, 196–99). But Gorgias is mistaken in thinking that poetical language is appropriate to oratory (III.1, 166). As a philosopher, Aristotle does not regard delivery as "an elevated subject of inquiry," insisting

> We ought in fairness to fight our case
> with no help beyond the bare facts.

But at least the speaker should try not to annoy the hearers, and a dramatic flair and good diction do favorably affect a speech's reception (III.1, 165–66).

As to arrangement, form follows function:

> A speech has two parts.
> You must state your case, and you must prove it.

Except for introduction and conclusion (epilogue), it needs nothing else (III.13, 199–200).

Though Aristotle's protest against stylistic fireworks persuaded few of the rhetoricians, his classification of the three kinds of rhetoric, his psychological analysis of audiences and the speaker's relation to them, and his procedures for developing arguments entered into the tradition.

Some two hundred years later Hermagoras of Temnos (2d century B.C.E.) produced an influential treatise that combined Aristotle's principles with the practical rhetoric of the old Athenians to produce a new system labeled "scholastic rhetoric." The manual soon came into use in Rome, where its influence began to counteract the florid Asianic style.

Rome: Greek Masters and Cato

After Crates of Mallos began public lectures on literature in Rome early in the second century B.C.E., the vogue of philhellenism led to an increasing demand for teachers from Greece. First came the *grammaticus,* often a slave, to tutor children in the works of the poets and interpret them, then the *rhetor* to instruct more advanced students in the art of speaking. With them came Greek textbooks, and soon the city was awash in alien culture. In 161 B.C.E. the Senate issued a decree "that no Philosophers or Rhetoricians be suffered at Rome."[8] Prohibition failed, and the rhetors kept on coming.

Trying a new approach, Cato the Elder worked up a Latin treatise on oratory for his son; its most notable contribution was its definition of the orator as "a good man skilled in speaking."[9] To the Censor, *ethos* was more than a matter of projecting an image; a speaker should actually be a virtuous person. That ethical concern would continue to echo through the great Roman treatises on the art.

The Roman Masters

Although Greek textbooks held the field yet awhile in Rome, more Latin authors tried their hands. The historian Livy (ca. 284–204 B.C.E.) composed rhetorical treatises early in his career and later followed Thucydides in writing masterful speeches for the characters in his histories.

Early in the first century B.C.E. a major work appeared called *Rhetorica ad Herennium.* Long mistakenly attributed to Cicero, but now ascribed by some to Cornificius, it employs standard principles from the Greek manuals illustrated by examples from the speeches of famous Romans.

It remained for the greatest of the Roman orators to replace the Greeks in teaching the art to his fellow citizens and to the Western world. Throughout his life (106–43 B.C.E.) Cicero composed several treatises on the subject. Those extant include a youthful *Rhetoric (De inventione)*; his mature works, *On Oratory, Brutus* (a reminiscent dialog concerning the famous orators of Rome), and *The Orator,* besides lesser pieces.

Marcus Annaeus Seneca (60 B.C.E.–ca. 37 C.E.), father of Seneca the moralist, came from Spain to teach rhetoric at Rome, and he composed a work on the art. In the twilight of the republic he heard all the most famous orators except Cicero; years later the old rhetor could recite verbatim long passages of their eloquence, and he loved to describe their mannerisms. *"Memini...,"* he would tell his students — "I remember..."[10]

First-century Romans

In the first century under the Caesars Roman interest in rhetoric continued unabated. Among the converts from rhetoric to philosophy,

Cornutus impressed his students with the Stoic zeal for truth and produced treatises on grammar and rhetoric. A Greek who came to teach in Rome in the time of Augustus, Dionysius of Halicarnassus, composed (besides inferior history) an impressive collection of *Rhetorical Writings (Scripta rhetorica).* A "writer of masterly competence,"[11] he showed insight into literary criticism and history; several of his pieces dealt with the Greek orators.

Another literary critic in Rome, the Sicilian Caecilius of Calacte, is the first writer extant to refer to the canon of the ten Attic orators.[12] A Greek by education, a Jew by faith, a Roman by residence, he pioneered the field of comparative literature, treating the written heritage of the three cultures known in his own experience. In addition, it is reported, he wrote a study on the art of rhetoric, a work on figures, and a lost piece on the sublime, *De sublimitate.*

"Longinus," known only by one title, also wrote *On the Sublime,* "probably the most influential work of literary criticism" in history.[13] He finds sublimity in five locations: great ideas, inspired emotion, well-constructed figures, noble diction, and dignity of composition. Among the pagan authors known to us he is the first to quote the Hebrew Scripture, citing Genesis 1:3 as an example of the sublime.[14]

Demetrius of Tarsus, who taught Greek at York about 80 C.E., wrote a treatise *On Style:* the elevated, the elegant, the plain, and the forcible. Dio of Prusa, it will be remembered, commended a selection of "Great Books" in his influential oration *On Training for Public Speaking.* The historian Tacitus (55?–117) composed *A Dialog on Oratory.* And the city's greatest teacher of the century, Quintilian (ca. 35–ca. 100)—like Seneca the Elder, a Spaniard—wrote *On the Education of the Orator (Institutio oratoria).* The younger Seneca, the moralist (4 B.C.E.?–65 C.E.), inherited the interest; in his epistles he frequently reflects on the rhetoric suitable for philosophical discussion.[15]

By their seriousness of purpose and depth of critical insight these authors brought the study of rhetoric to maturity for the education of public speakers and, after their own time, attracted gifted Christian preachers to their works.

THE CONTENT OF THE ART [16]

A Pervasive Theory

A proper understanding of the orations requires some grasp of the theory of classical rhetoric. It is likewise essential to an understanding of Hellenistic literature in general, the New Testament itself, and the Christian sermons of the first nineteen centuries. Quintilian organized his thinking on the discipline under three considerations, "the art, the artist, and the work":

> The art is that which we should acquire by study,
> and is the art of speaking well.
> The artist is the person who has acquired the art,
> that is to say, the artist is the orator whose task it is to speak well.
> The work is the achievement of the artist, namely good speaking.[17]

A few pages cannot do justice to a discipline developed by so many creative minds across a period of five hundred years, much less indicate the subtleties of difference among them, but a brief outline can suggest its general shape. *Technical* rhetoric concentrated on the *speech* as a production worked up according to the rules set forth by the teachers in the handbooks (*technai*); it gave attention to issues arising in the courts. *Sophistic* rhetoric put the emphasis on the mind and character of the *speaker;* idealizing the orator as leader and guide, it looked upon an effective address as a significant work of literature. *Philosophical* rhetoric was most concerned with the *message*, giving attention to the validity of the action advocated by the orator in deliberative speaking and to the speaker's engagement with the audience.[18]

The Three Functions

The philosopher Zeno had likened dialectic, the speech of his discipline, to a closed fist, the address of the orator to an open hand.[19] Yet in extending that open hand, the effective orator always keeps his purpose clearly in mind. Isocrates underscored that requirement:

> I always teach my pupils that, in composing a speech,
> the first thing needful is to define clearly the object
> which they wish the speech to effect;
> the next thing is to adapt the means to that end.[20]

In pressing toward the goal thus determined, the orator must know the audience, in order to discharge the three responsibilities of the speaker as noted by the rhetors: to *teach*, to *please*, and to *persuade*.

Teaching has to do with the substance of an address, with communicating facts and arguments that support the speaker's case. *Pleasing* the audience puts it in a receptive frame of mind; moreover, a proper concern that the hearers enjoy the speech will motivate the orator in the effort to avoid tediousness and to stave off boredom, perhaps with a dash of humor.[21] The chief function, however, is *persuasion,* moving the hearers to a course of action.[22] Everything in the speech should contribute to that end: the argument (*logos*), the perceived character (*ethos*) of the orator, the emotion (*pathos*) aroused by the speaker.

For each of the three functions a particular style or mode of expression was recommended: the plain (*tenue*) style for teaching, the tempered (*medium*) style for pleasing, the grand (*grande*) style for persuasion. Whether a speech was deliberative (political), forensic (judicial), or epideictic (ceremonial),[23] it was incumbent on the orator to teach, to please, and to persuade.

The Five Parts of Rhetoric

The teachers undertook to prepare students to perform well five different "tasks" of the orator: invention, arrangement, style, memory, delivery; Cicero hailed each of these as "in its own right a great art."[24] While the manuals concentrated on the first three, the classroom exercises also gave large attention to the final two, though some authorities argued that ability in these areas, since it depended largely on innate capacity, could not be taught.

INVENTION. "Discovery" (a literal translation of *inventio*) was the process of finding or thinking up the most telling arguments and materials to support one's case. Thanks to the rhetoricians, composing a speech had become a technical skill involving mechanical procedures for turning up the right material; no longer did it depend, like poetry, on the inspiration of the Muses. The manuals gave large attention to the most advantageous way of handling legal issues in the courts, with emphasis on the importance of *color,* the skillful manipulation of the facts in a case in order to present the most favorable interpretation.

But a large part of the instruction continued the tradition of Aristotle in analyzing general lines of argument and drilling students in the commonplaces or topics which might suggest usable substance for any speech, "as the letters do for writing the word."[25] (Cicero freely adapted Aristotle's treatise on *Topics.*) The commonplaces of praise or blame, for example, recommended for ceremonial orations, included the attributes of persons (name, nature, manner of life, fortune, habit, feeling, interests, purposes, achievements, accidents, speeches made), and extraneous virtues (public office, money, connections by marriage, high birth, friends, country, power, and other things). In preparing a speech, and especially in trying to think on one's feet in the rough-and-tumble of debate, the speaker could run through such memorized lists in search of topics suggesting useful material.

ARRANGEMENT. The task of *dispositio* involved the ordering of one's material for presentation. While some concession was made to the judgment of the orator, and while some manuals proposed slight variations, the rules commonly recommended a six-part ordering of the speech.

(1) The opening or introduction (*exordium*) should win the attention of the audience and a favorable attitude toward the speaker. Depending on circumstances, it might be straightforward or indirect.

(2) The statement of facts (*expositio, narratio*) set forth as favorably to the speaker's case as possible, the events leading up to the issue before the court or assembly or to the occasion for the speech.

(3) The partition (*divisio*) announced the argument to be advanced, either by stating the points the speaker intended to establish or by indicating the question being contested.

(4) The proof (*probatio, confirmatio*) of one's argument was the crucial section of the speech and ordinarily occupied most of the time.

(5) In any kind of debate, refutation (*confutatio, reprehensio*) of the opponent's argument involved pointing out fallacies in reasoning and disproving allegations.

(6) The conclusion (*peroratio*) ordinarily offered a recapitulation of the speaker's main points and undertook to arouse in the audience indignation or pity or some other emotion likely to lead to decision in favor of the speaker.

Besides these six standard parts, some rhetoricians commended the use of digression, the introduction of material not related to the case at hand, but deliberately brought in to relieve tension, divert attention from a damaging argument, "score points" with the hearers, or achieve some other end.

STYLE (*elocutio*). The use of words in an appealing and distinctive mode of expression offered the speaker the challenge of art. In contrast with the subdued charm of the philosopher in quiet discourse with other scholars, the eloquence of the orator required "vigour and sting" and fire to engage a popular audience.[26] The masters of eloquence also embellished their speech with "flowers of language and gems of thought," but cautioned against overdoing it.[27] Rhetoricians, speakers, and hearers all noted not only *what* was said but also *how* it was said; and they rated speakers on their mastery in handling words.

Of the four virtues of style—correctness, clarity, propriety, and ornament—it was ornament that presented the aesthetic challenge and rewards. The primary adornments were figures and tropes.

Figures of thought involve the calculated use of concepts or emotions to add force to one's presentation: questions, anticipating an objection, communication (seeming to take the adversary or the judge into consultation), the simulation of strong feeling by the use of exclamation, putting words into the mouth of an opponent or a historical or mythical personage (personification or *prosopopeia*), addressing such a person by name (*apostrophê*).

Figures of speech are various devices affecting the choice and arrangement of words for artistic effect: resorting to unusual or archaic grammatical forms, the doubling of a word or phrase, various kinds of wordplay, rhyme, ending a sentence in a particular rhythmic pattern (*clausula*), and many more.

Tropes include metaphor, simile, allegory, and all sorts of devices for adding vividness to speech. Various rhetoricians categorized the figures and tropes under different kinds of schemes. Each had a technical name, and the lists involving all the refinements of differentiation went on almost endlessly. A great part of the teaching of rhetoric was the presentation of examples of every kind of ornament from the masters of oratory and literature. No speaker trained in this culture of words could utter a line without conscious attention to such matters.

MEMORY, the ability to hold one's argument and all the supporting materials, including quotations, in one's head and to draw them out effortlessly so as to give the impression of speaking spontaneously, was highly prized. The rhetors set forth various aids for developing this skill, but recognized wide variations in natural ability. The topics or commonplaces, learned in order, provided a kind of mental filing cabinet for holding what one intended to say.[28]

DELIVERY (*actio* or *pronuntiatio*), the actual speaking of the piece before a live, perhaps hostile, audience, is the ultimate test of the orator; a story about Demosthenes, when asked to name the three most important things in oratory, reports his reply as "Delivery, delivery, and delivery."[29] Cicero regarded it as "the dominant factor in oratory,"[30] and the rhetoricians gave large attention to it in the schools. Work on voice production aimed for strength, durability, and flexibility (capacity to vary one's manner from conversational to argumentative to emotional). Much attention was given to bodily action and the mastery of gesture, and some would-be masters of an audience fell into overdoing it: Verginius Flavus once undertook to fluster a rival orator by asking how many miles he had declaimed.[31] Yet the listeners prized a dramatic delivery. Needing to reach large audiences without electronic aids for amplifying the voice or projecting a close-up picture of the speaker in action, the classical orators practiced a more exaggerated or flamboyant delivery than is common in the late twentieth century. Even so, delicacy of control could be as important as volume; Demosthenes twitted an opponent who prided himself on his "fine voice" about his "strength of lungs and lusty howling."[32]

Forms of Religious Address

Several distinct forms of address particularly identified with the philosophers and moralists were soon to be appropriated by the Christian preachers. The rhetorical treatises discuss some of these forms; others were newly emerging genres.

The EXAMPLE *(exemplum)* is a brief story about an event real or imagined (an illustrative parallel or a fable), or even the quotation of an apt saying from a particular person. (When such a dictum climaxed a pithy narrative about a philosopher or other hero, the illustration was termed a *chreia.*) Regarded in the manuals as one of the figures, the *exemplum* was used in secular address for embellishment, proof, clarity, vividness, or arousing emotion.[33] In Cicero's handbook for public officials (*De officiis*), it becomes a case study. Among religious teachers it is often a self-contained form, as in the parables of Jesus; because language about God is necessarily analogical, the *exemplum* or little story standing alone or appearing within a larger discourse to drive home a point is characteristic of the rhetoric of religion. In classical and medieval times the fondness of moral and religious teachers for biography frequently led them to employ this form in a chain or series of *exempla.*

Especially suited to popular discourse was the MAXIM,[34] a pithy, colorful statement of folk wisdom, such as a proverb, or perhaps of seemingly obvious truth in the orator's own formulation. Often a clever speaker employed a maxim as one premise in an enthymeme, a logical device less rigorous than a syllogism.[35] (In argument, an enthymeme could suggest probability, but not demonstrate truth; hence the philosopher's distrust of rhetoric.) Much more readily than a flight of eloquence or belabored argument, a pointed maxim could stick in memory to evoke recurring laughter or even (when spoken by a moralist or preacher) amendment of life. Fondness for the proverb made Greek and Roman oratory akin in that respect to the wisdom tradition of the East. (The memorable "one-liners" of Jesus are maxims.)

A device employed by the moralists was the CATALOG of virtues and vices. Such lists represented the application to ethics of a mode of development typical of classical thinkers; recall the catalogs already noted: lines of argument, commonplaces, figures, tropes, virtues of style, and so on. The rhetoricians even composed lists of the vices or flaws of style for their students to memorize and seek to avoid. Lists of ethical virtues and vices drawn up by the popular moralists were readily appropriated for Christian use and appear frequently in the New Testament.

Also favored by philosophers and moralists, especially the popular interpreters, the DIALOGUE used the form of an extended narrative for the unfolding of a discussion among several characters representing diverse points of view; it offered charm of characterization, the illusion of being "in on" an argument in a circle of celebrities, the fascination induced by clash of opinions, and the suspense of a good story. Masterfully developed by Plato, it was also employed by Cicero, Tacitus, Plutarch, Dio of Prusa, and other classical authors and was taken up by several early Christian writers. Written to be read rather than presented as a speech, it nevertheless carried the color and excitement of a debate among orators.

The DIATRIBE we have already noted as the prevailing type of speech used by the Stoic and Cynic orators. Originally the word had designated a "pastime," as verbal artists whiled away an idle hour improvising orations on some theme. In the practice of the popular moralists it became an epideictic speech with serious purpose, the commendation of a particular virtue or the censure of a vice, making full use of the topics of praise or blame. Recall Plutarch's *Virtue and Vice, How One Recognizes Progress in Virtue, Bravery of Women, Brotherly Love, Can Virtue be Taught?* or Seneca's *On Mercy*. Whereas it had once suggested a lighthearted diversion, infused now with the *parrhesia* of an earnest philosopher or moralist, diatribe had come to have the weight and intensity of a Puritan sermon.

The public CONVERSATION *(sermo)* evolved from a natural, less agitated mode of delivery. In rhetorical manuals *sermo* was the technical term for a casual manner. The title came to be applied also to a type of satire, dealing quietly with a serious matter, without the flamboyance or calculated rhetoric of an oratorical performance. Well suited to an earnest talk by a philosopher or moralist, the form readily lent itself to the purposive, frequently artless presentations of the earliest Christian witnesses. So the Greek word *homilia* and its Latin equivalent *sermo* passed into Christian usage as the customary title for a particular instance of preaching—the homily or sermon.[36]

Summary Comment

The outline here given is the mere skeleton, dry and meatless, like bones of a once-living art hanging gruesomely in a museum case. Remember, especially in the case of a master orator like Cicero, that the "speeches...were real speeches"[37] dealing with hotly contested issues before partisan crowds, who wanted to be amused and might possibly be persuaded. It was not enough to recall the formulas taught by the rhetors or to engage in the kind of textbook exercises assigned in the classroom. "The classical orator [was] a fighter in a lonely contest,"[38] who must know audiences, dare to stand alone before an unruly, unsympathetic, even hostile assembly, contrive to win a hearing, make one's case convincingly, and, in the end, *persuade.*

No wonder that rhetoric excited the leading citizens, challenged the brightest students, and engaged the favored members of society for ten brilliant centuries from Gorgias to St. Jerome, or that it continued to break out in new bursts of vitality in the later Middle Ages, the Renaissance, the eighteenth century, and the nineteenth century (with its "princes of the pulpit" and the platform), or that it has once again seized the attention of New Testament scholars. For every technical word from the manuals, here given only a definition or brief explanation, the authors of the rhetorical texts supplied pages of discussion animated with dazzling examples. Lacking acquaintance with this art, the reader cannot fully grasp the letters of the apostle Paul, the sermons of John Chrysostom or Augustine, the eloquence of the Vulgate. But this brief analysis suggests some elementary considerations essential to discerning the artistry of Christian preaching in a world which in its schooldays had rhetoricians for masters.

THE EDUCATION OF ORATORS[39]

A Culture of Words

For five hundred years before Jesus, Greco-Roman education had concentrated on the development of orators. When the sophists had begun the emphasis in Athens, it may well have seemed something of a vogue. But even in the time of Augustus and his imperial successors, with possibilities for a vital political oratory restricted and with many speakers limiting themselves to the empty eloquence of epideictic effusions, the popular delight in public speaking in no way abated; the golden-tongued orator was a celebrity.

Schools of rhetoric conducted by highly educated Greek scholars flourished in Rome and in the far-flung cities of the empire. Very few of these "Greeks," of course, were Athenians, but rather Hellenized children of the emerging *oikoumenē*, hailing from every part of Greece, from Macedonia, Asia Minor, Syria, Egypt, and the islands of the Mediterranean, to mingle in the capital with "Romans" from throughout Italy, Spain, Gaul, Africa, and far-off Britain. Even in undistinguished towns provincial schoolchildren began their progress through the grades, studying grammar first of all and then the basics of rhetoric; both these disciplines drew heavily on the literary heritage—especially poetry, history, and philosophy—to provide examples of every rule. More promising and more favored pupils went on to the great teachers of rhetoric in the cities. Thus a curriculum designed to produce effective public speakers operated—even in a time when Seneca the Younger lamented the decline of oratory under the Caesars—to produce a unity of culture throughout the empire. It was a culture of words.

Course of Study

Students were drilled in the theory and practice of the five tasks of the orator, memorizing lists of topics and tropes, reading and listening to accounts of past masters of the art, cultivating a critical ear for the speeches they heard, endlessly preparing exercises for presentation before their masters and peers, suffering criticism, or basking in acclaim. They worked up speeches for every conceivable circumstance, arguing now one side of a question, then the other, or contriving to treat the same theme in different ways. Their teachers assigned melodramatic situations for them to address forthwith in extemporaneous declamation:

> Scythians, return to your nomadic life.
> Aeschines, when the grain had not come.
> The adulterer unmasked.
> The instigator of a revolt suppresses it.
> The ravished chooses that her ravisher be put to death.
> The man who fell in love with a statue.
> Description of a peacock.[40]

With its highly wrought *suasoriae* and *controversiae* the school was an unreal, overheated world. It cultivated the artificiality and flamboyance so admired in some prestigious orators, concentrating on a highly ornamented style, and inculcating an unnatural mode of expression heavy with the affectations of poetry. Petronius (1st century C.E.) satirized the pedagogical decadence:

> It is my conviction that the schools are responsible
> for the gross foolishness of our young people,
> because, in them, they see or hear nothing at all
> of the affairs of everyday life,
> but only pirates standing in chains upon the shore,
> tyrants scribbling edicts
> in which sons are ordered to behead their fathers;
> responses from oracles delivered in time of pestilence,
> ordering the immolation of three or more virgins;
> every word a honeyed drop,
> every period sprinkled with poppy-seed and sesame.
> Those who are brought up on such a diet
> can no more attain to wisdom than a kitchen scullion
> can attain to a keen sense of smell or avoid stinking of grease...
> Young people did not learn set speeches
> in the days when Sophocles and Euripides
> were searching for words in which to express themselves...
> I do not find that either Plato or Demosthenes
> was given to this kind of exercise.[41]

Yet despite the foolishness of educators, the rhetorical curriculum served to stimulate imagination and a sense of the dramatic. It cultivated sensitivity to the psychology of audiences. It commended, when it followed Cicero, the discipline of writing as a means of achieving eloquence. It exalted the ideal of the learned speaker. It introduced young minds to philosophy. It kindled enthusiasm for a career as an orator.

Even though the accession of the Caesars resulted in turning over the major share of the oratorical field to epideictic or ceremonial speech, this eloquence of praise or blame could serve serious purposes; it is not to be identified with the pretentious grandiloquence of the declamations in the classroom. The high intent of philosophers, moralists, and preachers sometimes invested their utterance with dignity and majesty appropriate to the sublimity of their vision.

Tacitus gave memorable expression to the excitement of the orator's life:

What a delight it must be to rise and stand amid the hushed crowd,
every eye on him alone,
the people assembling and gathering round him in a circle,
and taking from the orator any emotion he has himself assumed...

If he produces a careful and well-prepared speech,
there is a solidity and stedfastness in his satisfaction,
just as there is in his style;
if, again, he offers his audience, not without some tremblings at heart,
the result of a fresh and sudden effort,
his very anxiety enhances the joy of success,
and ministers to his pleasure...
is there an accomplishment, the fame and glory of which
are to be compared with the distinction of an orator?[42]

Critique of Rhetoric

Rhetoric nevertheless troubled the minds of the thoughtful, from the time when Gorgias arrived on the scene. Annoyed by its preoccupation with style, Plato parodied its tricks of rhythm and other devices; its inversions of normal word order and other affectations he held to be unnatural.

More serious questions came from Socrates in the famous dialogue entitled *Gorgias*. Conceding that there is a rhetoric which "aims at the training and improvement of the souls of the citizens," the inquiring philosopher asks:

But have you ever known such a rhetoric?...
can you mention any one...
who may be said to have improved the Athenians,
who found them worse and made them better,
from the day that he began to make speeches?[43]

Pursuing his question with a wry skepticism, Socrates lays out a course for the right kind of speaking:

So we have temperance and justice; have we not?...
And will not the true rhetorician
who is honest and understands his art have his eye fixed upon these,
in all the words which he addresses to the souls of his hearers?...
Will not his aim be
to implant justice in the souls of his citizens and take away injustice,

to implant temperance and take away intemperance?
to implant virtue and take away every vice?[44]

Thus Socrates charts a course for the popular philosophers and moralists who soon will take philosophy to the people gathered in the marketplaces and describes an ideal that will guide Christian preaching when Greeks begin to proclaim the gospel. Even so, for all the charms of rhetoric, he considers philosophy "a finer kind of music."[45]

Aristotle's conviction that cases should be won by a blunt appeal to the facts and not by extraneous techniques of delivery elicited agreement from other serious minds. His refusal, moreover, to place either rhetoric or poetic within the realm of truth, in contrast to dialectic, which could demonstrate validity or falsity, touched the verbal art at a point of serious weakness.

The readiness of orators to present a plausible argument for a bad cause and of sophisticated speakers to manipulate their audiences by flattery continued to trouble the morally sensitive. Yet Aristotle recognized that though ethics was a discipline distinct from rhetoric it might still guide the orator. Even the archetypical critic of rhetoric and poetry, Plato himself, conveyed his most memorable teachings in *Dialogues,* which are carefully crafted works of art; in the *Phaedrus* he presents Socrates making light of writing and of formal speeches, yet insisting nonetheless:

> Only in principles of justice and goodness and nobility
> taught and communicated orally for the sake of instruction
> and graven in the soul...
> is there clearness and perfection and seriousness.[46]

The haunting questions lingered. Could rhetoric really teach skill in speaking? Even more crucial, could it produce goodness of character?

The Humane Ideal

The issue finally came down to the character of the orator, the kind of person issuing from the rhetorical schools. The critique of rhetoric voiced by their graduates and the involvement of the philosophers themselves in the education of the young indicate the presence of a corrective tendency within the tradition itself. The Greek ideal for education (*paideia*) avowed its concern for the development of character, while literary convention cast the poet in the role of ethical hero and model of public usefulness.[47] Even though the downfall of the city-states was hastened by a deficiency of virtue in their leaders, that failure stemmed from various causes; it cannot be charged against the schools or the rhetorical curriculum alone.

Among the Romans, who celebrated the sturdy virtues of their republican ancestors even after ceasing to practice them, that strain of rhetorical theory and practice represented by Cato, Cicero, and Quintilian concerned itself with goodness as essential to the ideal orator. In his emphasis on *humanitas* (the word he used to translate the Greek *paideia*),[48] Cicero gave larger attention to the cultivation of the orator's mind and spirit than did Aristotle. Though accounted a lightweight in philosophy, the Roman asserted a philosophical vision of the orator's calling as one responsible for elevating the common life, public taste, and general understanding. His work on the duties of public officials (*De officiis*) literally preached the Stoic virtues. And Quintilian climaxed the *Education of the Orator* with a book on the development of character. The ideals they commended persisted for centuries in the classical understanding of the liberal arts, the tradition of the "more humane letters." The orator's *ethos*, authentic, not merely perceived, was intended to prevent misuse of the art.

Ethical Commitment

The literature of the Hellenistic age, both Greek and Latin, manifests impressive ethical concern. Granted that a number of clever writers deal lightly with traditional morality and that self-indulgence, dishonor, and disdain for the public weal were widespread; still the longing for goodness to which the mystery religions appealed found expression in a number of authors. Satirists exercised their wit in behalf of virtue, historians moralized their narratives, and divers authors celebrated Stoic ideals. The poet Aratus of Soli (3d century B.C.E.) picked up the great line from the philosopher Cleanthes, "For we are also his offspring," which early found its way into Christian preaching (Acts 17:28).[49] The laureate of the Augustan age, the poet Virgil, exalted his hero's high sense of mission in contrast to the old, fateful concept of destiny.

In a literature which shows in every line the influence of the rhetorical schools, such a high degree of ethical concern argues against dismissing too lightly their emphasis on the character of the orator or attributing such concern entirely to the influence of the heavyweight philosophers. In the strictest sense, rhetoric and ethics were separate fields. But those teachers occupied solely with technique and those unprincipled speakers intent only to dazzle and deceive failed to comprehend the serious commitment of the orators whom Cicero termed "the players that act real life" in contrast with actors, "who only mimic reality."[50] The trivializers betrayed the great masters of the art who in their evident commitment to values, humane, aesthetic, and ethical, whatever their personal shortcomings may have been, clung to Cato's definition of the orator—a good man skilled in speaking. Hear the noblest of the Roman teachers:

> For my part, I have undertaken the task of moulding the ideal orator, and my first desire is that he should be a good man.[51]

The Significance of Hellenistic Oratory for Christian Preaching

As background and context for the emergence of Christianity as a universal faith, Hellenistic oratory and the culture of which it was an integral part exercised profound influence on the development of the church's preaching from the very beginning. Some aspects of that influence are here summarized.

1. The Greco-Roman world produced and disseminated the culture of Hellenism within which Christianity arose and spread. For centuries to come that culture shaped the life of Europe, the continent in which the new faith rooted most firmly, and it still shapes the life of the modern world in language, institutions, concepts, and ideals. In that pre-technological society oratory was the primary mode of public communication. So preaching became the primary medium for "publishing" or "broadcasting" the Christian gospel.

2. The unity of a common culture pervaded the *oikoumenē*, the inhabited "world" unified by government and commerce, promoting the ideal of universalism and interpretations of reality in harmony with that ideal. Preaching in Greek, the universal language, Christian missionaries could address audiences throughout the empire.

3. The institutions of government, Greek democracy and Roman republic, created by subjects claiming their rights as free citizens, fostered popular participation in arriving at political and judicial decisions. As the decisive instrument in the process, oratory achieved a position of cultural importance that continued even beyond the era of classical antiquity, though impaired by the replacement of free institutions with the new machinery of empire. Preaching the Christian gospel would give orators a new cause.

4. The educational ideal of the Hellenistic world (*paideia, humanitas*) projected a vision of the human spirit reaching for the fulness of its possibilities—intellectual, aesthetic, ethical, spiritual—which places a premium on cultivation of mind and body, development of sensitivity, and creativity. Though full participation in such a life was, with rare exceptions, severely limited for women and closed for the large majority of the population that did not enjoy the privileged position of citizens or leisure from hard physical labor, the vision of human possibility proved attractive even to many of these when circumstance opened the door. To the favored Greeks and Romans whose names we know, civilization is indebted for much of its intellectual, political, cultural, and artistic heritage. Early Christian preachers laid claim to that heritage and to a place within it.

5. The rise of Greek philosophy in the seventh century B.C.E. and the continued vitality of the philosophical tradition in the Hellenistic era gave impetus to the development of critical thought. As summarized in the ideals of truth, beauty, and goodness, classical philosophy ennobled human existence. In its insistence on asking hard questions and on rational analysis, philosophy rejected superstition, much popular religion, and even some answers advanced within its own domain to the insistent questions arising from human existence. It accelerated an inclination toward monotheism which, at least at the level of rationality, was beginning to displace the traditional belief in many gods. The Christian preachers took their stand alongside Stoics, Cynics, and Epicureans in rejecting superstition, even while asserting the superiority of the worldview they proclaimed over that of the philosophers.

6. The dominant figure in culture was the orator. People found amusement, intellectual stimulation, ethical inspiration, and aesthetic delight in listening to speeches, and skill in the art of public address opened the road to celebrity. Even though the death of the republic seriously reduced the scope of political oratory and limited that of judicial oratory, ceremonial or epideictic oratory flourished more than ever. Persons with a cause to promote or a desire for recognition mounted the rostrum and made a speech. The Christian preachers did likewise.

7. The desire for skill in oratory had called forth the discipline of rhetoric, with its precise analysis and program for producing effective public address. It cultivated an intense consciousness of style on the

part of speakers and listeners alike and, through its dominance of education, profoundly influenced all forms of literary expression. Christian preachers educated in the tradition inevitably employed the art.

8. Popular "preachers" appeared everywhere, addressing whatever crowds they could assemble on religious and ethical themes. For such communication the popular philosophers and moralists employed rhetorical forms well suited to it, forms which became models for Jewish and Christian sermons. Along with the mystagogues, they had developed audiences for speakers who dealt with the issues of life, people who, out of eagerness or curiosity or habit, would gather to hear some new thing, asking, "What does this babbler want to say?" (Acts 17:18). Such speakers were the prototype of the Christian preachers, who soon appeared among them.

9. A high level of moral insight and ethical concern characterized significant numbers of the philosophers, rhetoricians, and literary figures. Whatever the moral laxity of the powerful and the privileged or the squalor of the downtrodden, a genuine regard for virtue and a longing for uprightness sounded from many voices. While much of the emphasis fell on personal conduct, philosophers also projected the vision of a good society and enunciated principles of justice and equality based on natural law. The Christian preachers engaged this ethical concern.

10. It was a time of personal restlessness and spiritual questing, as old patterns of inner security broke down and a colorful religious pluralism swept an empire that by its conquests had brought many diverse peoples and cultures into one governmental fold. The Christian preachers spoke to that hunger.

11. Increasingly, in their spiritual search the people of Greece and Rome were turning to religions—some old, some new, some coming out of the East —which, in contrast with the official cult, dealt with personal needs and private anxieties. These "mysteries" set forth an offer of salvation, dazzled the impressionable with wonder-workers and holy gurus, overwhelmed the emotions with powerfully impressive rites of initiation and worship. In such a context people began to turn with wistfulness, even eagerness, to the missionaries of the new Christian faith.

12. If these developments seem a remarkable combination of circumstances that opened the world of the early Caesars to the preaching

of Christianity (and they did so impress the early Christians, most especially the church historian Eusebius), the philosophers and rhetoricians offered a concept for interpreting it all. The rational, purposive activity of God, which they designated as *Logos,* the Word, bore a striking likeness to the work of the orator in imparting understanding and persuading people to right decision. Some of the most attractive Christian thinkers seized on the concept of the Logos that enlightens every human being to explain what God had been doing in noble minds and spirits before the coming of Jesus the Christ.

13. To such minds, when the gospel preachers came on the scene, it must have been all but inevitable to perceive the work of preaching as an analogue of the divine activity. In the fear of God, they would undertake to persuade the men and women of the classical world.

+

To the world described in Part One, the Christian preachers appeared as heralds of good news, which one of them termed "the power of God for salvation" (Rom 1:16.) That gospel offered the assurance of divine deliverance to those who longed to be set free from their fears and guilt. It provided a powerful inner dynamic for the realization of that goodness after which the noblest spirits in Hellenism aspired. All this it put forward in the name of Jesus of Nazareth, whom the preachers presented as foretold by the prophets and whom they called the Christ.

Jesus of Nazareth? Foretold by the prophets? The Christ expected by the Jews? Was this new faith a form of Judaism?

Apart from its roots in that historic faith it cannot be understood. To a consideration of Judaism in the Hellenistic era, therefore, we now turn.

PART TWO

People of the Word

Jewish Preaching in Hellenistic Times

INTRODUCTION TO PART TWO

Declaring the Word of God

CHAPTERS

4. Judaism: The Preaching of Torah

5. Preachers in the Struggle for a People's Soul

6. The Homiletic of Judaism

CONCLUSION TO PART TWO

Preaching in Judaism: An Assessment

INTRODUCTION TO PART TWO

Declaring the Word of God

If the world of Hellenism, dazzled by oratory and schooled in rhetoric, was a culture of the word, Judaism could claim that title in quite a different sense. For here was a scattered people on the verge of losing every outward means of nationhood, yet finding ineradicable identity, unity, and indestructibility in a faith centered in the Word of God. The preaching of the synagogue would characterize and sustain this people through a tragic future.

In the first century of the Caesars Judaism gave an important place to preaching and employed characteristic modes for that art. It profoundly influenced the development of preaching within emerging Christianity.

Part Two will consider the rise of preaching in old Israel, representative types of sermons in the biblical tradition, and the veneration of Torah as Word of God so characteristic of early Judaism. That sacred esteem survived the ruins of the Jewish nation, animating the preaching throughout the dispersion that made of a once localized faith a worldwide religion. It will sketch the development of preaching, present notable preachers, outline their homiletic (exegesis, theology, and rhetoric), and assess the significance of Jewish religious address in the Hellenistic era.

CHAPTER 4

Judaism: the Preaching of Torah

SACRED SPEECH IN OLD ISRAEL[1]

An inscription from the first century C.E. on an old synagogue in Jerusalem dedicates it "for the reading of the Law and the teaching of the commandments."[2] The understanding of public worship as centering on instruction in the Torah culminated a long process in the development of biblical religion, a process marked by the emergence of various forms of "preaching" inculcating reliance on the Word of Yahweh.

Recital—the Old Creed

From its earliest days as a confederation of tribes occupying Canaan, Israel proclaimed its faith through a recital of Yahweh's saving acts on behalf of the chosen people. Offering the firstfruits at the shrine of Yahweh, the worshiper, not the priest, recited the old "creed":

> A fugitive Aramean was my ancestor,
> who went down into Egypt and lived there as an alien...
> The LORD brought us out of Egypt
> with a mighty hand and an outstretched arm.
>
> [Deut. 26:5–9 NRSV alt.][3]

Through all the centuries, Israel told and retold in varied ways the account of its deliverance. That provided the theme for liturgical celebration in Psalms (e.g., 66, 77, 78, 135) and for one of the most moving passages in the prophets (Hos. 11:1–11) Late in the second century B.C.E. the author of the apocryphal book of Judith put an impressive version of the recital in the mouth of an Ammonite commander (Judith 5:5–21). The texts of early Christian sermons in the book of Acts make use of this pattern (Acts 7:2–53; 13:16–41), and in more recent times the retelling by African American preachers has infused the "Genesis to Revelation sermon" with power.

The Old Stories[4]

Like people in oral cultures everywhere the Hebrews made use of *story* to enshrine common commitments and convey cherished values. From primordial times artists gifted in speech recounted old remembered tales as listeners waited—around the campfire, at the well, in the open square at the town gate, or in liturgical gatherings that celebrated notable events from the tribal past. Above all else, the cult of early Israel, periodically bringing the tribes together at the ancestral shrines, provided occasion for rehearsing the story of how they had become a people.

> Remember the days of old,
> Consider the years of ages past;
> Ask your father, he will inform you;
> Your elders, they will tell you.   [Deut. 32:7 Tanakh]

Narration of the old stories was a primordial form of preaching. Some legends honored the virtues of an ancestor, commending generosity and the nobility of living at peace.

> From Egypt, Abram went up into the Negeb, with his wife
> and all that he possessed, together with Lot.
> Now Abram was very rich in cattle, silver, and gold.
> And he proceeded by stages…as far as Bethel,
> to the…site of the altar that he had built there at first;
> and there Abram invoked the LORD by name.

> Lot…also had flocks and herds and tents,
> so that the land could not support them staying together…
> And there was quarelling between the herders…
> Abram said to Lot, "Let there be no strife beween you and me,
> between my herders and yours, for we are kindred.
> Is not the whole land before you?"…
> So Lot chose for himself the whole plain of the Jordan,
> and Lot journeyed eastward.
> Thus they parted from each other;
> Abram remained in the land of Canaan…

> And the LORD said to Abram…"Up, walk about the land,
> through its length and its breadth, for I give it to you."

And Abram…came to dwell at the terebinths of Mamre…
and he built an altar there to the LORD. [Gen. 13:2–18 Tanakh]

Here in brief, unadorned account the old storyteller has proclaimed (along with the status, magnanimity, and piety of their ancestor) the blessing and promise of Yahweh.

Recounting with matchless artistry the story of Abraham's sending his old servant back to the former home to find from among his own kindred a wife for his son Isaac (Gen. 24), one of the narrators packed into that suspenseful tale Israel's sense of being a distinct people in covenant with Yahweh, God's providential leading of the faithful, reliance on prayer, the patriarchal ideal of womanhood, the exquisite courtesy of the bedouin, and the deep joy of honorable marriage. Similar suspense marks the tale of Jacob's return, after years of exile, to the old home in Canaan, his dread of encountering the brother wronged so long ago, and Esau's unexpected generosity of spirit in meeting him with forgiveness (Gen. 32, 33). To that example of pardon the storytellers added another with an even greater build-up of suspense: their moving account of Joseph, the grand vizier of Egypt, disclosing his identity, hidden until now, in an act of reconciliation with the brothers who years before had sold him into slavery (Gen. 45).

The stories charmed and instructed—and lodged indelibly in the memory of those who heard them. Generation after generation recalled the tales of Adam and Eve, the brothers Cain and Abel, Noah and his floating menagerie riding out the great flood, the rivalry of Sarah and Hagar for Abraham's favor and of Leah and Rachel for that of Jacob, famished Esau's disregard for his birthright, the faithfulness and prudence of young Joseph, assailed despite his rectitude by successive troubles until his vindication in the providence of God. Later stories told of Miriam and Moses and Aaron and Yahweh's deliverance of the slaves from Egypt, of Joshua and Caleb and the conquest of the promised land, of Jephthah's rash vow and his daughter's doom, of Samson's strength and tragic folly.

Few of the stories have left a deeper impress on the language of faith than the account of Jacob's flight from the wrath of Esau. Alone, on his first night away from home,

He came upon a certain place and stopped there for the night
for the sun had set.
Taking one of the stones of that place, he put it under his head
and lay down in that place. He had a dream;

a stairway was set on the ground and its top reached to the sky,
and angels of God were going up and down on it.
And the LORD was standing beside him and He said,
"I am the LORD, the God of your father Abraham
and the God of Isaac;
the ground on which you are lying
I shall assign to you and to your offspring...
All the families of the earth shall bless themselves
by you and your descendants.
Remember, I am with you:
I will protect you wherever you go,
and will bring you back to this land..."
Jacob awoke from his sleep and said,
"Surely the LORD is present in this place...
This is none other than the abode of God,
and that is the gateway to heaven."   [Gen. 28:11–17 Tanakh]

A clump of marvelous tales clung to memories of the early prophets Elijah and Elisha. Imagination can picture the eyes of children widening in wonder and parental fingers wagging in admonition during the telling of one brief story:

Elisha...went up to Bethel.
As he was going up the road,
some little boys came out of the town
and jeered at him, saying,
"Go away, baldhead! Go away, baldhead!"
He turned around and looked at them
and cursed them in the name of the LORD.
Thereupon, two she-bears came out of the woods
and mangled forty-two of the children.   [2 Kings 2:23–34 Tanakh]

With intense human interest the oral tradition witnessed to God's faithfulness, the divine demand for righteousness, and the experiences of the chosen people; rising out of a dim and ancient time, it dominated the subsequent spiritual consciousness and preaching of Israel. When at last the narratives were written down, gathered, and arranged by unknown editors (whom scholars designate by alphabetical symbols—J, E, D, P), they were accorded a place in the canon of scripture. They have provided inspiration and substance for preaching among Jews and Christians ever since.

Fascination with Eloquence

Noteworthy in those old stories that scholars assign to the Elohist is their inclusion of speeches by the leading characters. One group, though showing no especially homiletical slant, suggests popular interest in the dynamics and content of a good public address:

Jacob's profession of innocence to Laban—Gen. 31:36–42
Joseph's account of his dreams—Gen. 37:5–11
Joseph's interpretation of the servants' dreams—Gen. 40:5–22
Joseph's interpretation of Pharaoh's dreams—Gen. 41:1–33
Jethro's description of upright judges—Ex. 18:13–26
Dathan and Abiram's complaint against Moses—Num. 16:12–14
Moses's plea for vindication against the rebels—Num. 16:15, 25–33.

As part of Israel's sacred history and in the recurring moralistic bent, these seven pieces may be considered akin to preaching in a broad sense of the word.

Fascination with eloquence—not only the enjoyment of an appealing style but also admiration for ingenuity in invention and for persuasive power—continued in Israel from earliest times right on into the Hellenistic era. Consider the apocryphal account of a debate held once upon a time in the Persian court as recounted in the first book of Esdras (late second century B.C.E.). Three young men of the king's personal bodyguard proposed a contest:

Let each of us name the thing he judges to be strongest,
and to the one whose opinion appears to be wisest
let King Darius give rich gifts and prizes:
he shall be robed in purple, drink from gold cups,
and sleep on a golden bed;
he shall have a chariot with gold-studded bridles,
and a turban of fine linen, and a chain around his neck.
His wisdom shall give him the right to sit next to the king
and to bear the title Kinsman of Darius.   [1 Esdras 3:5–7 REB]

One proposed

Wine is strongest.   [3:10]

A second affirmed,

The king is strongest.   [3:11]

The third asserted,

Women are strongest, but truth conquers all.   [3:12]

Bidden by the king to defend his proposition, each spoke with persuasiveness and charm. When the third had celebrated the power of women—without them there would be no wine, and they rule the hearts of kings—the dignitaries of the court "looked at one another," tacitly conceding victory.

Then Zerubbabel proceeded to speak of truth:

> With her there is no injustice.
> There is injustice in wine, and in kings, and in women,
> injustice in all mortals and their works...
> and in their injustice they shall perish.
> But truth abides and remains strong for ever;
> she lives and is sovereign for ever and ever....
> There is no favouritism with her, no partiality; ...
> in her judgments there is no injustice.
> Hers are strength and royalty,
> the authority and majesty of all ages.
> Praise be to the God of truth!   [4:37–40]

As Zerubbabel finished speaking, all the people shouted,

> "Great is truth: truth is strongest!"   [4:41]

To return now to the old stories of Israel's tradition, some offer speeches with a decidedly homiletical character. Of eight such included by the Elohist five are ingredient to the narrative:

> Joseph's self-disclosure to his brothers—Gen. 45:3–15
> God's command to Jacob to go to Egypt—Gen. 46:2–4
> Yahweh's command and promise to the people—Ex. 23:20–31a
> Yahweh's judgment on Israel's faintheartedness—Num. 14:22–25
> Moses's judgment speech on faintheartedness—Num. 14:41–43.

These homilies lovingly elaborate Israel's old creed in sermonic fashion as they emphasize God's providence and promise.

In condemnation of the fainthearted, trembling at the borders of Canaan, the very voice of Yahweh speaks in the form of a prophetic judgment speech:

> As I live and as the LORD's Presence fills the whole world,
> none of the people who have seen My Presence
> and the signs that I have performed in Egypt and in the wilderness,
> and who have tried me these many times and have disobeyed Me,
> shall see the land that I promised on oath to their ancestors;
> None of those who spurn Me shall see it.   [Num. 14:22–23 Tanakh]

A speech by Moses, using the same form, pronounces judgment with equal finality:

Why do you transgress the LORD's command?
This will not succeed...You will fall by the sword,
inasmuch as you have turned from following the LORD
and the LORD will not be with you.   [Num. 14:41–43 Tanakh]

Further indication of an emerging homiletical tradition in Israel occurs in the materials that scholars designate J2, regarding them as elements inserted by a northern editor into the Yahwist's account in order to affirm the common spiritual heritage of the separated kingdoms. These passages include a number of speeches:

Yahweh's dialog with Cain, including a curse—Gen. 4:9–16
Yahweh's appointment of Aaron as mouthpiece for Moses—Ex. 4:13–17
Sermon of Moses memorializing the exodus—Ex. 13:3–16
Yahweh's self-predication in instituting the Covenant—Ex. 34:6–7,
    10–27
Plea of Moses to Yahweh for mercy on the people—Num. 14:13–19
The angel's rebuke of Israel's sin—Judg. 2:1b–5a

These discourses suggest that as the traditions developed, the narrators tended to become more explicitly homiletical.

Even more important for their common rhetorical form is a group of three cultic covenant-formulations attributed to the three greatest figures of Israel's pre-monarchical past:[5]

The Covenant at Sinai (Moses)—Ex. 19:3–6
The Covenant at Shechem (Joshua)—Josh. 24:1–25
The Covenant at Gilgal (Samuel)—1 Sam. 12

The first of the three, decidedly briefer than the other two, sets forth the memorable Eagle Sermon of Moses.

The LORD called to [Moses] from the mountain, saying,
"Thus shall you say to the house of Jacob
and declare to the children of Israel:
    'You have seen what I did to the Egyptians,
    how I bore you on eagle's wings and brought you to Me.
    Now then, if you will obey Me faithfully and keep My covenant,
    you shall be My treasured possession, among all the peoples.
    Indeed, all the earth is Mine,

But you shall be to Me a kingdom of priests and a holy nation.'
These are the words that you shall speak
to the children of Israel."   [Ex. 19:3b–6 Tanakh]

Enclosed at beginning and end by the messenger-formula, the "sermon" proper opens with Yahweh's self-predication concerning his act of deliverance witnessed by Israel, a word made forever memorable by the soaring metaphor of the eagle, suggesting both the grandeur of the towering mountains in the wilderness and the parental tenderness of the majestic bird. The thought advances to an appeal for the people's response in freely given loyalty and love, the condition for the nation's unique destiny: *if* you will listen and keep my covenant, *then* you shall be my very own. In the third movement the Lord of all the earth sets forth the full meaning of the destiny to which Yahweh has called them: that of a priestly nation holy to God. Throughout, the divine word addresses the people directly, reinforcing intimacy by repetition of the personal pronouns, *you* and *I.* In spirit, language, and form, this brief passage establishes a pattern for Israel's speech concerning the covenant in narrative, psalm, and sermon.[6]

Song and Psalm

The old remembered *songs*, which break out now and again in the Pentateuch, joyfully declare the salvation wrought by God; they may be considered a primal form of preaching, some possibly as old as the events they celebrate. The song of the prophet Miriam exults in the deliverance of the Israelite slaves, brought safely through the sea just before it engulfs the pursuing troops of Pharaoh:

Sing to the LORD, for He has triumphed gloriously;
Horse and chariot He has hurled into the sea.   [Ex. 15:21 Tanakh alt.]

A much longer song (Ex. 15:1–18), composed somewhat later, but still considered quite old, elaborated Miriam's theme in an impressive poem; clearly the work of a preacher, it was attributed, like much else in the Exodus saga, to Moses, the towering figure of that event and Israel's "official leader."[7]

Another such paean is regarded as "the oldest surviving extended fragment of Heb[rew] literature";[8] the triumphant canticle of Deborah and Barak (Judg. 5:1–31) rejoices in victory over the Midianites:

I shall sing, I shall sing to the LORD,
making music to the LORD, the God of Israel.
LORD, when you set forth from Seir,
when you marched from the land of Edom,
earth trembled; heaven quaked;
the clouds streamed down in torrents.
Mountains shook in fear before the LORD, the LORD of Sinai,
before the LORD, the God of Israel.   [Judg. 5:3–5 REB]

A sermon known as the Song of Moses (Deut. 32:1–43) ranks with the most impressive poems of Israel's early cult. This majestic work, long regarded as a late composition, seems in recent analyses of vocabulary and style to belong to the eleventh century B.C.E. Clearly delivered in a liturgical setting, with affinities to the early hymns, it proclaims the deeds of Israel's God, condemns the people's faithlessness, and announces Yahweh's coming triumph.

The sermon begins with a solemn invocation and a series of similes in which the preacher acknowledges the sublimity of the kerygmatic task:

Give ear, O heavens, let me speak;
Let the earth hear the words I utter!
May my discourse come down as the rain,
My speech distill as the dew,
Like showers on young growth,
like droplets on the grass.   [Deut. 32:1–2 Tanakh]

The preacher then announces the theme: the incomparable nature of Israel's God:

For the name of the LORD I proclaim;
Give glory to our God!
The Rock! His deeds are perfect,
Yea, all His ways are just;
a faithful God, never false,
True and upright is He ...
Is not He the Father who created you,
fashioned you and made you endure?   [Deut. 32:3–4, 6c–d Tanakh]

Appealing to the congregation to remember Yahweh's dealings with Israel in days of old, the preacher evokes memories of the wilderness and the gift of the land, echoing two themes in Moses' covenantal address (the "Eagle Sermon"): this people's election as Yahweh's "possession" and the leading of divine love.

> The LORD's portion is His people,
> Jacob His own allotment.
> He found him in a desert region,
> In an empty howling waste.
> God shielded him and cared for him.   [Deut. 32:9–10 Tanakh alt.]

Here the preacher amplifies the memorable metaphor from Moses's sermon.

> As an eagle watches over its nest,
> hovers above its young,
> spreads its pinions and takes them up,
> and bears them on its wings,   [Deut. 32:11 REB]
> The LORD alone did guide him.   [Deut. 32:12 Tanakh]

From the high emotion of sacred memory the preacher moves with sternness and pathos to the rebelliousness of a people who have broken covenant:

> They forsook God their Maker
> And dishonored the Rock of their salvation.
> They roused his jealousy with alien gods.   [Deut. 32:15–16 REB]

Now the preacher's involvement carries him from the third person of narrative-recital to the second person of direct encounter:

> You neglected the Rock that begot you,
> Forgot the God who brought you forth.   [Deut. 32:18 Tanakh alt.]

Such a people God can only repudiate, and the preacher speaks fearsome words of divine rejection (vv. 19–21), followed by an eloquent prophecy of judgment (vv. 22–35). Yet if Yahweh were to forsake the chosen people utterly, their enemies would scoff at both them and their God. So God's purpose must triumph (vv. 36–38).

The sermon climaxes in Yahweh's self-predication, reminding Israel of God's sole deity and absolute sovereignty:

> Learn then that I, I alone am God,
> and there is no god besides me.
> It is I who bring death and life,   [Deut. 32:39a NAB]
> I wounded and I will heal:
> None can deliver from my hand.   [Deut. 32:39b Tanakh]

By God's own person Yahweh swears to make good the divine triumph:

> I raise my hand towards heaven and swear:
> As I live for ever,
> when I have whetted my flashing sword...   [Deut. 32:40–41a REB]
>
> I shall enforce justice.   [Deut. 32:32–42b NJB]

Concluding on the note of divine deliverance, the preacher solicits praise for Israel's judging and redeeming God:

> Exult with Yahweh, you heavens,   [Deut. 32:43a NAB alt.]
> bow down, all you gods...   [Deut. 32:43b REB]

Repeatedly using one of the most ancient names for deity (*Sur,* "Rock" or "Mountain"), the sermon breathes the bloodthirsty spirit of holy war and terrible judgment. Its warrior-God takes a Homeric delight in battle (v. 42). Yet in a time of terror the preacher apprehends Yahweh as a God of compassion toward Israel, faithful and demanding faithfulness. Contending eloquently for the worship of God alone and asserting the obligation of the covenant, founded on the deeds of Yahweh, the sermon conveys the spirit, content, and style of priestly preaching in the shrines of the tribal league. (Other such sermons would find their way into the Psalter. See below, "Sermons in the Temple Liturgy.")

Oracle

Almost as ancient in Israel as story and song was the *oracle* of Yahweh, a brief pronouncement of judgment received by a prophet in a state of ecstasy and delivered as a word literally spoken by God. Consider Elijah's encounter with King Ahab, who has ruthlessly taken over the ancestral vineyard of a small landholder. God commands:

> Say to him, "This is the word of the LORD
> Have you murdered, and seized property?"
> Say to him: "This is the word of the LORD:
> Where dogs licked the blood of Naboth,
> there dogs will lick your blood."   [1 Kings 21:19 REB]

In obedience the prophet confronts the unprincipled ruler.

Until the eighth century, prophetic deliverances normally came in such oracles, too cramped and unreflective to qualify as preaching in the common understanding of the term, but a forthright declaration of the divine will.

When the ancient priest consulted Yahweh by the sacred lot, Urim and Thummim, he too spoke in this oracular style. After the Philistines, in David's absence with his troops, had raided his base at Ziklag, put it to the torch, and taken captive the women and children, he sent for the priest Abiathar to come with the ephod. Then David consulted Yahweh:

"Shall I go in pursuit of these raiders? Will I overtake them?"

The answer came:

Pursue, for you shall overtake and you shall rescue.

[1 Sam. 30:7–8 Tanakh]

The oracular form also served the national liturgy, being well adapted to the assurance given in a royal Psalm:

This is the LORD's oracle to my Lord:
   "Sit at my right hand,
   and I shall make your enemies your footstool."   [Ps. 110:1 REB]

Presumably when a priest was asked for spiritual counsel or pastoral guidance, this terse style carried the ring of authority. An oracle was not a sermon nor a polished exercise in persuasion. It was heard as an authoritative word from God compressed into a single sizzling sentence.

EMERGENCE OF PREACHING[9]

From Inspired Prophecy to Reflective Address

Prophecy had begun with theophanies and visions; the prophet "saw" or "heard" a manifestation of Yahweh, imparting a command or oracle to be delivered to a ruler or to the people.[10] The narrators depicted Moses (13th century B.C.E.), after the encounter at the burning bush (Ex. 3), as a prophet, proclaiming to Pharaoh and the Hebrew captives Yahweh's word of deliverance from slavery and declaring the law received directly from God. In the ninth century Elijah and Elisha championed the cause of Israel's God against the deities of the surrounding polytheistic nations, and in the face of impending national crisis the eighth-century prophets (Amos, Hosea, Isaiah, Micah) spoke the divine word of judgment and hope. Despite the warnings of Jeremiah in the seventh century, Jerusalem fell, and its people went into exile. Yet in Babylon "Second Isaiah" proclaimed sublime assurance and Ezekiel saw visions of Yahweh's providence still at work.

Prophecy continued after the restoration in the pleas of Haggai and Zechariah to get on with the rebuilding of the Temple and in Malachi's effort to revive religious loyalty and righteousness as demanded by the covenant with Yahweh.

Eighth-century prophecy moved beyond the brief and often withering *oracle* direct from Yahweh to take on the form of an extended *poem;* inspiration led to meditation and reflection, and serious thought came to sublime expression through deliberate literary art.[11] While prophets still recounted a divine "call" or vision to establish their credentials, they now consciously employed creative artistry in communicating the vision they had seen or the word they had received: in the sixth century Jeremiah *acted out* the message as he went about Jerusalem bent beneath a yoke as sign of the nation's coming captivity (Jer. 27:2). More commonly and with deliberate use of "rhetorical" form, they turned the message into memorable poetic utterance. The prophet Isaiah composed a haunting song around an image that would continue to inspire preaching over the centuries:

> Let me sing for my beloved
> A song of my lover about his vineyard:
> My beloved had a vineyard
> On a fruitful hill.
> He broke the ground, cleared it of stones,
> And planted it with choice vines.
> He built a watchtower inside it,
> He even hewed a wine press in it;
> For he hoped it would yield grapes.
> Instead, it yielded wild grapes…
> For the vineyard of the LORD of Hosts
> Is the House of Israel,
> And the seedlings he lovingly tended
> Are the people of Judah.
> And He hoped for justice
> But behold, injustice;
> For equity,
> But behold, iniquity!   [Isa. 5:1, 2, 7 Tanakh]

The prophet recites a list of injustices in Israel; God's righteous anger must impose a terrible judgment, invasion by a faraway people:

> Anyone who looks over the land sees darkness closing in,
> and the light overshadowed by the gathering clouds. [Isa. 5:30 REB]

It was not possible for these messengers, believing themselves sent from God, to speak of Yahweh apart from public affairs, for they saw Yahweh as active in all human concerns. In impassioned eloquence the cry for justice rang through their preaching; prophecy was not the propaganda of a doctrinaire political liberalism, but the voice of spiritual identification with the divine *pathos*, God's unflagging empathy for the weak, the poor, and the downtrodden, and, concurrent divine wrath against wealth and privilege reared on a foundation of exploitation.[12]

But the prophets who denounced injustice with such burning anger could also preach assurance, comfort, and hope in time of disaster, responding to God's command to console and fortify:

Speak tenderly to Jerusalem.   [Isa. 40:2 Tanakh]

In immortal poetry inspired by sustaining faith in the living God, the prophet of the exile, "Second Isaiah," preached his strong word of hope.

All people are grass,
their constancy like flowers of the field.
Grass withers, flowers fade
When the breath of the LORD blows on them.   [Isa. 40:6–7b Tanakh]

surely the people are grass: [7c NRSV]
Grass withers, flowers fade—   [8a Tanakh]
But the word of our God will stand forever.   [Isa. 40:6b–8 NRSV]

Amos, Isaiah, Hosea, and Micah cast their preaching in immortal poetry. But later prophets, while sometimes retaining poetic form, commonly couched their deliverances in blunt prose, the product of intense reflection and moral fervor. Consider the forthright words of Malachi:

A son honors his father, and servants their master.
If then I am a father, where is the honor due me?
And if I am a master, where is the respect due me?
says the LORD of hosts to you,
O priests, who despise my name.   [Mal. 1:6 NRSV]

The prose of these later prophets rings with an unmistakably homiletical tone; some passages are doubtless brief homilies, while others appear to be digests of remembered preaching.

Sermon

In the preaching of Amos, Isaiah, Hosea, Jeremiah, Ezekiel, and other prophets, the *sermon* had arrived—a public address applying to a contemporary situation the preacher's reflection on a divine word or on the sacred tradition. In time their speeches were gathered into collections, e.g., "the sermon-book of the prophet Isaiah" (Lk. 3:4, Williams).[13]

Then prophecy ceased.[14] The Spirit of Yahweh no longer overcame chosen messengers with visions requiring them to cry out. A Psalmist lamented,

> We cannot see what lies before us,
> we have no prophet now. [Ps. 74:9 NEB]

Yet the living word of Yahweh continued to be spoken. In the seventh century a group of reformers committed to the righteousness and the spirituality at the heart of the sacred tradition gave it current relevance by rewriting it for their time. These "Deuteronomists" found places, in their book (Deuteronomy) and in the sacred history that they compiled, for more than a dozen of their sermons,[15] putting them into the mouths of Moses or Joshua or Samuel through *prosopopeia,* the preacher's favorite device for relating sacred tradition to contemporary conditions. Holding that true prophecy must conform to the teaching of Moses, the Deuteronomists warned against false prophets.

After them the priestly redactors who compiled and edited the older documents, gathering them, along with Deuteronomy, into "the Five Books of Moses," added an occasional sermon (e.g., Gen. 1:1– 2:4), though their primary interest was in law. The fifth-century chroniclers rewrote the national history with an eye to edification, filling their idealized narrative with psalms, prayers, and speeches (or sermon digests) attributed to David, Solomon, and lesser figures. The books of the prophets include not only the messages of those whose names they bear but also the homilies of lesser preachers among their disciples, adapting the tradition to new situations.

In the Hellenistic era a new genre of literature arose, discrete works attributed to one of the spiritual giants of former generations— Solomon, Jeremiah, Baruch, Daniel, Ezra—speaking in Greek rather than Aramaic, but with explicit reference to the sacred tradition and the situation troubling the faithful at the time of writing. In that broad sense they may be considered preaching, especially since in those days one rarely if ever sat alone perusing a scroll in silence, but rather heard it read aloud in a gathering of eager listeners. And some of the passages credited to an ancient worthy or an angel of God read very much like condensed sermons (2 Esdras, chaps. 1–4, contains a collection of such homilies), giving us the flavor of some Jewish preaching in the decades close to Jesus and the rise of the church. Incorporated into the Septuagint (LXX), the Greek version of Israel's scripture, they were regarded by the early Christians as divinely inspired and included in the Latin Vulgate; though not listed in the Jewish or Protestant canons, they may be found under the general title Apocrypha in various contemporary versions of the Bible.

The readiness of so many preachers—Deuteronomists, Chroniclers, disciples of major prophets, composers of apocryphal works—to accept anonymity, committing their proclamation to a place in the tradition without personal credit, suggests the high priority they placed upon the word itself.

Sermons in the Temple Liturgy

After the building of the Temple (10th century B.C.E.) its courts resounded with *psalms* (e.g., 44, 77) rehearsing in the liturgy familiar incidents from the old stories, elaborating the primal creed, reflecting on the sacred history. Psalm 78 preserves priestly preaching that ponders the riddles posed by the recital of the saving events and the twin mysteries of Israel's unfaithfulness and God's grace.

> My people, listen to my teaching,
> pay attention to what I say. [78:1 REB]
> I will open my mouth in story,
> drawing lessons from of old… [2 NAB]

> [The LORD] laid on Jacob a solemn charge [5a REB]
> and appointed a law in Israel,
> which he commanded our ancestors
> to teach to their children… [5b–d NRSV]
> They were charged to put their trust in God…
> and to keep his commandments… [7 REB]
> He split the sea and brought them through,
> made the waters stand up like a dam;
> He led them with a cloud by day,
> and all the night with the light of a fire. [13–14 NJB]
> But they went on sinning against him,
> rebelling against the Most High in the desert. [17 NAB]

Nevertheless, mused the preacher, God continued to lead and provide for the unfaithful wanderers in the wilderness.

He brought his people to his holy land...
and settled the tribes of Israel in their tents. [55 NJB]

And God refused to give up on them:

He chose David to be his servant
and took him from the sheepfolds...
to be the shepherd of his people Israel. [70–71 REB]

Read in full, the searching psalm runs longer than many a homily. Like the "Song of Moses" it represents a form of sermon which, centuries before the exile, played variations on the theme of Israel's ancient recital.

Running through the Psalms, as through the stories of the oral tradition, a central theme is obedience to the divine commandments. From the time of Moses, Israel is covenanted to live by the Law of Yahweh, the Torah.

Preaching in the Wisdom Tradition [16]

In addition to prophetic and liturgical sermons Israel had developed other forms of reasoned utterance. Priests offered practical counsel in a style more discursive than that of the oracle. "Elders" or judges handed down case-law, which was absorbed into the "law of Moses." But kings and sages gave impetus to a new style of speech, kings by bringing wise women and wise men to their courts to offer counsel, sages by providing instruction in reflective conduct. So arose the rhetoric of wisdom.

Constantly required to make fateful decisions like heads of state everywhere, the kings of Israel gathered about them the wisest counselors they could find. David (11th century B.C.E.) relied on an inner circle of advisers, and his successors followed suit. Some gained admission to the royal "brain trust" by achieving preeminence in a department of government: the army, public works, the chancery, the royal chapel or temple.[17] Others won their place primarily as intellectuals: Endowed with native shrewdness and wit, they had honed their mental powers in mastering the tradition of *wisdom*—a cover-all term in antiquity, somewhat comparable to our term "education."

The tradition flourished in Egypt, Arabia, Phoenicia, and Mesopotamia. Israel appropriated and refined it in the service of Yahweh, even claiming to have possessed it from the time of the nation's emergence; in a famous apology of the first century C. E. an eloquent Jew made the assertion with pride:

> Moses was educated [in] all the wisdom of the Egyptians.
>
> [Acts 7:22 NAB]

Devotees of this eastern *paideia,* which was older than Greek philosophy, sought to establish principles of sound public policy and personal prudence, and to epitomize them in aphorisms made memorable by the sparkling imagery and the insistent parallelism of Semitic poetry.[18]

David himself won a reputation for native wisdom and could point his speech with a folk-proverb (1 Sam. 24:13); some of the advisers he brought to his court must also have mastered wisdom in the technical sense, for his administrative organization followed Egyptian models.[19] The affairs of court required maintaining official records, tabulating census reports, transcribing laws, and preparing sundry documents; so David included among his officials a recorder and a secretary.[20] Solomon (962–922 B.C.E.) increased the size of the chancery, establishing in effect a royal school for scribes. At his court bright young men could learn the art of composition and study the lore of Eastern wisdom, sharpening their minds while earning a place in the cultural elite and in the expanding bureaucracy.[21]

Solomon's reputation for wisdom became legendary; in due course Israel attributed its literary corpus of this genre to him—just as it credited its body of law to Moses and of psalms to David, honoring in each instance a hero larger than life whose words had inspired the particular form of literature, attracting subsequent expressions to his own name.

Solomon liked the game of coining proverbs and patronized the collecting of wise sayings from various sources. Major sections of the biblical book of Proverbs date, at least in nucleus, from his reign (1:7–9:18; 10:1–22:16).[22] Although the origin of particular maxims is uncertain, the following sayings are typical:

> The thoughtful mind is eager to know more;
> the wise person longs to learn.   [Prov. 18:15 NTB]

> The mind of the wise makes their speech judicious,
> and adds persuasiveness to their lips.
> Pleasant words are like a honeycomb,
> sweetness to the soul
> and health to the body.   [Prov. 16:23–24 NRSV]

A mild answer turns away anger,
but a sharp word makes tempers rise.
The tongues of the wise spread knowledge;
the stupid talk a lot of nonsense.   [Prov. 15:1–2 REB]

Israel's fascination with persuasive speech—and mystification at its limitations—fashioned a couplet regarding lawsuits:

The one who first states a case seems right,
until the other comes and cross-examines.   [Prov. 18:17 NRSV]

A brace of aphorisms commends the cultivation of eloquence:

From the fruit of the mouth someone may live;   [NRSV, REB]
the yield of the lips brings satisfaction.
Death and life are in the power of the tongue,
and those who love it will eat its fruits.   [Prov. 18:20–21 NRSV]

The gift of judicious speech, while it might make a counselor rich, is a treasure in its own right.

Gold, wealth of rubies, jewels rare—
such are wise words.   [Prov. 20:15 BNT]

Eloquence in the offering of wisdom could match the most exquisite artistry of the goldsmith:

Like golden apples in silver showpieces
is a phrase well turned.   [Prov. 25:11 Tanakh]

But eloquence is not to be prized merely for aesthetic delight, for wisdom cherishes a commitment to justice that though not revolutionary, is as searching as that of the prophets.[23] In the second century B.C.E., Jesus ben Sira, one of this tradition's most attractive teachers, admonished his students:

Never remain silent when a word might put things right,
and do not hide your wisdom,
for it is by the spoken word that wisdom is known,
and learning finds expression in speech.   [Sir. 4:23–24 REB]

In the centuries after Solomon, ambitious young people looked upon wisdom as a promising *paideia* opening the way to honor and influence (as the mastery of rhetoric was understood to do in the Hellenistic world):

I determined to take [wisdom] home to live with me,
knowing that she would be my counsellor in prosperity
and my comfort in anxiety and grief.
Through her, I thought, I shall win fame in the eyes of the people
and honour among older men, young though I am.
When I sit in judgment, I shall prove myself acute,
and the great will admire me;
when I say nothing, they will wait for me to speak;
when I speak, they will attend
and, though I talk at some length,
they will lay a finger to their lips and listen.
Through her I shall have immortality and leave an undying memory
to those who come after me.   [Wis. 8:9–13 REB]

Even so, an air of humble piety pervades many of the sayings:

A human heart makes the plans,
Yahweh gives the answer.
A person's own acts seem right to the doer,
but Yahweh is the weigher of souls.
Commend what you do to Yahweh,
and what you plan will be achieved.   [Prov. 16:1–3 NJB]

The spirit of wisdom melds its piety with unblinking pragmatism. It sets forth sound advice on interpersonal relationships, just rule, moral uprightness, a prudential style of living, and the way to prosperity. Reflective rather than passionate, it upholds dignity and honor and casts shame on cunning and deceit.

Inevitably in Israel it inculcates respect for Yahweh, regarding such wisdom as any mortal might attain as an endowment of the divine Spirit.

I saw that there was no way to gain possession of [wisdom]
except by gift of God—
and it was itself a mark of understanding
to know from whom that gift must come.   [Wis. 8:21 NEB]

Wisdom honors Israel's sacred tradition of Law and cult and prophecy. At the same time it is far from ecstatic, its ethos more this-worldly than mystical. Only rarely does it speak of covenant, election, or God's purpose for the chosen people. Dominated by a mood of prudence and marked by an egalitarian individualism, it lays down principles for advancing within the established order, calling for justice and compassion without advocating radical social reform.[24]

One of the most striking developments in this school, fraught with significance for Hellenistic Judaism and early Christianity, came with the personification of Wisdom as an expression of the divine mind. Depicted already in Proverbs as a woman of effectiveness, stateliness and honor and presented as a character of surpassing grace, she speaks eloquently in some of the most impressive discourses in the writings of the "wise":

In the very first chapter of Proverbs she appears:

Wisdom cries out in the street;
in the squares she raises her voice.
At the busiest corner she cries out;
at the entrance of the city gates she speaks:
"How long, O simple ones, will you love being simple?...
Give heed to my reproof;
I will pour out my thoughts to you...
Those who listen to me will be secure
and will live at ease,
without dread of disaster."   [Prov. 1:20–22a, 23a, 33 NRSV]

This opening discourse is striking, the speech of a street-corner teacher of wisdom offered by a respectable woman in a public setting, who has come to seek justice and to judge[25]—an uncommon event in that time of patriarchy.

Delivered "on the heights, beside the way," (8:2) Lady Wisdom's next speech, after the conventional invitation to hear (vv. 5–6) and learn, surprises by her dazzling claim:

The LORD created me at the beginning of his work,
the first of his acts of long ago.
Ages ago I was set up,
at the first, before the beginning of the earth...
Before the mountains had been shaped,
before the hills, I was brought forth...
When he established the heavens, I was there...
when he marked out the foundations of the earth...
then I was beside him, like a master worker.   [Prov. 8:22–30 NRSV]

More than rhetorical personification has occurred here. A myth of Wisdom has been created which was destined for great significance in the Hellenistic era.

The teachers of wisdom hold importance for preaching at two additional points: (1) They concentrated their observations into pithy, memorable sayings, orally taught, readily remembered, and effectively quoted in spicing either private conversation or public admonition.[26] (2) Having little love for abstraction, they gave intense vividness to their expression of important principles by casting them in concrete terms. An idealized description of Solomon, embellished by later generations, catches this essential character of wisdom, suggesting a mode of picturesque speech to be cultivated by the preacher who would reach the popular ear:

> God gave Solomon very great wisdom,
> discernment, and breadth of understanding
> as vast as the sand on the seashore,
> so that Solomon's wisdom surpassed the wisdom
> of all the people of the east, and all the wisdom of Egypt...
> His fame spread throughout all the surrounding nations.
> He composed three thousand proverbs,
> and his songs numbered a thousand and five.
> He would speak of trees, from the cedar that is in Lebanon
> to the hyssop that grows in the wall;
> he would speak of animals, and birds, and reptiles, and fish.
> People came from all the nations to hear the wisdom of Solomon;
> they came from all the kings of the earth
> who had heard of his wisdom.   [1 Kings 4:29–34 NRSV]

Drawn from wisdom's international treasury, *proverbs* served as primary carriers of teaching and learning.

Along with such aphorisms, as brief and pungent as oracles, "the wise" also spoke in fables and parables, and in extended speeches on a theme, which by linking a series of proverbs constituted a sort of homily (e.g., Prov. 31:10–31). A few poetic addresses in the tradition of wisdom were claimed for Israel's psalter (e.g., Psalms 1, 19, 37, 104). The speeches of Job's friends also offer examples of preaching in this style.

+

Speeches composed in the manner of the sages take their place along with the preaching of the prophets (and of the Deuteronomists) as primal sermons within Judaism. Highly concentrated and condensed in comparison with the orotund eloquence of the Greeks and Romans, they represent a form of address growing out of deep reflection on the issues of life in the light of Israel's received faith. In keeping with the conventions of wisdom, their rhetoric is distinctive; like Lady Wisdom herself, their aim is not to assert power, but to establish authority, not to coerce but to persuade.[27] And their preaching is vital.

The full-blown sermon in our understanding of the term would emerge when Hellenistic Jews embraced classical rhetoric and put it to the service of proclaiming the divine Law. (See below, "Midrash: Interpretation of Torah.") But first we turn to the elevation of the Law itself.

TORAH, THE HEART OF JUDAISM[28]

Ezra

A dramatic scene set by the chronicler (Neh. 8—9), writing apparently in the 4th century B.C.E., signals the establishment of Judaism as a faith centered in Torah, written and oral. Like an enthusiastic director of epic films, the chronicler loved to picture spectacular occasions, massing a cast of thousands to give praise to God while a religious hero, larger than life, dominates the scene. In depicting the restoration after the Babylonian captivity, he portrays Ezra the scribe standing on a high wooden dais in Jerusalem (like his contemporary Pericles delivering the Funeral Oration to the citizens of Athens).

Having returned to the holy city with a company of former exiles, the priest rose up to read the Book of the Law of Moses "which the LORD had given to Israel" (Neh. 8:1). Gathered in the Water Gate Square, all the people stood while Ezra opened the scroll he had brought and listened as he "read from early morning until midday." Six Levites standing at his right and seven at his left "helped the people understand," reading clearly from that book containing the Torah of God, and giving the sense. Because Hebrew, the language of the sacred text, had given way in daily usage to Aramaic, the lingua franca of Mesopotamia, Syria, and Palestine, the task of the assistants was to supply a translation (Targum) of the scripture in the common idiom. Next morning, after an evening of feasting, the heads of families returned to Ezra "in order to study the words of the law" even further. Judaism had arrived.

The Written Torah

The holy book of the Law which Ezra the scribe brought from Babylon held the written Torah, the supreme priestly work of the exile. In the desolation of captivity, their temple destroyed and sacrifices suspended, the priests had clung tenaciously to the supreme treasure, their sacred scrolls, to survive the national catastrophe. Composed by various authors across the previous four centuries, these included documents that scholars ascribe to the Yahwist, the Elohist, the Deuteronomists, and a succession of editors. Conflating these documents, and incorporating material from the priestly tradition, the exilic scribes produced the Books of the "Law"—or "Instruction" or even "Revelation," as *Torah* might be more precisely rendered. From now on Jews would be "the people of the Book."

Other sacred writings had come to be revered along with the "books of Moses." Accordingly, the priestly editors in exile had associated with those five books, called the Torah, these other documents, known as the Early Prophets (Joshua, Judges, Samuel, Kings) and the Latter Prophets (Isaiah, Jeremiah, Ezekiel, and the "Book of the Twelve"—the so-called minor prophets). While not accorded the supreme measure of authority ascribed to the five books of Moses, they were widely held, at least as early as 200 B.C.E., to be divinely inspired. From then on "the Law and the Prophets" meant scripture.

Even newer books also came to command esteem as sacred writings, being read in the synagogues and revered by Jews willing to die as martyrs rather than surrrender them to the Syrian troops of Antiochus (2d century B.C.E.). By usage the Palestinian community generally included alongside the Law and the Prophets a collection broadly termed "the Writings." It contained three poetic works (Psalms, Proverbs, Job), five scrolls for various annual festivals (Song of Solomon, Ruth, Lamentations, Ecclesiastes, Esther), one apocalyptic prophecy (Daniel), and two historical writings (Ezra-Nehemiah and Chronicles).

When at the end of the first century C.E. the rabbis at Jabneh (Jamnia) fixed the (Palestinian) canon of the Hebrew Bible, they reckoned the total number of books at twenty-four. The Jewish community in Alexandria accepted a larger number of books, some of which have subsequently been termed apocryphal. Torah came to mean the entire corpus of sacred writings, as well as the authoritative oral interpretation of the Law; more commonly it meant the five "Books of Moses." Throughout Judaism, whatever sanctity was imputed to the larger collections of writings and the oral tradition, the Pentateuch held the place of preeminent authority.

Education in Torah

Torah comprised the chief subject of Jewish education, reflection, and intellectual activity. In the first century C.E. the synagogue school became an established feature of local Jewish life, teaching the boys of the community the sacred writings along with the rudiments of general learning. By the end of the century, perhaps as early as the time of Jesus' youth, Nazareth supported such a school. Is it possible that he may have attended it? Advanced rabbinical schools flourished in nearby Sepphoris, in Tiberias, and in Caesarea.

To the Jews, the discipline of life's difficult experiences, understood in the light of Torah as a mode of divine teaching, constituted *mûsar*—or as the Hellenistic Jews would say, *paideia*—i.e., education. The essence of such learning was meditation on Torah. The great prayer of love for the Law, Psalm 119, repeats in 175 of its 176 verses some term for divine Law: decree, precept, statute, commandment, promise, word, judgment, way. Torah was the heart of the life of the synagogue. The eloquent preacher of the second century B.C.E., Jesus ben Sira, declared,

> A sensible person puts his trust in the law,
> finding it reliable like the oracle of God.   [Sir. 33:3 REB]

Midrash: Interpretation of Torah[29]

A new element in the life of Israel now characterized synagogal discourse as over against that of the prophets: the preacher no longer claimed to speak under immediate divine mandate or to offer reflections on an oracle personally received by direct communication from God. By the beginning of the first century B.C.E. it was believed that prophecy had ceased. Yet God had not left this people without divine guidance. On the contrary, the divine Spirit had inspired Torah, the sacred scripture, speaking through prophets and priests and sages of old, and Israel's calling was to read and reflect on the inspired words; interpretations offered by respected rabbis and remembered by colleagues and disciples also came to be known as the *Oral Torah*, carrying authority like that of the scripture itself.[30] It was the glory of the faithful to meditate on Torah day and night and for the most learned among them to set forth a faithful commentary (*midrash*) that the word of scripture might become the message of God for the living present.

Whenever scripture is addressed to persons who do not speak the language of the text, translation is inescapable. Inevitably it requires paraphrase or explanation which, however faithful to the intention of the author, goes beyond the supplying of equivalent words, for literal translation often makes no sense when removed from the original context. The Targums needed explaining. Enter midrash.

The synagogue became the local venue for intensive Bible study, as a circle of men formed for their favorite enterprise, searching out the meaning of passage after passage in the Torah. While any of them might speak up to express an opinion regarding the passage under discussion, the words heard with greatest respect would be those of the reader most conversant with scripture as a whole, quick to mention other sentences in the holy writings in which the word under consideration also appears, and able also to recall insights spoken by others in the past. One who earned recognition for this kind of knowledge was popularly addressed by the title *rabbi*[31] and accorded particular deference in discussions. Thus the common memory preserved an increasing body of midrash.

In considering Exodus 13:17–18, e.g., "Now when Pharaoh let the people go, God did not lead them by the way of the land of the Philistines, although that was nearer...God led the people by the roundabout way of the wilderness toward the Red Sea,"it was remembered that Rabbi Eliezer (end of first century C.E.) had opined:

> *Way* indicates that He intended to tire them, as in the verse
> *He drained my strength in the way.*   [Ps. 102:23]

His contemporary, Rabbi Joshua, offered a different slant:

> *Way* (Ex. 13:18) indicates that He intended to give them the Torah as in the verses
> *Follow only the way*
> *that the LORD your God has enjoined upon you*   [Deut. 5:33]
> and
> *For the commandment is a lamp,*
> *and the teaching [Torah] a light*   [Prov. 6:23a NRSV]
> *and the way to life.*   [Prov. 6:23b NJB][32]

Remember that these rabbis did their exegesis without benefit of concordance, relying on memory to recall the use of a given word in various passages. It is also clear that allegorical interpretation disclosed edifying possibilities in verses where a literal reading would offer little in the way of spiritual guidance.

In the liturgy of the synagogue, midrash quickly developed from such brief, informal commentary into a homily or familiar lecture on the meaning of the scripture read in the sabbath service. In time a manner of sermonizing arose which no longer undertook a complete exposition of the passage, but strove to develop a particular line of thought suggested by it. Even a general reference to the tradition without citing a specific text might qualify as midrash. Thus the rabbis pioneered expository, textual, and topical preaching.

A common theme was the denunciation of idolatry; what appears to be a topical sermon of this sort from the second century B.C.E. is preserved among the apocryphal books.

> Clearly they are not gods;
> therefore have no fear of them.
> These gods, sitting in their temples,
> are of no more use than a broken pot.
> Their eyes get filled with dust
> from the feet of those who come in...
> They are like one of the beams of the temple,
> but...their hearts are eaten out,
> for creatures crawl from the ground
> and devour both them and their vestments
> without their being aware of it.
> Their faces are blackened by the smoke in the temple.
> Bats and swallows and birds of all kinds
> perch on their bodies and heads, and cats do likewise.
> From all this you may be sure that they are not gods;
> therefore have no fear of them.   [Let. Jer. 6:16–23 REB][33]

Synagogal preaching was controlled by a didactic purpose far more pronounced than that which marked the oratory of the Greeks and Romans, even the moralists among them. For the Jewish preacher was essentially a teacher of divine Law, involved by definition in the explication of scripture. Even so, the expositor was concerned, like the Hellenistic orators, to please and to persuade—and thus necessarily and self-consciously involved with rhetoric (and dialectic).[34] The rabbis consistently delighted their audiences with the proverbial form of their speech, their pointed and pithy commentary, their sly humor even in the discussion of sacred questions, and their gift for the perceptive story. (See "Forms of Religious Address" in chapter 6.)

Texts from Interpreters and Preachers

Repeated disasters overtook Israel in the first two centuries of the Common Era: first the destruction of Jerusalem in the year 70, putting an end to the temple cult; then the Roman crushing of the Jewish rebellion under Bar-Kochba in 135, the last futile effort to restore national independence. Judaism was left with only its people—and the Torah to enable them to maintain their identity. Through decade after decade of political helplessness, devotion to the Law, their sole abiding legacy from their days as a nation, flamed with undying fervor in the hearts of devout Jews.

In those perilous times the rabbis of the period devoted much energy to compiling the legal tradition that composed the Oral Torah; they were known as the Tannaim, a title derived from the Aramaic term meaning *to repeat* or *to hand down orally.*[35] About 200 C.E., Rabbi Judah the Holy (also remembered as Judah the Prince—or as Rabbi, with no name being necessary) completed the Mishnah in the Hebrew language.[36] The oldest such compilation extant, it spelled out precise rules for every kind of legal situation to which the Torah might apply, condensing the interpretations of the great rabbinic authorities of the past. Presuming knowledge of scriptural law, it does not ordinarily quote the sacred text; while failing to qualify as preaching in the usual sense, or even as biblical exposition, this digest of pronouncements by authorities on the Law nevertheless held immeasurable importance for the communities of Jews who sought to remain faithful after the loss of both temple and nation.

Sometimes the flame burned low among a disheartened people. To contend with growing ignorance of Torah toward the end of the second century C.E., Rabbi Hiyya undertook to rekindle the fire.

> To make sure the Torah would not be forgotten in Israel,
> what did I do? I sowed flax,
> and from the flax cords I made nets.
> With the nets I trapped deer,
> giving their meat to orphans to eat,
> and from their skins prepared scrolls.
> On the scrolls, I wrote the five books of Moses.
> Then I went to a town that had no teachers
> and taught the five books to five children,
> and the six orders of the Mishnah to six children.
> I instructed them,
>   "Until I return, teach each other the Torah and the Mishnah."
> And that is how I kept the Torah from being forgotten in Israel.[37]

The Amoraim (Speakers), as the rabbis in the century and a half after "publication" of the Mishnah are known, continued Israel's long devotion to the tradition of oral exegesis and succeded in committing a considerable body of midrash to writing. With great importance for the history of preaching, their work bore the simple title *Avot* ("Fathers"); preserving remembered utterances across a span of generations from the second century B.C.E.—and possibly earlier—up to the time of publication, about 250 C.E. it is commonly known as *Pirqe* (or *Pirke,* "Chapters") *Abot* (P. A.). These "Sayings of the Fathers" compress the application of a biblical text into an epigram or a brief paragraph of homiletic reflection, marked by wit, forthrightness, grace, and spiritual insight. Frequently a speaker enumerates three or seven or ten items of practice in a list to be remembered. Handed down orally for generations, some of the sayings are credited to a famous name when that of the person who first uttered them has been lost; in any event, the Amoraim remembered the teachings, as their predecessors had done.

Many a saying in *Pirqe Abot* contains a sermon in a nutshell, the essence of a rabbi's teaching; nearly all the dicta are capable of expansion by anyone with an iota of homiletical flair. For the history of preaching in Judaism during the centuries immediately before the destruction of the temple and the century that followed, they are our most important single source.

By 400 C.E. the rabbis had collected a much larger compilation of commentaries known as the Talmud of the Land of Israel, commonly referred to also as the Jerusalem (or the Palestinian) Talmud; two centuries after that the Babylonian Talmud was compiled.[38] On these works subsequent generations have depended for knowledge of classical midrash and of the rabbis who formulated the conclusions it contains. In these venerable digests of Jewish exegesis and preaching, assembled in commentaries on the various Books of Moses and other parts of scripture, we engage the inner life of Israel as the rabbis contended for the souls of their people and faithful Jews struggled to maintain the Covenant in a world that had radically changed.

Already in the first century B.C.E., when the Romans took over Palestine, Judaism was heir to a long and vigorous tradition of exegesis, commentary, and preaching. We proceed to note how the rabbis continued and enriched that heritage.[39]

CHAPTER 5

Preachers in the Struggle
for a People's Soul

A Scattered People at Worship[1]

The Dispersion

Strewn about the Mediterranean littoral and the Fertile Crescent by shifting tides of empire and the winds of commerce, children of Abraham and Sarah had established communities in every part of the *oikoumené*. Since their conquest by Babylon (597 B.C.E.) a number of Jews had lived in Mesopotamia and northern Syria, and from the days of Jeremiah (587 B.C.E.) a colony had flourished in Egypt; Philo of Alexandria (ca. 30 B.C.E.–40 C.E.) reckoned their number in his time at almost a quarter of a million. Their synagogues dotted Cyprus, Asia Minor, Macedonia, Achaia, North Africa, and Italy. The Greek geographer Strabo wrote, "They have penetrated...into every state."[2] In Rome, where their numbers probably exceeded 20,000, Cicero defended the proconsul Flaccus on charges of embezzling gold intended for the temple at Jerusalem; he feared to raise his voice above a whisper, he confided to his audience, lest he arouse the enmity of the large number of Jews present.[3] The book of Acts pictures Jews coming to Jerusalem from as far away as Phrygia, Libya, and Ethiopia. Because of the dispersion (Diaspora) of the Jews throughout the *oikoumené*, Judaism in the Hellenistic era was a worldwide faith.

The Temple at Jerusalem

Yet until the destruction of Jerusalem (70 C.E.) the thoughts of this scattered people turned to the Holy City, as they prayed with the psalmist,

> Gather us from among the nations,
> to acclaim Your holy name,
> to glory in Your praise.   [Ps. 106:47 Tanakh]

From every quarter Jews came on pilgrimage to the temple. After the splendid edifice erected by Solomon about 950 and destroyed by Nebuchadnezzar in 586 B.C.E. had lain in ruins for two generations, it was replaced by a modest sanctuary. Then about 20 B.C.E. the Roman puppet-king Herod built a magnificent new structure. "When the morning sun burst upon the white marble," Josephus rhapsodized, "Mount Moriah glittered like a hill of snow; and when its rays struck the golden roof of the edifice, the whole mount gleamed and sparkled as if it were in flames."[4]

Built with a series of commodious courts, porches, and colonnades surrounding the Holy Place and its great altar, the temple attracted persons coming for prayer or diversion; its courts offered ready audiences for discussions about Torah or harangues on religious themes. During the great feasts thousands of pilgrims crowded the sacred precincts, drawing preachers like a magnet.

The Synagogue, Center for Preaching

But regular preaching found a home in the synagogue, the congregation of Jews organized for instruction in the Law, even in localities far from Jerusalem. Like so much at the heart of Judaism, the synagogue may have come into being during the exile in Babylon (6th century B.C.E.) as a heartsick people, their temple destroyed, their holy city lying in ruins, turned to their sacred tradition. The oldest structures clearly identifiable as synagogues, however, date from first-century C.E. Palestine; the Gospels and Acts frequently mention synagogues there and throughout the Diaspora. Documents from the third century B.C.E. refer to Jewish *proseuchai* ("places of prayer," presumed to be synagogues) in Egypt.

Whenever and wherever local communities of Jews first established places of regular meeting for worship and reflection on the Law,[5] the synagogue has stood at the heart of Jewish life ever since. In reverence for the Law, in reading, hearing, and interpreting Torah as the divine Word, even in a strange land, Jews continued to worship the God whose glory had once filled the Temple. Instead of a sometime thing—a seasonal festival in Jerusalem attended perhaps once or twice in a lifetime if one lived in the Diaspora—communal worship in their own community became the climax of every week in the year, wherever Jews might find themselves. The name for their local meeting or gathering together (*synagogé* in Greek) soon attached itself also to the place where they assembled.

The building of the second temple after the return from Babylon (ca. 520 B.C.E.) and its splendid renovation by King Herod in no way diminished the synagogue's importance; rather it had become in the Roman era a significant institution both in the Diaspora and throughout Palestine. The regular gathering of a local congregation to ponder scripture and its meaning was a new thing in history, a revolution to rival the invention of printing. It set preaching squarely at the center of communal religious life.

The synagogue belonged to the people. Not dominated by a professional caste, as was the temple, a synagogue could be formed by as few as ten sons of Abraham. The "elders" of the community, presided over by a "ruler," ordered its life, but any man among the Jews could lead its simple services if requested to do so. Jerusalem boasted 400 synagogues, and many were to be found in Rome, Alexandria, and other cities. A sizeable synagogue normally supported a rabbi and possibly an associate to care for the school.

Within the building, minimally a rectangular hall,[6] benches were provided, including some that were elevated for the elders and the rich; a low screen separated women from men. The room had no altar. Its distinctive furniture—*béma* or platform, lectern, and *kathedra* or seat of Moses—served the reading and interpretation of scripture. Attention centered on an ark containing the sacred scrolls of the Torah, shielded by a veil or screen, and a holy light burned as symbol of the Law. Architecturally, the synagogue dominated its area, standing on high ground or at least projecting a pole from its rooftop to reach above surrounding buildings, thus asserting the transcendence of the divine Word.

Services were held at the three daily hours of prayer (9:00 a. m., noon, and 3:00 p. m.), the chief days of worship being the Sabbath, Monday and Thursday. The recitation of the *Shema*, the summation of the Law opened the service:

Hear, O Israel! The LORD is our God, the LORD alone... [Deut. 6:4 Tanakh]

There followed the eighteen blessings, psalms, and hymns, then readings from the Law and the Prophets, with translation into the common speech, Aramaic or Greek, and the midrash or homily. In an apology Philo of Alexandria characterized the proceedings:

They do always assemble and sit together,
most of them in silence

except when it is the practice to add something
to signify approval of what is read.
But some priest who is present or one of the elders
reads the holy laws to them and expounds them point by point
till about the late afternoon, when they depart
having gained both expert knowledge of the holy laws
and considerable advance in piety.[7]

The service concluded with a benediction and the congregational *Amen.*

Worship was preeminently the service of the Word, with the Law subdivided into portions for weekly reading; in Palestine the entire Torah would be read through in three years, in Babylonia in one year. About the end of the first century C.E., lections from the prophets were likewise scheduled. Any man in the congregation might be asked to read and, if considered capable, to comment on the passage for the day. The speaker stood to read, then—unlike the Hellenistic orators—seated himself to expound the scripture. (This custom may have set the pattern for the early Christian bishop, who delivered the homily while seated on the *kathedra* or throne behind the holy table.)

The synagogue produced a devoted company of commentators and preachers who shared their delight in the Law. Their careful exposition of the sacred text as guide for living and source of spiritual power gave Judaism its distinctive flavor. Commonly the preacher began by taking a question from the congregation concerning a passage in the scripture reading for the day (perhaps having been given advance notice of the question). Snatches of the preaching as recalled through the oral tradition may be discerned in the Talmud; one such deals with a question concerning the text, "And Moses took with him the bones of Joseph" (Ex. 13:19). Someone asks,

And how did Moses know where Joseph was buried?

The preacher has an answer:

They say, Serah, daughter of Asher, had survived of that generation,
and she showed Moses the grave of Joseph. She said to him,
    "The Egyptians made him a coffin of metal and sank it in the Nile."

Having let the congregation in on information derived from tradition, the preacher summons up his gifts of narration:

Moses came and stood at the bank of the Nile,
took a golden tablet, incised in it the Holy Name of God,
and threw it into the river, crying out,

"Joseph, son of Jacob, the time [has come] for fulfilling the oath
that the Holy One, blessed be He,
took to our father Abraham to redeem his children.
If you come up, well and good,
but if not, we are freed of the oath
that you have imposed on us."
Of a sudden the coffin of Joseph floated up, and Moses took it.

Having regaled his hearers with the tale of a miracle, the rabbi
now appeals to a standard form of argument to make it credible.

Do not find this matter surprising,
for lo, Scripture says, *"But as one was felling a beam...*
and the man of God said, 'Where did it fall?'"   [2 Kings 6:5–6]
Lo, this yields an argument *a fortiori:*
If Elisha, who was disciple of Elijah, made the iron float,
how much the more so Moses, the master of Elijah,
could do such a thing![8]

There are still more wonders. The preacher also recounts a different
miracle that enabled Moses to find Joseph's coffin, then imagines the
magnificent procession up from Egypt to the homeland:

The coffin of Joseph went
alongside the ark of the One Who Lives Forever.
And the nations of the world said to the Israelites...
    "What is interred in the ark of the corpse,
    that it goes along with the ark
    of the One Who Lives Forever?"[9]

In the old land of Israel and throughout the Diaspora rabbis proclaimed the righteousness and universal majesty of Jacob's God, preaching tens of thousands of sermons in the synagogues of Palestine alone
during the first four or five centuries C.E.[10] And faithful Jews found
strength in the promise of one of them:

Whenever ten people enter the synagogue,
the Divine Presence enters with them, as it is said
God stands in the divine assembly.   [Ps. 82:1][11]

CONFRONTATION WITH HELLENISM[12]

The Heel of the Conqueror

When Alexander the Great added Palestine to his skein of conquests (332 B.C.E.), a struggle for national survival began. That conflict

produced a series of glorious victories under Judas Maccabeus (d. 160 B.C.E.), followed by a succession of military disasters. In 63 B.C.E. Pompey raised the standard of Rome over Jerusalem; from then on imperial underlings governed the former Jewish nation. To put down rebellion the Emperor Vespasian laid Jerusalem under siege, and in 70 C.E. his son Titus destroyed the temple. The Arch of Titus in Rome still displays a weathered bas-relief depicting the soldiers in his triumph bearing the seven-branched candlestick seized from the sacred courts.

In one last revolt in 135 C.E. half a million rebels lost their lives. Forbidding Jews access to Mount Zion except once a year to bewail the temple, the Romans erected a shrine to Jupiter on that sacred site. The cult of the Aaronic priesthood vanished from history.

The Issue of Jewish Integrity

For five troubled centuries one central issue had agitated Judaism: the question of Jewishness. It confronted every Jew in the life of the mind and the inmost sanctuary of the spirit. When the conqueror undertook to stamp out the faith, as Antiochus IV of Syria (175–163 B.C.E.) attempted to do, heroic spirits resisted, and Judaism had its martyrs. The faithful fortified their own courage by recounting the steadfastness of ninety-year-old Eleazar, a leading teacher of the Law, who refused to save his life by violating the prescriptions of the Torah against eating pork; the old man spoke eloquently to his torturers:

> If I practiced deceit for the sake of a brief moment of life,
> I should lead [the young] astray and stain my old age with dishonour...
> If I now die bravely, I shall show that I have deserved my long life,
> and leave to the young a noble example;
> I shall be teaching them how to die a good death,
> gladly and nobly, for our revered and noble laws...
> [The LORD] knows...that in my soul I suffer gladly,
> because I stand in awe of him.   [2 Macc. 6:25–30 REB][13]

Along with his death Israel recalled the martyrdom of seven brothers, tortured one by one until they died, for refusing the demand to eat pork—each in his turn giving an eloquent testimony to his persecutors (2 Macc. 7).

More remarkable than these men was their mother, who stood by, exhorting each of her seven sons to hold fast in faith. Urged by the king to persuade her youngest to avoid death, she spoke to the lad in their native language:

Son, take pity on me,
who carried you nine months in the womb,
nursed you for three years,
reared you and brought you up to your present age.
I implore you, my child, to look at the heavens and the earth;
consider all that is in them, and realize
that God did not create them from what already existed
and that a human being comes into existence in the same way.
Do not be afraid of this butcher; accept death willingly
and prove yourself worthy of your brothers,
so that by God's mercy I may receive back
both you and them together.   [2 Macc. 7:27–29]

"Last of all, after her sons, the mother died" (7:41)—a faithful witness and courageous preacher.

When the Romans came, tolerating Judaism, the conquered people faced again the difficult question: To what extent might a Jew properly embrace the alien *culture*? To what degree did faithfulness to God require separation from the Gentiles, their customs, and their thought? The crisis proved far more intense than that which Philhellenism had precipitated in republican Rome. Some Jews, seduced by Hellenistic splendor, surrendered their ancient faith. Some chose a path of rigid separatism in loyalty to Torah. And some strove to worship the one God of their ancestors while adopting the culture of the new *oikoumenē*. In the midst of spiritual confusion preachers and commentators on scripture struggled for the soul of a people.

Parties within Judaism[14]

In diverse responses to Hellenism and its political embodiment in the Roman empire, distinctive movements arose among the Jews.

GROUPS DEFINED BY RESPONSE TO ROME.[15] Some Jews determined their stance with specific regard to imperial Rome. Herod and his retainers ingratiated themselves with the conquerors, affecting Hellenistic ways. Also out of necessity, the Sadducees cooperated with the occupation; Rome looked to the priestly establishment, considered by the Jews as ritually legitimate, to restrain popular turbulence. Conservative in any case, the chief priests pursued a policy of realism designed to secure as large an area of autonomy as possible.

The Zealots, by contrast, defined themselves as the resistance; ever ready to launch a new revolt, they sustained their hopes with apocalyptic expectations of intervention by God's anointed champion, the Messiah. A preacher invited death by agitating on the streets with such a message, but proclamations of this hope appeared in the literature of the underground.

> In those days the Elect One shall arise,
> And he shall choose the righteous and holy from among them:
> For the day has drawn nigh that they should be saved…
> And the earth shall rejoice,
> And the righteous shall dwell upon it,
> And the elect shall walk thereon.[16]

PHARISEES AND ESSENES. Concerned primarily with their religious calling, other Jews forsook politics and military plotting. In radical commitment to the Law, they set up a "cultural resistance" to the *status quo.* The Pharisees attempted to sanctify all of life by perfect observance of all the commandments and shunned all activities or persons likely to compromise that total obedience. They revered not only the Law *written* in the Books of Moses, but also the Law *spoken,* preserved in the oral tradition and applying the commands to every conceivable situation. High-principled and intently spiritual, the Pharisees pursued "the sainthood of exclusiveness"[17] in constant study of Torah.

Some religious communities withdrew into monastic colonies. Essenes pursued the quest for purity in various settlements; Qumran, above the shores of the Dead Sea, may have been one of these. Its recently discovered library has greatly enhanced our knowledge of Jewish life and thought at the time.[18]

A RELIGIOUS ARISTOCRACY. Under Roman occupation the righteous had no way of affecting public policy; holiness went individualistic, a pursuit for the privileged. That withdrawal into private probity by Pharisees and Essenes radically altered the character of biblical religion, for Law and Prophecy had addressed the *nation;* righteousness had been the quality of its common life. Now *individuals* with time and means to study Torah occupied themselves with its punctilious observance. Like political participation in Greek democracy, the way of the Pharisees opened only for a privileged minority (even though many rabbis lived simply). Pious acceptance of the *status quo* with hope for redress at the Last Judgment put the Pharisees on the side of social conservatism.[19]

Participation in Hellenistic Life

Yet the Jews of the Diaspora, though preferring Jerusalem above their chief joy, could scarcely avoid involvement with Hellenism.

Aggressive in business and the professions, and thriving as an influential minority in Alexandria, Antioch, Tarsus, Rome, and the lesser cities of the West, they readily adopted *koiné* Greek as earlier generations had taken up Aramaic. Their children studied in Greek schools, read Greek authors, wrote in Greek; even in their synagogues the *koiné* dialect replaced Aramaic as the language of worship, instruction, and preaching.

EDUCATION. Some Jewish lads received an education exclusively rabbinical. "Judaism adopted the most important idea of Hellenism, that of *paideia*, of perfection through liberal education." But there was a difference: for Judaism undertook to educate "the scholar versed in Holy Writ" rather than "the athletic gentleman of the gymnasium."[20]

Other Jewish boys were also exposed to Graeco-Roman culture and learned to synthesize with their biblical faith Hellenistic ideals that they found compatible with it. Philo in Alexandria and Josephus in Palestine must have studied in the rhetorical schools, and Saul of Tarsus showed an acquaintance with Greek philosophers and poets. Jewish moralists made use of Stoic concepts, and Jewish historians recounted their past in Hellenistic rhetorical style, complete with speeches for Abraham, Judah, Joseph, and others. Whereas the Maccabean heroes in their fight for freedom had resisted Hellenism in all its forms, Jews of the Diaspora two centuries later found in it great cultural attractiveness. Some were assimilated and even apostasized, but many retained their Jewishness. They kept the covenant in faithfulness to their God and obedience to the Law, while responding positively to the ecumenical culture, much as their sages since Solomon had participated in the international tradition of wisdom. Their involvement in Hellenism held large significance for the future of preaching.

NOTABLE JEWS IN HELLENISM. Some Jews won recognition within the general world of Hellenistic culture. Alityrus was one of Nero's favorite actors. Herod Agrippa I is said to have received extravagant acclaim for an oration he delivered at Caesarea (Acts 12:21–22). In Cyprus Elymas or Bar-Jesus held a position in the household of the Roman pro-consul. Aided by Greek secretaries, Josephus composed history in the prevailing fashion, and at least five Alexandrian Jews wrote in Greek about the early history of their people. Philo "the elder" and Theodotus undertook epic poems on the biblical story, and Ezekielos a drama on the Exodus.

The Sicilian rhetorician, Caecilius of Calacte, a proselyte to Judaism, went to Rome to teach late in the first century B.C.E. Born a slave, he composed a history of the slave rebellion on his island. He also wrote *On the Ten Attic Orators*, the earliest extant work to recognize the "canon" of the Ten; *Against the Phrygians*, an attack on the Asianic style; *On Figures;* an *Art of Rhetoric;* and comparative studies of famous orators, including one concerning Demosthenes and Cicero—the Greek like a thunderbolt, the Roman like a conflagration. He illustrated his work of literary criticism, *On the Sublime*, with passages from various works, including, apparently, translations from the Hebrew scriptures. By considering together exemplary selections from Greek, Latin, and Hebrew authors, he pioneered the discipline of comparative literature. It is thought that the more famous critic, Longinus (1st century C.E.) took his celebrated reference to Genesis 1, along with his title, from this intriguing convert to Judaism.

THE TORAH IN GREEK. To make the holy scriptures more readily accessible to Hellenized Jews, the Pentateuch was translated into Greek at Alexandria already in the third century B.C.E.–purportedly by seventy-two scholars, and consequently known as the Septuagint (LXX). Completed in the second century, this version came to include the Prophets and the Writings, as well as a number of more recent Jewish religious books, originally written in Greek and collectively designated Apocrypha. Accepted as scripture by the Hellenized Jews and the early Christians, the apocryphal books were eventually excluded from the canon of Judaism (and from Protestant Bibles).

The Septuagint version proved to hold considerable appeal for philosophers, seekers after Eastern wisdom, and other Greco-Roman intellectuals, including rhetoricians and devotees of literature. But a reverse influence also occured: inevitably it led Hellenistic Jews to think of their faith, not just in Greek *words*, but in Greek *categories of thought*, in terms of ideas formulated by the classic philosophers, for translation necessarily imports into a text conceptualities shaped by the alien culture.[21]

THE RHETORICAL SERMON. Under the rule of the Hellenistic powers the inhabitants of Palestine were exposed to oratory in the classical mode. A Jewish patriot writing late in the second century B.C.E. mentions opposition by the people of Ptolemais (now known as Acre) to concessions made by Antiochus V Eupator, the under-age Syrian ruler, in a treaty with the Jews. As the situtation threated to get out of hand, the king's vice-regent went to Ptolemais to confront the complainants. "Lysias took the platform, defended the treaty as well as he could, and won them over by persuasion" (2 Macc. 13:26 NAB)—here embodying the accepted ideal of the orator.

Given the dominance of classical rhetoric in Hellenistic education, it was bound to exert a profound effect on Greek-speaking preachers in the synagogues of Alexandria and elsewhere. A style of preaching emerged, quite distinct from the measured parallelism of the classic Semitic wisdom speech—and even more radically different from the gnomic dicta of the rabbis. In Hellenized circles rabbis schooled in Greek rhetoric attracted admiring audiences by their eloquence; they succeeded not only in holding bright young Jews to the ancestral religion, but also in commending the faith of Israel to Gentiles who heard them. One such preacher was Philo of Alexandria.

"A Light to the Nations" [22]

By entering the cultural dialogue, Greek-speaking Jews encountered in the philosophers high concepts with which Torah had long made them familiar—and they knew that Moses was more ancient than Plato. So the hypothesis arose that formative Greek intellectuals had learned these concepts from the Law and the Prophets. In Alexandria a Jewish priest named Aristobulus dedicated to Ptolemy VI Philometor (180–145 B.C.E.) a book that "proved" this very point.[23]

In any event, Jews succeeded in commending their faith among the Gentiles. It had no small appeal. At a time when traditional polytheism was weakening and people were drawn to universal ideals, the worship of one God made sense to ordinary persons as well as to philosophers. The symbolism of Sabbath, annual feasts, and ceremonial purification appealed to those attracted by rites from the East. Veneration for the Law, especially in its ethical emphasis, addressed concerns taken up by the Hellenistic moralists. The idea of a last judgment followed by everlasting reward or punishment met the longing for life after death.

All these emphases were enhanced by the appeal of the Hebrew scriptures, which were widely held in high esteem after their translation into Greek. Books that Greek-speaking Jews wrote for the religious instruction of their children were eagerly read by Gentiles, some of whom affected a superficial "Jewish chic"; here and there trendy converts, eager to accommodate biblical concepts to their polytheistic heritage, whipped up forms of syncretism.[24]

From their far-flung base in the Diaspora (estimated at about 7 per cent of the population of Greek-speaking areas) Jewish preachers vigorously proclaimed the message of one God and the biblical demand for righteousness, and their preaching attracted proselytes.[25] Even more "God-fearers" among the Gentiles frequented the synagogue, read the scriptures, and except for submitting to circumcision, clung to the faith of Judaism.

SCRIBES, SAGES, AND RABBIS [26]

Scribes and Sages: "The Wise"[27]

Across the world of Judaism, interpretation of Torah and exposition of the faith occupied the best minds. Once the Law was committed to writing, the hereditary priests, Israel's earliest teachers, limited their ministry to the cult and to lining out the ceremonial rules; now a new class had emerged as official exegetes of the legal requirements set forth in scripture. These professional lawyer-theologians were the *soferim*, the scribes.

Originally a *sofer* was one who had mastered the technology of writing and the complexity of bureaucratic regulations. Limited to an educated minority, such skills served an increasing demand as the red tape of obligations to the empire multiplied, and bewildered workers turned to scribes to interpret the rules and prepare proper documents. People also had questions regarding civil requirements of the Torah, and, except for cultic stipulations, turned to the scribes. At first the *sopherim* had come from the hereditary priesthood, as had Ezra, but by the first century C.E. members of various tribes studied Torah in advanced academies, following rigorous exegetical procedures. Granted formal standing by ordination, the scribes enjoyed prestige and power, the most distinguished interpreters of Mosaic Law being acclaimed as "the wise." Greatest influence among them was exercised by those who held membership in the Sanhedrin, the great court in Jerusalem. A majority of scribes were Pharisees.

The scribal schools continued the tradition of wisdom, characteristically receptive to international currents of thought, and the writings of "the wise" allude here and there to themes discussed by Greek poets and philosophers. Ethics was a major concern, and their pieces, sermonic in tone, call to mind the spirit of Hellenic sophists and moralists. Nevertheless, the scribes sunk their roots deep into scripture and nurtured their spirits in reverent recital of Israel's history.

Notable passages of wisdom literature celebrate the work of the teacher. The book of Job, perhaps written during the exile, expresses the genius of wisdom as it honors

the teaching of the sages,
those faithful guardians of the tradition.   [Job 15:18 JB]

It lists "orators" also among persons of importance to society (12:20). The book of Koheleth, "The Preacher" (Ecclesiastes), probably from the late third century B.C.E., likewise praises the sage (8:1).

Early in the second century, offering tribute to the "heroes" of Israel, Jesus ben Sira apostrophized Solomon as personifying the ideal cultivated by the sages:

Your mind ranged the earth...
and you were loved for your peace.
Your songs, your proverbs, your sayings
and your answers were the wonder of the world.   [Sir. 47:15–17 NJB]

He also celebrated the prophets:

Then the prophet Elijah arose like a fire,
his word flaring like a torch.   [48:1 NJB]

Like Isaiah before them, the "twelve prophets"

comforted Jacob and redeemed him in faith and hope.   [49:10 NJB]

Speaking to his own time, Ben Sira portrayed the idealized scribe as

one who concentrates his mind
and his meditation on the Law of the Most High...
He preserves the discourses of famous men,
he is at home with the niceties of parables...
At dawn and with all his heart...
he opens his mouth in prayer
and makes entreaty for his sins.
If such be the will of the great Lord,
he will be filled with the spirit of intelligence...
He will grow upright in purpose and learning...
taking his pride in the Law of the Lord's covenant.
Many will praise his intelligence,
and it will never be forgotten...
Nations will proclaim his wisdom.   [39:1–10 NJB]

In the first century B.C.E. the author of the "Wisdom of Solomon" affirmed faith in the work of the scribal exegetes:

In the greatest number of the wise
lies the world's salvation.   [6:24 NJB]

A psalm from the wisdom tradition pictures God in the role of the scribe:

Yahweh, the teacher of all people…
How blessed are those you instruct, Yahweh,
whom you teach by means of your law.   [Ps. 94:10–12 NJB]

By the first century C.E. a majority of the scribes were Pharisees.

Rabbis: Other Sages, Also Wise[28]

But Israel had other sages as well, who were not scribes and did not commit their work to writing but, for all that, were also hailed as "the wise" and were remembered by the honorific title of sage. They were the students and learned commentators on Torah who searched diligently for its *religious* meaning—as distinguished from the scribes, preoccupied with its application to legal situations, or those sages of the old wisdom tradition with their pragmatic this-worldly involvements. In the commentary of *these* sages, Torah *is* wisdom.

In every community of Judaism could be found a small company of inquiring minds and spirits whose favorite occupation was reflecting together on the scriptures and offering their interpretations in brief, often epigrammatic dicta. Students of the Book, these commentators did not *write* books, but expressed their conclusions orally, their work of exegesis being more commonly dialogical than declamatory. Their characteristic style, spare and terse, stands at the opposite pole from the flowery fulness of the eloquent Greeks and Romans; clearly not orations, their exegetical pronouncements hardly qualify as preaching. Yet midrash was a distinctive wisdom rooted in scripture, a careful setting forth of the divine word and its meaning for the interpreter's own times; attention to it is mandatory for anyone who would understand preaching in Judaism and in the early church. The remarkable power and pertinence of some pointed pronouncements caused the midrash to be remembered, attached to an honorable name, and preserved in the oral tradition.

The popular designation for *these* sages was *rabbi,* teacher.[29] (*Rab, rabban, rabbi* were all variants of the Aramaic term for "prince.") But the honorific was not reserved for graduates of schools, since good Jews everywhere loved to hear and to discourse about the Law. A well-known proverb promised,

Whoever walks with the wise becomes wise,   [Prov. 13:20 NRSV]

and faithful attendance at the synagogue became an instrument of education in the understanding of Torah. By faithfulness and diligent participation in the informal groups meeting for Bible study, a man of limited formal education could gain recognition among his peers for understanding of scripture, leading to an invitation on occasion to expound to the congregation the lesson for the day. Having won respect among those who knew them, such men were informally accorded the title rabbi. In local communities the rabbinate was an open aristocracy of merit to which any diligent student of Torah might aspire.

By the time of the Roman occupation well-esteemed rabbis also addressed congregations on sabbath or feast-day in extended sermons, and some won reputations for inspiring speech and spiritual insight. To their synagogues country folk flocked from the surrounding villages, daring to break the limits imposed by the Law for a sabbath day's journey, if only they might hear a favorite preacher. Speaking to popular audiences of women, children, and laborers without schooling, not just to a select group of serious-minded men such as gathered in small groups to study Torah, these popular speakers held their audiences with skilfully told stories, dramatic dialogue, and telling humor.[30] The acclaim of the crowds lured some rabbis to exchange the earnest preaching of Torah for the empty patter of cornball entertainers, exploiting antics used by some popular "philosophers" and mystagogues in Hellenistic circles. And they had their reward.

At its best the rabbinic ethos nicely balanced study with way of life. Rabbi Ishmael said,

> If one studies in order to teach,
> it is granted to him to study and to teach;
> but if one studies in order to practice,
> it is granted to him to study and to teach,
> to observe and to practice.[31]

Fixed as their concentration was on Torah and on God (whose word they held it to be), the rabbis were not theologians in the sense of scholars who discuss deity in abstract categories borrowed from the reigning philosophy. As students of scripture they were devotees of the great *I Am*, to whom the texts bear witness, and they perceived *ethical practice* as the appropriate response. Simeon son of Gamaliel (10 B.C.E.?–66) put their concern in a nutshell:

On three things does the world stand:
on justice, on truth, and on peace. As it is said,
   "Execute the judgment of truth and peace in your gates." [Zech. 8:16][32]

The rabbis followed a trade to support their families and lived simply in order that they might follow the ideal pattern for dividing their time: one-third of the day for prayer, one-third for work, and one-third for the study of the Law.[33]

That Law was the Jews' delight; whenever opportunity offered they repaired to the synagogue, the house of a rabbi, or the courts of the temple to discuss Torah. Rabbi Yose Ben Joezer said,

Let thy house be a meeting-place for the sages,
and sit in the very dust at their feet,
and thirstily drink in their words.[34]

Spiritual camaraderie rose at times to the level of veneration, and many of the remembered dicta preserve a generous tribute from one Bible student to another. About the turn of the century, from the first to the second, the young disciples of Rabbi Joshua went without him for a day in Jabneh. When in response to his persistent inquiry, they told him of the midrash they had heard from Rabbi Eleazar Ben Azariah, Joshua responded in elation:

This is indeed a new teaching.
Behold I am about eighty years old
and never had the privilege of hearing it until today.
Happy are you, our father Abraham,
that Eleazar b[en] Azariah descended from you.
The generation which has Eleazar b[en] Azariah in its midst
is not bereft![35]

But their highest praises were for the Torah itself.

Greater is Torah than priesthood or kingship.
For kingship is acquired through thirty virtues,
and priesthood through twenty-four,
but Torah is acquired through forty-eight. And these are they:—
By study, by the listening of the ear,
by the ordering of the lips, by the discernment of the heart,
fear, dread, humility, cheerfulness, purity,
attendance on the Wise, cleaving to associates,
discussion with disciples...[36]

and so on and on, through the forty-eight virtues, recalled without the aid of writing. For the heritage of midrash, the oral Torah, was laid upon the heart as divine word to the seeker after God's truth.

Making this treasure of revelation one's own required serious application. Rabbi Jose said:

> Dispose thyself to learn Torah, for it is not an inheritance.[37]

Nor was knowing it an occasion for arrogance. Rabbi Johanan ben Zaccai (1?–80? C.E.) admonished:

> If thou hast learned much Torah, take not credit to thyself,
> for thereunto wast thou created.[38]

The rabbis marveled at the riches to be found in the Torah by diligent searching. Ben Bag Bag's loving exclamation (end of first century B.C.E.) was not forgotten:

> Turn it and turn it for all is in it and look in it
> and grow gray and old in it, and turn not away from it,
> for there is no better rule for thee than it.[39]

Monastic Preachers

In faithfulness to the genius of Judaism, the community of ascetics at Qumran defined its life as centered in the divine word. The rule called for preaching by a priest "versed in the Book of Study and in all the regulations of the Torah, so as to be able to declare them on each appropriate occasion."[40] Its leader was honored as "the correct expositor" or "right-Teacher,"[41] in contrast to the "preacher of falsehood" and "prophets of deceit."

> It is his duty to enlighten the masses about the works of God,
> and to make them understand his wondrous powers.
> He is to tell them in detail
> the story of things that happened in the past.
> He is to show them the same compassion
> as a father shows for his children.
> He is to bring back all of them that stray,
> as does a shepherd his flock.[42]

God had appointed the preacher "as nurse unto them who open their mouths for [his] words, like sucklings."[43] (To the reader familiar with the New Testament the imagery seems to have a decidedly Christian ring, but it was common throughout the world among popular philosophers, rabbis, and apostles.)[44] For the sacred and demanding task the preacher was dependent wholly on God for insight and grace.[45]

Philo's treatise *On the Contemplative Life* offers an idyllic picture of an ascetic community he called the Therapeutae, describing the eagerness with which they gathered for worship and listened to the preaching:

> Every seventh day they meet together as for a general assembly
> and sit in order according to their age in the proper attitude...
> Then the senior among them
> who also has the fullest knowledge of the doctrines they profess
> comes forward and with visage and voice alike quiet and composed
> gives a well-reasoned and wise discourse.[46]

The scrolls in the library at Qumran included sketches of sermons[47] and a series of hymns or psalms for the spiritual meditation of the preacher.

> Blessed art thou, O Lord,
> Thou God of compassion and mercy,
> for Thou hast given me knowledge of Thy truth
> and insight to tell forth Thy wonders,
> unhushed by day or night.[48]

A non-canonical psalm from the Manual of Discipline expresses the preacher's high intent:

> With thanksgiving I will open my mouth,
> the righteous acts of God shall my tongue recount always
> and the faithlessness of men until their transgression is complete.
> Empty words I will banish from my lips,
> unclean things and perversions from the knowledge of my mind.[49]

Charismatics and Prophets[50]

Amid popular frustration and spiritual depression arising from the occcupation of the land by unbelievers, an occasional charismatic appeared, to rally faith in God by exhortation and convincing demonstrations of supernatural power. In the first century B.C.E. Honi the Circle-Drawer gained the veneration of the common people for his piety and efficacy in securing rain by his prayers; an anonymous midrash expresses the tribute of such folk:

No one has existed comparable to Elijah
and Honi the Circle-Drawer,
causing humanity to serve God.[51]

Josephus refers to him as Onias the Righteous, showing considerably more sympathy with him and his admirers than did the officials of the religious establishment. Seemingly a man of few words, he taught through his public prayers.

In the first century C.E. another charismatic held in popular esteem was Hanina ben Dosa, who came from a Galilean town about ten miles from Nazareth. He was reputed to have healed sickness at a distance by his prayers and to have survived the bite of a poisonous snake. When the people marveled at that, he proclaimed aphoristically:

It is not the snake that kills, but sin.[52]

The rabbis also remembered another of his pronouncements:

For anyone whose fear of sin takes precedence over his wisdom,
his wisdom will endure.
And for anyone whose wisdom takes precedence over his fear of sin,
wisdom will not endure.[53]

Along with such charismatics and holy men, excitement accompanying resistance to the Roman occupation during the last century of the temple called forth a number of prophets and pseudo-prophets, who played on popular resentments and hopes. Among these were Theudas and a rebel known as the Egyptian; the former announced that at his command the Jordan River would be parted, the latter that at his word the walls of Jerusalem would tumble down. And when the Romans had laid siege to the holy city the rebels found speakers who gave themselves out to be prophets and by their promises of divine protection lured their believers to bloody death.[54] In times not so dark, Jews had accepted, though with regret, the teaching of the rabbis that prophecy had ceased, but now fervent hope for divine intervention betrayed many into credulity—and disaster.

Women[55]

In Jewish society—patriarchal like that of Israel from the beginning—woman "was perceived as the indicative abnormality in a world in which men were perceived as normal."[56] The Law limited priesthood to males of the tribe of Levi, and practice customarily excluded women from religious leadership. A few exceptions marked the nation's history: Miriam, Deborah, Huldah, raised up by the Spirit of Yahweh in the long-ago time of ecstatics and prophets, sang or spoke the divine word to the chosen people. But the rabbis had now long held that prophecy had ceased.

In such a setting the book of Judith, evidently written in the late second century B.C.E., probably in Hebrew, presents a remarkable exception to the rule of male dominance. A stirring tale of deliverance in the long ago from an overwhelming force of Assyrian invaders, it takes for its hero a pious, resourceful, and beautiful Israelite widow, who with cunning and great boldness effects the death of Holofernes, the enemy commander, causing the rout of his army.

Equally as remarkable as her epic heroism in dispatching Holofernes is her boldness, prior to that risky venture, in dressing down the fearful elders of Bethulia for consenting to surrender their town without resistance; appealing for permission to undertake her secret mission, she speaks eloquently of God's power to deliver and of Israel's faithfulness in repudiating idolatry:

> At the present day
> there is not one of our tribes or clans, districts or towns,
> that worships man-made gods, or has done so within living memory…
> We…acknowledge no God but the Lord,
> and so have confidence that he will not spurn us,
> nor any of our nation.   [Jdt. 8:18–20 REB]

Here she commands the eloquence of a practiced deliberative orator:

> If we should lose Bethulia,
> then all Judaea will be lost; the temple will be sacked,
> and God will hold us responsible for its desecration.
> The slaughter and deportation of our fellow-countrymen
> and the devastation of our ancestral land
> will bring his judgment on our heads,
> wherever among the Gentiles we become slaves…
> There will be no happy ending to our servitude, no return to favour;
> the Lord our God will use it to dishonour us.   [Jdt. 8:21–23 REB]

In a stirring peroration she appeals for a decision to resist the invaders:

> My friends, let us now set an example to our fellow-countrymen,
> for their lives depend on us,
> and with us rests the fate of the temple, its precincts, and the altar.
> Despite our peril let us give thanks to the Lord our God,
> for he is putting us to the test, as he did our ancestors.

Remember how he dealt with Abraham, and how he tested Isaac,
and what happened to Jacob in Syrian Mesopotamia
while he was working as a shepherd for his uncle Laban.
The Lord is subjecting us to the same fiery ordeal
by which he tested their loyalty, not taking vengeance on us:
it is as a warning that he scourges his worshipers.

[Jdt. 8:24–27 REB]

Her "sermon" had the effect she hoped for. The elders reconsidered their decision, gave their consent to her daring venture, and asked for her prayers. And her perilous operation succeeded.

In the patriarchal culture of Israel, the book of Judith is noteworthy not only for its gripping story of a perilous operation carried out by a heroic widow of devotion and high character, but especially for assigning to this brave and beautiful woman a stirring sermon in the mode of a classical orator. Recall that this same book selects a *Gentile* to recite God's dealings with Israel in a rhetorical elaboration of the old creed; he was an *Ammonite* commander. (See "Recital—the Old Creed," in chapter 4.) The author obviously held impressive preaching in high esteem and regarded it as especially worthy of note when offered by an unconventional speaker; if no "properly qualified" preacher stepped forward to speak up for Yahweh, God had no hesitation in using an Ammonite warrior or a Jewish widow.

Roughly contemporaneous with the book of Judith is the "pathetic history" known as the Second Book of the Maccabees, compiled in Greek by an Epitomist late in the second century B.C.E., with a stirring account of Jewish resistance to Antiochus Epiphanes, including "invented speeches" for its exemplary figures, none more heroic or more eloquent than that of the mother who saw her seven sons go one by one to a cruel death rather than traduce the Torah. (See "The Issue of Jewish Integrity," above.)

Israel evidently had no lack of courageous women faithful to the Law, capable of inspiring loyalty to it, and gifted in the capacity for putting iron into the souls of their hearers. In the days of the monarchy certain "wise women" had earned a place among the sages. And in several remarkable passages by writers in the wisdom tradition (from Proverbs on to the apocryphal works in the first century B.C.E.) Sophia speaks, personified as a female figure of grace, charm, and eloquence. (See "*Sophia* and *Logos*, in chapter 6.) She is an idealized concept, inspiring the love and longing of the wise, but a model young women were not allowed to emulate as public teachers.

The rabbinate remained a male preserve. Those who would master Torah were admonished not to be diverted by conversations with women, the implication being that such talk must needs be idle. Making midrash was serious business. In the second century B.C.E. Rabbi Jose ben Johanan of Jerusalem prescribed proper behavior for a rabbi:

> Let thy house be opened wide,
> and let the poor be thy household,
> and talk not much with a woman.[57]

In general, the rabbis agreed:

> Everyone that talketh much with a woman causes evil to himself,
> and desists from words of Torah,
> and his end is he inherits Gehinnom.[58]

Yet the rabbis were too shrewd to identify virtue automatically with gender. Consider this story:

> It once happened that a pious man married a pious woman,
> and they did not produce children.
> They said, "We are of no use to the Holy One, Blessed be He,"
> and they arose and divorced each other.
>
> The man went and married a wicked woman,
> and she made him wicked,
> while the woman went and married a wicked man,
> and she made him righteous.
> This proves that all depends on the woman.[59]

Rabbi Eliezer commented intriguingly on the giving of the Law:

> The Holy One, Blessed be He, said to Moses,
> "Go speak to the daughters of Israel
> [and ask them] whether they wish to receive the Torah."
> Why were the women asked first?
> Because the way of men is to follow the way of women.[60]

An occasional rabbi eased the customs of patriarchy by sharing his knowledge of Torah with a daughter or wife, and in the house of such a man a well-informed woman might even venture to offer an interpretation of scripture. In the second century C.E., Beruria (Valeria), daughter of the martyred Rabbi Hananiah ben Teradion and wife of Rabbi Meir, listened eagerly, learned well, and in her comments showed rare pastoral and spiritual insight. The Talmud tells of a time when her husband, aggrieved by the behavior of lawless men living nearby, prayed for their death.

> His wife, Beruria, exclaimed, "What thinkest thou?
> Is it because it is written, '*Let sinners cease out of the earth*'?
> But has the text *hatta'im*? It is written *hata'im*.
> Glance also at the end of the verse,
> '*And let the wicked be no more*,' [Ps. 104:35]
> that is, when sins will cease, then the wicked will be no more.
> Rather shouldst thou pray that they repent, and be no more wicked."
> Then R. Me'ir offered prayer on their behalf, and they repented.[61]

Though she is honored here and elsewhere in the Talmud, some later rigorists impugned both the permissiveness of those who admitted her to the rabbinic discussions and her character.[62]

One fanciful tale in the tradition pitted Caesar against the *daughter* of Rabban Gamaliel.

> Caesar said to Rabban Gamaliel,
> "You maintain that the dead will live.
> But they are dust, and can the dust live?"[63]

After asking her father's permission, the daughter said to Caesar:

> "There are two potters in our town,
> one who works with water, the other who works with clay.
> Which is the more impressive?"
> He said to her, "The one who works with water."
> She said to him, "If he works with water,
> will he not create even more out of clay?"

But such stories are few and far between. *Midrash* was a man's game.

NOTABLE PREACHERS AND COMMENTATORS [64]

Jesus ben Sira[65]

The best known preacher from the Wisdom tradition in the Hellenistic era, Jesus son of Sira(ch), combined eloquence and poetic gifts with a cultivated mind and evident devotion to the religious heritage of Israel. He taught in Jerusalem, where he may have known the author of Ecclesiastes, early in the second century B.C.E., leaving a compilation of his work that his grandson took to Alexandria and translated into Greek. Given a place among the apocryphal books under the title Ecclesiasticus, it is a noble and inspiring opus, integrating faith and reason, aesthetic sensitivity and commitment to justice, in forceful and memorable utterance by a master of the style of the wisdom speech.

This preacher fervently celebrated Israel's tradition of covenant and cult and prophecy:

> [God] let Moses hear his voice
> and brought him into the dark cloud,
> where face to face he gave him the commandments,
> law which is the source of life and knowledge,
> so that he might teach his covenant to Jacob,
> his decrees to Israel.　[Sir. 45:5 REB]

The life of the covenant people sank its roots deep into the liturgy of tabernacle and temple:

> [God] raised up Aaron of the tribe of Levi,
> a holy man like his brother.
> He made an everlasting covenant with him,
> conferring on him the priesthood of the nation.
> He honoured and adorned him, clothing him in splendid vestments...
> adorned with embroidery, gold and violet and purple;
> the oracle of judgment with the tokens of truth　[Sir. 45:6–10 REB]

The preacher also composed an encomium on a high priest whom he is thought to have known, Simon son of Onias (50:1–21); and he honored Israel's prophets and sages. Speaking to his own time, he portrayed the idealized scribe:

> He concentrates his mind and his meditation
> on the Law of the Most High...
> He preserves the discourses of famous men...
> 　he is at home with the niceties of parables...
> At dawn and with all his heart...
> 　he opens his mouth in prayer
> 　and makes entreaty for his sins.
> If such be the will of the great Lord,
> 　he will be filled with the spirit of intelligence...
> He will grow upright in purpose and learning...
> 　taking his pride in the Law of the Lord's covenant.
> Many will praise his intelligence,

and it will never be forgotten…
Nations will proclaim his wisdom.   [Sir. 39:1–10 NJB]

In the mind of this preacher, wisdom and eloquence were closely linked.[66] He commended humility and diligence in study. And his poetic mind bequeathed to his hearers a metaphor beloved by generations of the faithful:

Like clay in the hands of a potter,
to mold as it pleases him,
so are human beings in the hands of their Maker.   [Sir. 33:13 NJB]

The Long Chain of Rabbis

The religious discourse of emerging Judaism centered in the Torah ("instruction"). The term referred primarily to the Law, given by God to Moses on Mount Sinai; secondarily to the "Five Books of Moses," the foundational scripture; but thirdly and equally to the oral Torah handed down by generations of faithful rabbis. Their "midrash begins when the writing of Scripture ends."[67] A modern Jewish scholar writes of the Mishnah and subsequent collections of rabbinical sayings as "integral components of the oral part of the one whole Torah that God gave to our rabbi, Moses, at Sinai."[68] It was held that every truth offered by one of the sages in setting forth the meaning of scripture was given to Moses at the beginning and consequently is part of Torah. "The midrash itself is revelation, just as the verse it comments on is revelation."[69]

The rabbinic exegesis of Torah was preserved for centuries primarily as oral tradition. Whenever Jews gathered to discuss the Law, they recalled the words of authoritative rabbis, though the particular utterance might be attributed now to one, now to another. The process put a premium on compression, for a bold and pithy form contributed to retention of the sayings in memory. Rabbi Eliezer Ben Hyrcanus embodied the ideal: he was characterized as "a plastered cistern which loses not a drop."[70]

At least as early as the first century C.E. the rabbis began to collect and order the vast body of midrash.[71] In the next century Rabbi Akiba and his successors published a compilation under the title *Mishnah*—it meant *Repetition*—and that "publication" was oral.[72] Preserved in Palestinian and Babylonian versions of the Talmud, which were reduced to writing only in the fifth century, it gives the flavor of rabbinic discussions rather than a body of sermons. Nevertheless, the names and the very words of notable rabbis were remembered and cherished, as were their interpretations of specific passages of scripture, and in the Talmud their distinctive voices are still heard.

For the period from the late third century B.C.E. on for 200 years, the tradition concentrated on a succession of five *Zûghôth* or "Pairs" of rabbis who frequently disagreed with each other. Their remembered comments provided the starting point for new discussions of Torah. The preeminent rabbinical "pair" in the first century B.C.E. were Hillel and Shammai.

Shammai

Rabbi Shammai was the great conservative, champion of the traditional ways of rural Palestine. Compressed into three brief admonitions, his message ran:

Make of thy Torah study a fixed practice;
say little and do much;
and receive all men with a cheerful countenance.[73]

His disciples and those of the more liberal Hillel took contrary positions regarding a number of small matters of practical piety:

These are the things that are between the House of Shammai
and the House of Hillel in [regard to] the meal:
The House of Shammai say, "One blesses over the day,
and afterward one blesses over the wine."
And the House of Hillel say, "One blesses over the wine,
and afterward one blesses over the day"...
The House of Shammai say, "Who created the light of the fire."
And the House of Hillel say, "Who creates the light of the fire"...
He who ate and forgot and did not bless [say Grace]—
The House of Shammai say,
"He should go back to his place and bless."
And the House of Hillel say,
"He should bless in the place in which he remembered."[74]

There is more. But large as such matters loomed in sectarian squabbling, and fascinating as such arguments were to religious partisans, they were not preaching.

Hillel

Rabbi Hillel (ca. 60 B.C.E.–20 C.E.), the voice of less rigid interpretation, spoke for the townsfolk of the new commercial age. An admiring legend linked him with Moses in its claim that he lived 120 years—forty years without learning, forty years as a student, and forty years as a teacher. While he held it illegal to eat an egg laid on the sabbath, he normally was mild in interpretation and gentle in spirit; he has been likened to Seneca. For generations after him rabbis recited his remembered maxims:

> Do not walk out on the community [congregation]
> And do not have confidence in yourself until the day you die.
> And do not judge your companion until you are in his place.
> And do not say anything which cannot be heard,
> for in the end it will be heard.
> And do not say, When I have time, I shall study,
> for you may never have time…
>
> A coarse person will never fear sin,
> nor will an *am ha-Aretz*[75] ever be pious,
> nor will a shy person learn,
> nor will an ignorant person teach,[76]
> nor will anyone too occupied in business get wise.
>
> In a place where there are no individuals,
> try to be an individual.
>
> Lots of meat, lots of worms;
> lots of property, lots of worries;
> lots of women, lots of witchcrafts;
> lots of slave girls, lots of lust;
> lots of slave boys, lots of robbery.
> Lots of Torah, lots of life;
> lots of discipleship, lots of wisdom;
> lots of counsel, lots of understanding;
> lots of righteousness, lots of peace.
>
> If one has gotten a good name,
> he has gotten it for himself.
> [If] he has gotten teachings of the Torah,
> he has gotten himself life eternal.[77]

Hillel's rhetoric is not the fulsome eloquence of the Attic orator, but rather the aphoristic compression of the sage in the wisdom tradition of Israel. Another example:

> If I am not for myself, who is for me?
> And when I am for myself, what am I?
> And if not now, when?[78]

An oft-told story has it that a certain Gentile agreed to become a proselyte if, while he stood on one leg, Shammai could teach him the entire Law. Driven away, the inquirer went to Hillel, who replied,

> What is hateful to you, do not to your neighbor.
> That is the entire Torah; the rest is commentary; go and learn it.[79]

Gamaliel

Hillel's grandson Gamaliel (Gamliel), the most distinguished rabbi in Jerusalem just before the destruction of the city, was the first to be hailed as *Rabban,* "our Master." The conventional term, *Rabbi,* meant "my Master," but Rabban signified greatness; regard for his learning and generous spirit accrued to the esteem of liberal Pharisaism. Gamaliel commended the rabbinic ideal:

> Fitting is learning in the Torah along with a craft,
> for the labor put into the two of them makes one forget sin.
> And all learning of the Torah which is not joined with labor
> is destined to be null and causes sin.
> And all who work with the community—
> let them work with them for the sake of Heaven.
> For the merit of the fathers strengthens them,
> and the righteousness which they do stands forever.[80]

Some of his dicta are conventional rabbinic commentary:

> Whosoever has not said [the verses concerning] these three things
> at Passover has not fulfilled his obligation.
> And these are they: Passover, unleavened bread, and bitter herbs:
> "Passover"—because God passed over
> the houses of our fathers in Egypt;
> "Unleavened bread"—because our fathers were redeemed from Egypt;
> "bitter herbs"—because the Egyptians embittered
> the lives of our fathers in Egypt.[81]

Later generations told of Gamaliel's ready sympathy:

A woman in the neighborhood of Rabban Gamaliel,
whose child died...was weeping by night on account of the child.
Rabban Gamaliel heard her voice and cried with her,
until his eyelashes fell out.[82]

Those who came after also recounted that his generous nature found expression in a final act of sympathy with the poor:

At one time funerals in Israel became so costly that the expense was harder for some relatives to bear than the death itself.
Some relatives even abandoned the corpse and ran away.
Such desertions ended when Rabbi Gamaliel left orders
that his body be carried to the grave in a simple linen garment.
From then on, everyone followed Rabbi Gamaliel's example.[83]

Gamaliel's reputation is celebrated in the book of Acts as a counselor of the Sanhedrin and teacher of Saul of Tarsus.

When the destruction of the Temple put an end to the sacrificial cult (70 C.E.), Rabbi Johanan Ben Zakkai reestablished the Sanhedrin at Jabneh (Jamnia) and guided his colleagues in defining the Judaism that continued after that disaster.

Preachers at Qumran

In the desert above the Dead Sea a community of sectarian Jews in the second century B.C.E. dug cisterns to collect water from Wadi Qumran, pitched their tents for sleeping nearby, erected common rooms for meeting, eating, and copying manuscripts, built up a library of religious works, and lived together under a monastic rule. When the Romans, after putting down the rebellion under Bar Kochba (135 C.E.), began systematically destroying everything Jewish, the people of Qumran sealed their precious manuscripts into large clay jars and hid them in caves in the cliffs behind their settlement, there to be forgotten until discovered in the twentieth century—the largest known body of literature in Hebrew and Aramaic from the period 200 B.C.E. to 200 C.E.

The scrolls include various books of scripture, commentaries, the rule of the community, interpretations of the Law, edifying stories that embroider portions of the sacred narrative, pseudonymous works attributed to biblical characters, apocalyptic visions, eschatological declarations, apocryphal psalms, hymns and other liturgical materials, "mysteries," and various types of literature in the wisdom tradition. Not a few of the texts, homiletical in tone and hortatory in approach, impress the reader as preaching; if not a distillation of sermons preached, such passages would still have been *heard* as homilies when read and could well have provided ideas and inspiration to those responsible for preaching to the assembly.

Now and again the documents refer to the "Teacher of Righteousness," thought by some scholars to have been the great formative figure of the community, a powerful preacher who led a company of rigorists in separating from the larger body of Essenes known to us through Philo. Other scholars regard the establishment as a regular house of Essenes and the "Teacher of Righteousness," not as its founder, but as an influential leader who put his impress on it in the second century B.C.E. In either case, for the community at Qumran he typified the ideal spiritual militant, embodying assurance of the triumph of truth in the spiritual battle of the last days.[84]

The Manual of Discipline provided that wherever ten men had formally enrolled in the community "there is not to be absent from them one who can interpret the Law to them at any time of day or night."[85] Though the context allows the passage to be understood as calling not so much for a rabbi as for a scribe, the community regarded attention to Torah as a compelling duty.

The abundance of verse-by-verse commentary on books of the Bible found in the caves, with occasional passages clearly sermonic, offers precious remnants of Jewish religious discourse before 70 C.E. Excepting those who preached and wrote in Greek, rabbis outside the monastery relied for the most part on oral tradition for the preservation of their work; if they wrote sermons, their manuscripts have disappeared, and whereas maxims and numerical sayings stuck in the memory of hearers, passages of sermonic eloquence faded beyond recall. But scraps of the preaching heard at Qumran survive,[86] even though the scrolls have suffered the ravages of time, transcriptions are necessarily fragmentary, and texts in translation are pocked with ellipses. The fragments have a representative importance surpassing their minimal exegetical, theological, or literary appeal to contemporary readers, with no small significance for the history of preaching.

One of the wisdom texts includes a series of beatitudes:

[Blessed is the one who speaks the truth] with a pure heart,
and does not slander with the tongue.
Blessed are those who adhere to God's laws,
and do not adhere to perverted paths.

Blessed are those who rejoice in her,
and do not explore insane paths.
Blessed are those who search for her with pure hands,
and do not importune her with a treacherous heart.
Blessed is the man who attains Wisdom,
and walks in the law of the Most High.[87]

A passage about the people on whom the Teacher of Righteousness turned his back in order to seek a haven for the righteous breathes the sectarian spirit of the rigorous preacher of judgment:

They sought easy interpretations, chose illusions,
scrutinised loopholes, chose the handsome neck,
acquitted the guilty and sentenced the just,
violated the covenant, broke the precept,
colluded together against the life of the just man,
their soul abominated all those who walk in perfection,
they hunted them down with the sword....
And kindled was the wrath of God against his congregation.[88]

Then in gentler tone the preacher turns to his hearers:

And now, my sons, listen to me, and I shall open your eyes
so that you can see and understand the deeds of God,
so that you can choose what he is pleased with
and repudiate what he hates,
so that you can walk perfectly on all his paths
and not follow after the thoughts of a guilty inclination
and lascivious eyes.[89]

Philo of Alexandria [90]

Whereas the Palestinian rabbis and the "Teacher of Righteousness" preached in Aramaic, exposition of the Torah also flourished in the Diaspora. Around the Mediterranean, where Greek prevailed as the language of commercial and intellectual exchange, many Jews spoke it as their native tongue and cherished Hellenistic cultural values; they did so especially in Alexandria, the thriving young city at the mouth of the Nile with its large Jewish colony. Celebrated for its magnificent library, the place had come to rival Athens as a center of learning and creative thought, and Jews took an active part in its intellectual life. There in the third century B.C.E. they translated the Pentateuch into Greek, and in the second century the remainder of the Hebrew scripture. The sacred text was now accessible to inquiring pagans searching for wisdom in the lore of the East, but also for many Jews who no longer understood Hebrew. Increasingly the study and preaching of Torah went on here in Greek.

Best known among the Greek-speaking exegetes is Philo of Alexandria (20? B.C.E.–42? C.E.), learned member of a distinguished family, and courageous advocate who led a delegation to Rome to plead successfully before the imperial authorities the rights of his co-religionists.[91] Impressive for piety and love of scripture, Philo engaged the intellectual and mystical tradition of the Greeks in the firm belief that Moses "had attained the very summit of philosophy, and…had been instructed in the greater and most essential part of Nature's lore."[92] Endeavoring to relate the Jewish heritage to the Hellenistic mind and spirit, Philo ventured to interpret the sacred texts of Judaism through Greek philosophical concepts, particularly those of Middle Platonism. Thus he affirmed to the intellectual world a strong faith in the transcendent God of the Bible.[93] (Even so, in considering woman as "incomplete and in subjection" to the male, belonging "to the category of the passive rather than the active," he succumbed to prevailing notions of patriarchy, failing to discern in scripture the idea of equality enunciated by the philosophers.)[94]

In addition to extended commentary on the books of Moses, Philo composed moralizing and apologetic pieces on themes the philosophers had addressed. Studding his discourse with gems from both scripture and the classical poets, he authored treatises *On the Creation, On the Unchangeableness of God, On Sobriety, On Dreams, On the Virtues, On Rewards and Punishments,* and *On Providence,* as well as a complementary pair: *Every Wicked Man Is a Slave* and *Every Good Man Is Free* (the latter includes a homily on "Repentance").[95] These works doubtless suggest the tone of his preaching, which, however, he addressed to simple as well as learned hearers.

Philo's midrash differed notably from that of the Aramaic-speaking rabbis; "virtually obsessed" with Greek ideas, he pondered the doctrines of the philosophical schools; and despite holding the secret rites of the mystery religions in contempt, he dealt with various notions to which they had given intellectual currency.[96] His intention was to reconcile biblical and philosophical thought in a synthesis acceptable to both traditions. The dualism of Greek thinkers presented a problem, but Philo found help in the idea of the Logos. "Here in one concept are fused the Jewish *memra*, the word of God…, the late Jewish Wisdom…, the Platonic doctrine of Forms, the Aristotelian doctrine of the Divine Intellect, and the Stoic Divine Reason; the ambiguity of meaning in Logos between word and reason made it an especially convenient term."[97] The concept was destined for a large part in Jewish thought and Christian preaching.

But more than love for Plato was at work in Philo. A notable reason for his appeal was his formation by the rhetorical tradition. True, like Socrates in Plato's *Apology,* he professed the ideal of pursuing truth unhampered by the distractions and distortions of eloquence; he celebrated the Essenes as "athletes of virtue produced by a philosophy free from the pedantry of Greek wordiness."[98] Even so, "his discourse was profoundly rhetorical."[99] He employed simultaneously "a philosophical conceptualization and…an exposition both aesthetic and structurally rhetorical."[100] Accordingly, he "read the sacred text in the Greek version of the Septuagint as if it itself were a rhetorically structured document."[101]

In his encomium *On Abraham,* Philo's exuberant rhetorical style contrasts strikingly with the restraint and calculated compression of rabbinic midrash spoken in Aramaic. He declaims:

> Abraham… filled with zeal for piety,
> the highest and greatest of virtues,
> was eager to follow God and to be obedient to his commands…
> Under the force of an oracle which bade him
> leave his country and kinsfolk and seek a new home,
> thinking that quickness in executing the command
> was as good as full accomplishment, he hastened eagerly to obey,
> not as though he were leaving home for a strange land
> but rather as returning from amid strangers to his home.
> Yet who else would be likely to be so firm and unmoved of purpose
> as not to yield and succumb to the charms of kinsfolk and country?[102]

With that the orator takes flight on the theme of "no place like home," proposing (in what seems like an exercise from the rhetorical schools) that the sentence of banishment is worse than capital punishment,

> since death ends our troubles, but banishment is not the end
> but the beginning of other new misfortunes
> and entails in the place of the one death which puts an end to pains
> a thousand deaths in which we do not lose sensation.[103]

To amplify the theme, Philo describes travelers who go abroad on business or government service or for the "love of culture to see the sights," willing in their hopes for profit or advancement to stay away from home for a time.

> Yet all these are eager to see and salute their native soil,
> and to greet their familiars
> and to have the sweet and most desired enjoyment
> of beholding their kinsfolk and friends.[104]

Then the preacher makes his point with emphasis:

> But Abraham, the moment he was bidden, departed...[105]

Philo's venture in reconciling the message of scripture with the axioms of philosophy and the flourish of the rhetoricians had considerable theological significance. It was a profound effort at translation, not merely linguistic, but also conceptual and cultural, of biblical history into the thought-forms of Hellenism. Philo achieved his purpose by means of *allegorical interpretation*.[106]

Such ingenious biblical exegesis attracted proselytes, who "by a beautiful migration" came to the worship of the one true God.[107] In his sermon on "Repentance" Philo characterizes conversion as a passage "from sin to a blameless life."[108] Its essential intellectual component is a turning from superstition, idolatry, and polytheism to monotheism by converts

> who did not at first acknowledge their duty
> to reverence the Founder and Father of all,
> yet afterwards embraced the creed of one
> instead of a multiplicity of sovereigns.
> [This is] the first and most essential form of repentance,
> but one should show repentance
> not only for the delusions under which one long laboured
> in revering things created before the Creator and Maker,
> but also in the other fundamental concerns of life.[109]

For conversion has ethical and social components,

> passing, as it were, from mob-rule, which is the vilest of misgovernments,
> into democracy, the government in which good order is best observed.
> This means passing from ignorance to knowledge of things
> which it is disgraceful not to know,
> from senselessness to good sense, from incontinence to continence,
> from injustice to justice, from timidity to boldness.
> For...where honour is rendered to the God who is,

the whole company of other virtues must follow in its train,
as surely as in the sunshine the shadow follows the body.
The proselytes become at once temperate, continent, modest,
gentle, kind, humane, serious, just, high-minded,
truth-lovers, superior to the desire for money and pleasure.[110]

Evidently attracted by such preaching, numbers of Gentiles in Alexandria were turning to Judaism.[111] Philo admonishes his fellow Jews that all such proselytes

must be held to be our dearest friends and closest kin.
They have shown the godliness of heart
which above all leads up to friendship and affinity,
and we must rejoice with them,
as if, though blind at first they had recovered their sight
and had come from the deepest darkness
to behold the most radiant light.[112]

So Philo's venture in reconciling the scriptures of Judaism with the high philosophical tradition of the Greeks had a double appeal. It drew serious-minded pagans to the ethical monotheism of the Torah, even as it strongly attracted those Jews lured by the intellectual splendor of Hellenism. His exegesis was destined to influence mightily both Jewish and Christian preaching.

THE EFFECT OF THE PREACHING

A touching rabbinic parable tells of a ruler who gave his only daughter in marriage to a king from far away. On being asked to allow her to return with her husband to his distant kingdom, the king replied:

"She...is my only daughter; I cannot bear to be separated from her;
yet I cannot say, 'Do not take her,' for she is your wife."

Accordingly, the father-in-law asked for the promise of a room

"so that I may stay with you,
for I cannot bear to be separated from my daughter."[113]

So the Holy One said to Israel:

"I gave you the Torah. I cannot separate myself from it;
yet I cannot say to you, 'Do not take it.'
So wherever you travel make me a home to live in."

For it is said:

> "And let them make me a sanctuary
> that I may live among them."   [Ex. 25:8]

The Jews of the Diaspora did carry the Torah with them wherever they went, and loving commitment to it impelled rabbis and preachers to tell forth its teaching; the elation sung by the psalmist was also theirs.

> My God, I have always loved your Law
> from the depths of my being.
> I have always proclaimed the righteousness of Yahweh
> in the Great Assembly.   [Ps. 40:8–9 JB]

Though the temple was gone, the synagogue remained as "the sanctuary of Israel"—"throughout his endless wanderings a visible token of the presence of God in the midst of the people."[114] There eager hearers listened attentively to respected rabbis. Though the gnomic speech of midrash was not oratory, no history of preaching would be complete without taking account of these interpreters who studied the scriptures so eagerly and spoke of their meaning for life with such delight. After the sacrificial system ended in the smoking ruins of the temple, faithful Jews continued to find in the word of God an enlightening and purifying power. Their gathering-place stood "as the champion of justice and brotherhood and peace," conveying to worshipers "the beauty of holiness."[115] Meditation on the Law, guided by the words of the Tannaim and of faithful preachers, still made God present to them.

> In the place out of which God's Lordship is spoken,
> there the Lord is.[116]

CHAPTER 6

The Homiletic of Judaism

The work of the preacher within the biblical tradition involves three kinds of tasks. *Exegesis* is the faithful discovery of the original intention of the text. As soon as the preacher moves to the situation of the hearers, *theology* comes to the fore; it is critical reflection on the faith received through the tradition in the effort to relate it to contemporary categories of thought. (Theologizing about the process of moving from text to application is called "hermeneutic.") *Rhetoric* is the art of formulating the message so derived and delivering it in persuasive address. Together these three ventures constitute the discipline of homiletics, the art of making a sermon. Under these three rubrics we now consider Jewish preaching.

Modes of Exegesis[1]

If Judaism's commitment to Torah linked the faith firmly to a text out of the sacred past—the conservatism of the scribes literally conserved the Jewish people and their religion—it nevertheless enabled the unchanging word to speak freely and freshly in the present. Though commonly tending toward literalism and traditionalism, the rabbis managed to relate ancient passages to new needs. The task of drawing from Torah a contemporary message called for interpretation, namely, *targum* (translation) and *midrash* (commentary). (Recall the discussion of *midrash* in chapter 4.)

Peshat and Midrash

The rabbis conceived of Torah as eternal and unchanging. Hence the first task of interpretation was to "make plain" the precise meaning of a passage; this was *peshat*, the work of scholars. But once the definition of the words was clear and their content understood, it was still necessary to "inquire" or "search into" their relevance to perplexing new situations; this was interpretation, midrash. Halakah expounded the legal passages with great seriousness because of the conviction that the law of God must be obeyed.

Paradoxically, however, though the law as stated in the written text was regarded as fixed, in actual practice "the oral tradition forced the tradition to remain flexible and made it easier to add, adapt, accumulate, and keep ever fresh and open-ended."[2] The process was endless.

In distinction from the legal concern of Halakah, the rabbis characterized the other chief form of exegesis as Haggadah; focusing on the biblical narrative, it was more homiletical, celebrating God's redemptive acts and commending exemplary figures out of Israel's past. It often explained a Bible story by retelling it in contemporizing fashion or with a shift of emphasis to explain or eliminate some problem in the text. It involved application to immediate situations.

Rabbinical Rules (middoth)

The rabbis undertook to systematize responsible exegesis. The *Tosephta* records seven exegetical principles (*middoth*) which Hillel commended to the elders at Petherah:

(1) "light and heavy" [arguments from the less to the greater and from the greater to the less]

(2) analogy

(3) a standard conclusion based on one passage [of scripture]

(4) a standard conclusion based on two passages

(5) general and particular—particular and general

(6) analogy with another passage

(7) proof from the context.[3]

Rabbi Ishmael (d. 135 C.E.) expanded the number of *middoth* to thirteen; for example, if two passages of scripture appeared to be contradictory, the problem might be cleared up by a third passage.[4] At the end of the second century Rabbi Eliezer ben R. Jose the Galilean ran the total up to thirty-two. The rabbinical rules of exegesis resemble those of Greek grammarians and rhetoricians, from whom some rabbis began to draw suggestions even before Hillel.

The midrash of the Tannaim has been characterized as possessing five distinctive qualities: (1) collectivity, (2) multiplicity, (3) retention of the original meaning, (4) expansion and openness, (5) text centeredness.[5] Yet it also had an eye to the present; because of this concern with current application, it gives insight into conditions in the time of the rabbis.

Simple Allegory

In their search through the ancient writings for contemporary meaning the interpreters resorted to simple allegory, identifying a biblical word or event symbolically with something in the experience of the hearers. This is the literal meaning of allegory: taking one thing to mean another. Sometimes the process involved no more than hearing a word addressed to ancient Israel as a divine word to the living present. So in commenting on Exodus 14:15 ("Then the LORD said to Moses, 'Why do you cry out to Me? Tell the Israelites to go forward"), Rabbi Joshua maintained simply:

> The Holy One said to Moses,
> "Moses, all Israel has to do is *to go forward!*"[6]

Somewhat less obviously, an expositor at Qumran moralized Numbers 21:18 as praising men of discernment and wisdom:

> And these men "*dug the well*"—that well whereof it is written,
> "*Princes digged it, nobles of the people delved it,*
> *with the aid of* mehôqeq."
> The "well" in question is the Law.
> They that "digged" are those of Israel who repented
> and departed from the land of Judah
> to sojourn in "the land of Damascus."
> God called them all "princes" because they went in search of Him...
> The term *mehôqeq* [which can mean "lawgiver" as well as "stave"]
> refers to the man who expounds the Law.
> Isaiah has employed an analogous piece of imagery
> when in allusion to the Law he has spoken
> of God's "*producing a tool for His work*" [Cf. Isa. 54:16].[7]

While maintaining the principle that "the verse never abandons its fundamental meaning,"[8] the rabbis could, with only a little imagination, transform an ancient story into a word for the living present. The hermits described by Philo were not unique among the Jews in taking the scripture allegorically, "thinking that the words of the literal text are symbols of something whose hidden nature is revealed by studying the underlying meaning."[9] In early Christian exegesis, Paul the apostle, schooled by rabbis, would deal with the biblical narrative in the same way:

> Now this is an allegory. [Gal. 4:24 NRSV]

Etymology and Arithmology

The expositor's playing with the word *mehôqeq* illustrates the interest in etymology, tracing the meaning of a term by analyzing its component parts or its history in linguistic development. Such analysis could be naive and unscientific, as in the explanation of patriarchal names (Isaac = Laughter) by the old story-tellers in Genesis. It could involve the kind of punning which, as we have just seen, enables the interpreter to offer a plausible allegory (stave = lawmaker). The practice of transcribing only the consonants in written Hebrew, leaving the vowels to be supplied by the reader, made the exegete easily aware of puns and ready to use those which suggested an edifying application. Thus in the second century C.E. Rabbi Jehoshua ben Levi, commented on Ex. 32:16 ("The tablets were God's work, and the writing was God's writing, incised upon the tablets"):

> Read not *haruth* (graven [= incised]) but *heruth* (freedom),
> for none is your freeman
> but one who is occupied with the study of Torah.[10]

At Qumran a commentator on Micah broke down the name Jerusalem into its components, *y-r-h* = 'teach,' and *shalom* = 'peace,' to suggest that the true sanctuary is built by the righteous teachers, who thus become the means of its peace and safety.[11] It should be obvious that a "teacher who taught [such] lesson[s] did so as a religious instructor not as a grammarian dealing with a text."[12]

Closely related to etymology was arithmology, the study of the symbolism of numbers. So in exegeting Genesis 14 with its account of a battle involving nine kings and Abraham's rescue of his nephew Lot from the captors, Philo reads the prevailing psychology:

> Of those nine kings, four are the power exercised within us
> by the four passions, pleasure, desire, fear, and grief,
> and...the five are the five senses,
> sight, hearing, taste, smell, and touch.[13]

Alexandrian Exegesis

In describing the gatherings of the Essenes or Therapeutae Philo's treatise on the contemplative life characterizes the preaching as "exposition of the sacred scriptures [that] treats the inner meaning conveyed in allegory."[14]

Allegorizing as practiced under the influence of Alexandria had become a far more sophisticated and complex process than that which marked the inferences of folk-interpretation (simple allegory), with its use of intuitive insight to come up with convincing and edifying applications. That method of reading symbolic meanings from a passage, as just noted, occurred within the cultural continuum of Judaism and involved little more than employing good intentions and a bit of ingenuity to uncover useful ethical admonition or spiritual encouragement.

In a radically different cultural and intellectual context, the Alexandrian Jews sought to fling a bridge between two worlds, the world of revealed truth that they cherished in scripture and the world of philosophical truth that they had accepted in the Hellenistic schools. For them, the sacred narrative of the Bible became the story of the soul—as the epic of Odysseus had become for the Greek philosophers.

But pursuing such insight proved a more complex task, its conclusions less self-evident than might at first have appeared, for the biblical account *had* been regarded as the *history* of a *people*. Now it was seen as containing "stories of the god(s) and heroes."[15] Only after such a remarkable change of perception, hardly possible except for persons schooled in Hellenism, were the stories "translated" into ethical and metaphysical categories. The allegorizing of a text was a carefully contrived hermeneutic, making it possible to relate an old tradition to a radically different culture, in the thinking of persons who valued them both. "Without allegory there could hardly have been a Hellenistic Judaism."[16]

Careful analysis of Alexandrian exegesis has discovered several distinct modes of approach:[17] (1) All anthropomorphic language about God was flatly declared to be poetic imagery; for obvious theological reasons it was not to be taken literally. (2) A biblical story was retold in such a way as to emphasize the virtues of the patriarchs and to minimize their shortcomings—a procedure already well established by the Haggadists. (3) In many instances where allegorizing occurred, a consistent pattern was followed: (a) quoting the text, (b) directing attention to specific words or raising the question of meaning, (c) asserting the (allegorical) meaning, (d) providing reasons for the meaning indicated, (e) giving examples or illustrations or biblical parallels for the "truth" asserted, (f) exhortation or application; the process has been termed "reasoned allegory." (4) In other instances, the procedure just indicated was omitted and the meaning merely asserted—as in the process referred to as "simple allegory." (5) A theme would be developed by tracing references to it through many passages of scripture. (6) Some texts were dealt with by straightforward exposition of their literal meaning.

By this hermeneutic the Alexandrian interpreter was able to maintain integrity as a devout Jew who loved scripture and the discourse of the rabbis, at the same time making connection with Hellenistic thought, especially the ideas of the philosophers.[18] Making it his habitual mode of exegesis, Philo was forthright enough concerning the process:

> Let us not...be misled by the actual words,
> but look at the allegorical meaning that lies beneath them.[19]

Accordingly, in his sermon on Abraham's setting out from Chaldea, Philo maintains:

> His emigration was one of the soul rather than the body,
> for the heavenly love overpowered his desire for mortal things.[20]

After a rhetorical flourish emphasizing Abraham's departure from all that had been near and dear, the preacher begins to draw out the meaning just stated.

> The migrations as set forth by the literal text of the scriptures
> are made by a man of wisdom, but according to the laws of allegory
> by a virtue-loving soul in its search for the true God.
> For the Chaldeans were especially active in...astrology
> and ascribed everything to the movements of the stars.
> They supposed that the course of the phenomena of the world
> is guided by influences contained in numbers
> and numerical proportions.
> Thus they glorified visible existence,
> leaving out of consideration the intelligible and invisible...
> They concluded that the world itself was God,
> thus profanely likening the created to the Creator.[21]

But God's call drew Abraham away from the deceptions of the creed he had been taught by the Chaldeans.

> Then opening the soul's eye as though after profound sleep,
> and beginning to see the pure beam instead of the deep darkness,
> he followed the ray and discerned what he had not beheld before,
> a charioteer and pilot presiding over the world
> and directing in safety his own work...
> And so...the Holy Word...[says] to him,

"Friend, the great is often known by its outlines
as shown in the smaller, and by looking at them
the observer finds the scope of his vision infinitely enlarged.
Dismisss then the rangers of the heavens
and the science of Chaldea, and depart for a short time
from the greatest of cities, this world, to the lesser,
and thus you will be better able
to apprehend the overseer of the All."
This is why he is said to emigrate first from the land of Chaldea.[22]

Thus Philo finds in the ancient saga of the ancestor of the faithful—composed long before Diotima and Socrates and Plato—instruction in the mystical ascent from the visible to the Invisible.

This way of interpreting scripture suited well the intellectual and spiritual task Philo had set for himself. Just as the Greek sophists had read the archaic tales of gods and heroes allegorically, to draw out metaphysical meaning and spiritual instruction concealed beneath outward events, Philo assiduously developed this exegetical tradition. Reading scripture in this way, finding hidden within the events of the biblical story ultimate philosophical and religious truth, enabled the preacher to reconcile Moses and Plato, Torah and philosophy.

The allegorists' pattern of thinking will doubtless strike the modern reader as irresponsible, even quaint, just as the apologists' argument—that Pythagoras and Socrates learned the evident truths they taught from Moses himself on their travels to Egypt—seems naive. But Philo and the Alexandrian Jews had no doubts as to the legitimacy of allegorical exegesis, expounding Torah through a conceptual, not merely linguistic, translation; moreover, the enterprise of correlating scripture and philosophy called forth the best powers of impressive minds, moving them from the exegesis of the sacred documents straight into the work of theology. Most Christian interpreters of the Bible for centuries to come would feel no uneasiness about allegorizing. Philo's work, and that of other Alexandrian rabbis, established North Africa as a major force in preaching; it would hold that leadership until its life was disrupted by the invasions of the barbarians four hundred years after Philo.

THEOLOGY AND ETHICS[23]

The Palestinian rabbis, occupying themselves almost totally with the text and taking little account of philosophic systems, were less concerned to correlate exegesis with secular thought. A twentieth-century Jewish scholar has characterized their outlook as "extraordinarily limited."

> They had no interests outside Religion and the Law. They had lost all historic sense. They had no interest in art, in drama, in *belles lettres*, in poetry or in science (except, perhaps, in medicine). They had no training in philosophy. How enormously they might have benefitted if, under competent teachers, they had been put through a course of Greek philosophy and literature. They had no training in rhetoric or the art of composition. That is one reason why the written precipitate of their teachings and discussions is so formless and shapeless. The Old Testament was practically the only book they possessed, but of an appreciation of the Hebrew Bible as literature we notice little. For them the Bible is a collection of texts and isolated utterances, of injunctions, proofs, and teachings. Yet this Bible, with all that it implied, is their world, their one overmastering interest.[24]

Intellectually barricaded within Jewish culture, the rabbis' zeal was heightened in intensity by their exclusive concentration on the sacred tradition.

For these rabbis in Israel, and even for the synthesizing thinkers of Alexandria, theology was clearly subordinate to exegesis, while ratiocination regarding religious ideas yielded to the priority of ethics as the measure of faithfulness. Even so, their constant and critical reflection about elemental religious concepts involved them in formulating theology in their own distinctive manner.

The Understanding of God[25]

The rabbis assumed monotheism. This doctrine, with its emphasis on the divine creation of all things and its clear implication of the universal validity of biblical truth, looms large in the Wisdom literature, in Midrash, and in the rhetorical preachers of the Hellenized Jews.

The most difficult issue in thinking about God, from the exile right on through the final destruction of Jerusalem in 135 C. E., was the question of theodicy, to which the later prophets and the Wisdom writers had repeatedly returned. Increasingly, Jews spoke of evil in mythical language, picturing a cosmic spirit of darkness—variously called Belial, the Satan (the Adversary), Angel of Darkness—at war with the God of light. This less-than-ultimate dualism, while careful to protect the final sovereignty of the one God, helped both to explain evil and to arm the faithful for spiritual battle. Dualism had great appeal to the Hellenistic age; it found various expression in the mystery religions, in Platonism and in Gnosticism, while Judaism became increasingly preoccupied with the conflict between Good and Evil.

Yet the rabbis affirmed God's sovereignty and ultimate triumph. That faith rings through the preaching of Rabbi Eleazar ha-Kappar (second century C.E.) as he declares that every soul must give account at the judgment:

> They that live (again) are to be judged;
> to know, to make known and to be made aware that He is God,
> He is the Maker, He the Creator, He the Discerner,
> He the Judge, He the witness, He the adversary and He will judge;
> blessed be He in whose presence there is neither obliquity
> nor forgetfulness, nor respect of persons nor taking of bribes...
> For not of thy will wast thou formed
> and not of thy will dost thou die,
> and not of thy will art thou to give just account and reckoning
> before the King of the kings of the kings, the Holy One,
> Blessed be He.[26]

Bringing solemn urgency to the warning of judgment to come, the preacher was compelled to speak of the majesty of God.

A certain mystical tendency is present in the rabbis (though little spoken of), in the preaching at Qumran, and especially in Philo. It is a mysticism of identification with the divine purpose made known in the Law. Rabbinic reflection on the nature of God led (early in the third century C.E.) to the assertion that God prays. The insight is anthropomorphic but nevertheless insightful—and touching:[27] What is God's prayer? A rabbi pictured God praying thus:

> May it be my will that my compassion overcome mine anger,
> and that it may prevail over my attributes [of justice and judgment],
> and that I may deal with my children
> according to the attribute of compassion,
> and that I may not act towards them
> according to the strict line of justice.

How could the divine pathos be expressed more succinctly or more eloquently?

In the third century C.E. Rabban Gamaliel (the eighth to bear that honored name) summed up the spirituality that thought of God in such a way:

> Do his will as though it were thy will
> so that he may do thy will as though it were his will:
> undo thy will for the sake of his will
> so that he may undo the will of others for the sake of thy will.[28]

The witness of scripture and of the rabbis emphasized the abiding reality of God in the experience of Israel. An unnamed preacher said it eloquently:

> You find: Every place where Israel was exiled,
> the Divine Presence was with them.
> They were exiled to Egypt, the Presence was with them.
> They were exiled to Babylon, the Presence was with them.
> They were exiled to Elam, the Presence was with them.
> They were exiled to Rome, the Presence was with them.
> And when they shall return,
> the Presence, as it were, will be with them.[29]

Anyone with even a slight awareness of rhetoric can analyze the artistry of this affirmation. But in the experience of the faithful there was more than art in what the preacher said.

Anthropology[30]

The rabbis' canny insight into human nature issued more commonly in admonitions to right action than in disquisitions on anthropology. Their realism enabled them to hold in tension the grandeur and the misery of the human species. Late in the first century C.E. Akabya Ben Mahalalel admonished forthrightly:

> Mark well three things, and thou wilt not fall into the clutches of sin.
> Know whence thou art come, whither thou art going,
> and before whom thou art destined to give an account and reckoning.
> "Whence thou art come?" From a putrid drop.
> "Whence thou art going?" To a place of dust, worm, and maggot.
> "And before whom thou art destined
> to give an account and reckoning?"
> Before the King of Kings, the Holy One, Blessed be He.[31]

The tradition is uncertain as to the identity of the rabbi who first patterned a dictum on life's stages, a theme that had fascinated moralists (and would inspire Shakespeare to his lines on the "seven ages"). But some preacher proposed an analysis closely tied to the ideals and practices of Judaism:

> At five years old one is ready for the scripture,
> at ten years for the Mishnah,
> at thirteen for the commandments,
> at fifteen for Talmud, at eighteen for marriage,
> at twenty for pursuit of righteousness,
> at thirty for full strength, at forty for discernment,
> at fifty for counsel, at sixty for old age,
> at seventy for gray hairs, at eighty for "labor and sorrow"   [Ps. 90:10],
> at ninety for decrepitude,
> at one hundred he is as though he were dead,
> and had passed away and faded from the world.[32]

Devoted to the life of the mind, Israel's wisdom teachers had faced mortal limitations without blinking; they had shown "a sometimes almost uncannily clear knowledge of the limits of human understanding and a knowledge of the ambiguity of phenomena."[33] That insight also guided those other sages, the exegetes who came after them. As to the mystery of human freedom and divine omniscience, Rabbi Akiba (ca. 50–ca. 135) simply accepted the paradox:

> Everything is foreseen, yet freedom of choice is granted;
> in mercy is the world judged;
> and everything is according to the preponderance of works.[34]

The limits he perceived to mortal understanding did not induce despair. Said he in an affirmation of human dignity:

> Beloved is man, for he was created in the Image.
> Extraordinary is the love made known to him
> that he was created in the Image, as it is said,
> *For in the image of God made He man.*   [Gen. 9:6][35]

Eschatology[36]

The ascetics at Qumran and other apocalypticists expected an imminent end of the present age, and their preaching undertook to prepare the faithful for the final battle against the hosts of evil. The scribal rabbis tended to take a less cataclysmic view of things, but— like Rabbi Eleazar ha-Kappar—to urge preparation for divine judgment on each life. His contemporary Judah the Holy admonished:

Mark well three things, and thou wilt not fall into the clutches of sin:
Know what is above thee—an Eye that sees, an Ear that hears,
and all thine actions recorded in the Book.[37]

Though the religion of early Israel looked on death as the end of any significant human existence, for an increasing number of Jews after the exile a hope for continuing life with God grew into a sure confidence. Perhaps influenced by a belief in immortality among Gentiles, this faith found authentic rootage in Israel's religion in the prophets' plea for justice on the ground of every person's supreme value to God; internalizing that sense of worth, more and more of the faithful came to believe that God would not allow the crown of creation, the highest work of the divine hand, to fall into nothingness.[38] In the time of Jesus and Paul, faith in the resurrection of the dead was still an issue for dispute between Pharisees and Sadducees. But strong voices among the rabbis warned of divine judgment and spoke of bliss after death for the righteous. Early in the second century C.E. Rabbi Jacob was fond of saying:

This world is like a vestibule before the world to come;
prepare thyself in the vestibule
that thou mayest enter into the banquet hall.[39]

He also taught:

Better is one hour of repentance and good works in this world
than all the life of the world to come;
and better is one hour of calmness of spirit in the world to come
than all the life of this world.[40]

Confidence in life beyond death rested on faith in the eternity of God.

Commenting on God's word to Moses, "Behold thy days draw near to die" (Deut. 31:14), Samuel bar Nahmani asked rhetorically, "Do *days die?*"—then answered with his understanding of the text:

It means that at the death of the righteous,
their days cease from the world, yet they themselves abide,
as it says, "*In whose hand is the soul of all the living.*"   [Job 12:10]
Can this mean that the living alone are in God's hand,
and not the dead? No, it means
that the righteous even after their death may be called living,
whereas the wicked, both in life and in death, may be called dead.[41]

Sophia and Logos

A highly creative thrust in Jewish theologizing after the exile was the filling out of the concept of Wisdom[42] —an enterprise carried forward in rhetorical and exegetical (rather than philosophical) mode, which is to say, advanced in the mode of the preachers. For Koheleth (3d? century B.C.E.), *wisdom* designates the intellectual tradition of inquiry and reflection, and it has its limits:

> Having applied myself to acquiring wisdom
> and to observing the activity taking place in the world…
> I have scrutinized God's whole creation:
> You cannot get to the bottom of everything
> taking place under the sun;
> You may wear yourself out in the search,
> but you will never find it.
> Not even a sage can get to the bottom of it,
> even if he says that he has done so.   [Eccl. 8:17 NJB]

World-weariness nevertheless gave way to affirmation in the sober *joie de vivre* which came to characterize the "wise," who found increasing delight in speaking of Wisdom (Sophia) as an expression of the divine mind. The first of all Yahweh's creatures, she is his companion and agent in creation; in God's providence she is the source of all knowledge and understanding. In the writings of the "wise," she delivers sermons of haunting beauty and insight.[43] These affirm the unique glory and power of God in creation and covenant with Israel, yet concurrently claim truths taught by the sages of other peoples— whom she has also enlightened.

If such imagining began as rhetorical personification and even took on mythical dimension,[44] this way of thinking about Wisdom came to serve as a significant instrument of theological reflection. With no hint of polytheism or idolatry, the Jewish sages and preachers could speak of Sophia in familiar, though respectful, terms at a time when veneration for the divine Name had led to an etiquette of reserve in referring to God.

About the end of the third century B.C.E. a psalmist linked wisdom both to the praise of God and to Torah:

> Wisdom has been granted so that YHWH's glory can be proclaimed
> and so that God's many deeds can be recounted
> has she been taught to humanity:
> so that God's power can be proclaimed to ordinary people…

Her voice is heard in the gates of the just
and in the assembly of the devout, her song…
their meditation is on the Law of the Most High,
their words, to proclaim God's power.[45]

Here wisdom is seen as enabler of worship, preaching, and meditation on Torah.

Perhaps a generation later (about 180 B.C.E.) Ben Sira began his
book with a celebration of wisdom:

All wisdom is from the Lord;
she dwells with God for ever…
Wisdom was first of all created things;
intelligent purpose has existed from the beginning…
One alone is wise, the Lord most terrible,
seated upon the throne.
It is God who created her, beheld and measured her,
and infused her into all his works.
To everyone God has given her in some degree,
but without stint to those who love him.   [Sir. 1:1, 4, 8–10 REB alt.]

Then about mid-century a poet or preacher identified wisdom with
Torah:

This is he who is our God;
there is none to compare with him.
Every way of knowledge God found out
and gave to Jacob his servant,
to Israel whom he loved.
After that, wisdom appeared on earth
and lived among people.
She is the book of God's commandments,
the law that endures for ever.   [Bar. 3:35–4:1 REB alt.]

The theological possibilities implicit in the myth of wisdom led
Jewish thinkers to equate Sophia with the Stoic concept of Logos or
universal Reason, "which is the same as God."[46] (Recall Philo on the
Logos.) Thus with undeviating adherence to their Judaic heritage and
the truth revealed in Torah they established a theological principle by
which they could legitimately appropriate the wisdom of the philosophers. Here was a theological basis for the equivalences between
Moses and Plato that Hellenistic Jewish preachers asserted in their

allegorical exegesis. The sages began to speak of the divine Word in language paralleling both their personification of Wisdom (Sophia) and the rhetoric of Greek philosophical preachers about the Logos.[47] An Alexandrian Jew of the first century B.C.E. discoursed glowingly of Wisdom as

> a clear effluence from the glory of the Almighty   [Wis. 7:25 REB]

and dramatically of the Logos:

> When peaceful silence lay over all,
> and night had run half of her swift course,
> down from the heavens, from the royal throne,
> leapt your all-powerful Word;
> into the heart of a doomed land
> the stern warrior leapt.   [Wis. 18:14–15 JB]

Such theological reflection on Sophia=Logos affirmed the divine origin of the scriptures in a way that also kept open for the preachers the treasures of secular learning, even from Greek and Roman sources. For the preaching that participates in the dialogue between religion and culture, this was a development of highest importance. It encouraged intellectual receptivity and creativity while retaining the profound spiritual depth of traditional Jewish piety:

> As for Your intention,who could have learnt it,
> had you not granted Wisdom and sent your holy spirit from above?
> Thus have the paths of those on earth been straightened
> and people been taught what pleases you,
> and saved by Wisdom.   [Wis. 9:17–18 JB alt.]

Ethics[48]

In contrast with the Greeks, the fundamental genius of the Jews was ethical rather than speculative, and the burden of their preaching had to do with righteousness before God. Philo took pride in maintaining that as philosophers the Jews were not much involved with logic or science, but studied ethics industriously.[49] The early wisdom tradition commended "the common virtues that build a healthy society": sober speech, forbearance, honesty, self-control, industry, intelligence, humaneness, good will, patience, philanthropy, tractableness, reverence, justice, modesty, humility, and fidelity.[50] In the second-century B.C.E. an author had his fictional hero, Tobit, a dying exile in eighth-century Assyria, summarize the ethic in admonishing his beloved son:

> Serve God in truth, and do what is pleasing to him.
> Teach your children to do what is right and give alms,
> to be mindful of God and praise his name sincerely
> at all times and with all their strength.   [Tob. 14:8–9 REB]

A century later, Rabbi Shemaiah counseled simplicity without self-seeking:

> Love work, hate lordship,
> and seek no intimacy with the ruling powers.[51]

The great third-century B.C.E. Rabbi Simeon the Just compressed the essence of righteousness into a single sentence he repeated often:

> Upon three things the world standeth;
> Upon Torah, upon worship and upon the showing of kindness.[52]

Rabban Simeon Ben Gamaliel (10 B.C.E.–66) epitomized ethical counsel:

> By three things is the world sustained:
> by justice, by truth, and by peace, as it is said,
> *Truth and justice and peace judge ye in your gates.*   [Zech. 8:16][53]

The rabbis delighted to group ideas thus in tens, sevens, fours, and threes.

> Every one in whom there are these three things
> is of the disciples of Abraham our father.
> And every one, in whom are three other things
> is of the disciples of Balaam the wicked.
> A good eye, a lowly spirit and a humble mind
> are the marks of the disciples of Abraham our father.
> An evil eye, a haughty spirit and a proud mind,
> are the marks of the disciples of Balaam the wicked.[54]

The pressure of Roman occupation worked to constrict the preaching of morality into narrow channels of personal decision-making; private virtue offered the primary area of ethical practice open to the faithful. Hillel said,

> Be of the disciples of Aaron, loving peace and pursuing peace,
> loving humankind and drawing them to the Torah.[55]

Early in the second century C.E. Rabbi Ishmael taught:

> Be submissive to the ruler, patient under oppression;
> and receive everyone with cheerfulness.[56]

That commitment to peace, combined with the predisposition of the Sadducees, led his contemporary, Rabbi Hananiah, prefect of the priests, to admonish:

> Do thou pray for the welfare of the Empire,
> because were it not for the fear it inspires,
> every one would swallow one's neighbor alive.[57]

Yet total obedience to divine Law remained a Jew's supreme obligation, and the practice of virtue involved reflection. In the mind of the rabbis,

> Lovingkindness is greater than charity in three ways.
> Charity is done with one's money, while loving-kindness
> may be done with one's money or with one's person.
> Charity is given only to the poor, while loving-kindness
> may be given both to the poor and to the rich.
> Charity is given only to the living, while loving-kindness
> may be shown to both the living and the dead.[58]

While some rabbis, like some people devoted to scripture in nearly every time, insisted on the letter of the Law, the wisdom of others included a dash of realism, as in the moderating principle:

> The saving of life supersedes the Sabbath.[59]

A persisting preoccuptation of "the wise" was to compress the fulness of Torah into its very essence. Hillel had condensed it into a single prohibition; both Jesus and the apostle Paul would do similarly.[60] In the third century C.E. Rabbi Simlai pointed out landmarks in the process:

> Six hundred and thirteen commandments were given to Moses…
> David came and reduced them to eleven. For it is written…
> (1) *Whoever walks blamelessly,*
> (2) *and does what is right,*
> (3) *and speaks truth from the heart;*
> (4) *who does not slander with the tongue,*
> (5) *and does no evil to a friend,*
> (6) *nor takes up a reproach against a neighbor;*
> (7) *in whose eyes a reprobate is despised,*

(8) *but who honors those who fear the Lord,*

(9) *who swears to one's own hurt and does not change;*

(10) *who does not lend...money at interest,*

(11) *and does not take bribe against the innocent.*

Whoever does these things shall never be moved...　　[Ps. 15:2–5]

Isaiah came and reduced them to six, for it is written:

(1) *Whoever walks righteously*

(2) *and speaks uprightly;*

(3) *...who despises the gain of oppressions,*

(4) *who shakes the hands, lest they hold a bribe,*

(5) *who stops the ears from hearing of bloodshed,*

(6) *and shuts the eyes from looking upon evil...*　　[Isa. 33:15]

Micah came and reduced them to three, for it is written:

He has showed you, O mortal, what is good;
and what does the Lord *require of you but*

(1) *to do justice,*

(2) *and to love kindness,*

(3) *and to walk humbly with your God.*　　[Mic. 6:8]

Isaiah came again and reduced them to two, for it is written:

Thus says the Lord*: Keep justice and do righteousness.*　　[Isa. 56:1]

Amos came and reduced them to one, for it is written;

For thus says the Lord *to the house of Israel:*
Seek me and live.　　[Amos 5:4][61]

In every way the good Jew clung to the admonition at the heart of rabbinical preaching:

Make a hedge about the Torah.[62]

Reflections on Preaching

The preeminence of the Torah was so self-evident, as was the duty of the interpreter to make its meaning plain, that no elaborate theory of preaching was articulated. A prayer from the first century B.C.E. expresses the conviction of what Israel needs to learn:

that it is not the production of crops that feeds humankind
but that your word sustains those who trust in you.　　[Wis. 16:26 NRSV]

All the deliverances of the early rabbis arose from a lifetime of reverent reflection on scripture and on the demands of God there revealed. Even so, they did not require specific textual authority for every precept they laid down. In all their discussion they thought of themselves as teaching the Torah, whether or not their words in the Mishnah appealed to a biblical "proof text."[63]

Later generations attributed (perhaps mistakenly) to Rabbi Meir (mid-second century C.E.) the pronouncement:

> Everyone who is occupied with Torah for its own sake
> is worthy of many things...He is called friend, beloved,
> one that loves God and that loves humankind,
> that makes glad both God and humankind.
> And it clothes him with humility and fear
> and fits him to be righteous, pious, upright, and faithful.
> It keeps him far from sin and brings him near to virtue.
> People are benefitted by him with counsel
> and sound knowledge, discernment and strength...
> It makes him great and lifts him above all things.[64]

Yet Rabbi Jehudah warned that the task was not to be taken lightly:

> Be cautious in teaching;
> for error in teaching may amount to intentional sin.[65]

And Hillel insisted that the work required constant application:

> Say not when I am at leisure I will study—
> perchance thou wilt not be at leisure.[66]

The Zadokite Document from Qumran speaks disparagingly of "the babbling preacher,"[67] citing the prophet Micah as source of the characterization:

> Babble-babble shall they preach.   [Mic. 2:6, Gaster]

The rabbis warned against putting the words of the Law to personal profit. So Rabbi Zadok said of the words of Torah,

> Do not make them a crown for self-exaltation
> nor a spade to dig with.[68]

A good rabbi would earn a living with his own hands.[69] Teaching scripture was a sacred privilege. So Rabban Gamaliel, the son of Judah the Prince, urged in the third century C.E.:

> Let all who labour with the congregation
> labour with them for the name of Heaven.[70]

In the same spirit Rabbi Hillel warned,

> Whoever puts the crown to one's own use shall perish.[71]

With insight into human nature to match their devotion to Torah and to the service of their community, the rabbis counseled sensitivity to the condition of those whom they would teach:

> Soothe not thy associate in the hour of his anger,
> and console him not in the hour when his dead lies before him;
> and question him not in the hour of his vow,
> and seek not to see him in the hour of his disgrace.[72]

It was understood among them that

> A wise man does not speak
> in the presence of one who is greater than he in wisdom,
> and does not interrupt the words of his associate,
> and does not hasten to reply.
> He questions according to the subject and answers according to rule.
> He speaks of the first things first, and of the last things last,
> and concerning what he has not heard he says I have not heard.
> He acknowledges the truth.[73]

In the study of scripture the life of the student—and of the exegete—must accord with the scripture one would learn or teach.

> A parable: A man came to a shopkeeper to buy a measure of wine.
> The shopkeeper said to him: Bring me your vessel.
> But the man opened his bag.
> Then he said to the shopkeeper: Give me some oil.
> The shopkeeper said to him: Bring me your vessel.
> But the man opened the corner of his garment.
> Said the shopkeeper to him:
> How can you buy wine and oil if you have no vessel at hand?
> Similarly: God says to the wicked:
> You have no good deeds with you—
> how then do you wish to learn Torah?[74]

As to skill in communicating insight into Torah, the rabbis recognized, like the generations of "the wise" before them, that ability to compress an insight into a memorable maxim was a divine gift.

> A mortal may order the thoughts,
> but the LORD inspires the words the tongue utters.   [Prov. 16:1 REB alt.]

The Law was to be accorded absolute veneration amounting to fear. Yet it was the path to freedom and fulfilment. Rabbi Joshua Ben Levi's remembered homily makes these points, even while illustrating the rabbinical mode of interweaving sentences of scripture into the preaching:

> Every single day a *bat kol* [heavenly voice] goes forth
> from Mount Moriah, proclaiming as follows:
> "Woe to humankind for their contempt of the Torah!"
> For whoever does not study the Torah is called Nazuf [Reprobate],
> As it is said, *As a ring of gold in a swine's snout,*
> *so is a fair woman that turneth aside from discretion.*   [Prov. 11:22]
> And it says, *And the tables were the work of God,*
> *and the writing was the writing of God, graven upon the tables.*
> [Ex. 32:16]
>
> Read not "Harut" (graven) but "Herut" (freedom),
> for thou wilt find no free person
> save one who is engaged in the study of Torah,
> But whoever is always occupied with Torah is surely exalted,
> as it is said, *And from the gift, one's heritage is God,*
> *and from the heritage of God, one is raised to high places.*   [Num. 21:19][75]

From God's abode in the heavens Sophia had come to earth to teach the human race. In this world the divine Word engaged human minds and hearts as Sophia invited hungry spirits to a feast surpassing all others. Through the study and preaching of Torah, people entered the very presence of God; early in the second century C.E. Rabbi Halafta of Kefar Hananiah declared it:

> When ten sit studying the Torah, the Shekinah resides in their midst,
> as it is said, *God standeth in the congregation of God.*   [Ps. 82:1][76]

FORMS OF RELIGIOUS ADDRESS[77]

The rabbis in Judea and Babylon who spoke Aramaic loved to engage in dialog about the scripture as they met to discuss its meaning, either indulging in their favorite enterprise with a knot of Bible-loving cronies or addressing the congregation in the synagogue. The sharp-eyed expositors favored a form of speech that honored the art of the terse, witty aphorism, preferring the quick jab of the rapier to the rolling periods of the eloquent orator. Idealizing the Essene preacher, Philo dismissed rhetoric as of little concern to the expositor of scripture, who

> does not make an exhibition of clever rhetoric
> like the orators or sophists of today
> but follows careful examination
> by careful expression of the exact meaning of the thoughts,
> and this does not lodge just outside the ears of the audience
> but passes through the hearing into the soul,
> and there lodges securely.[78]

The listeners, Philo added, paid quiet attention, giving assent "by their looks or nods"—i. e., not by tumultuous demonstrations of applause like those offered by the Greek samplers of discourse. (Striking such a pose of lofty disdain for the art of oratory had become a commonplace among philosophers.)

The religious discourse of the rabbis—whether interactive dialog with other students of Torah or public address from the chair on the *bema* to the waiting congregation—was for the most part unaffected in tone, employing a casual manner not unlike that of a Greek or Roman speaker involved in "public conversation" about an issue of importance. (Recall that the Latin designation for such a speech was *sermo*, from which *sermon* derives.) In the broad meaning of the term their speech in the synagogue was *preaching*, even when it did not assume the proclamatory mode of the herald or announcer.

Though unschooled in classical rhetoric, the rabbis at Bible study showed concern for style as well as content; true to the insights of the wisdom tradition, they obviously gave thought to the effectiveness of their pronouncements,

> The wise of heart is called perceptive,
> and pleasant speech increases persuasiveness...
> The mind of the wise makes their speech judicious,
> and adds persuasiveness to their lips.   [Prov. 16:21, 23 NRSV]

Some of the preachers, moreover, enjoying the rapt attention of popular audiences, as already noted, aspired, despite Philo's disclaimer, to the dazzling eloquence prized in Hellenistic circles.

Rabbinic discourse followed for the most part those rhetorical forms found in scripture or developed tendencies already present there.

Dialogue and Disputation[79]

Discussions among the rabbis took on excitement from the air of friendly argument as minds well versed in Torah sought to sharpen understanding of the Law. Later generations recalled the gist of a disputation in the first century C.E.:

Rabban Johanan said to them: Go out and see
which is the right way to which a person should cleave.
Rabbi Eliezer replied: A liberal eye.
Rabbi Joshua replied: A good companion.
Rabbi Yose replied: A good neighbor.
Rabbi Simeon replied: Foresight.
Rabbi Eleazar replied: Goodheartedness.
Said Rabban Johanan Ben Zakkai to them:
I prefer the answer of Eleazar Ben Arak,
for in his words your words are included.[80]

For hearers who followed such an exercise, it carried the appeal
of a riddle and the excitement of a contest. Despite the warning of
Rabbi Akiba against laughter and levity as conducive to immorality,[81] the disputations were characterized by a wry humor that could
evoke a smile if not a guffaw. Rabbi Eliezer's counsel is a case in
point:

Repent one day before thy death.
And keep warm at the fire of the sages,
but beware of their glowing coal lest thou be scorched...
All their words are like coals of fire.[82]

Salty wit often combined with clear insight into the workings of
the psyche. Rabbi Nathan (second century C.E.) cautioned:

Don't upbraid your fellow for a blemish that disfigures yourself.[83]

As that warning suggests, all-too-human rivalries among rabbis straining for status could distort the beauty of the spiritual quest. According to one story, Rabbi Eliezer, Rabbi Joshua, and Rabbi Nathan
became involved in an unseemly contest for recognition, each calling
for a miracle (which was granted) as a sign of divine approval on his
interpretation. But turning the making of midrash into that kind of
game was disturbing to one of the onlookers:

Rabbi Nathan met the prophet Elijah. He asked him,
"What was the Holy One, blessed be He, doing in that hour?"
Said Elijah, "He was laughing and saying,
'My children have defeated me, my children have defeated me.'"[84]

More troubling than the foibles of the rabbis, serious issues of
faith were at stake, and faithful Jews devoted to Torah could not help
disputing with the Almighty, as Job had dared to do. After the Roman

destruction of Jerusalem and the temple, the unknown author of
2 Esdras addressed the Most High in anguish:

> My Master and Lord, out of all the forests on earth,
> and all their trees, you have chosen one vine;
> from all the lands in the whole world you have chosen one plot;
> and out of all the flowers in the world you have chosen one lily.
> From all the depths of the sea you have filled one river for yourself,
> and of all the cities ever built you have set apart Zion as your own.
> From all the birds that were created
> you have named for yourself one dove,
> and from all the animals that were fashioned you have taken one sheep.
> Out of all the countless nations, you have adopted one for your own,
> and to this chosen people
> you have given a law approved above all others.
>
> Why then, Lord, have you put this one people
> at the mercy of so many?...
> Those who reject your promises have trampled on the people
> who put their trust in your covenants.   [2 Esd. 5:23–29 REB]

An angel sent to instruct him opens with a counter-question:

> Do you love Israel more than Israel's Maker does?   [5:33 REB]

For all the intensity of exegetical study and theological dialog, the
suffering of Israel remained an inexplicable mystery.

Maxim and Word-Play

Even so, the rabbis loved to play with words. In Aramaic as well
as in Greek their speaking manifested deliberate artistry, well-honed
by the preachers and for its form gratifying to the hearers. The tradition of wisdom knew well that

> The ear is a judge of speeches,
> just as the palate can tell one food from another.   [Job 34:3 JB]

They took pleasure in tossing off puns,[85] and delight in playing with
words prevailed to such an extent that often they deliberately
manipulated passages of scripture to produce effective phrases and
tropes.

The love for wordplay found a ready vehicle in aphorism. From
much practice after much listening, these rabbis spoke in maxims, as
if by second nature. Theirs was the rhetoric of the condensed, biting,
proverbial utterance; it had marked the wisdom tradition from its

origins. The disciples of Qoheleth (Ecclesiastes) held him up as an example:

> Besides being a sage,
> Qoheleth also taught his knowledge to the people,
> Having weighed, studied, and amended a great many proverbs.
> Qoheleth tried to write in an attractive style
> and to set down truthful thoughts
> in a straightforward manner.   [Eccl. 12:9–10 JB]

A series of connected maxims on a common theme was commonly presented as an extended wisdom speech.

Ability to speak in maxims did not come easily. Jesus Ben Sira did his best to put a positive spin on the tedium involved:

> Happy heart, cheerful expression;
>   but wearisome work, inventing proverbs.   [Sir. 13:26 NJB]

Determined speakers nevertheless mastered the form. Consider Rabbi Tarfon:

> The day is short, the work is plentiful,
> the laborers are sluggish, and the reward is abundant,
> and the master of the house presses.[86]

The spirit of serious play that found delight in maxims also made a game of collecting ideas in tens, sevens, fours, and threes. In discussions with those who cherished an extensive oral tradition and relied on writing only minimally (if at all), the practice served as an aid to memory.

The mystery of creativity intrigued the rabbis, as it had peoples devoted to artistic expression throughout the ancient world. Israel's wisdom tradition regarded it, as we have seen, as a gift from God (Prov. 16:1). For creative artistry the wise looked not to the Muses, but to God the Creator.[87]

Exemplum and Application

The vividness of the Bible itself and consequently of biblical preaching springs from the preponderance of narrative involving scores of vivid characters. The preachers drove home their points by brief references to exemplary figures from scripture and to incidents, including their own experience, from which lessons could be drawn.

Typical of the genre is the testament of the dying Mattathias, father of the Maccabees, set forth as a speech to his sons:

> Remember the deeds performed by your ancestors,
> each in his generation,
> and you shall win honor and everlasting renown.
> Was not Abraham tried and found faithful,
> was that not counted as making him just?
> Joseph in the time of his distress maintained the Law,
> and so became lord of Egypt.
> Phinehas, our father, in return for his burning fervour
> received a covenant of everlasting priesthood.
> Joshua, for carrying out his task,
> became judge of Israel.   [1 Macc. 2:51–61 JB]

The exhortation continues on through Caleb, David, Elijah, Hananiah, Azariah, Mishael, and Daniel, in a pattern that has persisted down the centuries; in folk preaching the cadences can still be heard. Frequently the exemplary figures provided cumulative illustrations for a particular theme, in this case faithfulness. Like the Palestinian rabbis, the popular philosophers of their own day, and the classical orators before them, the preachers among the Jews of the Diaspora made frequent use of *exempla.*

Rabbi Joshua ben Hananiah, who late in the first century C.E. followed the school of Hillel, drew on personal experience to make a point at his own expense; he recounted losing an argument three times in his life: once to a woman, once to a small boy, and once to a little girl. Here is one of the stories:

> I was once walking down a road, and there was a path
> that led through a [privately owned] field. I used that path.
> Then a little girl called out to me. "Master, is this not a field
> [... forbidden for you to use without permission]?"
> "No," I replied, "it is obviously a well-trodden path."
> "Robbers like you have made it into such." she said to me.[88]

In the second century C.E. during a governmental roundup of Jews, Rabbi Akiba was imprisoned for violating an edict against teaching the Law. Comparing the offenses which had led to their arrests, Pappus ben Judah exclaimed,

> Happy are you, Rabbi Akiba,
> that you have been arrested because of Torah!
> Woe to Pappus who was arrested for worthless reasons.[89]

Beneath the unmistakably Jewish content of the story, the reader discerns a form like the classical Greek *chreia*, an incident involving a notable person or persons, coming to a climax in a telling declaration by the principal character.

When, after the revolt of Bar Kochba in 135 C.E., the Romans ordered a company of rabbis to be executed, tradition recalled, one was troubled in spirit:

> Rabbi Simon said to Rabbi Ishmael:
> Rabbi, my heart is consumed,
> for I do not know why I am to be executed.
> Rabbi Ishmael said to Rabbi Simon:
> Perhaps a man once came to you to hear judgment,
> or to consult you about something,
> and you let him wait until you had emptied your goblet,
> or fastened your sandals, or put on your cloak?
> The Torah says: *"If thou afflict them in any wise."* [Ex. 22:22]
> It counts the same whether you afflict them greatly or only a little!
> Then the other said to him, You have consoled me, Rabbi![90]

Further bite was given to sermons by pointed application to specific situations. This was achieved by Haggadah—retelling a biblical story in such a way as to give it contemporary relevance. The "Testament of Job" presents the great sufferer, after his vindication and a long life of prosperity, addressing his children, recounting once again the experiences he has endured, and admonishing them to faith and charity.

Some rabbinic stories show delicacy of sensitivity, keenness of insight, and unshakeable faith in God; notable among these is an account from the Midrash on Proverbs, telling of a trial that befell wise Beruria and her husband:

> R. Me'ir sat discoursing on a Sabbath afternoon in the House of Study.
> While he was there, his two sons died. What did their mother do?
> She laid them upon the bed and spread a linen cloth over them.
> At the outgoing of the Sabbath R. Me'ir came home,
> and said to her, "Where are my sons?"
> She replied, "They went to the House of Study."
> He said, "I did not see them there"…
> Then she gave him to eat, and he ate and said the blessing.
> Then she said, "I have a question to ask you."
> He replied, "Ask it."
> She said, "Early today a man came here,
> and gave me something to keep for him;
> now he has come back to ask for it again.

Shall we return it to him or not?"
He replied, "One who has received something on deposit
must surely return it to its owner."
She replied, "Without your knowledge I would not return it."
Then she took him by the hand, and brought him up to the bed,
and took away the cloth, and he saw his sons lying dead upon the bed.
Then he began to weep, and said about each,
"O my son, my son; O my Rabbi, my Rabbi!...
My sons...gave light to their father's face
through their knowledge of the Law."
Then his wife said to him,
"Did you not say to me that one must return a deposit to its owner?
Does it not say, '*The Lord gave, the Lord took,
blessed be the name of the Lord'?*"   [Job 1:21]
So she comforted him and quieted his mind.[91]

Figures: Metaphor, Simile, et al.

In holding the attention of hearers, vividness of imagery also kept the mind's eye constantly engaged. Simile and metaphor abound in oral literature, and in the preaching of the rabbis those forms readily lent themselves to their teaching purpose. Judah Ben Tema marshalled a series of similes to say:

Be strong as the leopard, swift as the eagle,
fleet as the gazelle, and brave as the lion,
to do the will of thy Father who is in heaven.[92]

A wisdom-preacher of the first century B.C.E. used an extended metaphor to picture God as a mighty warrior:

The Lord will take...zeal as his whole armor,
and will arm all creation to repel his enemies;
he will put on righteousness as a breastplate,
and wear impartial justice as a helmet;
he will take holiness as an invincible shield,
and sharpen stern wrath for a sword...   [Wis. 5:17–20 NRSV]

Preachers would play variations on that metaphor for centuries to come.

The same preacher made effective use of *sorites,* a figure which the Stoics also liked to use. It linked arguments in a chain to wrap up a case:

The beginning of wisdom is the most sincere desire for instruction,
and concern for instruction is love of her,
and love of her is the keeping of her laws,
and giving heed to her laws is assurance of immortality,
and immortality brings one near to God;
so the desire for wisdom leads to a kingdom.
Therefore if you delight in thrones and scepters,
O monarchs over the peoples, honor wisdom,   [Wis. 6:17–21 NRSV]

The reader will also recognize in this passage the figures of personification and apostrophe.

Story and Parable[93]

The imaginative preacher could easily extend simile or metaphor into a parable, a story with a teaching purpose:

There are four types among those that sit in the presence of the sages:
the sponge, the funnel, the strainer, and the sifter.
The sponge soaks up everything.
The funnel takes in at one ear and lets out at the other.
The strainer lets pass the wine and retains the lees.
The sifter holds back the coarse and collects the fine flour.[94]

Actually, the "parable" just quoted is quite devoid of narrative; its charm lies in the striking pictures and soul-searching comparisons evoked by the vivid metaphors. Other rabbinic parables employed this same technique.[95]

Parables could also be composed by elaborating into narrative a metaphor found in scripture[96] or putting memory or imagination to work to produce a brief story that would vivify a dictum in the Torah. This latter technique became a favorite mode of haggadic exposition.[97] (Both patterns may be discovered in the parables of Jesus in the gospels.)

The rabbis also worked up parables with a flavor reminding one of Aesop's fables.[98] One who did so was Rabbi Akiba (early second century C.E.), who, on continuing to teach Torah publicly despite an imperial decree forbidding Jews to study it, was asked if he was not afraid of the government:

I will answer you with a parable.
A fox was once walking alongside a river,
and he saw fishes anxiously swimming from place to place.

He said to them, "From what are you fleeing?"
The fishes answered, "From the nets cast for us by men."
The fox said, "Why do you not come up and find safety on land,
so that you and I can live together [in peace]...?"
But the fishes replied,
"Are you the one they call the most clever of animals?
You are not clever, but foolish.
If we are afraid in the one element in which we can live,
how much more would we have to be afraid
in the element in which we would certainly die?"

So it is with us. If we are in such danger
when we sit and study the Torah, of which it is written,
"For thereby you shall have life, and shall long endure,"   [Deut. 30:20]
how much worse our situation will be
if we were to neglect the Torah![99]

The rabbis told stories about human characters, too, stories now
and again touched with pathos to match their spiritual insight. They
also liked to spin yarns with mordant humor to elicit knowing smiles
from the hearers. In Babylon they were fond of recalling Rabbi Beroka
of Hoza, who in the marketplace frequently received a visit from the
prophet Elijah. The ancient prophet would point out to him Jews
looked down upon by the more religious for failure to observe punc-
tiliously the fine points of the Law, yet assured of a place in the
World-to-Come because of a virtue not perceived by their critics. As
they conversed, two others walked by.

Elijah remarked, "These two also have a share in the World-to-Come."
Rabbi Beroka asked them, "What is your occupation?"
They replied, "We are comedians.
When we see people who are depressed, we cheer them up;
also when we see two people quarreling,
we strive hard to make peace between them."[100]

Literary Forms Influenced by Preaching[101]

Jewish literature produced in the Hellenistic era gives prominence
to preaching and to sermonic passages. The fascination with eloquence
on the part of sages and composers of inspirational histories moved
them to fill their works with speeches on religious themes.

Books of various literary genres, which began now to appear under
the names of Israel's patriarchs and saints, imitated the preaching in
scripture; these pseudepigrapha offered messages from ancient

worthies addressed to current crises. A Letter of Jacob, for example, directed ethical preaching to the Jews of the Diaspora, and the Testaments of the Twelve Patriarchs similarly addressed all Israel. The "Second Book of Esdras" has Ezra the priest discussing with God, or with God's angel, in a vision the troubling conditions that were disturbing the faithful late in the first century C.E. and presents a series of divine discourses offering explanation and encouragement.

More fanciful than these was a class of elaborately symbolic messages presented as reports of visions received by revelation (*apocalypse*). In the train of Israel's classic prophets (Amos, Isaiah, Ezekiel) the pseudonymous authors of these fantastic works "preached" the doom of Judah's oppressors and God's imminent intervention to deliver the righteous. The book of Enoch, the Assumption of Moses, the Prophecy of Daniel have survived, the latter in the canon; the Dead Sea Scrolls also contain literature of this sort.[102]

By their effect on sermonic style and by setting scenes for impressive religious speeches, all these literary forms testify to the importance of preaching in Jewish life.

Sermon Types and Forms

In contrast to the compression of aphorism, Jewish preachers also made use of extended speeches or sermons. True to the genius of their faith these addresses explained, expounded, and applied passages in the Torah; even the Hebrew word for sermons (*derashot*) has the same root (*d-r-sh*) as *midrash*.[103]

One type of sermon followed the immemorial biblical pattern of the *recital* or summary of God's dealing with the covenant people, urging the hearers to repentance.[104] Another linked together a *succession of maxims*; sometimes the advice was disconnected, as in the "string of beads" (*charaz*). A variation presented combinations of related maxims in groups of threes, fours, sevens, or tens; one numerical scheme listed forty-eight requisites for acquiring Torah.

More extended was the *thematic speech* in the tradition of wisdom. "The Futility of Riches" (Ps. 49) is a suggestive example. The familiar wisdom theme of the reversal of situations, illustrated in hymnic form in Ps. 107:33–43, provided ideal opportunity for rhetorical development; some of the speeches in Job, such as Elihu's meditation on the mysteries of God's power in nature (36:22–37:24) also suggest the type. Thematic sermons are also found in the documents at Qumran.

Appealing less to reason than to imagination and emotion was the *report of a divinely given vision* in imitation of the classical prophets. Preachers like Amos, Isaiah, and Ezekiel may actually have experienced the visual splendors or horrors they recounted, but the genre soon led to a literary pose (mentioned in the previous section) as gifted writers described marvelous sights they had "seen and heard"; such preachers with vivid powers of imagination could strike emotional depths in their hearers. Apocalyptic (visionary) literature like the book of Daniel and and the Greek book of Second Esdras suggests the power of the form.

Anyone who has listened much to gifted speakers and reflected on their power as compared with others whose talk is dull, even though both serve the same cause, perceives that the former clearly make conscious and deliberate use of rhetorical artistry. They do it for the sake of the message, to convey it with greater force; consequently, they are troubled when sophisticated sermon-tasters knowingly analyze this or that aesthetic touch while showing little regard for the moral and spiritual content of their sermons. Such preachers find themselves in the position of the prophet Ezekiel, whom God consoled:

> [Your people who talk about you say to one another]
> "Let us go and see what message there is from the LORD"…
> They will sit down in front of you, and hear what you have to say,
> but they will not act on it.
> "Fine words!" they will say with insincerity,
> for their hearts are set on selfish gain.
> To them you are no more than a singer of fine songs
> with a lovely voice and skill as a harpist.   [Ezek. 33:30–32 REB]

Yet despite the shallowness of hearers preoccupied with form rather than substance and the danger that the rhetorical game may turn even the mind of the preacher from the urgency of the message to frivolities of style, nevertheless prophet, scribe, rabbbi, and Christian preacher have necessarily—and gladly—given attention to the artistry of effective religious speech.

Hellenistic Models

In the Greek-speaking communities, especially the great centers of Alexandria and Antioch, rabbis and other *literati* took over Hellenistic forms to proclaim the faith. Like the Aramaic pseudepigraphists they also wrote pieces in the name of biblical worthies; but they took the process a step further in producing treatises "by" classical poets and philosophers upholding the morality taught in the Hebraic tradition. In the second century C.E. they composed a book of "Sibylline Oracles" (into which the Christians later inserted their own propaganda), a compilation of "pagan" prophecies honoring the one God and the divinely chosen people, the Jews.

The speeches with which pious authors filled their histories (2 Esdras, Maccabees, the chronicles of Josephus), narratives (Tobit), and books of wisdom (Wisdom of Solomon) present the heroes and heroines of faith as stirring orators in the classical mold. The "Letter to Aristeas," an apology for Judaism, used the form of an epistle for which the rhetoricians had prescribed rules paralleling those for oratory. Josephus's apology *Ad Apion* likewise adopts and adapts an accepted literary form that originated in the courts, the judicial speech of defense.

The most striking and fateful borrowing from Hellenism was the appropriation of classical rhetoric for preaching. The informal commentary of the rabbi on a passage of scripture, the homily, now took on the color and richness of oratorical style with the use of the many figures that both speaker and hearers had learned in the rhetorical schools. Even the *form* of a classical speech was adopted, with reliance on the techniques of invention by prepared lists of topics (including catalogs of vices) and the rules of partition laid down in the manuals. Diatribe became as characteristic of Hellenistic rabbis as of Stoic and Cynic moralists. The encomium or panegyric lent itself to ceremonial occasions honoring Israel's past; Fourth Maccabees may well have been such an oration, delivered perhaps at Antioch, to eulogize the martyrs of the faith. By wedding classical rhetoric to the proclamation of biblical religion, the Alexandrian rabbis invented the standard form of sermon that would flourish in the synagogue—and in the church—for centuries. A "new art" had come to birth, "that of pulpit oratory."[105]

Preaching in Judaism:
An Assessment

For the history of preaching, developments in Judaism during the Hellenistic era are of monumental importance—for that majestic faith and for Christianity as well.

1. The faith of Judaism affirmed the transcendence of the one God, a theme grander and more sublime than the political disputes and judicial arguments that preoccupied the classical orators. The Jews resisted, often at the cost of life itself, the pretensions of political power or of totalitarian culture and heroically maintained the principle that loyalty to the divine will take precedence over every other demand.

2. The form of congregational worship followed in the synagogue gave primacy to the reading and exposition of scripture. Judaism taught children and adults to love the Word of God made known therein and to rejoice in biblical exegesis, *midrash* (Ps. 1:2). Unlike other religions contesting for adherents in the Roman Empire, and unlike the great world faiths of the East that have subsequently become known to the West, it was a religion of the book;[1] it flourished by speaking the words and the meaning of the sacred text. *Midrash* became *derash*—sermon or biblical preaching.

3. Preaching to the congregation had gained great popular prominence in the synagogues in the first century of the Common Era. Though the rabbis had preached tens of thousands of sermons by the fifth century C.E., virtually no manuscripts have survived.

4. The scriptures set forth the sacred story of God's dealings with Israel, impressing on biblical preaching a lively narrative character.

5. Jewish preaching embodied four traditions: recital (with its mutation into narrative concerning exemplary figures), prophecy

(speaking under divine inspiration), discourse in the wisdom tradition (setting forth reflections on situations in life, with use of figures and parable), and midrash (biblical exposition). (All four would enter into Christian preaching, with Jesus favoring the way of wisdom, the apostles relying in large measure on recital, and the early church moving within decades from living prophecy to reliance on exposition.)

6. The Jewish community accorded veneration to the learned interpreter of Torah, the rabbi, whose manner of life was expected to conform with his knowledge of scripture.

7. The nonprofessional rabbinate, open to students who achieved the ability to interpret Torah, effectively shifted religious leadership from the Levitical priesthood to the laity before the destruction of the temple in 70 C.E. brought an end to the cult.

8. The establishment of synagogues in all the communities of the Diaspora, the translation of the scriptures into Greek (the Septuagint), and the activity of Jewish missionaries and apologists gained a respectful hearing for Judaism in many parts of the empire. It pointed them toward an understanding of God at once monotheistic, universal, and personal, and toward an ethic of righteousness demanded by a just and compassionate deity both transcendent and immanent.

9. While maintaining loyalty to the divine Law, Hellenistic Judaism participated sympathetically in the cultural as well as the commercial life of the larger world. In the great Jewish communities of Alexandria, Antioch, and Rome, an openness to intellectual and aesthetic movements among the Gentiles made possible a two-way traffic of the spirit. Jewish thinkers gladly took over insights from the classical philosophers, especially Plato and the Stoics.

10. Jewish interpreters developed methods of biblical exegesis designed both to deal seriously with the text and the sacred history it narrated and also to address the new situation of the hearers. The rabbinical "rules" and the sophisticated allegorizing of the Alexandrians put the authority of scripture at the service of preachers in proclaiming the divine word to Jew and Gentile.

11. The rhetoric of the wisdom tradition intended to persuade the hearer, and the rhetoric for preaching worked out by the rabbis drew on forms developed in that tradition, appropriating also those taught in the Hellenistic schools. Sacred rhetoric, melding biblical and classical aspects of the art, would long persist in Western culture.

12. The glory of Judaism, the Law, which in its moral sublimity appealed to many high-minded Gentiles, nevertheless proved a liability in the mission to win universal acceptance for the faith. Even among Gentiles who frequented the synagogues and revered the God of Abraham, the ceremonial law gave the appearance of a burden, which most of them were unwilling to assume, and they were loath to adopt the covenant-sign of circumcision. Judaism attracted more "proselytes at the gate" than were drawn within the fold.

13. A more serious limitation, discerned by the great prophets and notable rabbis (a tendency that shows itself in other great religions) was an inclination toward a formalism preoccupied with the external demands and minutiae of the Law and too often failing to carry out the divine intention toward justice and mercy. Criticism of this inclination arose repeatedly within Judaism to reassert the ethical genius of the Law.

14. In working out a theology of Wisdom as the divine Reason—active in creation, imparting guidance through scripture, and granting understanding to those diligent in seeking—and in equating Sophia with the Logos of Hellenistic philosophy, Jewish theologians opened the entire world of intellectual and spiritual truth to the preacher. They established a conceptual base for proclaiming a message of universal validity and appeal.

+

From the synagogue as from no other single source the Christian church derived the shape of its preaching. Here was the regular reading of holy scripture to a waiting congregation, followed by the sermon, the interpretation of that scripture in the proclamation of the divine word. The first preacher of the gospel, both in point of time and in supremacy, was Jesus of Nazareth, a child of the synagogue. To his preaching we now turn.

PART THREE

Preacher of Good News

Jesus of Nazareth

Good News of Jesus Christ

In the days of the Caesars a new band of religious advocates from the homeland of the rabbis appeared throughout the *oikoumené,* calling themselves messengers of good news. For these speakers, the word *preaching (kérygma,* "heralding") denoted their proclamation, both the action and the content. The term, though not widely used until then, already meant *publishing* or *broadcasting,* but their appropriation of it would give to it a distinctive importance in Christian circles and invest it with the meaning which from that time forth would be its primary connotation. For the Christian gospel (*euaggelion*) announced salvation, and *preaching* was the announcement—directed to the situation of the hearers.

What made the word of the Christian missioners news was its report about Jesus of Nazareth, a Jew only recently executed by the Romans. Some of the preachers had known him. Now they declared him to be the Son of God, saying that God had raised him from the dead. In his name they offered salvation.

Even though *salvation* was a term these new missionaries shared with rabbis, apocalypticists, mystagogues, and even philosophers, *preaching* soon came to have a distinctively Christian ring. In time this new faith prevailed over the old paganism, the philosophies of the contending schools, and the various mysteries. With an aggressiveness exceeding that of the Jewish witness among the Gentiles, Christianity took up the mission of bringing the nations to biblical monotheism and soon surpassed Judaism as the chief instrument in that task.

The evangelists proclaimed their Savior as Messiah, ("Christ"— God's Anointed or Chosen). This Jesus of Nazareth had himself been a preacher and teacher, they said, and they related parables, pronouncements, and other teachings attributed to him. In proclamation as in all else, they held him up as their exemplar and model.

For our knowledge of the preaching of Jesus, as for everything else about him, we are dependent on the preaching of these disciples. Secular writers ignored him. Jewish authors took little notice. Our sources come almost entirely from the early Christian community. Its first documents to survive, the letters of Paul the apostle, give almost no information about Jesus' life and refer to only a very few of his words.

The source of virtually all that is known about Jesus is a four-part work in the New Testament entitled *The Gospel* ("The Good News").[1] That title must be noted. It designates preaching. Across a long generation after Jesus, prior to the composition of the gospels, information about him was cherished and preserved in the reminiscent conversations of believers and the discourse of their preachers and teachers. Matthew, Mark, Luke, and John were not written as biographies or as history. Rather, each sets forth the *evangel* compiled from the oral tradition of the church, that is, the witness of the early heralds of the glad message; and each is given distinctive shape by the author's special interests, goals, and theological perspective.

The modern critical historian asks: Out of all this preaching what kernels of assured fact can we responsibly affirm as the words of the historical Jesus? But the Christian preachers prior to the four gospels worked with a different intention. Faith in him was the issue: Jesus had lived, preached, died, and been raised from the dead. He was the center of the good news they proclaimed, and without its basis in history and their own experience they would have considered their message vain. Likewise, the evangelists who composed the gospels intended to declare the good news. They did not fancy themselves annalists setting down incidents in an orderly chronology, much less critical historians of past events writing an impartial account, distanced from their own involvement, for the sake of the record. Rather, they, too, were proclaiming *evangel* to bring hearers to faith. The apostle Paul had already declared:

> Faith comes from what is heard,
> and what is heard comes by the preaching of Christ.   [Rom. 10:17 RSV]

Accordingly, the first of these literary evangelists opened his book with the words,

> The beginning of the good news of Jesus Christ,
> the Son of God. [Mk. 1:1 NRSV]

And the last of the four to complete his account said straightforwardly,

> Now Jesus did many other signs in the presence of his disciples,
> which are not written in this book.
> But these are written so that you may come to believe
> that Jesus is the Messiah, the Son of God,
> and that through believing
> you may have life in his name. [Jn. 20:30–31 NRSV]

Even though *we read* their words from a book, *they* are preaching. Whatever our interest in Jesus of Nazareth, it is only through the words of the preachers that we can get back to him and his gospel.

The chapters of Part Three consider the portrait of the preacher set forth in the gospels and the way in which the oral tradition of the early Christian communities used the preaching of Jesus. They examine his message, his rhetoric, and his commitment to preaching, concluding with an assessment of his contribution as a preacher.

At this point it is sufficient to continue to understand preaching as the discussion of religious and ethical themes in public address. Sometimes the earliest Christian sources clearly differentiate between preaching and teaching, as we shall see; at other times they use the terms synonymously. These chapters denominate as preaching all the public discourse of Jesus.

As to chronology, a complex, technical issue on which the reader may consult a Bible dictionary, we will assume that Jesus was born in 8–6 B.C.E., baptized late in 27 C.E. or early in 28 C.E., and crucified on April 7, 30 C.E.[2]

CHAPTER 7

Portrait of the Preacher

JESUS THE PREACHER[1]

Overture

We begin with the picture presented by the evangelists.

The Gospel of Mark opens in Judea with a stir of excitement about preaching. After the long silence of prophecy in the age of the scribes, the word of Malachi and Isaiah sounds again, its promise come to fulfillment:

> "See, I am sending my messenger ahead of you,
>   who will prepare your way;
> the voice of one crying out in the wilderness:
>   'Prepare the way of the Lord, make his paths straight.'"

[Mk. 1:2–3 NRSV]

A new prophet appears in the wilderness, John the baptizer "preaching a baptism of repentance for the remission of sins" (Mk. 1:4 RSV).

The stage is now set for Jesus. He comes to John for baptism, the Spirit descends like a dove, a voice from heaven pronounces him "my beloved Son," and he retires to the wilderness to face temptation. Excitement mounts. Then comes the real entrance.

"Jesus Came Preaching"

A palpable thrill runs through the words of the evangelist, still cast in the form of preaching:

> Now after John was arrested,
> Jesus came into Galilee, preaching the gospel of God, and saying,

"The time is fulfilled, and the kingdom of God has come near;
repent, and believe in the good news." [Mk. 1:14–15 NRSV, JS–b][2]

The Gospel according to Matthew, at this point, conveys a similar
sense of high drama:

From that time Jesus began to preach.   [Mt. 4:17 RSV]

After a day filled with demonstrations of compassion in healing
power, Jesus withdraws alone very early the next morning to pray.
Finding him at last, his followers press him to return to Capernaum,
the scene of yesterday's triumphs, but he responds:

Let us go on to the next towns, that I may preach there also;
for that is why I came out.   [Mk. 1:38 RSV, JS–g]

Matthew summarizes the sequel:

And he went about all Galilee, teaching in their synagogues
and preaching the gospel of the kingdom...
And great crowds followed him.   [Mt. 4:23–24 RSV]

The Overwhelming Response

The evangelists unite in asserting that this preacher was unlike
any other. (Once again their words echo the accents of the oral tradition.) Mark pictures the crowds pressing around Jesus so eagerly that
he and his companions had no chance to eat (Mk. 3:20; cf. 2:2).
Matthew portrays him preaching to thousands and notes the response
to his "Sermon on the Mount":

The crowds were astounded at his teaching,
for he taught them as one having authority,
and not as their scribes.   [Mt. 7:28–29 NRSV]

As Jesus preached in the synagogue at Nazareth, Luke writes,

All spoke well of him and were amazed
at the gracious words that came from his mouth.   [Lk. 4:22 NRSV]

When Jesus disputed *midrash* with the scribes in the temple, Mark
notes,

The large crowd was listening to him with delight.   [Mk. 12:37 NRSV]

The Fourth Gospel offers a similar picture. The temple police sent by
the chief priests to arrest Jesus return without a prisoner, exclaiming,

Never has anyone spoken like this! [Jn. 7:46 NRSV]

A clearly homiletical pericope affirms its theology through symbolic narrative, claiming for the preaching of Jesus a divinely attested authority above that of the Law and the prophets. On the Mount of Transfiguration the apostles hear a voice from the cloud:

This is my Son, the Beloved; listen to him! [Mk. 9:7 NRSV]

Settings for Preaching

Accompanied by a retinue of followers, including a company of women, Jesus itinerates throughout Galilee and the surrounding provinces, then carries his message to Jerusalem. He preaches and teaches in all kinds of settings, formal and informal, in the manner of a wandering Hellenistic philosopher.[3]

In the early days of his ministry he preaches in synagogues at Capernaum, Nazareth, and elsewhere. Often he preaches in the open air—on a mountainside, along the Sea of Galilee, from a boat anchored just offshore, in the streets and marketplaces, in the atriums of large houses, in the courts of the temple. As a dinner guest he makes his point with memorable table talk. Whenever he speaks, he responds easily to questions or objections from his hearers and engages in frequent disputations with the "scribes and Pharisees." Unlike Moses and the prophets, however, he does not accost kings or political rulers; when at last he is haled before the Roman procurator and the Jewish puppet-king he declares no word from the Lord, but holds his peace.

Preaching as a Theme in the Gospels

In the Gospel according to Mark, preaching is a persistent theme. As Luther observed, Jesus did not write; he spoke.[4] "Preaching is by its nature an acoustical event, having its home in orality not textuality."[5] Mark early says of Jesus:

He appointed twelve...to be with him,
and to be sent out to preach. [Mk. 3:14 RSV]

He is taken by the public for a preacher; a blind beggar addresses him as rabbi (Mk. 10:51). After his death, the women who discover that his tomb is empty receive good news to proclaim:

He has been raised; he is not here...
But go, tell his disciples and Peter. [Mk. 16:6–7 NRSV]

The final words of the risen Lord admonish the young church:

Go into all the world and preach the gospel.   [Mk. 16:15 RSV][6]

Very clearly the tradition, both oral and written, expressed in this gospel, arises out of a community that sees preaching as essential action in its life and appeals to the example of Jesus for its centrality. The Gospels according to Matthew and Luke enhance the emphasis by incorporating extensive blocks of teaching preserved in the community as words of Jesus. As radically different from the first three (Synoptic) Gospels as the Fourth Gospel is, it resembles them in also presenting Jesus as an impressive preacher and teacher, interspersing its narrative with discourse. Throughout the four-part work Jesus' preaching is a central and characteristic thrust of his ministry.

THE SOURCES AND THE SOURCE[7]

The Church's Faith

In order to examine the preaching of Jesus, it is necessary to sketch the oral transmission of his words and accounts of his actions. Before the completion of the four gospels it was the preachers and teachers of the young Christian community who preserved and shaped the tradition about Jesus. They first taught in Aramaic (as he had done) until the Jewish revolt that brought on the Roman destruction of Jerusalem in 70 C.E. scattered the believers across a world that spoke Greek.[8] Translated now into the language of Hellenism, the tradition soon passed over into writing, and Greek was the language of the gospels. They took form, not as historical archives, but as the preaching of the church's faith.

Preachers' Sequences

As the Christian speakers told and retold stories of Jesus, the heart of their gospel, they began to link separate incidents into sequences. First they gave shape to the passion narrative, with its extended account of Jesus' conflict with the authorities, arrest, trials, condemnation, crucifixion, and death—events remembered annually by the Christians in the paschal season. It was, in effect, a ceremonial sermon on the passion. In the three Synoptic Gospels the story of these events follows the same general pattern, with considerable variation in materials. Each evangelist preceded this large coherent block with other traditions circulated by the preachers concerning the life and teachings of Jesus and followed it with brief narratives proclaiming faith in his resurrection.

Sequences of Teaching

In much the same way the church's teachers arranged the remembered words of Jesus in sequences, which circulated first in Aramaic, and soon also in Greek translation. Frequently a bare saying or pronouncement was preserved, with no accompanying details as to context or application—much as compressed digests of the teachings of various rabbis were, at the same time, being handed down in Judaism. Consequently, the didactic purpose of the teacher affected the order and arrangement of the separate sayings.

Sometimes a number of sayings on a common theme were gathered into a series, not unlike the thematic sermons in the wisdom literature; Mark's sequence on discipleship is a good example:

> If any want to become my followers, let them deny themselves
> and take up their cross and follow me.
> For those who want to save their life will lose it,
> and those who lose their life for my sake,
> and for the sake of the gospel, will save it.   [JS–b]
> For what will it profit them to gain the whole world
> and forfeit their life?
> Indeed, what can they give in return for their life?   [JS–g]
> Those who are ashamed of me and my words
> in this adulterous and sinful generation,
> of them the Son of Man will also be ashamed when he comes
> in the glory of his Father with the holy angels.
>
> [JS–b] [Mk. 8:34–38 NRSV]

Alternatively, various sayings might be gathered in "chains" (*catenae*), a word near the end of one saying suggesting another, perhaps unrelated, saying in which that word appeared near the beginning:

> Have faith in God.
> Truly I tell you, if you say to this mountain,
> "Be taken up and thrown into the sea,"
> and if you do not doubt in your heart,
> but believe that what you say will come to pass,
> it will be done for you.
> So I tell you, whatever you ask for in prayer,
> believe that you have received it, and it will be yours.
> Whenever you stand praying, forgive.   [Mk. 11:22–25 NRSV, JS–g]

It was only natural, then, to combine some of these sequences or other types of materials with a common form, like parables, into extended "discourses" or "sermons." Best known of these is Matthew's "Sermon on the Mount" (chaps. 5—7), with which Luke's "Sermon on the Plain" (6:17—49) provides an instructive comparison, illuminating the process here described.

Flexibility in Application

In any retelling of remembered events or sayings, variations arise; gradual elaborations occur, as details are added to a story in the manner of rabbinic Haggadah. The texts of the written gospels illustrate the process. Matthew elaborates material given in Mark (cf. Mk. 8:29, Mt. 16:16) and adds details to the scene so that events are shown to "fulfill" pictures given by the prophets.

Moreover, homiletical comments made by the preacher are not always clearly distinguished from the words of Jesus himself, and the hearers might later repeat them as dominical utterances. A case in point is the conclusion to Jesus' parable of the unrighteous manager:

> And the master applauded the dishonest steward
> for acting so astutely.   [Lk. 16:8 REB, JS—r]

Are these words part of Jesus' parable? Or some unknown preacher's explanation of its meaning? And is "the master" the rich man in the story whose steward schemed so dishonestly? Or is the term a preacher's designation for Jesus? It appears that an occasional interpretation of a parable has become so closely attached to the story as to be understood as an explanation offered by Jesus himself (Mk. 4:13—20; Lk. 16:9).

"The Word of the Lord"

Preaching draws its life, as *midrash* or commentary, from a process that causes historians to despair. Its interest in a text is not antiquarian but existential; by accent in reading, by slight variations in wording to make a point, by juxtaposing a traditional word with a contemporary situation, the preacher speaks to the present moment. As already noted, many of Jesus' sayings were recalled in isolation from any context. Consequently, different preachers made quite different applications. Consider the words:

> Nothing is covered up that will not be uncovered,
> and nothing secret that will not become known.   [Lk. 12:2 NRSV, JS—p]

Mark understands the saying as a declaration that the meaning of the parables will be hidden only for a time (Mk. 4:22; cf. Lk. 8:17),

Matthew that the disciples are to proclaim publicly what Jesus has taught them in private (Mt. 10:26), Luke that the hypocrisy of the Pharisees will be exposed (Lk. 12:1); each evangelist applies the words as though directed to a different situation in the writer's own time and place.

Moreover, in the Christian homilists' use of *prosopopeia*, the rhetorical figure in which the speaker supplies the words that a famous person from the past might be expected to address to the speaker's audience in their particular situation, rhetoric and theology combined to provide a form of great vitality for bringing the church a living word from its risen Lord—"And now the Lord says to us: '...'." The Christian prophets likewise brought oracles to present situations in his name. As he continued to speak through the preachers of the post-resurrection church, some counsels—for example, "Every Christian must expect to carry a cross"—were read back into the tradition of Jesus' teaching. Such homiletical creativity inevitably distorted the view of the historical Jesus as it passed down through the tradition. The "Little Apocalypse" in Mark 13 appears to be a sermon by a Jewish apocalypticist attached to words of Jesus as a "text"; despite making a somewhat different point from his words, it was attributed to him. The result is confusion as the historian undertakes to determine what Jesus taught about the Last Days.

Law of Internal Correction

Because oral transmission both preserves and adapts tradition, it is difficult to assign particular sayings to Jesus with assurance that they contain his words precisely as spoken. Some scholars conclude that nothing may be attributed to him with historical certainty. Yet such total skepticism needs to be tempered by regard for the Law of Internal Correction formulated by folklorists: the community will permit a storyteller some leeway but only within limits; if the narrator wanders outside the bounds of the tradition as the community understands it, they will disown the tale being told. (Something like this happened in the church's rejection of the so-called apocryphal gospels.)

To the extent one agrees that oral transmission tends to work in this way, one may place confidence in the general tenor of the gospel tradition. It must be recognized, however, that radical changes in a community's experience may induce new ways of thinking that allow, perhaps do not even recognize, shifts in the tradition—as the sermon of the apocalypticist just mentioned came to be regarded as expressing the teaching of Jesus.

Collection and Publication

The preachers' need for words from Jesus led to the collection of sayings attributed to him. Within a generation after Jesus, compilations were circulating in Syria. But preachers who had not seen the Lord "in the days of his flesh" and who lacked continuing access to those who had known him needed an account also of his mighty works, his passion, and his transforming influence in the lives of persons. In response, a new form of literature emerged—the Gospel according to Mark, written in koiné Greek about 70 C.E. to set forth the good news in a narrative of Jesus' public ministry interspersed with brief snatches of his preaching, teaching, and conversation as handed down in the oral tradition.

Two larger works in the new genre, Matthew and Luke, followed within a generation, each incorporating along with material from Mark large numbers of sayings from the collections; these included identical passages from a common "Sayings-Source" which scholars refer to as Q.[9] (In German, *Quellen* = Source.) Besides these three "Synoptic Gospels," the Gospel according to John appeared, using a different chronology and a distinctive homiletical elaboration of words attributed to Jesus. Each of the evangelists addressed the needs of the church in the light of conditions in a particular Christian community and the author's theological stance; both of these affected the way in which words and deeds of Jesus were presented.[10]

Sayings outside the Four Gospels

Meanwhile an occasional word from Jesus had already been incorporated into earlier forms of Christian literature. The apostle Paul, in writing to a congregation about divorce, cited a pronouncement of Jesus as authoritative (1 Cor. 7:10–11); his approach here suggests the manner in which preachers and teachers must have drawn on the remembered sayings. And long after the publication of the canonical gospels, the oral tradition perpetuated other unwritten sayings (*agrapha*), some of which found their way into Christian literature written in the second, third, and fourth centuries. The most striking example of such materials is a large collection of sayings attributed to Jesus in the Gospel of Thomas, one of the documents discovered at the ancient Gnostic Christian library in Nag Hammadi, Egypt, in 1945. Some of these sayings duplicate or parallel those found in the canonical gospels, some are also known from other extra-biblical literature, and some have not been preserved in any other known work. The evident Gnostic slant suggests that they have been colored by the views of the preachers who used them and gives force to the question raised about all the sayings it attributes to Jesus: Can our sources take us back to the source?

The Distinctive Voice of Jesus[11]

Criterion of Dissimilarity

Using a test developed by historical criticism, the criterion of dissimilarity, scholars attribute a presumption of genuineness to sayings credited to Jesus which have no known parallel in prior literature and no evident application to the peculiar problems of the early Christian community. Such sayings would have been preserved for one primary reason, their derivation from Jesus. This highly restrictive criterion cannot disprove the authenticity of all other reported sayings, but it establishes a minimal core. Examination of the sayings thus accounted genuine indicates several distinctive features.

A Distinctive Style

Jesus' teaching of the imminence of the kingdom of God, which at its coming would radically reverse present conditions—a theology of "eschatological polarity"—found expression in a distinctive form of speech addressing the present in the light of the new age just at hand:

> Blessed are you who weep now,
> for you will laugh.   [Lk. 6:21 NRSV, JS–r][12]

Jesus' characteristic term of address to God—Aramaic *Abba* ("Papa") one of the first words of a little child babbled in response to its father—seems to have been unique with him. So central was it to his speech in prayer that it carried over into the early Christian liturgy, even in Greek-speaking communities (Gal. 4:6; Rom. 8:15). The gospels report in Aramaic a few other words from Jesus that had stuck in the memories of those who heard.

Some crucial assertions Jesus underlined by a unique characteristic of his style, the frequently repeated formula,

> Truly I tell you…   [Mk. 3:28 NRSV, JS–b]

This formula consistently appears in Aramaic:

> *Amen* = truly [or verily]

and is now and then doubled:

> *Amen, Amen* = truly, truly [or verily, verily].

The expression appears repeatedly with the words of Jesus in all four gospels.[13]

Jesus' most memorable mode of preaching was the parable, a brief story to make a point and a favorite device of the rabbis. Numerous parables attributed to Jesus deal with his overriding theme, the reign of God, and thus can be distinguished from the rabbinic pieces. A phrase commonly occurring in Jesus' parables and analogies, "Which of you...?" has no rabbinic parallel. At the same time, his stories may be distinguished from early Christian formulations by their refusal to explain or to allegorize; instead they challenge. Illustrating the same themes and showing a similarity of style and temper to the sayings of Jesus already isolated with some degree of certainty, the parables considerably enlarge the body of material which can with confidence be assigned to him.

Genuine Sayings

Sayings marked by the distinctive style of Jesus may be accepted as quite probably genuine, even if they do not qualify under the canon of dissimilarity. By extension, other passages coherent in tone and manner, especially if attested by more than one source,[14] may be distinguished from secondary material. For technical studies of the problems involved and analysis of individual passages, the reader is referred to the large body of material by biblical scholars.[15]

Given the nature of our primary documents, the gospels as faith-statements—even as preaching addressed to the needs of the Christian community at the time of their publication—and as presentations clearly shaped by the theology of the particular evangelists, we cannot avoid the question: *How reliable, historically, are their accounts of Jesus' preaching and their representation of his words?* Drawing on the work of biblical scholars across the past two centuries, the Fellows of the Jesus Seminar worked from 1985 until 1991 to arrive at a common decision on that question. After thorough discussion of each saying attributed to Jesus by the four evangelists and in the recently discovered Gospel of Thomas, the Fellows voted, in each instance reaching one of the following judgments, made visible by the color of type used in printing the text:[16]

Red: Jesus undoubtedly said this or something very like it.
Pink: Jesus probably said something like this.
Gray: Jesus did not say this, but the ideas contained in it are close to his own.
Black: Jesus did not say this; it represents the perspective or content of a later or different tradition.

Throughout Part Three of this book, for the information of the reader, the judgments of the Jesus Seminar are indicated for each saying quoted.

With regard to the authenticity of particular passages, reputable biblical scholars by no means always agree. In each instance, the Fellows of the Jesus Seminar found it necessary to vote, and some respected scholars have taken vigorous exception to both their process and their judgments.[17] Not being a certified member of the guild of textual critics, this writer regards the seminar's work with respect, if not always convinced of the conclusions. It appears, for example, that the black designation has been given to sayings that do not require the judgment it carries. Even if an observation was not original with Jesus, but derived from the common stock of ideas and expressions at the time, some persons in the community of disciples could have heard it first from him and could have remembered hearing him say it. (Consider how many churchgoers in our time have heard first from their own preacher, and from no one else, an idea picked up from Fosdick or Wesley or Luther and presented without attribution. Obviously, such a saying might not merit the designation "red," but the judgment that their preacher "did not say this" would be totally unwarranted.)

It can hardly be expected that Jesus would have tagged his speech with such comments as "in the words of Ben Sira" or "as our well-known proverb has it." How many preachers in our time have quoted without specific attribution, or have paraphrased, a passage from Shakespeare or Lincoln or even a popular song, seizing on words which carry emotional overtones, even if not all the hearers consciously identify the original source. An additional formula (with a distinctive color) might have served the Jesus Seminar well, carrying some such designation as "This saying was not original with Jesus, but there is no reason to believe he would not have said it." Some passages quoted in this chapter and the two that follow, though designated "black," seem to accord with his message and style as presented in the gospels. Hypothetical premises can lead to unduly skeptical conclusions.

In any case, the image of Jesus as preacher projected by the four evangelists has had far larger importance throughout the entire history of preaching than might ever have been expected from the considerably reduced figure sketched by some of the more skeptical scholars. It is the Jesus of the gospels whom the preachers have made central in their proclamation.

The ensuing treatment of Jesus as preacher, while committed to taking current scholarship into account, relies heavily on the portrait derived from the gospels. It will make use of sayings commonly regarded as primary, without here arguing technical details. In these passages, it has been said, we hear the distinctive voice of Jesus. And we shall draw upon sayings discounted by some scholars when the rejection seems less than convincing or the words appear harmonious with utterances accounted historically authentic.

We move on now to pay close heed to what Jesus preached.

announcing that God's reign can begin whenever and wherever eager hearts prepare in repentance and receive it gladly. God's glorious future can become present! And God is at the point of inaugurating the divine rule everywhere—with great joy for all who are willing to receive it, with righteous judgment on those who refuse it.

The long silence of the Spirit has come to an end. God is dealing directly with God's people once again.

> The law and the prophets were in effect until John came;
> since then the good news of the kingdom of God is preached.
>
> [Lk. 16:16 NRSV alt., JS–g]

Along with his announcement through preaching, the mighty works wrought by Jesus in the healing of the sick proclaimed the reality of God's rule and the overcoming of Satan's power (Mk. 3:27, JS–p). The inauguration of the new age was an occasion for unbounded gladness (Mt. 13:44–46, JS–p).

Present and Future

Rather than identifying the kingdom of God with the end of the world or the final page of history, Jesus interpreted it as the initiation of God's rule in earthly human experience. In place of a frantic search for "signs" of its coming, he commended a quiet faith in God, whose silent work was under way (Mt. 13:33). Instead of trying to discern the mysteries of apocalyptic visions, he called on people, as the prophets had done, to repent—and to open their lives to the reign of God. The preaching of the kingdom was itself sign enough. Because it had been proclaimed, its dawn had already broken:

> The kingdom of God is not coming with things that can be observed;
> nor will they say, "Look, here it is!" or "There it is!"
> For, in fact, the kingdom of God is among you.
>
> [Lk. 17:20–21 NRSV, JS–p]

The coming of God's New Day would be as silent as the work of leaven or the growth of a seed. And its coming was certain:

> Truly I tell you: there are some of those standing here
> who will not taste death before they have seen the kingdom of God
> come with power.   [Mk. 9:1 REB, JS–g]

Because of the hardness of their hearts some who heard the announcement resisted the advent of God's reign, and in their blindness others failed to discern its imminence. On them it would come in judgment, as unexpectedly as a thief in the night. The preaching was an urgent call to prepare for what God is ever ready to do. So he taught his disciples to pray,

> Your kingdom come.... [JS–p]
> And forgive us our sins.   [JS–g] [Lk. 11:2, 4 NRSV]

Where God's rule prevails the kingdom is already present; where God's rule is thwarted, the kingdom is imminent—as both threat and promise.

The Great Reversal
Where God reigns, the structures of the old evil age are over-turned.

> The last will be first, and the first will be last.   [Mt. 20:16 NRSV, JS–p]

That means a radical reordering of society in favor of the weak and most helpless:

> Let the little children come to me…
> it is to such as these that the kingdom of God belongs.
> [Mk. 10:14 NRSV, JS–p]

The preacher's harshest words fell on those who of all his fellow Jews were closest to him in their commitments, the scribes and the Pharisees, like him devoted to the rule of God. He faulted them, not for their devotion, but for their self-seeking, for their lives of comfort-able privilege achieved at the disadvantage of the common people above whom these paragons of piety had managed to raise them-selves. Jesus' vocabulary teemed with words indicating concern for the downtrodden, the oppressed, the captive, the helpless, the lame, the blind, the sinful, the outcast. The coming of the kingdom would turn the tables.

> Blessed are you who are poor, for yours is the kingdom of God.
> [Lk. 6:20 NRSV, JS–r]

By unexpected contrast,

> It will be hard for a rich person to enter the kingdom.
> [Mt. 19:23 NRSV, JS–p]

Jesus clearly expected an imminent change in human affairs, radi-cal in its reversals, all-inclusive in its scope, dramatic in its sudden-ness. In supreme confidence he announced the kingdom's certain coming:

It is like a mustard seed, which, when sown upon the ground, is the smallest of all seeds on earth; yet when it is sown it grows up and becomes the greatest of all shrubs. [Mk. 4:31–32, JS–p]

So the preacher sowed the seed.

GOOD NEWS OF GOD

The Divine Parent

The announcement of God's rule was good news because Jesus brought good news about God. In its basic elements his doctrine of God was scarcely novel. What was fresh, even unsettling to the religious establishment, was the emphasis Jesus made and the inferences he drew from the intensity of his communion with God. Like the rabbis, he confessed God's righteousness, power, and goodness, and like them he pondered the witness of the scriptures. Moreover, he frequently employed the rabbinical etiquette of reticence regarding the divine name, using the passive voice to speak of divine action, or roundabout terms like "before the angels" in place of "God," and he included an ascription of holiness in the prayer ever since known as his:

Hallowed be your name. [Lk. 11:2 NRSV, JS–p]

On his lips such language did not imply vast distance; rather it had the effect of emphasizing God's nearness. Most striking was his unheard-of use of the term *Abba,* the first burble of Jewish baby-talk for the human parent, to address God in prayer, and his constant reliance on the image of Abba for God in place of such conventional terms as Creator, Judge, Holy One of Israel, Lord, or King. Without in any way denying the divine attributes and prerogatives suggested by those titles, he opened the door to a new understanding of God's relationship with the humblest and most unworthy person by the simple word,

When you pray...say: [JS–b]
Father... [JS–r] [Lk. 11:2 NRSV]

Imagery and Gender

It should hardly be necessary to observe that the emphasis in Jesus' use of the term Father falls on the familial and personal relationship expressed in the cry "Abba" and not on any presumption that deity is innately masculine rather than feminine. Though Wisdom had been personified as female, the entire tradition of Jewish piety used masculine nouns and pronouns for deity. Jesus' innovation in looking to God as Abba, rather than accenting maleness, emphasized parental tenderness, insight, and care for a child in its helplessness and utter dependency. He readily used feminine imagery, though not feminine titles, in speaking of God, as in Mt. 13:33 (JS–r) and Lk. 15:8–9 (JS–p), and he gave women a new importance as his spiritual associates and helpers.

God's Generosity toward All

In contrast with conventional piety, which saw prosperity as a sign of divine favor and adversity as punishment for sin, Jesus celebrated the generosity of the Father in heaven toward all:

> He causes his sun to rise on the bad as well as the good,
> and sends down rain to fall on the upright
> and on the wicked alike.   [Mt. 5:45 NJB, JS–p]

In the Synoptic Gospels Jesus speaks neither of God's love nor of God's righteousness, but rather of God's care and constant readiness to forgive. Repeatedly he announces forgiveness for the outcast—publicans, prostitutes, persons of no consequence, and especially the poor. He brings the sublimest themes into the humblest and most sordid circumstances. He associates with the disreputable and the reprobate, even eats with them; by example and by word he insistently affirms God's forgiveness, extending the call and the promise of a better life. That is his good news of God.

Good News as Call and Confrontation[3]

Call to Love and Forgiveness

As example-books of early Christian preaching, the four gospels tell of all sorts of persons to whom Jesus brought the call of the kingdom. As herald of God's forgiveness the preacher declares:

> I have come to call not the righteous, but sinners.   [Mk. 2:17 NRSV, JS–g]

Responding to the call requires living out with one's whole being one's love toward God and toward other persons, even the most difficult:

> Do not resist those who wrong you.
> If anyone slaps you on the right cheek,

turn and offer him the other also.
If anyone wants to sue you and takes your shirt,
let him have your cloak as well.   [Mt. 5:39–40 REB, JS–r]

God's perfection demands perfection in God's children (Mt. 5:48, JS–g). So the preacher insists:

Love your enemies [JS–r], do good to those who hate you,
bless those who curse you, pray for those who abuse you.

[Lk. 6:27–28 NRSV, JS–g]

Character of such wholeness and generosity is not achieved by the keeping of the Law; rather it represents a surpassing order of righteousness (Mt. 5:20). So Jesus has been called a supra-legalist.[4] The quality of life he enjoins is not a matter of keeping score on a tally-sheet of comparative morality, but of forgiving others in love as full as one's love for oneself. How can such an impossibly demanding ethic be denominated good news? Because it springs from the forgiveness of God,

There must be no limit to your goodness,
as your heavenly Father's goodness knows no bounds.

[Mt. 5:48 REB, JS–g]

Yet God can forgive only those who stand on forgiving ground:

When you stand praying,
if you have a grievance against anyone, forgive…,
so that your Father in heaven may forgive you.   [Mk. 11:25 NEB, JS–g]

The dictum has a rabbinic flavor, like the word of Jesus's contemporary, Rabbi Gamaliel:

So long as you are merciful, God will have mercy upon you,
and if you are not merciful, He will not be merciful unto you.[5]

Like the rabbis, Jesus also is reported to have encapsulated all the commandments in a single admonition:

Always treat others as you would like them to treat you: [JS–g]
that is the law and the prophets.   [JS–b] [Mt. 7:12 REB]

Yet Jesus seems to have been less concerned to propound general rules than to address the particular situation with a specific word. His discerning and compassionate eye constantly studying the faces before him, he spoke precisely to the needs he discerned. In the informal setting of outdoor preaching he took interruptions in stride and responded memorably to questions called out to him. He showed far more interest in the people crowding around him than in any schedule or homiletical game plan—much less sermon manuscript! Knowing God as Abba, feeling the burdens of the people, and eagerly expecting the advent of God's reign on earth, he spoke from the depths of mind and spirit.

A Spiritual Offensive

In pressing the invitation to life in the kingdom, Jesus simply admonished,

Follow me.   [Lk. 9:59, JS–r]

No obligation could take priority over commitment to God's purpose.

Let the dead bury their own dead;
but as for you, go and proclaim the kingdom of God.

[Lk. 9:60 NRSV, JS–p]

Jesus did not propose a political program in the common understanding of that term. He had no privileged access to the circles of power, and he recruited no army of guerillas. (How else could a Galilean artisan hope to influence Herod or Caesar?) He was only a wandering preacher. But he made it disturbingly clear that the radical onset of the kingdom would totally transform the structures of power on which the world's rulers relied. With their profane view of greatness he contrasted the disciples' obligation to esteem the humble and to serve the lowly (Lk. 22:25–27, JS–g), and he demonstrated that esteem and service in ways that shocked the guardians of community standards and religious propriety.[6]

Jesus' utterances have been worn so smooth by much hearing that we scarcely feel in them the rough edge of subversion and the hard smash of iconoclasm that struck his first listeners with such force. If we were more sensitive to the patriarchy prevailing in first-century Palestine and the rigor of official religious concern for ceremonial purity, we might hear the gasps of disbelief and feel the shock of consternation when people heard his confident words:

The kingdom of heaven is like yeast that a woman took
and mixed in with three measures of flour
until all of it was leavened.   [Mt. 13:33 NRSV, JS–p]

The good Jews who heard him had rigorously observed, every year of their lives, the Passover tradition of scouring through the house to throw out any leaven (Ex. 12:14–20), and their Law forbade bringing bread or cake made with leaven as an offering to God (Lev. 2:11). Yet Jesus dared to liken the coming of God's reign to a woman's working yeast into dough.

And when he answered an inquirer's question,

"And who is my neighbor?" [Lk. 10:29 NRSV]

by recounting his unforgettable story of a traveler who fell among thieves, why did he choose a priest and a Levite to represent failure to observe the Law's requirement to love the neighbor? And why, above all, did he select as hero—*a Samaritan?* (Lk. 10:23, JS–r). Jesus' spiritual offensive carried unavoidable offense to those committed to customary ways of doing and thinking.

As to the struggle between faith and culture, between Judaism and Hellenism, he said nothing that has survived. But with regard to the leaders of the religious institution into which he was born he spoke words of scathing denunciation. Like the prophets before him he drew his indictment from the sacred tradition itself; rather than repudiate it, he spoke in its name. The essence of his accusation was the charge that the leaders served themselves rather than the people they were sent to serve. His excoriation of the spiritual establishment took off the hide:

Beware of the scribes, who like to walk around in long robes,
and to be greeted with respect in the marketplaces,
and to have the best seats in the synagogues,
and places of honor at banquets!   [JS–p]
They devour widows' houses
and for the sake of appearance say long prayers.
They will receive the greater condemnation.   [JS–g] [Mk. 12:38–40]

Caesar's dominance left Jesus no option of launching an outright political program. But his gospel implied no acceptance of the status quo. Rather, he forthrightly repudiated every system of human domination, political or religious. Urgently he called for a totality of radical repentance, by which alone the kingdom could be entered:

Enter through the narrow gate;
for the gate is wide and the road is easy that leads to destruction,
and there are many who take it.   [Mt. 7:13 NRSV, JS–g]

The Scandal of the Gospel

Though Jesus repudiated the apocalyptic notion of an end to history, his preaching of the kingdom had a profoundly eschatological character. It confronted the hearer with the urgency of God's radical demands and the necessity of decision "with no reserve and no delay." The choice had eternal implications. The word he preached inevitably provoked resistance and—unless the heart of the hearer melted in repentance—a hardened opposition to God's will. For the kingdom and its demands could not be easily accommodated in the old, comfortable way of doing things.

> No one puts new wine into old wineskins;
> otherwise, the wine will burst the skins,
> and the wine is lost, and so are the skins;
> but one puts new wine into fresh wineskins.   [Mk. 2:22 NRSV, JS–p]

His preaching sounded a call for radical change.

> I came to bring fire to the earth,
> and how I wish it were already kindled!   [Lk. 12:49 NRSV, JS–g]

The scribal guardians of the Law, both Pharisees and Sadducees, took issue with his radical program and pursued him with mounting opposition; despite the effect of later rivalry between Christianity and Judaism in heightening the gospel accounts of their hostility, the opposition seems well-enough established, even though some individual scribes responded wholeheartedly to Jesus.

In time his popular following fell away, perhaps from disappointment at his failure to launch a rebellion against Rome or to inaugurate the new age as soon as he had led them to expect it. Resistance to his preaching evoked the lament:

> From the days of John the Baptist until now
> the kingdom of heaven has suffered violence,
> and the violent take it by force.   [Mt. 11:12 NRSV, JS–g]

For all his offer of forgiveness and the winsomeness of his speech, his blunt insistence on the demands of the kingdom brooked no compromise. His stern words of judgment aroused intense hostility and hastened him to his death. In the end unforgettable preaching, enthusiastic crowds, and even changed lives gave no assurance of success, or even safety. Hounded by the religious establishment, rejected by the people, and sent off to execution by imperial Rome, the preacher of

God's imminent rule on earth was nailed to a wooden cross and died forsaken, refusing to break faith with the gospel he had proclaimed.

THE PLACE OF JESUS IN THE GOOD NEWS[7]

The Problem

The most difficult aspect of Jesus' own preaching to disentangle from the interpretation of the early Christian preachers that entered into the gospels is his understanding of himself and his place in the kingdom. Of all the words that he spoke, none would have been so subject to heightening in transmission as any reference to himself. Virtually every first-person saying attributed to him incorporates in its present form concepts from a later stage in the development of doctrine concerning his person. Even so, such a saying may point to interpretations of his ministry expressed by him in less dogmatic terms.

The Decisive Messenger

Jesus came as the decisive messenger of the good news, his mission being to proclaim the gospel of the kingdom (Mk. 1:38, JS–g). He carried this role in evident humility as one without status (Lk. 22:27, JS–g) and characterized it in a saying that now reads:

> The Son of Man came not to be served but to serve,
> and to give his life… [Mk. 10:45 NRSV, JS–g]

He associated gladly with outcasts and sinners and, when criticized for it, countered with a neat riposte:

> It is not the healthy who need a doctor, but the sick. [JS–p]
> I came to call not the upright, but sinners. [JS–g] [Mk. 2:17 NJB]

His lifestyle devoted to that end prompted criticism by the religious, as did his comment:

> The Son of Man came eating and drinking, and they say,
> "Look, a glutton and a drunkard,
> a friend of tax collectors and sinners!" [Mt. 11:19 NRSV, JS–g]

The Preacher as Scandal

Confronting his hearers by preaching the imminence of the kingdom, its coming the decisive event in history, Jesus laid down stern demands:

> Follow me, and let the dead bury their own dead. [Mt. 8:22 NRSV, JS–p]

That word was a hard one, and he made no attempt to soften his demands or to curry favor by the way he handled scripture.

His practice in exegesis presents a difficult historical question, for surely the process of oral tradition presented no other opportunity for embellishing his words to match the inclination of early Christian preachers to import familiar verses from the Hebrew scriptures, either to enforce a point in their preaching or to contrast them with the words of Jesus. Even so, it would appear overly rigorous to dismiss all biblical passages as subsequent insertions.

What does seem clear is that Jesus was not commonly an exegetical or expository preacher. His characteristic mode of speaking was parable or aphorism dealing with a life-situation, not commentary on a text. When the Jesus of the gospels deals with scripture, his method contrasts strikingly with that of the rabbis. Their custom was to conclude discussion of a problem with the clincher,

It is said,

followed by a verse from the Torah quoted as final authority. By contrast, Jesus is reported as saying,

You have heard that it was said,
"An eye for an eye and a tooth for a tooth."
But I say to you,
Do not resist an evildoer.
But if anyone strikes you on the right cheek, turn the other also;
and if anyone wants to sue you and take your coat,
give your cloak as well.   [Mt. 5:38–40 NRSV, JS–r]

It is hard for one who has not read a good deal of rabbinic dialog to realize the shock such words would have carried when first spoken. A well-informed scholar has observed, "No rabbi would do that."[8] Yet careful reading indicates that Jesus was not here setting up his authority against that of scripture. Rather, his insight pierced to the heart of the matter, concerned less with the overt expression of sin than with the hidden springs of motivation. For anyone to speak in such bold and radicalizing fashion, appearing to the casual hearer to claim priority over the Torah, would surely antagonize the recognized guardians of tradition in Judaism. The preaching of Jesus appears to have done precisely that.

Little wonder that the first Christian preachers included among his sayings a bold beatitude:

Blessed is anyone who takes no offense at me.   [Mt. 11:6 NRSV, JS–b][9]

Predictions of Suffering

But take offense they did. The scandal of his challenge provoked violent opposition, foreshadowing rejection and suffering (Mk. 8:31, JS–b; 9:31, JS–b; 10:33, JS–b). The Jesus of the gospels foresees it all.

> The Son of Man must undergo great suffering,
> and be rejected by the elders, the chief priests, and the scribes,
> and be killed, and after three days rise again.   [Mk. 8:31 NRSV, JS–b]

This saying and its recurring parallels, their present form plainly shaped by the event and the faith of the early church, point to an effort on Jesus' part to prepare his disciples for the coming disaster. Despite the warning, they could not see the inevitable outcome until the last minute. The preacher spoke with ultimate pathos:

> They that are with me have not understood me.[10]

Vulnerable Human Being

The supreme conviction of the early Christians—that God had vindicated Jesus as the Anointed (=Messiah=Christ) by raising him from the dead—they inevitably read back into the events they recounted in their preaching. It is not certain that Jesus applied Messianic titles to himself, or regarded himself as Messiah, or intended to make any such claims. The designation Son of Man (which the early Christians understood as a Messianic title belonging to Jesus) appears in all the separate sources of the tradition, and for them it also carries overtones of his mission as Savior. The recurrence of the term in the sayings with such frequency indicates that Jesus must have used it in speaking of himself. But in those instances that show least evidence of heightening in transmission and which in their original intent most clearly refer to him, the phrase suggests a different meaning. Rather than a title of Messianic office, it is an assertion of common humanity unsupported by official status; it is Aramaic idiom for "man" or "a man." A human being may forgive sins (Mk. 2:10), humanity is lord over the Sabbath (Mk. 2:28), this human being has nowhere to lay his head (Mt. 8:20). *Son of Man* has been rendered as *Son of Adam*[11] and as the *Human One*.[12] Jesus apparently used the term to express his solidarity with all people, especially the needy, but all his expressions of self-understanding have been filtered through the oral and written tradition passed on by followers who had come to perceive him as divine.[13]

Crisis for the Hearers

Jesus' sayings about himself indicate that his preaching precipitates a crisis for those who hear. In deciding for or against him they decide for or against God. Through his proclamation God's New Age draws near.

CHAPTER 9

The Rhetoric of Jesus[1]

To speak of the rhetoric of Jesus is simply to recognize that any effective speaker, especially one so conscious of form as Jesus evidently was, makes use of procedures and devices of oral communication that can be analyzed. It is not to imply that Jesus affected the mannerisms of classical rhetoric or even that he had any formal knowledge of the discipline, even though vigorous Hellenistic intellectual and cultural activity flourished in Galilee. Yet the evangelists, writing in a culture of oratory, present him as a man of "pleasing speech" (Lk. 4:22), who attracted crowds of hearers.

If perhaps limited in formal education (presumably Jesus was not a graduate of the rabbinic academies, though possibly of a local synagogue school), he had yet learned much from observation, from discussions of the rabbis, and from reflecting on the scriptures. His sayings manifest a conscious affinity with the traditions of religious speech in Judaism, especially prophecy and wisdom and rabbinic discourse.

Prophetic Proclamation[2]

Prophetic Self-Consciousness

With the coming of John the Baptist and the preaching of the kingdom's imminence, both by John and by Jesus, the age of prophecy had been renewed. Jesus' disciples believed, as did he, that he spoke in the power of the Spirit, and the popular mind took him for a prophet. Though in the gospels he recounted no experience of prophetic call to validate his ministry, the synoptic accounts of his baptism and temptation serve such a purpose, clearly indicating that they had such a meaning for him.

The numerous statements of personal mission that affirm a divine commission—"I have come...," "The Son of Man has come...," "I am among you as...," and so forth—suggest a mode of speech that Jesus might conceivably have used, though these assertions lack other marks that characterized his style. Unlike most of the prophets, the Jesus we find in the gospels does not undertake to validate his message by revelations or visions; the language of vision occurs only in a rare revelation-oracle (Lk. 10:18, JS–p). Customarily he bases his declarations on his understanding of the divine nature that derives from a striking sense of intimacy with God; his reported sayings on this matter have obviously been colored by the christological interests of the preachers.

Prophetic Witness

Jesus' self-understanding as a prophet shines forth clearly in his preaching of judgment and his call for repentance. It is evident in his insistence on inward obedience rather than outward ceremony. After quoting Isaiah he adds his own stern word:

> Woe to you, scribes and Pharisees, hypocrites!
> For you clean the outside of the cup and of the plate,
> but inside they are full of greed and self-indulgence.
> You blind Pharisee! First clean the inside of the cup,
> so that the outside also may become clean.   [Mt. 23:25–26 NRSV, JS–g]

It appears also in his attitude toward religious institutions:

> The sabbath was made for humankind,
> and not humankind for the sabbath.   [Mk. 2:27 NRSV, JS–p]

His deliberate ignoring of the laws governing Sabbath-observance and ceremonial purity and his expulsion from the temple of the animals on sale for sacrifice magnified the scandal of his prediction that the temple would be destroyed (Mk. 14:58, JS–g). Of his own destiny, the evangelist Luke pictures him saying:

> It is impossible for a prophet
> to be killed outside of Jerusalem.   [Lk. 13:33 NRSV, JS–b]

Jesus' distinctive terminology for his announcement of the kingdom—*preaching, proclaiming, heralding, speaking the word*—suggests a sense of kinship with the prophets.

Patterns of Prophetic Speech

Jesus made effective use of forms of speech favored by the prophets. He improvised a telling *song:*

> We played the flute for you, and you did not dance;
> we wailed, and you did not mourn.   [Mt. 11:17 NRSV, JS–g]

He delivered stern *pronouncement-sayings:*

> Truly I tell you,
> whoever does not receive the kingdom of God as a little child
> will never enter it.   [Mk. 10:15 NRSV, JS–g]

He pronounced *woes* on the hypocritical (Mt. 23:16–19, 23, JS–b; 23:24–26, JS–g). The evangelist Matthew attributes to him kindly words of *invitation:*

> Come to me, all you that are weary and carrying heavy burdens,
> and I will give you rest.   [Mt. 11:28 NRSV, JS–b]

He employed *dynamic action* to dramatize the teaching and to give it greater impact, setting a child in the midst as model for those who would enter the kingdom (Mt. 18:2–3), washing the disciples' feet as a lesson in humility (Jn. 13:1–11), healing the sick as demonstration of God's concern for the outcast and of the binding of Satan's power at the advent of the kingdom (Mk. 3:27, JS–p). And he devised *parables* by weaving narratives on prophetic models (Mk. 12: 1–8, JS–g). It is evident why the people thought of Jesus as a prophet.

THE RABBINIC MANNER[3]

The Tradition of Wisdom

Jesus' use of parable, allegory, maxim, rhetorical question, and other devices of speech characteristic of Wisdom associates him, along with the rabbis, with that tradition also. His fondness for these modes of address indicates familiarity with the literature of the tradition and an affinity for its manner of expression, an affinity likely more a response of personal temperament than the product of schooling. The words of Jesus show little concern with the speculative interests that characterized Hellenistic wisdom or with the prudential considerations that received so much attention in the tradition of the Middle East. But the close observation of nature and of human behavior, the moral forthrightness, the shrewdness of thinking, and the biting humor that characterized the school appear consistently in his words, as do reflection on the tragic aspects of life and the affirmation nevertheless of confidence in the goodness of God. His sayings chide his hearers for foolishness rather than for sinfulness, though he rarely addresses them either as sinners or as fools.

A number of his pronouncement-sayings take the form of the beatitude, a form characteristic of wisdom.

Yet despite his fondness for the rhetoric of this tradition and his words that seem to identify him with it, Jesus' manner is hardly that of the conventional sage.

Rabbinic Dialogue

More than through formal schooling or private study, Jesus must have learned his characteristic manner of preaching from observing and perhaps participating in the discussions of the rabbis. His way of preaching and style of speech bear many obvious similarities to theirs, but at no point is the likeness more striking than in his practice of engaging in dialogue with those who questioned or interrupted him. The "Socratic style"—better, in his case, the "rabbinic style"—that responds to a question with a counter-query and then involves the questioner in digging a grave for his own folly characterizes Jesus' interaction with his audiences. A question designed to entrap him, "Is it lawful to pay taxes to the emperor, or not?" (Mk. 12:14), he deftly turned on the schemers by demanding a coin and asking,

> Whose head is this, and whose inscription?   [Mk. 12:16 REB, JS–b]

Their one-word admission, "Caesar's," made it impossible for them to escape the judgment in his pronouncement,

> Pay Caesar what belongs to Caesar,
> and God what belongs to God.   [Mk. 12:17 REB, JS–r]

The gospels present a significant number of Jesus' sayings under the form of controversy with scribes, Pharisees, Sadducees, Herodians, even disciples of John the Baptist, most of them dealing with issues over which the early Christian community found itself in conflict with Judaism. By use of the dialogic method Jesus is pictured as drawing out a good answer (Lk. 10:26, JS–b) and commending a sincere inquirer (Mk. 12:34, JS–g).

Maxims

In the give-and-take of disputation Jesus demonstrated mastery of the rabbis' aphoristic technique. In the retentive minds of hearers schooled in a culture still dominantly oral, his proverbial sayings stuck, as they were designed to do:

No one can serve two masters.   [Mt. 6:24 NRSV, JS–p]

In everything do to others
as you would have them to do to you.   [Mt. 7:12 NRSV, JS–g]

Even the hairs of your head are all counted.   [Mt. 10:30 NRSV, JS–p]

What will it profit them to gain the whole world
and forfeit their life?   [Mk. 8:36 NRSV, JS–g]

In the excitement of the demonstration that initiated his last appeal to Jerusalem and doubtless alarmed the authorities into taking final action against him, some members of the establishment warned him to rebuke his disciples. As Luke would have it, he replied,

I tell you, if my disciples are silent
the stones will shout aloud.   [Lk. 19:40 REB, JS–b]

Analogy and "Light and Heavy"

Rabbinic reasoning made large use of analogy to clarify the understanding of God, and Jesus did likewise. Indeed, the good news of the kingdom, that God is about to take up sovereignty in the experience of the hearers, employs an analogy from civil government; Jesus gives it point by working up parables that elaborate the image: "The kingdom of heaven is like…" His gospel of God's readiness to forgive, with unwavering determination to seek out and find the offender, also rests on analogy, as is evident in three of his most familiar parables:

Which one of you, having a hundred sheep, and losing one of them,
does not leave the ninety-nine in the wilderness
and go after the one that is lost until he finds it?
                                            [Lk. 15:3–4 NRSV, JS–p]

Or what woman having ten silver coins,
if she loses one of them…?   [Lk. 15:8 NRSV, JS–p]

There was a man who had two sons…   [Lk. 15:11 NRSV, JS–p]

So he comes to the very center of the Good news, the knowledge of God as Abba, loving Father. And from this analogy he reasons by the rabbinical rule of "light and heavy," from the less to the greater.

Is there anyone among you who,
if your child asks for bread, will give a stone?

Or if the child asks for a fish, will give a snake?
If you then, who are evil, know how to give good gifts to your children,
how much more will your Father in heaven give good things
to those who ask him!   [Mt. 7:9–11 NRSV, JS–p]

Speaking in Specifics

By suggesting specific application, Jesus, like the rabbis, gives point to the discussion of a principle and drives it home. Particularity illuminates the abstraction of the principle, thus making it more compelling. The admonition,

Beware of practicing your piety before others
in order to be seen by them.   [Mt. 6:1 NRSV, JS–b]

he illustrates with vivid caricatures of spiritual phonies advertising their almsgiving, praying, and fasting (6:2–18, JS–b, –g, –p, –r). In showing how a doctrine is lived out, he avoids both abstraction and legalism. He uses specificity for illumination in the exegesis of scripture, as we shall shortly see.

Appeal to the Hearers

In the free-and-easy interchange of an outdoor setting or in the tense, sometimes hostile atmosphere of disputation, Jesus kept his hearers engaged. Delight in his stories was not permitted to distract the hearers from the call and confrontation ever at the heart of the preaching:

Which one of you…?   [Lk. 15:4 NRSV, JS–p]
Or what woman…?   [Lk. 15:8 NRSV, JS–p]
If you then…?   [Lk. 11:13 NRSV, JS–g]
What do you think…?   [Mt. 18:12 NRSV, JS–p]

Jesus' Debt to the Rabbis

These examples clearly indicate Jesus' indebtedness to the rabbinic preaching. His rhetoric involves more than familiarity with the scriptures and the use of biblical forms of expression. Jesus was a Jew in the last days of the temple. The Judaism in which he was reared nourished his mind and spirit. More than that. It shaped the distinctive mode of his preaching and that of the church that came after him.

MATERIALS FOR PREACHING[4]

Rhetorical Invention

For Jesus the process of rhetorical "invention" or discovery of materials seems to have involved an almost intuitive insight rather than a labored effort to come up with something to say. He knew his message. And everywhere he turned he found analogies, images, stories, arguments to serve as carriers of the gospel. The freshness of his preaching persists after nearly twenty centuries, repeatedly breaking through the dullness induced by familiarity, the insufferable stodginess of homiletical abstraction, and the oppressive predictability of routine sermonizing, which have so often seemed designed to smother interest. That lively bloom that does not fade appears to have sprung naturally from the soil of the preacher's spirit without labored effort or studied artificiality.

Perhaps the impression belies the toil and pain that hold the secret of great art. Perhaps Jesus' freshness of speech sprang from much observation and reflection during unspectacular years as a carpenter prior to his public ministry. Perhaps the gospel references to his spending the night hours in prayer recall times of arduous struggle in thinking through his message for the coming days. Perhaps the almost unnoticed preface to some of his parables,

> What is the kingdom of God like?
> And to what should I compare it?   [Lk. 13:18 NRSV, JS–p]

represents not conventional introduction but the preacher's struggle even at the moment of delivery to find the right image. About such matters we can only speculate. But we can suggest the sources where Jesus found the materials that gave such freshness to his preaching.

The Immediate Situation

Again and again the words of Jesus suggest an offhand response to an immediate situation, a mastery of improvisation that the archaic English of the traditional versions of the Bible tends to obscure. Granted that the "Sermon on the Mount" represents compilation by the redactor of the first gospel, the memory of outdoor preaching to throngs of people must still be authentic. Bearing in the mind's eye the hillside setting under an open sky, recall the following words:

> A city built on a hill cannot be hid.   [Mt. 5:14 NRSV, JS–p]
>
> Look at the birds in the sky!   [Mt. 6:26 NAB, JS–p]

> Learn from the way the wild flowers grow.
> They do not work or spin.
> But I tell you that not even Solomon in all his splendor
> was clothed like one of them.   [Mt. 6:28–29 NAB, JS–p]

Possibly the ruins of a house built too near a streambed and recently destroyed by flood, along with the stability of a nearby house with its foundations set on solid rock, suggested the parable of the wise and foolish builders (Mt. 7:24–27, JS–b).

Mark pictures Jesus seated in a boat anchored just offshore speaking to the crowd seated in the natural amphitheater around the cove. Surveying that rural landscape, Jesus says,

> Listen! A sower went out to sow!   [Mk. 4:3 REB, JS–p]

In the same setting Matthew includes another parable, which might even then have been unfolding before the eyes of preacher and hearers:

> The kingdom of heaven is like a net that was thrown into the sea
> and caught fish of every kind.
> When it was full, they drew it ashore, sat down,
> and put the good into baskets but threw out the bad.
>
> [Mt. 13:47–48 NRSV, JS–b]

Unperturbed by activities in the background that catch people's attention, resiliency of spirit turns distractions into parables. From the color of the passing scene and the vitality of life going on before their eyes, Jesus draws materials for his preaching to the crowds. "The world is seen in the light of the rule and will of God. Thus it becomes a parable."[5]

Common Experience

Jesus had a discerning eye for the texture of everyday experience as it could suggest an understanding of life in the kingdom. He drew on the most common articles of domestic life, saying to his disciples:

> You are salt to the world.   [Mt. 5:13 REB, JS–b]

> You are the light of the world...   [JS–b]
> No one after lighting a lamp puts it under the bushel basket,
> but on the lampstand.   [Mt. 5:14–15 NRSV, JS–p]

> The kingdom of heaven is like a mustard seed.   [Mt. 13:31 NRSV, JS–p]

Recall also the shocking image of leaven, cited previously (Mt. 13:33).

References to wandering sheep, lost coins, patches on old clothes, crooked managers, overambitious builders, improvident party-goers, presumptuous dinner guests, merchants, housekeepers, fishers, farmers, day laborers, the idle rich and the wretched poor—the list could be extended—indicate the preacher's zest for the tang of daily life, the quirks of human nature, and the foibles of society. He used them all to help people grasp the earthy nature of the good news.

Current Happenings

Dramatic occurrences in the news of the day found their way into Jesus' preaching, not as diversions, but as points of engagement between the gospel and the life of the hearers. On being told that Pilate had slain some Galileans (doubtless Zealots), mingling their blood with that of their sacrifices, Jesus asked,

> Do you suppose that because these Galileans suffered this fate,
> they must have been greater sinners than anyone else in Galilee?
> No, I tell you; but unless you repent,
> you will all come to the same end.   [Lk. 13:2–3 REB, JS–b]

One of his parables he began with the words:

> A man of noble birth went to a distant country
> to be appointed king and then return.   [Lk. 19:12 NJB, JS–b]

The story calls to mind the incident on which it must surely have been based, the journey of Herod's son Archelaus to Rome to negotiate for appointment as his father's successor. The event occurred during the childhood of Jesus and his contemporaries, and its color lingered in imagination.

Several other parables, rather than emerging as products of sheer fantasy, may have been suggested to Jesus, at least in germ, by occurrences well known to him and his hearers: the man who discovered a buried treasure (Mt. 13:44, JS–p), the builder who began a tower he could not afford to finish (Lk. 14:28, JS–b), the king with a small army who must sue for peace before his opponent with superior forces (the Romans?) crushes him in the field (Lk. 14:31–32, JS–b), the rescue on the Jericho road of a traveler wounded and robbed by muggers—rescue by a Samaritan! (Lk. 10:30–35, JS–r). Who knows but that the story of the boy who set out for a far country, squandered his share of the inheritance, and returned to his father as a beggar (Lk. 15:11–24, JS–p) may have occurred within the circle of

Jesus' acquaintances? Since events of this character recur in every generation and every community, specific instances known to Jesus may well lie back of a number of parables; it is clear that he appropriated current happenings, without fatuous comment, as material for his preaching.

Literature[6]

A preacher with Jesus' feel for a story or a pointed saying might be expected to draw on literature. The striking parallels between his words (or in any case those of the tradition) and a wide range of the literature known at the time suggests that he mined this resource. One cannot demonstrate that Jesus had read a great deal of this material or that many of his hearers had done so. Books were expensive and rare, and knowledge of literature came largely from oral transmission, but good stories and pithy sayings circulated even among those with little opportunity to read. While a specific allusion may not be certain, the occurrence of many parallels indicates openness on Jesus' part to such material. Similarities have been noted to the Targums, the Aramaic translations and explanations of biblical texts, to the "apocryphal" books of Tobit and the Wisdom of Jesus the son of Sirach, to the Testaments of the Twelve Patriarchs, to current proverbs, to the sayings of the rabbis, and to the liturgy of the synagogue. Some of Jesus' parables depict situations similar to those in popular Egyptian literature, especially the Wisdom of Ahiqar. These many allusions, clear enough in the gospels, may trace in a number of instances to the words of Jesus himself.

Scripture and Its Exegesis[7]

Foundational to the preaching and teaching of the rabbis was the holy scripture; their midrash was offered as commentary on the meaning of particular passages, their sermons as reflections drawn from the larger sweep of the sacred story with application to the situation of their hearers. Within limits, the same observation may be made regarding the preaching of Jesus, although his use of scripture is a particularly difficult aspect of his preaching to treat historically, for here the Christian preachers of the generation after him have obviously colored the tradition. Virtually all the specifically exegetical activity attributed to him occurs in controversy with the scribes (or in Luke's resurrection narrative).

Yet the general approach to the text attributed to him in the gospels—apart from those passages supporting controversial positions of the developing church and its growing christology—suggests a distinctive way of interacting with scripture. He speaks as a devout Jew, with biblical phrases and images coming naturally to his lips. Yet there is a difference of emphasis. The color of his language, tinged by the reality of everyday experience, draws its tones from scripture without falling into religious or theological jargon. He picks up phrases from the Law and the prophets and the Writings, deftly expanding a point or amplifying an image into narrative to produce a parable.[8] Like the rabbis, he uses biblical commonplaces and examples, reminding his hearers of incidents involving Noah, Lot, Moses, David, Elijah, Elisha, and the later prophets.

The essence of Jesus' gospel, however, is the *contemporary* activity of God. He comes heralding the good news of God's present and imminent action—the God who has been made known in the history of Israel and to whom the scriptures bear witness. It appears that he seldom preached by taking a text and expounding it through a sermon. His mode was to begin with the present, assuming a general knowledge of Israel's God as context for the proclamation.

In the interpretation of particular texts, he does not follow the prevailing pattern, but consistently probes beneath the literal crust to demonstrate what the scribes have missed in the passage under dispute; he looks not for regulations, but for the action of God, whom he proclaims in his gospel. Accordingly, he proposes that Moses legalized divorce, not as a matter of fulfilling divine intention but because of human hardheartedness (Mk. 10:5–9, JS–g). David, when his troops were hungry, did not hesitate to feed them with the consecrated bread from the altar, thus subordinating cultic propriety to human need (Mk. 2:25–27, JS–b). The prophetic vision of the temple as a house of prayer for all people justifies clearing its courts of the animal market and financial exchange which have grown up around the sacrificial cult (Mk. 11:15–17, JS–g). His understanding of God as known in Israel's faith and in his own experience determines his approach to a particular text.

In these instances Jesus showed himself no cavalier antinomian or iconoclast, but rather a "supralegalist" concerned for a right relationship with God and guided by emphases in the scriptures that point in that direction. A saying not found in most manuscripts of the New Testament expresses this attitude. On seeing a man breaking the Sabbath by working, Jesus said,

> If you are doing this deliberately, you are blessed;
> but if you are acting out of ignorance,
> you are transgressing the law and are accursed.[9]

The total witness of scripture to the power and purpose of the living God occupies Jesus rather than disputation about the fine points of particular texts. He finds biblical support for the resurrection of the dead, despite the lack of explicit passages on that theme, in the nature of the Eternal One as confessed in the Torah:

> the God of Abraham, the God of Isaac,
> and the God of Jacob.   [Mk. 12:26–27, JS–g]

Only once in the gospels is a formal sermon as exposition of a passage of scripture attributed to Jesus. Occurring in Luke 4, it fits the pattern of the evangelist's fondness for set pieces featuring impressive orations in dramatic settings. In the synagogue at Nazareth Jesus reads Isaiah 61 from the prophetic scroll and proclaims:

> Today this scripture has been fulfilled in your hearing.
>
> [Lk. 4:21 NRSV, JS–b]

His elaboration of the passage, recalling God's actions through Elijah and Elisha in behalf of foreigners, offends his hearers, who drive Jesus from the synagogue. The pericope is consistent not only with Luke's interest in the mission to the Gentiles, but also with other reported examples of Jesus' exegesis.

Jesus' understanding of God as Father, caring for the least and the despised and ever ready to receive the outcast, enabled him to draw inferences from the scripture that literalists, for all their study and disputation, failed to see. The early Christian assertion of his authority over the scriptures (Mt. 17:3–5) may well derive from this approach, as does the word in Matthew that he has come not to destroy the Law and the prophets but to fulfil them (Mt. 5:17, JS–b). Certainly the early Christian community read the scriptures in a new way in the light of Jesus. At no point is this more evident than in the bold merging of two heretofore contradictory notions: the promise of the Messiah, God's Chosen and Anointed (Isa. 11:1–5, 32:1; Jer. 33:14–26), and the haunting vision of God's Suffering Servant (Isa. 52:13–53:12). The early church preached Jesus the *crucified Christ* as the heart of its gospel. That paradox goes back to what they had seen and heard in his ministry, perhaps even to an understanding on his part of his mission as Servant.

Out of his deep familiarity with the scriptures, new insights into passages commonly overlooked, and discernment of the purpose and nature of God revealed in the broad sweep of the sacred story, Jesus practiced a brand of preaching that was at times intensely biblical, though seldom textual. To the interpretation of scripture as to every other aspect of his preaching, he brought freshness, vitality, and personal authority.

STYLE[10]

Distinctiveness

As already noted, Jesus spoke with a distinctiveness of style which, along with the uniqueness of his message, serves as criterion of his genuine sayings. Because of the passage from the Aramaic in which he spoke to the *koiné* Greek in which the gospels set forth his preaching to the English in which the readers of this book hear his words, some color of his style is lost. Yet striking aspects of it survive translation.

Poetic Structure

As a devout young Jew with a sensitivity to language, growing up in the atmosphere of the synagogue and loving the poets and prophets of the Bible, Jesus would quite naturally have adopted the fundamental pattern of Semitic poetic speech, that of *synonymous parallelism:*

> Ask, and it will be given you;
> search, and you will find;
> knock, and the door will be opened for you.
> For everyone who asks receives,
> and everyone who searches finds,
> and for everyone who knocks,
> the door will be opened.   [Mt. 7:7–8 NRSV, JS–p]

Scholars assume that a saying recorded in such a pattern retains the form in which Jesus spoke it, whereas a saying of only a single member or stich may very well have suffered alteration, even if it preserves an authentic element of Jesus' teaching.

Even more characteristic of Jesus is the poetic structure of *antithetic parallelism,* which occurs 138 times in the sayings reported in the Synoptic Gospels.[11] The form lends itself to forceful expression of the eschatological polarity in Jesus' thinking about the dramatic reversals to be expected in the kingdom of God.

> All who exalt themselves will be humbled,
> and all who humble themselves will be exalted.
> [Mt. 23:12 NRSV, JS–g]

It could also express the darker moods arising from Jesus's prescience of coming suffering and death:

> The wedding guests cannot fast
> while the bridegroom is with them, can they?
> As long as they have the bridegroom with them,
> they cannot fast.   [Mk. 2:19 NRSV, JS–p] .

This mode of sharp contrast between *now* and *then,* more than any other single element, characterizes the style of Jesus. The style itself dramatically represents the substance of thought that it expresses.

Jesus showed a fondness of *rhythm* in speech, a basic element in Semitic poetry and a device carefully cultivated by the Greek and Roman orators. By translating the sayings of Jesus from Greek back into Aramaic, several common patterns have been noted: two-beat sayings, abrupt and urgent, carry the central ideas of his message; four-beat lines, matter-of-fact and unhurried, impart instruction and consolation; three-beat lines, the pattern most frequently used by Jesus, carry important sayings and maxims; the *kina* metre (3 + 2 beats, with occasional variations of 2 + 2 and 4 + 2), used in Jewish lament, expresses intense emotion; Jesus uses its elegiac accents for "laments, warnings, threats, admonitions and summons, as well as beatitudes and messages of salvation."[12]   It is difficult to transpose the effects of these patterns to English, though the two-beat line may be suggested by the words:

> Freély ye recéived,
> freély gíve.   [Mt. 10:8 ASV, JS–b]

Rhetorical Devices

Some devices of Jesus' rhetoric also elude the modern reader, especially the various kinds of *wordplay* that draw their effectiveness from the sound of the spoken Aramaic. These include alliteration, assonance, punning (paronomasia), onomatopoeia, and occasional rhyme.[13]

Evident in translation is the effect of *repetition* sounding like an alarum bell throughout the urgent admonition (emphasis added):

> Take heed, *watch;*
> for you do not know when the time will come.   [JS–b]
> It is like a man going on a journey,
> when he leaves home and puts his servants in charge,
> each with his work,
> and commands the doorkeeper to be on the *watch.*
> *Watch* therefore—

for you do not know when the master of the house will come...

[JS–g] .

And what I say to you I say to all: *Watch.*   [Mk. 13:33–37 RSV, JS–b][14]

The same word *watch* recurs three times with evident pathos in the conversations of Jesus with his disciples in the Garden of Gethsemane (Mk. 14:32–42, JS–b).

Also obvious in translation is Jesus' recurring use of *rhetorical questions,* one of the surest marks of a speaker's intent to keep a dialog going with the hearers. Putting an enthymeme in this form doubles the effect of its logic, for it demands the assent of the listener:

You will know them by their fruits.   [JS–g]
Are grapes gathered from thorns, or figs from thistles?

[Mt. 7:16 NRSV, JS–p]

We saw earlier how Jesus repeatedly put questions to an audience as a mode of appeal. Some were designed to drive the hearer to intense searching of heart:

If they do this when the wood is green,
what will happen when it is dry?   [Lk. 23:31 NRSV, JS–b]

Tropes and Figures

In Jesus' lavish use of *tropes* and *figures* he establishes himself as incomparable poet-preacher. In his mind's eye vivid pictures crowded one upon another, and in his speech they issued as a succession of images.

The *metaphors* of Jesus can hardly be forgotten. When a theoretical question is put to him, which the self-assured among the religious love to discuss, "Will only a few be saved?" he turns the answer into a disturbing admonition:

Strive to enter through the narrow door;
for many, I tell you, will try to enter
and will not be able.   [Lk. 13:24 NRSV, JS–p]

The urgent metaphor carries the total discussion.

Jesus compressed into minimal words—*salt, light, leaven, seed*—endless possibilities for meditation and sermonizing. Even in the names he gave his disciples he indulged a playfulness that amuses but also inspires, naming Simon the fisherman Cephas (Peter=Rock) (Mt. 16:18, JS–b; Jn. 1:42, Js–b)[15] and calling the sons of Zebedee Boanerges (Sons of Thunder) (Mk. 3:17).

Simile abounds in the speech of Jesus, constantly flashing pictures, imparting emotional overtones to the preaching, repeatedly moving from tableau to narrative in the briefest of parables.

> The kingdom of heaven may be compared
> to someone who sowed good seed in his field.   [Mt. 13:24 NRSV, JS–g]

> The kingdom of heaven is like a mustard seed.   [Mt. 13:31 NRSV, JS–p]

> The kingdom of heaven is like yeast.   [Mt. 13:33 NRSV, JS–r]

> The kingdom of heaven is like a merchant
> in search of fine pearls.   [Mt. 13:45 NRSV, JS–p]

> The kingdom of heaven is like a net that was
> thrown into the sea.   [Mt. 13:47 NRSV, JS–b]

The vividness of an extended simile carries great pathos.

> Jerusalem, Jerusalem…
> How often have I longed to gather your children together,
> as a hen gathers her brood under her wings,
> and you refused!   [Lk. 13:34 NJB, JS–b]

To impress on his hearers the radical reversals implicit in the coming of God's kingdom, Jesus used the language of *paradox*.

> Those who want to save their life will lose it,
> and those who lose their life for my sake will find it.
>
> [Mt. 16:25 NRSV, JS–g]

With this figure he also described the radical transformation of religious concern brought about by the gospel. All the scribal disputations regarding ceremonial uncleanness were beside the point:

> There is nothing outside a person that by going in can defile,
> but the things that come out are what defile.   [Mk. 7:15 NRSV, JS–p]

The vigor of Jesus' style broke into frequent *hyperbole,* a prodigal extravagance that by evident exaggeration drives home the point.[16] Like his use of paradox, it intensified the teaching. The rabbis loved to explain difficult concepts by using hyperbole. Requiring considerable skill, it occurs with surprising frequency in the preaching of Jesus:

> If your hand causes you to stumble, cut it off;
> it is better for you to enter life maimed
> than to have two hands and to go to hell.   [Mk. 9:43 NRSV, JS–g]

Truly I tell you, if you say to this mountain,
"Be taken up and thrown into the sea,"
and if you do not doubt in your heart,
but believe that what you say will happen,
it will be done for you.   [Mk. 11:23 NRSV, JS–g]

The form lent itself especially to declaring the demands of the kingdom.

Whoever comes to me and does not hate father and mother,
wife and children, brothers and sisters, yes, and even life itself,
cannot be my disciple.   [Lk. 14:26 NRSV, JS–p]

The searching earnestness of such sayings could hide at times under the camouflage of humor:

It is easier for a camel to go through the eye of a needle
than for someone who is rich
to enter the kingdom of God.   [Mk. 10:25 NRSV, JS–p]

Humor[17]

Glints of humor sparkle through the words of Jesus, often unexpectedly. This aspect of Jesus' style is often hidden from congregations and from cinema audiences attending biblical epics, concealed by the lugubrious manner in which readers intone his words, by the sanctity imputed to the archaism of the *King James Version* of the Bible, and by solemn presuppositions concerning Holy Scripture which induce blindness to the drama of its actual content. Perhaps only a few of the sayings, when spoken naturally rather than in a "holy" tone, may prompt laughter, but scores of them will elicit smiles of delight and even a chuckle or two.

How is this overflow of humor in Jesus to be understood? Humor is sometimes explained as the means by which an ill-adjusted or lonely person copes with life and earns a degree of acceptance. For those who have been badly wounded or who feel threatened, especially by an inferior, it serves as a weapon for inflicting cruel cuts. More cerebrally, it has been seen as similar to that philosophy which views everything *sub specie aeternitatis;* such humor is not vicious, but rather restores perspective and proportion. In a mature and jocund spirit it reflects a glad acceptance of life and of human beings with all their frailties, foibles, and frustrations. Here we come close to the humor of Jesus.

Much of his humor reveals his keen eye for the comical situations in everyday life: the irascible father who has just got the babies to sleep awakened by the insistent rapping of a neighbor who will not stop until he gets out of bed and brings bread from the pantry (Lk. 11:5–8, JS–p); an unprincipled judge, not cheaply bought, who settles the petition of a poor widow simply to rid himself of her constant nagging (Lk. 18:2–5, JS–p), a defendant under subpoena frantically negotiating a settlement with the plaintiff on the way to court (Lk. 12:58–59, JS–p), a sower prodigally scattering seed with no regard to the kind of soil on which it falls (Mk. 4:3–8, JS–p), a dishonest manager too weak to earn an honest living whose shrewdness matches the occasion when he is fired (Lk. 16:1–7, JS–r), a social climber who presses too hard and in the sight of all is humiliated by being directed to yield the seat at the head table to someone more important (Lk. 14:7–11, JS–b, g), giddy bridesmaids who go to welcome the bridegroom without taking oil for the lamps they have brought to carry in the nocturnal procession (Mt. 25:1–12, JS–g). Amusing as these situations are, Jesus uses each of them to yield some insight into the ways of God's kingdom.

Again, Jesus uses humor to help people laugh at themselves and so amend their ways. Sayings of this type picture someone staggering about with a beam lodged in an eye officiously trying to remove a speck from a neighbor's eye (Mt. 7:3–5, JS–p), a group of blind persons trailing behind a guide who also turns out to be blind so that all tumble into a ditch (Mt. 15:14, JS–g), the conscientious Milquetoast of a servant who never dares use the entrusted talent of limited ability but scrupulously returns it neatly wrapped in a napkin, just as it was received long ago (Mt. 25:24–28, JS–p), the show-off who begins to build on a grand scale, is forced by financial reality to suspend operations, and remains a laughingstock whenever people look at the unfinished tower (Lk. 14:28–30, JS–b), the spoiled children who don't want to play wedding and won't play funeral (Mt. 11:17, JS–g).

Jesus delights in exaggerating to make a point.

> If you are presenting your gift at the altar
> and suddenly remember that your brother
> has a grievance against you,
> leave your gift where it is before the altar.
> First go and make peace with your brother;
> then come back and offer your gift.   [Mt. 5:23–24 REB, JS–g]

When Jesus' humor bites, it chews on privileged persons who

lord it over others, especially in religion. He makes fun of punctilious types who make a production of straining a gnat from the broth, then swallow a camel (Mt. 23:24, JS–g), who publicly flourish their tithing of herbs from the garden but pay no attention to weightier matters of the law (Mt. 23:23, JS–b), who cross sea and land to make a single proselyte, then turn their convert into a worse child of hell than themselves (Mt. 23:15, JS–b); of the hypocrites who present a beautiful appearance like yonder whitewashed walls in the sunlight, dazzling charnel houses, grisly on the inside with the bones of the dead despite their stunning exterior (Mt. 23:27–28, JS–b); of pretentious champions of religious Law who pile burdens on the weak and poor and will not lift a pious finger to help lighten the load (Mt. 23:3–4, JS–b); of the "good" boy whose correct behavior yields so little happiness that even when his lost brother comes back from the far country he cannot enter into the festivities and share the father's joy (Lk. 15:25–30, JS–p).

This extended list by no means exhausts the sallies of humor in the sayings of Jesus. Their abundance is made all the more remarkable by the relative dearth of such passages in the rest of the New Testament and in the Bible as a whole, outside the Wisdom literature. The very extent of these risibilia indicates a streak of merriment in the preacher akin to that of the more scintillating rabbis. Without losing sight of his goal or swamping his message under a spate of one-liners, he could keep an audience of all ages and types fascinated by the hour. And more than fascinated. This humor sustains no comfortable illusion of distance between hearer and message. Rather, it shatters the shield of pretense and opens a way for the good news.

Cumulative Effect

Jesus' style of speech comes through to hearers as strikingly natural and fresh, vivid, direct, and unadorned. It features strong nouns, active verbs, and remarkably few adjectives and adverbs. (It has been noted that the Lord's Prayer contains only one adjective.)[18] His is in no sense a special "holy language," but rather the colorful idiom of everyday used with suppleness and grace to reveal the mysteries of God. It conveys a glad sense of spontaneity and unstudied naturalness: "Jesus spoke as the birds sing."[19] Though he used many of the devices that the rhetoricians commended in their textbooks, he avoided the windy eloquence that lured so many orators into insincerity. Heeding his admonition against idle or careless words (Mt. 12:36, JS–b), he made "no display of oratory."[20]

Jesus could package both judgment and hope into a short saying:

If you had faith the size of a mustard seed... [Lk. 17:6 NRSV, JS–g]

And in a single parable he could compress powerful dramatic contrast:

Two people went up to the temple area to pray;
one was a Pharisee and the other was a tax collector.
The Pharisee took up his position and spoke this prayer to himself,
"O God, I thank you that I am not like the rest of humanity—
greedy, dishonest, adulterous—or even like this tax collector.
I fast twice a week, and I pay tithes on my whole income."
But the tax collector stood off at a distance
and would not even raise his eyes to heaven
but beat his breast and prayed, "O God, be merciful to me a sinner."
I tell you, the latter went home justified,
not the former.   [Lk. 18:10–14a NAB, JS–p]

The parable demonstrates not only the immediacy of Jesus' speech, but the technique known in sports as "blindsiding": the hearer, with attention focused on the story, does not see the blow coming until too late to dodge.

Jesus' preaching exemplifies the way in which style, far from adding unessential adornment to content, is ingredient to the message it conveys.

PREACHING IN PARABLES: THE CREATIVE ARTISTRY OF JESUS[21]

The Nature of Parable

In one aspect of his preaching Jesus' rhetorical art manifests itself preeminently: "He did not speak to them except in parables" (Mk. 4:34; cf. Jn. 16:25). The word means *figure, illustration, story.* The parable has a long tradition in Judaism, occurring in the preaching of the prophets and also of the sages; the rabbis brought it to a point of high artistry, but Jesus is unsurpassed.

To Mark, an analogy is a parable, as is even a paradox. Luke includes allegory as well, but it appears that Jesus did not favor this form; the pressing of some of his stories in that direction occurred in cases when his followers had lost the original context or application. In any event, as we have seen, Jesus drew on every aspect of human experience to illustrate the workings of the kingdom of God.

Parabolic Form

All of Jesus' parables are brief, some remarkably so. All are un-pretentious, yet fascinating. Sometimes they occur in pairs, making a similar point, one about a man, the other about a woman. No rigid or standard form marks them all, though a number follow a consistent pattern: (1) an introductory question or statement; (2) a brief analogy or story answering the question or reinforcing the assertion; (3) a concluding formulation of the point in language of authority: a sentence of scripture, a popular proverb, or perhaps an Oriental maxim. It may be that these conclusions, especially those using biblical passages, were added by the early preachers as they recounted Jesus' parables. In any case, most of these pieces as reported in the gospels consist only of part 2, a compelling story or the briefest of analogies.

It would appear that Jesus rarely if ever composed a formal oration or sermon with a carefully wrought-out structure, but that his preaching proceeded informally through a series of maxims or other sayings, rejoinders to arguments, and responses to the particular situation. And always there were parables, sometimes, it would appear, a succession of parables.

Purpose of the Parables

Given the great attractiveness of the parables and their apparent genius in communicating profound insights to simple minds, Mark's understanding of their purpose comes as a shock. For he regards them as intended to hide the truth, so that, in the words of the prophet (Isa. 6:9–10),

> they may look and look, but never perceive;
> listen and listen, but never understand;
> to avoid changing their ways and being healed.   [Mk. 4:12 NJB, JS–b]

Mark portrays Jesus as guarding the secret of his Messiahship, speaking to the crowds in dark language, explaining the real meaning privately to his disciples; the mystery is revealed to the public only after his resurrection.

Mark's theory is disturbing for anyone who understands preaching as proclamation and regards Jesus as master preacher. It must be noted, however, that others have spoken with deliberate obscurity—the apocalyptists of Mark's own time, the Provençal poets of the late Middle Ages, and some twentieth-century poets as well. It must be further admitted that on occasion, at least, Jesus spoke in riddles, apparently with deliberate intent.[22]   Certainly if he saw himself as

Messiah, the claim had to be advanced with either the greatest of care or the most reckless abandon, for it was sure to arouse the apprehension of the authorities. Indeed, it was the charge on which Jesus was crucified.

Jesus' Purpose

Yet on hearing most of the parables, who can deny that the one who first preached them must have intended above all else to make clear to his hearers the message they so plainly convey? He came, he said, to proclaim a message, the good news of the kingdom (Mk. 1:38, JS–g), and "the parables are the preaching itself."[23] However we deal with this difficult question of Jesus' intention during his ministry, veiled as the evidence inevitably is by the understanding of the early preachers and the writers of the gospels, we are forced to the conclusion that the parables actually function to illuminate Jesus' preaching.

Creative Artistry

A brief analysis will suggest the way in which Jesus' creative artistry operated in the composition of the parables.

(1) It began with the poet's mode of perception, the "direct insight"[24] of pictorial thinking, perhaps even "eidetic imagery," for the poet, retaining one of the striking gifts of childhood, "feels and even sees his thoughts,"[25] thinking in percepts, not concepts. In this respect, Jesus' metaphors are poetic, not didactic.

(2) It proceeded by "imaginative playfulness"[26] to amplify the picture into a story; many of the parables, as already noted, are simply images expanded into narratives—figures from familiar experience, from scripture, from other literature. Consider how Jesus so vivified a biblical proverb (Prov. 15:33) as almost to make a story from it (Lk. 14:7–11, JS–b, g) or elaborated a legal provision (Deut. 24:5) into a discerning and disturbing tale (Lk. 14:15–23, JS–p).

(3) The preacher's artistry vitalized and actualized the story by making it existential. Jesus contemporized the symbols, some of which were primordial archetypes (light, water, tree) by bonding them to reality in the secular present.

(4) The point Jesus wanted to make connected with the experience of the hearers, his mode of communication relying on a story or image seen and felt, vibrant with emotion, and applying specifically to their lives. "The down-to-earth dimensions of the stories" convey "the concrete involvement they intend."[27]

(5) His artistry, by achieving memorability, stamped the story or image indelibly in the mind of the hearer. In part, he achieved this end by setting forth unforgettable situations (rich fool, waiting father, good Samaritan, last judgment), in part by compression. "The original parable [of the lost sheep] may have been less than forty words; enough on his lips to tell the whole story of earth and heaven."[28] Far more memorable than a long, discursive tale, the incident thus compressed waited to explode into story, drama, song, or sermon. So Matthew applied to Jesus the prophecy,

> I will open my mouth in parables,
> I will announce what has lain hidden
> from the foundation of the world.   [Mt. 13:35; cf. Ps. 78:2 NAB]

JESUS' COMMITMENT TO PREACHING

His 'Doctrine' of Preaching[29]

A DIFFICULT PROBLEM. Only with some tentativeness may a statement be advanced as to Jesus' doctrine of preaching, for two reasons. First, he was not a systematician given to the definition of abstract concepts and the fabrication of these into a tight conceptual structure. Rather, he was a poet bent on conveying the insights he saw so clearly and felt so keenly. Second, so much of the reflection about preaching that we find in the gospels springs from or interacts with the experience of the early church that trying to delve through to Jesus' own thought on the point becomes highly complex. Nevertheless, a few possibilities may be suggested.

PREACHING AS IMMINENCE OF GOD'S NEW AGE. Through the preaching of the good news of God's kingdom, that kingdom confronts the hearers as imminent actuality. The announcement with which Jesus begins his ministry opens up the possibility of the divine rule wherever the hearers heed his urgent call for repentance. With his preaching God's reign has appeared; it is "among you" (Lk. 17:21, JS–p). The broadcasting of the good news belongs among the signs of the kingdom:

> The blind receive their sight, the lame walk,
> the lepers are cleansed, the deaf hear, the dead are raised,
> and the poor have good news brought to them.   [Mt. 11:5 NRSV, JS–b]

The announcement itself should be enough to convince the people of the kingdom's imminence and to convict them of their sin.

> The queen of the South will rise at the judgment
> with the people of this generation and condemn them,
> because she came from the ends of the earth
> to listen to the wisdom of Solomon,
> and see, something greater than Solomon is here!
> The people of Nineveh will rise up at the judgment
> with this generation and condemn it,
> because they repented at the proclamation of Jonah,
> and see, something greater than Jonah is here!
>
> [Lk. 11:31–32 NRSV, JS–b]

THE RESPONSE OF THE HEARERS. Jesus lays squarely upon the hearers full responsibility for accepting or rejecting the announcement. This point receives fullest development in his parable of the sower and the soils (Mk. 4:3–8, JS–p). The same good seed is scattered broadcast and springs up in various kinds of lives; now the harvest depends on the soil. No matter how artful the rhetoric or persuasive the preacher, the response ultimately requires a decision on the part of the hearer.

> Blessed are those
> who hear the word of God and observe it!   [Lk. 11:28 NAB, JS–g]

THE VITALITY OF THE WORD. Nevertheless, the effect of the preaching derives from the life inherent in the word itself. In the parable of the sower and the soils, the seed is the word that is preached (Mk. 4:14, JS–b); in other parables it is the kingdom (Mk. 4:26–29, JS–p). This virtual equivalence of kingdom and word implies much about the nature of preaching.

> The kingdom of God is like this.
> A man scatters seed on the ground;
> he goes to bed at night and gets up in the morning,
> and meanwhile the seed sprouts and grows—how he does not know.
> The ground produces a crop by itself, first the blade,
> then the ear, then the full grain in the ear.   [Mk. 4:26–28 REB, JS–p]

Given the power inherent in the word, proclamation takes precedence over persuasion, taught by the rhetoricians, as the preacher's primary task.[30] Even so, the style of the preaching remains integral to the proclamation. Jesus' evident concern with the form in which the

Word is presented indicates keen insight into the dynamics of oral communication. The hearers must be enabled to "see," feel, and grasp the word proclaimed—and be grasped by it. Consequently, he was ever concerned with simplicity, clarity, vividness, with catching the attention and holding the interest of the listeners.

PERSONAL DISCLOSURE. Given the primacy of the word, the speaker's ethos itself takes on undeniable importance, for it must accord with the proclamation. Apparently the person perceived by the listeners was a major factor in the impressiveness of Jesus' preaching; though that preaching in the Synoptics contains few self-references, it tells us much about him. In it we see his instant sympathy, his sparkling imagination, his playfulness, his humor, his keen eye for human nature, his responsiveness to earth and sky and sea. More profoundly, we see his trust in God, his uncompromising insistence on God's will, his total faithfulness to it, his urgent call for repentance, his assurance of divine forgiveness to the penitent. Without referring to himself, he implies that a person's speech involves self-disclosure:

> Good people draw what is good
> from the store of goodness in their hearts;
> bad people draw what is bad from the store of badness.   [JS–g]
> for the words of the mouth flow out of what fills the heart.
>
> > [Lk. 6:45 NJB, JS–b]

In his gracious invitation, reminiscent both of the prophets and the wisdom writers, Jesus speaks directly:

> Take my yoke upon you, and learn from me;
> for I am gentle and humble-hearted;
> and you will find rest for your souls.   [Mt. 11:29 REB, JS–b]

In the act of preaching one necessarily discloses oneself.

> I am among you as one who serves.   [Lk. 22:27 NRSV, JS–g]

+

If these suggestions provide something less than a complete doctrine of preaching, they nevertheless point to its essential shape in the ministry of Jesus.

Jesus' Appointment of Preachers[31]

All four gospels relate that Jesus appointed preachers with responsibility to spread the good news; this unanimous witness points convincingly to such an action on his part. The calling of the first disciples to be made to "fish for people" (Mk. 1:17 NRSV, JS–g) and the appointment of twelve apostles "to be sent out to proclaim the message" (Mk. 3:14 NRSV) represent on his part a commitment to preaching as essential means for spreading the word of the kingdom. In a programmatic passage Luke also recounts the appointment of seventy-(two) others to share in the task (Lk. 10:1–24), with Jesus saying,

> Whoever listens to you listens to me,
> and whoever rejects you rejects me,
> and whoever rejects me rejects the one who sent me.
>
> [Lk. 10:16 NRSV, JS–g]

As to the responsibility of hearers to proclaim the good news, the gospels present a varying picture. Some persons healed by Jesus were bidden to keep silent (Mk. 7:36); in such accounts the evangelists hold to the doctrine of the Messianic secret. But others were enjoined,

> Go home to your friends, and tell them
> how much the Lord has done for you,
> and what mercy he has shown you.   [Mk. 5:19 NRSV, JS–b]

The evangelists picture Jesus as envisioning a mission to continue his own ministry. They present this development as foreseen by him, or even intended, during his lifetime, as in his saying about the woman who had just anointed him with costly ointment:

> Wherever the gospel is proclaimed throughout the world,
> what she has done will be told as her memorial.   [Mk. 14:9 REB, JS–b]

It is only to be expected, after Jesus' death, that the disciples who had convincing experience of his resurrection should find their living Lord setting them to the task to which he had given himself in the days of his flesh. Each of the gospels concludes with stories that depict the risen Jesus commanding his followers to preach the gospel to all the nations (Mk. 16:15; Mt. 28:19–20; Lk. 24:48; Jn. 20:21). Faith in Jesus' resurrection called the church to engage in that work which had held a central place in his ministry—the preaching of the good news. So began the mission of the church.

CONCLUSION TO PART THREE

The Significance of Jesus' Preaching

Any assessment of the preaching of Jesus must take into account the following considerations:

1. In his remarkable ministry as set forth in the four gospels, Jesus of Nazareth made preaching his central and characteristic action.

2. Jesus spent his entire life within Judaism, and as a devout child of the synagogue he acquired from his brother-and-sister Jews a profound love for scripture. Its accents sound repeatedly through his sayings, at least in the form in which they come to us, and he drew upon it lovingly to illuminate his preaching about God and the life of the child of God.

3. While the four gospels depict Jesus as cherishing the scriptures of Judaism—making clear their prophetic message in the synagogue, calling on their words in time of personal trial, in controversy, and in his last hour—they do not depict him as an exegetical preacher. Rather, in his open-air ministry, he addressed an immediate need, responded to the situation at hand, or spoke in parables drawn from life.

4. The burden of Jesus' preaching was the imminence of God's reign, the reordering of personal life by repentance and divine forgiveness, and the transformation of social relationships in accordance with God's righteous will. He saw the kingdom coming through his preaching, announcing it with such urgency and forthrightness that the attention gained for his message forced the hearers to a decision for or against.

5. The good news of his proclamation presented God as divine Parent who cares for all creation, provides for human need, persistently seeks for God's lost and wandering human children, freely

forgives the penitent, restores them to their intended place as daughters and sons of God, and sustains them in hope.

6. The person of Jesus, projected as the ethos of the preacher, drew people to him in great numbers as they made him the focus of their hopes and longings. Many found healing of body and spirit, their lives transformed by the encounter. His words remain the best explanation of his life, his life the best illustration of his words.

7. His authority for preaching was rooted in his knowledge of God, and his gospel was an offer which the hearer would either accept or reject. Despite the power of God at work in the proclamation, the free response or refusal of each listener determined the outcome.

8. The preaching of Jesus won a large and interested hearing. In a time of eager expectation of the Messiah, it aroused great excitement, at least for a while.

9. Jesus combined in his public ministry the work of preaching and teaching (as these are sometimes differentiated), announcing the imminence of the divine reign and making clear its demands for the life of the disciple. By familiarity with the major traditions of religious speech in Israel, both prophecy and wisdom, by emulation of the trenchant utterance of the rabbis, and by the working of his own genius, he fashioned a rhetoric of unique power for the proclamation.

10. His uncompromising message of divine judgment fell most heavily not on publicans and sinners, but on those very persons whose love for the Law, commitment to righteousness, and joy in the praise of God would seem to have bound them to the preacher in close spiritual kinship, namely, the scribes and Pharisees. His call for a righteousness that exceeds the most conscientious obedience of religious rules made him unacceptable to the best people of his time, just as it has continued to disturb and judge the most devout religionists of subsequent generations.

11. His unswerving demand caused most of his hearers to turn away. This was true of his once great popular following and also of the religious leaders. For all the attractiveness of their piety and the devoutness of their meditation on Torah, the religious establishment joined with the political realists, whether Sadducees or Romans, in the repudiation of the Nazarene as a blasphemer and disturber of the peace. Only a few from the rabbinic community responded to the word he preached. Even his closest disciples failed him or

misunderstood. "He had to discover that the world is more difficult to redeem than he imagined."[1]

12. As his popular following began to dwindle and opposition by the religious and political establishment to increase, a note of melancholy entered his preaching in contrast to the high confidence with which he began his ministry. But despite the scandal of his preaching and the outcome so clearly foreseen, his faithfulness to God did not fail.

13. Despite the winsomeness and power of his preaching, and the large popular following he attracted for a time, he was sentenced to public execution. By his cross he demonstrated that God's last appeal is that of helplessness—a persuasive plea before which the hearer remains totally free, yet bound by the necessity to decide.

14. Though repudiated and sentenced to death, Jesus launched a movement that spread by preaching, the method of ministry that he himself had chosen. The preachers who came after him cherished his words, repeated them lovingly, elaborated them in countless sermons, and thus preserved the materials incorporated into the fourfold gospel, the preaching of the early church.

15. Through the color and pictorial liveliness of his speech Jesus contributed countless elements to the basic imagery of the art, literature, music, and liturgy of subsequent centuries, as the remaining chapters of this study will suggest. The church Fathers, the early medieval hymnodists, the cathedral builders of the Middle Ages, the painters of the Renaissance, Dante and Milton, Bach and Rembrandt, and other artists on six continents have woven his themes and figures into the texture of the cultural heritage.

16. Jesus released into the common life a spiritual force which, however misunderstood, distorted, and diminished, has worked to reclaim those who knew themselves lost, to elevate morals, to challenge injustice, and to bring inspiration and hope to thousands from his time to our own. From Saul of Tarsus to Francis of Assisi to Toyohiko Kagawa to Martin Luther King, Jr., to Mother Teresa, his words and work have exercised a redemptive and transforming influence.

17. In his own life and person Jesus so fully incarnated the gospel of the kingdom and the good news of God that he himself came to hold a central place in the preaching of his disciples and of the church that came after him. The gospel they proclaimed—his words and deeds, his life and death, his resurrection and abiding presence—

which they believed consistent with his own, became the gospel of Jesus Christ.

To the preaching of those earliest witnesses we now turn.

PART FOUR

Witnesses of Jesus Christ

The First Christian Preachers

The Earliest Christian Preaching

Preaching Jesus as Risen Christ

Shortly after the death of Jesus the disciples who had companied him began proclaiming a message that made three astounding claims. This Jesus who was crucified is alive, for God has raised him from the dead. This crucified and living Jesus is the Messiah, for by raising him God has vindicated him as the anointed Deliverer. This Jesus will return soon to take up his reign, to initiate the kingdom of God.

Gathering a sizeable company of persons attracted during his ministry in Galilee and a rapidly growing number of new believers who responded to their message, the disciples shared a life of worship and service in a new community that they soon came to call the church. And when opposition hardened into persecution, forcing them to flee to other places, they "went about preaching the word" (Acts 8:4 RSV).

Growth of the Church[1]

The earliest strength of the young church lay in Palestine and Syria, spreading out from the regions where Jesus himself had proclaimed the kingdom of God. In Jerusalem, their first major center, some of his apostles and James his brother guided the new company by their teaching. Times were turbulent in Palestine. When anti-Roman sentiment exploded into revolt, the imperial legions retaliated by destroying the temple in 70 C.E. Two generations later, a final rebellion proved even more disastrous: crushing Jewish life and institutions, Rome eliminated Palestine as a center for Judaism and consequently for Christianity as well.

Meanwhile, preachers of Jesus had begun to proclaim the gospel to Gentiles and to baptize them into the faith without requiring adherence to Jewish ceremonial law. Thriving Christian churches sprang up around the eastern Mediterranean, in Asia Minor, Macedonia, Greece, Italy, and Egypt. Antioch, Ephesus, Rome, and Alexandria became important centers of the faith. When in 64 C.E. the Emperor Nero sought a convenient scapegoat to blame for the great fire at Rome, he accused the Christians, a minority already well known—and feared by outsiders.

The Early Preaching: Sources

Appearing in synagogue, market-square, and other public places, Christian evangelists turned up alongside rabbis, mystagogues, and sophists to proclaim the new way of salvation and call their hearers to repentance. Gathering believers into congregations, which met in private homes, a diverse company of prophets, teachers, and exhorters spoke oracles from their living Lord, recalled sayings of Jesus, and encouraged the faithful to endure despite persecution and the delay in the Lord's return. By public preaching, communal recollection, and personal witness the church grew in numbers, capacity to withstand opposition, and insight into its unexpected destiny in unterminated history.

Echoes of the preaching resound in numerous letters, in the four Gospels, and in other Christian tracts that were subsequently assembled as the New Testament; some of these books were written shortly after mid-century, within two or three decades of Jesus, some toward the end of the century, or even later. Though other literary remains from the church of the apostolic era are minimal, the documents that survive as scripture provide considerable information about the first Christian preaching.

Overview of Part Four

This part of our study (chapters 10–13) will consider the preaching of the first Christian century, noting the various persons and offices committed to the ministry of the word, the central elements in the gospel that they made known, representative sermons or sermon-digests, and the historical significance of this preaching.

CHAPTER 10

Servants of the Word

THE UNKNOWN PREACHERS[1]

A Witnessing Community

Scarcely twenty-five years after the death of Jesus, his followers had already condensed the good news into a formalized tradition, received and handed on:

> that Christ died for our sins in accordance with the scriptures,
> and that he was buried,
> and that he was raised on the third day
> in accordance with the scriptures,
> and that he appeared to Cephas, then to the twelve.
> Then he appeared to more than five hundred brothers and sisters
> at one time, most of whom are still alive...   [1 Cor. 15:3–7 NRSV]

Despite the silence of this tradition (for whatever reasons), all four Gospels narrate the first announcement of the resurrection as being given to the women who came to Jesus' tomb to anoint his body; against all expectation, they became the first witnesses and preachers of his rising from the dead. Soon they were joined by the men named in the tradition. Through corporate life and worship and through individual testimony, they proclaimed his resurrection.

Believers who had heard him in the flesh, whether they had experienced a resurrection appearance or not, attested to the "great salvation" (Heb. 2:3). By preaching and teaching, disciples shared the faith and sustained remembrance of Jesus over a period of years, as we have seen, before some believers began to commit their accounts to writing.

247

Handing on the Oral Tradition [2]

Even though students of the New Testament know these facts, and though scholars repeatedly mention *oral tradition* and the *transmission of the passion narrative* by the community, few readers seem to form a vivid picture of *persons speaking to other persons* or of *preachers and teachers* at work with such energy as to bring numerous churches into existence and to continue addressing their members on many occasions.

The announcement of the gospel by these preachers and teachers, especially their repeated recounting of incidents in the ministry of Jesus gave shape to the story. Stereotyped forms developed for rehearsing accounts of healings he had performed, or of his encounters with sinners in need of forgiveness. Some of these narratives followed the pattern of incidents in the Hebrew scriptures. Sometimes an isolated saying of Jesus was added to the account of an incident, serving as a "tag" or "memory verse"—what Hellenistic rhetoricians called a *chreia*.[3] Each incident was boiled down to its essentials, each segment shaped in such a way that the very telling of the story became proclamation of the gospel in a nutshell.

It is not now possible to isolate the work of individual speakers or to assign names to them; whenever we open one of the gospels, we find a compilation edited with a distinctive theological slant and with no little acumen. But between the obvious seams in the grand narratives we can still catch glimpses of the sermonizing of these unknown preachers.

Teachers

In preserving the tradition, the church's teachers played a crucial part. The range of persons covered by this title must have been broad, from the storyteller repeating with unflagging wonder the reminiscence of an eyewitness, to the "scribe...trained for the kingdom of heaven" (Mt. 13:52 NRSV, JS–b) meticulously analyzing the sayings of Jesus in the manner that their counterparts in the rabbinic tradition had long employed to interpret Torah.

Many of the stories about Jesus accord an important place to women. With no argument or declaration that this is something new, even revolutionary, they depict the circle of the Master's immediate disciples as a company differing remarkably from the typical gathering of rabbis in their male sanctum or from a group of Greek men (perhaps accompanied by *hetairai*) in a philosophical symposium. Again and again the gospels name women honored in the Christian community as followers and companions of the Lord. Consider the story of the woman who, a short time before Jesus' death, anointed him with ointment of pure nard, and the commendation lovingly repeated:

> Truly I tell you, wherever the gospel is preached in the whole world, what she has done will be told in memory of her. [Mk. 14:9 RSV, JS–b]

The key involvement of women in so many events of Jesus' public ministry implies a significant role for them as transmitters and guardians of the gospel tradition. The Fourth Evangelist clearly pictures women as preachers.[4]

Besides the well-loved stories, the teachers also conveyed in the Christian *paideia* sayings of Jesus remembered apart from any contextual narrative. One cluster of logia from the tradition occurs in a letter written by Clement of Rome to the church at Corinth near the end of the first Christian century:

> Show mercy, that you may be shown mercy.
> Forgive, that you may be forgiven.
> As you behave to others, so they will behave to you.
> As you give, so will you get.
> As you judge, so you will be judged,
> As you show kindness, so will you receive kindness.
> The measure you give will be the measure you get.[5]

Scribal *midrash* by Christian teachers sometimes attached itself to sayings in the oral tradition:

> Do you not see
> that whatever goes into a person from outside cannot defile...?
> (Thus he declared all foods clean.) [Mk. 7:18–19 NRSV, JS–g]

Digests of homilies by the teachers appear in the tradition as secret explanations of the parables (Mk. 4:13–20; Mt. 13:10–23, 36–43), their exhortations as favorite connecting formulas:

> Let anyone with ears hear! [Mt. 13:43 NRSV, JS–g]

Tradition had Jesus saying to his followers:

> Take my yoke upon you, and learn from me. [Mt. 11:29 NRSV, JS–b]

Then in a time when the disciples themselves were suffering persecution, a vital hermeneutic had the Lord say more pointedly to would-be disciples:

> Let them deny themselves and take up their cross
> and follow me.   [Mk. 8:34 NRSV, JS–b]

The most majestic contribution of the teachers is the passion narrative. Shaped by the annual remembrance of its events in the liturgy, given intensity by early experiences of martyrdom, it attains an elegiac sublimity by its quiet restraint and incorporation of emotionally charged motifs from the Hebrew scriptures. The effect of the entire narrative is overpowering. Even brief incidents convey the somber tone:

> Then the soldiers led him into the courtyard of the palace
> (that is, the governor's headquarters);
> and they called together the whole cohort.
> And they clothed him in a purple cloak;
> and after twisting some thorns into a crown, they put it on him.
> And they began saluting him, "Hail, King of the Jews!"
> They struck his head with a reed,
> spat upon him, and knelt down in homage to him.
> After mocking him, they stripped him of the purple cloak
> and put his own clothes on him.
> Then they led him out to crucify him.   [Mk. 15:16–20 NRSV]

The unpretentious eloquence of unknown teachers fixed in a form of words impossible to forget the story of Jesus' passion. Though thousands of human beings have suffered unjustly, the narrative of *this* suffering claimed the center of the gospel of salvation.

In the earliest days of the church, leading figures in the story would be known to the hearers, at times even telling the tale. Later on, after the community had grown and scattered, the teachers still related their account to persons whom the hearers knew:

> They compelled a passer-by, who was coming in from the country,
> to carry his cross; it was Simon of Cyrene,
> the father of Alexander and Rufus.   [Mk. 15:21 NRSV]

So the tradition linked the community through a chain of flesh and blood to the crucial event of their faith-story.

Prophets and Other Charismatic Speakers[6]

A different kind of contemporaneity occurred in the utterances of prophets. Probably of greater importance than the teachers in the church's first decade or two, they appear more clearly in the record, with occasional snatches of their speech.[7] Some early Christian prophets are known through accounts from hearers; a few are remembered by name, while others are known only by their imprint on the gospel tradition. Under immediate impulse of the divine Spirit, it was believed, they spoke to the community: "For those who bear witness to Jesus have the spirit of prophecy" (Rev. 19:10 REB). In the early Christian gatherings for worship, each member had opportunity to contribute "a hymn, some instruction, a revelation, an ecstatic utterance, or its interpretation" (1 Cor. 14:26 REB). Women enjoyed this opportunity and along with men spoke the word of the Lord to the assembly.[8] Believers were urged to desire the prophetic gift (1 Thess. 5:20; 1 Cor. 14:39), though it could not be achieved by the mere exercise of human will (2 Pet. 1:21).

A related kind of Spirit-prompted utterance was speaking in tongues, glossolalia, a gift prized by many. Paul accepted it as a manifestation of the Spirit and practiced it, but to circumvent the disorder it tended to produce, he sought to limit the number speaking in this fashion and insisted that in every case someone interpret; he understood this capacity to tell the meaning as also a spiritual gift, necessary if the exercise was to make for edification (1 Cor. 14:2–5; cf. 12:7–11). Prophecy he accounted a superior charism, so long as the prophets kept a rein on their eagerness to speak and disciplined themselves to prophesy only one at a time.

Prophets tended to declaim in apocalyptic terms, picturing the end of the age, and some such oracles—in the name of the living Lord—entered the gospel tradition, handed on as words of Jesus.[9]

> If they say to you, "Look! He is in the wilderness," do not go out.
> If they say, "Look! He is in the inner rooms," do not believe it.   [JS-b]
> For as the lightning comes from the east and flashes as far as the west,
> so will be the coming of the Son of Man.   [JS-g] [Mt. 24:26–27 NRSV]

The Revelation to John, the supreme literary example of such apocalyptic "preaching" in the early church, contains numerous references to prophets.[10]

Prophecy also dealt with practical concerns of the ongoing church, such as designating a person to be ordained for ministry (1 Tim. 1:18; 4:14). As the church developed from informal community to ordered institution, the ebullient expression of spiritual gifts was brought under restraint and emphasis was placed on orderly process as the proper channel for the Spirit. The necessity of dealing with false prophets gave impetus to the transition (1 Jn. 4:1–3). Still, the church honored the memory of those who had spoken the living word, associating prophets with apostles and teachers among its divinely given founders.[11]

A sublime oracle from a prophet was incorporated into the infancy narrative of Luke's Gospel:

> Now, Lord, you are releasing your servant in peace,
> according to your promise.
> For I have seen with my own eyes the deliverance
> you have made ready in full view of all nations:
> a light that will bring revelation to the Gentiles
> and glory to your people Israel.   [Lk. 2:29–32 REB]

Ministers of Encouragement

Alongside teaching and prophecy, another kind of speaking dealt with the experience of the believers in the living present and concentrated on motivation. It was *paraklēsis,* which involved exhortation, consolation, and encouragement and can hardly be translated by one word alone. The New Testament uses no noun to designate a disciple as an exhorter or encourager, perhaps for two reasons: (1) All Christians were expected to offer this ministry constantly to one another (1 Thess. 5:11; Heb. 3:13) and (2) the title *Paraclete,* at least in some circles, designated the Holy Spirit (Jn. 14:16) or the living Christ (1 Jn. 2:1). But *paraklēsis* required a number of individual voices, each speaking in personal exhortation (Rom. 12:8), and we cannot adequately picture an early Christian meeting without portraying a speaker or succession of speakers earnestly offering their discourses of admonition and hope. The epistles of the New Testament normally include a section of exhortation near the end, and these suggest well enough the flavor of such address.[12] The gospel tradition also shows a tendency in recounting events in Jesus' life to apply them to problems of Christian living that had subsequently arisen within the community.

The preachers spoke in admonition, urging Christians to maintain their distinctive lifestyle in a pagan world in the face of the Lord's delay in coming. Before impending persecution, they rallied the spirits of believers. Even in undramatic situations there were always some who needed "upbuilding and encouragement and consolation" (1 Cor. 14:3 NRSV). Hence the apostolic counsel:

> We urge you, friends, to rebuke the idle, encourage the faint-hearted,
> support the weak, and be patient with everyone.   [1 Thess. 5:14 REB]

The name that the community gave to Barnabas—"Son of Encouragement"—indicates particular effectiveness in this ministry. (See Acts 4:36, 11:23.) It was akin to teaching and prophecy in being like them a spiritual gift and sharing with them a common purpose:

> You can all prophesy, one at a time,
> so that all may receive instruction and encouragement.
>
> [1 Cor. 14:31 REB]

Teaching and motivation were the intention of that ministry of the word to the faithful that claimed so much of the energy of the apostles and their coworkers in the gospel.

Missionary Heralds

In its primary sense, however, preaching meant announcing the good news to those on the outside. The apostles, in the literal meaning of their title, were persons who had been sent on this mission; evangelists were the carriers of the gospel; preachers were its heralds. Some of these, to be considered momentarily, are well known to us through documents describing their work. Some have been commemorated in local legends concerning the pioneers of the word of salvation in a particular place. So, it is piously said, the apostle Thomas took the gospel to India, the evangelist Mark to Egypt, the disciple Joseph of Arimathea to Britain. Each of the apostles holds a place of honor in some such legend, which in some instances may enshroud a relic of authentic history.

In any case, the documents in the New Testament clearly attest to the existence of Christian communities from Palestine on around the northeast quadrant of the Mediterranean to Italy and imply others reaching from Mesopotamia to Ethiopia and along the coasts of North Africa, while Paul the apostle long cherished the purpose, perhaps realized, of taking the gospel to Spain. Within two generations after Jesus, thousands of religious seekers, even in remote regions of the Hellenistic world, had responded to the missionaries of this new and demanding faith. Among the many ways of salvation offered by the philosophical schools and mystery religions, Christianity had become one of the strongest contenders. Hundreds of congregations formed a network spread across the *oikoumené* to "shine like stars in a dark world" (Phil. 2:15 REB).

The remarkably rapid rise of so numerous a community of adherents to a new faith, with strength of conviction sufficient to survive the destruction of its original base in Jerusalem and to withstand two Roman persecutions before 100 C.E., points to a large company of mobile and persuasive preachers vigorously at work throughout the empire.

For the spread of the gospel they relied on the spoken word and acts of human helpfulness inspired by the love of Jesus Christ. The literary remains of their preaching are limited to particular pericopes that can be isolated within the gospel tradition, to the highly programmatic account in the Acts of the Apostles, and to sections of the New Testament epistles; these letters remain close to oral discourse, some of them at least having been dictated to a scribe and nearly all having been designed to be read aloud to congregations. (All that was lacking was the personal presence and impulsive delivery of the sender.).

The letters of the apostle Paul suggest the flavor of the missionary preaching, its evangelistic appeal being suggested by a snatch from a Christian hymn:

> Sleeper, awake! Rise from the dead,
> And Christ will shine on you.   [Eph. 5:14 NRSV]

Something of the content of a gospel addressed to inquirers in search of salvation echoes through another hymn, which honors Christ Jesus as "the mystery of our religion":

> He was manifested in flesh, vindicated in spirit, seen by angels;
> he was proclaimed among the nations,
> believed in throughout the world,
> raised to heavenly glory.   [1 Tim. 3:16 REB]

The missionary preachers had limited success in Galilee and among Jews generally, but the response of Gentiles was so large and continuous that they soon outnumbered Jewish Christians within the church. As a result, the missionaries very early began to use concepts and imagery from Hellenistic thought and the vocabulary of the mystery religions as well as from the Hebrew scriptures, as Jewish missionaries and Alexandrian exegetes had done before them. In the books of the New Testament, though this development had not yet gone far, one can hear echoes of Platonic, Aristotelian, and Stoic teachings—not systematic arguments addressed to professional philosophers, but ideas and phrases that popular audiences would have heard from traveling sophists.[13]

The distinctive plea of the Christian missionaries is suggested by Paul's summary characterization:

We are…Christ's ambassadors.
It is as if God were appealing to you through us:
We implore you in Christ's name, be reconciled to God!

[2 Cor. 5:20 REB]

As we turn now to a consideration of some of the more famous teachers and missionaries, it is fitting to remember the immense activity of the scores of unknown preachers who carried the word of Jesus to speech-loving crowds across the *oikoumené* and left new companies of believers in their wake.

APOSTLES AND OTHER REMEMBERED PREACHERS[14]

Outstanding in the ranks of the earliest preachers a few will be remembered so long as Christianity endures. Set apart, as they believed, by their particular charisms or gifts from the Spirit of the living Lord, by the providential circumstances of their lives, and by their faithfulness, they were uniquely endowed for preaching.

The Women at the Tomb

Prominent in all four Gospel accounts of Jesus' resurrection are the women who, on the first day of the week, just after his crucifixion and burial, first discovered that his body was not in the tomb. In the Gospel according to Mark a young man meets them at the sepulcher with a stupendous announcement, imposing on them the first commission to preach it:

Do not be alarmed;
you are looking for Jesus of Nazareth, who was crucified.
He has been raised; he is not here.
Look, there is the place they laid him.
But go, tell his disciples and Peter…   [Mk. 16:6–7 NRSV]

In the oldest extant text of Mark this commission is the only one reported after the resurrection.

The Gospel according to John names Mary Magdalene as the first person to whom the risen Jesus appeared, and Matthew recounts an appearance to the group of women. These first appointed preachers of the risen Lord are listed by Mark as Mary Magdalene, Mary the mother of James, and Salome. (16:1) According to John, Mary Magdalene first proclaimed the incredible event in the words,

I have seen the Lord!   [Jn. 20:18 REB]

Even though the early tradition cited by Paul does not mention the women by name, it is notable that the four evangelists subsequently concur in listing them as the first witnesses of the resurrection, the first to announce the amazing good news, and that both Mark and Matthew recount an angelic commission to them to proclaim it. In the secure house where the apostles, all males, still cowered in sorrow and fear, these women were the first Christian preachers. They must have preceded all the others. In a society bound by the presuppositions and customs of patriarchy, who would have *invented* primacy for *them*—and why?—unless they had been first with the news?

Simon Peter

Singled out by the new name Jesus had given him—it persisted in the tradition also in its Aramaic form, Cephas—was Simon Peter, foremost among the disciples in the days of Jesus' ministry and in the early years of the church.

In the stories about the inner circle around Jesus, told as part of the gospel tradition, Peter repeatedly speaks for the group. In the first half of the Acts of the Apostles (written near the end of the first century) he is the leader of the new Christian community, its first and foremost public preacher (see chapter 12). The First Epistle of Peter offers his pastoral counsel to the scattered churches, and the Gospel according to Mark (about the year 70) was believed by Papias (second quarter of the second century) to have reported the gist of his preaching. He was remembered as speaking in the distinctive accent of Galilee (Mt. 26:73).

The Twelve

With Peter the early traditions associated the other leading men among Jesus' disciples as "The Twelve." Each of the Synoptic Gospels, as also the book of Acts, in reporting that Jesus "appointed twelve" to preach, gives a list of names, though there is variation among them.[15]

The brothers James and John, along with Simon Peter and his brother Andrew, all fishers at first, form the inmost circle among the disciples and figure prominently in the early chapters of Acts. James was beheaded by Herod Agrippa I in the earliest persecution in Jerusalem. Several books of the New Testament bear the name of John, though scholars divide in their conclusions as to whether or not any of these derive from the apostle by that name. As to other members of the Twelve (aside from Judas Iscariot, who committed suicide after betraying Jesus), the only information about their preaching is legendary. Christian usage early came to denominate these men as the "twelve apostles," but in the first years of the church the title *apostle* was a more inclusive term; certainly this was true in Paul's usage, as it appears to have been in the reference (cited above) to "all the apostles." In any case, those who bore the title were preachers.

The Brothers of the Lord

Never mentioned in the gospels as a disciple during Jesus' lifetime is his brother James, who according to the attestation in the tradition received an appearance of the risen Lord and who soon came to share with Simon Peter the supreme leadership of the church in Jerusalem. The Acts of the Apostles includes a deliberative speech attributed to James (15:13–21), and the publication of an epistle bearing his name further suggests his importance. Paul lists "the brothers of the Lord" along with the apostles as leaders of the church during the first generation (1 Cor. 9:5), and Mark gives their names as James and Joses and Judas and Simon (6:3), but nothing is known of their preaching.

Paul's Coworkers in the Gospel

By far the best known of the early preachers, because of his extensive correspondence preserved in the Christian scripture, is the apostle Paul; through his letters we catch glimpses of an impressive company of coworkers in the gospel.

Barnabas labors alongside Paul in Antioch and accompanies him to Jerusalem,[16] as does Titus, a Greek.[17] Silvanus (Silas) (1 Thess. 1:1; 2 Cor. 1:19) and Timothy[18] travel with him on a mission through Macedonia and Achaia, the latter commuting among the churches as Paul's representative; through the years, writes the apostle, "like a son with a father he has served with me in the work of the gospel" (Phil. 2:22 NRSV). After Paul's establishment of a church in Corinth, Apollos labors there to build it up (1 Cor. 1:12; 3:4–8; 4:6; 16:12). Prisca (Priscilla) and Aquila are leaders of a church that meets in their house; they have "risked their necks for my life" (1 Cor. 16:19; Rom. 16:3–4). All of these except Titus also appear as significant figures in the book of Acts, even though the author indicates no familiarity with Paul's letters.

The roll call of Paul's fellow preachers has scarcely begun. It includes, unnamed, "the brother who is famous among all the churches for his preaching of the gospel" (2 Cor. 8:18 RSV). "Our sister Phoebe" is a minister (*diakonos*) of the church at Cenchreae and a helper of the apostle (Rom. 16:1, 2). Andronicus and Junia [Julia], also imprisoned along with him, are "eminent among the apostles and were Christians before I was" (Rom. 16:7 REB).

Several are mentioned as "workers": Mary, Urbanus, Tryphaena and Tryphosa, Persis (Rom. 16:6, 9, 12), Demas, Luke (Philem. 24). Did their hard work include preaching? Epaphras, a faithful minister of Christ, is also Paul's fellow prisoner (Col. 1:7, 4:12; Philem. 23). So likewise is Aristarchus, who along with Barnabas's cousin Mark and Jesus called Justus represents the Jewish Christians in working with Paul during the latter days of his ministry (Col. 4:10). Nympha heads a house church (Col. 4:15), as do Philemon and Apphia (Philem. 1, 2). Archippus is Paul's "fellow soldier" (Col. 4:17; Philem. 2). Tychicus serves as representative of the imprisoned Paul in strengthening (exhorting) the churches (Col. 4:7). Epaphroditus of Philippi is Paul's "brother and co-worker and fellow soldier" who "nearly died" in Christ's service (Phil. 2:25–30; 4:18 NRSV). The women Euodia and Syntyche have labored side by side with Paul in the gospel (Phil. 4:2–3 RSV), as has Clement, his coworker (Phil. 4:3).

The names of a number of these preachers turn up in the late Pastoral Epistles, which appear to have been written in Paul's name by one of his disciples and helpers some years after his death, but also preserve authentic reminiscences. In addition to preachers already named, these letters link with him in the work of the gospel Artemas (Titus 3:12), Zenas the lawyer—was he an orator?—(Titus 3:13), Crescens (2 Tim. 4:10), Erastus, and Trophimus (2 Tim. 4:20).

Whatever the "office" or ecclesiastical status of these people, here are more than thirty Christians mentioned individually by Paul as working with him in the gospel (read *preaching*—or, perhaps, *witnessing*). Perhaps yet other persons whom he names in his letters but whose work he does not identify should be added to this impressive list. One of these, doubtless, is Onesimus, the slave (possibly a runaway) whom he converted in prison and sent back, with a touching letter, to Philemon and Apphia and the church in their house. At the end of the century the church at Ephesus had a bishop named Onesimus, possibly this same person.

Preachers in Acts

The Acts of the Apostles recounts the preaching activity, not only of Peter and John, James the brother of the Lord, Paul, Barnabas, Silas, and others mentioned in connection with Paul, but a number of impressive preachers besides.

Stephen appears as the first to die for the faith, being stoned in the presence of Saul of Tarsus just before the latter's conversion (chaps. 6, 7). Philip evangelizes Samaria and the Mediterranean coast (chap. 8). Ananias of Damascus takes the word of the Lord to Saul after his encounter with the risen Jesus and restores his sight (9:10–19). Refugees from the persecution over Stephen preach in Antioch, converting Gentiles as well as Jews (11:19–26).

Agabus (11:28; 21:10–11), the four daughters of Philip the evangelist (21:9), and Judas called Barsabbas (15:22–23) are prophets. In Antioch Symeon called Niger and Lucius of Cyrene—were these men black?—and Manaen, along with Barnabas and Saul, are "prophets and teachers" (13:1). Erastus is a helper of Paul (19:22), as are Gaius of Derbe and Aristarchus from Macedonia (19:29; 20:4), Sopater of Beroea, Secundus of Thessalonica, and Trophimus the Ephesian (20:4; 21:29). Here are seventeen additional persons beyond those mentioned in the letters.

Besides all these, the unnamed elders of the church at Ephesus are bidden to "feed the church of the Lord" (20:28 RSV).

Preaching Offices

The activity of so large a company of remembered persons indicates the importance of the ministry of the word in the church of the first century. The community used many names to denote aspects of this work, including *prophets, evangelists, teachers, preachers (heralds, announcers, proclaimers), ministers of the gospel or of the word, exhorters, counselors, leaders* (these were speakers), *witnesses, speakers in various kinds of tongues, interpreters of tongues, ambassadors for Christ.* Ministry of the word was clearly a major responsibility of the key offices in the young church: apostles, the Twelve, the Seven, pastors or shepherds of the flock, elders or presbyters, guardians or overseers or superintendents or bishops, rulers or leaders, workers. While some of these preachers earned their living by a craft or trade, after the manner of Paul and the Jewish rabbis before him, it was taught as a command of the Lord that

> those who preach the gospel
> should get their living by the gospel.   [1 Cor. 9:14 REB]

PAUL'S ACCOUNT OF HIS WORK AS A PREACHER[19]

The Correspondence

Moving through the host of unknown preachers and the impressive company now remembered only by name was the indefatigable missionary Paul. His care for the young churches established by his preaching led to repeated visits and to an extensive correspondence, prized and preserved by the community—to become Christian scripture. In them we have a full-length self-portrait of one of the chief preachers of the apostolic age, and certainly the best known, whose influence over subsequent preaching has been unsurpassed.

The following chronology, or one very similar, is widely accepted:

1 Thessalonians (50 C.E.)
2 Thessalonians (50–51)
1 Corinthians and Galatians (54–55)
2 Corinthians (55)
Romans (56)
Colossians, Philemon, and Philippians (59–61).

Other letters bearing Paul's name (Ephesians, 1 and 2 Timothy, Titus) appear to have issued from disciples of the great apostle seeking to guide the churches some decades later by his mind and spirit. From the earlier, generally accepted letters, and without appealing to the idealized picture in the book of Acts, we can draw the following portrait of the preacher.

"Entrusted with the Gospel"

Paul understands himself as a preacher and commends himself to others under that title. He, Silvanus, and Timothy "have been entrusted with the gospel" (1 Thess. 2:4 REB). God has assigned parallel and complementary destinies to him and to Cephas: "For the same God who was at work in Peter's mission to the Jews was also at work in mine to the Gentiles." (Gal. 2:8 REB). Having received

> the privilege of an apostolic commission to bring people of all nations
> to faith and obedience in his name   [Rom. 1:5 REB]

Paul can say :

> I have an obligation to Greek and non-Greek,
> to learned and simple;   [REB]
> so I am eager to preach the gospel.   [RSV] [Rom. 1:14–15]

He calls himself "a minister of Christ Jesus to the Gentiles in the priestly service of the gospel of God" (Rom. 15:16). With the other preachers he has an obligation to act "consistently with the truth of the gospel" (Gal. 2:14 NRSV). They are "stewards of God's mysteries" (1 Cor. 4:1 NRSV).

Upbringing in Judaism

Born and nurtured in Judaism, Paul can claim the signs of prestige in that community:

Circumcised on my eighth day, Israelite by race,
of the tribe of Benjamin, a Hebrew born and bred;
in my practice of the law a Pharisee,
in zeal for religion a persecutor of the church,
by the law's standard of righteousness without fault. [Phil. 3:5–6 REB]

In the same vein he claims:

In the practice of our national religion
I outstripped most of my Jewish contemporaries
by my boundless devotion to the traditions. [Gal. 1:14 REB]

The book of Acts presents Paul as also a Roman citizen, brought up among the Hellenistic Jews of Tarsus, a sizeable city of Asia Minor, and given advanced education in the academy of Rabbi Gamaliel. The forthright quotation of Hellenistic authors attributed to Paul in Acts may constitute part of the color supplied by the author in keeping with the manner of Hellenistic historians, but in the epistles Paul uses enough catch phrases from the sophists and mystagogues to indicate familiarity with the intellectual and spiritual currents of the times without falling in behind any of the popular philosophers as an intellectual or spiritual disciple. In this respect he resembles the Palestinian rabbis. Chronological possibility and cultural probability make for an interesting game of imagining particular philosophers or moralists Saul may have heard as a youth in Tarsus or books he may have read in school, but we can only say, "Perhaps." After his conversion, he avows,

All such assets I have written off because of Christ. [Phil. 3:7 REB]

and he mentions no mentors—pagan, Jewish, or Christian.

Conversion and Commission

Paul recites no account detailing a colorful life as a sinner or testifying to dramatic details of his conversion. He simply affirms that the crucified and risen Christ appeared to him "last of all" (1 Cor. 15:8). In handing on the tradition concerning the resurrection, with its list of witnesses, Paul stakes his own claim to membership in that company; though he did not become a disciple until some time after those appearances, he boldly adds his own name to the list in the early tradition:

> Last of all, as to one untimely born,
> he appeared also to me.   [1 Cor. 15:8 NRSV]

The risen Christ has ranked him among the apostles because he has seen "Jesus our Lord" (9:1), not during the days of his earthly ministry but after the resurrection. That encounter effected not only his conversion but also his commission as an apostle and preacher:

> God, who had set me apart before I was born,
> and called me through his grace,
> was pleased to reveal his Son to me,
> so that I might proclaim him among the Gentiles.   [Gal. 1:15–16 NRSV]

In this decisive act God had commissioned him (2 Cor. 1:21 RSV) and empowered him to be the minister of a new covenant (3:6 REB), which he understands not as a repudiation of Judaism, but as a fulfilment of the promises given in the scriptures (Rom. 1:1–6). The totality of spiritual transformation by which "Christ Jesus has made me his own" (Phil. 3:12) beats at the heart of Paul's gospel (Gal. 2:20 REB):

> I have been crucified with Christ: the life I now live
> is not my life, but the life which Christ lives in me;
> and my present mortal life is lived by faith in the Son of God,
> who loved me and gave himself up for me.   [Gal. 2:20 REB]

Paul insists that he received this knowledge of Christ from no one else, but directly from the living Lord (Gal. 1:11–12). After that event he went off to Arabia and then returned to Damascus; only after three years did he go to Jerusalem to visit with Cephas for fifteen days, during which he also saw James, the Lord's brother. It is possible that from them or previously from others Paul received some of the content of the Christian tradition that he handed on (1 Cor. 11:23–25; 15:3–7), but, instead of providing information on that score, he insists that his apostolic authority came directly from Christ.

Work as a Preacher
Whether or not the new convert preached during his three years in Arabia and Damascus, he does not say, though we may readily infer that he did. After his visit to Jerusalem he evangelized in Syria and Cilicia, the province where Tarsus was located, evoking wonder in the Christian congregations that "our former persecutor is preaching the good news of the faith which he once tried to destroy" (Gal. 1:23 REB).

He spent some time in Antioch, where the conversion of many Gentiles caused such disturbance in the Christian community at Jerusalem that Paul went with Barnabas and Titus, one of his converts, to lay before the church there the gospel he preached, with the result that James and Cephas and John publicly commended his mission. When Cephas on a follow-up visit to Antioch first ate with the Gentiles there, then drew back after a delegation of hardliners came from Jerusalem, Paul opposed him before the church, continuing to proclaim his inclusive gospel (Gal. 2).

Paul now enlarged the geographical scope of his mission. Despite a severe physical ailment, perhaps an affliction of the eyes, he preached in Galatia (Gal. 4:12–15), calling churches into being "in the grace of Christ" (Gal. 1:6). Soon he had made his way to Macedonia. After suffering and shameful treatment in Philippi, he and Silvanus and Timothy moved on to declare the gospel of God at Thessalonica in the face of great opposition (1 Thess. 2:1–2). Turning from idolatry enough converts to establish a new church, the evangelists cared for them, like a nurse or a father looking after children, meanwhile working to earn their own living (1:9; 2:7–9). When opposition brought suffering to the church and drove the missionaries from the city, they proceeded to Athens (and then to Corinth, to add a detail from Acts 18:1), but Paul's concern for the young church moved him to send Timothy back for a visit and then to write a letter, First Thessalonians, probably composed in 50–51, a mere two decades after Jesus' death.[20]

In Corinth also Paul preached and baptized, suffering want until the church in Macedonia sent a contribution for his support. After traveling back to Asia (presumably Ephesus) he kept in touch with the Corinthians through a succession of letters and return visits.

Meanwhile Paul had launched a demanding venture that consumed much of his time and energy, the collection of a great offering from the Gentile churches for the poor in Jerusalem. This project involved him in extended correspondence and travel among the churches he had founded in Macedonia and Achaia. Before leaving with representatives from these churches to take their gift to Jerusalem he wrote, however, to the church in distant Rome, expressing his hope of visiting them after returning from Judea—*on his way to Spain.*

To the Romans he summarized the sweep of his missionary work:

> In Christ Jesus I have indeed grounds for pride in the service of God.
> I will venture to speak only of what Christ has done through me
> to bring the Gentiles into his allegiance, by word and deed...
> I have completed the preaching of the gospel of Christ

from Jerusalem as far round as Illyricum.
But I have always made a point of taking the gospel to places
where the name of Christ has not been heard...
as scripture says, *Those who had no news of him shall see,*
and those who never heard of him shall understand.   [Rom. 15:17–21 REB]

Paul's work as a preacher involved him in toil, hardship, and suffering, which he bore with steadfast endurance:

in affliction, hardship, and distress;
when flogged, imprisoned, mobbed;
overworked, sleepless, starving.
We recommend ourselves...by gifts of the Holy Spirit,
by unaffected love, by declaring the truth, by the power of God...
Honour and dishonour, praise and blame, are alike our lot:
we are the impostors who speak the truth...
poor ourselves, we bring wealth to many;
penniless, we own the world.   [2 Cor. 6:4–10 REB]

Despite a physical affliction, which he termed a "thorn in the flesh" (2 Cor. 12:7) and which repeated prayer did not remove, he endured the constant pressure of "anxiety for all the churches" (2 Cor. 11:28). But now he must journey back to Jerusalem.

Imprisoned yet again "for the defense of the gospel" (Phil. 1:16), Paul continued to preach through personal conversation and correspondence, converting the slave Onesimus (Philem. 10) and spreading some knowledge of Christ among his guards (Phil. 1:12–13). A late letter of the Pauline school attributes to him in his last imprisonment words that may well have come from the aging apostle:

As for me, my life is already being poured out on the altar,
and the hour for my departure is upon me.
I have run the great race, I have finished the course,
I have kept the faith.   [2 Tim. 4:6–7 REB]

No other preacher of Jesus Christ has done more or exercised so large an influence.

CHAPTER 11

"Power of God for Salvation"

"THE GOSPEL OF GOD, THE GOSPEL CONCERNING HIS SON"[1]

What Was It?

What was the good news proclaimed by the great company of preachers? It was so rich, so extensive, so transforming, and was preached with such variety of emphasis that any effort to reduce it to a phrase or simple formula serves only to conceal its fulness and thus to misinterpret it. The effort once made to isolate the essential elements in the apostolic preaching as *kerygma,* in sharp distinction from the ethical teaching, *didache,* commended to believers after their conversion, oversimplifies and distorts.[2] To answer the question here we shall consider the earliest extant written evidence, the letters of Paul, not as theological essays nor even as presumed summaries of his proclamation, but as historical documents that repeatedly specify what the churches had heard him preach.

The Early Tradition

Writing to the Corinthian church about 54–55, Paul reminds them of the evangel he brought to them when he handed on the tradition that he had also received and by which they were saved (1 Cor. 15:1). We have already noted that tradition (chapter 10), thought to be one of the earliest summary confessions of Christian faith. This central content of his message Paul could condense even further, for he reminds the same Corinthians:

> I resolved that while I was with you I would not claim to know anything but Jesus Christ—Christ nailed to the cross. [1 Cor. 2:2 REB]

Yet writing from Corinth to the church at Rome only a few months later, Paul gives a carefully wrought summary of his evangel without specifically referring to the crucifixion:

> This gospel God announced beforehand in sacred scriptures...
> It is about his Son: on the human level he was a descendant of David,
> but on the level of the Spirit—the Holy Spirit—he was proclaimed
> Son of God by an act of power that raised him from the dead:
> it is about Jesus Christ our Lord.   [Rom. 1:2–4 REB]

The one common element in the three summaries is their reference to Jesus Christ and his death. Evidently when Paul spoke of Christ, the name implied the fulness spelled out in the traditional confession, whether each particular element was specified or not, as it also implied Christ's expected coming again, to which none of these summaries alludes. This fulness of faith was implicit in the very term *gospel*, which Paul used to catch up the essence of his preaching, even when he made no mention of any of the particular elements.

> For I am not ashamed of the gospel; it is the power of God for salvation
> to everyone who has faith, to the Jew first and also to the Greek.
> For in it the righteousness of God is revealed,
> through faith for faith.   [Rom. 1:16–17 NRSV]
> (*or:* beginning in faith and ending in faith.   [REB])

But Paul's preaching included much more than these nutshells could hold.

The Word in Thessalonica

Paul's stay at Thessalonica was brief (Acts 17:1–10), and he wrote his first letter to the church there within weeks of his departure. He filled it with references to what he had shared with them, as "our message of the gospel came to you" (1 Thess. 1:5). In response to the preaching,

> You turned from idols to be servants of the true and living God,
> and to wait expectantly for his Son from heaven,
> whom he raised from the dead,
> Jesus our deliverer from the retribution to come.   [1 Thess. 1:9–10 REB]

Even though the letter has been prompted by questions that have been disturbing the Thessalonians concerning the coming of the Lord, Paul asserts that they have no need of explanation with regard to times and seasons:

> For you yourselves know perfectly well
> that the day of the Lord comes like a thief in the night.
> While they are saying, "All is peaceful, all secure,"
> destruction is upon them,
> sudden as the pangs that come on a woman in childbirth;
> and there will be no escape.
> But you, friends, are not in the dark:
> the day will not come upon you like a thief.
> You are all children of light, children of day.
> We do not belong to night and darkness,
> and we must not sleep like the rest, but keep awake
>
> [1 Thess. 5:2–6 REB]

Both Paul's assurance that his converts already know clearly about the parousia and his reiteration of assurance concerning it indicate what a large place the expectation has held in his preaching. The language and imagery here are closer to that of the gospel tradition than almost any other passage in Paul.[3] Both that tradition and the apostle couch their eschatological hope in the idea of Jesus' coming again rather than in his expectation of the kingdom of God.

Confusion continued among the Thessalonians, and within a few months Paul wrote them again to try to settle their thinking. Again he refers to his preaching among them: "I told you these things when I was still with you" (2 Thess. 2:5). So now he reminds them about "the day":

> That day will not come unless the rebellion comes first
> and the lawless one is revealed,
> the one destined for destruction.   [2:3–4 NRSV]

Concerning the lawless one, the Thessalonians also know

> what is now restraining him,
> so that he may be revealed when his time comes.   [2:6 NRSV]

That the excitement about the coming of the Lord flared up at Thessalonica *after* Paul's departure suggests that his preaching there evidently had included, but not majored in, the theme. His comment about praying for the Thessalonians makes this fact clear:

> We must always give thanks to God for you,
> brothers and sisters beloved by the Lord,
> because God chose you as the first fruits for salvation
> through sanctification by the Spirit and through belief in the truth.

> For this purpose he called you
> through our proclamation of the good news,
> so that you may obtain the glory of our Lord Jesus Christ.
> So then, brothers and sisters, stand firm and hold fast
> to the traditions that you were taught by us.   [2 Thess. 2:13–15 NRSV]

A benediction follows, calling on

> our Lord Jesus Christ himself and God our Father,who loved us
> and through grace gave us eternal comfort and good hope.
>
> [2 Thess. 2:16 NRSV]

The tradition handed on by Paul dealt with conduct as well as belief in God.

> These are our instructions to you...
> hold aloof from every Christian who falls into idle habits,
> and disregards the tradition you received from us...
> Already during our stay with you we laid down this rule:
> anyone who will not work shall not eat.   [2 Thess. 3:6–10 REB]

In this matter as in other aspects of behavior the Thessalonians know—that is, they have been told by the preachers—

> how you ought to follow our example: you never saw us idling;
> we did not accept free hospitality from anyone;
> night and day in toil and drudgery we worked for a living,
> rather than be a burden to any of you...
> to set an example for you to follow.   [3:7–10 REB]

The code of conduct was plainly taught:

> we appealed to you, we encouraged you, we urged you,
> to live lives worthy of the God who calls you
> into his kingdom and glory.   [1 Thess. 2:12 REB]

Despite the brevity of his stay in Thessalonica, the evangelist reminds the converts,

> You know what instructions we gave you   [NRSV]
> in the name of the Lord Jesus.   [REB]
> This is the will of God, that you should be holy:
> you must abstain from immorality;   [RSV]
> that each one of you must know
> how to control your own body in holiness and honor,   [NRSV]
> not giving way to lust like the pagans
> who know nothing of God.   [REB]   [1 Thess. 4:2–5]

The code also had a positive side:

> You are yourselves taught by God to love one another,
> and you are in fact practicing this rule of love
> toward all your fellow-Christians throughout Macedonia.
> Yet we appeal to you, friends, to do better still.
> Let it be your ambition to live quietly
> and attend to your own business;
> and to work with your hands, as we told you,
> so that you may command the respect
> of those outside your own number,
> and at the same time never be in want.   [1 Thess. 4:9b–12 REB]

Yet neither belief in the gospel nor exemplary living would guarantee freedom from suffering.

> For when we were with you we warned you
> that we were bound to suffer hardship;
> and so it has turned out.   [1 Thess. 3:4 REB]

All these admonitions, Paul specifically reminds the Thessalonians, were part of his message to them when he brought them the gospel. Repeatedly he buttresses his exhortation with terms like "you know," "I told you," "I taught you the tradition"[4] If one were to read the letters carefully to lift out everything which is assumed as already part of the Thessalonians' faith or a clear implication of what they were told at the beginning, considerably more material could be added. The echoes here cited, however, indicate the range of Paul's gospel made known during a very brief mission as well as the considerable emphasis he evidently had laid on the coming of the Lord.

The "traditions" that Paul specifically recalls in this correspondence have more to do with conduct than with the confession of faith, showing kinship with both the rabbis and the popular moralists, the orators most concerned with ethics. Yet a broad understanding of and love for Father, Son, and Spirit are assumed. The elements of "the *kérygma*" once listed by C. H. Dodd and other New Testament scholars as central to the preaching are nowhere brought together in the Thessalonian correspondence, and some are scarcely even implied.[5]

Interestingly enough, Paul does not use either of the two chief verbs for preaching in these letters. "To bring good news" (*euangelizesthein*) appears once in its original secular sense (1 Thess. 3:6), but does not refer to proclamation. "To preach" (*kérussein*) occurs not at all. Yet the passages we have cited clearly constitute, at least in part, the gospel Paul proclaimed during his brief mission in Thessalonica (1 Thess. 1:5). That preaching echoes hauntingly through the letter.

The Gospel in Galatia

The gospel that Paul recalls having preached to the Galatians has a different emphasis. Without our analyzing it at comparable length, its essence is clear. It is Paul's message to the Gentiles, by which they were "called...in the grace of Christ" (1:6) and from which they have turned to "a different gospel."

> You foolish Galatians! Who has bewitched you?
> It was before your eyes
> that Jesus Christ was publicly exhibited as crucified.   [Gal. 3:1 NRSV]

The gospel Paul had preached was a call to freedom from the Law, but not a freedom to be misused as opportunity for self-indulgence (5:13). Against such permissiveness the preacher had warned them clearly enough:

> Now the works of the flesh are obvious:
> fornication, impurity, licentiousness, idolatry, sorcery,
> enmities, strife, jealousy, anger, quarrels, dissensions, factions,
> envy, drunkenness, carousing, and things like these.
> I am warning you, as I warned you before:
> those who do such things
> will not inherit the kingdom of God.   [Gal. 5:19–21 NRSV]

Faithful to the gospel he has preached to them, Paul reminds the Galatians:

> Christ redeemed us from the curse of the law.   [Gal. 4:13 NRSV]

He surprises with a touching image expressing both his purpose in preaching and the agony of his heart:

> You are my children, and I am again in the pain of childbirth
> until Christ is formed in you.   [Gal. 4:19 REB, NRSV]

The Preaching at Corinth

Paul uses a similar figure, this time with male rather than female imagery, in addressing his converts in Corinth:

> In Christ Jesus I became your father
> through the preaching of the gospel.   [1 Cor. 4:15 NRSV, REB]

To them he recalls his preaching at some length (1 Cor., chaps. 1–4), with the clear indication that they know this message well. He contrasts it with what they might hear from sophists, scribes, and other wandering disputants whose teachings have no power to save (1:25–30).[6]

To the Corinthian church Paul has delivered the traditions (11:2). He repeats those dealing with the Lord's supper (11:23–26) and the summary confession (15:3–7) and implies also those setting forth the code of behavior. Their range is suggested in one passage by a repeated question reminding them of his message:

> Do you not know that the saints will judge the world?...
> Do you not know that we are to judge angels?...
> Do you not know that wrongdoers will not inherit the kingdom of God?...
> Do you not know that your bodies are limbs and organs of Christ?...
> Do you not know that whoever is united to a prostitute
>   becomes one body with her?...
> Do you not know that your body is a temple
>   of the indwelling Holy Spirit? [1 Cor. 6:2–19 NRSV alt.]

These questions recall what even the dullest Corinthian ought to be able to remember from the apostle's message, the essence of his preaching on eschatology, ethics, spirituality, and life in the Christian community. It is all part of the gospel.

> So we preach and so you believed. [1 Cor. 15:11 RSV]

The Fullness of the Preaching

The few passages in which Paul specifically recalls the message he has communicated in establishing three new churches indicate the fulness of his gospel. No one phrase or sentence specifies it all; each phrase or sentence implies it all.

The epistles build upon and amplify what the new believers already know. Nowhere does the apostle suggest that in writing he is admitting them to secrets previously withheld, even though he chides the Corinthians as "infants in Christ," able to handle only milk, not solid food (1 Cor. 3:2).

Nowhere does Paul indicate a sharp distinction between preaching (*kérygma*) and teaching (*didaché*), between his missionary preaching and his pastoral exhortation. He preaches Jesus Christ, "born of a woman" (Gal. 4:4), "who for their sake died and was raised to life" (2 Cor. 5:15 REB), "in accordance with the scriptures" (1 Cor. 15:3-4), who is coming to reign (1 Cor. 15:23–25). He says little more of the life and the teachings of Jesus. He preaches the indwelling Spirit who sanctifies the believers and unites them in the church. He preaches the manner of life to which Christians are called.

All the elements of his gospel Paul sees as according with the purpose of God to justify both Jews and Greeks who respond in faith to its proclamation. So he preaches in gratitude:

> I am always thanking God for you.
> I thank him for his grace given to you in Christ Jesus;
> I thank him for all the enrichment that has come to you in Christ.
> You possess full knowledge and you can give full expression to it,
> because what we testified about Christ
> has been confirmed in your experience...
> It is God himself who called you to share in the life of his Son,
> Jesus Christ our Lord; and God keeps faith.   [1 Cor. 1:4–6, 9 REB]

This summary sketch of Paul's preaching as the apostle himself recalls it warns us against any attempt, including his own (1 Cor. 2:1), to condense it all into a single phrase or idea. The fullness of his gospel was too great to be caught in the net of a single concept or precept. It began with God. It centered in the grace of Jesus Christ. It was empowered by the Holy Spirit. It broke the power of sin over ordinary people. It called believers to a new life in Christ, and gave direction for clean, ethical, loving, joyous behavior. It brought the church into being. Quietly it portended a new social order, not by publicly setting the axe of protest to the root of systemic evil, but by awakening in the hearts of believers a new vision and directing the Christian community to new kinds of relationships. It offered hope of personal resurrection in the final reign of Christ. It redeemed, enlarged and ennobled the lives of those who heard it. It dealt in faith, hope, love—and joy.

We do not really have a sermon from Paul, though he packaged seeds for thousands of them. We can only imagine his presence, his voice, his mannerisms as a preacher. We can conclude a good deal about his rhetoric from the style of his letters and the way he argued in them. We can try to work out a systematic summary of his theology. But if we want to hear him preach, the best we can do is to work through the recollections he calls to mind for those new communities of faith in Christ that he brought into being by his missionary work. We can look beneath the surface of his letters to see what reminders he presses or assumes that the recipients already know. Uncovering what the great apostle took for granted in the memory of these new believers brings us as close to his preaching (and to that of the earliest Christian missionaries) as we are likely to come.

"IN ACCORDANCE WITH THE SCRIPTURES" [7]

"Promised Beforehand"

The tradition that Paul taught the Corinthians as summary of the Christian confession twice asserts (1 Cor. 15:3, 4) that the events at the heart of the gospel occurred "in accordance with the scriptures," that is, the authoritative sacred writings of Judaism. The Christian preachers made this claim with respect to the death of Christ "for our sins" and to his resurrection on the third day. At the outset of his letter to the Romans, Paul introduces himself to a church he has not yet visited, as a "servant of Christ Jesus, called by God to be an apostle and set apart for the service of his gospel" (Rom. 1:1 REB). Immediately he follows with his familiar claim:

> This gospel God announced beforehand in sacred scriptures.
>
> [Rom. 1:2 REB]

The tradition concerning Jesus proclaimed by the unknown preachers and variously accented by the evangelists who wrote the gospels repeatedly links the words and actions of Jesus with passages in the Jewish Bible. The practice recurs in virtually every book of the New Testament.

Here is one of the characteristic marks of the apostolic preaching: Jesus Christ is understood as the fulfilment of Israel's hope, and the old scriptures glow with a new luminescence in the light of Jesus Christ. The Christians now look back on the history of Israel from the highest peak of God's revelation and see it all in new perspective. Their risen Lord becomes for them not only the key to the biblical story, but its chief interpreter. In Luke's resurrection narrative Jesus preaches to the disciples from "the law of Moses, the prophets, and the Psalms":

> Thus it is written, that the Messiah is to suffer
> and to rise from the dead on the third day,
> and that repentance and forgiveness of sins
> is to be proclaimed in his name to all nations. [Lk. 24:46–47 NRSV]

Meditating on the ancient words of promise in the presence of the living Lord, the believers see it all clearly now:

"Were not our hearts burning within us...
while he was opening the scriptures to us?"   [Lk. 24:32 NRSV]

Christian Midrash

Schooled both formally and informally in the rabbinic mode of interpretation, the earliest Christians took over from Judaism that familiar process of explicating the sacred text. Doubtless some of their exegetical insights regarding the Messiah were not original with them but were appropriated from current targums and midrash.

In some cases they simply provided a brief Christian comment on selected verses, frequently drawn together from more than one biblical author. In this manner Paul climaxes his great passage on the resurrection by picking up a verse from Isaiah 25:8 and one from Hosea (13:14):

> When this perishable body has been clothed with the imperishable
> and our mortality has been clothed with immortality,
> then the saying of scripture will come true:
> "Death is swallowed up; victory is won!"
> "O Death, where is your victory?
> O Death, where is your sting?"
> The sting of death is sin, and sin gains its power from the law.
> But thanks be to God! He gives us victory
> through our Lord Jesus Christ.   [1 Cor. 15:54–57 REB]

In this case, as in much Christian midrash, the scriptures cited from the prophets are not so much texts to be carefully exegeted as they are stimuli for the preacher's proclamation, providing the power of phrases from the sacred tradition for the heralding of the good news.

Some Christian *midrash,* however, expounds a biblical text at some length in the light of the gospel. Twice Paul develops an extended reflection or homily on Genesis 15:6, quoted by him to read:

> "Abraham put his faith in God,
> and that faith was counted to him as righteousness."   [Rom. 4:3 REB]

These words, says Paul,

> were meant to apply not only to Abraham but to us;
> our faith too is to be "counted,"
> the faith in the God who raised Jesus our Lord from the dead;
> for he was given up to death for our misdeeds,
> and raised to life for our justification.   [Rom. 4:23–25 REB]

In the other homily he proclaims

> In Christ Jesus you are all children of God through faith.
> As many of you as were baptized into Christ
> have clothed yourselves with Christ.
> There is no longer Jew or Greek, there is no longer slave or free,
> there is no longer male and female; for all of you are one in Christ Jesus.
> And if you belong to Christ, then you are Abraham's offspring,
> heirs according to the promise.   [Gal. 3:26–29 NRSV]

Two other such "homilies" appear in the New Testament. They might be entitled "He Gave Them Bread from Heaven" (Jn. 6:31–58) and "A Priest Forever after the Order of Melchizedek" (Heb. 7:1–10; cf. 5:5–6).

Still another form of midrash, Jewish as well as Christian, developed a meditation on a biblical person or event rather than on a verse of scripture. Paul was fond of this mode. He uses it in meditations on "Adam and Christ" (1 Cor. 15:21–22, 45), "The Veil over Moses' Face" (2 Cor. 3:7–18), and "Abraham's Two Sons" (Gal. 4:21–31). In these instances he uses the method he calls "allegory" (Gal. 4:24), also known as typology, regarding events in the story of Israel as signs or symbols or types of realities (the antitypes) known most fully in Christ. In his most elaborate development the preacher says:

> Let me remind you, my friends,
> that our ancestors were all under the cloud,
> and all of them passed through the Red Sea;
> so they all received baptism into the fellowship of Moses
> in cloud and sea.
> They all ate the same supernatural food,
> and all drank the same supernatural drink;
> for they drank from the supernatural rock
> that accompanied their travels—and that rock was Christ.
>
> [1 Cor. 10:1–4 REB]

Thus, Gentile Christians and their spiritual ancestors in Israel's exodus were united in baptism and sacred meal.

"It Is Written"

Within the young church Jesus Christ became "the great midrash" by which the purpose of God, running through all the scriptures, was now clearly understood.[8] Believing that the intention of God in Israel's election was fulfilled in him and that the whole story of the chosen people pointed toward him, they found everywhere in the sacred writings texts hitherto unnoticed that now glowed with meaning. Their appropriation of these in preaching may have sometimes had the quality of a literary allusion, pleasing by a certain aptness, but their conviction that "the prophets...prophesied of the grace that was to be yours" (1 Pet. 1:10 NRSV) led them to discover in scores of passages hopes and promises that they saw fulfilled in Jesus Christ. Again and again in their preaching—both in the gospel tradition and in the epistles—occurs the phrase *it is written,* followed by a verse from prophecy or psalter.

Jewish exegetes had already compiled collections of Messianic texts, and there is reason to believe that the Christians early put together a "Book of Testimonies" which contained scriptures they understood as referring to the Christ. As Jews who confessed him to be Messiah and Lord, they found in such passages a profound appeal, and their involvement with the Bible may have colored the tradition, as in the story of Jesus' temptations or placing his birth in Bethlehem. The argument that the prophecies had been fulfilled in him became a major claim in their missionary propaganda, both with Jews and with Gentiles.

The authors of the various books in the New Testament commonly quote from the Septuagint, the standard Greek version of the Jewish scriptures, despite its frequent variance from the Hebrew text; only rarely do they alter this version in order to conform more closely to the Hebrew original. Some of their quotations, however, may come from translations not otherwise known to us, or perhaps were cited from memory. The Alexandrian version included books not admitted to the Palestinian canon by the rabbis at Jabneh in 90 C.E., and the authors of the New Testament cite as scripture useful verses from such apocryphal books (Ecclesiasticus, 2 Maccabees, Wisdom of Solomon), and even from the pseudepigrapha (Enoch, Apocalypse of Elijah, Assumption of Moses.)

"Ministers of a New Covenant"

Thus, the early Christians distinguished their faith from Judaism and, at the same time, claimed to participate in all God's promises to the children of Abraham. The first Christian communities were, of course, totally Jewish in membership; not only did they honor the scriptures now "fulfilled," but they continued to honor the Sabbath and to observe the moral Law. Some kept the ceremonial Law as well, including its taboos regarding foods, but the presence in the gospel tradition of numerous stories recounting Jesus' challenge to such prohibitions indicates that some communities of his disciples no longer observed these latter provisions.

The book of Acts tells of early tensions at Jerusalem between the main body of Palestinian disciples and the Hellenists; both groups had come out of Judaism, but their problems may have been rooted in linguistic and cultural differences. After the preachers began bringing in Gentile converts on a large scale, sharper controversy developed: some insisted that by faith in Christ the Gentiles had become children of Abraham with no need for first converting to Judaism, while the "Judaizers" held them obligated to keep the law of Moses in its entirety. Paul's Letter to the Galatians reveals the sharpness of this conflict, whereas the book of Acts, written much later, pictures a rational, idyllic compromise (Acts 15:1–35). It also reports the first use of the name Christian at Antioch to designate the mixed company of disciples, both Jews and Gentiles (Acts 11:19–26).

Even in the first century the relationship between Christianity and Judaism manifested a paradoxical character that has marked it ever since, often with tragic consequences. On the one hand, as we have seen, Paul declared to the Gentile disciples,

> If you belong to Christ, then you are Abraham's offspring.
>
> [Gal. 3:29 NRSV]

In this sense Christians counted themselves "heirs according to the promise" fulfilled in Christ. On the other hand, the eucharistic tradition received by Paul and handed on by him within twenty-five years of Jesus' death reports the Lord as saying,

> "This cup is the new covenant in my blood."   [1 Cor. 11:25 NRSV]

Paul described himself and Timothy as

> ministers of a new covenant, not of letter but of spirit;
> for the letter condemns to death, but the Spirit gives life.
>
> [2 Cor. 3:6 REB]

Thus, Paul saw the Judaism in which he had been nurtured as not repudiated but fulfilled in a new spiritual dispensation The old legalism, which in his understanding of the Law had so oppressed him, was replaced by a new motivation and inward power. He earnestly longed for his fellow Jews to find the new life that had come to him in Jesus Christ. Yet he categorically denied that, in not confessing Jesus as Lord, they had been rejected by God or excluded from the promises (Rom. 11:1–2). On the contrary, he joyfully argued that Gentiles had been *included with them* in the grace of God, accepted simply for their faith and not by works of the Law. He proclaimed a new humanity in Christ, with all the old distinctions erased (Gal. 3:27–28). Paul's letter to the Romans, his most extended piece of theologizing, and also the final chapter of the book of Acts, represents him in his most audacious ecumenical venture: seeking to bring both Jews and Gentile Christians into unity as the one people of God, and at the same time longing for his fellow Jews to come to faith in Christ, even while he regards them as fully embraced within the covenant of God's faithfulness.

Despite the inclusiveness of Paul's vision, Christianity and Judaism became distinct faiths marked by unseemly and ultimately tragic rivalry. Unable to reconcile his christology with the monotheism of the Torah, many Jews took deep offense at Christian disregard for the Law, even as many zealous disciples became frustrated over the large number of Jews who would not confess Jesus as Lord. Rivalry sharpened into controversy and colored a good deal of the early preaching, becoming fixed in the gospel tradition. Then controversy escalated into hostility.

Yet, while the bitterness arising from rivalry and frustration came to ugly expression, the Christian preaching of the first century is not *in principle* anti-Semitic, even though the gospels clearly represent the high priests and leaders of the religious establishment as plotting the death of Jesus, and the term used in the Fourth Gospel as shorthand for opposition to him, namely "the Judeans" (*hoi Judaioi*), came to be understood in the setting of the Gentile mission as meaning "the Jews." That reading portended alienation and atrocities to come. The inability of the preachers to lead the young church into a positive relationship with continuing Judaism (the faith of Jesus himself) and to an acceptance of the Jews, his own people, as their brothers and sisters in him—an inability that grew ever more stubborn as rivalry flared into hostile polemic—is the most tragic failure of first-century preaching.[9]

"We Preach Jesus Christ as Lord"

Yet from the religious vocabulary of Judaism in their time and particularly from the scriptures, the Christian preachers and inteppreters of the apostolic age drew the titles that they applied to Jesus and the concepts by which they attributed to him a unique dignity in relationship to God. These titles and concepts constitute the most radical distinction between Christianity and Judaism and an offense to those Jews who have not confessed faith in Jesus. In this respect also, the gospel of the young church goes beyond the gospel that Jesus himself preached,[10] though the early Christians believed that the development wholly accorded with the meaning of his life, death, and resurrection and of the words he had spoken.

The primitive confession "Jesus is the Christ" hails him as God's Messiah, God's Chosen, the One whose coming has been so long awaited. In time the preachers added other titles, understood as virtual synonyms for Messiah or Christ: the Son of Man, the Son of David, the Holy One of God, the King of the Jews, God's Servant, God's Beloved. All are biblical phrases, though the fully developed Messianic hope—preached by the Christians, who claim Jesus as its fulfillment—finds expression not so much in the Law and the prophets as in the apocalyptic writings being produced among the Jews in the time of Jesus and the early Christians.

The concept is so central to the church's gospel and is preached of Jesus so consistently that *Christ,* the Greek translation of *Messiah,* moves rapidly from title to proper name. They preach him as Jesus Christ, Christ Jesus, or simply Christ.

They draw on many other biblical concepts and images to express his significance, presenting him as lawgiver, prophet, teacher, faithful witness, root of David, lion of the tribe of Judah, and morning star. In more exalted terms he is the holy and righteous one, the wisdom of God, the prince of life, the firstborn from the dead, the second Adam, God's agent in creation. He is the lamb of God, the Savior of the world, the perfect sacrifice whose blood was offered for the world's sin, the ransom for many, the apostle and high priest of our confession. He is the Son of God.

Clearly these Christian preachers have moved far beyond the theological limits of Judaism, even though they draw these titles from the scriptures and lovingly repeat the texts in which they find them. They push the boundaries of their thinking even farther. To Paul, Christ the beloved Son is the image of the invisible God, the first-born of all creation.

In him the whole fullness of deity dwells bodily.   [Col. 2:9 NRSV]

To the author of the Fourth Gospel he is the Logos, who was with God and who was God, made flesh in Jesus Christ the Son (Jn. 1:1, 14).

The term the preachers use more than any other (standing alone or in combination with the name Jesus) is the title *Lord*. The word covers a great range of meanings, being sometimes used in polite conversation as an indication of respect, much like "Sir" or "Rabbi." In the Hellenistic world *lord* is a common referent for the savior-gods of the mysteries, and among the Jews it is the name used for God in order to avoid pronouncing the sacred Tetra-grammaton, YHWH (Yahweh). In the first century C.E. imperial Rome boldly adopts the title as an honorific for the deified emperor; a decree of Domitian at the end of the century began, "Our lord and god commands..."[11]

Holding stubbornly to the monotheism of the Hebrew scriptures, and of Jesus himself, the early Christians permit no such use of the title for a mere mortal. But they employ it in a radically new way in their bold confession:

> For us there is one God, the Father,
> from whom are all things and for whom we exist,
> and one Lord, Jesus Christ,
> through whom are all things, and through whom we exist.
>
> [1 Cor. 8:6, RSV]

That confession is the center of their gospel:

> What we preach is not ourselves, but Jesus Christ as Lord,
> with ourselves as your servants for Jesus' sake.   [2 Cor. 4:5 RSV]

"THE CLIMAX OF HISTORY"[12]

Accepting Historical Existence

With eager expectation the early preachers proclaimed the imminent return of the Lord. The radical eschatological language that Jesus had used to herald the impending advent of the kingdom of God they took over to announce his speedy parousia. That understanding pervaded the gospel tradition, doubtless coloring the memory of many of Jesus' sayings, certainly putting a "spin" on their interpretation. It dominated Paul's earliest preaching and preoccupied his Thessalonian converts; some even gave up their daily work to spend their full time looking for the Lord's advent.

As the Lord did not return, the preachers gradually worked through to a new apprehension of the gospel and of the church's continued existence in a world with an ongoing history. They did not achieve such a revised understanding of the faith all at once, but we may trace the process through the fragments of their preaching left to us, noting first a gradual change of mood and finally a profound restatement of Christian hope.

Twenty years after Jesus, Paul has preached the Lord's coming to the Thessalonians, with the results we have noted. About four years later, when he writes to the Corinthians, the focus has shifted to the preaching of the cross, to issues of Christian life and worship, and to the resurrection of the dead, the context within which the parousia is briefly mentioned. Paul still holds to the hope of the Lord's return.

> Listen, I will tell you a mystery! We will not all die,
> but we will all be changed, in a moment, in the twinkling of an eye,
> at the last trumpet.   [1 Cor. 15:51–52 NRSV]

The emphasis now falls on the victory over death.

In 2 Corinthians Paul is preoccupied with the immediate concerns of the churches, particularly the offering for the poor in Jerusalem, and with Christian discipline. In the letters to the Romans and the Galatians he centers on grace, the life of faith, freedom in the Spirit, and the indwelling Christ. These epistles scarcely suggest the expectation of the parousia, yet they indicate no awareness on Paul's part of any change in his gospel.

In the later letters, Philemon, Colossians, and Philippians, the hope persists, being briefly mentioned, but the emphasis falls on the person of Christ and the Christian's relation to him. These letters grapple with the common problems of life and of threatening death in a spirit of profound serenity:

> It is my confident hope that nothing will daunt me
> or prevent me from speaking boldly;
> and that now as always Christ will display his greatness in me,
> whether the verdict be life or death.
> For to me life is Christ, and death is gain.   [Phil. 1:20–21 REB]

A similar shift may be traced in the gospel tradition, from an early emphasis on the coming of the Son of Man to a later restatement. Matthew presents in his Gospel a concern for the institutional life of the church, and Luke ascribes to false prophets announcements that

> "The time is near!"   [Lk. 21:8 NRSV]

John has abandoned all language about the coming of the Son of Man or of a future kingdom; rather, he speaks of eternal life, which for the believer has already begun:

Whoever believes in the Son has eternal life.   [Jn. 3:36 NRSV]

The other New Testament books from late in the century show a similar trend. While some of them still mention the parousia as an element in the preaching, major attention has shifted to the Christian life now, in the light of what God has done in Jesus Christ. The preacher who spoke in the "letter" to the Hebrews sees Christians standing at "the climax of history,"[13] because they live in the time in which God "has spoken to us by a Son" (1:2 NRSV). The accent on the risen and ascended Christ falls not on some future encounter but on his continuing ministry, ever living "to make intercession for" those who draw near to God through him (7:25).

Thus, through three generations of preaching after Jesus, the mood shifts from future expectation to present involvement with the living Christ, whose lordship penetrates every aspect of daily experience.

What has not changed across the decades is the spirit of joy, amounting to elation, which lilts through all the preaching. It sounds through the tradition of his first announcement of the kingdom, through the parables, through the old stories of his healing the sick and forgiving the sinful. It sings in the announcement of the resurrection and in the early hope of the Lord's speedy return. It pervades the ministry of the great apostle, whose letters so often burst into doxology, as his preaching also must have done. It soars to majestic chorus in the visions proclaimed by the seer of the Apocalypse. It echoes through the hymns and narratives celebrating the birth of the Messiah. It settles serenely over the later books in the New Testament, with their echoes of homilies addressed to newly baptized converts and to Christians facing persecution. This joy derives from and centers in the Lord whom they preach and follow,

> eyes fixed on Jesus, the pioneer and perfecter of faith.
> For the sake of the joy that lay ahead of him,
> he endured the cross, ignoring its disgrace,
> and has taken his seat at the right hand of the throne of God.
>
> [Heb. 12:2 REB]

The Holy Spirit in the Church

The church began not only with hope but "with joy inspired by the Holy Spirit" (1 Thess. 1:6), for the gospel was preached "in power and in the Holy Spirit" (1:5). In the earliest days prophets uttered inspired oracles, some Christians spoke in tongues when they gathered for worship, and others interpreted; these powers and the various other charisms for the upbuilding of the church were regarded as the Spirit's gifts.

Over the years, as ecstasy yielded to more sober rationality and order, belief in the presence and power of the Spirit continued. Paul held that the Spirit enables the believers to cry, "Abba! Father!" and intercedes for them when they do not know how to pray. John interpreted the Spirit as the presence of the living Christ, who would bring his words to remembrance and guide the disciples in understanding their meaning (Jn. 14:26). He used for the Spirit the name *Paraclete* (Counselor or Advocate or Comforter); the term comes from Hellenistic legal process, an image from the practice of rhetoric. In the Pastoral Letters, the Spirit is conveyed by ordination and the laying on of hands (2 Tim. 1:6–7). Luke also sees the Spirit at work in the orderly processes of the church, speaking through the community or its prophets and teachers. His picture of the descent of the Spirit upon the church at the first Pentecost after the resurrection represents the glossolalia not as "unknown tongues" but as the open preaching of the gospel in the world's many languages.

The early Christian community regarded the Holy Spirit as empowering its fellowship in the various aspects of its worship, witness, and life (Eph. 4:4–6; 5:18–20).

Preaching in Christian Worship

For the young Christian congregations, their meetings became occasions for sharing life in the Spirit through worship and the ministry of the word. Their gatherings on the first day of the week, in celebration of the Lord's resurrection, appropriated the familiar liturgical pattern of the synagogue to surround their observance of the Lord's supper. As many of them had previously done in the synagogue, believers sang "psalms and hymns and spiritual songs" (Eph. 5:19), offered prayers, read passages of scripture, and expounded them.

Here they made another crucial addition. Besides hearing the sacred texts received from Judaism, they also listened to stories of Jesus or a recital of his sayings and to homilies based on these. If there was a letter from an apostle, even a copy of a letter sent to another church, they would attend to readings from it (1 Thess. 5:27; Col. 4:16). Gradually a body of Christian literature began to be built up: The sayings of Jesus were compiled, as in Q, the passion narrative was rehearsed, and the evangelists composed their various gospels. Toward the end of the first century these scattered writings began to be collected.

The term *scripture*, which still meant the Bible of Judaism, was not yet applied to this new corpus of Christian literature—nor had such a term as *The New Testament* come into use. But its components were gaining wider circulation and use, being accorded the weight of authority because of their testimony to Jesus Christ. As the original eyewitnesses passed from the scene this emerging body of scripture-in-the-making furnished the distinctively Christian substance for teaching, exhortation, and preaching, both in the mission to unbelievers and in the worship of the church.

"THE MINISTRY OF THE WORD" [14]

Action of the Church

The church took its existence from the gospel and continued to exist by proclaiming and hearing the good news. The preaching of Christ by word and deed was the distinctive action of the Christian community. The believers expended little effort on defining what the church is; rather, they involved themselves in the activity of preaching, which, according to their understanding, is preeminently what the church does. This is the work of the church, early and late; note how the labor of preaching is exalted in every part of the tradition gathered in the New Testament. The book of Acts pictures the apostles as appointing the Seven to relieve them from the serving of tables so that they might pursue their primary task:

> Then we can devote ourselves to prayer
> and to the ministry of the word.   [Acts 6:4 REB]

Missionary Proclamation

The original essence of preaching was the proclamation of good news to those who had not heard it. This character of announcement marked the preaching of Jesus and of the earliest church.

The Christian vocabulary of proclamation carried this note of address to outsiders: to deliver a message as a lowly herald (*kerussein*), to publish the good news (*euangelizesthai*), to proclaim (*katangelo*), to bear witness (*martyrein*), to speak (*lalein*), to tell (*legein*), to persuade (*peitho*). The task was to make known neither a philosophical truth nor a mystagogic myth, but an *event experienced* by those most closely associated with Jesus: his life, death, and resurrection; it was to proclaim him as Christ and with boldness to assert his lordship over all. This was the action that evoked faith:

> You have been born again...
> through the living and enduring word of God...
> this "word" is the gospel which was preached to you.
>
> [1 Pet. 1:23–25 REB]

The Word to Believers

The public declaration of the gospel proved as crucial for sustaining the day-by-day life of the believing community as it was for evangelism. Apostles and prophets, pastors and teachers guided and inspired the church by a constant ministry of the word. For this activity the vocabulary was also large: to teach (*didaskalein*), to exhort or encourage or console (*parakalein*), to command (*parangelein*), to prophesy (*propheteuein*), to speak in a tongue (*lalein glossei*), to interpret (*diermeneuein*), to discourse (*homilein*), to hand on a tradition (*paradidesthai*), and, of course, to tell (*legein*).

The intense involvement of the preachers with the word had numerous facets. It included recounting remembered incidents or sayings of Jesus (Acts 11:16; 20:35). It involved counsel as to appropriate conduct in particular circumstances (1 Cor. 7:25). It embraced deliberation as to policy to be followed by the church (Acts 11:1–18; 15:1–29). It included the rebuking of inappropriate behavior or deviant doctrine (1 Tim. 1:3). It was essentially a ministry of teaching, for Christians had *their* distinctive *paideia*[15] : a training in righteousness (Heb. 12:11).

This large educational task within the church, like the teaching in the synagogue before it, had its roots firmly set in the sacred writing of Israel:

> All inspired scripture has its use
> for teaching the truth and refuting error,
> or for reformation of manners and discipline in right living.
> So that everyone who belongs to God   [NRSV]
> may be capable and equipped for good work of every kind.
>
> [REB] [2 Tim. 3:16–17]

Preaching: An Inclusive Term

By the end of the first century the duties of a minister[16] clearly centered in the ministry of the word:

> Attend to the public reading of scripture,
> to preaching, to teaching.   [1 Tim. 4:13 RSV]

Our English word *preaching* in this passage designates action within the Christian community. Though the Greek term in this passage (*paraklesis*) carries the distinctive meaning of *exhortation* (NRSV, REB), it appears here to designate *preaching* (as the RSV renders it) with a somewhat broader intention, that is, the continuing and authoritative ministry of the word by which the church lives.

Preaching has had that larger meaning in the Christian community ever since, with *encouragement,* however, remaining an essential element. Even earlier the term had been used in this pastoral, as well as in a missionary, sense, as in Paul's moving ascription:

Now to God who is able to strengthen you
according to my gospel and the preaching of Jesus Christ,   [RSV]
according to the revelation of the mystery...   [NRSV] [Rom. 16:25]

In this instance *preaching* renders the Greek *kerygma*, in its original secular meaning the *announcement* brought by a herald. But by the time Paul wrote to the Romans the word had become well established in the Christian vocabulary to designate the speaking of Israel's prophets and the church's apostles. It referred both to the public broadcasting and to the content, the message. While the emphasis originally fell on the action of declaring the good news to those who had not heard it, the work of the missionary or evangelist, it came to be used also for address to the believing congregation, reminding them of the gospel that they had first heard and confessed. In common usage in the modern church, *preaching* embraces both the notions of such a public witness and the exhortation or encouragement implicit in that witness.

In the gospel tradition and elsewhere *preaching and teaching* often occur together, used almost synonymously rather than discriminately. Without forgetting the missionary imperative, the church knew that not only did it come to belief by preaching but also that God continued by it to sustain its life.[17] If the Pastoral Epistles reflect already an "early catholicism," it is more concerned with the ministry of the word than with sacraments. So the minister receives the solemn charge to "preach the word" (RSV):

Proclaim the message, press it home
in season and out of season,
use argument, reproof, and appeal,
with all the patience that teaching requires.   [2 Tim. 4:2 REB]

CHAPTER 12

First-Century Sermons and Homilies

The Available Texts

The literature we have examined up to this point is the distillation of first-century preaching (the gospel tradition) and the correspondence of preachers. What about actual texts of homilies or sermons? While these terms themselves were not used, so far as we know, by Christians in the time of the apostles, we do find in the literature several samples of their preaching. These include the orations ("sermons") in Luke-Acts, the discourses in the Gospel according to John, and some apparent homilies preserved in the New Testament under the title of epistles.

The Sermons in Luke–Acts[1]

Manual for Mission

Written near the end of the century, the two-part work, Luke-Acts, is a manual for mission in a world radically different from that in which the church began. After the passage of decades, the hope for the kingdom of God has not been fulfilled, nor has the risen Lord returned. Neither has Israel in significant measure accepted the gospel, but rather the lines between Christianity and Judaism have hardened, and Jerusalem, the spiritual center of both faiths, has been destroyed.

The church now finds itself in an alien culture. It confronts the massive political power of the Roman Empire, before which it must defend itself against charges of sedition. Its lot is now cast among the urban masses of tradespeople and slaves, its strongest base apparently located at Antioch, the third largest city of the *oikoumenē*. While

Paul had already effected the transformation of the church into a cosmopolitan community of urban people, increasingly it encounters the pressure of the contest with idolatry and superstition on the one hand, with Hellenistic philosophy and culture on the other. It must now pursue its mission among a people not formed by the scriptures nor animated by the Messianic hope, as the earliest believers had been.

To guide the church in its mission, Luke writes his Gospel and its sequel, an account of the first decades of the church, advancing his theological position by the way in which he presents the story of the past. He emphasizes the vocation of Christianity as an emerging world religion, the power of the Holy Spirit and of prayer, and the need of institutional structures for the continuing Christian community. Above all, he emphasizes the message of salvation. And he exalts the preaching of the gospel as the supreme task of the missionary church.

Preoccupation with Oratory

As a typical Hellenistic man of letters, Luke is preoccupied with oratory. He uses the vocabulary of rhetoric and approaches the world oratorically, presenting his case through a series of speeches or sermons which provide the "big moments" of the book and advance its argument. Rather than narrating the advance of Christianity he writes of the triumph of "the word of God." He chooses that term for the message of Jesus, that of the apostles, and also the witness of the church: "The word of God continued to advance and gain adherents" (Acts 12:24 NRSV). His periodic summaries refer again and again to the preaching.

Luke presents in Acts an album of stirring oratorical scenes, with great crowds, eager and intent, with impressive speakers standing up in temple or Sanhedrin, stoa, or governor's palace, to extend the hand, command attention by personal presence and strength of voice, and present a case with reasonable, persuasive, artistic words. The preachers win dazzling triumphs as thousands believe, the number of reported converts in Jerusalem amounting to a fifth of the city's normal population.

When Moses is called to mind, he appears as an orator. The prophet Jonah is recalled as converting the city of Nineveh by his preaching. Jesus begins his ministry with an impressive sermon in the synagogue at Nazareth.[2]

For their preaching the apostles are haled before the high court in Jerusalem; yet, after injunction to silence, they nevertheless preach all day long in the temple and in private houses (Acts 5:42). Paul's career is an impressive sequence of missionary journeys studded with dramatic sermons; whereas in his letters his mode of thought is thoroughly rabbinic and professedly non-rhetorical, here he appears as a master of the dais, pointing his speeches with apt allusion to classical literature and philosophy. He makes the grandest gesture available to a Roman rhetor:

> I am now standing before the emperor's tribunal....
> I appeal to Caesar!   [Acts 25:10–11 REB]

The book rises to its climax with a fond picture of Paul standing at last in Rome, preaching the gospel in Caesar's own city.

Luke crowds his stage with bit players in oratorical roles: the Jewish high priest; the celebrated Rabbi Gamaliel; Herod Agrippa I, whose oration evokes blasphemous acclamation from the boot-licking crowd:

> "The voice of a god, and not of a mortal!"   [Acts 12:22 NRSV]

a rabble-rousing entrepreneur, the silversmith Demetrius; a would-be orator in Ephesus frustrated by the obstructionist misbehavior of an anti-Jewish mob; a formidable and reasonable town clerk whose personal presence restores order in the amphitheatre; a Roman tribune speaking through a rhetorical letter; a rhetor named Tertullus retained by Paul's accusers; the lawyers (*dynatoi*) representing the parties in a court of law.

He brings on other distinguished persons with ties to the world of culture: Sergius Paulus the successor of Cicero as proconsul of Cyprus; a company of Epicurean and Stoic philosophers in Athens; Gallio the proconsul of Achaia who was son to the rhetorician Seneca the Elder, brother to the philosopher Seneca the Younger, and uncle to the poet Lucan; Felix and Festus, the Roman governors of Syria; Drusilla, the Herodian princess and wife of Felix; Agrippa II, the last Jewish king and great grandson of Herod the Great; his sister and consort Bernice, widow of another king, and later mistress to the Emperor Titus; Publius, the chief official of the island of Melita; and, just off stage but ever an influential presence, the Emperor Nero himself. A company of lesser Roman officials moves through the book—the centurions Cornelius and Julius, a jailer in Philippi, the Asiarchs of Ephesus—and groups of noble women.

The writer sets his scenes in the most celebrated venues: the temple and the Tower of Antonia at Jerusalem; a centurion's private quarters in Caesarea; the Agora in Philippi; the Athenian Areopagus in the shadow of the Parthenon and its adjacent temples; the bustling seaport of Corinth; the school of Tyrannus in Ephesus and then its amphitheater within sight of the celebrated Temple of Artemis, the seventh wonder of the world; a score of lesser cities and harbor towns; and finally the capital of the empire.

Luke links his book to the high culture of the time with quotations from the Septuagint, references to philosophers, and allusions to literature and drama. (He also presents encounters with popular superstition.) Without the slightest diminution of the apostolic gospel, but rather as a means of exalting its supreme importance and unique appeal, Luke presents the Christian mission as moving dramatically to the major centers of Hellenistic intellectual and cultural life. The readers he primarily targets will recognize without explanation the secular personalities he brings on stage, will have visited or at least heard about the locations where he sets his scenes, will note the literary and philosophical allusions without a tutor or commentator. And Luke himself is such a mind.

A Gallery of Christian Preachers

As for the Christian community, scores of preachers crowd the pages, heralding the word of God. At the birth of Jesus and his forerunner John the Baptist, pious Jews prophesy concerning the mission of these two children of promise, and a messenger (angel) of the Lord announces the Savior's advent. In the wilderness John proclaims the coming one and preaches good news to the people. Jesus preaches to multitudes and sends out the Twelve to broadcast the imminence of the Kingdom. Later he appoints seventy others to go out as preachers in an enlarged phase of the mission.

After the ascension of the risen Lord, Matthias is chosen to take the vacant place of Judas among the Twelve as witnesses to the resurrection. With the descent of the Holy Spirit on the day of Pentecost and a memorable sermon by Simon Peter that wins converts from near and far the church comes into existence three thousand strong. In succeeding days the great company continues in the apostles' teaching. Peter and John preach boldly in the temple. So that the apostles may not be diverted from their responsibility for preaching, the Seven are appointed to attend to the feeding of the needy, but two of them, Stephen and Philip, emerge forthwith as powerful preachers. Philip's daughters and the prophet Agabus prophesy.

Saul of Tarsus receives a dramatic call to preach, thrice recounted in the book, and Barnabas the Son of Exhortation enlists this new convert to join him in teaching at Antioch, along with the other prophets and teachers there. Soon Saul and Barnabas are sent on a missionary journey, and Saul becomes Paul. Judas Barsabbas and Silas travel from Jerusalem to Antioch to prophesy and exhort. Paul enlists Timothy to assist in the mission. Apollos, the eloquent Jew from Alexandria, speaks with power in the synagogue at Ephesus, proving from the scriptures that Jesus is the Christ. Even to such an illustrious orator, Priscilla and Aquila expound the way of the Lord more accurately. Because they do not believe in Jesus, some wandering Jewish exorcists are confounded in their attempts to appropriate his name as a word of power. And before setting out for Jerusalem Paul announces his grand intention,

> After I have gone there, I must also see Rome. [Acts 19:21 NRSV]

The journey to the capital of the empire is a perilous voyage fraught with adventure. But the book of Acts reaches its climax with a picture of the great apostle preaching unmolested in Caesar's city, sought out by many.

Only a writer who loved oratory, who believed profoundly in the high significance of preaching, and who felt the drama of conversion as preachers of conviction heralded the word of God, would have recounted the course of the Christian church in the first generation of its development with such dramatic emphasis on the proclamation of the gospel. Thus, Luke set the stage for a series of dramatic sermons.

Model Sermons

At times Luke merely indicates the action of preaching—members of his heroic company testify or prophesy or exhort. Occasionally he condenses an extended speech into a few words:

> Save yourselves from this corrupt generation. [Acts 2:40 NRSV]

But Luke gives over a large part of his narrative to extended reports of sermons; though obviously condensed, they are carefully developed and are reported at some length. Have we in these digests a treasure trove of the earliest apostolic preaching? Or has Luke, following the confessed practice of Hellenistic historians, himself contrived appropriate orations for his characters at crucial points in the history? Or has he given literary form to summaries of genuine sermons remembered in the tradition? A lively debate among biblical scholars leaves the third option quite tenable.

In any case, one thing is clear: Luke offers these speeches, not as relics, but as *models* for the preachers of his own time. He provides outlines, with appropriate scriptures and exempla, for sermons on various occasions and to all kinds of audiences. The speeches may be classified, for the most part, as "evangelistic, deliberative, apologetic, and hortatory."[3] We shall discuss them as addressed to three types of audiences.

SERMONS TO JEWS. The action in the book really begins with Peter's sermon to a great assembly of Jews from across the *oikoumené*, gathered in Jerusalem for the feast of Pentecost. Other sermons to Jews, some evangelistic, some apologetic, soon follow: three more by Peter, one each by Stephen and Philip, and three by Paul. In content, the sermons all proclaim the Messiahship of the crucified and risen Jesus, calling the hearers to repentance, promising forgiveness of sins and salvation in him; in mood, structure, and style they vary considerably.

Peter's Sermon on Pentecost. The proclamation by the spokesperson for the apostles forty days after the resurrection (Acts 2:14–40) has dramatic importance as the first public announcement of the Christian message. Its rush of power and overwhelming urgency command attention, but the simple artistry of its format contributes to the total effect. With only the briefest of introductions, the preacher moves quickly to testimonies from scripture, declaring their fulfilment in Jesus and moving step-by-step to an ever higher level:

> (1) Jesus of Nazareth, a man attested…by God, …
> you crucified and killed.
> (2) This Jesus God raised up…
> and having received from the Father the promise of the Holy Spirit,
> he has poured out this that you both see and hear…
> (3) Let the entire house of Israel know with certainty
> that God has made him both Lord and Messiah,
> this Jesus whom you crucified.   [Acts 2:22–36 NRSV]

Interrupted by cries for guidance from penitent hearers, Peter calls for action:

> Repent, and be baptized, every one of you,
> in the name of Jesus the Messiah;
> then your sins will be forgiven
> and you will receive the gift of the Holy Spirit.
> The promise is to you and to your children and to all who are far away,
> to everyone whom the Lord our God may call.   [Acts 2:38–39 REB]

Stephen's Sermon. Quite a different mood pervades Stephen's sermon (chap. 7). Haled before the Sanhedrin on charges of attacking the temple and the Law, he offers a long apology for the gospel in the pattern of a *recital* of sacred history, a pattern conventional enough in Jewish preaching. But instead of celebrating God's redemptive acts, the sermon picks up the dark thread of the people's recurrent and consistent refusal to obey God. The preacher quotes Isaiah 66 to argue that the temple was built on human initiative and that God has no need of it, then launches a scathing *indictment*:

> How stubborn you are, heathen still at heart and deaf to truth!
> You always resist the Holy Spirit.
> You are just like your ancestors.
> Was there ever a prophet your ancestors did not persecute?
> They killed those who foretold the coming of the righteous one,
> and now you have betrayed him and murdered him.
> You received the law given by God's angels
> and yet you have not kept it.   [Acts 7:51–53 REB alt.]

Turning against his accusers the charge of unfaithfulness to the Law that they have leveled against him, the preacher concludes with a *vision* :

> Look, I see the heavens opened
> and the Son of Man standing at the right hand of God.
>
> [Acts 7:56 NRSV]

Then as the stones thud against Stephen's body, he dies with a prayer on his lips:

> Lord, do not hold this sin against them.   [Acts 7:60 NRSV]

Already in Jerusalem, so soon after Pentecost, the preaching of the gospel to the Jews, undertaken with such high hopes, has failed with the great majority. Later incidents in the book repeat this theme, so that a tragic gulf widens between Christianity and Judaism, and Christian frustration turns to bitterness, which will be escalated by succeeding generations. Later preachers, filled with hatred, will seize upon the words of Peter and Stephen to support anti-Semitic dogma and condemn the entire Jewish people as Christ-killers. That is to miss the point of these sermons, even while quoting some of their words.

Both Peter and Stephen, themselves Jews, address their hearers as "Brothers." They speak in Jerusalem to persons of power who have taken part in turning Jesus over to "those outside the law" (Acts 2:23) for crucifixion. The charge they press of resistance to God's will is the theme of all the prophets, an indictment not against Jews, but against blind wilfulness in those who claim to be the people of God.

Paul's Addresses to Jews. So long as they have access to Jewish audiences, the missionaries plead their cause, as Paul does in the synagogue at Thessalonica, arguing that

it was necessary for the Messiah to suffer and to rise from the dead,

and concluding,

This is the Messiah, Jesus, whom I am proclaiming to you.

[Acts 17:2–3 NRSV]

In Philippi, which has no synagogue, Paul seeks out a place of prayer by the riverside and sits down to speak to a group of women assembled there to keep the sabbath. The book of Acts offers no suggestion as to his sermon.

In the last scene in the book Paul is in Rome, where he calls together the leaders of the Jewish community, addresses them as brothers, asks for a hearing, and, when they have brought an audience, undertakes to convince them about Jesus from the Law and the prophets.

The sermons to Jews that we find in Acts carry not the slightest suggestion that the hearers have imposed any guilt on their descendants. The intensity of the language, which may appear anti-Jewish, reflects the mystification of the preachers at the large-scale rejection of the gospel by their own people, as well as the animosity exacerbated by the rivalry between the two biblical faiths. The language is part of the apologetic of Christians claiming the authority of scripture for their message, an apologetic prompted by the refusal of the people whose scriptures they quote to accept the message. That refusal the Christians use as part of their rationale for turning to the Gentiles.

SERMONS TO GENTILES. The Gentile mission was a radical departure, totally unimaginable at the beginning, and a cause of intense controversy within the church. Though that conflict colored the early epistles of Paul, and though controversy continued until the Judaizers were hopelessly outnumbered, only Luke suggests how the preaching to the Gentiles began.

Peter is the key figure. In response to a special revelation, he goes to Caesarea to preach to the household of Cornelius, a Roman centurion. The sermon begins with a pronouncement:

> I now understand how true it is that God has no favourites.
>
> [Acts 10:34 REB]

The preacher then commends to the God-fearers, Gentiles though they are, the word God has sent to Israel:

> how God anointed Jesus of Nazareth with the Holy Spirit and with power;
> how he went about doing good and healing all who were oppressed...
> They put him to death by hanging him on a tree;
> but God raised him on the third day...
> He commanded us to preach to the people and to testify
> that he is the one ordained by God as judge of the living and the dead.
> All the prophets testify about him
> that everyone who believes in him
> receives forgiveness of sins through his name.   [Acts 10:38–43 NRSV]

When the Holy Spirit falls on the hearers and they speak in tongues, Peter commands them to be baptized. Then he goes to Jerusalem to rehearse the event to the church, and his critics are silenced.

Other preaching to Gentiles follows. To hearers who know nothing of the coming Messiah, the scattered preachers tell "the good news of the Lord Jesus" (11:20 REB). Summaries of the message are suggested from time to time (14:15–17; 16:31; 24:25).

Luke's great set piece is Paul's sermon in Athens to a company of philosophers (17:22–31), the preacher appearing in the likeness of Socrates. It is an urbane and reasoned discourse dealing in philosophical axioms and citing classical poets, including Paul's fellow Cilician, Aratus.

All this differs radically in style from the Paul we know through the epistles; the sermon, of course, addresses quite a different kind of audience from the young congregations to whom he has written. These hearers have no knowledge of the scriptures, to which he makes no appeal. The climactic summary, nevertheless, is consistent with the gospel preached throughout the book of Acts:

> Now God commands all people everywhere to repent,
> because he has fixed a day on which he will have the world judged,
> and justly judged, by a man whom he has appointed,
> and of this he has given assurance to all
> by raising him from the dead.   [Acts 17:30–31 NRSV alt.]

The scoffing of the sophists at the idea of the resurrection of the dead breaks off the sermon before the name of Jesus can be spoken. But Luke implies that the failure must be charged to the attitude of the hearers, not to any deficiency of the preaching.

The most stirring of the sermons to Gentiles, quite different in tone from those already examined, is Paul's defense before King Agrippa and a glittering company of notables in the audience hall of the Roman governor at Caesarea, the provincial capital (chap. 26). Like the other Herodides, Agrippa formally professed the Jewish faith out of deference to his subjects, but he was thoroughly Hellenized by education, disposition, and open liaison with Bernice.

In Luke's dazzling set piece, the royal pair enter the courtroom with high pomp, accompanied by military tribunes and prominent men of the city. Dramatically, the governor, Porcius Festus, gives orders that the prisoner Paul be brought in. This high Roman official presents the missionary to the last puppet-king over the Jews with the explanation that, though he must send the prisoner to Caesar on appeal, no proper charges have been preferred in the case.

At a signal from the king, Paul speaks in the forensic rhetoric of apology:

> I consider myself fortunate that it is before you, King Agrippa,
> I am to make my defense today...   [Acts 26:2 NRSV]

He narrates his manner of life in Judaism as a Pharisee.

> And now I stand here on trial on account of my hope
> in the promise made by God to our ancestors.   [Acts 26:6 NRSV]

The preacher recounts his opposition to "the name of Jesus of Nazareth," his persecution of the saints, his journey to Damascus (which he has previously narrated to a hostile mob in Jerusalem), and the fateful encounter on the road when he saw a light from heaven and heard a voice saying,

> I am Jesus whom you are persecuting...
> I have appeared to you for a purpose:
> to appoint you my servant and witness...
> I will rescue you from your own people
> and from the Gentiles—to whom I am sending you.
> You are to open their eyes and to turn them
> from darkness to light, from the dominion of Satan to God,
> so that they may obtain forgiveness of sins

and a place among those whom God has made his own
through faith in me.   [Acts 26:15–18 REB]

Paul has not been disobedient to the heavenly vision, but has preached repentance, testifying to what the prophets and Moses foretold:

> that the Messiah must suffer,
> and that, by being the first to rise from the dead,
> he would proclaim light both to our people
> and to the Gentiles.   [Acts 26:23 NRSV]

Interrupted by Festus, who considers him mad for speaking of the resurrection of a dead man, Paul turns to the guest of honor:

> King Agrippa, do you believe the prophets?
> I know that you believe.   [Acts 26:27 NRSV]

The playboy king replies noncommittally:

> Are you so quickly persuading me to become a Christian?
>
> [Acts 26:28 NRSV]

The prisoner-preacher replies with a dramatic gesture,

> Whether quickly or not, I pray to God
> that not only you, but also all who are listening to me today
> might become as I am—except for these chains!   [Acts 26:29 NRSV]

The prisoner is led away for his journey to Rome, while the king declares to the governor that, except for his appeal, he might have been set free.

Paul's apologia is a compelling testimony and a masterful oration. It is as though, deprived by historical fact of the grandest imaginable scene—that of Paul making his defense before Nero Caesar—Luke has given us here the sermon that the great missionary would have presented to the emperor himself.

SERMONS TO CHRISTIANS. Throughout his book Luke depicts a constant occupation in the church with oral address—teaching, deliberation as to policy, exhortation. As noted already, this continuing ministry of the word may fairly be called preaching (following the practice of later generations), though Luke nowhere uses that term for it.

The first preacher to the church is the Lord Jesus himself. Luke's Gospel, of course, contains a number of discourses—the sermon at Nazareth, the "Sermon on the Plain," the "Apocalyptic Discourse," and others. But the risen Lord continues to preach to the church, as we have seen. During a period of forty days after the resurrection he appears to the disciples, "speaking about the kingdom of God" (Acts 1:3). All through the book the Lord continues to address his people—through vision and audition, through angelic messengers, through the Holy Spirit. Some of these oracles were doubtless delivered by Christian prophets.

Most of the exhortations of the preachers to the community are only lightly sketched. Peter speaks of the need to fill the place vacated by Judas (1:15–22), the Twelve request the appointment of the Seven to serve tables (6:1–6), Peter recounts to the Jerusalem church the vision that prompted him to preach to Cornelius and to offer baptism to Gentiles (11:4–17). Barnabas exhorts the disciples at Antioch to remain faithful to the Lord (11:23), Peter narrates his deliverance from prison (12:17), Paul and Barnabas visit among the churches "encouraging them to be true to the faith" and warning that

> To enter the kingdom of God
> we must undergo many hardships.   [Acts 14:22 REB]

The two missionaries return to Antioch to declare all that God has done through them and how he has thrown open the gates of faith to the Gentiles (14:27 REB). At the so-called council of Jerusalem Peter speaks once more of God's acceptance of believers in Christ who have not first been Jews:

> We believe that we will be saved through the grace of the Lord Jesus,
> just as they will.   [Acts 15:11 NRSV]

James delivers a slightly more extended address proposing concessions by both parties, to which they agree (15:13–21).

Finding at Ephesus some disciples who have not yet received the Holy Spirit, Paul explains:

> John baptized with the baptism of repentance,
> telling the people to believe in the one who was to come after him,
> that is, in Jesus.   [Acts 19:4 NRSV]

The prophet Agabus foretells Paul's imprisonment (21:10–11), and Paul resolutely replies:

> I am ready not only to be bound but even to die in Jerusalem
> for the name of the Lord Jesus.   [Acts 21:13 NRSV]

In the holy city at last Paul relates to James and all the elders the things that God has done among the Gentiles (21:18).

Only one sermon to Christians in the book of Acts bears the marks of a dramatic production that Luke loved so well. It is delivered at the port of Miletus, where Paul's ship has stopped briefly on his final voyage to Jerusalem. At his request, the elders of the church at Ephesus have come to meet him for a last reunion, and the venerable missionary delivers a farewell sermon (20:18–35). He recalls how he went about among them "preaching the kingdom" (20:25 RSV):

> I did not shrink from doing anything helpful,
> proclaiming the message to you,
> and teaching you publicly and from house to house,
> as I testified to both Jews and Greeks about repentance toward God
> and faith toward our Lord Jesus.   [20:20–21 NRSV]

Despite coming imprisonment and afflictions (for the Spirit has warned him), the preacher declares,

> I do not count my life of any value to myself,
> all I want is to finish the race,
> and the ministry that I received from the Lord Jesus,
> to testify to the good news of God's grace.   [Acts 20:24 NRSV alt.]

Solemnly he declares,

> I am not responsible for the blood of any of you,
> for I did not shrink from declaring to you
> the whole purpose of God.   [Acts 20:27 NRSV]

Now he charges the elders:

> Keep watch over yourselves and over all the flock,
> of which the Holy Spirit has made you overseers,
> to shepherd the church of God
> that he obtained with the blood of his own Son.   [Acts 20:28 NRSV]

Paul warns of false teachers to come. He commends the elders to God "and to the word of his grace" (20:32 REB). Once again he protests his own innocence. He reminds them how he has toiled with "these hands of mine" (20:34 REB) to care for his needs. Reminding them to help the weak, he concludes with a saying from the Lord not found in the gospels:

Keep in mind the words of the Lord Jesus, who himself said,
"Happiness lies more in giving than in receiving."   [Acts 20:35 REB]

They all, writes Luke, knelt down and prayed. They wept and
embraced and kissed in sorrowful farewell. "Then they brought him
to the ship" (20:38 NRSV).

MODELS FOR PREACHERS. This collection is a remarkably varied, yet
consistent compilation of homiletical models for the church in its
mission as it enters the second century. Here are sermons for various
audiences. Here is great diversity of form and mode of development.
Here is forthright recognition that even the greatest of preachers are
not successful—as Jesus himself was not—with all who hear. Here is
unreserved conviction as to the overwhelming importance of preaching and the glory of the task. One may easily see Luke-Acts as the
first of many compilations put together in succeeding years as guides
for preachers. It may appropriately be called (fifteen centuries before
Thomas Cranmer), the First Book of Homilies. The Hellenistic author
of Luke-Acts has firmly established in the Christian tradition the ideal
of the preacher as orator in the classical mold—and in the tradition of
the prophets.

THE DISCOURSES IN THE FOURTH GOSPEL[4]

Sermons of the Glorified Lord

As the decades passed, it fell to the preachers to bring the gospel
as a living word to new generations in new settings. They attributed
their power to do this to the working of the Holy Spirit. By the gift of
prophecy they spoke the word of the Lord directly into the present.
But the contemporizing of the gospel was a work of reflection, not of
inspiration alone. A striking example of the process is the Gospel
according to John, evidently written near the end of the century, and
especially the discourses of Jesus found there.

These dialogues and homilies differ noticeably in style from the
saying of Jesus in the Synoptic Gospels and the agrapha. Here are no
parables. Instead, extended allegories explain the true significance of
his miracles—for example, feeding the hungry multitude, healing a
man blind from birth, raising Lazarus from the dead. Frequently the
narrative leads up to a declaration by Jesus in the form, "I am..." So
he says:

I am the bread of life,   [Jn. 6:35 NRSV]

I am the resurrection and the life.   [Jn. 11:25 NRSV]

In these utterances the Jesus of the gospel story speaks with the voice of the risen and glorified Lord. Without parallel in the Synoptics, they disclose an understanding of Jesus' significance gained from a lifetime's meditation.

In such passages, it appears, we have the preaching of a thoughtful disciple to whom the believers look for a word from the Savior. Frequently the discourse seems to grow out of a seminal saying – handed down in the oral tradition, perhaps spoken as a prophetic oracle—now amplified into a homily. The sermons in John constitute the most insightful, enduring, and spiritually satisfying example in all Christian preaching of the bold use of *prosopopoeia* or personification in answer to the question: what is Jesus Christ saying to us now?

THE OPEN DISCOURSES. The significant number of discourses set during Jesus' public ministry is suggested by the following list:[5]

Discourse with Nicodemus: Dialog and Homily (3:1–21)
Dialog with a Samaritan Woman (4:7–30, 39–42)
Dialog with the Disciples (4:31–38)
Discourse on the Father and the Son (5:17–47)
Discourse on the Bread of Life (6:25–59)
Series of Controversial Dialogs (7:14–8:58)
Dialog concerning a Man Born Blind (chap. 9)
Discourse on the Shepherd and the Flock (10:1–21)
A Controversy with the Jews (10:22–39)
Dialog, with Miracle, on Death and Resurrection (11:1–44)
Discourse on Jesus' Impending Death (12:20–36)

At the end of the public ministry Jesus cries out in words that briefly reprise the preaching set forth in this gospel:

Whoever believes in me
believes not in me but in him who sent me.
And whoever sees me sees him who sent me.
I have come as light into the world, so that everyone who believes in me
should not remain in the darkness.
I do not judge anyone who hears my words and does not keep them,
for I came not to judge the world, but to save the world.
The one who rejects me and does not receive my word has a judge;
on the last day the word that I have spoken will serve as judge,
for I have not spoken on my own,
but the Father who sent me has himself given me a commandment
about what to say and what to speak.
And I know that his commandment is eternal life.   [Jn. 12:44–50 NRSV]

THE FAREWELL DISCOURSES. Like the synoptic evangelists, the author of the Fourth Gospel also represents Jesus as imparting some of his teaching to his disciples in secret; unlike them, he reserves all of this private instruction for a series of farewell discourses during his last supper with them. These extended discussions may be represented as follows:

Dialog on Jesus' Departure and Return (13:31–14:31)
Dialog on Jesus' Continuing Relationship with the Disciples (chaps. 15, 16)
Christ's Prayer for the Disciples (chap. 17).

The Message of This Preaching

The Christ who speaks through the Johannine discourses presents himself as the supreme Revealer of God, and the content of his revealing is no hidden *gnosis* of esoteric doctrine, but simply himself. In the understanding of John, God has entered visibly and decisively into human life in Jesus, God's ultimate gift. In this gospel alone Jesus uses the word *love* to denote God's attitude to humanity, and it is love that Jesus himself manifests. The cross on which he is lifted up becomes the means of drawing all humanity to him. Though he dies, he lives forever, as do all who believe in him. The *parousia* is not some distant future event to be awaited, for the living Christ has already come to be with his people, that is, the resurrection and the coming are one.

To the preacher, Jesus is the divine Logos become flesh, the preexistent Wisdom of God. Therefore, all that he says is ultimately and profoundly true. Scripture is to be understood in the light of his ministry, for it points to him. Yet his words, like the scriptures, are not understood by many. But because the words are true, those who refuse or resist them are judged by them. They force a decision:

Those who believe in him are not condemned;
but those who do not believe are condemned already,
because they have not believed in the name of the only Son of God.
[Jn. 3:18 NRSV]

Just as the revelation in Christ becomes an address by God to all who encounter Jesus, so the promised Spirit will address the world through the disciples, for the knowledge given by the Paraclete leads to witness. The purpose of the preaching is the same as that of the gospel itself:

that you may come to believe that Jesus is the Messiah, the Son of God, and that through believing you may have life in his name.

[Jn. 20:31 NRSV]

OTHER FIRST-CENTURY HOMILIES[6]

Sermons in Another Guise

Besides the impressive number of sermons in Luke-Acts and of discourses in John, a few other first-century homilies are available to us, in form not far removed from that in which they were preached. Since, however, homily or sermon was not yet a recognized form for publication, these works have come down to us in the guise of epistles.

Preaching Preserved as Correspondence: The First Epistle of Peter

The author of the letter known as 1 Peter describes it as a brief work of encouragement and testimony (5:12). If composed by the apostle, it must be dated before 67 C.E., and even if pseudonymous—scholars are divided over the question—it must still be dated within the first century. Although the view that it is essentially a homily delivered during the baptismal liturgy has gone out of favor, its dominantly sermonic character is evident. If the message was formulated by the author but given its written form by Silvanus (Silas) (5:12)—since, it is presumed, the Galilean fisher was not expert in literary Greek—its nature as homily is all the more understandable. The document contains no other references to particular persons.

The work opens with an ascription of praise:

> Blessed be the God and Father of our Lord Jesus Christ!
> By his great mercy he has given us a new birth into a living hope
> through the resurrection of Jesus Christ from the dead.

[1 Pet. 1:3 NRSV]

The preacher exhorts the hearers to stand fast in their trials and admonishes them to Christian living. He holds forth the calling of the church as

> a chosen race, a royal priesthood, a dedicated nation,
> a people claimed by God for his own,
> to proclaim the glorious deeds of him who has called you
> out of darkness into his marvelous light.   [1 Pet. 2:9 REB]

Urging "good conduct among the Gentiles" (2:12 RSV), the preacher closes on a note of "eternal glory" (5:10). The work is a beautiful and unpretentious example of early *paraklésis*.

A Compilation of Sermons: The "Letter" to the Hebrews

The so-called Letter to the Hebrews names neither its author nor its recipients; the sole epistolary characteristic, a brief paragraph of greetings at the end, begins:

I appeal to you, brothers and sisters,
bear with my word of exhortation.   [Heb. 13:22 NRSV]

This characterization by the author, the recurrent use throughout of terms for oral address, the frequent shifting in personal pronouns ("you," "we," "I"), the repetition of a clear pattern—stating a theme, supporting it by scripture with an allegorical or typological exegesis, then moving to a word of exhortation—the refined style of expression, and other marks of spoken delivery suggest that the author has compiled and slightly edited a group of sermons and posted them off as a letter.

The first thematic division of the book (1:1–4:13), an exegetical homily on "The Superiority of Christ over Angels and Moses," can be marked out as the first sermon. Other major divisions do not show such clear homiletical seams, but the arrangement suggests a series of topical addresses:

Jesus Our High Priest   [4:14–7:28]
Christ the Mediator of a New Covenant   [8:1–10:39]
A Sermon on Faith   [11:1–13:16].

The last named deliverance, particularly, is marked by moving *exempla* and urgent exhortations.

This book of sermons probably derives from the final two decades of the century. It has been termed "the finest example of Greek prose in the New Testament,"[7] and some scholars have proposed Paul's coworker Priscilla as its author.[8]

A Christian Diatribe: The "Letter" of James

More rhetorical than any other extant homily of the first century, and written in an eloquent Greek style which, at the same time, contains an abundance of Semitisms is the "Letter of James." Its obvious intention to correct a popular misunderstanding about faith and works, with insistence on the latter as evidence of the former, leads some scholars to regard it as designed to correct a misuse of Paul's letters and so to place it as late as the second quarter of the second century, but again scholarly opinion divides and certainty eludes.

Drawing heavily on modes of thought employed in the schools of wisdom and showing sympathy for attitudes expressed in the primitive tradition of Jesus' sayings, the author is an ardent advocate for the poor. He presents his case in the style of the diatribe, using wordplay, alliteration, *exempla*, and other devices of the popular moralists. Without christological or "kerygmatic" elements, except for a brief reference to "the coming of the Lord" (5:7–8), the work is oriented toward practice, like the Sermon on the Mount. Typical is the declaration:

> Religion that is pure and undefiled before God, the Father, is this:
> to care for orphans and widows in their distress,
> and to keep oneself unstained by the world.   [Jas. 1:27 NRSV]

It is not enough to hear the preaching.

> Only be sure you act on the message,
> and do not merely listen, and so deceive yourselves.   [1:22 REB]

Carrying no personal references—a fact that does not rule out its being an epistle—the work is patently sermonic, its form that of an ethical homily. The author refers to himself as a teacher (3:1).

We have noted the central convictions of the earliest preachers as well as the urgency and thoroughness with which they conveyed their understanding of the Way. It is important also to give attention to the arguments to which they appealed, the style of their utterance, and the form they gave their addresses. So we move on to consider their rhetoric.

CHAPTER 13

The Preaching of the First-Century Church

THE HOMILETIC[1]

A brief commentary on the homiletic of the preachers, based on their practice as it may be analyzed from the available texts, will conclude our consideration of the apostolic age.

Forms of Public Discourse

The preachers took over both Jewish and Hellenistic forms of discourse and developed new forms of their own. Apart from the gospel tradition itself, which readily absorbed some of their utterances, no effort to imitate the homiletic of Jesus is discernible. As they worked out ways to present with greatest urgency the evangel of his death and resurrection, they seized rather on the Judaic mode of *recital*, climaxing the story of God's saving acts in Israel with the account of Jesus' dying and rising again. They also succeeded in conveying the essence of the good news in one after another of the many brief *stories* they told about his ministry, whether recounting one of his mighty acts of power or reciting a snatch of *dialog* in which he engaged another. Sometimes the preachers spoke searching words of admonition leading up to a call for repentance, or they extended an invitation to sinners to receive the salvation offered in his name.

Address directed to believers included the *revelation* or *oracle* of Christian prophets, *utterance* in tongues, and *interpretation* of tongues. Forms used for teaching and encouragement were closer to those of traditional rhetoric. *Encomium* commended a particular virtue (love, faith) or the Christian way of life. *Homily* lent itself to an informal if fervent talk about the Christian way, enlarging on words of scripture or a remembered saying of the Lord. *Diatribe* furnished a rhetorical pattern for inveighing against sin or false teaching. Such practical discussions would be filled with references to *exemplary figures* from the biblical narratives and soon (as in the First Epistle of Clement, written near the end of the century) to the apostles and martyrs of Christ Jesus.

A characteristically Christian mode of speech, calling the believers to ponder their own story of salvation through the gospel, set forth a sharp *contrast* between the *then* of their past existence in sin and despair and the *now* of their present life in Christ:

> You who were once estranged and hostile in mind, doing evil deeds,
> he has now reconciled in his fleshly body through death,
> so as to present you holy and blameless
> and irreproachable before him.   [Col. 1:21–22 NRSV]

The scriptural mode of *testament* or *farewell address* lent itself to powerful use (e.g., Acts 20:17–35; 2 Tim. 4:6–8), as did *quotations* or *allusive echoes* from scripture.[2]

Like the rabbis seeking to summarize the essence of the Law, and Jesus in setting forth the "Golden Rule" (Mt. 7:12), the earliest preachers also resorted to *compression*, undertaking to reduce the practice of the Christian life to an aphorism (Rom. 13:9–10; Jas. 1:27).

In all these forms of practical discourse two different moods constantly interplay: an uncompromising reminder of the demanding way of life Christians are expected to follow, and a joyful sense of the divine presence to inspire, guide, and empower them—referred to as God, or as living Lord, or as the Holy Spirit.

Rhetoric in Practice

The Christian missionaries believed that they had received a message to be delivered. They possessed a vital stock of material in the growing tradition, new to many of their hearers. They proclaimed the fulfillment of scriptural promises in Jesus, some account of his life, death, and resurrection, his exaltation as Lord and Christ, his giving of the Holy Spirit, his expected coming in judgment and triumph—all leading to a call to repentance coupled with the offer of forgiveness in him. These elements, received, handed on, and to some degree reinterpreted by each of the preachers, constituted an essential part of the preaching or *kérygma,* but by no means all of it.

"Material" for amplifying these elements came both from the gospel tradition with its stories and sayings and from the testimonies of scripture, frequently applied allegorically. In making their case, the preachers might resort to one or another of the formal arguments set forth in the rhetorical manuals. Or they might follow the methods of the rabbis.

As to the delivery of the preachers, we have little information, apart from references in Acts, perhaps idealized, to Peter or Paul, speaking "in a loud voice" (2:14; 14:10). Both Jews and Gentiles were accustomed to impressive public utterance with the high degree of animation characteristic of the Mediterranean peoples. We are advised in imagining their preaching "to think of the way in which Vachel Lindsay read or of the appropriate reading of James Weldon Johnson's *God's Trombones*."[3] Yet in writing to the Corinthians Paul cannot hide his sensitivity to the criticism that he lacks impressive presence as an orator, perhaps in contrast to Apollos.[4]

As to style, we have closer access to the preachers. Few of them echo the colorful "down home" accents of Jesus' sayings, but their words are forthright, lively, and clear, with an occasional rhetorical flourish. They use telling phrases and devices from scripture, the liturgy of the synagogue, and the literary practice of contemporary Judaism, as well as from the oratorical technique of the popular philosophers. They heighten impact by repeating key words or phrases. Only by analysis of passages do we discern the considerable degree to which they have deliberately worked for telling effect.

The preachers reached into one aspect of common experience after another, into the Jewish scriptures, into the joyous hymnody already emergent in the Christian movement, even into the vocabulary of the mysteries, to find vivid similes and metaphors for the new relationship of the believers with God. Because of the novelty of the Christian message, such imagery possessed remarkable freshness, its impact enhanced by the force of spiritual conviction: in Christ all who responded in faith were *acquitted* or *justified* by grace, *redeemed* or *emancipated,* their sins *expiated* or *paid for by the sacrifice* of Jesus Christ (Rom. 3:24–25; Gal. 3:13). They had been *bought with a price* (1 Cor. 6:20), a *ransom* (Mk. 10:45). God had *canceled the bond* against them, *forgiving* their *trespasses* (Col. 2:13–14), *reconciling* them to himself or *setting things right* between them (2 Cor. 5:18). They had experienced a *new birth* (1 Pet. 1:3). They were now a *new creation* (2 Cor. 5:17). They had received the assurance of *adoption* as *God's own children* (Gal. 4:5). They were *heirs* of God and *fellow heirs* with Jesus Christ (Rom. 8:17). They were *members of God's household* and *fellow citizens with the saints.* (Eph 2:19). They were like *living stones in God's temple* (1 Pet. 2:5). They were

> a chosen race, a royal priesthood,
> *a holy nation, God's own people* .   [1 Pet. 2:9 NRSV]

Now they were called to *keep in step with the Spirit* (Gal. 5:25 NIV).

In their ability to command the attention of a street corner crowd, the preachers matched the popular sophists, moralists, and missionary rabbis, even in the use of irony and satire. But their overriding concern was the good news of salvation, and they were remembered for their power to convert or exhort, not for oratorical virtuosity. Even in such a setting, however, Apollos of Alexandria—the city where Jewish intellectuals had most successfully adapted classical rhetoric for preaching in the synagogue—was celebrated for eloquence. (Isa. there perhaps an allusion to rhetoric in his being linked with Zenas the lawyer in Titus 3:13?) Unfortunately, none of his preaching survives (unless, as some have surmised, the "epistle" to the Hebrews is his creation).

Reflections on Rhetoric[5]

When some Christians who had listened with admiration to Apollos in Corinth demeaned the apostle Paul for his lack of impressiveness as a speaker (2 Cor. 10:1, 9–11), he showed sensitivity to the charge (2 Cor. 11:5–6; cf. 1 Cor. 1:17). Was the presumed defect a matter of delivery associated with weakness induced by his physical affliction? It can hardly be put down as deficiency in style. A speaker with the force of spirit evident in Galatians, the power of argument manifest in Romans, the eloquence of 1 Corinthians 13 and 15, and the recurrent attention to rhetorical form that an analysis of his writings reveals could hardly be dismissed as inexpert in these matters, even though he made no display of sophistic virtuosity. Stung by the criticism, he disavowed any intention of relying on persuasive words of human wisdom.

Though itself patently rhetorical in style, Paul's apparent dismissal of rhetoric (1 Cor. 1–4) has often been misconstrued as literal and absolute repudiation, not only of human wisdom but of the forensic art as well. Such a conclusion with regard to rhetoric is hardly convincing when we examine with care what the apostle actually says regarding the issue, especially if we also reflect on the implications of the manner in which he says it:

> Christ did not send me to baptize, but to preach the gospel,
> and not with eloquent wisdom,[6]
> so that the cross of Christ might not be emptied of its power.

For the message about the cross is foolishness
to those who are perishing,
but to us who are being saved it is the power of God...
For since, in the wisdom of God,
the world did not know God through wisdom,
God decided, through the foolishness of the preaching,[7]
to save those who believe.
For Jews demand signs and Greeks desire wisdom,
but we preach Christ crucified,
a stumbling block to Jews and foolishness to Gentiles,
but to those who are the called, both Jews and Greeks,
Christ the power of God and the wisdom of God.
For God's foolishness is wiser than human wisdom,
and God's weakness is stronger than human strength...

I did not come in such a way
as to distinguish myself in eloquence or wisdom,
in order to proclaim to you the testimony of God.
For I decided to know nothing among you except Jesus Christ,
and him crucified.
And I came to you in weakness and in fear and in much trembling.
My speech and my proclamation
were not with plausible words of wisdom,
but with a demonstration of the Spirit and of power,
so that your faith might not rest on human wisdom,
but on the power of God.   [1 Cor. 1:17–2:5 NRSV alt.]

A careful reading of the text indicates that it is a forceful repudiation of human wisdom or philosophy as having any power to save, and not a discussion of rhetoric, except for the implication that some of the street-corner philosophers may use the tricks of the oratorical trade to lend an appearance of plausibility to their presentations. Since, however, the passage has been made *locus classicus* by theorists of Christian preaching who regard any concern with rhetoric as theologically unacceptable, some comment is in order here.

Committed to the folly of God, the apostle rejects the notion that any human power can bring salvation. Only the grace of God in the cross of Jesus Christ can save, and it is the task of the preaching to make it known. The power of the proclamation is of a totally different order from dialectical reasoning or rhetorical eloquence. It is a hard fact that not many philosophers or orators (*dynatoi*) have been called (1:26). The pretensions of the world—here used in the sense of the world at enmity with God—cannot deal with the ultimate human need; therefore Paul cannot stake his ministry on any aspect of human culture, for "the present form of this world is passing away" (1 Cor. 7:31 NRSV). Nor can he indulge in the empty sport of those for whom rhetoric is a game, nor approve the smooth talk of those who lead the simple-minded astray (Rom. 16:18), nor deflect attention from the gospel to fancy phrases.

If driven to choose between substance and form in the old conflict between philosophers and rhetoricians, he would doubtless side with the former. But here he sides with neither. Actually, it is the philosopher whom he rejects with the greater force. For philosophy cannot save, and in repudiating the word of human wisdom he dismisses not only the form but also the substance. Yet Paul does not sacrifice reason or learning; he simply will not stake his faith on any human power, but on God alone, as made known in Jesus Christ nailed to the cross.

Note, however, that in practice, if not in specific theory, the apostle grants a legitimate place to rhetoric: He insists that the Corinthians have heard the testimony of Christ "in all eloquence" (1:5),[8] and the rhetorician Augustine of Hippo will later turn to Paul as a model of Christian speech.[9]

Why then does Paul use rhetorical artistry? To *please*? If so, he does not admit it, though anyone who turns a phrase with the skill he commands[10] must derive at least a twinge of delight from the exercise. To *teach*? Certainly. If everything is to be done for edification, he will instruct his hearers in the most effective way available to him. To *persuade*? No and Yes!

The cross itself is the central and essential and effectual mode of persuasion; in that respect, the answer is No. But the preaching of the cross is spoken necessarily in a form of words, and in that respect the answer must be Yes:

> It is with the fear of the Lord always in mind
> that we try to win people over.　[2 Cor. 5:11 NJB]

Obviously, Paul will not compromise the preaching by pleasing people with what they want to hear (Gal. 1:10; 2 Cor. 4:2) or by chasing after celebrity for his eloquence. All his achievements he has counted as loss for the sake of Christ (Phil 3:7–8). But having the gift of speaking, by endowment and by education, will he not use it (Rom. 12:6–8)? With every power that he has he will address his appeal to men and women, doing his best to persuade others (2 Cor. 5:11 NRSV).

Paul nowhere avows, or even admits to, the use of rhetoric—or of philosophy or hermeneutic—but if he is to speak at all, he must employ some form of words. What he does use is far more self-conscious, far more sophisticated, than the so-called "natural rhetoric" of an untrained provincial, however ingenious. In truly important passages he marshals the devices of artistic and persuasive speech to make his point with maximum effectiveness. Some of these passages, for their beauty and force, have earned a high place in world literature, but he did not write them in pursuit of that goal. Rhetoric is ancillary and functional:

> All I do is done for the sake of the gospel.
>
> [1 Cor. 9:23 NRSV, alt.]

The apostle's preoccupation is not artistic declamation, but the good news of salvation. As its herald he commends himself in every way:

> by innocent behaviour and grasp of truth,
> by patience and kindliness, by gifts of the Holy Spirit,
> by unaffected love, by declaring the truth, by the power of God.
> We wield the weapons of righteousness in right hand and left.
>
> [2 Cor. 6:6–7 REB]

THE EXALTATION OF PREACHING[11]

The Essence of Preaching

Preaching in the first century is a personal encounter between hearers in need of the gospel and a witness to the power of the living Lord. It is not primarily a matter of *form,* though without form it cannot occur. Neither is it a matter of closely defined *content,* as though it must transmit a particular verbal formulation of the gospel, or as though its intent were to induce intellectual assent to specific dog-mas—or even facts. In the First Letter to the Corinthians Paul can define his gospel as the preaching of Christ crucified; in the Letter to the Romans, written soon afterward, he can give his most carefully wrought statement of his gospel without mention of the cross or cru-cifixion. Yet if no specific verbal formulation or structure of doctrine is essential to qualify a given utterance as preaching, it is obvious that it as surely requires content as it does form and that both of these must be consistent with its essential action: that is, *speaking which in personal engagement with the hearers makes known the reality of Jesus Christ.*

The preaching may recite the sacred story of God's dealings with Israel, which have come to their climax in him. It may set forth the promises made through the prophets, and their fulfillment, offering "the encouragement of the scriptures" (Rom. 15:4 NRSV). It may set forth some of Jesus' own words and apply them to the present situation of the hearers, may recall a particular incident of his ministry, may rehearse the narrative of his passion. It may speak primarily in terms of natural theology concerning God as Creator, but warn of coming judgment by the One whom God has raised from the dead. It may relate one's own personal encounter with the risen Lord. It may testify to the kingdom of God. It may admonish the hearers concerning specific sins and call for repentance. It may exhort to the pattern of living expected of Christians. It may rehearse familiar ethical admonitions popularized by philosophers and moralists. It may deal with a particular problem confronting the community of believers.

The preaching we have examined manifests such variety of content as to defy any effort to delimit a narrow range of ideas or any particular formulation of the gospel as alone appropriate to the action. What is essential is faithful testimony to Jesus as the living Christ:

> It is he whom we proclaim,
> warning everyone and teaching everyone in all wisdom,
> so that we may present everyone mature in Christ.   [Col. 1:28 NRSV]

As a trusty witness, the preacher makes it possible for the listener who responds in faith to encounter the Lord who commissioned the preaching and the God who sent both the Son and the preacher: Had he not given his promise?

> Whoever listens to you listens to me...   [Lk. 10:16 REB]
> To receive you is to receive me,
> and to receive me is to receive the One who sent me.   [Mt. 10:40 REB]

The Problem of Rejection

But the response to the preaching also had a darker side, for many who heard did not believe. Some merely drifted away to listen to other speakers and perhaps profess some other faith. But some who disbelieved the gospel threw themselves into active opposition to it. The preachers expected heckling and public debate; these were the lot of the street-corner missionary. But some opponents of the gospel stirred up mobs to violence or turned the public authorities against the preachers. They were sentenced to flogging and imprisonment, and some of their leaders were executed. Yet they counted persecution their glory rather than cause for complaint, linking them with the prophets and with their Lord himself.

But they could not fail to puzzle over the great conundrum: How was it that people could neglect so great a salvation? And how especially could Israel, the chosen people of God, reject the good news of the Christ?

Jesus' parable of the soils locates the deficiency in the heart of the hearer without explaining why some respond and some do not. Paul traces belief and unbelief to the inscrutable mystery of divine election (Rom. 9:14–18). Luke concludes the book of Acts with a pertinent testimony from the prophet Isaiah (Acts 28:26–27; cf. Isa. 6:9–10); had he quoted it in full, he would seem to have concurred with Paul's explanation, but by omitting a tricolon in the center of the passage, he presents a view harmonious with that expressed in the parable of the soils.

In whatever way the refusal might be explained, it had the same effect, described in the Lord's saying:

> whoever rejects you rejects me.
> And whoever rejects me rejects the One who sent me.
>
> [Lk. 10:16 REB]

Faithfulness to the Gospel

Even within the church the love of some grew cold, the "good message of God" (Heb. 6:5 JB) lost its appeal, and they fell away. Even some who preached lost contact with the gospel proclaimed by Peter and Paul and their coworkers. Paul's Letter to the Galatians invokes anathemas on any one who distorts the preaching:

> Even if we or an angel from heaven should proclaim to you
> a gospel contrary to what we proclaimed to you,
> let that one be accursed!   [Gal. 1:8 NRSV]

Everywhere the leaders show concern about false prophets and teachers—in the gospel tradition, in Paul, in Acts, in the Johannine literature, in the Pastoral Epistles. The authentic gospel is seen as deriving from Jesus Christ himself:

It was there from the beginning; we have heard it;
we have seen it with our own eyes;
we looked upon it, and felt it with our own hands:
our theme is the Word which gives life.   [1 Jn. 1:1 REB]

By the end of the century the church was struggling to find effective criteria for faithful preaching. Those who undertook the work
were admonished to do it with full seriousness:

Whoever speaks must do so
as one speaking the very words of God.   [1 Pet. 4:11 NRSV]

The Supreme Task

By such preaching, with all that it implied for personal and corporate life within the church, the Christian mission went forward, exult-
ing in both the message and the action of proclamation. Repeatedly
Jesus was remembered as a preacher.[12] As for the calling of the heralds, Paul expressed it memorably:

I cannot help myself;
it would be agony for me not to preach.   [1 Cor. 9:16 REB]

CONCLUSION TO PART FOUR

First-Century Preaching: An Assessment

The significance of Christian preaching in the first century of our era may be suggested by the following considerations:

1. By the end of the century the preachers had spread both the knowledge of Jesus and faith in him as Christ and Lord across a large part of the world known to them, from Mesopotamia (and perhaps farther east) to Spain. The movement grew both by conversational testimony or intimate dialog and by public proclamation. Christians sometimes came first to the attention of others by their distinctive manner of life or their care for the helpless, but that fuller knowledge of the gospel and that conviction that led to faith came from the work of the preachers and teachers.

2. The preaching brought into existence believing communities in hundreds of localities and sustained them in a hostile world. Their fellowship included both Jews and Gentiles, slaves and free persons, "Greeks" and "barbarians"—that is, persons within the sphere of Hellenistic culture and persons beyond—a few from conditions of privilege and a multitude of the exploited and oppressed. Statistical estimates as to the number of Christians vary widely, but the total evidently ran into the thousands. They thought of the church as one and universal.

3. The preaching of the first century fixed the life of the church in a living relationship with the transcendent "word of God." That term designated the revelation of God in the witness of the scriptures and supremely in Jesus Christ; it referred to the preaching; it signified the Christian cause. Through the proclamation, they believed, the God who had addressed Israel through the prophets and through the Son continued to speak to all who heard the proclamation of judgment

and grace, which they now offered in the name of the Lord Jesus. Their responsibility as they saw it was to make known "the whole counsel of God."

4. Relating their experience of the living Christ and evoking it in others, the preachers conveyed, shaped, and established the normative content of the Christian message as it would be confessed by the church for generations. They preserved the tradition of Jesus' ministry and teachings, death and resurrection. They handed on the forms of confession witnessing to the faith that would later be crystallized by formulation into the "catholic" creeds. Their metaphors, abstracted as formal metaphysical terminology and hardened into legalism, furnished the working vocabulary for theology for centuries to come.

5. In the light of their experience with Jesus and their faith in his resurrection, the preachers appropriated and redefined the familiar vocabulary of Judaism to express the new relationship they had found with God through him. The term *Messiah,* so powerfully expressive of Israel's hope, they made central in its Greek form *Christ* as title and name for Jesus, proclaimed by them as initiator of a new covenant. The great old terms for God's action in behalf of Israel—*election, deliverance, salvation, redemption*—they applied to the work of Jesus Christ accomplished by his death and resurrection. They proclaimed him the second Adam and all who believed as constituting a new humanity in him.

6. Thus, like Israel before them, the preachers "mythicized history" (a modern, not an apostolic, notion) by attributing divine and ultimate meaning to events that had occurred in their own place and time and experience. In their preaching, their interpretation of the cosmic significance of the coming of the Savior—of his life, death, and resurrection among them—overwhelmed in importance any concern about the details of his career as a historical figure. Insisting that he had lived among them as a real person—they had heard and seen and touched with their hands the one whom they preached—the element they made crucial in their proclamation was his coming as revealer and mediator of God, as the word of life (1 Jn. 1:1–3).

7. The missionary task undertaken so effectively by the preachers of the apostolic era combined with the emphasis of classical rhetoric on persuasion to imbue preaching with a spirit of urgency, calling hearers to repentance and to new life in Christ—even though reliance on authority and grace to a large extent displaced the topics of the schools in moving hearts and minds to respond to the gospel.[1] Until

the Theodosian establishment of Christianity as the faith of the Roman Empire, evangelical urgency would continue to characterize the work of the church's orators, seeking audiences outside the cult, and from time to time far down the centuries it would spring up anew in the spirit of earnest preachers and the excitement of revivals to bring many to conversion.

8. The work of the first two generations of Christians established preaching as the generative and defining action of the church. Practiced at first by women and men alike, it became the means of their missionary evangelism. It assumed a central place in the cult and functioned as the primary mode of Christian *paideia* or education. It served as a major outlet for the witness of disciples generally, as the rabbinate had done in Judaism. It assumed priority among the responsibilities of ministerial office.

9. Emerging within a patriarchal culture that assigned roles of leadership to men and kept women subservient if not silent, the early church continued the practice of Jesus in according to women a position of honor and responsibility in its common life, including significant participation in the task of preaching. In addition to their initial role as first heralds of the resurrection, women were acknowledged as prophets, teachers, ministers, and coworkers of the apostles, though this original participation in the tasks of preaching was soon obscured, then forgotten, and for centuries denied, by the triumph of patriarchy within the church.

10. The moral earnestness of the preachers charged their *paranesis* with the call to newness of life in Christ and repeated exhortation to Christians to walk worthily of their calling in him. Had it not been for their emphasis on *agapé*-love as made known in the Lord Jesus, their repeated admonitions and warnings might well have sounded moralistic, but the patterns of behavior they commended were presented as their expression of devotion to him rather than subservience to law. Though the ethical concern of the preachers had much in common with that of the rabbis and of the popular moralists, their proclamation set it forth as it had been embodied in the person of the Lord Jesus. Moreover, in making love the supreme excellence, they substituted a democratic spiritual ideal for what was originally an aristocratic ideal in Hellenism. Their ethical preaching attracted converts.

11. The preaching, however, resulted in an ambiguous relationship between Christianity and Judaism. Beginning with the proclamation of the risen Jesus as Messiah, the church was first of all a movement

within the household of Israel, hoping to bring to that whole people the joy of the promise fulfilled. Opposition from temple authorities, apparently quite early, and the quite unexpected opening of the church to Gentiles, who quickly came to outnumber the original Jewish Christians, soon resulted in rivalry, suspicion, and mounting mutual hostility. It was, however, Christians of Jewish blood and heritage, not Gentiles, who first recounted the repudiation and crucifixion of Jesus at the instigation of their religious leaders—a point made not to express anti-Semitism but to evoke repentance. In a later situation of religious competition which waxed bitter on occasion, some Gentile Christians, even in the first century, heard this charge as propaganda directed against Jews generally, a misperception compounded by the Fourth Gospel's use of the term "Judeans"—unfortunately translated as "Jews"—to denote the opponents of Jesus.

But a more conciliatory and inclusive spirit was also at work in the preaching, represented by Paul in his insistence that God remains faithful to the covenant with Israel, with whom, by the mystery of grace, the Gentile Christians have also been united as children of Abraham by faith. So also the Letter to the Ephesians celebrates the breaking down of the wall of hostility between Jews and Gentiles; through the death of Christ, both have been made one people in the inclusive household of God.

By the end of the first Christian century, the relationship had not been clearly worked out. Christianity prized the legacy it received from Judaism: the faith in one God, the transcendence of the word of God, the holy scriptures, the weekly gathering of the congregation for worship centered in exposition of scripture, the ethical understanding of the call to holiness, the hope it saw fulfilled in Jesus Christ. In their missionary ventures the Christian preachers turned to the synagogues of the Diaspora to find audiences most likely to respond to the gospel; many of their first adherents were devout Jews or God-fearing Gentiles who had been instructed by the rabbis. The Christians adopted Jewish modes of exegesis and, perhaps as early as Apollos of Alexandria, took over the Jewish use of classical rhetoric in preaching. The leading Christians in the first two generations were Jews, including all the writers whose work found a place in the New Testament, except for Luke.

12. The preachers engaged the high culture of classical antiquity in profoundly important ways. They challenged its idolatry, superstition, immorality, and reliance on wealth and power. They addressed

its spiritual need with their gospel of hope. They spoke to it in its own mode of communication, oratory, if not on its own terms. They released a new spiritual dynamic which, after some generations of contention and uneasiness, would in the fourth century effect a synthesis between classical culture and Christian faith destined to transform the intellectual life of Europe and of all the world affected by the European heritage.

13. The preachers, in their struggle to understand the meaning of the gospel for the unexpected situation in which they found themselves, carried the church onward, from a widely held expectation of the imminent end of the present age in the coming of the Lord, to a living belief in the Lord as present through the Holy Spirit, ever with the church as it fulfilled its ministry within the ongoing history of the world. Their work of "edification" consolidated the church as a continuing community, developing institutions for its life in society and no longer regarding its message as essentially apocalyptic. Their emphasis on the lordship of Christ, not only over private conduct but over the whole world, set the focus once again on the central element in Jesus' own preaching: the reign of God. Any program for the renovation of the social order, however, remained implicit in their confession that "Jesus is Lord" and their continued emphasis on the final triumph of God's kingdom. They launched no direct assault on specific political or societal ills—not yet an option, given the massive magnitude of the empire and their own limited numbers and social power.

14. The preaching, especially of the first generation, shaped the form of the classical literature of the Christian movement, which first emerged in occasional letters of exhortation and witness. In time certain writings from the first century would be canonized as the New Testament and incorporated with the scriptures of Judaism into the Christian Bible. This development gave the world a new form of literature, the four Gospels, which bind together the commonplace and the sublime.[2] As condensation of the original preaching, epistle and gospel formed the substance of the subsequent preaching of the church.

15. Preaching was established within the church as a personal mode of conveying the knowledge of the person of Jesus Christ, the supreme revealer of a personal God. Public address was, of course, the common means of communication within the prevailing culture, as it had been the method employed by Jesus. But any theory of

communication that fails to note the essentially personal encounter between speaker and hearer necessitated by this mode ignores the essentially dialogic nature of the preaching of Jesus and the Christian heralds. This fact, which the historian can point out, is a key point for reflection in formulating a theology of preaching.

16. Not all who heard the proclamation answered in faith, but the preachers saw whatever response was made—whether Yes or No—as a response to God, who had chosen to be made present through the preaching.[3] The divine vulnerability in electing to rest the issue on the decision of the hearer might seem at first nothing less than heavenly foolishness, a show of weakness in a world that measured deity in terms of strength and might. But just as the ultimate theophany shining through the helplessness of a crucified Savior excelled all human power and wisdom, so God's folly, in relying on the preaching of the cross to touch and persuade and attract and change human hearts, proved stronger than mortals and wiser than mortals.

17. The preachers of the first century established within the church the message and the action that would repeatedly serve across subsequent centuries as the means and source of its renewal. Again and again in times of spiritual debility a revival of Christian faith and life would come with a new upsurge of power in preaching. It would be marked not only by the method of public proclamation but by a new engagement with the apostolic message. That story will unfold in subsequent chapters of this study.

+

With the death of the apostles and eyewitnesses to the ministry of Jesus and then of the generation who had received the gospel through their preaching, an era came to an end. And a new era had begun. The church was launched on a perilous and uncertain history in a world that waited for its message, yet met it with hostility. Not until the second decade of the fourth century would the preachers and their hearers be free from the threat of persecution. Yet throughout the second and third centuries they would continue to proclaim the gospel of Jesus Christ and to draw increasing numbers of persons to profess faith in him. We now proceed to consider the preaching of those advocates of an illicit faith.

PART FIVE

Advocates of an Illicit Faith

Preachers of the Second and Third Centuries

INTRODUCTION TO PART FIVE

A Continuing Apostolic Mission

Mandate to Preach

The old manuscripts of the Gospel according to Mark terminate so abruptly as to suggest the loss of a final column or page; the briefest of the various endings found in the most ancient texts concludes its report of the empty tomb of Jesus with this sentence:

> And afterward Jesus himself sent out through them, from east to west, the sacred and imperishable proclamation of eternal salvation.
>
> [Mk. 16, THE SHORTER ENDING, NRSV]

The Christian scribe who composed those lines encapsulated the church's understanding of its mission in the second and third centuries. With the death of the apostles and of those who had heard them, new generations of Christians continued preaching, both to the masses, and to the intellectual elite, and despite intense opposition the church continued to grow. The high culture that had put Jesus to death turned on his followers with violence, and recurrent persecution periodically drove the church underground. For a time its future looked uncertain, but it gained strength while political confusion mounted, until in his bid to pacify the empire, Constantine sought the support of the Christians. In 311 his celebrated Edict of Toleration ended the persecutions. Still a small minority, the Christians were nevertheless widely dispersed; moreover, they were respected by many, both for the temper of their lives and the witness of their preachers.

Overview of Part Five

The period of some two hundred years covered in these chapters, from about 100 C.E. to 311, involves a time span comparable to that from the Declaration of Independence to the present. Allowance must therefore be made for striking differences of circumstance and mood within these twenty-one decades, and the relative chronology of persons and events must be kept in mind as, for the sake of order, we follow a topical outline. We will briefly observe the world of the second and third centuries, the witness of the martyrs, and the defense of the gospel addressed by the apologists to the makers of public opinion. We will consider the preaching, often secret, that sustained the beleaguered community of Christians and will analyze development in the art. We will conclude by assessing the significance of the era for the history of preaching.

CHAPTER 14

Witnesses in a Hostile World

THE WORLD OF LATE ANTIQUITY[1]

The Roman Empire

After the death of Domitian (81–96 C.E.), who had expelled the philosophers from Rome and perhaps also exiled John of the Apocalypse to Patmos, Nerva (96–98) initiated the line of the "five good emperors." Each of his four immediate successors reigned for approximately two decades with intelligence and equity, giving the world from Armenia to Britain a period of peace and justice that translated Stoic ideals into political actuality.

The foremost minds of the time celebrated the empire, and the eloquent preacher Tertullian (ca. 160–220) praised Trajan and Marcus Aurelius, even though they had persecuted the Christians. But after 180 a long period of blood and iron disrupted the peace. Rival commanders seized the imperial purple by force of arms, frequently attempting radical changes in policy and often ruling only briefly. Constantine's grant of toleration to the Christians in 313 was part of his successful bid to restore stability to the Roman world.

It was a world that confronted emperors and peasants alike with problems and ordeals. During the first three centuries of the common era rural people were migrating on a large scale to the cities, where hard, impersonal actuality more often than not dashed unrealistic hopes. Then, in the second and third centuries, recurrent epidemics of malaria broke out, striking terror and wasting population. Times were hard, physically, economically, emotionally for multitudes, both small and great.

Offering splendor amid disorder, the emperors patronized sculpture and architecture on a grand scale. Literature was pretentious, imitative, and for the most part forgettable. Early in the second century Juvenal composed his bitter satires and Suetonius his collection of biographies, *De viris illustribus.* A bit later Babrius, writing in Greek as was the mode, versified scores of Aesop's fables. Roman culture followed the roads and the sea lanes to the far reaches of the empire but had virtually no influence beyond its boundaries.

Oratory

Oratory continued to enjoy more prestige than vitality. Though Nerva and Trajan (98–117) allowed speakers greater freedom than had been tolerated during the first century, public deliverances were overloaded with adulation of the emperor, and there was little deliberative oratory before assemblies of citizens. Yet Tacitus (ca. 55–ca. 117) and Pliny the Younger (62?–113) deserve to be noted as speakers of integrity.

The most illustrious orator of the century was the Numidian M. Cornelius Fronto (ca. 100–ca. 167), tutor to Marcus Aurelius and literary arbiter of the era.[2] A lover of early Roman literature, he sought to popularize the authors of the republic and, like them, to root the language of literature in the common speech. The "new Latin"—*elocutio novella*—which began to emerge as a result became the universal tongue of Western learning until the end of the Middle Ages, but no revival of letters occurred.

Another Numidian, Lucius Apuleius, gained fame as a traveling commentator and lecturer. He brought out two dozen of his pieces under the title *Florida,* and his romance *The Golden Ass (Metamorphoses)* remained a "best seller" for centuries. Apuleius was a man of many-sided interests with a flair for popular address.

Rhetoric

Despite the widely lamented decline of oratory, rhetoric continued to dominate education and to enjoy imperial patronage. The favored teachers—five in the major cities, three in smaller towns—were granted immunities from taxation like those allowed to the priests of the ancestral religion and in subsquent centuries to the Christian clergy. In the schools the practical department dealt with pleading in the courts, but the sophistic department, which treated speaking as an art, enjoyed greater prestige, and its leading teachers lived ostentatiously. The rhetoric known as the second sophistic, which flourished from the second to the fourth century, emphasized stylistic flourish and showmanship. Lucian of Samosata (120–190) wrote on "How to Become a Perfect Orator" and gave attention on the relation of rhetoric to the work of the historian. Hermogenes of Tarsus (2d cent. C.E.) compiled a digest of scholastic rhetoric from the time of Hermagoras (2d cent. B.C.E.); it remained authoritative in the schools until the fourth century.

Philosophy and Personal Salvation[3]

Meanwhile, conditions continued to diminish the sense of personal worth. Decisions that determined one's destiny resided with Caesar—still remote from the faceless masses, no matter how benevolent his intentions, or at least his carefully crafted image. Confrontations with death accompanied every new epidemic, as malaria wasted the population. Engulfed in the great urban masses, men and women who had left the countryside with little reason to believe that they were valued in the vast human scheme of things turned increasingly to reflecting on their own lives and fates. The mood of individualism so evident in the first century intensified in the second.

In increasing numbers seekers looked to philosophy, and philosophy itself moved toward a concern with individual salvation. Near the middle of the second century a revival of Epicureanism began, lasting for about a hundred years; hailed as *Soter* (Savior), Epicurus delivered many from their fears. Stoicism inspired others to introspection and the quest for virtue; the Emperor Marcus Aurelius (161–180) himself devoted the quiet hours at the end of the day to such self-examination, recorded in his *Meditations.* Responding to Stoic doctrines of human equality, the Emperor Commodus in 212 extended citizenship to all freeborn men living within the empire. The Hermetic literature enjoyed widespread popularity. Scores of wandering philosophers continued to harangue the crowds with aggressive street-corner rhetoric, making the most of their well-rehearsed humor, abrasive arguments against other schools, and unabashed appeals for donations.

Because of the skeptical arguments popularized by Cicero and not yet answered, many intellectuals found it impossible to embrace any philosophical system. To the widespread uncertainty a powerful and appealing rejoinder emerged in the Neoplatonism of Plotinus (205–270) and his disciple Porphyry (ca. 232–ca. 304). After studying in Alexandria and venturing as far as Mesopotamia to seek the wisdom of the East, Plotinus came to Rome to advocate the certainty arising from mystical union with God and to commend the life of contemplation as the means of releasing spirit from matter. His teachings were edited by Porphyry under the title *Enneads.* Though these mystical philosophers opposed the Christian faith, both had much in common with it and exercised considerable influence over the thinking of the young church. It was not uncommon for outsiders with a superficial knowledge of Christianity to think of it as yet another philosophy, and its preachers (e.g., Tertullian) did not hesitate to present it as such; critical thinkers saw it as superstition.

The Religious Scene[4]

Preoccupation with personal issues reached beyond philosophy with an openness to popular religion. In the second century Artemidorus wrote on the interpretation of dreams, and the mystery cults continued to exert a wide appeal. The celebrated orator Aelius Aristides (129–189) testified in his *Sacred Discourses* to the healing power of Asclepius over a disease from which he had suffered for thirteen years. As emperors both Hadrian (117–138) and Antoninus Pius (138–161) received initiation into the Eleusinian mysteries, and many of the Senators identified with the mystery cults, especially those of Mithras and Dionysus. Funds from the public treasury financed the construction of magnificent temples to the gods. The uncertainties of the third century intensified personal anxiety and with it religious interest.

Gnosticism reached its peak in the second and third centuries. This highly eclectic movement counterposing matter and spirit, as already noted (see chapter 2), appropriated concepts and vocabulary from various schools of philosophy and assorted religions as far away as India. Popular preachers representing its numerous sects offered salvation through secret knowledge. One of them pleaded:

> Release yourselves, and that which has bound you will be dissolved.
> Save yourselves, in order that it may be saved.
> The gentle Father has sent you the savior and given you strength.
> Why are you hesitating? Seek when you are sought;
> when you are invited, listen. For the time is short.[5]

Zealous advocates mingled their collection of notions with Neoplatonism and Christianity, producing Gnosticized versions of both movements that proved highly attractive, until the latter rejected them as heretical. Something of Gnosticism's appeal lay in its air of the occult and its eastern aura, emanating from Zoroastrian sources.

Under a tolerant, even inquiring, attitude in both popular and official circles, both Christianity and Judaism had prospered for a time, but now their situation had radically changed. The Jewish wars against Rome undercut the appeal of their missionaries, even as the conflict intensified Jewish antipathy toward Hellenism. By the middle of the second century, Hellenistic Judaism collapsed; the memory of Philo and his Alexandrian colleagues, suppressed in the Talmud, persisted only among the Christians. The base of Jewish Christianity was also fatally weakened; the future belonged to the Gentile mission.

But just as public opinion began to realize that Christianity and Judaism were two different faiths,[6] official policy turned against the Christians. The orator Fronto himself, in intimate contact with the imperial court, leveled charges against them.

THE WITNESS OF THE MARTYRS[7]

Two Centuries of Persecution

Prejudice in the intellectual establishment against the Christians rested on a popular base. Tacitus wrote that they were "hated for their vicious crimes."[8] Pliny considered them victims of "depraved and excessive superstition,"[9] and Lucian dismissed them as deluded "wretches" who had turned against the gods to "worship that crucified sophist, and live according to his laws."[10] By their determination to have nothing to do with idolatry, they cut themselves off from socializing with unbelievers and from public festivities, for nearly all meat came from animals sacrificed in the temples of the ancestral gods; and the rituals associated with the games, like those attesting political loyalty, involved religious ceremony.

The reclusiveness practiced by the followers of Jesus, their secret meetings, the growing strength of their organization, their frequent attack on traditional belief and popular custom made them suspect. Although the patience of Roman officials finally gave out before the Christian refusal to obey a simple order, they generally protected this strange community from hostile mobs throughout the second century, unwilling to act on anonymous charges against believers or to track them down systematically. Yet no emperor formally reversed Nero's policy of regarding a Christian profession as a crime in itself, and when charges were pressed against a bishop or other leader, refusal to sacrifice to the gods of the empire led automatically to execution.

Ignatius of Antioch[11]

About 110 C.E. the bishop of Antioch in Syria was sentenced to "fight with beasts at Rome."[12] Chained to his military guard, Ignatius turned his long overland journey to the capital into a moving pageant, exhorting his brother bishops and even companies of Christians who boldly came to meet him in the various cities along the way. To churches that had greeted him through their bishops he dictated letters asking their continued prayers and encouraging them to faithfulness; in one of these he recalls an instance of prophesying in the Spirit:

> I cried out while I was with you,
> I spoke with a great voice,—with God's own voice,—
> "Give heed to the bishop, and to the presbytery and deacons."
> ...the Spirit was preaching, and saying this,
> "Do nothing without the bishop, keep your flesh as the temple of God,
> love unity, flee from divisions, be imitators of Jesus Christ,
> as was he also of his Father." [Ign. Phila., VII. 1, 2, LCL, *Ap F,* I:245, 247]

Called *Theophorus,* "God-inspired," Ignatius writes as he prophesies, with great earnestness; yet his intensity of spirit does not prevent him from striking off one rhetorical phrase after another. He shows a particular fondness for metaphor and paradox, figures which must also have abounded in his homilies:

> There is one Physician, who is both flesh and spirit,
> born and yet not born, who is Deity in humanity, true life in death,
> both of Mary and of God, first passible and then impassible,
> Jesus Christ our Lord. [Ign. Eph. VII. 2, LCL, *Ap F,* I:181, alt.]

Ignatius insists that this one in whom God was fully present was indeed human in a complete sense, standing against those who viewed him as a purely spiritual being:

> For I know and believe that he was in the flesh
> even after the Resurrection. [Ign. Smyrn., III. 1, LCL, *Ap F,* I:255]

The condemned bishop implores the Christians at Rome to do nothing to prevent his impending death, for he sees it as a proclamation of the gospel:

> For if you are silent concerning me, I am a word of God;
> but if you love my flesh, I shall again be only a cry...
> God has vouchsafed that the bishop of Syria shall be found

at the setting of the sun, having fetched him from the sun's rising.
It is good to set to the world towards God,
that I may rise to him.   [Ign. Rom., II. 1, 2, LCL, *Ap F,* I:227–29][13]

Polycarp of Smyrna

Nearly half a century later (155), the venerable bishop of Smyrna, who had embraced Ignatius on his journey to Rome, was haled before the proconsul for refusing to say *"Kyrios Kaisar"*—"Caesar is Lord." Pressed by the patient and humane official to cry, "Away with the atheists," a label applied to the Christians because of their disbelief in the traditional gods, Polycarp ironically complied—by pointing to the bloodthirsty mob in the arena and speaking those words. But when the proconsul again urged him to take the loyalty oath and revile Christ, he replied,

For eighty and six years I have been his servant,
and he has done me no wrong,
and how can I blaspheme my King
who saved me?   [Mart. Polyc., IX. 2, 3, LCL, *Ap F,* II:325]

Still pressed by the proconsul, he answered,

Listen plainly; I am a Christian.   [X. 1, LCL, *Ap F,* ibid.]

The narrator of Polycarp's death added a dramatic touch, noting that the proconsul "sent his herald into the midst of the arena to announce three times":

Polycarp has confessed that he is a Christian.   [XII. 1, LCL, ibid., 327, 329]

The words for *herald* and *announce* were *kēryx* and *kēryssein.* The official voice of Roman authority had become a preacher, preaching the unconquerable word!

The death of the faithful bishop, long honored in his city, impressed pagans as well as believers. "He was not only a famous teacher," wrote a disciple, "but also a notable martyr [the word means *witness*], whose martyrdom all desire to imitate, for it followed the gospel of Christ."[14]

Perpetua and Eulalia[15]

Half a century later in Carthage a young Christian mother and her brother were arrested. When the governor ordered, "Offer the sacrifice for the welfare of the emperors," she responded, "I will not." Then to his inevitable question, "Are you a Christian?" she replied, "Yes, I am."[16] For that public word she was executed in March 203.

A century after Perpetua's witness a young Christian girl of twelve named Eulalia escaped from her parents' home in Lusitania, found her way through the night to the town of Merida, and at dawn appeared at the magistrate's court, challenging the imperial guards and facing down the Roman prefect to protest devotion to gods chiseled from stone, the work of the Creator:

> Miserable men, for the Christians you search!
> Lo, I am one of that odious race,
> Foe to your fiendish idolatrous rites.
> Witness to Christ with my heart and my lips,
> Under my feet I will trample your gods.
>
> Isis, Apollo, and Venus are nought,
> Nought is Maximian, lord of the world;
> Nought are those deities fashioned by hand,
> Nought is the one who pays homage to them—
> Vanity all of these, nothingness all.
>
> Mighty Maximian is but a slave
> Subject to meaningless idols of stone.

[Prudentius, "Hymn...Eulalia," 71–82, FC 43:131–32][17]

Seized by the soldiers at the order of the prefect, the girl was given a last chance to save herself by offering incense to the gods; refusing, was dragged immediately to bloody torture and death. She had learned well the lesson taught by the preachers and was able to proclaim it herself, as did countless other Christian women in those grim decades of persecution.

Martyrdom Itself as Proclamation

The faithfulness of Christian women and men, even children, ready to die for their confession, gave new and particular meaning to the familiar word "witnesses," *martyres.* Now it came to have the special meaning of *martyrs,* persons who had given up life itself in their refusal to deny Christ as Lord. Their example became a powerful force in Christian self-consciousness, just as the constant possibility of death turned aside potential converts who might otherwise have lightly made a profession. Throughout the second and third centuries preachers undertook to prepare their people for that ultimate decision when any Christian might be called to submit to the final test: Deny the Lord Jesus or give up life forthwith. The martyrs' willingness to let their own blood be shed by the sword of Caesar's magistrate proved the most convincing preaching of all. The public examination and execution of a believer became *martyria,* a witness or demonstration, a dramatic proclamation of the gospel.

Narratives of martyrdom soon formed an established genre of Christian literature, modeled after earlier Jewish and even pagan narratives of ultimate faithfulness.[18] Some include a "sermon" to the hostile authorities, which prompts the judgment of death;[19] others simply recount the official interrogation and the fateful words of testimony to Christ as sole and supreme Lord. Under the circumstances, even the plainest of utterances functioned as a powerful mode of Christian preaching. When persecution raged with full force, that last testament, sealed in the martyr's blood, was the only form of *public* proclamation to be heard.

And it was remembered. Born a generation after Constantine's Edict of Toleration, the Christian poet Prudentius (348–ca. 410) composed a sequence of hymns on *The Martyrs' Crowns,* celebrating fourteen who died as faithful witnesses. In "The Passion of Cyprian" he praises both the eloquence and the unfailing courage of the great preacher and bishop of Carthage:

> Yet he still hovers over the world and on earth is always present,
> Ever discoursing, exhorting, expounding, instructing, prophesying.[20]

Such a witness was not a matter of rhetoric, as Ignatius himself observed:

> Christianity is not the work of persuasiveness, but of greatness,
> when it is hated by the world.   [Ign. Rom. III. 3, LCL, *Ap F,* I:229]

CHAPTER 15

"The Defense of the Gospel"

CONVERSION OF A GENRE

Christians could die bravely, and some even courted martyrdom, but whenever conditions permitted, a company of thoughtful and eloquent speakers raised their voices to commend the faith—despite Ignatius's bold claim, by *persuasion.* In a tradition as old as forensic oratory, the apology or defense was a recognized genre of public address and, in its published form, of literature. Those of Isocrates and Demosthenes were classics studied in every school. Since Plato's "Apology of Socrates" the genre had had links to philosophy; Hellenistic Jews had used it to contend for biblical monotheism, and the author of Luke-Acts had twice (chaps. 22, 26) pictured the apostle Paul making speeches of this type under dramatic circumstances.

Christian preachers of the second century seized on the form for presenting their case to the public; virtually all the church's literature addressed to outsiders that remains from the two centuries before Constantine consists of apologies. Such defenses were needed in a time when traditional art, public ceremony, and glamorous celebrities celebrated the deities of polytheism: the eloquent Maximos of Tyre, tutor to Marcus Aurelius, delivered an oration "In Defense of Idols," and the urbane and witty Lucius Apuleius speculated in his picaresque novel *The Golden Ass* that all the supreme goddesses are actually one, though known under various names. Philosophers wrote in criticism of Christian belief, the Platonist Celsus late in the second century and the Neoplatonist Porphyry in the third, and preachers undertook to answer their charges.

EARLIEST CHRISTIAN APOLOGISTS[1]

Apology as Preaching

Some apologists saw attack as their best defense; they assailed idolatry and superstition by an appeal to common sense and rejected polytheism on philosophical grounds. Others argued the reasonableness of the Christian faith. Some preachers commended its way of life; a few entered stirring pleas for religious liberty. All appealed to the goodwill and intelligence of the audience, and the extant pieces show considerable rhetorical polish. Through a dedication to the Roman Senate or the Emperor, some made a bid in pamphlet form for an audience the preacher had no other way of addressing. Others apparently represent speeches actually delivered in public to a general audience.

The arguments that run through the apologies indicate the approach taken by the preachers in their address to outsiders during the two centuries when Christianity was an illicit faith. For the missionary preaching of the era these documents constitute our chief source.

Quadratus: "Letter to Diognetus"

In the third decade of the second century, while the Emperor Hadrian was in Asia Minor, two Christians named Quadratus and Aristides appealed to him on behalf of their fellow believers, who were then suffering persecution.

The text of Quadratus's apology, long lost except for a brief citation by Eusebius in his *Ecclesiastical History* (4.3), written in the fourth century, has now been identified with the first ten chapters of the so-called "Letter to Diognetus." Though scholars are not unanimous in supporting this conclusion, the arguments are persuasive. Aside from his appeal to Hadrian, virtually nothing is known of this Quadratus, but he is presumed to have hailed from Asia Minor and is therefore not to be confused with the Athenian bishop of the same name later in the century.

In customary rhetorical fashion, the speaker begins with an appeal for openmindedness on the part of the hearer,

as one...about to listen to a new story.   [Ep. Diog. 2. 1, LCL, *Ap F,* II:353]

The preacher reasons against gods of stone and metal and wood and pottery:

Are they not all dumb? Are they not blind?
Are they not without souls? Are they not without feeling?

Are they not without movement?
Are they not all rotting? Are they not all decaying? ...
Is this the reason why you hate the Christians—
that they do not think that these are gods?

[Ep. Diog. 2. 4–6, LCL, Ap F, II:353]

After this paraphrase of Psalm 135:15–18 in the rhetorical style of the Second Sophistic, the preacher moves on to explain why Christians do not worship in the same way as Jews, dismissing any need of God for sacrifices and discounting the scruples of the ceremonial Law. He praises the life of the Christians:

They live in their own countries, but only as aliens...
They busy themselves on earth, but their citizenship is in heaven.
They obey the established laws,
but in their own lives they go far beyond what the laws require.
They love all people, and by all people are persecuted...
They are put to death, and yet they are brought to life...
To put it simply, what the soul is in the body,
that Christians are in the world.

[Ep. Diog. 5. 5, 9–12; 6.1, LCC, I:217–18, alt.]

Despite opposition, argues our orator, Christians increase (6.9). This is because God has sent the "truth from heaven," the holy Logos (7. 2), whose preexistent glory the preacher hymns and whose saving mission he also celebrates:

He sent him out of kindness and gentleness,
like a king sending a son, who is himself a king.
He sent him as God;
He sent him as a human being to human beings.
He willed to save by persuasion, not by compulsion,
for compulsion is not God's way of working.
In sending him God called, but did not pursue;
he sent him in love, not in judgment.
Yet he will indeed send him someday as our Judge,
and who shall stand when he appears?   [Ep. Diog. 7. 4–6, LCC, I:219, alt.][2]

Insisting on the necessity of divine revelation, the apologist dismisses the "idle nonsense" of the philosophers (8.2), then, without naming the name of Jesus or Christ, commends the love of God:

God did not hate us or drive us away, or bear us ill will.
Rather, he was long-suffering and forbearing.

In his mercy, he took up the burden of our sins.
He himself gave up his own Son as a ransom for us—
the holy one for the unjust, the innocent for the guilty,
the righteous one for the unrighteous,
the incorruptible for the corruptible, the immortal for the mortal.
For what else could cover our sins
except his righteousness?   [Ep. Diog. 9. 2–3, LCC, I:220]

To those who love the only-begotten Son, God will give the kingdom of heaven (10.2). And by their love they will imitate the example of God's goodness (10.4).

The sermon has been hailed for its beauty and dismissed as an immature rhetorical exercise lacking in profundity. Not a work of formal theologizing, it does not engage metaphysical principles in the mode of abstraction; that kind of depth it lacks. But taken for what it is, a public presentation of Christian faith to a Hellenistic audience, it deserves recognition for raising crucial issues, affirming the gospel in the idiom of the hearers, and attaining a pitch of eloquence appropriate to the material. As a rhetorical address after the manner of the popular philosophers and with no pretensions as a work of dialectic, this earliest extant post-biblical sermon directed to persons outside the faith occupies a memorable place in the history of preaching.

Aristides of Athens

Also mentioned by Eusebius as presenting an apology to the Emperor Hadrian is the philosopher Aristides of Athens. With no more than a formal address to the emperor, the Christian sophist launches immediately into his argument:

Having contemplated the heavens and the earth and the seas,
and beheld the sun and the rest of the orderly creation,

[*Apol.*, 1, Harris, 78][3]

as so many philosophers since Anaxagoras (ca. 500-428 B.C.E.) had done, the Christian perceives behind these phenomena their original Mover who

is God of all, who made all.   [*Apol.*, 1, Harris, 79]

He then offers a description of deity to which many of his fellow-philosophers would also subscribe

Now I say that God is not begotten, not made;
a constant nature, without beginning and without end;

immortal, complete, and incomprehensible...
There is no deficiency in Him, and He stands in need of nought,
but everything stands in need of him...
He has no name;
for everything that has a name is associated with the created;
He has no likeness, nor composition of members...
He is not male, nor is He female:
The heavens do not contain Him.   [*Apol.*, 1, Harris, 80]

(It became standard practice for Christian apologists to affirm as a fundamental proposition the monotheistic understanding of God commonly advocated by Stoics and other popular philosophers—and thus to claim a place alongside the most highly regarded thinkers of the time.)

Aristides moves quickly from God to the human race:

This is plain to you, O king, that there are four races...in this world;
Barbarians and Greeks, Jews and Christians.   [*Apol.*, 2, Harris, 81]

After a brief definition of each, he characterizes the Christians in words that seem to enlarge only slightly on a simple baptismal creed:

The Christians reckon...the beginning of their religion
from Jesus Christ, who is named the Son of God Most High;
and it is said that God came down from heaven,
and from a Hebrew virgin took and clad Himself with flesh,
and in a human daughter there dwelt the Son of God...
He was pierced by the Jews; and He died and was buried;
and they say that after three days He rose
and ascended to heaven.   [*Apol.*, 2, Harris, 82 ff.]

Through the preaching of his disciples, our preacher affirms, many have believed, and they are called Christians.

The apologist now takes up the religion of each of the four races in turn. The barbarians have erred (chaps. 3–7)

in serving elements subject to dissolution,
and dead images.   [*Apol.*, 7, Harris, 92]

The Greeks (and the Egyptians) have made an even more severe mistake in worshiping "many gods that are made" (chaps. 8–13): the myths concerning their gods are "flimsy words." The Jews are "much nearer the truth" (chap. 14), but in their observances they have "gone astray" and they do not follow them perfectly.

In contrast to the other races, Christians "have found the truth":

> For they know and believe in God, the Maker of heaven and earth...
> from whom they have received those commandments
> which they have engraved on their minds, which they keep
> in the hope and expectation of the world to come.
>
> [*Apol.*, 15, Harris, 105]

Aristides describes the ethic of this new people, characterizing them as upright, chaste, and helpful to the oppressed, their lives marked by constant praise and prayer:

> And because they acknowledge the goodness of God towards them,
> lo! on account of them there flows forth the beauty that is in the world...
> And I have no doubt that the world stands
> by reason of the intercession of Christians.   [*Apol.*, 16, Harris, 109, 111]

Repeatedly the apologist urges the emperor and, by implication, all who may be reached by his address, to inquire into the faith:

> Truly divine is that which is spoken by the mouth of Christians,
> and their teaching is the gateway of light...
> Let all those then approach thereunto who do not know God,
> and let them receive incorruptible words,
> those which are so always and from eternity:
> let them, therefore, anticipate the dread judgment which is to come
> by Jesus the Messiah upon the whole human race.
>
> [*Apol.*, 17, Harris, 113f.]

Using a vocabulary more Hellenistic than biblical, Aristides affirms a theology found in all its particulars in the New Testament; his argument is essentially an amplification of that in Romans 1. Confining himself largely to the moderate style of the teacher rather than the grand style used with such flourish by Quadratus, he employs much the same argument. His address progresses neatly, with signposts along the way, and he makes his case with clarity.

This apology, long lost, then rediscovered and published in the late nineteenth century, has been dismissed by some historians of dogma as naive. Certainly it shows little subtlety of thought and none of the spirit of "dialogue with living faiths." It is a forthright declaration of conviction, a rhetorical refutation of the "errors" espoused by others, an elementary exposition of the church's faith, drawing on its simple baptismal formula and also on current philosophical commonplaces—in short, just such a presentation of the Christian faith as might be expected from a sophist of that illicit new persuasion. Its style is clear, though the movement is occasionally awkward; the tone is often winsome.

In the apology of Aristides and the companion piece by Quadratus we have the earliest surviving examples of preaching to outsiders by Christians who had been educated in the rhetorical schools and who used the skills there acquired to set forth the gospel in their own cultural idiom. These two sermons therefore hold a significant place in homiletical history, exemplifying the state of preaching a hundred years after Jesus of Nazareth.

LATER GREEK APOLOGISTS[4]

A New Generation

In the latter half of the second century an impressive group of apologists spoke out in defense of the faith. Intellectuals with a philosophical bent and a solid education in rhetoric and literature, they had thought deeply about the issues involved in the engagement of Christianity with classical culture and had sharpened their wits in academic disputation. Possessed of profound piety and high courage, which in some instances issued in martyrdom, they betrayed no sense of standing over against the church or above the common run of Christians, most of whom were slaves and members of the lower classes, but rather demonstrated a strong sense of solidarity with them and of pride in their faithfulness. We consider first the apologists who spoke and wrote in Greek.

Justin, Philosopher and Martyr[5]

At mid-century the philosopher Justin (ca. 100–165), who was to earn the title Martyr, was a Christian teacher in Rome. Well versed in the scriptures, he had considerable knowledge of Judaism acquired in his native Samaria, as well as a thorough schooling in the classical intellectual tradition. In an idyllic account of his conversion, Justin tells of his search for the true philosophy, unsatisfied by any of the various schools of thought, and of an encounter, while walking along the seashore, with an aged man who told him of the prophets: Long before the philosophers, these blessed men spoke by the inspiration of the Holy Spirit to predict events subsequently fulfilled, and their writings could still be read.

> They…exalted God, the Father and Creator of all things,
> and made known Christ, His Son,
> who was sent by Him.   [Justin, *Dial. Trypho,* 7, FC 6:159]

Convinced that the way of Christ "was the only sure and useful philosophy,"[6] Justin eagerly confessed it. His account of the incident exemplifies the significance of personal witness as a form of missionary preaching.

The young intellectual spent the rest of his life expounding his new faith. Wearing still the pallium, the cloak of the wandering philosopher, he engaged in public disputations, debating (as one of them observed) "with many persons on every possible topic."[7] At Ephesus he engaged Trypho, a Jew, and at Rome Crescens, a Cynic. For some years he conducted a school in the capital city, reasoning with inquirers concerning Christianity. Probably most of those who attended his sessions, which were not secret, had already heard the gospel and came to him for instruction before baptism.

Showing little rhetorical interest, he apparently did not seek recognition as an orator, and he left no homilies or cultic sermons. Nevertheless, Eusebius was right in thinking of him as a preacher.[8] His subsequent influence on the church derived from his apologies, written necessarily in the form of orations.

Running to approximately fifty printed pages and clearly intended to be read, his First Apology strikes the reader as a compilation of his teachings in his school. It represents the content, if not the precise form, of the oral witness of this influential philosopher of the Way of Christ.

Justin quickly rebuts the charge of atheism repeatedly brought against the Christians:

> We certainly confess we are godless with reference to beings like these
> who are commonly thought of as gods,
> but not with reference to the most true God,
> the Father of righteousness…who is untouched by evil.
> Him, and the Son who came from him, and taught us these things,
> and the army of the other good angels who follow him
> and are made like him,
> and the prophetic Spirit we worship and adore.   [*1 Apol.,* 6, LCC, I:245][9]

Celebrating the manner of life followed by ordinary Christians, the preacher recalls and expounds a number of the "fair commands of Christ" (14), then ridicules religions that go unpersecuted:

Others everywhere worship trees and rivers, mice and cats
and crocodiles, and many kinds of irrational animals.

[*1 Apol.*, 24, LCC, I:257]

Justin now turns to the argument that convinced him:

We find it predicted in the books of the prophets
that Jesus our Christ would come, born of a virgin, grown to manhood,
healing every sickness and every disease and raising the dead,
hated and unacknowledged and crucified, dying and rising again
and ascending into heaven,
both really being and being called Son of God.
[We find also that] certain persons sent by him
would proclaim these things
to every race of humankind.   [*1 Apol.*, 31, LCC, I:261, alt.]

Justin contrasts Christian truth with the familiar "mythical stories
about the so-called sons of Zeus" (*1 Apol.* 53, LCC, I:276). No matter
how these may be interpreted, he argues, they are not proofs like the
demonstrations from the prophetic books that he offers for inspection.

The apologist esteems his intended audience—the Emperor
Antoninus Pius, his sons, and the Roman Senate—as philosophers
and lovers of culture, cherishing only the truth (*1 Apol.* 2, LCC, I:242).
He therefore engages some issues that strike him as having philosophical importance. First, he argues a point we have seen made
earlier by the Hellenistic Jews of Alexandria:

Moses was earlier than Plato and all the Greek writers.
And everything that philosophers and poets said
about the immortality of the soul, punishments after death,
contemplation of heavenly things, and teachings of that kind—
they took hints from the prophets
and so were able to understand these things.   [*1 Apol.*, 44, LCC, I:270]

The apologist advances to profounder argument, based on his doctrine of the Logos (which he has mentioned earlier),

Reason himself, who took form and became man
and was called Jesus Christ.   [*1 Apol.*, 5, LCC, I:245]

Now he boldly asserts,

Christ is…the Reason [*Logos*] of whom all humankind partakes.
Those who lived in accordance with Reason are Christians,
even though they were called godless, such as,

among the Greeks, Socrates and Heraclitus and others like them;
among the barbarians, Abraham…and Elijah,
and many others.   [*1 Apol.*, 46, LCC, I:272, alt.]

Here the teacher of the illicit faith, appropriating the doctrine of the 'seminal word' (*spermatikos Logos*) enunciated in Alexandria by Philo Judaeos, boldly affirms on the basis of theological principle a catholicity of mind that will characterize the most influential preachers of the next three centuries. As a Christian he is sure of his own ground, the truth brought by Christ and announced in scripture. Any teaching compatible with that, whatever its source, he can acknowledge and can claim as common property with its proponents, for (he maintains) they have also been instructed by Christ the Logos.

Yet he glories chiefly in the cross, the "greatest symbol" of the power and authority of Christ. He points to its presence everywhere (55, LCC, I:278)—in the masts of ships, plows, spades, and other tools, the human figure, the human face, even the standards of the imperial armies. But whereas the wealthy and the mighty thus testify unknowingly to Christ, the humblest Christian understands:

Among us you can hear and learn these things
from those who do not even know the letters of the alphabet—
uneducated and barbarous in speech, but wise and faithful in mind…
These things are not the product of human wisdom,
but are spoken by the power of God.   [*1 Apol.*, 60, LCC, I:281]

Justin's Second Apology, addressed to the Roman Senate and more tightly organized than its predecessor, sounds more like preaching from the Christian counterculture with the hope of persuading or converting outsiders. Once again Justin describes the upright lives of believers, but for most of the speech he returns lovingly to his concept of the *spermatikos logos*, "the seminal Divine Word" or "generative Divine Reason" as the source of those truths found in Plato and the Stoics, the poets and the historians, but announced long before by the prophets, and now professed by the Christians.[10] Since all truth comes from Christ, Justin boldly lays claim to it all:

The truths which people in all lands have rightly spoken
belong to us Christians.
For we worship and love, after God the Father,
the Word who is from the Unbegotten and Ineffable God…
Indeed, all writers, by means of the engrafted seed of the Word

which was implanted in them,
had a dim glimpse of the truth.   [*2 Apol.,* 13, FC 6:133–34, alt.]

Justin's penultimate sentence conveys the ethos of the preacher:

And now, having done the best we could,
we conclude with a prayer that the people of every land
be deemed fit to receive the truth.   [*2 Apol.,* 15, FC 6:135, alt.]

So far as is known, Justin Martyr held no office in the church, acceptance as a teacher being still tacit and informal. As a philosopher he engaged other philosophers on their own ground and in their own mode of disputation; as a lover of truth and freedom he exposed himself to danger, badgering the authorities in behalf of his co-believers. His courageous refusal to stay out of sight led to trial and conviction as an enemy of the state; along with six other Christians he was scourged and beheaded in the reign of Marcus Aurelius, noblest of the philosopher-emperors. The preacher proved true to his bold declaration:

Even under the threat of death
we do not deny His name.   [*Dial. Trypho,* 30, FC 6:192]

Though Justin's debates with reigning intellectuals and his appeals to the civil power failed of his highest hopes, his preaching guided the thinking of the Christian community, even as his defiant boast strengthened its resolution:

I am proud to say that I strove with all my might
to be known as a Christian.   [*2 Apol.,* 13, FC 6:133]

Athenagoras of Athens

Perhaps a dozen years after Justin's death, the most eloquent of the apologists, Athenagoras of Athens, addressed a plea in behalf of the Christians to Marcus Aurelius and his son Commodus; he praises them under the same title he claims for himself—*philosopher*. Eclectic rather than systematic, embellishing his piece with selections from the *florilegia,* he nevertheless marshals his arguments in good order.

Masterful in rhetoric, he pleads with an elegance of style that does not fall into excess. It would be stirring to imagine a polished Athenian orator delivering his impressive plea before the emperor, like Paul before Agrippa; the scenario appealed to the preacher himself, but circumstances made this a merely literary "oration," submitted to the authorities as a document. Even so, it dramatically illustrates the way in which a Christian sophist could argue his case when preaching to a cultivated audience of outsiders.

Athenagoras begins by noting three charges brought against the Christians but devotes most of his oration to the first, the allegation of atheism. He answers with the most majestic and philosophical formulation of Christian theology yet advanced:

> We acknowledge one God, who is uncreated,
> eternal, invisible, impassable, incomprehensible, illimitable.
> He is grasped only by mind and intelligence,
> and surrounded by light, beauty, spirit, and indescribable power.
> By him the universe was created through his Word...
> The Son of God is his Word...the Father and the Son being one.
> And since the Son is in the Father and the Father in the Son
> by the unity and power of the Spirit,
> the Son of God is the mind and Word of the Father...
> Indeed we say that the Holy Spirit himself,
> who inspired those who utter prophecies, is an effluence from God,
> flowing from him and returning like a ray of the sun.
> Who, then, would not be astonished to hear those called atheists
> who admit God the Father, God the Son, and God the Holy Spirit,
> and who teach their unity in power and their distinction in rank?
>
> [Athenagoras, *Plea*, 10, LCC, I:308–9][11]

The preacher contrasts his sublime philosophical concept of God with the old myths of the Olympian deities and argues that once these tales have been rationalized their protagonists are no longer gods. He concludes:

> Therefore, we are not atheists, since we worship God
> the creator of this universe, and his Word. [*Plea*, 30, LCC, I:335]

Much more briefly Athenagoras discusses the lifestyle of the Christians:

> We realize that God is a witness day and night
> of our thoughts and our speech, and that by being pure light
> he can see into our very hearts. [*Plea*, 31, LCC, I:335]

Refuting charges of incest and cannibalism at their secret meetings, he declares:

> We are altogether consistent in our conduct.
> We obey reason and do not override it. [*Plea*, 35, LCC, I:339]

He links Christian faith and conduct to belief in the resurrection of the dead, then concludes with an affirmation of the Christians' political loyalty.

Athenagoras manifests a rhetorician's gift for epigram:

Names do not deserve to be hated.   [*Plea*, 1, LCC, I:301]

No Christian is wicked unless that one is a hypocrite.

[*Plea*, 2, LCC, I:302, alt.]

Wrath, lust, passion, and procreation
are not appropriate to God.   [*Plea*, 21, LCC, I:319]

God…is perfect goodness and is always doing good.

[*Plea*, 26, LCC, I:329]

It is nothing surprising that our accusers should invent
the same tales about us that they tell of their gods.

[*Plea*, c. 32, LCC, I:336]

The orator's arguments are original, the style fairly gleams with rhetorical gloss, and an ethos of nobility, both in mind and character, pervades the whole. In eloquence and clarity the apology shows a striking appropriation of the vocabulary and thought-patterns of the popular philosophers, a tendency also evident in Justin and in the other Christian thinkers of the time; they seem altogether un-selfconscious about their shift from biblical to academic modes of discourse about God. Yet how strikingly this language differs from that used by Jesus scarcely 140 years earlier!

For reasons now unknown, Athenagoras's work was not much used by other Christians in their long struggle for legal recognition. It nevertheless contains moving intimations of the power of Christian preaching when rhetors and sophists began to profess the gospel.

Other Apologists of the East

In the closing decades of the second century an impressive number of other Christians composed apologies—and orally delivered some of them. Pionius boldly confessed the faith before "the people and the rulers" of Smyrna.[12] Theophilus of Antioch wrote three books to Autolycus; the first is almost diatribe—he calls it homily—and concludes with an invitation to receive God's oil of anointing, chrism, with baptism. Miltiades, a rhetor of Asia Minor, wrote three apologies no longer extant. Apollinaris, bishop of Hierapolis, wrote four, also lost.

Melito, bishop of Sardis, addressed an apology to Marcus Aurelius. Clement of Alexandria composed a rhetorical plea called *Protreptikos, An Exhortation to the Greeks.* The Christian scholar Origen issued a reply to the attacks on Christianity by the philosopher Celsus. Writers now unknown put forth three apologetic pieces in the name of Justin Martyr, using titles of genuine but lost works; one of these, *Discourse to the Greeks,*[13] is a fervent evangelistic appeal, concluding with an invitation:

> Therefore, my Greek friends, come and share in unrivalled wisdom, and receive the teaching of the Divine Word.   [*Discourse,* 5, FC 6:435]

Tatian, a student of Justin's, after returning to his native Syria and inaugurating a sect that mingled Gnostic and Christian principles, prepared an *Oration to the Greeks;* in contrast with his teacher, he repudiates the totality of Greek civilization with a point-by-point critique of its "mythology, philosophy, poetry, rhetoric, and art."[14] In striking contrast, a third-century apologist, in a work on *The Monarchy or the Rule of God* (preserved by mistaken attribution to Justin Martyr), undertook to prove monotheism from passages in Greek literature.[15]

The diversity of intellectual outlook among the champions of the faith becomes further evident as we consider those apologists who wrote and preached in Latin.

LATIN APOLOGISTS[16]

A Literary Polemic

The gospel continued to win new believers in Italy and the western parts of the Empire—by the powerful witness of the martyrs, by quiet conversation in safe seclusion, by a strategy deliberately aimed at the intellectual elite, and perhaps by occasional missionary preaching when circumstances permitted. The Latin apologists were skillful rhetoricians, forced by persecution to preach *in absentia* through their books the gospel they wished to proclaim openly. While they offered a stirring plea for toleration on grounds of Roman justice, there is no evidence that the officials paid any attention to their apologies, which did, however, fortify the Christians with arguments supporting their cause.

The Latin apologies continue the tradition of forensic oratory in the service of the church. At least to a hypothetical audience of nonbelievers they present the message for which Christians were dying. We rightly consider them a form of preaching and briefly note their plea.

Tertullian

Incorrigible rhetorician and erudite polemicist, Tertullian of Carthage (ca. 150–ca. 220) turned his pyrotechnic style and intense temperament to the defense of the gospel against enemies outside the church and heretics within. A jurist by education and perhaps a distinguished commentator on Roman law—someone named Tertullian, possibly this preacher, is quoted as authority in the later Justinian code—he was converted in midlife, by the constancy of the martyrs, to the faith he henceforth so vigorously espoused.

Certain weaknesses of manner sometimes undercut the effectiveness of his presentation—a readiness to distort the position of an opponent, an uncritical acceptance of evidence apparently favorable to his case, occasional use of flimsy argument which could be made to sound superficially plausible, a fondness for *ad hominem* tactics. Though these standard faults of rhetoricians rendered his work "dazzling rather than convincing,"[17] they did not entirely vitiate it.

Tertullian's colorful style, ability to oppose a strong Christian position against a damaging weakness of the accepted philosophers, and the force of his moral earnestness enabled him to strike some telling blows. His espousal in his later years of the Montanist heresy qualified his subsequent influence in the church. But his plea for freedom is memorable:

> This empire…is a government controlled by free citizens,
> not by tyrants.   [Tertullian, *Apol.,* 2 (14), FC 10:13][18]

> It is not proper for religion to compel people to religion.
> [*To Scapula,* 2, FC 10:152, alt.]

Tertullian contrasts the gospel's accessibility to everyone with the uncertainty of elitist philosophy:

> Any Christian laborer at all finds God, makes Him known,
> and consequently assigns to Him in actual deed
> everything which a human being seeks in God;
> though Plato asserts that the Maker of the universe is not easily found,
> and, when found, is with difficulty made known
> to all people.   [*Apol.,* 46 (9), FC 10:112–13, alt.]

He discusses this God in sublime and moving terms:

> The object of our worship is the one God,
> who, out of nothing, simply for the glory of His majesty,
> fashioned this enormous universe
> with its whole supply of elements, bodies, and spirits,

and did so simply by the Word wherewith He bade it,
the Reason whereby He ordered it,
the Power wherewith He was powerful.   [*Apol.*, 17 (1), FC 10:52]

He declares with bravado,

I will not call the emperor God.   [*Apol.*, 33 (3), FC 10:89]

and taunts his opponents with the Christian's disregard of death:

We fear God, and not the proconsul.   [*Apol.*, 45 (7), FC 10:110]

He boasts of the unyielding faith of the martyrs:

Crucify us—torture us—condemn us—destroy us!
Your iniquity is the proof of our innocence...
By recently condemning a Christian maid
to the *pander* rather than to the *panther*,[19]
you confessed that among us a stain on our virtue is considered worse
than any punishment or any form of death.
Yet, your tortures accomplish nothing...
We become more numerous every time we are hewn down by you:
the blood of Christians is seed.   [*Apol.*, 50 (12, 13), FC 10:125]

We shall return to Tertullian to consider his preaching to the
church.

Minucius Felix

Despite the rumors everywhere repeated about the Christians,
the low social standing of most of them, and the prospect of action at
law, by the turn of the second century to the third, they were attracting cultivated Romans of wealth and standing to the still illicit faith.

A charming little book called *Octavius* testifies to this development. Written by Minucius Felix as a memorial to his friend named in
the title, it recounts an idylllic outing at the seashore shared by these
two and a third friend, Caecilius. All three were lawyers of standing,
the first two having converted to Christianity. (Caecilius was a not
uncommon name in Rome, but here it subtly and playfully suggests
someone still "in the dark.")

Displeased when Octavius lightly chides him for a gesture of honor
to a statue of the god Serapis, Caecilius proposes a debate on religion,
with Minucius serving as moderator and judge. Two speeches follow,
at once hard-hitting and urbane, controversial in substance but friendly
in spirit, in the best tradition of rhetorical and philosophical dialogue.

Caecilius leads off with a critique of Christianity as a superstition of the ignorant; he lightly dismisses their faith in God and hope of life after death. Alluding to the persecutions, he asks:

Where is this God of yours, who can come to your rescue
in the future life but cannot in this? [Minucius, *Octavius,* 12 (4), FC 10:342]

He advises his friends to have done with religious illusions and settle for a gentle philosophical skepticism. Except for the wholly amicable setting, it is the kind of speech that his fellow Numidian Fronto and other orators were making against the Christians.

Octavius's speech in reply is a reasoned and eloquent apology for the Christians and their faith. He argues from the order and beauty of the created world for belief in one God, a belief that implies a high regard for human nature:

Above all, the very beauty of the human form
proclaims the creative genius of God:
our carriage erect, our countenance uplifted,
our eyes fixed on the very heights as though in a watchtower,
and all the other organs of sense arranged
as though a citadel. [*Octavius,* 17 (11), FC 10:351]

He cites an array of poets and philosophers in support of his argument, then affirms:

one might think that either the Christians of today are philosophers
or that the philosophers of old were already Christians.

[*Octavius,* 20 (1), FC 10:359]

Ridiculing traditional polytheism and idolatry, Octavius denies rumors about the Christians' secret rites, upholds their belief in resurrection, praises the nobility of their ethic, declares their love of the world and its beauty, and concludes:

Why are we ungrateful, why unjust to ourselves,
if the true idea of the godhead has come to maturity in these our days?
Let us enjoy our happiness...
Superstition should be repressed, impiety done away with,
and true religion kept untouched. [*Octavius,* 38 (7), FC 10:400–401]

Convinced by the argument, Caecilius congratulates his friends:

We have both won...
As he gained a victory over me, so I gained a triumph over error...
I acknowledge Providence, agree with you on the concept of God,

and recognize the moral purity of the religion
which has just become my own.   [*Octavius,* 40 (1, 2), FC 10:401]

Written some years after the event, when both of the debaters
have died in the faith, the *Octavius* suggests the kind of preaching
that seemed to prove most effective with Roman intellectuals.
Ciceronian in form and argument as well as in style, it relies on truth
and natural reason, without appeal to scripture or miracle, without
discussion of atonement. According to some definitions of the gospel,
this seems a strangely philosophical and unevangelical approach. Yet
it, too, produced Christians willing to risk the peril of confessing the
illicit faith.

The Great Persecutions

The disorders of the third century occasioned by struggles within
the military for control of the empire and the frantic effort of insecure
rulers to provide stability led some of them to launch general
persecutions.

Trajan's policy laid down in 112 still stood: A Christian brought
before the magistrate and refusing to offer the sacrifice of the imperial cult was to be sentenced to death. While he and his successors
until Marcus Aurelius (161–180) had generally desisted from track-
ing down Christians, efforts to do so throughout the empire were
now initiated from time to time. Bishops were put to death, church
buildings expropriated, scriptures and liturgical books publicly burned,
and the property of wealthy Christians confiscated.

Though not sustained in duration, these persecutions were bloody.
Public appearances by advocates of the faith virtually ceased. In the
Octavius innuendo lurks in Caecilius's question concerning the
Christians:

Why do they never speak in public, never assemble in open?

[*Octavius,* 10 (1), FC 10:338]

Octavius answers plainly enough:

We…recognize God and call Him the Father of all,
but we never speak of Him in public,
unless questioned by a judge on that account.   [*Octavius,* 19 (15), FC 10:358]

Nevertheless, the "secrecy" of Christians fed suspicion. Even the publication of apologies in the form of orations abated.

Early in the fourth century, however, two distinguished rhetoricians, both converts to the faith, composed sizeable volumes in its defense. Arnobius of Sicca, a Numidian, wrote *Against the Gentiles,* and his student Lactantius, also a North African, who later would be hailed as "the Christian Cicero," wrote his *Divine Institutes.* Each of these works consisted of seven books, amplifying with rhetorical flourish the arguments of earlier apologists. Though not possessing a full and profound command of Christian doctrine—the towering theologians of the ancient church had not yet come on the scene—these two rhetors converted in mature life boldly took their stand. "The first systematic presentation in Latin of the main teachings of the Christian faith," the work by Lactantius was a "vindication of faith and reason, of culture and Christianity."[20]

Discussing the celebrated thinkers of the classical world, Lactantius quotes Cicero's dictum that "philosophy shrinks from the crowd," accusing them of elitism:

> How will the untutored understand...perplexing and involved things
> which even educated men scarcely grasp?...
>
> What place is there for the inexperienced and unlearned?...
> They never taught any women to be philosophers
> except one from all memory, Themistis,
> nor any slaves except one, Phaedon.

> [Lactantius, *Institutes*, Bk. III, 25, FC 49:232]

With such limitations the preacher contrasts the gospel's power to change lives:

> What those men realized under the power of nature ought to be done,
> but which they themselves...were not able to do,
> and which they saw could not be done by the philosophers,
> this heavenly doctrine accomplishes, because it alone is wisdom...
> But daily experience shows how much the commands of God,
> since they are simple and true, accomplish in human hearts.
> Give me a person who is wrathful, evil speaking, uncontrolled;
> with very few words of God I will render him "as gentle as a lamb."

> [*Institutes*, Bk. III, 26, FC 49:233, alt.]

Then the rhetorician takes flight, describing change in the avaricious, the person "fearful of pain and death," the lustful, the cruel, the unjust, the foolish, the sinner. Each such person can be transformed at once, Lactantius preaches:

> So great is the power of divine wisdom that,
> once infused into the human breast,
> it expels folly, the mother of transgressions, at one blow,
> and there is no need of pay, of books, or of night work and long study…
> Only let the ears be opened, and let the heart thirst for wisdom…
> The font of God, very rich and exceedingly full, lies open to all,
> and this celestial light arises for all…who have eyes.
>
> [*Institutes,* Bk. III, 26, FC 49:233–34, alt.][21]

Lactantius's appealing exposition celebrates the courageous faith of the martyrs and decries the persecutions, offering an implicit plea for toleration:

> We do not ask that anyone against his will
> should worship our God, who is the God of all,
> whether they wish it or not.   [*Institutes,* Bk. V, 20, FC 49:383]

His arguments may have influenced Constantine to grant religious freedom.

The Coming of Toleration

Despite official violence, the faith grew until, in 311, Galerius, Licinius, and Constantine extended toleration to the stubborn Christian minority. Two years later, with the western half of the Empire in hand, Constantine issued the Edict of Milan, decreeing a general religious amnesty and ordering the return of their churches to the Christians. Lactantius now revised his *Divine Institutes* to include panegyrical passages dedicating the work to Constantine:

> Now, all fictions have been laid to rest, Most Holy Emperor,
> from that time in which the Most High God raised you up
> for the restoration of the domicile of justice
> and the protection of humankind…
> Under your rule of the Roman state,
> we who are the worshipers of God
> are no longer regarded as criminal and wicked.
> Now, the truth is coming forth into the clear light.
>
> [Lactantius, *Institutes,* Bk. VII, 27, FC 49:537–38][22]

Before following the preachers into the new era of freedom, we conclude this volume by considering the ministry of the word within the Christian community during the two centuries of persecution.

CHAPTER 16

Diverse Preaching and Apostolic Tradition[1]

A Changed Situation

With the elapse of a century since the ministry of Jesus, and then of yet more decades rapidly passing, Christians found themselves in a different world from that in which the church had begun. In the preaching of the apologists, along with the recurrence of themes sounded by Jesus and Paul and John, we have encountered novel elements of vocabulary and imagery, conceptuality and emphasis. To point out such variations is not to decry them. As a word of faith to persons in new times and circumstances, preaching is inevitably marked by change.

Such change can be avoided only by repeating unaltered the formulas of an earlier day and so denying the essential character of preaching as address to the present. Even though Christian speakers continued to announce the end of the current age and the imminent return of Christ, the nature of expectation could not be the same as in the early days at Thessalonica. Though followers of the Way professed and followed a distinctive lifestyle, the temper of radical asceticism tended to abate within many disciples of the third or fourth generation.

After the creative accommodation represented by Luke to the demands of a continuing mission within history, the renunciation of the culture and thought-forms of this world could scarcely be total. The catholicizing tendency of Justin and most of the apologists to claim common ground with the philosophers made for an appropriation, in varying degrees of classical learning, popular modes of thought, and prevailing social custom. Some Christians resisted the trend. Others eagerly embraced prevailing ideologies. After his claims to be the Christ of the Second Coming found few believers, Peregrinus left the church to become a Cynic philosopher of some repute, then committed suicide.[2] Diverse movements developed into sects preaching variant doctrines. The church entered a period of painful struggle to vouchsafe its faithfulness to the gospel.

PREACHERS OF VARIANT GOSPELS[3]

Marcion

A Christian intellectual from Asia Minor who came to Rome about 137 raised questions of profoundest consequence about the church's sacred writings. This was Marcion, able theologian and impressive teacher, whose psychological "hang-up"—he was nauseated at the thought of sex—comported with his quest for a religion of pure spirit. Excommunicated by his own bishop of Sinope, but hospitably received by the Roman Christians, he attracted a considerable following until declared heretical in 144.

Marcion spoke his view of the faith with moving fervor:

> O wonder beyond ecstasy, might and astonishment is it,
> that one can say nothing about the Gospel,
> nor think about the same, nor compare it with anything else.[4]

This gospel of the gracious, kindly God who had appeared in Jesus Christ differed so radically from all other ideas of God that Marcion rejected Judaism and its scriptures out of hand, as well as those Christian writings, including some of the most venerated, that he regarded as distorted by Jewish notions. These he held erroneous in their teaching that God had created the material world. In accordance with the dualism taught by Platonists, Gnostics, and others, Marcion believed that matter is necessarily evil and only spirit is good. Therefore the biblical Creator-God who brought the evil world into being and gave the Law to Moses was at war with the good God of Jesus.

Marcion accepted as scripture only the ten epistles of Paul (excluding Hebrews and the Pastorals) and the Gospel according to Luke, heavily excised. Jesus Christ should be proclaimed, with no need of prophetic testimony.

Marcion's radical rejection of the God of wrath and of Torah drove the church to define its position on the issues he had so forcefully raised. Against the prevailing mood among intellectuals, the church that, resisting Marcion, claimed the title "holy, catholic, and apostolic," opted for a God of judgment as well as love; of creation as well as redemption; and a canon of scripture that continued to link its preachers to the spiritual heritage from Judaism.

The New Prophecy: Montanus

Primarily ecstatic rather than theological, a movement of New Prophecy, soon to be known as Montanism, sought to recall the church to the intensity of life in the Spirit that had marked its earliest days. Rising in Phrygia, it spread from Asia Minor to North Africa, where it recruited the aging Tertullian, and won adherents as far away as Italy and Gaul.

The name derived from Montanus, a Christian prophet, who about 157 began to proclaim that the Age of the Paraclete had come: the promised Comforter had appeared in him and his followers, consummating the stages of divine revelation. He presented himself as the instrument through which the Holy Spirit spoke:

> The man himself is a lyre,
> and I am the plectrum which causes him to vibrate...
> I am not an angel, nor a messenger...
> I am the Lord, the Almighty.[5]

Now that the Paraclete had come, the parousia of the Lord was imminent. A host of believers gathered in the "wilderness" to await the appearance of the Son of Man on clouds of glory. Their mood sustained at high pitch by the frenzy of ecstatic prophets, they practiced a rigid asceticism. Montanus instituted obligatory fasting, forbade second marriages, imposed permanent excommunication for serious offenses, prohibited flight in time of persecution, and glorified martyrdom. He held that martyrs and prophets had power to forgive sins. So great was the excitement that, it was said, in some villages of Phrygia not a single Christian remained at home.

Maximilla and Priscilla

Two charismatic women forsook their husbands in order to exercise a ministry of New Prophecy; historians and polemicists have traditionally pictured them as taking their stand alongside Montanus, though a plausible case suggests *their* priority, with Montanus joining them.[6] In any event, the ecstatic utterances of Maximilla and Priscilla kindled great zeal among the believers gathered in the desert. They denied that their message was their own. Maximilla said it plainly:

> Do not listen to me, but listen to Christ.[7]

Montanists held that their three prophets were the last of a succession reaching back through Quadratus (probably not the apologist) and Ammia of Philadelphia, yet another female preacher of whom we know virtually nothing, to Agabus, Judas, Silas, and the daughters of Philip in the earliest days of the church.

To await the descent of the holy city from heaven, the expectant company retired to Pepuza, now renamed Jerusalem in accordance with a vision announced by Priscilla:

> Christ came to me in the form of a woman in shining garments
> and taught me wisdom and revealed to me that this place is holy
> and that here Jerusalem will come down from heaven.[8]

Among the Montanists, women enjoyed complete religious equality with men, serving as presbyters and bishops, celebrating the eucharist, receiving honor as spiritual and doctrinal leaders. In an annual rite of later years, seven virgins dressed in white wept over the sins of the world, melting the congregation to tears. Tertullian's Montanist community in North Africa included "a sister with wonderful gifts of revelation" experienced in ecstasy while the church was at worship:

> She converses with the angels and, sometimes, with the Lord Himself.
> She perceives hidden mysteries
> and has the power of reading people's hearts
> and of prescribing remedies for such as need them.
> In the course of the services, she finds the matter of her visions
> in the Scripture lessons, the psalms, the sermon, or the prayers.
> One time I happened to be reading about the soul
> when she became rapt in ecstasy...She reported,
> 'I have seen a soul in bodily shape.'
>
> [Tertullian, *On the Soul*, FC 10:197, alt.][9]

Attack on the New Prophecy

Montanist enthusiasm and millennialism troubled those more sober leaders of the church who maintained that the Spirit works through duly appointed and ordered offices. Though they continued for a while to tolerate prophesying by women they regarded as orthodox, they could not accept the claim of the "Phrygians" to a superior level of spirituality, much less the insistence that everyone obey their prophets or that the Paraclete, speaking through them, could annul the words of the apostle Paul. To have yielded here would have subordinated ecclesiastical officials and the apostolic writings to anyone who could make a convincing claiming of speaking by the Spirit.

When the Montanists appointed bishops of their own, other Christians, fearing that schism would weaken the church, launched an attack. Disturbed also at the prominent leadership of ecstatic women, some bishops undertook to exorcise them and forbade that women should write books.[10] Leading preachers assailed the teachings of the New Prophecy—among them Irenaeus of Lyons, Apollinaris of Hierapolis, and Melito of Sardis, as well as the rhetor Miltiades and Appolonius. Some Christians calling themselves Alogi even repudiated the Fourth Gospel and the Apocalypse because of the Montanists' appeal to these writings.

Journeying from Phrygia, Praxeas persuaded the Bishop of Rome to withdraw letters of conciliation toward the Montanists, prompting Tertullian to protest that Praxeas had driven away prophecy and put the Paraclete to flight. The church insisted that the age of prophecy had closed with the last of the apostles.

Not long before her death in 180, Maximilla the lone survivor of Montanism's three leading prophets, spoke for the Holy Spirit:

I am driven away from the sheep, like a wolf.
I am not a wolf. I am word and spirit and power.[11]

Tertullian protested the growing emphasis on ecclesiastical order.

The Church will indeed pardon sins,
but the Church which is spirit, through a spiritual man,
not the Church which is a collection of bishops.

[Tertullian, *De pudicitia*, 21, LCC, V:77]

In time prophetic ecstasy and millenarian enthusiasm subsided, but throughout the third century Montanists pressed their call for ascetic rigor, and scattered companies persisted in remote places even longer. Their preaching strengthened the moral fibre of their hearers and for yet a while gave women a continuing place in the ministry of the word.[12]

Christian Gnostics[13]

A more intense struggle arose over the effort to proclaim the Christian faith in Gnostic terms. The great vitality and appeal of Gnosticism made it natural for spiritually minded intellectuals to attempt a correlation with Christianity (a development as understandable as the preoccupation of twentieth-century preachers with psychotherapy). Both movements spoke of a cosmic warfare between light and darkness, both appealed to the primacy of spirit over flesh, both proclaimed Christ as redemptive mediator between God and humanity, both offered salvation by restoring the soul to its right and original relationship with God.

In the second century Basilides, Valentinus, Bardesanes, and other Christian Gnostics gathered large followings, prompting a widespread polemic against them by Irenaeus, Tertullian, Clement of Alexandria, and other defenders of that gospel which, by prevailing, won the name of orthodoxy. The victors destroyed such literature of the Gnostics as they could get their hands on, and the rival teaching was lost, except as fragments were quoted or their teachings were summarized (and exaggerated if not distorted) in hostile tracts.

Irenaeus digests the preaching of a Gnostic named Cerdo who came to Rome shortly before the mid-point of the second century:

> The one who was proclaimed as God by the Law and the prophets
> is not the Father of our Lord Jesus Christ.
> The God is known; the Father is unknown.
> The former is just, while the latter is good.
>
> [Irenaeus, *Advers. Haeres,* 27, 1, Grant, 44]

And Clement's summary of a homily by a Gnostic teacher suggests the appeal to the seeker, the sentimentality, and the presumed philosophical tone of their preaching:

> From the very beginning you are immortal
> and children of eternal life.
> You wished to distribute death among yourselves
> in order to consume it and spend it,
> so that death might die in you and through you.
> For when you destroy the world but are not destroyed yourselves,
> you are rulers over the creation and over all decay.
>
> [Clement, *Stromateis,* IV. 89. 1–3, 6, Grant, 144, alt.]

The recovery in 1945 of the library of a Christian Gnostic community at Nag Hammadi in upper Egypt has made available to us a Gospel (Thomas) and a corpus of preaching otherwise unknown. Some of this literature is Gnostic-in-general, without a distinctive Christian emphasis, sugggesting a desire within the community to offer a philosophical basis of their theology.[14] Some is Christian in the broad sense, without elements peculiar to Gnosticism, demonstrating the essentially evangelical appeal of some preachers in the movement, even though the emphasis on secret, saving knowledge is present. In these recovered texts the preachers speak for themselves.

The Gospel of Thomas, composed in the second century, sets forth the "secret sayings" of Jesus (including a number found also in the canonical gospels and other sources). While a few retain their well-known form, most have undergone change in passing through the Gnostic oral tradition:[15]

> The person old in days
> won't hesitate to ask a little child seven days old
> about the place of life, and that person will live.
> For many of the first will be last.   [Th. 4:1–2 (*5 Gospels*, 473)]

> I am not your teacher.
> Because you have drunk, you have become intoxicated
> from the bubbling spring that I have tended.   [Th. 13:5 (*5 Gospels*, 480)]

> I disclose my mysteries to those
> who are worthy of my mysteries.   [Th. 62:1 (*5 Gospels*, 507), alt.]

> Lord, there are many around the drinking-trough,
> but there is nothing in the well.   [Th. 74 (*5 Gospels*, 514)]

> Woe to the flesh that depends on the soul;
> woe to the soul that depends on the flesh.   [Th. 112, *NH*, 129]

In the enlargement of some sayings, perhaps original at the core, the *midrash* of the Gnostic preachers is evident:

> I am the light that is over all things.
> I am all: from me all came forth, and to me all attained.
> Split a piece of wood: I am there.
> Lift up the stone, and you will find me there.   [Th. 77 (*5 Gospels*, 515)]

Such dicta have the aphoristic vividness if not the eschatological urgency of the canonical sayings of Jesus. The Gospel of Thomas includes several parables found in the New Testament, some slightly reshaped to give them a Gnostic twist,[16] some not otherwise known.[17]

No little artistry and narrative skill characterize a moving allegorical tale entitled "The Acts of Peter and the Twelve Apostles" found at Nag Hammadi. In a city called Habitation where the apostles have journeyed to preach the gospel, a pearl merchant named Lithargoel directs them to go on to his own city; there they will see and receive as a gift a great pearl. Arriving after many hardships, they are met by Lithargoel disguised as a physician; at length he makes himself known as Jesus Christ and sends them back to the city of Habitation with a commission:

The preachers give expression to the Gnostic abhorrence of matter and of its Maker, a power lamentably inferior to the true God:

> The world came through a mistake.
> For he who created it wanted to create it imperishable and immortal.
> He fell short of attaining his desire.
> For the world never was imperishable,
> nor, for that matter, was he who made the world.
> For things are not imperishable, but sons are.
> Nothing will be able to receive imperishability
> if it does not first become a son.[22]

The gospel of the preachers conveys the gift of secret knowledge that renders the hearer a sexless or androgynous Gnostic, though the person raised to this state is commonly designated by a masculine image such as "son."

Yet feminine imagery is also used for the spiritual powers, customarily discussed in a dazzling counterpoint of antithesis and paradox that emphasizes the ineffability of the transcendent. By revelation a female prophet speaks in this vein—though it is not certain that she was either Gnostic or Christian. The preacher's mind is so absorbed into the consciousness of the divine that it is difficult to differentiate one from the other:

> I was sent forth from the power,
> and I have come to those who reflect upon me,
> and I have been found among those who seek after me...
> Do not be ignorant of me. For I am the first and the last,
> I am the honored one and the scorned one.
> I am the whore and the holy one. I am the wife and the virgin.
> I am the mother and the daughter...
> I am the barren one and many are her sons...
> For I am knowledge and ignorance. I am shame and boldness...
> And they will find me...and they will live, and they will not die
>   again.[23]

The Gnostic preachers celebrate a secret knowledge that assures salvation. This *gnosis* involves the names of archons and aeons and angels, as well as the repetition of mystic syllables—occult lore which presumably sends thrills of spiritual elation through the initiate and may strike the non-Gnostic as moonshine. One preacher has the resurrected Christ revealing to John the mystery of the divine creation of Adam, with the assistance of the heavenly powers:

And the powers began...
The first one began to create the head:
Eteraphaope-Abron created his head;
Meniggesstroeth created the brain;
Asterechme the right eye; Thaspomocha the left eye;
Yeronumos the right ear; Bissoum the left ear; Akioreim the nose...[24]

and so through all the parts of the body, not forgetting tonsils and uvula, spleen and kidneys, shin-bones and toes, or any other part, nor failing to name the host of powers who contributed to the project.

This is the number of the angels: together they are 365.
They all worked on it until, limb for limb,
the psychic and material body was completed by them.
Now there are other ones...[25]

Besides meditating on such heavenly intelligence, the devout Gnostic could ponder the mystic meaning of the letters of the alphabet (they are the same in Coptic as in Greek) and spiritually significant combinations thereof:

Bagadazatha, begedezethe, bégédézéthé, bigidizithi, bogodozotho...[26]

and on through all the vowels. But, the prophet explains:

the rest are different: abebébibob,
in order that you might collect them,
and be separated from the angels.[27]

All this is part of the knowledge that brings the believer to the perfect state of salvation. The preacher does not hesitate to amplify the language of the apostle Paul by a climactic addition to his triad of abiding realities:

faith, hope, love, and knowledge.[28]

Thus the Gnostic *midrash* overrules the word of the apostle who taught:

as for knowledge, it will come to an end...
And now faith, hope, and love abide.   [1 Cor. 13:8, 13 NRSV]

APPEAL TO THE APOSTOLIC PREACHING

The varied gospels proclaimed by diverse schools of Christian Gnostics, Montanists, Marcionites, and others precipitated a crisis for preaching. Ignatius had already warned against teachers of heresy who mix "a deadly poison...with honeyed wine."[29] Throughout the worldwide church troubled believers were asking: What is the authentic Christian message? and how is it to be known? Ignatius had put the issue in a nutshell:

> Give heed to the prophets and especially to the Gospel,
> in which the Passion has been revealed to us
> and the Resurrection has been accomplished.
>
> [Ign. Smyrn., vii. 2, LCL, I:259–61]

Among the bishops and teachers who addressed the crucial questions, Irenaeus of Lyons (ca. 130–ca. 200) proved most incisive and influential. A native of Asia Minor who had listened to the sermons of Polycarp and studied with Justin in Rome, he became a presbyter and then bishop of the important imperial city in southern Gaul. Finding his own people disturbed by the advocates of divergent teachings and himself alarmed at their widespread influence, he addressed the problem in his preaching and pressed his case in several works, chiefly "The Refutation and Overthrow of the Knowledge Falsely so Called" ("Against Heresies") and "The Demonstration of the Apostolic Preaching."

Irenaeus, the first biblical theologian, argues by analogy:

> As God's creature, the sun, is one and the same in the whole world,
> so also the preaching of the truth shines everywhere...
>
> [Irenaeus, *Ag. Heresies*, I. 10. 2, LCC, I:360]

the same in Germany, among the Iberians and the Celts, in Egypt and Libya, and among those "in the middle parts of the world." The "plan of our salvation" came to us from the apostles to whom the Lord committed "the power of the gospel."[30] What they preached, Irenaeus maintains, they wrote in the four Gospels and the epistles, which he cites as scripture; he and Hippolytus and others take it as axiomatic that all the apostles taught the same thing.

He also appeals to the tradition of those who like Polycarp had known the apostles and to the succession of bishops in the oldest churches which go back to them. By way of example he provides a list of the bishops at Rome from the start:

> In this very order and succession
> the apostolic tradition in the Church and the preaching of the truth
> has come down even to us.   [*Ag. Heresies*, III. 3. 3, LCC, I:373]

By contrast the heretics are upstarts:

> There were no Valentinians before Valentinus,
> or Marcionites before Marcion.   [*Ag. Heresies,* III. 4. 3, LCC, I:375]

Apparently quoting a Christian tract, the pagan critic Celsus mentions other sects:

> Marcellians who follow Marcellina, and Harpocratians who folow Salome, and others who follow Mariamme, and others who follow Martha.[31]

(Evidently women who aspired to spiritual leadership were finding opportunity to preach in Christian groups outside the mainstream, which the guardians of orthodoxy sought to demean because they were led by women; their preaching we know, if at all, only through such passing references, too often libelous.)

Against all such sectarian "mystagogues"[32] Irenaeus sets the writings of the apostles and the words of the Lord; "orthodoxy" (as it would come to be called) is "in his bones"; he knows the gospel when he hears it. Called "the founder of Christian theology,"[33] he reasons with fervor, rather than the tools of dialectic, in unwavering commitment to his primary concern: the good news to be preached in the church. The Christians he mentions among the barbarians, despite their inability to read Latin, have come to faith (obviously through hearing it preached) and to a manner of life pleasing to God; they too know the gospel when they hear it:

> If anyone should preach to them the inventions of the heretics,
> speaking in their own language, they would at once stop their ears
> and run far, far away, not enduring even to listen
> to such blasphemous speech.
>
> [Irenaeus, *Ag. Heresies,* III, 3. 4. 2, LCC, I:375]

(Folklorists term the process the law of internal correction.)

A vigorous growth of theological literature now sprang up. Tertullian issued his *Prescriptions against the Heretics;* Clement of Alexandria (V. 17. C. iii) and Origen (V. 17. C. iv) wrote extensively against those they considered to have departed from the faith.

The understanding of the gospel advocated by such teachers came to prevail within the church as orthodoxy. Rallied by their bishops to uphold the apostolic faith, the main body of Christians repudiated Montanism, Marcionism, Gnosticism, and other rival doctrines as heresies. Irenaeus eloquently summarized the essence of authentic preaching as received from the apostles:

Diligently following the old tradition,
they believe in one God,
maker of heaven and earth and all that is in them,
through Christ Jesus the Son of God,
who on account of his abundant love for his creation
submitted to be born of a virgin,
himself by himself uniting humanity to God,
and having suffered under Pontius Pilate, and risen,
and having been received up into splendor,
is to come in glory as the Savior of those who are saved,
and the judge of those who are judged,
and will send into eternal fire those who alter the truth,
and despise his Father and his coming.

[*Ag. Heresies*, III. 4. 2, LCC, I:375, alt.]

On such preaching the church staked its future.

THE ORDERING OF THE PREACHING[34]

In their frequent gatherings, open or secret as necessity required, Christians found their safest opportunity for preaching and listening to the gospel. Laypersons still had a part in the ministry of the word—in the reading of the scripture, in teaching, and, yet for a time, in prophecy, regarded as a gift of the Spirit that "blows where it chooses." Wandering prophets made their way from church to church, living on the hospitality of the faithful and presenting the pastors with increasing problems. Some who called themselves prophets were moochers and rogues; others whose manner of life was exemplary in ascetic rigor delivered oracles not only ecstatic, but erratic, in the judgment of the bishops and their supporters. Early in the second century Christians began to develop procedures for testing and regulating prophecy, and after the Montanist experience, they accepted it no longer. Regulations for the ordering of ministry increasingly prevailed.

In the emerging pattern of institutional life the bishop became established as the key leader of the Christian community in each place—its chief preacher, supervisor of discipline, and celebrant of the eucharist. (The faithful in Smyrna remembered and revered Polycarp as "an apostolic and prophetic teacher and bishop."[35]) Associated with him in his liturgical and pastoral ministry were the elders or presbyters (Tertullian calls them priests), who assisted by giving instruction to catechumens or preaching to the Christian assembly; in the idealism of Ignatius, they were "attuned to the bishops as the strings to a harp."[36] Deacons served in the care of the poor, pastoral ministry, and administration. In making preaching and teaching the particular prerogative of bishops, or of ordained presbyters or deacons responsible to them, the church drew a line of distinction between clergy and laity.

Persons duly approved were admitted to these orders by ordination, an act of authorization, consecration, and spiritual empowerment. A disciple who had been imprisoned for the faith was honored with the title of confessor and acknowledged as a presbyter without the laying on of hands, "for he has the honor of the presbyterate by his confession."[37] Although women had been prominent in the early days as teachers and prophets and even bishops, the ordained ministry of the orthodox community became a male preserve. Early in the fourth century age requirements for ordination were set: thirty years for presbyters and fifty for bishops.

As early as the end of the second century the instruments of church order were well established: the bishop as guardian of the faith, the collaboration of bishops in maintaining unity of witness throughout the universal body, the scriptures as the authoritative Christian literature, tradition as "our teacher" regarding the apostolic message,[38] the local baptismal confession as the canon or rule of faith.

The strength of the churches in the western reaches of North Africa, Italy, and Spain created a need for the scriptures in Latin, Greek being generally unknown there. (After the death of Hippolytus, ca. 236, no significant writer of the Roman church was writing in Greek.)[39] Already in the second century "Old Latin" translations had begun to appear, serving the common people but lacking in the stylistic polish esteemed by the educated. These rough-and-ready translations were made from the Greek text of the Septuagint (LXX) rather than from the original Hebrew.

A rigorous course of instruction for catechumens, required after preliminary examination to spend three years as "hearers of the word,"[40] explained such basic essentials as the rule of faith, the Lord's Prayer, the Ten Commandments, principles of morality and discipline, the meaning of baptism and eucharist. Early in the second century a well-known Jewish treatise on "The Two Ways" had already been adapted for this purpose, several similar but varying versions with Christian interpretations being in use, notably "The Letter of Barnabas" (xvii–xxi) and "The Didache" (i–vi). By the end of the century, bishops, presbyters, and certain unordained teachers were presenting carefully prepared catechetical lectures, some in polished rhetorical form akin to the diatribes and encomia of the moralists.

The developments here sketched marked the emergence of early catholic Christianity. While the reasons for their acceptance were manifold, their importance for our study is their concern for faithful preaching: they were designed to assure the integrity of the gospel.

CHAPTER 17

Preaching within the
Christian Community

PASTORAL AND CULTIC PREACHING[1]

The Living Tradition

By the beginning of the second century the church was already a community with a history, proclaiming a gospel it had received by faith on the testimony of others. None were now preaching who themselves had heard Jesus, and the number who had heard the apostles was diminishing. About 130 the Bishop of Hierapolis, named Papias, gave a touching account of his effort, through oral history, to snatch from oblivion whatever might be remembered by his elders about the preaching of a time now gone:

> If ever anyone came who had faithfully followed the presbyters,
> I inquired as to the words of the presbyters,
> What Andrew or what Peter said, or what Philip
> or what Thomas or James,
> or what John or Matthew or any other of the disciples of the Lord,
> and what Aristion and the presbyter John,
> the Lord's disciples, were saying.[2]

Among the preachers from whom he had heard accounts he listed the daughters of Philip the Evangelist, who were traveling Christian prophets.

Such eagerness for every opportunity to hear the "living and permanent voice" from the Christian past was shared by others. Toward the end of the century in barbarian Gaul, Irenaeus used to recall his youthful days in far-off Asia Minor, when he listened to the preaching of Polycarp, who in turn had listened to John, the disciple of the Lord.

For Papias and Irenaeus and their Christian contemporaries, "living tradition" was the message brought in the beloved quaver of an aged voice, rising with animation as involvement in sacred reminiscence imparted power to preach the good news yet one more time. When they asserted the apostolic tradition as a canon of orthodoxy, they affirmed their ties with the gospel that had been preached from the beginning and their intention to set it forth as the basis of the church's faith.

However the accents might have changed with the passing decades, the Christian community located the center of its life in the primal story. About the end of the second century, in dismissing criticism, Tertullian appealed to apostolic tradition:

> Lest the well-known variety within this Christian religion
> should seem to anyone to put us in the same class
> with the philosophers...
> we promptly place against our corruptors the formal reply
> that there is one rule of truth, which proceeds from Christ
> and has been transmitted through His companions;
> and these conflicting interpreters will be found
> to be of somewhat later date than they.
>
> [Tertullian, *Apology*, 47 (9), FC 10:116]

The Liturgical Context of Preaching

The Christians held their meetings in private houses, with spacious atriums offering seclusion from the noise of the streets and the curiosity of potential accusers. In intervals of peace they erected more commodious buildings, which were destroyed during the persecutions under Diocletian in 303. At times of extreme peril they met in secret hideaways like the catacombs, Christianity going literally underground. They gathered for their principal meeting on "the Lord's Day" to celebrate the resurrection of Jesus, recalling also that the divine creation of light had likewise occurred on the "first day."

In a service of the word much like that of the synagogue they listened to readings from "the memoirs of the apostles or the writings of the prophets ... as long as time permits," followed by "a discourse" urging and inviting them "to the imitation of these noble things."[3] (Appropriating for the work of the preacher a classical motif in celebration of the philosopher, bas-reliefs on Christian sarcophagi from early in the third century depict the bishop seated among believers and holding an opened scroll; for a while Jesus was depicted in the same fashion.)[4] After prayers, bread and wine and water were offered in thanksgiving and received by the people, who responded with voluntary gifts for the care of the poor.

Justin's account of the practice of the church at Rome about 150, which we follow here, names the person delivering the discourse and the eucharistic prayers the "president," perhaps a neutral term chosen for an audience of outsiders. Across the two centuries we are considering, these responsibilities ordinarily devolved upon the bishop as chief pastor of the Christian community in a city or rural area; he did not yet have responsibility for looking after or administering a congeries of ecclesiastical communities spread over a sizeable area.

Ordinarily the bishop was a revered and beloved figure. Irenaeus looked back on the days of his youth, recalling

> the place where the blessed Polycarp sat and talked...
> and the appearance of his body,
> and the discourse which he gave to the multitude,
> and how he reported his living with John
> and the rest of the Apostles who had seen the Lord,
> and how he remembered their words...
> about His miracles and about His teaching,
> how Polycarp received them from eyewitnesses of "the word of life,"
> and proclaimed them all in harmony with the Scriptures.[5]

With such a man presiding over the Christian community, "the bishop's seat came...to be at once a doctoral [magisterial] chair, a liturgical bench, and a judicial throne."[6] His dignity was not unlike that of the pastor of a large black congregation in twentieth-century urban America, except that his was the only church in town. He was expected to embody the faith and life set forth in the preaching, and believers were admonished

> to love him, and...to resemble him.   [Ign. Eph., i. 3, LCL, *Ap F,* I:175]

Tertullian remarks on the atmosphere of intimacy, even informality, at the evening meetings for the *agape* or "love feast":

> We nourish our faith with holy conversation,
> we uplift our hope, we strengthen our trust, intensifying our discipline
> at the same time by the inculcation of moral precepts...
> There are words of encouragement, of correction, and holy censure.
> Then, too, judgment is passed.   [*Apology,* 39 (3, 4), FC 10:98]

Hippolytus indicates that the bishop—or in his absence, a presbyter or deacon—teaches while the people eat in a spirit of praise, breaking their silence only to respond to questions put by him; they converse, says Tertullian as those "who know that the Lord is listening" [*Apol.* 39 (18), FC 10:101]. Clement of Alexandria observes that Christians joyfully "chant psalms to the lyre or lute,"[7] but in the mystic discourse of prayer, directed by reason and offered in sincerity, he sees the essential character of their worship:

> The church's sacrifice is indeed speech rising,
> like incense, from holy souls,
> while every thought of the heart is laid open to God
> along with the sacrifice.   [Clement, *Strom.*, VII. vi. 32, LCC, II:112]

Sunday not yet being a legal holiday, Christian services were held at early morning or late evening when people had some time free from their work. The same thing was true of the daily assembly of deacons and presbyters to receive their assignments and to offer instruction to the people who came for it. When a visiting teacher was announced, all the faithful were admonished to attend. Children also listened to this Christian *paideia.* The community was tightly knit, for the sake of its members' safety and the maintenance of discipline. Christian women had no reason to appear in public, one of their teachers told them, except to visit the sick, attend the eucharist, or "listen to the word of God."[8]

Second-Century Homilies[9]

The oldest surviving Christian homily outside the New Testament, long unrecognized as such, is known as "Clement's Second Letter to the Corinthians" because it was early linked with a first true letter to that church. Preached by a presbyter now unknown, perhaps in Alexandria before the middle of the second century, it is an informal but earnest discourse without rhetorical pretensions exhorting the hearers to zealous devotion. In a moving passage the preacher contrasts their old existence with the new life they have received in Jesus Christ:

> We were maimed in our understanding, worshiping stone, and wood,
> and gold, and silver, and copper, the works of human hands
> and our whole life was nothing else than death.
> We were covered with darkness, and our eyes were full of mist;
> but we have received our sight,
> and by his will we have cast off the cloud which covered us.
> For he had pity on us, and saved us in his mercy...
> for he called us when we were not, and it was his will
> that out of nothing we should come to being.
> [2 Clement, I. 6, LCL, *Ap F,* I:129, alt.]

The preacher introduces numerous sayings of the Lord, some taken from the "Gospel of the Egyptians," some from sources not known to us. He uses several extended metaphors, not original in themselves, but developed in his own way: life as a sojourn in this world, sailing abroad to run in a contest, clay in the potter's hand. He concludes with a doxology glorifying "God, the father of truth" and "the Saviour and prince of immortality."

Other snatches of preaching addressed to congregations are embedded in the relatively scant sermonic literature of the second century.[10] About mid-century in Rome a simple Christian of active but limited imagination, whose name was Hermas, compiled a book of visions and exhortations entitled *The Shepherd.* It contains a number of "mandates" and rather wooden "parables" interpreted allegorically after the Markan pattern of parable-followed-by-secret-explanation. It has the feel of a scrapbook kept by a prophet and teacher through a lifetime of ministry and minimally revised for publication. Irenaeus (whose collection of sermons has been lost), Tertullian, and Origen regarded the book as Christian scripture.

A company of notable preachers are remembered only by their names. Let them be represented here by Musanus, whose "very eloquent discourse"[11] still circulated a hundred years later and was known to Eusebius.

Melito of Sardis

A full-scale appropriation of classical rhetoric—the earliest known instance in an address to a Christian congregation—occurs in an Easter sermon entitled "On the Pasch" (commonly but debatably translated "Passover") by Melito of Sardis. Already mentioned among the apologists, he published a number of works, including sermons.[12] The text of his paschal homily, preached about 170, was recovered in 1940. Using the form and style of a carefully planned and highly artistic ceremonial oration in the tradition of the Second Sophistic, the bishop draws his theme from scripture: the account of the exodus and the institution of Passover, which he sees as presenting types of Christ:

> For instead of the lamb, a son is come and instead of the sheep, a man, and in the man, Christ, who comprises all things...
> For, born as a son, and led forth as a lamb, and sacrificed as a sheep, and buried as a man, he rose from the dead as God, being by nature God and Man.
>
> [Melito, *On the Pasch*, 5, 8, White, 17, 18][13]

The orator employs the most impressive devices of epideictic declamation: parallelism, antithesis, anaphora, homoteleuton, exclamation, question, apostrophe, prosopopoeia, and carefully contrived cadences:

> It is he, led away as a lamb, and sacrificed as a sheep,
> who delivered us from bondage to the world as from the land of Egypt...
> It is he who rescued us from slavery to liberty, from darkness to light,
> from death to life, from tyranny to everlasting sovereignty,
> and made us a new priesthood and a chosen people forever.
> He is the passover of our salvation...
> It is he who was slain.   [*Pasch*, 67–69, 72, White, 36–38]

Mention of the passion launches the preacher into a tirade against "iniquitous" and "ungrateful" Israel for rejecting and crucifying Jesus. Under the form of apostrophe, he addresses that people in the most scathing manner of the prophets, demanding repentance. But the plea rings false: in a situation of rivalry and alienation, it feigns an appeal to a people not present; it fails to call on the Christian hearers, who believe they are now God's Israel, to apply the prophetic denunciation to their own lives. The preacher avoids using the term "Jews" and urges no action against them; he is content to announce divine judgment on absent Israel.

The sermon closes on a note of grace, offered by the glorified Christ in an extended *prosopopoeia*:

> Therefore come, all families of humankind, sullied by sins,
> and receive remission of sin, For I am your remission,
> I am the passover of salvation, I am the lamb sacrificed for you,
> I am your ransom, I am your life, I am your light, I am your salvation,
> I am your resurrection, I am your king.   [*Pasch*, 102, White, 50, alt.]

This first known work to exploit rhetoric to the hilt for the celebration of the cross and resurrection brought a noble art before the altar and offered a brilliant composition which, representing its genre, might have stood with the classic "passions" of Christian painting and music produced many centuries later. Yet the familiar patterns of *this* art, with its flights of reprehension, lured the preacher into a misdirected reading of the drama of rejection; instead of moving his hearers to search their hearts, he laid the burden of guilt on another people.

Melito was not only a virtuoso of rhetoric; he was a Christian prophet who himself had known the certainty of delivering the word of the Lord received in ecstasy. But now the prophet-who-stood-over-against-Israel like the classic giants of scripture, though their words echoed through his accusation, no longer spoke like them from *within* Israel. Unlike them, he did not bring his own auditors under judgment. His vituperation fed the broadening stream of alienation dividing Christians from Jews and thus contributed to the bitterness and demonic cruelty of later centuries.[14]

Sadly, it must be noted that the first dedication of the classical art of eloquence to the preaching of the gospel by an accomplished rhetorician was tragically flawed. Even so, in parts, it was not without magnificence.

PREACHERS OF THE THIRD CENTURY[15]

In the third century the church's foremost preachers were products of the rhetorical schools and, in some cases, former teachers of the art. A significant legacy of sermonic literature survives, commonly unrecognized as such because editors have chosen such designations as "essay," "treatise," or "tractate" for these works. In the Latin west Tertullian and later Augustine used the word *tractatus* for "sermon"; it is the equivalent of the Greek *homilia* (originally = "conversation"), used in the Eastern church for a popular lecture or sermon delivered *ex tempore* and not uncommonly taken down by stenographers, often without revision by the preacher.[16] Tertullian also referred to a speech in church as *allocutio*, the term for a hortatory address. (In today's seminaries, educating students for ministry, historians and theologians, thinking like scholars rather than pastors, rarely label such works as preaching.)

Tertullian

The Carthaginian presbyter and apologist, Tertullian[17] left rhetorical sermons on "Prayer," "Baptism," "Patience," "Penance," "Women's Dress" (two discourses), "The Virgin's Veil," "The Soldier's Crown" (an argument against military service by Christians), "Idolatry," "To the Martyrs," and "Exhortation to Chastity." His work entitled "Spectacles," which inveighs against the hippodrome, the gladiatorial games, and the theater, appears to be a compilation of speeches edited into a unified piece. The various titles here listed were prepared for the most part as lectures to catechumens, but some addressed mature Christians as well; the earliest comes from about 197. After Tertullian went over to the Montanists, he preached sermons on "Monogamy," "Fasting," "Chastity," "Flight in Persecution," and some others now lost—"Fate," "Paradise," "The Christian's Hope," and "Ecstasy."

Marred by an impulse toward specious exegesis, the sermons also show the flaws we have observed in the preacher's apologetical works: frequent rhetorical excess and occasional flimsy argument. His uncompromising spirit and crabbed scrupulosity tend to antagonize modern readers. Yet Tertullian's intensity of conviction, the cumulative force of his argument (most of which was not specious), his familiarity with scripture, his effective use of literature and philosophy to substantiate his position, his gift for illustration and imagery, his constant application of his theme to daily experience, his telling sarcasm, his dialogic response to objections, and his undeniable eloquence make him a preacher of power.

Not only rigor but also nobility of thought characterize Tertullian's deliverances, notably in his celebration of "Jesus Christ our Lord," whom he characterizes as

> the Spirit of God and the Word of God and the Reason of God—
> the Word [which expresses] the Reason,
> and the Reason [which possesses] the Word,
> and the Spirit of both.   ["Prayer," 1 (1), FC 40:157][18]

Christ is "a perfect teacher," and "God's teachings" received through revelation greatly simplify the mysteries discussed by philosophers.[19]

Tertullian coins memorable aphorisms and strikes off eminently quotable passages:

> Nowhere and never is there any exemption from what God condemns;
> nowhere and never is there any permission
> for what is forbidden always and everywhere.
>
> ["Spectacles," 20 (5), FC 40:92]

> The Holy Spirit does not acknowledge an impure spirit,
> neither is a sad spirit recognized by the Spirit of Joy,
> nor a spirit that is bound by one that is free.
>
> ["Prayer," 12 (1), FC 40:169]

> We who are united in mind and soul
> have no hesitation about sharing what we have.
> Everything is in common among us—except our wives.
>
> [*Apology*, 39 (11), FC 10:99–100]

Even the birds, upon rising in the morning, mount into the sky
and stretch their wings as a cross in place of hands
and say something which might seem to be a prayer.

["Prayer," 29 (4), FC 40:187–88]

We [Christians are] the future comrades of the angels.

["Prayer," 3 (3), FC 40:161]

With rigor he upholds his ethical ideal of simplicity.

In practically every passage of the holy Scripture
one is admonished to despise the world
and no greater exhortation is there to an indifference toward money
than that our Lord himself is without it.
He always justifies the poor and condemns the rich.

["Patience," 7 (2–3), FC 40:205]

His social critique condemns not only wealth but military power.

Even when He is betrayed… He did not approve of an avenging sword
on the part of even one of His disciples.
It was the forbearance of the Lord that was wounded in…Malchus.
And so He actually cursed for all time
the works of the sword.   ["Patience," 3 (7–8), FC 40:196–97]

His rhetorical ship scudding along under full sail, Tertullian lauds
patience by reprehension of its opposite:

Impatience is, as it were, the original sin in the eyes of the Lord.
For, to put it in a nutshell, every sin is to be traced back to impatience.
Evil cannot endure good.
No unchaste person but is intolerant of chastity;
no scoundrel but is irked by righteousness;
no negligent person but resents his obligations;
no agitator but is impatient of peace.   ["Patience," 5 (21), FC 40: 202]

Tertullian's eloquence was a function of his intensity, marked by
a tendency toward extravagance as well as absolutism, and it led him
into legalism—a legalism from which Western Christianity has not
always managed to escape.[20] Yet he is a preacher to remember, a
rhetorician who brought his art, with its failings as well as its strengths,
to the service of the gospel.

Cyprian

Third-century pastoral preaching culminated in the majesty given it by Cyprian (c. 200–258), bishop of Carthage and martyr under Valerian. No less rigorous than Tertullian, he was more even-tempered; fully as eloquent, he was not swept off his feet by the torrent of his own rhetoric, nor given to specious argument. He thought through his position carefully and coolly, established it in the plain sense of scripture and undeviating adherence to the gospel's demand, pondered its meaning with remarkable pastoral insight and compassion, and only then called on oratorical skill to present the message with maximum force and appeal. His art, "governed" (as he said prayer should be) "by restraint and possessing a quiet modesty,"[21] served the preaching without luring him into traps. He did not, of course, persuade all his contemporaries, nor did the church of later centuries endorse his stand at every point. But his thought is clear, his ethos engaging, his style alluring.

Born into a home of wealth and culture and favored with a first-rate education, Cyprian practiced as a rhetor and lawyer. Converted in midlife and baptized on Easter Eve, probably in 246, he gave away a sizeable fortune; less than three years later he was made bishop of the chief see in Latin Africa.

In a ten-year ministry Cyprian guided the church through a series of persecutions, dealt with serious schisms, rallied a people devastated by successive plagues, corresponded and published extensively, defied the proconsul's demand for the names of his presbyters, suffered a year's banishment, then was sentenced to execution as a Christian.

Celebrated among the faithful for his preaching, Cyprian worked over a number of his sermons for publication. Some of these deal with familiar topics: "The Good of Patience," "Jealousy and Envy," "The Dress of Virgins," "Works and Almsgiving," "Mortality," "An Exhortation to Martyrdom." His meditation on "The Lord's Prayer," which reads more like an address to disciples generally than a lecture to catechumens, has been declared "the best work on the subject in the long history of Christianity."[22] He highly esteemed Tertullian and freely borrowed ideas from the writings of the "master," yet reworked them so that his preaching bore the stamp of originality, as can be seen from a comparison of their sermons on patience or prayer. He is vigorous and direct, "going straight to the point."[23]

Two declarations read by Cyprian at the Council of Carthage, which brought together the African bishops in the spring of 251,

demonstrate his impressive powers of thought and his carefully reasoned ecclesiastical statecraft. In "The Unity of the Church" he holds
doggedly to the visible and institutional integrity of the one body:

> If you leave the Church of Christ you will not come to Christ's rewards,
> you will be an alien, an outcast, an enemy.
> You cannot have God for your father
> unless you have the church for your mother.
> The faithful have no home but the one Church.
>
> [Cyprian, *Unity,* 6, 8, LCC, V:127–29]

Simple and consistent rather than subtle or conciliatory, the address
flatly denies any legitimacy to separatist groups. It strengthened emerging catholicism, though the church in the next century revised the
sermon's hard line regarding baptism received from schismatics.

No surviving work of the first three centuries more effectively
combines careful Christian thought with classical rhetoric in addressing an issue under debate than Cyprian's second great oration to the
council, a declaration on "The Lapsed." It deals with a vexing problem. During the Decian persecution, when Cyprian had followed the
dominical injunction to flee for safety, a majority of the Christians
remaining in Carthage had either sacrificed to the gods of the empire
or had managed to secure documents falsely certifying that they had
met the requirement. After the persecution had ended, a number of
the confessors—now acknowledged as presbyters—granted a speedy
pardon to those who had lapsed, while the rigorists maintained that
they could never be restored. What should be the bishops' stand?

Cyprian's sermon, an orator's address to issues much discussed in
his letters, charts a mediating policy requiring a lengthy penance designed to secure full commitment. He lauds the martyrs and confessors. Without rancor and with pastoral sensitivity he chastens those
who have compromised the faith. And he seeks to strengthen the
community for trials yet to come:

> Does one think oneself a Christian
> who is either ashamed or fears to be a Christian?...
> Let us weep as greatly as the extent of our sinning.
> For a deep wound let there not be lacking a careful and long cure;
> let the repentance be no less than the crime...
> If anyone performs prayer with one's whole heart,
> if anyone groans with genuine lamentations and tears of repentance,
> if by continuous just works one turns the Lord

to the forgiveness of one's sin,
such can receive His mercy, who has offered His mercy…
The soldier will seek the contest again…
who by repentance for one's deed, who by shame for one's sin
has conceived more of both virtue and faith
from the very sorrow of one's lapsing,
after being heard and aided by the Lord…
and will merit not alone the pardon of God but a crown.

["The Lapsed," 28, 35, 36, FC 36:82, 86–88, alt.]

The African bishops adopted Cyprian's policy of firmness with compassion, and he went on to martyrdom only a few years later. His works circulated widely, as many early manuscripts, still extant, attest. In the next century the church's master rhetoricians, Augustine and Jerome, hailed him as the supreme model of Christian eloquence. (In his sermons he seems more lovable than in his letters.) As with other notable preachers, some of his passages transcend time and circumstance to speak, even now, a clear, convincing word; a modern writer characterizes his "elevated discourse" ("On Good Works and Almsdeeds") as "a perfect example of pure and simple Gospel preaching."[24]

In his "treatise" on the Lord's Prayer Cyprian addresses the spiritual seeker "who has begun to be a disciple of Christ" [*The Lord's Prayer*, 19, FC 36:143] in a searching discussion of a Christian life-style:

The will of God is what Christ both did and taught.
Humility in conversation, steadfastness in faith, modesty in words,
justice in deeds, mercy in works, discipline in morals,
not to know how to do an injury and to be able to bear one done,
to keep peace with the brethren, to love the Lord with a whole heart,
to love Him in that He is Father, to fear Him in that He is God,
to place nothing at all before Christ,
because He placed nothing before us,
to cling inseparably to His love,
to stand bravely and faithfully at His cross;
when there is a struggle over His name and honor
to exhibit the constancy in the speech with which we confess,
under investigation the confidence with which we enter combat,
in death the patience for which we are crowned;
this is to wish to be co-heir with Christ;
this is to do the commandment of God;
this is to fulfill the will of the Father.   ["The Lord's Prayer," 15, FC 36:140]

Cyprian's disciple Pontius lamented the world's deprivation in being denied opportunity to listen to such an orator. We can almost hear his wistful sigh:

If the pagans could have heard him on their rostrums...[25]

Other Preachers and Their Sermons

A few other examples of third-century pastoral preaching survive. A festal homily, probably for Epiphany or perhaps Easter, occupies the two final chapters of the "Letter to Diognetus"; it is widely ascribed to Hippolytus of Rome (ca. 160–236). A "Homily on the Pascha," pseudonymously attributed to the same author, makes a display of Asianic rhetoric and shows some affinity with the sermon of Melito already noted. A collection of Armenian homilies preserves some of the Eastern preaching of the period. Appended to the apocryphal book of 2 Esdras, chapters 15 and 16 are considered the work of a Christian prophet, about 250, pronouncing woes and destruction on all manner of sinners; while ostensibly addressing the evil powers of the world, it was apparently directed to Christians for their encouragement.

An impressive mode of episcopal discourse is exemplified in a disputation conducted by Dionysius of Alexandria, bishop of the leading see of Greek-speaking Africa from ca. 247 to 264. Finding many of the people in the district of Arsinoë excited by the hope of a literal "millennium of bodily luxury on this earth,"[26] which they had deduced from their literal reading of the Apocalypse of John, and seeking to arrest defection from the church, he summoned presbyters, teachers, and rank-and-file Christians to a public discussion.

The disputation provided opportunity for the millennialists to make their case, and the bishop undertook to listen with openness, "accepting whatever was established by the proofs and teachings of the holy Scriptures." Some came armed with a book by Bishop Nepos, recently deceased, which argued for their chiliastic notions. Whereupon Dionysius, who respected Nepos for his life but not for his doctrine, "sat with them for three consecutive days from morning until night," going through the book and trying "to set right what had been written." At last, the millennialists were convinced, and the bishop rejoiced in the restoration of harmony.

Apparently an effective teacher, Dionysius was also a gifted administrator. Head of the famous catechetical school at Alexandria from 231, he retained that post while serving as bishop. Some of the most impressive preachers of the third century were teachers in that school and its counterpart at Antioch. To them we now direct our attention.

SCHOOLS OF FAITH: ACADEMY AND DESERT[27]

The Rise of Christian Schools

The new Christian schools gave expression to an impulse present in Christianity from its beginnings. Teaching was so closely akin to preaching that one could not be separated from the other. We have observed this linkage in Israel and in Jesus, and developments in Christian thought and proclamation during the second and third centuries gave it further importance as the church exalted the unique dignity of Christ. Hear Cyprian on the theme:

> God wished many things ...to be said and heard
> through the prophets, His servants;
> but how much greater are the things which the Son speaks,
> which the Word of God, who was in the prophets,
> testifies with His own voice...
> He Himself coming and opening and showing the way to us,
> that we who thus far have been wandering
> in the shadows of death, improvident and blind,
> illumined by the light of grace, may hold to the way of life
> with the Lord as our leader and guide.   ["The Lord's Prayer," 1, FC 36:127]

As their supreme Teacher Christians looked to the Logos, the Word and Reason of God.

Already by the end of the first century, the ministry of the Word was idealized as a combination of preaching and teaching. Paul the apostle was venerated as saying:

> For this gospel I was appointed a preacher and apostle and teacher.
>
> [2 Tim. 1:11 RSV]

Christians of the second century continued to regard ability to teach as one of the *charismata*, like prophecy and healing, except that in this case emphasis did not fall on ecstasy. Rather a teacher was a Christian informally recognized by the community for knowledge and understanding of the tradition and ability to make it plain to others— much in the way that acknowledgment as rabbi had been accorded in the synagogue in the time of Jesus.

Possession of the gift of teaching was an important qualification for bishops and presbyters, but the work was broader than a particular function of ecclesiastical office. The rigorous preparation of

catechumens for baptism, with their three-year course of study, necessitated the enlistment of teachers in every church, many of these
being unordained persons; naturally the task appealed to intellectuals
converted to the faith. The teachers known to history are marked
both by their readiness to think through the Christian message in the
light of scripture and contemporary thought and by their sense of
involvement with their fellow disciples.

Already by mid–second century Justin's school at Rome was something more than a catechetical class, and a generation later the Christian school at Alexandria had become an impressive center of learning.
Other significant schools flourished at Caesarea and Antioch. The
one at Caesarea developed a notable library of Christian manuscripts,
which Eusebius consulted and quoted at length when, near the end
of our period, he began to write his history of the church.

The teachers who conducted these schools rank among the foremost interpreters of the gospel, distinguished for their classroom lectures, their writing, and their preaching. Excluded from the recognized
system of secular learning, the schools functioned somewhat in the
manner of a "free university" (or college), offering courses in Christianity to persons motivated to study for the learning itself rather
than for any degree or mark of public distinction. Directed toward a
general Christian audience, and particularly toward the inquiring minds
within the church, their design did not focus narrowly on the education of ministers. Even so, some of the leading preachers of the third
and fourth centuries studied in these centers.

The Issue for Christian Intellectuals

Christian converts from the ranks of the intelligentsia faced a
perplexing practical issue: How were they to use their education?
Tertullian counted the profession of schoolteacher unsuitable for a
Christian, along with that of gladiator, actor, soldier, lawyer, or judge;
he had in mind, of course, the secular schools catering to the general
populace. Like persons in the other occupations noted, public teachers
were expected to pay ceremonial deference to the ancestral gods (in
the Roman version of prayer in the schools). Moreover, the literature
in the accepted curriculum referred repeatedly to these deities, including stories about all kinds of immorality. He conceded that a
Christian might continue in this work only if no other means of live-
lihood was available.

Not everyone in the church held so rigorous a view. The apologist Aristides of Athens identified himself as a philosopher, Justin

continued to wear the philosopher's *pallium,* and his school was avow-edly Christian; even Tertullian whimsically defended his own right to go about in the recognized mantle of an intellectual. In third-century Antioch, Malchion practiced as a public teacher of rhetoric and boldly instructed bishops on questions of orthodoxy. Yet Christian teachers obviously had freer range in institutions serving their own religious community than in those for the general public. Even there, however, they faced an issue far deeper than the question of dress: *What were they to do with the secular learning that the philosopher's mantle represented?*

Every believer willing to die for the faith, including many a "heretic," recognized a fateful line excluding practices and ideas totally unacceptable to the Christian community. Persons not willing to hold to the unique demands of the gospel simply reverted to the old religions; in Alexandria the philosopher Ammonius Saccas (175–244), brought up as a Christian, and sought out as a teacher by such brilliant minds as Origen and Plotinus, found greater attraction in Plato and Aristotle, working out an eclectic mystical philosophy that addressed some of the same issues as did the gospel. Known as Neoplatonism, this school of thought proved among intellectuals a formidable rival of Christianity.

For the church it was difficult to conclude just where to draw the line in the ideological sand. Christians attracted by particular features of one philosophy or another were tempted to compromise the apostolic tradition in order to accommodate the concepts they found appealing; accordingly, Tertullian dubbed the philosophers the "patriarchs of the heretics."[28] An anti-intellectual Christian populism endorsed his rhetoric, which repudiated secular learning out of hand:

> What has Jerusalem to do with Athens,
> the Church with the Academy, the Christian with the heretic?...
> I have no use for a Stoic or a Platonic or a dialectic Christianity.
> After Jesus Christ, we have no need of speculation,
> after the Gospel no need of research.   [*Prescr. ag. Heret.* 7, LCC, V:36]

Yet even Tertullian balked at following to its logical conclusion the extreme course avowed in such rhetoric. Though he held that there was no salvation in pagan thought and that Christ came to bring truth to even the most cultivated minds, deceived by their own sophistication, he conceded that Christian children needed a general education. In his preaching he habitually drew on his knowledge of philosophy and literature, as well as of scripture.

Justin claimed the great philosophers as Christians before Christ, and other apologists, from Aristides to Minucius Felix, appropriated much of the secular tradition. For the most part these preachers acted intuitively in claiming for their proclamation elements of the cultural heritage deemed congruous with the faith. As we have seen, Justin began to formulate a rationale for the correlation of philosophy and revelation, both deriving from the Logos. That correlation reached its apex in Alexandria, where the tradition of Philo's exegesis had been taken up in the Christian school. Its two great teachers, Clement and Origen, directly engaged the issue of the relation between revealed truth and the truth of philosophy. Their work held massive importance in raising theology to new levels of precision and in relating preaching to the major intellectual currents of the time.

Clement of Alexandria

The first great Christian scholar and "formal champion of liberal culture in the church,"[29] both a teacher and a preacher, was Clement of Alexandria (ca. 150–ca. 215). Born a Greek, perhaps an Athenian, near the middle of the second century, he pursued his education in his native land, in Magna Graecia (southern Italy and Sicily), and in Egypt, studying under a cosmopolitan succession of teachers from Assyria, Coele-Syria, and Palestine, one of whom was a Jew. But his master was Pantaenus, Christian missionary, former Stoic philosopher, and earliest known teacher in the catechetical school at Alexandria. Throwing in his lot with Pantaenus about 180, Clement began to teach and succeeded to the headship of the school. The time of his conversion is unknown, but his remarkable familiarity with scripture as well as the classical authors suggests that it was early.

Clement's work as a preacher resulted in sermons on the Passover, providence, fasting, and slander; an "Exhortation to Patience," addressed to the newly baptized; and a homily, "What Rich Man Shall be Saved?" The last named holds that sin, not wealth and culture, excludes from salvation. He composed commentaries on various portions of scripture. But his best known works are *Exhortation to the Greeks (Protreptikos), Christ the Educator (Paidagogos),* and *Miscellanies (Stromateis)*; like the Puritan divines of the seventeenth century who reworked a series of sermons into books of impressive intellectual weight, Clement revised his classroom lectures into important treatises. In a time when persecution was always a possibility, the classroom offered a relatively protected forum for thinking through Christian faith with a trusted audience. Given the circumstances, we are justified in seeing this winsome intellectual as one of the first "university preachers."

Clement presents Christ as the supreme teacher, who leads the diligent disciple to perfect *gnosis*—that is, knowledge, understanding, insight, and a fitting pattern of life. While the term was central to the vocabulary of Gnosticism, Clement wrote vigorously against that system and against those thinkers—he regarded them as heretics—who accommodated Christianity to it. His use of *gnosis* (as of the term Christian *gnostic* to describe the perfect disciple) was unconfused in his own mind; in his intellectual milieu it was analogous to a believer's use of the term *truth*. To the well-to-do Greeks, women as well as men, who attended his classes he presented an engaging picture of Christ as the perfect mentor, an image taken from the rhetorical and philosophical schools:

> The all-loving Word, anxious to perfect us
> in a way that leads progressively to salvation,
> makes effective use of an order well adapted to our development;
> at first, He persuades, then He educates,
> and after all this He teaches.   [Clement, *Paidagogos* I. 1 (3), FC 23:5]

The persuasion of Christ produces saving faith. His education sets forth a way of life. His teaching imparts understanding of truth.

The "education" given by Christ the pedagogue begins at the most elementary level, with instruction in behavior and character reminiscent of that recommended by Quintilian for the tutoring of a young child, then leads on to the life of the mature disciple. The Lord as Educator uses encomium, the rhetorical mode of rebuke and praise, to instill right behavior:

> As there is one sort of training for philosophers,
> another for orators and another for wrestlers,
> so, too, there is an excellent disposition
> imparted by the education of Christ
> that is proper to the free will loving the good.
>
> [*Paidag.* II. 12 (99), FC 23:88]

This tutelage deals with voice, walk, dress, table manners, rules for sleep, marital relations, consideration for slaves, concern for the poor and helpless, prayer—everything from etiquette to interpersonal ethics to spirituality.

A gem is not worth much, nor is silver, nor clothes, nor beauty of body,
but virtue is, because it is reason translated into deeds
under the guidance of the Educator.   [*Paidag.* III. 6 (35), FC 23:228]

Clement's ideal of Christian gentility is addressed to an obviously cultured and privileged clientele. But the courage of the martyrs runs through it, as does a practiced simplicity of life and commitment to a distinctive morality:

We have the Cross of the Lord as our boundary line,
and by it we are fenced around
and shut off from our former sins.   [*Paidag.* III. 12 (85), FC 23:263]

When in the *Miscellanies* he contends with the Gnostics, he faults them less on theological than on ethical grounds.[30]

Clement did not produce his intended climactic work on Christ the Teacher. Some pieces of what he had projected for this third phase of his program appear, however, in the *Miscellanies (Stromateis),* a "book" executed less artistically than he had hoped, but nevertheless systematically in treating the ideas he takes up. Clement observes that in addressing Greek philosophical minds concerning the faith, it is necessary to use some words "different from the Lord's Scriptures," but hastens to add:

It is from the Scriptures that they draw their life and breath, and…
it is their object, taking these as their starting-point, to set forth,
not their phraseology, but their meaning only.

[Clement, *Stromateis,* VII. 1. 1, LCC, II:93]

Thus neatly describing the task of the teacher—we would say "theologian"—he follows Philo in taking the story of Hagar and Sarah to signify allegorically that philosophy serves as handmaid to Christian thought (theology).[31] In his works he quotes more than 360 profane authors; while obviously making use of *florilegia* or compilations of useful passages, he cites the material with the assurance of one who has read the literature discerningly. Always his priorities are clear:

Only the beautiful is good…only the Lord is beautiful,
and God alone is good and is alone to be loved.

[*Strom.,* III. v. 43, LCC, II:60][32]

God has been at work in human culture to draw humanity to Christ:

By giving to the Jews commandments and to the Greeks philosophy...
he leads human beings by both ways of advance,
whether Greek or barbarian,
to the perfection which is through faith.   [*Strom.*, III, 10, 11, LCC, II:9][33]

This preacher whose supreme loyalty is pledged to Jesus Christ is at home both with scripture and with the classical intellectual tradition:

He who of all philosophers so praised truth, Plato,
gave new life to the dying ember of Hebrew philosophy...
Surely, Plato was not unacquainted with David.

[*Paidag.* II (18), FC 23:109]

In the next paragraph Clement cites Aristotle and the comic poet Epicharmis. That perfection which unites the mystical knowledge of God with an active love for humanity is served in the divine economy by the classical intellectual tradition, placed here by Clement alongside revelation in bold allusion to the apostle Paul's picture of the Law leading a child by the hand to go to school to Christ (Gal. 3:24).

His affection for persons, created in God's image, recurs again and again.

There is a certain lovableness in humanity,
which is the very quality inbreathed into it by God.

[*Paidag.* III (7), FC 23:9, alt.]

Centuries before Shakespeare's *Hamlet*, Clement celebrated the divine endowment and glorious potential of the human creature:

By nature, man is a noble and majestic animal who seeks the beautiful,
simply because he is a creature made by the only true Beauty.

[*Paidag.* III. 7 (37), FC 23:230][34]

Though he does not expound a theory of atonement as the doctrine was developed by later theologians, he sounds a winsome evangelical note:

We need the Saviour, for we are sick; the Guide, for we are wandering;
Him who gives light, for we are blind;
the life-giving Spring, for we are parched with thirst;
and, once we have tasted of it, we will never thirst again.
We are in need of Life, for we are dead;
of the Shepherd, for we are sheep;
of the Educator, for we are children.
In a word, throughout the whole of our human lives we need Jesus
that we may not go astray.   [*Paidag,* I. 9 (83), FC 23:74]

Claiming the world of culture while proclaiming grace and faith, Clement "walked the straight road" of truth, and like his ideal Christian gnostic, "grown old in the study of the...Scriptures,"[35] he commended the gospel to the intelligentsia. He attracted hearers by the largeness and openness of his mind, his devotion to liberal culture, the gladness of his gentle spirit, his genuine love for persons, and his unabashed commitment to Christ. After persecution drove him from Alexandria about 202, his most brilliant student succeeded him at the "school of the sacred faith"[36] as an even more influential teacher.

Origen [37]

The most celebrated preacher in the first centuries was also the church's foremost intellectual, heard by many outside the Christians' circle and singled out for attack by opponents among the philosophers. He was Origen (ca. 185–ca. 254), whose one avowed goal was to declare the biblical message. Soundly educated in liberal studies, he received from his father a profound love for the scripture and from Clement instruction in doctrine. Deprived of both his spiritual tutors in the same persecution—his father was martyred—Origen was appointed by his bishop to preside over the catechetical school; he was eighteen years old.

Abandoning secular study, disposing of his books of literature, deliberately cultivating a non-rhetorical style, Origen tirelessly expounded the scriptures. His keenness of mind, honesty of thought, and earnest piety attracted inquiring pagans "to him to hear the word of God."[38] Some entered the catechumenate, and within a short time seven of his pupils died as martyrs. A wealthy pupil named Ambrose became the scholar's literary patron, providing seven amanuenses to take down his lectures and seven calligraphers to turn their shorthand into finished manuscripts. Hence Origen's amazing "literary"— actually, homiletical—productivity. Of his two thousand titles noted by Eusebius at the end of the century, virtually all were biblical studies of some sort—scholia or brief explanations of difficult passages, commentaries on books of the Bible, a comparative study of various translations of the sacred text, and more than five hundred homilies.

Origen zealously instructed the catechumens as various groups came throughout the days and into the nights. He studied, though he did not master, Hebrew. He traveled to Caesarea, Ephesus, Athens, and Rome, where he heard Hippolytus preach. Two, probably three, times he was called to Arabia to settle theological controversies; the transcript of one of these disputations was recovered in mid-twentieth century.[39]

On Origen's second visit to Caesarea (about 231), the local bishop ordained him a presbyter and, when the Bishop of Alexandria protested, the Christian scholar settled in Caesarea, establishing there a new catechetical school that drew students from afar. During an interval of official leniency toward Christians, he was bidden by Mamaea, mother of the emperor, to come to Antioch and explain the faith to her. At the appointment of the bishop, he preached daily in the church at Caesarea, and his published homilies derive from this period. The first preacher to produce a major corpus of sermonic literature, he left homilies on virtually all the "historical" books in the Old Testament, on Job, Psalms, Canticles, Isaiah, Jeremiah, on Luke, 1 Corinthians, Hebrews, and other books. In addition he left an "Exhortation to Martyrdom"; an apology answering the charges of the pagan intellectual Celsus; a deeply spiritual work "On Prayer"; and the earliest manual of dogmatics, entitled "On the Principal Doctrines" (*Peri archon, De principiis*).

Firmly believing that "every word of Jesus is true,"[40] Origen diligently studied and prayed for a right understanding of the scriptures. Often he quoted them from memory but never ceased to study the text. When exegeting the Lord's Prayer he examined the Hebrew scripture with unusual care,

> to see if it is possible to find anywhere in it
> a prayer in which someone calls God "Father."
>
> [Origen, *On Prayer*, XXII. 1, LCC, II:280]

He could not discover one instance. As a biblical theologian he sought to understand the text in faithfulness to apostolic tradition:

> My wish is to be truly a man of the Church,
> to be called by the name of Christ…
> which is blessed all over the earth;
> I desire to be, and to be called, a Christian,
> in my works as in my thoughts.[41]

Though Origen's exegetical method, following in the tradition of Philo's allegorical interpretation, learned in Alexandria, drove him to prize the "spiritual" meaning beyond the literal reading, he gave close attention to the text, putting to it the same sort of fundamental questions that an intelligent modern reader might ask.

> Let us ask when our Saviour spoke these words,
> and to whom, and in what connexion.　[Origen, *First Principles*, I. 4:9][42]

His Platonism accentuated the compulsion to "spiritualize," and his boldness of thought as a pioneer in Christian theology led him to some positions later declared unorthodox. (Such are the perils of the explorer who ventures into new territory before trails have been marked.)[43] Despite the popularity of Origen's writings, a strong reaction set in; two centuries after his time the authorities ordered his works destroyed, undoing the generous patronage of Ambrose and the foresight of Pamphilius, Origen's admirer and head of the school at Caesarea, in collecting his manuscripts for its library. Only fragments survive from this most productive preacher and biblical theologian.

Though Origen worked out his exegetical method with great care, his allegorizing appeals only to those committed, like so many of his generation, to the discovery of hidden meanings;[44] it strikes others as fanciful and excessive, and the Neoplatonist philosopher Porphyry chided him for it. Consider his ploy, already hoary in Alexandria, for interpreting Exodus 11:2. Moses' instructions to the Israelites to borrow jewelry and fine clothing from their neighbors before departing into the wilderness, Origen counsels, are not to be taken as divine orders to practice dishonesty and theft; rather, Christians are to use the philosophy of the pagans in the service of the one true God, thereby "spoiling the Egyptians."[45] Thus Origen rationalizes a Christian appropriation of pagan learning. Yet in contrast with his teacher Clement, he almost never displays such a "jewel" from "Egypt."

Instead Origen gives himself to the hard work of wrestling out the meaning of the text, however difficult, and he commends the struggle involved—

> When you are reading Scripture,
> and you seek with pain to find the meaning within it,
> not that you think that the Scripture has erred,
> or narrated something wrongly,
> but you strive to find the truth that is hidden there.[46]

Sometimes he painstakingly reflected in varying meanings that could be drawn from the text, depending on one's conclusion as to how it should be punctuated (as his manuscripts of the scriptures were not).[47] When at last the spiritually-minded exegete discerned the "true" intent of the text, it was like being present at the Lord's transfiguration:

> Where any one discerns a spiritual significance in the Law,
> or Christ's wisdom hidden in the prophets,
> such a one sees Moses and Elias in glory with Jesus.[48]

His devotion never faltered. Preaching on Mary's word to the child Jesus in the temple, he admonishes:

> Let us seek Him in much labouring, and with sorrow of spirit,
> and then we shall be able to find Him Whom we seek.
> For not idly was it written: *Thy father and I have sought thee sorrowing.*
> Whoever seeks Jesus, let that one not seek carelessly, or casually,
> or for the passing moment; as many seek Him, and so cannot find Him.
> Let us however say to Him: We have sought Thee sorrowing.
> And when we have said this, He will make answer
> to our labouring soul that has sought him with anguish.[49]

The life of reason was an essential element of his spirituality.

> Thus alone can we accept *"Pray without ceasing"* as a practicable saying if we speak of the whole life of the saint as one great unbroken prayer.
>
> [Origen, *On Prayer*, XXX, 2, LCC, II:262]

As a youth Origen had longed for martyrdom, and in response to Matthew 19:12—read quite literally—he had surgically rendered himself a eunuch for the sake of the kingdom. (It was his mutilated physical condition which, in the opinion of Alexandria's bishop, rendered him unfit for ordination.) In the persecutions beginning in 249 the old man was thrown into prison; though tortured for days, he rallied his fellow Christians by words of encouragement. Released unmartyred, but devastated in body, he died not long after. One of Origen's converts, whom he had also attracted to the ministry, Gregory Thaumaturgos (ca. 213–275) noted his death with a panegyrical oration, a full-scale appropriation of epideictic rhetoric to the praise of Christianity's first intellectual celebrity and, up to his time, most prolific preacher.

Clement and Origen, the two greatest teachers of Alexandria's catechetical school, commended the faith to the intelligentsia by interpretation harmonious with the best thought of the time. Both were Christians of earnest piety as well as of profound intellect, but because they offended the guardians of that orthodoxy formulated by a later generation, neither has received the title "Saint," which has been awarded to their less creative predecessor Pantaenus. Yet their lives and their preaching did much to commend the ascetic ideal to the third-century church. As that ideal caught hold, a new pattern of discipleship seized the imagination of many believers. The desert came to rival the academy as a school of faith, and the hermit became the great penitential preacher.

Voice from the Wilderness[50]

The most serious interpreters of the gospel in the second and third centuries, especially the Africans, regarded it as a call to self-denial. Justin Martyr (in Rome), Tertullian and Cyprian in Carthage, Clement and Origen in Alexandria commended marital chastity, but celebrated virginity as a higher calling, and many groups considered heretical—Marcionites, Montanists, Encratites, and a broad variety of Gnostic Christians—tolerated only virginity. All these gave full force to numerous passages in the New Testament to which moderns have paid little heed.[51]

Platonic idealism transmuted into neoplatonic mysticism furnished Christian intellectuals with presuppositions that strengthened the tendency toward *askésis,* for in the transfer of its intellectual leadership from Jew to Greek, Christianity tended at times to lose touch with the feeling for creation as good. In seeking to maintain among the disciples the high pitch of commitment necessary to remain faithful under persecution, the preachers called upon them to despise the world and to give their posssessions to the poor. One strain of Hellenistic popular religion honored renunciants, virgins, and *castrati* as holy, and even Judaism had produced communities of ascetics like the Essenes.

With persecution still a grim reality, Paul of Thebes[52] (mid–3rd cent.), Anthony (c. 251–356), and other Egyptian Christians withdrew to the desert to practice solitary rigors of self-denial and prayer. Rumors of their remarkable sanctity drew others after them in search of spiritual counsel, and the erstwhile hermits found themselves presiding over growing companies of disciples. In the fourth century, with the cessation of persecution, gifted ascetics succeeded in ordering these communities in monasteries under the rule of abbots, and monasticism became a major institution of Christianity.

About 357 Athanasius composed his *Life of St. Anthony,* a book unsurpassed in influence in the entire history of the church. Believing that "the life of Anthony is for monks an adequate guide in asceticism,"[53] he pointed his treatise to that end. We consider here that fateful period of the hermit's long life that falls within our period, for it includes the beginning of his preaching.

Two features of this idealized biography have importance for our study of third-century preaching in the Christian community. First, Athanasius emphasizes the child Anthony's being taken to church by his pious Christian parents; there he paid "close attention to the passages read aloud,"[54] many of which he would never forget. Avoiding association with other children, he refused to attend school, confining his life to home and church. Second, the author features the crucial role of that pericope which, more than any other, would for the next thousand years convey to listeners beyond counting the call to the monastic life. (We have already observed its effect on Cyprian.) Not long after the death of Anthony's parents, the youth at church heard the Lord's words in the Gospel:

> If you wish to be perfect, go, sell your possessions,
> and give the money to the poor, and you will have treasure in heaven;
> then come, follow me.   [Mt. 19:21 NRSV][55]

Anthony gave his parents' estate to the villagers, keeping back only a little for the support of his sister, then devoted a solitary life to labor, to fighting temptations, and to vigils. At about age thirty-five he left his village for the wilderness, to continue his legendary struggle with those temptations that have fascinated artists, poets, and psychologists less spiritually inclined. When twenty more years had passed, people began streaming into the desert to see this prodigy, to seek healing, and to hear his words. So he began to preach, comforting, reconciling, exhorting—and persuading not a few to take up the life of solitude.

In his own youth Athanasius, the great fourth-century theologian, followed the hermit as a disciple, and he fills pages of the *Life* with the substance of the hermit's preaching. Spoken "in the Egyptian tongue" (Coptic), it makes no pretension to rhetorical form, but rambles on like an extended conversation. Not a man of books, Anthony nevertheless remembered much scripture from hearing it read, lacing his homilies with appropriate citations:

> Do not be fearful when you hear of perfection,
> nor be surprised at *the word*, for it is *not far from us*,
> nor does it exist outside of us...
> The Greeks go abroad, even crossing the sea to become learned,
> but we have no need to go abroad
> for the sake of the kingdom of heaven,
> nor need we cross the sea for the sake of perfection;
> the Lord has already told us: "*The kingdom of God is within you.*"[56]

Anthony could even fashion a parable in the manner of Jesus:

> Though we were lords of even the whole earth and gave it all up,
> it would be as nothing compared to the kingdom of heaven.
> It is as if a person should disregard one bronze coin
> in order to gain a hundred gold ones;
> so a person who renounces the whole earth, though being ruler over it,
> gives up little and receives a hundredfold in return.[57]

In Anthony's preaching the "will to perfection," expressed through rigorous asceticism, keeps the soul in "its natural state," just as it was created, beautiful and upright.[58]

During the persecution under Maximinus in 310—how could the Christians know that toleration was so close at hand?—Anthony hastened to Alexandria. With a boldness born of longing for martyrdom, he "ministered to the confessors in the mines and in the prisons,"[59] stood by the believers in court, and accompanied them to the end, speaking words of encouragement and faith. When the persecutions at last were halted, he returned to the wilderness to continue daily "as a martyr to conscience in the sufferings he endured."[60] For yet another forty years he would preach to the throngs who sought him there, continuing at the task until his death, at an age well beyond a hundred years. He was the memorable prototype of the anchorite preachers who for centuries to come would sustain the spirituality of the church, their undeniable power deriving from the *ethos* of total renunciation.

As his greatest disciple put it, "The Lord also gave Anthony grace in speech."[61] And the desert became a school of faith.

CHAPTER 18

The Work of Preaching

INTERPRETING THE REVEALED WORD[1]

Christian Familiarity with Scripture

Preachers as diverse as Anthony the unschooled villager and Origen the erudite scholar spoke from minds saturated in scripture. The discourses of the hermit who was not a man of letters are known to us only by courtesy of his disciple who was—a fact which reminds us that the vast majority of the population could not read. Many Christians, doubtless including most teachers in the villages, depended on *hearing* and *remembering* for their knowledge of the sacred word. Yet without aid of concordance (a late medieval contrivance), the memories of the preachers, learned *and* unlearned, called up obscure verses from scripture containing the precise word or image that bore most cogently on the issue at hand. They had *listened* to the sacred word.

With its strength in the cities, Christianity drew an impressive company of leaders from the educated classes. Yet even in urban churches the number of persons able to read well in public was limited; the office of reader [*lector*] carried distinction, signified at Rome by the action of the bishop in ceremonially handing over the sacred scrolls to the person being appointed for that responsibility in the liturgy.

Copies of the biblical manuscripts were so scarce and expensive that only the wealthiest Christians could own even one gospel or epistle. And the preacher who undertook to bring the message to outsiders must deal with a vacuum of total ignorance of the sacred text; though some philosophers had passed on the judgment, probably based on hearsay, that the scriptures of the Jews were to be

401

esteemed for their teaching of ethical monotheism, intellectuals commonly despised books written by barbarians and unread in their own tradition. Consequently, Lactantius faulted Cyprian for his reliance on scripture in an apology offered to a hostile magistrate:

> He did not use his material as he should have,
> for not by the testimonies of the Scriptures
> which that one thought of as empty, fictitious, deceitful
> was he to have been refuted,
> but by argumentation and reason.   [*Inst.* V. 4, FC 49:338][2]

In commending the scriptures to unbelievers, the apologists most commonly appealed to prophecy as a foretelling of the future,[3] esteeming the prophets less for their witness to justice than for predictions they interpreted as fulfilled in Christ.

The Canon of Scripture

In the church from its beginning the scriptures of Judaism were read, as in the synagogue. In the Hellenistic communities the so-called Septuagint (LXX) became the standard text for Greek-speaking preachers; it contained not only the Law and the Prophets, but also the Writings, including the apocryphal books excluded from the Palestinian canon by the rabbis at Jamnia. The Christian practice, begun already in the first century, of reading from an apostolic letter during the liturgy became firmly established, and the epistles attributed to Paul were soon brought together. When the four gospels became available, they provided matter for yet another reading. Liturgical practice thus established the pattern of three lections—"prophecy," epistle, and gospel. It standardized the body of Christian writings regarded as scripture and ultimately declared canonical.

Educated Romans with pretensions to high culture, esteeming Greek as the language of serious literature and philosophy, naturally read the Septuagint (as well as the Christian texts) in that language, and readers made off-hand translations into Latin for unlettered listeners. And already in the second century North Africa had a Latin Bible, made from the Septuagint rather than from the original Hebrew.[4]

The Two Testaments[5]

With the acceptance of a distinctive body of scripture written by Christian authors, a new terminology evolved. Preachers began to speak of scripture as composed of two parts, united by the one divine purpose and revealed by the divine Logos. Clement of Alexandria firmly declared:

The Old and the New Testaments proclaim the same God...
The author of the law and the gospel is the same.

[Clement, *On Marriage*, III. 83, LCC, II:79]

Consequently, Tertullian believed that "Holy Scripture is never contradictory."[6]

The Christian appropriation of Israel's scriptures involved a decision on theological principle, clarified in the church's deliberate rejection of Marcion's bid to repudiate them. In claiming these sacred writings the orthodox preachers implicitly accepted the spiritual heritage of Jesus and the apostles, preeminently Judaism's sublime faith in one God. At the same time, their assumption that that ancient book had been divinely inspired with the primary intention of foreshadowing in minute detail the life and ministry of Jesus Christ resulted in their misreading of much of its message. Preoccupied with typology, they named the Hebrew scripture the Old Testament and prized it chiefly for what they found in it of him. The term and its implications involved the doctrine of supersessionism, with its notion that God had repudiated Judaism and set the church in its place as the chosen people. (Even without that inference, many Jews have found the appellation offensive.) For all his spirituality and his liberality of spirit, Origen could exegete Luke 11:24 to mean:

> Those who are of Israel...have now retained nothing of God
> within them, having forsaken, and no longer dwelling, in His house.[7]

The comment found its way into one of the earliest forms of homiletical helps, the Christian equivalent of the literary *florilegium* (collection of famous quotations); linking digests of comments from various exegetes on one Gospel verse after another to form a "chain," the *catena* enabled the preacher to pass on the insights and *dicta* of earlier Christian scholarship. Catenae in Greek began to circulate in the fifth century, in Latin two centuries later; through that medium Origen's harsh conclusion about Israel was passed down for generations—and still appears in "aids for preachers."[8]

Spiritual Exegesis[9]

Typological interpretation had, of course, been used by the apostle Paul and other New Testament writers (Rom. 5:14; 1 Cor. 10:1–6; Heb. 3–9). Clement of Alexandrria flatly states his own motivation in using it:

> There is life in the law in that it is spiritual
> and is to be gnostically understood.　[Clement,*On Marriage*, III. 83, LCC, II:79]

But this exegesis, so severely criticized after the Protestant Reformation, was far more than a device for drawing explicitly Christian readings from the Old Testament. It was the established hermeneutic in the philosophical schools; by its use Greco-Roman intellectuals drew from their own ancient literature wisdom applicable to current problems. Refined as a methodology for biblical study by the Hellenized Jewish exegetes of Alexandria, known to us preeminently through Philo, it exerted an attraction that the new company of Christian scholars found almost irresistible.

Origen, that early Christian champion of allegorical interpretation, formalized an exegetical method in keeping with his Platonist psychology, which understood human nature to consist of body, soul, and spirit:

> The simple person may be edified by what we may call the flesh
> of the scripture, this name being given to the obvious interpretation;
> While the person who has made some progress may be edified
> by its soul, as it were; and the person who is perfect...
> [here he quotes 1 Corinthians 2:6–7 on God's secret wisdom]
> —this person may be edified by the spiritual law,
> which has *"a shadow of the good things to come."*   [*Peri archon*, IV. ii. 4, alt.][10]

In instances that offended moral sensibility or taxed belief, Origen held that the obvious meaning was not to be taken seriously:

> these are figurative expressions
> which indicate certain mysteries through a semblance of history
> and not through actual events.   [*Peri archon*, IV. iii. 1, 288]

In its denial of some incidents narrated in "sacred history," this earliest Christian effort at "demythologizing" scripture was to turn later expositors against Origen, particularly those after the Reformation who disapproved his spiritual conclusion.

Exegesis in Preaching

Many passages, however, are clear enough to require no spiritualizing, especially the ethical admonitions that the preachers apply with forthright literalism—selections from the Law, the Sermon on the Mount, the letters of Paul. Even Origen explains many difficult mandates logically, illuminating them by other scriptures literally understood and without recourse to allegorical interpretation. Tertullian in his preaching calls upon Christians to think clearly about the relevance of the command to love one's neighbor:

Now, no utterance of the Holy Spirit should be restricted
only to its present matter,
but must be directed and referred to every occasion
to which its application is useful.   [*Apparel of Women*, II. 2 (5), FC 40:132]

From that it is only a short step to allegorizing.

Some spiritual renderings established early are still familiar today, being homiletically useful despite radical changes in worldview. Tertullian observes:

It was not to prevent Herod pursuing them that the Magi were warned
in a dream…to return to their own country another way…
The true meaning was that they should not walk
in their former way of life.   ["On Idolatry," 9, LCC, V:91]

The exegesis of other passages helped establish long-prevailing dogmas, as in Clement's reading of Psalm 51:

When David says: "In sin I was born…"
he says in a prophetic manner that Eve is his mother.
[*Stromateis*, III. 16, 100, LCC, II:87]

The belief that the essence of prophecy was the foretelling of Christ, both in literal prediction and in typological foreshadowing, led the preachers to love the Old Testament and to quote from it endlessly, as Justin did in his dialogue with Trypho, offering a Christian *midrash* on scores of texts.

Not until the end of the second century, however, did the preachers begin to focus a sermon exegetically on a specific portion of scripture. Most discourses throughout our period are thematic, developed after established rhetorical patterns, and using scattered biblical passages to prove or illuminate a particular point before moving on to another. Initiating a new development, Clement's sermon on "What Rich Man Shall be Saved?" addresses a difficult text. Cyprian's discourse on the Lord's Prayer presents an orderly exposition, moving from clause to clause in a straightforward, literal reading.

The growing preoccupation with spiritual interpretation, however, inspired ever more zealous study of the sacred writings; this exegesis was not an evasion of scripture (as those in later times who opposed to it would charge) but an effort to uncover the fullness of its hidden meaning. Origen appears to have been the first Christian preacher who made it a regular practice to devote an entire homily to a given verse or cluster of verses and to work through a portion of the Bible in a series of discourses. Judged on the basis of early homilies extant, we may designate him both the originator of the textual sermon and the founder of expository preaching.

The Church's Scriptures

Authority for Christian proclamation derived from the assertion

It is written.   [Rom. 3:10; cf. Mt. 4:4, 7, 10]

The preachers filled their sermons with well-loved examples from the biblical story; in time Eve, Noah, Abraham, Hannah, Job, and a vast gallery of other characters from the Old Testament almost totally displaced the exemplary figures that pagan moralists had made so familiar to Hellenistic audiences. We may assume that the Christians had heard the stories from their teachers, for Cyprian makes his point by brief allusion:

> When did it happen that resources could fail a just man,
> when it is written,
> *"The LORD will not afflict the soul of the just with famine."*
> Elias in the desert is fed by ministering ravens,
> and a meal is prepared in heaven for Daniel
> when he was inclosed in a den of lions… ;
> and you fear lest food be lacking for you.
>
> ["Works and Almsgiving," 11, FC 36:237]

Tertullian roundly proclaims that scripture belongs to the church, not to any idiosyncratic interpreter, and Clement of Alexandria faults the heretical Gnostic Christians for their exegesis, by which, he says, they abolish both law and gospel. Interpreted by the church in the light of apostolic tradition, scripture is at the same time a crucial carrier of that tradition.

When the most intense persecutions broke out, a well-informed imperial policy undertook to destroy the sacred writings. But the preachers held the Christians on a steady course:

> We must follow where the word leads…
> by following the divine scriptures.
>
> [Clement, *Stromateis*, III (5). 42, LCC, II:59]

THE MESSAGE OF THE PREACHERS [11]

Proclamation Prior to Formal Theology

The message they proclaimed was a powerfully appealing corre-lation of biblical witness with the religious longing of the times. The reigning philosophies provided vocabulary and concepts for conveying the meaning of scripture—words and ideas sometimes deliberately chosen for comparison or contrast with the Christian faith, but just as often, it appears, springing automatically to the lips of thoughtful and educated preachers for whom such language had become the normal mode of speech.

The message, delivered long before Christian theology had worked out its classic formulations in the fourth century, now read in cold print, sometimes appears deficient to partisans of orthodox dogma, blessed with 20/20 hindsight, to modern liberals, or to evangelical advocates of grace alone.[12] Yet, whatever its insufficiency, it sustained these preachers and their people through two fearful centuries and brought the church to the new era of freedom in a condition of spiritual power. Their work—primarily proclamation, apology, and exhortation—necessarily involved the preachers in theologizing. Their attempts, at first more intuitive than systematic, took paths that despite a show of promise sometimes led to dead ends. But in the third-century Christian schools, Christian thinking reached impressive heights.

To reduce their discourse to abstract notions charted on a trajectory of developing systematics radically alters its nature, distorts the mode of witness, stifles its existential quality, and obscures its vitality. But because their preaching made a crucial contribution to the development of Christian thought, we suggest the main lines of the preachers' witness.

Father, Son, Holy Spirit

They proclaim one righteous God, maker of all things. Hence the created world is good, birth is holy, and life in the flesh is not to be despised. As righteous Father, God has patiently endured human sin and has sent the Son to lead humanity to righteousness before the final judgment.

The preachers celebrate the Son as the divine Logos, characteristically referring to him as Teacher or Guide or Truth or Wisdom (*Sophia*), who has set forth the true philosophy. Many sermons treat some aspect of this distinct way of life, pointing to the cross as the supreme evidence of divine mercy and the measure of the demand made on the Christian. Grace is God's kindness in making known the truth—or imparting the spiritual gift—that enables the interpreter to understand scripture. Though they use Logos or Son or Teacher as titles far more than Christ or Savior and only rarely employ the name

Jesus, they evince an intense devotion to his person and a warm response to incidents of his earthly ministry. They commonly speak of him as God, and Origen uses the expression *God-Man.*

Repeatedly the gospel is rehearsed in brief rhetorical variations on the primitive confession of 1 Corinthians 15, paralleling the witness of the liturgy and the baptismal creeds. So *grace* refers to incarnation, death, and resurrection; to the coming of the Son to save; to the divine love beyond measure manifested in him. But the preachers elaborate no theory of atonement or justification, nor do they focus on it as the theme of a doctrinal sermon. Neither do they offer a major treatment of the Holy Spirit, whom they sometimes identify as the eternal Christ. They know the term Trinity, but use it rarely. In preaching to the church, as in their apologies to the world, monotheism and ethics loom as major topics.

"Enemies of Christ"

In contrast to the truth of the one God, the preachers constantly attack polytheism and all the ideas and customs associated with it. They commonly regard the gods of the pagans as genuine beings but view them as unclean demons subject to the power of Christ. That power works through the word of preaching as well as the word of exorcism to cast out the demons, imparting to believers bodily health, mental composure, and spiritual victory over sin.

The prince of the demonic powers is the devil, the fallen angel taken over from late Judaism, who constantly besets the Christian with temptations but cannot hope to match the Son of God. Origen permits himself to express the opinion that at the consummation of all things even the devil may be saved, so that God may be all in all. But most of the preachers stay close to that biblical imagery that depicts final judgment, everlasting punishment of the devil and his angels, and the casting into hell of all who have not believed in the Son of God nor walked in the way of righteousness taught by him. Yet despite the zeal of the preachers, the threats and the promises, not all who hear them find the *kērygma* persuasive.[13]

The Chosen People of the scripture become the stock example of disbelief and its attendant punishment. Justin's dialogue with Trypho the Jew is conducted with great courtesy on both sides, but the Christian debater perceives Israel as wilfully stubborn in refusing to believe—a view strengthened in the context of continuing rivalry between the two religions by a literal reading of numerous passages from both the Old and the New Testaments. Although Christians claim the scriptures of Israel, they have lost all sense of kinship with the continuing people. Their attitude toward the Jews parallels closely their posture toward the pagan majority, and especially the Romans, who are also understood as perverse in their disobedience of God. Unless they repent, unbelievers will be cast into the lake of fire, Jew and Gentile alike. Their only hope is to accept the gospel; then God will forgive.

The Christian Way [14]

The dominant note in the early preaching is ethical, whether apology, liturgical homily, or catechetical lecture. Scripture is read as divine demand. The Law and the Prophets inculcate moral rigor. The Logos (Christ) has declared and embodied the way of righteousness. The apostle Paul has delivered admonitions regarding behavior, to which these preachers allude far more often than to his theology. In contrast with the blatant sensuality of many pagans and the "puritanical," old-Roman sternness of those who cherish traditional values,[15] the Christian stands out by the quality of an upright life and the joy found in the Way—a pilgrim and stranger in a hostile world. The homilists constantly accent chastity, prayer, honesty, humility, consideration for the helpless, hospitality, generosity toward the poor; the self-denial they preach does not burden, but rather issues in true freedom.

The preachers' primary social ethic operates in the limited space of liberty open to Christians to follow new patterns of behavior—relationships in the household, including both relatives and slaves, and in other limited areas of personal choice. They openly deplore the bloodlust of the gladiatorial games, the lewdness of the theater, the irresponsibility of the ruling classes, the widespread cruelty and corruption. They preach a universal human equality akin to the vision of the Stoics,[16] and some teach pacifism. For the most part, their social witness is implicit in their confession of one God and their refusal to acknowledge Caesar or any earthly power as Lord, and their vision of the ultimate triumph of the divine kingdom.

A major reason for the long course of required catechesis is to impress upon candidates for baptism the real change involved in conversion, to stress the difficulty of the demands, and to provide a term of probation, so that they may be admitted to the church "intent only upon salvation."[17] Always the possibility of arrest and examination, to be followed by torture and death, looms before them. Even the practice of the distinctive Christian virtues requires courage. Constantly the preachers stress the demands of the Christian life, exceeded only by their emphasis on the promise of eternal glory. The greatness both of the pressure and the hope makes for a preaching of striking intensity.

Life in the Church

Christians share their glorious calling within the unity of the church, their spiritual mother. The preachers idealize the days of its beginning under the apostles and celebrate its present calling. Far more important than the place of meeting—for which, however, the term *church* is commonly used—the Christian orators hail the congregation of the saints. In this communion believers receive baptism, are signed with the cross, unite in common prayer, partake of the eucharist, and strengthen the bonds of that life together which moves outsiders to exclaim of them, "See, how they love one another!"[18] With the triumph of autocracy in the political sphere, many persons find in the church an air of freedom, "its free and democratic organization a spiritual, human, and collective substitute for the Latin liberties lost to the hated imperial autocracy."[19] Together believers advance undismayed through the "storms of a turbulent world,"[20] preparing for its end, which cannot be much longer delayed. They cultivate that life in the Spirit that leads to the unclouded vision of the pure in heart, being perfected in the likeness of their Teacher. In this company they find both the courage to face impending martyrdom and that joy in God which makes "all our life … a festival."[21]

PREACHING AS AN EXPLICIT CONCERN

The Appropriation of Rhetoric [22]

Of the many themes treated in the sermons, preaching itself is one of those most often mentioned. Its prominence as a concern in the minds of the preachers signals a significant synthesis of commitment to the gospel, handed down from the primitive church, with the classical vision of the orator as the good person of broad education using one's skill in persuasion for the betterment of society. Christian converts brought up in Hellenism naturally assume two axioms: (1) the gospel is to be preached, and (2) rhetoric provides the appropriate instrument. The first axiom they constantly verbalize. Taking the second for granted, they rarely discuss it; they just practice it.

Given the nature of Greco-Roman schooling and the entrance of so many educated persons into the church, such a development was to be expected. We have noted a similar phenomenon in Judaism. A number of the most prominent preachers—Arnobius the Elder,

Cyprian, and Lactantius in North Africa, Minucius Felix in Rome[23] — had earned their living as rhetoricians, and Tertullian had been a lawyer. The appropriation of rhetoric was heightened by the move on the part of ecclesiastical authority to clamp down on "prophecy," which subsided after the rejection of Montanism. As a charismatic mode of speech, prophecy had employed such eloquence as "came naturally"; but as deliberate, prepared, and scheduled address, preaching inevitably went rhetorical, making use of the mode in which people had been taught to engage an audience.

Granted the preachers' zeal for Christian truth, we might have looked for the unpretentious mode of informal conversation—*homilia*: a "talk"—to have dominated preaching, to the exclusion of any move toward calculated oratory, particularly in the light of the apostle Paul's professed disavowal of persuasive words. That is not what occurred. The artless homily continued, of course, in familiar sessions and in the counsel of the anchorites. But among the "Greeks" a studied disregard for rhetoric did not manifest itself until Clement and Origen, in whom the concern for more systematic theological discourse took over; and even they, despite professed disdain for artistry in speech, could not help talking at times like graduates of the schools.

The old habits took over, as with Tertullian when he defended himself for long-windedness:

> Verboseness, though a fault at times,
> is no fault when it tends to edification.
>
> [Tertullian, "Patience," 5 (1), FC 40:199]

And opponents of the third-century Bishop of Palmyra, Paul of Samosata, who charged him with heresy, added further disgrace by faulting him for crudeness in delivery.

Deliberately chosen rhetorical form, for all the vigorous protestations to the contrary, is a striking feature of most Greek and Latin preaching from these early centuries after the apostles. Such a concern is to be expected in the apologies and in the appeals for conversion (*protreptikoi*) addressed to cultivated outsiders. Yet it also dominates the bulk of the surviving sermonic literature addressed to Christians, except only for the homilies of Origen. Athenagoras, Melito of Sardis, Tertullian, Cyprian, even Clement, cut off though they are from access to large public audiences, rank with the most accomplished orators of the time. The full range of epideictic expression marks not only the preaching for the great liturgical festivals—Epiphany and the Pasch, the latter combining Passover and "Easter"—but also the lectures to catechumens. Preachers of the second and third centuries inaugurated a tradition of Christian eloquence that would come to flower in the church's magnificent orators of the fourth century, for whom the pagans would have no match. The secular rhetorical education of the preachers in most cases preceded their conversion; they brought the art with them as one of the chief "spoils" taken from "the Egyptians."

Even the church's catechetical schools showed the marks of the prevailing style of education. Clement's Christ the Educator talks like an idealized rhetor, offering instruction in how a Christian should speak; Book One of the *Paidagogos* gives attention to a rhetoric of reproof, sets forth methods of offering advice, and argues the need for praise and blame, the old stock-in-trade of epideictic oratory. In the *Miscellanies (Stromateis)* Clement also turns occasionally to the discourse of the Christian teacher,[24] but neither work is in any sense a technical manual of speech-making. Primarily concerned with *ethos,* Clement conveys by example a mode of Christian persuasion. The power of his ideal Christian, whom he terms the true gnostic, is evident in three achievements:

> (1) in the knowledge of the facts of the Christian religion,
> (2) in the accomplishment of whatever the Word enjoins,
> (3) in the capacity to impart to others in a godly manner
> the hidden things of truth.[25]

Whimsically he observes,

> We must provide a large variety of baits owing to the varieties of fish.[26]

In seeking to impart the secrets of divine truth, the preachers sometimes made common cause with other advocates of monotheism, as we have noted. But despite their readiness to despoil Stoics, Platonists, and even Gnostics of thought-forms deemed useful to the proclamation, the Christian thinkers never forgot their calling to an exodus from "Egypt" nor their involvement in a fight to the finish against polytheism. To the modern liberal mind they frequently appear intolerant as well as unfair in the way they lampoon other positions—heresy, Judaism, the popular religions, philosophy. The historian may well ask, however, if a more tentative rhetoric, a genteel readiness to state opposing arguments as strongly as possible, could have been expected from, or could have been expected to sustain, a community under persecution for its faith. The preachers argued like rhetoricians, and more of the dust of Egypt remained on them than they knew. Again, to the modern mind some of their positions seem deficient in critical judgment. Yet comparison with current popular religion and philosophy—presented in the prevailing high-flown pattern of speaking—makes the preachers sound sober and restrained. In them Cicero's dream has come to fulfilment: in a manner he could not have imagined, philosophy has been married to rhetoric, and substance to practice.

Forms of Christian Discourse[27]

By inductive analysis of the sermonic literature it is possible to suggest a variety of forms used by the preachers. The APOLOGY or defense adapted the familiar pattern of forensic oratory to plead for justice toward the Christians, to defend the faith against misconceptions and false charges, to argue its superiority against rival religions and philosophies. A form used in public evangelistic appeal was the PROTREPTIKOS, a speech designed to persuade and convert, taken over from the wandering philosophers; it included arguments for the truth of the Christian position along with an urgent plea to accept it. When persecution drove them from the streets, Christians sought audiences for these oral forms by circulating them in writing.

Another literary genre essentially rhetorical was the DIALOGUE, an effective and popular means of making one's case against opponents. Two forms of address to outsiders were in most cases less "artistic." (1) The TESTAMENT or final declaration of a martyr might consist of only a few words authenticated by faithfulness to the death, although in some cases the Christian prepared a fullblown apology and undertook to deliver it so that it might be written into the record. (2) The personal witness or TESTIMONY of the individual Christian to a friend, fellow prisoner, or guard was perhaps the dominant form of speech to outsiders. Much of this would have been rudimentary, unsystematic, direct from the heart. But the formalized nature taken on by testimony in modern times and the heavy reliance on coaching personal evangelists suggest that dialogues like Justin's disputation with Trypho and the *Octavius* of Minucius Felix, as well as some of the ostensibly forensic apologies, may well have been designed to offer guidance in discussing the faith with nonbelievers.

In address to the church, PROPHECY had fallen into disrepute by mid-second century, but Montanists and Gnostic Christians prized the REVELATION-DISCOURSE, whether received in ecstasy or conventionalized. With the conclusion by the orthodox party that the age of prophecy had ceased, charismatic utterance yielded to non-ecstatic preaching which was, in the nature of the case, rhetorical.

HOMILY was the first term commonly used for a discourse preached within the Christian community. While the word originally designated an informal talk, as we have seen, it came to imply what *sermon* means today, an address set in the context of liturgy.[28] The term embraced a variety of forms: the rambling *speech* spontaneously moving by free association from one notion to another, the *diatribe* or rhetorical discussion of a theme, the *encomium* or declamation praising a virtue or decrying a vice. The teachers delivered *lectures* to catechumens, using essentially the various forms taken by homily. Before our period ended, Christians had taken over the PANEGYRIC or funeral oration, and it had become customary to deliver a sermon of this type at the tomb of a martyr on each "birthday" or anniversary of death; rehearsed in the liturgy, this annual retelling of the story established itself early as a moving form of address to the congregation; in the tradition of those accounts in the apocryphal books that tell of faithful Jews who endured suffering and gave up life itself rather than violate the sacred Law, it became a stylized literary genre.[29]

Some figures or devices so pervade the preaching as to merit designation as subordinate forms of Christian address, recurring within the various types already mentioned. More characteristic of the folk-preachers than of the rhetors is *symbolic narrative*, sometimes called *parable*, and occasionally expanded to fill an entire sermon. The "then …now" scheme of *contrast* used by some New Testament writers continues to be employed effectively. Hermas gives the name *mandate* to a homiletical paragraph amplifying a command of the Lord. A *series of exempla*, setting forth a succession of biblical characters who illustrate or embody the preacher's theme, appears in almost every sermon. The ancient form of *wisdom sayings* continues, but is no longer a major type. *Paradox*, a figure prized by sophistic orators and audiences alike, enables the preachers to spread their rhetorical wings in celebrating the central affirmations of the gospel, for example, "the Creator created," or "by death life." The homilists add dramatic intensity to their words through *prosopopoeia*, which represents them as being spoken by God the Creator, by the Son, by the devil, by an exemplary figure, or by a personified virtue such as Patience. An effective variation of this figure is *sermocinatio* or *discussion*, in which the preacher states a question or objection offered by an imaginary critic in the audience and then proceeds to answer it.

The style of the preachers ranges from the unschooled talk of Hermas or Anthony and the studied artlessness of Origen to the high-flown rhetoric of Melito or Tertullian. In general, the preachers practice greater restraint than the sophistic orators, a tendency enhanced by their Christian seriousness of purpose. With Clement of Alexandria, such simplicity is a matter of principled conformity to the "plain style of the Holy Spirit."[30] With Irenaeus or Cyprian it is perhaps more a matter of temperament and involvement in the substance of the message. In contrast with the popular address of the Stoic and Cynic philosophers[31] and of Jesus, few sallies of humor appear in the extant sermons, except for the frequent use of irony. But the preachers do not come across as grim; on the contrary, a mood of joy pervades their speech. All in all, they automatically express themselves as men who have gone to school to the classical rhetors. Even Clement terms his work on *Christ the Educator*

> our panegyric of the Word.   [Clement, *Paidog.*, XII (101), FC 23:275]

The Glory of Preaching

The ministry of preaching never fails to stir excitement in the Christian speakers and writers. They see it as the typical and essential work of God's people from the beginning. They laud Noah and Elijah and other preachers of old Israel. They honor John the Baptist as a preacher. They recall Jesus as engaged in this gracious task:

> While teaching Israel and doing such great signs and wonders
> he preached to them and loved them greatly.
>
> [Ep. Barnabas, v. 8, *Ap F*, LCL, I:357]

Repeatedly they celebrate his descent into hell to preach to patriarchs and prophets so that they too might believe and be saved by the gospel that their words and deeds had foreshadowed. His preaching continues to instruct and strengthen the church.

Time and again the preachers refer to the Lord's appointment of apostles to carry on his work of preaching, as the prophets had foretold. Clement notes that while the apostles gave themselves unreservedly to this task, their wives labored as "their fellow-ministers in dealing with the house-wives":

> through them the Lord's teaching penetrated also the women's quarters
> without any scandal being aroused.   [Clement, *Stromateis*, III. 53, LCC, II:65]

The Gnostic Gospel of Mary depicts the Mother of Jesus exhorting and instructing even the apostles, "proclaiming" through a revelation-discourse the words of her glorified Son.[32] Hermas has the apostles continuing to preach in Hades after their deaths.[33] And their successors are the preachers now on earth. That kerygmatic title is good enough for them; rarely, if ever, do they refer to themselves as orators.

Memories of the great bishops and martyrs center on their preaching, cherishing not the actual words, now faded from recall, but the abiding image of the beloved figures engaged in the glorious work of declaring the apostolic gospel. Pontius reported Cyprian's love for this task: he prayed to be granted "the grace to be put to death in the very act of preaching, while speaking of God."[34]

Reflections on preaching recur as a persistent theme in the sermons and other forms of Christian literature, though no treatise devoted completely to kerygmatic theory or technique is known from our period. Aristides hails it as "a gateway of light in corruptible words,"[35] and Quadratus glories in its reliance on persuasion, not compulsion.[36] At a time when famous orators in the secular world repeated their best speeches all over the Empire,[37] the preachers celebrated the power of the Christian proclamation as deriving not from rhetorical eloquence, but from "the magnificence of the word"[38] and the work of the Holy Spirit.

> As...the remotest particle of iron is drawn by the influence
> of the magnet extending through a long series of iron rings,
> so also through the attraction of the Holy Spirit the virtuous
>
> [Clement, *Stromateis*, VII. ii. 9, LCC, II:98][39]

are prepared for their heavenly habitation. Accordingly, Origen looks upon biblical preaching as sacramental, the Word being incarnate in the flesh of the text.[40]

Ignatius insists that the teacher match deeds to words.[41] Justin asserts Christian preaching's congruity with scripture:

> I can persuade...even those of weak intellectual faculties,
> for the words which I use are not my own,
> nor are they embellished by human rhetoric,
> but they are the words as David sang them,
> as Isaias announced them as good news,
> as Zacharias proclaimed them,
> and as Moses wrote them. [*Dial. Trypho*, 29, FC 6:191)

This ministry is not for personal display; at the Synod of Antioch, ca. 265, the bishops dismiss any notion that the heretical Paul of Samosata is entitled to serious consideration by characterizing him as a vainglorious man of affairs who preaches for vulgar acclaim.[42] Clement of Alexandria celebrates meetings of the Christians as feasts of reason and the *agape* or "love-feast" as a banquet of the Word.[43] To Origen, Christ's kingdom means the words of salvation; he characterizes the preaching as like a fruitful rain, and undertakes to shape his discourses to heal; indeed, preaching is an allegory of the body and blood of Christ, which believers received "when we accepted his words, in which is life."[44] Christianity retains a sacramental understanding of preaching, which the author takes over from the rabbis:

> Where the Lord's nature is spoken of, there is he present.[45]

A full-blown rhetorical *protreptikos* from about the end of the second century, preserved in mistaken attribution to Justin Martyr, plays with the multiple meaning of *Logos* in Christian discourse, referring primarily to the Christ, but with overtones that suggest scripture and even more the glory of preaching:

> Therefore, my Greek friends, come and share in unrivalled wisdom,
> and receive the teachings of the divine Word,
> while you become acquainted with the immortal Sovereign...
> For our Leader, the divine Word, does not demand a strong body
> and beautiful countenance, or high and noble birth,
> but a pure soul, well-grounded in holiness.
> He demands the password of our Sovereign, namely, divine deeds,
> for the power to perform such deeds is transmitted...through the Word.
> This power of the Word does not make us poets,
> or learned philosophers,
> or fluent orators, but it does make us immortal...
> Come, therefore, and be instructed.
> Become as I am, for I was once as you...
> The divinity of the doctrine and the power of the Word
> have conquered me.   [Pseudo-Justin, *Discourse to the Greeks*, FC 6:435–36, alt.]

The Bitter Contest

The preachers saw the glory of their work in the splendor of the message, not in the prospect of acclaim or ease. Even when persecution subsided for a time, Christians were a despised minority, regarded as ignorant, antisocial, and subversive. Defenders of the old order blamed them for disasters, whether military or natural. Celebrated orators praised the worship of the traditional gods as demonstrating loyalty to the state; Maximos of Tyre had a famous speech "In Defense of Idols," and in his romance Lucius Apuleius interpreted all the supreme goddesses as one, known under varying names. Celsus and Galen characterized the Christians as superstitious and anti-intellectual, accusing them of pleading:

> Do not ask questions, only believe. Faith will save you.[46]

In rejoinder, the frustrated Christians could only ask for a fair fight, with a chance to make their case in the open. So Cyprian challenged:

> Destroy faith, conquer, if you can, by discussion,
> conquer by reason.   [Cyprian, *To Demetrian*, 13, FC 36:179]

On occasion a Christian orator could come out to raise his voice in behalf of the helpless. During a revolt in 262, when part of Alexandria was under siege, Anatolius negotiated a safe-conduct for noncombatant refugees; in an appearance before the municipal assembly he persuaded its members to allow everyone not needed for the army to cross the lines. Later he was credited with saving many lives, including all the Christians.

But persecution had not yet ended. Under Emperor Diocletian, Eusebius later wrote, "the prisons everywhere...were then filled by bishops and presbyters and deacons and readers and exorcists, so that there was no longer any place left...for those condemned for wrong-doing."[47] As late as 312 the principal of the Christian school at Antioch was beheaded for the faith.

The Triumph of the Preaching

Yet the preachers interpreted the apostolic mission and their part in continuing it as the triumph of the word of God changing lives throughout the whole world. When the Christians were banished from Egypt to Libya, Bishop Dionysius reported that "there God opened a door for speech,"[48] and the word was brought to many who had not received it before. Constantly the Christians gloried in the universal spread of the faith, boasting as early as Justin:

> There is not one single race of people—
> whether barbarians, or Greeks, or persons called by any other name,
> nomads, or vagabonds, or herdsmen dwelling in tents—
> among whom prayers and thanksgivings are not offered
> to the Father and Creator of the universe
> in the name of the crucified Jesus.   [Justin, *Dial. Trypho*, 117, FC 6:329, alt.]

In the decade before the grant of toleration, offered throughout the empire in 313 by the commanders Constantine and Licinius during their struggle for control of the state, Christian sympathizers, perhaps even catechumens, within the imperial household were pleading their cause, and Helena, the mother of Constantine, had embraced the faith.

It was a believer who, in recounting Cyprian's earlier martyrdom in 258, boasted that his execution occurred

> under the emperors Valerian and Gallienus,
> but in the reign of our Lord Jesus Christ.[49]

Even when these witnesses went to their death, they saw their final testimony as a vindication of the preaching.

Preaching before Constantine: An Assessment

In assessing the preaching of our period, we are limited for the most part to texts from orthodox, or nearly orthodox, Christians, the attacks by critics and heretics having been for the most part destroyed in the interest of religious uniformity. Generally speaking, the relatively few homilies extant come from the most honored voices; a small fraction of the total preaching, they probably represent it at its best. Though they obviously idealize the cause they regard as righteous and the struggle they see as heroic, when read along with other historical evidence and approached with a not too suspicious hermeneutic, they provide a basis for analyzing the achievement of those who preached in a critical time for the church.

1. Across more than two centuries of social repression and intermittent governmental persecution, the preachers gave voice to Christian faith; in the face of intense opposition, their preaching attracted, instructed, motivated, and sustained a growing company of believers gathered from all ranks of society throughout the *oikoumenē.* They inspired commitment and held the church together in disciplined strength until leading contenders for control of the Roman empire, bidding for Christian support, abandoned the struggle.

2. Many of the preachers authenticated their words by laying down their lives for the gospel. The bloody opposition they faced and resisted through eight generations of imperial hostility from Nero to Diocletian impressed upon the preaching an unimpeachable authenticity, for it delivered the preachers from the temptation to offer cheap grace, to court popularity by empty rhetoric, to play to the gallery, to forget even for a moment their seriousness of purpose. Transcendent

demand sounded through their proclamation. In later, easier times the legacy of the martyrs intensified the zeal of the church; century after century it aroused in some preachers a readiness to stand against popular pressure and hostile authority.

3. The preaching of transcendent divine demand imbued the church with an intense conviction of distinctiveness from the larger society. Christians refused to take part in the rituals of the imperial cult or in public religious ceremonies in the schools and at the theater, regarding these as offensive to the one true God. They flatly rejected the popular culture represented by the gladiatorial games and the contests in the arena, abhorring the passionate excitement and blood lust aroused by such spectacles—of which many believers became victims.

4. The apologists formulated persuasive and principled arguments for religious liberty, stated with an eloquence reinforced by their absolute refusal to compromise their allegiance to one God. Though the church of later centuries would often enter into alliance with "friendly" governments to make doctrine, worship, religious instruction, even support of ecclesiastical budgets, concerns of the state, these early Christian pleas for toleration hold a significant place in the literature of freedom.

5. With regard to the cultural and intellectual tradition, the stance over against the world was not hard and fast, ranging from Tertullian's rejection of "Athens" in favor of "Jerusalem" to Origen's eager "spoiling of the Egyptians." The diverse attitudes toward the high culture advocated by various preachers converged, however, in fully acknowledging supreme allegiance to God alone.

6. Addressing the thought-world of the time, the Christian preachers engaged the philosophical tradition, finding in it more resources for their ministry—and in their contemporaries among the philosophers, more challenging resistance—than was offered by the mystagogues. The apologists cast their rejection of idolatry and polytheism in language taken from the Hebrew prophets, the Psalms, and the tradition of wisdom, even as they made use of concepts and arguments made current by the street-preachers of the various theological schools.

7. Finding their point of contact with philosophy in the concept of the divine Word or Reason, the Christian preachers followed the prologue to the Gospel of John in proclaiming Jesus Christ as the Logos who enlightens everyone coming into the world, who became flesh

and lived among us. They made that idea central to their apologetic and evangelism. Heavy reliance on the Logos notion led some to an "intellectualist" presentation of Christianity, offering Jesus as the perfect Teacher and the Christian Way as the true philosophy. (Remember that philosophy was commonly seen as a way of living.)

8. The preachers gave comparatively less attention to soteriology and speculations regarding biblical images of atonement, perhaps because the prominence of similar language in the mysteries inevitably colored and commonly distorted the popular understanding of such terms and their connotations. The preachers have consequently been charged with a defective understanding of grace. They emphasized the salvation imparted by Christ the Truth, the Teacher, and Shepherd. Salvation occurred in the new lives of upright living and joyful hope to which the Logos led them.

9. The call to conversion sounded repeatedly in the appeals of the apologists and in the *protreptikoi* or rhetorical appeals designed to persuade unbelievers to receive the Christian gospel and accept the new faith. As with the apologies, it is likely that these invitations were commonly circulated as literature to be read rather than proclaimed as speeches in the forums, given the danger of hostile action by the government. Even so, being cast in the form of a public appeal, they are to be understood as preaching.

10. The gospel concerning Jesus Christ the Word of God spoke to the sorrows, fears, needs, and longings of the nameless people struggling in the great cities to come to terms with life; Christian preachers had the insight and courage to point out the the limitations of the popular philosophies, the delusions of idolatry, and the emptiness of the pleasures through which many sought to find meaning or escape.

11. The preachers put forth special efforts to attract intellectuals to the faith, seeking to make the gospel convincing by presenting the essence of Christian belief in terms of the most respected thought-forms of the time. Although some outspoken members of the intelligentsia failed to respond to their apologetic, it dealt with the issues in such a way as to convince impressive numbers of educated persons.

12. The missionaries and teachers of the Christian faith, when conditions permitted, gladly made use of the primary means of "mass communication" in the Mediterranean world, namely the oration or public address. Even when driven from the public square and, during times of greatest danger, into secret meetings, the preachers continued to assume the role and manner of classical orators.

13. It should not be forgotten, however, that person-to-person testimony, which often served as the leading edge of witness, was itself a form of preaching; inquirers who had been thus attracted to the faith went on to a fuller understanding communicated by teachers, presbyters, and bishops.

14. Though the preachers best known to us had enjoyed the privilege of a good education and undertook to win their intellectual peers to the faith, they honored their Christian sisters and brothers among the lower classes—the ignorant, the poor and the enslaved—striving to make the promises and demands of the gospel clear to all. Without hesitation they took up basic intellectual, ethical, and spiritual issues in their sermons to rank-and-file Christians, standing shoulder to shoulder with them against the pretensions of the world, the worship of the gods, and the demands of the state.

15. The church's first theologizing, accordingly, was missionary and pastoral. In their apologies and *protreptikoi* addressed to outsiders evangelists and teachers explained the new faith, answered objections, and appealed to them to take the dangerous step of claiming Jesus Christ as Lord; in their homilies during worship they addressed questions that had literal life-and-death implications. Christian theology was not an occupation for the ivory tower; it was the work of missionary preachers.

16. If the preachers and teachers of the second and third centuries did not carry the enterprise of theology to a final conclusion with regard to major issues confronting Christian thought after their work was done (how many theologians have ever managed that trick?), they fairly launched the venture. They adopted positions the church of subsequent centuries would sustain with regard to God as Creator (against the Gnostics), to Jesus Christ as truly human (against the Docetists) and truly divine, to scriptures of the Old Testament (against Marcion) and the New as the source of normative guidance from the Spirit, as well as other issues.

17. The preachers commended to their hearers in their day-by-day existence a rigorous ethic, ascetic lifestyle, and active concern for the poor and helpless. Even though the general level of believers' conduct fell short of the apologists' idyllic representation and though some communities claiming the Christian name may have practiced scandalous behavior, the high standards of morality commended by the preachers generally contributed largely to the appeal of the faith.[1]

18. Though their exaltation of love (*agapê*) toward all and their commitment to the neediest members of society represented a shift from prevailing ideals that was little short of revolutionary, the Christians mounted no rebellion against the empire or any attempt to overthrow it.

19. By universal custom and conviction the church established preaching as integral and essential to public worship, its major instrument of Christian teaching, motivation, and discipline, as well as of evangelism. Along with the eucharist, the ministry of the word (even when reduced to the briefest of homilies) proved to be the necessary carrier of Christian understanding and devotion.

20. To maintain the fidelity of the preaching, the church invoked scripture and tradition as canons for determining faithfulness to the gospel. Tradition, its champions maintained, pointed to the essence of the apostolic preaching as summarized in the local baptismal confessions and the writings attributed to the apostles. An enlarged understanding of holy scripture as including, along with the sacred texts of Judaism, the four Gospels and the apostolic epistles committed the preachers to a specifically Christian New Testament; before the end of the second century Irenaeus was working with it as the accepted guide to Christian teaching. United with the older Testament received from Israel, it completed the church's supremely authoritative canon.

21. The need of the churches in the west (North Africa, Italy, Gaul, and Spain), where only a few of the academically elite understood Greek, led to the translation of the scriptures into Latin. The "Old Latin" translations (from the LXX), which began to appear in the second century, lacked rhetorical elegance but served the needs of those preachers whose opportunities for education had been limited and the plain people who came to hear them. Translations were also produced in Armenian and other indigenous languages.

22. Except for bishops, presbyters, lectors, and some deacons and teachers, knowledge of the text of scripture came from *hearing*. Few private persons owned or even had access to the sacred books, every expensive copy of which had had to be laboriously transcribed by hand. Yet the people of that highly oral culture possessed a well-developed auditory memory in contrast with moderns constantly assailed by the sounds of the electronia media—who unconsciously protect themselves by an involuntary reflex of shutting out much of the clamorous assault on the ears. In the second and third centuries,

many preachers could repeat a striking number of passages that they had never read.

23. The emergence across North Africa of the church's most flourishing communities, led by its most notable converts, won for that continent the foremost place in the development of preaching and Christian thought (as well as of Latin letters).[2] (In later times the most prominent bishop in Africa would glory in the title of "Patriarch of Alexandria…and of all the Preaching of St. Mark.")[3]

24. Distinctive modes of discourse inherited from the synagogue came to characterize life within the church—the homily on a text and the extended course of expository sermons. The establishment of the Christian sermon-form—as a face-to-face engagement of preacher and people with the word of scripture, in quest of light on their particular situation and need—would profoundly affect the subsequent history of preaching.

25. The preachers' appropriation and adaptation of classical rhetoric as the instrument of proclamation took place almost by conditioned reflex (as it had done among the educated rabbis in Hellenistic Judaism); they made effective use of the forms and manner of speech in which they had been schooled. Their work offers virtually no theoretical reflection on this development, except for the insistence that the power of the preaching derives from the majesty of the divine word, not from human artifice. But it does not repudiate rhetoric in the sweeping fashion that later became a Christian commonplace. The practice of educated preachers indicates simply that, with the notable exception of Origen, they consistently used it. Their occasional attacks on the empty rhetoric of the sophists and other pagans address an issue quite different from a total renunciation of the art, linking them with the most honored of the philosophers.

26. At a more subtle level, the reliance of rhetoric on "proof" (*probatio*) tended to shift the emphasis in preaching from proclamation to demonstration, too often subtly transmuting scripture from witness to proof-text.

27. The appropriation of rhetoric and of the manner of the classical orators made for a pronounced (though well-intentioned—even unconscious) departure from the mode of speaking that had characterized Jesus (and the rabbis before him). The unaffected naturalness of his aphorisms and parables and his direct engagement with simple folk gave way before torrents of pretentious "eloquence" cultivated

as schoolboys. In part the change was a matter of cross-cultural adaptation, Hellenized preachers "talking the language" of Hellenized hearers. The more serious fault lay in the tendency of self-consciously rhetorical speakers to assume an ethos befitting the orator-as-master-of-the-assembly, the self-image of one in a position of importance "talking down" to lesser folk. With good reason to forswear rhetoric of that sort, Origen and the anchorite preachers maintained a capacity for speaking person-to-person on level ground before the word of scripture. But even good bishops who loved their people and bravely died for the faith too easily fell into the mode of speaking they had been taught, unintentionally turning hearers into inferiors and sermons into lectures.

28. The remarkable success of the Gentile mission, along with the devastation of the Palestinian communities, both Jewish and Christian, by Roman legions in the second century made for a dominance of the Hellenistic mentality in the church, at the expense of Hebraic modes of thought. Philosophical presuppositions as to the nature of divine perfection, for example, prevented the preachers from imagining any limitation on God's arbitrary power, or of attributing "passibility" (the capacity for feeling and suffering) to God—even though the scriptures clearly do so. In ways that Christians did not perceive, Greco-Roman thought-forms shaped the preaching.

29. The rivalry of Christianity with Judaism, the preachers' single-minded compulsiveness about converting the Jews, and their typological understanding of the Old Testament as primarily concerned with foreshadowing the Christ precluded the opening of any genuine dialogue between the two faiths. Moreover, the declamatory mode of classical rhetoric—and the habit it instilled in those who practiced it of needing to score points in debate—lured such gifted orators as Melito and Tertullian into excesses of reprehension, upsetting their balance in their discussion of Israel. Alienation deteriorated into the bitter spirit of anti-Semitism.[4]

30. The crucial importance of preaching led to the church's ordering of its public ministry by the attribution of authority to its bishops as chief exponents and guardians of the apostolic gospel, entrusted with the exercise of oversight over the preaching and teaching.

31. The decision to commit to the bishops responsibility for good order and for adherence to the apostolic faith effectively eliminated "prophecy" from the life of the Christian community. With rare

exceptions in the subsequent history of the church persons announcing that they were possessed by the divine Spirit would be restrained by ecclesiastical control.

32. Christian ministry emerged from this period as an order limited to males, even though for a time women had served the church as prophets and teachers, presbyters and bishops. The extant sermons do not contend over the exclusion of women from leadership; they simply operate from assumptions of patriarchy. In openness to the public ministry of women certain "heretical" movements may have arisen as efforts of feminist protest; if so, that factor may have figured even more largely in their repression than their alleged departures from the faith of the apostles. In any case, the orthodox line virtually eliminated for centuries to come any churchly prospect for women to serve as preachers.

33. Later generations of Christians began to honor the preachers of the second and third centuries as Fathers of the Church. In falling short of inclusiveness that title obscures the significant contribution of women to the ministry of the word in the early days of the faith and the firm fidelity of many of them in going to death rather than deny their Lord. At last historians are beginning to realize that, along with the "Fathers," there were Mothers of the Church as well, spiritual ancestors of all subsequent generations of believers.

34. The quality of second-and-third-century preaching must be measured both by pragmatic considerations and by criticism, theological as well as rhetorical. Though by today's standards these Christian orations may seem wooden in form and overblown in style, they contain passages of genuine beauty and moving eloquence, and in the light of the then-prevailing canons of effective speech, they are impressive.

35. Because the most serious orators outside the church, on whose work and mode of speech the preachers drew most heavily, were moralists, and because Christians were committed to ethical rigor, the preaching tended to emphasize law more than grace. That trait, along with the avowal of theological positions that the later church considered immature (after it had had time to reach a more advanced stage in its dogmatic thinking), has resulted in some disparagement of the preaching of our period—anachronistic criticism offered at a safe distance. Certainly the remembered preachers of these two centuries demonstrated an intention toward faithfulness to the gospel—in proclamation, manner of life, and readiness to die for their confession.

36. Preaching held a place of primacy in the church's understanding of its vocation and mission. The great Christian names of these two centuries, as of the two that followed, are preachers. Their "books" are sermons or other types of preaching, perhaps slightly reworked for publication. Their theological reflection deals with the content of the preaching, their concern for order and apostolic tradition with its faithfulness. They glory in the work of preaching and in its triumphant progress. They think of it as a sacramental act.

This massive fact about the church and the writers of the patristic era—the centrality of the ministry of the word in their witness and thought—has been too largely neglected, as has the influence of the preaching on the Christian community and the larger society. Church historians tend to emphasize dogmatic and institutional developments, without noting the involvement of these "writers" in proclamation. Anthologies of preaching commonly ignore or pass over this period, even as collections of readings on church history conceal the fact that many of the selections, usually entitled tractates or treatises, are in fact sermons. Only by reading these works attentively and noting the constant recurrence of "preaching" as a theme does one come to realize its large place in the thought and affection of those who witnessed to the foolishness of the cross in a time when Caesar was god.

+

Across two perilous centuries the minds and spirits mentioned in these chapters, as well as hundreds of women and men whose very names have been forgotten, exercised a decisive influence as martyrs, prophets, evangelists, pastors, and teachers in the service of the gospel, handing on Christian faith to their spiritual descendants in a new era of freedom. Their lives and preaching and deaths offer eloquent commentary on the word of the apostle:

> The message of the cross is sheer folly
> to those on the way to destruction,
> but to us, who are on the way to salvation,
> it is the power of God...
> Where is your wise one now, your man of learning,
> your controversialist of this present age?...
> The world failed to find God by its wisdom,
> and God chose by the folly of the preaching
> to save those who have faith...
> We proclaim Christ nailed to the cross,
> and though this is an offence to Jews and folly to Gentiles,

yet to those who are called, Jews and Greeks alike,
he is the power of God and the wisdom of God.
The folly of God is wiser than human wisdom,
and the weakness of God stronger than human strength.

[1 Cor. 1:18–25 REB, alt.][5]

NOTES

Preface

[1]Richard R. Niebuhr, "A Power and a Goodness," *The Christian Century,* 72:48 (Dec. 1, 1965), 1472.

[2]Albert C. Outler, "A Way Forward from Lund," *Ecumenical Review,* 5:1 (Oct., 1952), 61–62.

[3]See "The Study of the History of Preaching" in *The Preaching of Chrysostom: Homilies on the Sermon on the Mount,* ed. Jaroslav Pelikan (The Preacher's Paperback Library, Philadelphia: Fortress Press, 1967), 1–5.

[4]See Ronald E. Osborn, "A Functional Definition of Preaching: A Tool for Historical Investigation and Homiletical Criticism," *Encounter,* 37:1 (Winter 1976), 53–72.

[5]John Killinger, "Homiletical Hoard," a review of *20 Centuries of Great Preaching,* Vol. 8, ed. Clyde E. Fant, Jr., and William M. Pinson, Jr., (Word Books), in *The Christian Century,* 89:5 (Feb. 2, 1972), 148–50.

[6]See Ross Shepard Kraemer, *Her Share of the Blessings: Women's Religions among Pagans, Jews, and Christians in the Greco-Roman World* (New York: Oxford University Press, 1992), 1–10.

[7]Quintilian, *Institutio oratoria,* X. i. 37 (LCL, IV, 25).

[8]See "Rhetoric, Public Address, and History," chapter 2 in Marie Hochmuth Nichols, *Rhetoric and Criticism* (Baton Rouge: Louisiana State University Press, 1967), 19–33.

[9]Phillips Brooks, *Lectures on Preaching Delivered before the Divinity School of Yale College in January and February, 1877* (New York: E. P. Dutton & Company, 1877), 108 ("The Idea of the Sermon").

[10]*Metropolitan Seminars in Art #2: Realism* (New York: Metropolitan Museum of Art, 1958), 5ff.

[11]Alexander Phimister Proctor, *Sculptor in Buckskin: An Autobiography,* edited and with a foreword by Hester Elizabeth Proctor (Norman: University of Oklahoma Press, 1971), 3–4.

PART ONE. CONTEXT OF ORATORY
Introduction to Part One

[1]*Gnomologium Vaticanum* 7, cited by Hans Dieter Betz, *Galatians: A Commentary on Paul's Letter to the Churches in Galatia.* Hermeneia — A Critical and Historical Commentary on the Bible (Philadelphia: Fortress Press, 1979), 55, n. 110.

Chapter 1: A Tradition of Eloquence

[1]See Werner Jaeger, *Paideia: The Ideals of Greek Culture,* Vol. 1 (2d ed.) translated from the Second German Edition, Vols. 2 and 3 from the German manuscript, by Gilbert Highet (New York: Oxford University Press, 1943–1945); George Kennedy, *The Art of Persuasion in Greece* (Princeton, N. J.: Princeton University Press, 1963); George Kennedy, *The Art of Rhetoric in the Roman World, 300 B. C.–A. D. 300* (Princeton, N. J.: Princeton University Press, 1972).

Additional works consulted: Charles Sears Baldwin, *Ancient Rhetoric and Poetic* (New York: The Macmillan Company, 1924); M. L. Clarke, *Rhetoric at Rome* (London:

Cohen and West Ltd., 1953); Moses Hadas, *A History of Greek Literature* (New York: Columbia University Press, 1950); *A History of Latin Literature* (1952).

[2]Albert B. Lord, *The Singer of Tales* (New York: Atheneum, 1971); for Homer, see 124–97. Cf. Werner Jaeger, *Paideia*, 1, chaps. 2–3.

[3]Compare Murray B. Emeneau, "Oral Poets of South India—The Todas," in Dell Hymes, *Language in Culture and Society: A Reader in Linguistics and Anthropology* (New York: Harper & Brothers, 1964), 330–43.

[4]For counsel and persuasion offered by speakers in Assyria and Babylonia (and its depiction in the Gilgamesh epic), see Thorkild Jacobsen, "Primitive Democracy in Ancient Mesopotamia," *Journal of Near Eastern Studies*, 2 (1943), 158–72.

[5]Homer, *The Iliad of Homer*, trans. Robert Fagles (New York: Viking, 1990), Bk. II, lines 161–77 (104).

[6]Jaeger, *Paideia*, 1:xxvii, 76, 219.

[7]Ibid., Introduction, chap. 1.

[8]Pindar, *Nemean Odes*, IV, 7; quoted by Jaeger, *Paideia*, 1:210.

[9]Hadas, *Greek Literature*, 67–68; cf. Jaeger, *Paideia*, 1:62, 67, 121, 123.

[10]Cf. Kimon Friar, "Attic Apophthegms," *Saturday Review*, May 20, 1961, 40–41.

[11]"The Fox and the Crow" as quoted in *The Book of Virtues: A Treasury of Great Moral Stories*, ed. William J. Bennett (New York: Simon & Schuster, 1993), 66. Cf. the more archaic translation in *The Fables of Aesop* (New York: Quality Paperback Book Club, 1995).

[12]See Whitney J. Oates and Eugene O'Neill, Jr., eds., *The Complete Greek Drama: All the Extant Tragedies of Aeschylus, Sophocles and Euripides, and the Comedies of Aristophanes and Menander, in a Variety of Translations*, 2 vols. (New York: Random House, 1938); cf. Bernhard Zimmerman, *Greek Tragedy: an Introduction*, trans. Thomas Marier (Baltimore: The Johns Hopkins University Press, 1991); Hadas, *Greek Literature*, chap. 8, "Drama."

[13]Sophocles, *Oedipus the King*, 882 ff., strophe 2, trans. R. C. Jebb, in Whitney J. Oates and Eugene O'Neill, Jr., eds., *The Complete Greek Drama* (New York: Random House, 1938), 1:396. [Trying to recast this in gender-neutral language, hardly intended by the playwright, has left me baffled.]

[14]Durant, *The Life of Greece*, 106.

[15]See Acts 8:29; cf. vv. 28–30, REB.

[16]See Homer, *The Iliad*, Bk. II (ML, 20–31, 41, 46–49), Bk. XIX (Modern Library, 315–35). Cf. Virgil, *The Aeneid*, Bk. XII, lines 220–450. Cf. Curtius, *European Literature in the Latin Middle Ages*, 176. Recall note 4, above.

[17]For a description of the conduct of business and speechmaking see Will Durant, *The Life of Greece* (New York: Simon and Schuster, 1939), 256.

[18]Ibid., 216–17.

[19]J. Huizinga, *Homo ludens: A Study of the Play-Element in Culture* (Boston: The Beacon Press, 1955), 178.

[20]Quintilian, *The Institutio Oratoria of Quintilian*, III, vii, 1–28, trans. H. E. Butler, 4 vols. (Cambridge, Mass.: Harvard University Press), LCL, I, 465–79.

[21]Jaeger, *Paideia*, 1:9.

[22]For the Greek orators, see Hadas, chap. 11; Edith Hamilton, *The Echo of Greece* (New York: W. W. Norton & Company, 1957), chaps. 4, 5; R. C. Jebb, *The Attic Orators from Antiphon to Isaeos* (London: Macmillan and Co., 1876).

Additional works consulted: Marie Hochmuth Nichols, *Rhetoric and Criticism* (Baton Rouge: Louisiana State University Press, 1963); J. W. Mackail, *Latin Literature* (London: John Murray, 1919); W. S. Teuffel, *A History of Roman Literature*, 2 vols. (London: George Bell and Sons, 1873); Clovis Lamarre, *Histoire de la littérature Latine depuis la fondation de Rome jusqu'à la fin du gouvernement républicain* (Paris: Librairie

Jules Lamarre, 1901); Will Durant, *The Life of Greece, Caesar and Christ* (New York: Simon and Schuster, 1944); Albert A. Trever, *History of Ancient Civilization,* 2 vols. (New York: Harcourt, Brace and Company, 1939).

23"Isocrates is the conscious voice of the Athenian upper class," Charles Edson, review of *Isokrates: Seine Anschauungen im Lichte Seiner Schriften* (Helsinki, 1954), in *AHR,* 61, 2 (Jan. 1956), 434.

24Jaeger, *Paideia,* 1:391–92; A. J. Woodman, *Rhetoric in Classical Historiography: Four Studies* (Portland: Areopagitica Press, 1988).

25Pericles, "Funeral Oration on the Athenians Who First Fell in the Peloponnesian War" [from Thucydides, *History of the Peloponnesian War*], *A Library of Universal Literature,* Part 3, Vol. 1, *Greek Orations* (New York: P. F. Collier and Son, 1900), 2–11.

26J. W. H. Atkins, *Literary Criticism in Antiquity: A Sketch of Its Development,* 2 vols. (Cambridge: University Press, 1934), 1:22.

27Cicero, *De oratore,* I, xlix, 216, 2, xxxii, 93 (LCL, I, 153, 267).

28Nichols, *Rhetoric and Criticism,* 19–20, citing *Selections from the Writings of Walter Savage Landor,* arr. and ed. Sidney Colvin (London: Macmillan & Co., 1882), 276–77.

29Durant, *The Life of Greece,* 248.

30Plato, *Menexenus,* 237, from *The Dialogues of Plato,* trans. B. Jowett (New York: Random House, 1937), II, 778.

31Ibid., 238, II, 779.

32Ibid., 246–47, II, 785 ff.

33Isocrates, *Antidosis* (No.15, 293–94) in George Norlin, *Isocrates with an English Translation,* Loeb Classical Library, 3 vols. (New York: G. P. Putnam's Sons, 1929), II, 347–49.

34Isocrates, *Nicocles,* 7 = *Antidosis.* 255, in H. I. Marrou, *A History of Education in Antiquity* (New York: Sheed and Ward, 1956), 90.

35Isocrates, *Antidosis,* 81 (LCL, II, 229).

36Marrou, *History of Education,* 80.

37Demosthenes, "The Third Philippic," *Library of Universal Literature,* Part 3, Vol. 1, *Greek Orators,* 312.

38Ibid., 313.

39Cyril E. Robinson, *A History of Greece* (New York: Thomas Y. Crowell Company, 1929), 352.

40Quintilian, *Institutio oratoria,* XI, iii, 54, 68 (LCL, IV, 271, 273, 281).

41Hadas, *Greek Literature,* 181.

42For the Latin orators, see Cicero, *Brutus* (LCL); Hadas, *A History of Latin Literature,* chap. 7.

43Cicero, *Brutus,* xix–xxvi (LCL, 422–28).

44Wilhelm Sigismund Teuffel, *Teuffel's History of Roman Literature,* revised and enlarged by Ludwig Schwabe. Trans. from the fifth German edition by George C. W. Warr, 2 vols. (London: G. Bell & Sons, 1891–1892), 1:153.

45Marcus Portius Cato, "Speech Delivered in the Roman Senate on the Treatment of the Catilinarian Conspirators," in *A Library of Universal Literature,* Part 3, *Orations,* 2:63.

46*Plutarch's Lives,* trans. Bernadotte Perrin (New York: The Macmillan Co., 1914), (LCL, II, 323). Another translator renders the phrase, "to make speeches to the belly."

47Livy, *Annals,* 34.2.14–34.3.3, quoted by Ross Shepard Kraemer, *Her Share of the Blessings: Women's Religions among Pagans, Jews, and Christians in the Greco-Roman World* (New York: Oxford University Press, 1992), 58.

[48]Albert A. Trever, *History of Ancient Civilization*, Vol. 2, *The Roman World* (New York: Harcourt, Brace and Company, 1939), 115, quoting the Latin original, here given a different translation than in Trever.

[49]Quintilian, *Institutio oratoria*, XII, x, 39 (LCL, IV, 471).

[50]Ibid., XII, x, 11 (LCL, IV, 455).

[51]Valerius Maximus, *Factorum et dictorum memorabilium libri novem*, VIII. 3. 3, quoted in Teuffel, 1, 360.

[52]*The Satires of Juvenal*, trans. Rolef Humphries (Bloomington: Indiana University Press, 1958), 72.

[53]Cicero, *Brutus*, xliii (LCL, 139).

[54]For Cicero's reflections on religion, see his *De natura deorum* (LCL).

[55]Cicero, *De officiis*.

[56]Cicero, *De amicitia*, 17 (LCL, 127).

[57]Ibid., 40 (LCL, 151).

[58]Cicero, *De senectute*, 15 (LCL, 25).

[59]Ibid., 17 (LCL, 27).

[60]Ibid., 28 (LCL, 37).

[61]Ibid., 44 (LCL, 55).

[62]Ibid., 71 (LCL, 83).

[63]For the influence of Cicero through the centuries see A. C. Clark, "Ciceronianism," in G. S. Gordon, collector, *English Literature and the Classics* (New York: Russell and Russell, 1912; reissue, 1969), 118–45.

[64]Cicero, *Brutus*, xcvi, 328 (LCL, 287).

[65]Ibid., xcvi, 330 (LCL, 287).

[66]Quintilian, *Institutio oratoria*, X, i, 118 (LCL, IV, 67, 69); XII, x, 11 (LCL, IV, 455) passim.

[67]Ibid., X, i, 86 (LCL, IV, 49).

Chapter 2: Philosophers, Mystagogues, and Moralists

[1]See Werner Jaeger, *Paideia: The Ideals of Greek Culture*, translated from the German manuscript by Gilbert Highet, Vol. 2, *In Search of the Divine Centre* (New York: Oxford University Press, 1943), 27–76, "Socrates the Teacher."

Additional works consulted: Herschel Baker Atkins, *The Dignity of Man* (Cambridge, Mass.: Harvard University Press, 1947); C. K. Barrett, ed., *The New Testament Background: Selected Documents* (New York: Harper & Row, Publishers, 1962), 54–79; Charles Boyer, *L'idée de vérité dans la philosophie de Saint Augustin*. Deux. ed. (Paris: Beauchesne et Ses Fils, 1940); *The Five Gospels: The Search for the Authentic Words of Jesus*. New translation and commentary by Robert W. Funk, Roy W. Hoover, and the Jesus Seminar (New York: The Macmillan Company, 1993), 287; Abraham J. Malherbe, *Paul and the Popular Philosophers* (Minneapolis: Fortress Press, 1989); C. C. McCown, lecture at University of Oregon (March 3, 1949); Gilbert Murray, *Stoic, Christian, and Humanist* (London: C. A. Watts & Co., 1940); Chester G. Starr, *Civilization and the Caesars: The Intellectual Revolution in the Roman Empire* (Ithaca, N. Y.: Cornell University Press, 1954).

[2]Barrett, 75.

[3]For comments by Nicias, participant in dialogue with Socrates, see Plato, *Laches, or Courage*, 187–88, *The Dialogues of Plato*, trans. B. Jowett, 2 vols. (New York: Random House, 1937), 1:63–64. Cf. Jaeger, *Paideia*, 2:18, 34–36, 87–91, 169–170, 380, nn. 141–42.

[4]From speech of Alcibiades in Plato, *Symposium*, 221–22, in *The Dialogues of Plato*, 1:344.

[5]Plato, *Apology,* 29–30, *The Dialogues of Plato,* 1:412–13.

[6]For the tradition of the symposium in the Greco-Roman world see Dennis E. Smith and Hal E. Taussig, *Many Tables: The Eucharist in the New Testament and Liturgy Today* (Philadelphia: Trinity Press International, 1990), chaps. 2, 3.

[7]Jaeger, *Paideia,* 2:41.

[8]Ibid., 2:40; cf. 39–47, 104; 376, nn. 64, 65; 3:192.

[9]Ibid., 3:156.

[10]Ibid., 2:85, 192; 295; 417, n. 77; 321; 3:242.

[11]See "Self-Definition among the Cynics," in Malherbe, *Paul and the Popular Philosophers,* 11–24; Barrett, *The NT Background,* 61–70, 75–77.

Additional works consulted: Curtius, *European Literature in the Latin Middle Ages;* Bernard Frischer, *The Sculpted Word: Epicureanism and Philosophical Recruitment in Ancient Greece* (Berkeley: University of California Press, 1982).

[12]Diog. B 5, quoted by Werner Jaeger, *The Theology of the Early Greek Philosophers: The Gifford Lectures, 1936* (London: Oxford University Press, 1947), 165–66.

[13]Hadas, *Greek Literature,* 187.

[14]Barrett, 75.

[15]Jaeger, *Paideia,* 2:55–57.

[16]Quintilian, *Institutio oratoria,* XII, 3, xii (LCL, IV, 407).

[17]Epicurus, "Principal Doctrines," XVII, in Saxe Cummins and Robert N. Linscott, eds., *Man and Man; The Social Philosophers,* unnumbered volume of *The World's Great Thinkers* (New York: Random House, 1947), 231.

[18]Ibid., XXXIII, 232.

[19]Ibid., VIII, 230.

[20]Ibid., V, 229.

[21]Epicurus, *Fragments,* LXXIV, in Cummins and Linscott, *The Social Philosophers,* 239.

[22]Lucretius, *De rerum natura,* i. 62–79, in Barrett, 72–73.

[23]Cleanthes, *Ode to Zeus,* in Frank H. Marshall, *The Religious Backgrounds of Early Christianity* (St. Louis: The Bethany Press, 1931), 61.

[24]W. B. Sedgwick, "The Origins of the Sermon," *Hibbert Journal,* 45 (1946–1947), 158–64.

[25]Georgia Harkness, *The Sources of Western Morality* (New York: Charles Scribner's Sons, 1954), 206.

[26]For Augustine's reflections on Stoicism, see his *The City of God,* Bk. XIV, chaps. viii, ix.

[27]Quintilian, *Institutio oratoria,* X, i, 84 (LCL, IV, 49).

[28]Thom. 13:3. See *The 5 Gospels: The Search for the Authentic Words of Jesus,* new translation and commentary by Robert W. Funk, Roy W. Hoover, and the Jesus Seminar. A Polebridge Press Book (New York: Macmillan Publishing Company, 1993). The Gospel of Thomas, thought to have been composed before 200 C.E. and from which only Greek fragments had been known, was discovered in its entirety in Coptic as part of the Gnostic library at Nag Hammadi, Egypt, in 1945.

[29]Strabo, *Geography,* 1. 2. 8, in Will Durant, *The Story of Civilization,* 1, 56.

[30]Works consulted: Joseph Cullen Ayer, *A Source Book for Ancient Church History from the Apostolic Age to the Close of the Conciliar Period* (New York: Charles Scribner's Sons, 1924); John Baillie, *And the Life Everlasting* (New York: Charles Scribner's Sons, 1933); Barrett, *The NT Background;* Walter Burkert, *Ancient Mystery Cults* (Cambridge, Mass.: Harvard University Press, 1987); Christopher Dawson, *Religion and Culture* (London: Sheed & Ward, 1948); Marshall, *Religious Backgrounds;* Richard Reitzenstein, *Hellenistic Mystery Religions,* trans. John Steely (Pittsburgh: Pickwick Press, 1978); Rose, *Ancient Roman Religion;* Willoughby, *Pagan Regeneration;* Ben Witherington III, *Women and the Genesis of Christianity,* ed. Ann Witherington

(Cambridge: Cambridge University Press, 1990); C. C. McCown, public lecture at University of Oregon, March 3, 1949.

[31]Saint Augustine, *The City of God,* IV. 8 (FC 8:200–202).

[32]Considerable, but not unanimous, scholarly opinion holds to the judgment that this was a time of spiritual anxiety. See Ross Shepard Kramer, *Her Share of the Blessings: Women's Religions among Pagans, Jews, and Christians in the Greco-Roman World* (New York: Oxford University Press, 1992), 75. Cf. Carlin A. Barton, *The Sorrows of the Ancient Romans: The Gladiator and the Monster* (Princeton: Princeton University Press, 1993).

[33]George Mylonas, "Mystery Religions of Greece," in Vergilius Ferm, ed., *Ancient Religions* (New York: The Philosophical Library, 1950), 181.

[34]Witherington, *Women and the Genesis of Christianity,* 24.

[35]Kramer, *Her Share of the Blessings,* 75.

[36]George Mylonas, "Mystery Religions," in Ferm, *Ancient Religions,* 184.

[37]Plato, *Symposium,* 202–12, Jowett, *Dialogues,* 1:327–35. For commentary, see Jaeger, *Paideia,* 2:178–97.

[38]Frederick C. Grant, *Hellenistic Religions: The Age of Syncretism* (Indianapolis: Bobbs-Merrill, Liberal Arts Press, 1953), 131–33, quoted by Marvin W. Meyer, ed., *The Ancient Mysteries, A Sourcebook: Sacred Texts of the Mystery Religions of the Ancient Mediterranean World* (San Francisco: HarperSan Francisco, 1987), 172–73.

[39]G. H. C. Macgregor, "The Acts of the Apostles," *Interpreter's Bible,* 9, 110.

[40]For an account of one such in the early days of Christianity, see Lucian of Samosata, "Alexander the Oracle-Monger," in LCL.

[41]The phrase is Burkert's in *Ancient Mystery Cults,* 31.

[42]Works consulted: Robert M. Grant, ed., *Gnosticism: A Sourcebook of Heretical Writings from the Early Christian Period* (New York: Harper & Brothers, 1961).

[43]*Poimandres,* 27ff., in Barrett, *The NT Background,* 88, g. 89.

[44]Cicero, *De legibus,* ii. 14, in Willoughby, *Pagan Regeneration,* 64.

[45]See John Ferguson, *The Religions of the Roman Empire,* 194–97, "Epictetus."

Additional works consulted: Ayer, *A Source Book for Ancient Church History;* Barrett, *The New Testament Background;* John W. Cunliffe and Grant Showerman, eds., *Century Readings in Ancient Classical and Modern European Literature* (New York: D. Appleton–Century Company, 1925); Hadas, *Greek Literature;* Edith Hamilton, *The Echo of Greece* (New York: W. W. Norton & Company, 1957); J. W. Mackail, *Latin Literature* (London: John Murray, 1919); Teuffel, *A History of Roman Literature;* Quirinus Breen, classroom lectures at University of Oregon.

[46]*De consolatione,* Seneca, *Moral Essays,* trans. John W. Basore (Cambridge: Harvard University Press, 1935), LCL, II, 429ff.; cited by William Baird, *The Corinthian Church—A Biblical Approach to Urban Culture* (Nashville: Abingdon Press, 1964), 18.

[47]Cicero, *Brutus,* xxx (LCL, 433).

[48]Seneca, *Epistulae morales* (LCL, I, 133–35).

[49]For a thorough study see Miriam T. Griffin, *Seneca, A Philosopher in Politics* (Oxford; The Clarendon Press, 1976).

[50]Philostratus, *Life of Appolonius,* Bk. 4, c. xxxi (New York: G. P. Putnam's Sons, 1917–1921), 419, 449.

[51]Philostratus, *Life of Appolonius,* i. 17, in Barrett, *The NT Background,* 76.

[52]Philostratus, *Life of Appolonius,* Vol. 3, Bk. V, c. viii, 477.

[53]Appolonius of Tyana, *Epistle* iii, in Barrett, *The NT Background,* 79.

[54]Appolonius of Tyana, *On Sacrifice,* quoted (via Eusebius) in Ferguson, *Religions of the Roman Empire,* 181.

[55]Dio of Prusa, *Discourses,* No. 18.

[56]Hadas, *Greek Literature,* 249.

[57]For an extended discussion, see Samuel Dill, *Roman Society from Nero to Marcus Aurelius* (London: Macmillan & Co., 1920), 367 ff.

[58]Plutarch, "Marcus Cato," in Cunliffe and Showerman, *Century Readings in Ancient Classical and Modern European Literature,* 273.

[59]Plutarch, *Moralia.* Cf. Hans Dieter Betz, ed., *Plutarch's Ethical Writings and Early Christian Literature* (Leiden: E. J. Brill, 1978).

[60]Plutarch, *Isis and Osiris,* in Barrett, *The NT Background,* 92.

[61]John T. McNeill, *A History of the Cure of Souls,* Harper Torchbooks (New York: Harper & Row, 1965), 37.

[62]Epictetus, *The Manual,* 8, 11; in Cummins and Linscott, *Man and Man,* 256.

[63]Ibid., 6.

[64]Frederic W. Farrar, *Seekers after God* (New York: A. L. Burt, 1902), 221.

[65]Epictetus, *Discourses,* III, xxii, in Barrett, *The NT Background,* 76.

[66]George A. Kennedy, *Classical Rhetoric and Its Christian and Secular Tradition from Ancient to Modern Times* (Chapel Hill: The University of North Carolina Press, 1980), 10.

Chapter 3: Rhetoric and Humane Education

[1]See Aristotle, *Rhetoric;* Cicero, *Brutus;* Tacitus, *A Dialogue on Oratory;* George A. Kennedy, *Classical Rhetoric and Its Christian and Secular Tradition from Ancient to Modern Times* (Chapel Hill: The University of North Carolina Press, 1980); Burton L. Mack, *Rhetoric and the New Testament* (Minneapolis: Fortress Press, 1990), chaps. 1, 2.

Additional works consulted: J. W. Atkins, *A History of Literary Criticism in Antiquity,* 2 vols. (Cambridge: University Press, 1934); Baldwin, *Ancient Rhetoric and Poetic;* Clarke, *Rhetoric at Rome;* J. D. Denniston, *Greek Prose Style* (Oxford: The Clarendon Press, 1952); Durant, *The Story of Civilization,* Vols. 2, 3; Hadas, *Latin Literature;* Vernon Hall, Jr., *A Short History of Literary Criticism* (New York: University Press, 1963); Sir Richard Claverhouse Jebb, "Rhetoric," *Encyclopaedia Britannica,* 11th edition (1911); Mackail, *Latin Literature;* Edouard Norden, *Die antike Kunstprosa* (Leipzig, Berlin: B. G. Tuebner, 1923); Teuffel, *Roman Literature,* Vols. 1, 2; Trever, *Ancient Civilization,* 2.

[2]For a classical summary of the history, see Quintilian, *Institutio oratoria,* III, i, 1–ii, 4 (LCL, I, 371–83).

[3]Werner Jaeger wrote, "In Greek oratory we find the same principles of form as in Greek sculpture and architecture…[Their] ability to carry out a complex plan and create an organic whole out of many parts proceeded purely and simply from a natural perception, increasingly sharpened, of the laws which govern feeling, thought, and speech—the perception which finally…created logic, grammar, and rhetoric" (*Paideia,* 1:xx, xxi).

[4]See Jaeger's chapter on "The Sophists," *Paideia,* 1, Part 2, chap. 3). For Plato's critique of the sophists, see *Paideia,* 2:263, 270, 318.

[5]Ernst Robert Curtius, *European Literature and the Latin Middle Ages.* Translated from the German by Willard R. Trask. Bollingen Series 36 (New York: Pantheon Books, 1953), 388. With characteristic irreverence, Harry Elmer Barnes characterizes such speech as "a Hellenic elaboration of shamanistic incantations," adding more comment in the same vein; see his *A History of Historical Writing,* 2d rev. ed. (New York: Dover Publications, 1963), 337.

[6]Ross Shepard Kraemer, *Her Share of the Blessings,* 7, citing Susan Guettel Cole, "Could Greek Women Read and Write?" *Women's Studies,* 8 (1981): 129–55;

reprinted in Helene P. Foley, ed., *Reflections of Women in Antiquity* (New York: Gordon and Breach, 1981), 225.

⁷References are to Aristotle, *Rhetoric,* trans. W. Rhys Roberts (New York: The Modern Library, 1945). See for comparison, *Aristotle on Rhetoric: A Theory of Civic Discourse,* newly translated with Introduction, Notes, and Appendixes by George A. Kennedy (New York: Oxford University Press, 1991).

⁸Paul Monroe, ed., *Source Book of the History of Education for the Greek and Roman Period* (New York: The Macmillan Company, 1906), 262.

⁹Cato, quoted by Quintilian, *Institutio oratoria,* XII, i, 1 (LCL, IV, 355).

¹⁰J. Wight Duff, *A Literary History of Rome in the Silver Age* (London: T. Fisher Unwin Limited, 1927).

¹¹Hadas, *Greek Literature,* 235.

¹²W. Rhys Roberts, "Caecilius of Calacte: A Contribution to the History of Greek Literary Criticism," *American Journal of Philology,* 18:3022–3312.

¹³Ibid., 236.

¹⁴Longinus, *On the Sublime,* 9.9. See the translation by O. A. Prickard (Oxford: Clarendon Press, 1906).

¹⁵E.g., Seneca, *Epistles,* 6, 40, 64, 75. See Abraham J. Malherbe, *Moral Exhortation, A Greco-Roman Sourcebook,* Library of Early Christianity (Philadelphia: The Westminster Press, 1986), 43–45, 64–66, 69–71.

¹⁶See the classical manuals mentioned in the text; also Richard A. Lanham, *A Handlist of Rhetorical Terms* (Berkeley: University of California Press, 1969); Lester Thonssen and A. Craig Baird, *Speech Criticism* (New York: The Ronald Press, 1948), chaps. 2, 3. This section relies heavily on Clarke, *Rhetoric at Rome.* For a brief summary, see Curtius, *European Literature and the Latin Middle Ages,* 68–71, "System of Antique Rhetoric."

Additional works consulted: Baldwin, *Ancient Rhetoric and Poetic;* Hans Dieter Betz, *Galatians,* in *Hermeneia* (Philadelphia: Fortress Press, 1979); John F. D'Alton, *Roman Literary Theory and Criticism* (New York: Russell & Russell, Inc., 1962); H. Munro and Nora K. Chadwick, *The Growth of Literature,* 3 vols. (Cambridge: University Press, 1932 seq.); W. B. Sedgwick, "The Origins of the Sermon," *Hibbert Journal,* 45 (1946–1947), 158–64; George L. Trager, "Paralanguage: A First Approximation," in Dell Hymes, *Language in Culture and Society: A Reader in Linguistics and Anthropology* (New York: Harper & Row, Publishers, 1964), 274–88; Willoughby, *Pagan Regeneration.*

¹⁷Quintilian, *Institutio Oratoria,* II, xiv, 5 (LCL, I, 299–301).

¹⁸For technical, sophistic, and philosophical rhetoric, see Kennedy, *Classical Rhetoric and Its Christian and Secular Tradition,* 16–87.

¹⁹Cicero, *Orator,* 113 (LCL, 389); cf. Quintilian, *Institutio Oratoria,* II, xx, 7 (LCL, I, 353). George A. Kennedy suggests the relationship of the speaker to the audience as a factor in the difference; see *Classical Rhetoric and Its Christian and Secular Tradition,* 250, n. 16.

²⁰Isocrates, *To the Children of Jason* [Ep. 6], in R. C. Jebb, *The Attic Orators from Antiphon to Isaeos* (London: Macmillan and Co., 1876), 2:243.

²¹See Irene Nye, "Humor Repeats Itself," *Classical Journal,* 9:4 (January 1914), 162. For philosophical reflection on laughter as an expression of intellectual freedom see "The Comic Poetry of Aristophanes," Bk. 2, chap. 5, in Jaeger, *Paideia,* especially 359, 364.

²²For an overview of the concern with persuasion in the classical rhetoricians, see Quintilian, *Institutio Oratoria,* II, xv, 1–22 (LCL, I, 301–11).

²³For reflections on deliberative speaking, see Cicero, *De partitione oratoria,* XXIV, 83–97 (LCL, 373–83); Quintilian, *Institutio oratoria,* III, viii, 1–70 (LCL, I, 479–515). For forensic speaking, see Cicero, *De part. orat.,* XXVIII, 98–138 (LCL, 383–

419); Quintilian, *Inst. or.*, IX, 1–28 (LCL, I, 515–37. For oratory of praise and blame (epideictic), see Cicero, *De part. orat.*, XXI–XXIII (LCL, 363–73); Quintilian, *Inst. orat.*, III, vii, 1–28 (LCL, I, 465–79).

[24]Cicero, *Brutus*, VI. 25 (LCL, 37).

[25]Cicero, *De oratore*, II. xxx, 130 (LCL, I, 291), xxxix, 162–xli, 176 (LCL, I, 315–23); cf. *De partit. orat.*, II, 5–8 (LCL, I, 313–17); see Stanley Frederick Bonner, *Roman Declamation in the Late Republic and Early Empire* (Liverpool: University Press of Liverpool, 1949).

[26]Cicero, *Orator*, 62 (LCL, 351–53).

[27]Cicero, *De oratore*, III, xxv, 96 (LCL, II, 77).

[28]Cicero, *De partitione oratoria*, VII, 26 (LCL, 331).

[29]Quintilian, *Inst. orat.*, XI, iii, 6; cf. Kennedy, *Classical Rhetoric*, 98.

[30]Cicero, *De oratore*, III, lvi, 213ff. (LCL, II, 169–83). Cf. *Brutus*, XLIII, 158 (LCL, 137); *Orator*, XVII, 55–60 (LCL, 347–51); *De partit. orat.*, VII, 25 (LCL, 331).

[31]Quintilian, *Institutio Oratoria*, XI, iii, 126 (LCL, IV, 311).

[32]Demosthenes, "On the Crown," in Cunliffe and Showerman, 236–37.

[33]Jaeger, *Paideia*, 1:27.

[34]Kennedy, *Classical Rhetoric and Its Christian and Secular Tradition*, 13, 66, 164; cf. Kennedy, *New Testament Interpretation through Rhetorical Criticism* (Chapel Hill: The University of North Carolina Press, 1984), 17, 60; Aristotle, *Rhetoric*, 2, 21 (LCL, 278–89); *Rhetorica ad Herennium*, IV, 17, 27 (LCL, 289–93, 297).

[35]For the enthymeme, its structure, and use, see Aristotle, *Rhetoric*, Bk. II, cs. 21–26 (LCL, 288–343); Bk. III, cs. 10, 27 (LCL, 396–99).

[36]For *sermo* as a genre, see D'Alton, *Roman Literary Theory*, 53–56.

[37]Clarke, *Rhetoric at Rome*, 623.

[38]Kennedy, *Classical Rhetoric*, 10.

[39]See H. I. Marrou, *A History of Education in Antiquity* (New York: Sheed and Ward, 1956), Part 2, chap. 10; Part 3, chaps. 6, 7; Werner Jaeger, *Paideia: The Ideals of Greek Culture*, trans. Gilbert Highet, 2d ed., 3 vols. (New York: Oxford University Press, 1945 seq.).

Additional works consulted: Aristotle, *Rhetoric;* Cicero, *De officiis, De oratore;* Quintilian, *Institutio oratoria;* L. F. Anderson, "A Study of the Prototypes of the Modern Non-Professional School among the Greeks and the Romans," *The Pedagogical Seminary*, 14 (1907), 1–38; J. W. H. Atkins, *Literary Criticism in Antiquity;* Erich Auerbach, *Dante: Poet of the Secular World*, trans. Ralph Manheim (Chicago: The University of Chicago Press, 1961), 152–56, 161–64; Hershel Clay Baker, *The Dignity of Man* (Cambridge, Mass.: Harvard University Press, 1947); Clarke, *Rhetoric at Rome;* Curtius, *European Literature and the Latin Middle Ages;* Georges Gusdorf, *Speaking*, trans. Paul T. Brockelman (Evanston: Northwestern University Press, 1965); Hadas, *Greek Literature;* J. W. Mackail, *Latin Literature* (London: John Murray, 1919); John J. Mood, "Poetic Language and Primal Thinking," *Encounter* 26, 4 (Autumn, 1965), 417–33; Nichols, *Rhetoric and Criticism;* Teuffel, *Roman Literature;* Karl Vossler, *The Spirit of Language in Civilization* (London: Routledge & Kegan Paul, 1932).

[40]Charles Sears Baldwin, *Medieval Rhetoric and Poetic* (New York: The Macmillan Company, 1928), 10–11, 18. Cf. George Saintsbury, *A History of Criticism and Literary Taste in Europe from the Earliest Texts to the Present Day* (Edinburgh: William Blackwood and Sons, 1900), 1: 230–32; D'Alton, *Roman Literary Theory* (London: Longmans, Green and Co., 1939), 439–40.

[41]Petronius Arbiter, *The Satyricon* (New York: Liveright Publishing Corp., 1943), chaps. 1, 2: 42–43.

[42]Tacitus, *A Dialog on Oratory*, 6, 7, in *The Complete Works of Tacitus* (New York: The Modern Library, 1942), 738–39.

[43]Plato, *Gorgias,* 503 (*DP,* I, 564); cf. Kennedy, *Classical Rhetoric and Its Christian and Secular Tradition,* 51.

[44]Ibid., 504–5 (*DP,* I, 566). Socrates pursues such questions throughout much of the rest of the dialogue.

[45]Quoted by Irwin Edman, *Arts and the Man* (New York: W. W. Norton & Co., 1939), 113.

[46]Plato, *Phaedrus,* 278 (*DP,* I, 281).

[47]Mary R. Lefkowitz, "The Poet as Hero: Fifth-Century Autobiography and Subsequent Biographical Fiction," *Classical Quarterly,* 28:2 (1978), 459–69.

[48]H. I. Marrou, *A History of Education in Antiquity,* trans. George Lamb (New York: Sheed and Ward, 1956), 99.

[49]Aratus, *Phaenomena,* exordium 1–6, in Hadas, *Greek Literature,* 212.

[50]Cicero, *De oratore,* III, lvi, 214 (LCL, II, 171).

[51]Quintilian, *Institutio oratoria,* II, xv, 33 (LCL, I, 315).

PART TWO. PEOPLE OF THE WORD
Chapter 4: Judaism: The Preaching of Torah

[1]See Martin Buber, "'Upon Eagle's Wings,'" in his *Moses* (Oxford: East and West Library, 1946), 101–109; James A. Sanders, *Torah and Canon* (Philadelphia: Fortress Press, 1974), 30–53. Additional works consulted: Karl Barth, *Church Dogmatics,* Vol. 1. *The Doctrine of the Word of God* (New York: Charles Scribner's Sons, 1936); *IDB*; Joachim Jeremias, *New Testament Theology* (New York: Charles Scribner's Sons, 1971); Arthur Vogel, *MPNT* 4; *IB,* 7:12.

[2]C. K. Barrett, ed., *New Testament Background: Selected Documents* (New York: Harper & Row, 1959), 51, g. 50.

[3]Reading "fugitive" with The Tanakh instead of "wandering" in NRSV. *Tanakh* is an acronym made up of the initial letters of the three major parts of the Jewish Scriptures: the Pentateuch (*Torah*), the Prophets (*Nevi'im*), and the Writings (*Kethuvim*). The translation designated *Tanakh* in this chapter is copyrighted by the Jewish Publication Society (1985). For Israel's "creed" see Gerhard von Rad, *Old Testament Theology* (New York: Harper & Row, Publishers, 1962), 1:4.

[4]Samuel Sandmel, "The Haggada within Scripture," in Sandmel, ed., *Old Testament Issues* (New York: Harper & Row Publishers, 1968), 99–116; Sigmund Mowinckel, "Tradition, Oral," *IDB, IV,* 684; D. N. Freedman, "Pentateuch," *IDB, III,* 714, 725–26; Eduard Nielsen, *Oral Tradition: A Modern Problem in Old Testament Introduction,* with a Foreword by H. H. Rowley. Studies in Biblical Theology (London: SCM Press, 1954), 48–49; Hermann Gunkel, *The Legends of Genesis,* trans. W. H. Carruth (Chicago: Open Court Publishing Co., 1901), 39–42, 130–32.

[5]James Muilenburg, "The Form and Structure of the Covenantal Formulations," *Vetus Testamentum,* 9 (1959), 351–57. Scholars commonly regard these formulations as probably belonging to the Elohistic source.

[6]This primal covenant-sermon, made vivid by artistic compression, is "*in nuce* the *fons et origo* of the many covenantal pericopes which appear throughout the Old Testament" writes Martin Buber in *Moses,* 101.

[7]Walter Brueggemann, "The Book of Exodus: Introduction, Commentary, and Reflections,"*The New Interpreter's Bible* (Nashville: Abingdon Press, 1994), 1:799.

[8]M. Jack Suggs, Katherine Doob Sakenfeld, and James R. Mueller, eds., *The Oxford Study Bible: Revised English Bible with the Apocrypha* (New York: Oxford University Press, 1992), annotation *in loc.*

[9]For brief but insightful reflections, see Kennedy, *Classical Rhetoric*, 120–25, "Old Testament Rhetoric."

[10]For the *eidetic vision* of children and poets who *feel* and even *see* their thoughts, see René Wellek and Austin Warren, *Theory of Literature* (New York: Harcourt, Brace and Company, 1949), 77; for their use of this concept Wellek and Warren cite W. Silz, "Otto Ludwig and the Process of Poetic Creation," *PMLA*, 60 (1945), 860–78, and Erich Jaensch, *Eidetic Imagery and Typological Methods of Investigation* (London, 1930).

[11]See Claus Westermann, *Basic Forms of Prophetic Speech*, trans. Hugh Clayton White (Philadelphia: The Westminster Press, 1967).

[12]See Abraham J. Heschel, *The Prophets* (New York: Harper & Row, Publishers, 1962), chaps. 12–18.

[13]Charles B. Williams, *The New Testament: A Translation in the Language of the People*. NRSV reads "the book of the words of the prophet…"

[14]1 Macc. 9:27; Geza Vermes, *Jesus the Jew: A Historian's Reading of the Gospels* (Philadelphia: Fortress Press, 1973), 90–94.

[15]G. von Rad, "Deuteronomy," *IDB*, I, especially 834–37; Russell Fuller, "Deuteronomic History" and Ronald E. Clements, "Deuteronomy, the Book of," in Bruce M. Metzger and Michael D. Coogan, eds., *The Oxford Companion to the Bible* (New York: Oxford University Press, 1993), 163–68.

[16]See Gerhard von Rad, *Wisdom in Israel* (Nashville: Abingdon Press, 1972).

[17]2 Sam. 8:15–18; 1 Chr 27:1–34; Nielsen, *Shechem* (Denmark: Aarhuus Stifts Bog Trykkerie, 1955), 179–80, 194; S. H. Blan, "Wisdom," *IDB*, IV, 854; John Bright, *A History of Israel* (Philadelphia: The Westminster Press, 1959), 184; P. A. H. deBoer, "The Counsellor," *Supp. Vetus Testamentum*, 3 (1955), 42–71.

[18]William L. Reed, "The Bible and North Arabia," *Encounter*, 26:2 (Spring, 1965), 143–153. Charles T. Fritsch, "The Book of Proverbs," 4:4, 767, 769.

[19]Bright, 184; Weiser, *The Old Testament* (New York: Association Press, 1961), 17; Martin Noth, *The History of Israel* (New York: Harper & Row, 1960), 192–93, 213.

[20]2 Sam. 8:16–17; 20:24–25; 1 Chr. 27:32; William Foxwell Albright, *From the Stone Age to Christianity: Monotheism and the Historical Process*, 2d ed. (Garden City, N.Y.: Doubleday & Company, 1957), 253–54; Noth, 215.

[21]1 Kings 4:1–6; Sigmund Mowinckel, "Literature,' *IDB*, III, 139; Noth, 217–18.

[22]Fritsch, "Proverbs," *IB*, 4:774–75; Bright, *History of Israel*, 199; Norman H. Snaith, "The First and Second Book of Kings," *IB*, 3:39, 43.

[23]See, e.g., The Wisdom of Solomon 6:1–11.

[24]Fritsch, "Proverbs," *IB*, 4:772–73, 776–77; John T. McNeill, *A History of the Cure of Souls* (New York: Harper & Row, [1951] 1965), 6.

[25]See Claudia V. Camp, *Wisdom and the Feminine in the Book of Proverbs* (Decatur, Ga.: The Almond Press, 1985), 131.

[26]Nielsen, *Oral Tradition*, 59–60; Fritsch, *IB*, 1:776–77.

[27]Paraphrasing Camp, *Wisdom and the Feminine*, 130.

[28]Works consulted: James A. Sanders, "Biblical Criticism and the Bible as Canon," *Union Seminary Quarterly Review*, 32:3, 4 (1977); Sanders, *Torah and Canon;* Sachar; Schaff; *IB*, 1:287; *IDB*; *JB*.

[29]See Reuven Hammer (translation, introduction, and commentaries), *The Classic Midrash: Tannaitic Commentaries on the Bible*, preface by Judah Goldin, The Classics of Western Spirituality (New York: Paulist Press, 1995); Jacob Neusner, *A Midrash Reader* (Minneapolis: Fortress Press, 1990); Elias J. Bickerman, *The Jews in the Greek Age* (Cambridge, Mass.: Harvard University Press, 1988), chap. 20, "The Midrash."

[30]Jacob Neusner, *Scriptures of the Oral Torah: Sanctification and Salvation in the Sacred Books of Judaism: An Anthology* (San Francisco: Harper & Row, 1987), 1–15.

[31]Pierson Parker, "Rabbi, Rabboni," *IDB,* R–Z, 3.

[32]Reuven Hammer, trans., *The Classic Midrash* (The Classics of Western Spirituality), 70.

[33]Some versions of the Apocrypha present this sermon under the title, "A Letter of Jeremiah," as a separate work; others attach it to the book of Baruch as chapter 6. The fourth book of Maccabees is also a sermon, probably originating in Alexandria in the first century C. E. (see Rylaarsdam, *Revelation in Jewish Wisdom Literature,* 45).

[34]See chap. 6, especially the section on "Forms of Religious Address." For an analysis of the characteristic rhetoric, logics, and dialectic of midrash, see Neusner, *Introduction to Rabbinic Literature,* chaps. 2–4.

[35]I. Epstein, "Talmud," *IDB,* R–Z, 512.

[36]Nahum N. Glatzer, *The Judaic Tradition: Texts Edited and Introduced* (Boston: Beacon Press, 1969), 184; Jacob Neusner, *The Mishnah, Introduction and Reader* (Philadelphia: Trinity Press International, 1992), 5–6.

[37]Babylonian Talmud, *Bava Mezia,* 85b (as cited by Telushkin, *Jewish Wisdom,* 338).

[38]Neusner, *Introduction to Rabbinic Literature,* xx–xxi.

[39]Because this study focuses on the rise of Christian preaching, attention to Jewish preaching is directed largely to developments contributing to the heritage of Jesus; its scope does not permit systematic attention to Judaism beyond the second century C.E. But passages are quoted from Pirqe Abot and a few other books in the Talmud to represent the genius of Jewish sacred discourse and the flavor of rabbinic eloquence, rooted as it was in a living tradition.

Chapter 5: Preachers in the Struggle for a People's Soul

[1]See Hershel Shanks, ed., *Christianity and Rabbinic Judaism: A Parallel History of Their Origins and Early Development* (Washington, D.C.: Biblical Archaeology Society, 1992). Additional works consulted: W. D. Davies and Louis Finkelstein, eds., *The Cambridge History of Judaism* (Cambridge University Press, 1989), Vol. 2, *The Hellenistic Age;* Arnaldo Momigliano, *Essays on Ancient and Modern Judaism,* ed. Silvia Berti; trans. Maura Masella-Gayley (Chicago: The University of Chicago Press, 1994); J. Andrew Overman and Robert S. MacLennan, eds., *Diaspora Jews and Judaism: Essays in Honor of, and in Dialogue with, A. Thomas Kraabel* (Atlanta Ga.: Scholars Press, 1992); Lee I. Levine, ed., *The Synagogue in Late Antiquity* (Philadelphia: The American Schools of Oriental Research, 1986); Donald E. Gowan, *Bridge between the Testaments: A Reappraisal of Judaism from the Exile to the Birth of Christianity* (Allison Park, Pa.: Pickwick Publications, 1986); Book of Acts; *IDB 1;* Yngve Brilioth, *A Brief History of Preaching* (Philadelphia: Fortress Press, 1965); Nathaniel Micklem, ed., *Christian Worship* (London: Oxford University Press, 1954); Philip Schaff, *A History of the Christian Church* (reprint, Grand Rapids: William B. Eerdmans Publishing Co., 1960); Williston Walker, *History of the Christian Church,* 3d ed. (New York: Charles Scribner's Sons, 1970).

[2]The *Geography* of Strabo, quoted in Abram Leon Sachar, *A History of the Jews,* 3d ed. (New York: Alfred A. Knopf, 1948), 78.

[3]Cicero, *Pro Flacco;* cited in Sachar, 111.

[4]Josephus, *Antiq.,* XV. xi. 1 ff.

[5]See Gowan, *Bridge Between The Testaments,* 218–20, for a brief discussion of the various theories of origin.

[6]For diagrams of various structures see Lee I. Levine, ed., *The Synagogue in Late Antiquity*, A Centennial Publication of The Jewish Theological Seminary of America (Philadelphia: The American Schools of Oriental Research, 1987), 189–213.

[7]Philo, *Hypothetica*, 7.13 (LCL, IX, 433). Cf. Eugene J. Fisher, ed., *The Jewish Roots of Christian Liturgy* (New York: Paulist Press, 1990) and Paul F. Bradshaw, *The Search for the Origins of Christian Worship: Sources and Methods for the Study of Early Liturgy* (New York: Oxford University Press), both of which sketch the pattern of worship in the synagogue, but with minimal reference to preaching.

[8]*Mekhilta according to Rabbi Ishmael: An Analytical Translation*, trans. Jacob Neusner (Atlanta, Ga.: Scholars Press, 1988), Beshallah, chap. 1, 20, A–K. Vol. 1 (*Pisha, Beshallah, Shirata, and Vayassa*), 128. Joseph Heinemann in *Encyclopedia Judaica* mentions this passage as a snatch of synagogue preaching preserved in the oral tradition.

[9]Ibid., 22. B–E, 1:129.

[10]The figure is proposed by Heinemann in *Encyclopedia Judaica*, 13:996.

[11]Exodus 10:21, Mekhilta Bahodesh 11, II, 287, in Hammer, *The Classic Midrash*, 168.

[12]See Elias J. Bickerman, *The Jews in the Greek Age* (Cambridge, Mass.: Harvard University Press, 1988).

[13]It is of course probable that the historian, after the custom of the times, invented this speech and those which follow for the edification of the readers—who in keeping with Hellenistic practice expected eloquence at crucial moments. See *The Oxford Study Bible: Revised English Bible with the Apocrypha*, introductory note to The Second Book of Maccabees.

[14]See George W. Nickelsberg and Michael E. Stone, *Faith and Piety in Early Judaism: Texts and Documents* (Philadelphia: Fortress Press, 1983), 1–49.

[15]Works consulted: Atkins, *Literary Criticism in Antiquity*, 2; F. F. Bruce, *The Speeches in Acts* (London: The Tyndale Press, 1942); Rudolf Bultmann, *Primitive Christianity in its Contemporary Setting*, Living Age Books (New York: Meridian Books, 1956); F. J. Foakes-Jackson, *Josephus and the Jews*; Hadas, *A History of Greek Literature*; Gregory Vlastos, "Jesus' Conflict with the Pharisees," *Christendom* (Winter, 1937), 86–100; Walker, *A History of the Christian Church*; *IDB*; *IB*, 1:36; 433–34; 9:162–63, 169; 12:656–57.

[16]Book of Enoch, chaps. 85–90, from Nahum N. Glatzer, *The Judaic Tradition*, rev. ed. (Boston: Beacon Press, 1969), 62–65, "The Day of Judgment" and "The Victory of the Righteous."

[17]G. George Fox, "Essential Judaism," a review of *The Pharisees and other Essays* by Leo Baeck, *The Christian Century*, May 5, 1948, 417.

[18]Scholars are not unanimous in regarding Qumran as an Essene community.

[19]See Marcus Borg, *Jesus, A New Vision: Spirit, Culture, and the Life of Discipleship* (San Francisco: Harper & Row, 1987), 88–90; Borg, *Meeting Jesus Again for the First Time: The Historical Jesus & the Heart of Contemporary Faith* (HarperSanFrancisco, 1994), 50–53.

[20]The quotation is from E. Bickerman, "The Historical Foundation of Postbiblical Judaism," in L. Finkelstein, ed., *The Jews, Their History, Culture, and Religion* (1940), 1:70–114, as quoted by Momigliano, *Essays on Ancient and Modern Judaism*, 57.

[21]C. K. Barrett, *The New Testament Background: Selected Documents*, Harper Torchbooks (New York: Harper & Row, 1961), 208–21.

[22]The notion of missionary Judaism and of "God-fearers" among the Gentiles, deriving ultimately from Matthew and Acts, and held by a large number of scholars, both Jewish and Christian, has recently been called into question. See Scot McKnight, *A Light among the Gentiles: Jewish Missionary Activity in the Second Temple Period* (Minneapolis: Fortress Press, 1991); Martin Goodman, "Jewish Proselytizing in the

First Century," in Judith Lieu, John North. and Tessa Rajak, eds., *The Jews Among the Pagans and Christians in the Roman Empire* (New York: Routledge, 1992), 53–78. Cf. R. S. MacLennan and A. T. Kraabel, "The God-Fearers—A Literary and Theological Invention," in J. Andrew Overman and Robert S. MacLennan, eds., *Diaspora Jews and Judaism: Essays in Honor of, and in Dialogue with, A. Thomas Kraabel* (Atlanta, Ga.: Scholars Press, 1992), 131–43. For a rejoinder, see J. Andrew Overman, "The God-Fearers: Some Neglected Features," ibid., 145–52.

[23]Suggs, Sakenfeld, and Mueller, *The Oxford Study Bible: Revised English Bible with the Apocrypha,* note to 2 Macc. 1:10.

[24]Ferguson, *The Religions of the Roman Empire,* 222–24.

[25]For confidence that "All the nations in the whole world will be converted to the true worship of God" see Tobit 14:6–7; this apocryphal book is thought to have been written in the second century B.C.E. For rabbinical commendation of proselytes, see Telushkin, *Jewish Wisdom,* 374–81.

[26]See Pirqe Abot, a classic collection of rabbinical sayings found in various editions of the Mishnah and so in those of the Talmud, e.g., Jacob Neusner, trans. and ed., *Scriptures of the Oral Torah: Sanctification and Salvation in the Sacred Books of Judaism* (San Francisco: Harper & Row, 1987), 70–95 [The Fathers, Pirqe Abot]); R. Travers Herford, ed., trans., *Pirke Aboth; The Ethics of the Talmud: Sayings of the Fathers* (New York: Schocken Books, 1962), with commentary. Portions from "The Sayings of the Fathers" are read in the afternoon services for the Sabbath, from the Sabbath after Passover until the Sabbath before the Feast of Weeks; see *The Union Prayerbook for Jewish Worship,* newly revised edition, edited and published by the Central Conference of American Rabbis (New York, 1961), 165–78. See also Gerald M. Phillips, "The Practice of Rhetoric at the Talmudic Academies," *Speech Monographs,* 26 (1959), 37–46. Additional works consulted: *IDB;* Jeremias, *Wisdom in Israel;* The Jerusalem Bible; McNeill, *A History of the Cure of Souls;* Rosemary Ruether and Eleanor McLaughlin, *Women of Spirit* (New York: Simon and Schuster, 1979); Schaff, 1; *IB,* 1:406–10; *IB,* 7:97.

[27] See Elias J. Bickerman, *The Jews in the Greek Age* (Cambridge, Mass.: Harvard University Press, 1988), 161–76.

[28]Some biographical material on leading rabbis was handed down, along with their teaching, in the oral tradition later preserved in the Talmud. For reflections by a 20th-century Jewish man of letters on their personalities and dicta, see Elie Wiesel, *Sages and Dreamers: Biblical, Talmudic, and Hasidic Portraits and Legends* (New York: Summit Books, 1991), Part 2, "The Talmud."

[29]The Greek text for the NT uses *rabbi, rabbonia, rabbouni;* also *didaskalos* (teacher, doctor, master), *epistates* (master), *grammateis* (scribe), *nomikos* (expert in the law), and *nomididaskalos* (teacher of the law). Cf. Schaff, 1:148, n. 3.

[30]J. Hei, "Preaching in the Talmudic Period," *Encyclopedia Judaica,* 13:994ff.

[31]Pirqe Abot IV. 6 (Goldin, 93).

[32]Pirqe Abot I. 18 (Neusner, *Scriptures of the Oral Torah,* 78).

[33]Cf. Rabbi Gamaliel's dictum on a life devoted to labor and the study of Torah, Pirqe Abot II. 2.

[34]Pirqe Abot I. 4, Judah Goldin, trans. *The Living Talmud: The Wisdom of the Fathers and Its Classical Commentaries* (New York: The Heritage Press, c. 1960), 9.

[35]Exodus 13:1, Mekhilta Pisha 16, I, 131, as found in Hammer, *The Classic Midrash,* 61–62. For other instances of rabbinic tributes, see Pirqe Abot II. 11, 13; IV. 1, 15; VI. 3, 8.

[36]Pirqe Abot VI. 6 (Herford, 157). For other examples of praise for Torah, see II. 19; III. 4, 9, 21; IV. 8, 12; VI. 1, 5.

[37]Pirqe Abot II. 17 (Herford, 58); cf. III. 10 (ibid., 74–75).

[38]Pirqe Abot II. 9 (Herford, 49).

[39]Pirqe Abot V. 25 (Herford, 145).

[40]The Zadokite Document, IV. xiv. 3–12, in Theodor H. Gaster, *The Dead Sea Scriptures in English Translation*, Doubleday Anchor Books (Garden City, New York: Doubleday & Company, 1956), 83; cf. 81.

[41]Gaster insists on this translation rather than "Teacher of Righteousness," which implies a single figure in the tradition. Cf. *The Dead Sea Scriptures*, 5, 13, 29.

[42]Zadokite Document, III. xiii. 7–19, Gaster, 81; Commentary on the Book of Micah, I (5), Gaster, 239; Book of Hymns, 8, Gaster 142–43; Commentary on the Book of Habakkuk, chaps. 1, 2, Gaster, 249–55.

[43]Book of Hymns, No. 11, Gaster, 162.

[44]See "'Gentle as a Nurse': The Cynic Background to 1 Thessalonians 2" in Abraham J. Malherbe, *Paul and the Popular Philosophers* (Minneapolis: Fortress Press, 1989), 35–48.

[45]Book of Hymns, No.19, Gaster, 184.

[46]From *De vita contemplativa*, in Glatzer, *The Judaic Tradition*, 93.

[47]See "Exhortation Based on the Flood," in Florentino García Martínez, *The Dead Sea Scrolls Translated: The Qumran Texts in English*, trans. Wilfred G. E. Watson (Leiden: E. J. Brill, 1994), 224–25; "Words of Moses," ibid., 276–77; "Mysteries," 399 ff.

[48]Book of Hymns, 16 (X, 14–XI, 2) in Gaster, 174.

[49]"From the Source of His Knowledge: A Psalm" (From the Manual of Discipline), in Glatzer, *The Judaic Tradition*, 79.

[50]See Geza Vermes, *Jesus the Jew: A Historian's Reading of the Gospels* (Philadelphia: Fortress Press, 1973), chap. 3, "Jesus and Charismatic Judaism."

[51]*Genesis Rabbah* 13:7 (alt.), from Vermes, *Jesus the Jew*, 72.

[52]*Berakhoth (Benedictions)*, 33a (found in the Babylonian Talmud), cited by Vermes, 74.

[53]Pirqe Abot III. 9A (Neusner, *Oral Scriptures of the Torah*, 84). Herford lists this as III. 11.

[54]For these latter-day prophets, some mentioned both in the New Testament and by the Jewish historian Josephus, see Vermes, *Jesus the Jew*, 98.

[55]Works consulted: Ben Witherington III, *Women and the Genesis of Christianity*, ed. Ann Witherington (Cambridge, Mass.: Cambridge University Press, 1990, 6–9); Rosemary Ruether and Eleanor McLaughlin, *Women of Spirit: Female Leadership in the Jewish and Christian Traditions* (New York: Simon and Schuster, 1979), 17.

[56]Jacob Neusner, *The Mishnah: Introduction and Reader* (Philadelphia: Trinity Press International, 1992), 175.

[57]Pirqe Abot I. 5 (Herford, 24).

[58]Ibid.

[59]*Genesis Rabbah* 17:7 (Telushkin, *Jewish Wisdom*, 116).

[60]*Pirkei d'Rabbi Eliezer*, chap. 41 (Telushkin, *Jewish Wisdom*, 116).

[61](*Ber.* 10*a*), in C. G. Montefiore and H. Loewe, *A Rabbinic Anthology: Selected and Arranged with Comments and Introductions* (Meridian Books, 1938), 461 (1291); cf. 616, 673.

[62]See Ross Shepard Kraemer, *Her Share of the Blessings*, chapter 8, "Jewish Women's Lives in Rabbinic Sources." Cf. Wiesel, *Sages and Dreamers*, 286–98, "Rabbi Meir and Brurya."

[63]*The Bavli*, XI (Neusner, *Scriptures of the Oral Torah*, 238).

[64]See Burton L. Mack, "Philo Judaeus and Exegetical Traditions in Alexandria," *Aufstieg und Niedergang der roemischen Welt: Religion II* (Berlin: de Gruyter, 1980). Additional works consulted: Barrett, *IDB;* Jeremias; Burton L. Mack and Roland Murphy, "Wisdom Literature," in *Early Post-Biblical Judaism and Its Modern Interpreters*, ed. Robert A. Kraft and W. E. Nickelsburg, SBL Centennial Publications 2

(Missoula, Mont.: Scholars Press, 1980); Massey H. Shepherd, Jr., "Philo and His Times," review of *An Introduction to Philo Judaeus* by Erwin R. Goodenough, *The Christian Century,* Dec. 4, 1940.

[65]See Von Rad, *Wisdom in Israel,* 241–306; Rylaarsdam, *Revelation in Jewish Wisdom Literature,* 27–40.

[66]Sir. 15:1–10; 50:27–28; 51:22.

[67]Hammer, *The Classic Midrash,* "Introduction," 16.

[68]Jacob Neusner, *Studying Classical Judaism: A Primer* (Louisville, Ky.: Westminster/John Knox Press, 1991), 13. Note the oral tradition regarding the rabbinic succession in *Pirqe Abot,* chap. 1.

[69]Hammer, *The Classic Midrash,* "Introduction," 19.

[70]Pirqe Abot 2 (Goldin, 44).

[71]Hammer, *The Classic Midrash,* "Introduction," 15.

[72]For a critical analysis of the oral tradition, with conclusions, see Jacob Neusner, *The Pharisees: Rabbinic Perspectives* (Hoboken, N.J.: KTAV Publishing House, copyright E. J. Brill, 1973).

[73]Pirqe Abot I.15 (Goldin, 23).

[74]Mishnah Tractate Berakhot, 8:1, 5, 7 (Neusner, *Introduction to Rabbinic Literature,* 135–36).

[75]The *am-ha-Aretz* were the poor 'people of the land', generally dismissed as ignorant, and looked down on especially by the scribes for their ignorance of Torah; here Neusner translates as 'boor'.

[76]Goldin translates the line: "The short-tempered cannot teach" (*The Wisdom of the Fathers,* 40).

[77]Pirqe Abot II. 4–5, 7 (Neusner, *Scriptures of the Oral Torah,* 79–80). Cf. Glatzer, *The Judaic Tradition,* 191–98.

[78]Pirqe Abot I. 14 (Neusner, *Scriptures of the Oral Torah,* 78).

[79]Glatzer, 197.

[80]Pirqe Abot II. 2 (Neusner, *Scriptures of the Oral Torah,* 78–79).

[81]From Mishnah Pesahim (Glatzer, *The Judaic Tradition,* 189).

[82]The Bavli, CXCVI (Neusner, *Scriptures of the Oral Torah,* 351).

[83]Babylonian Talmud, *Ketubot* 8b (Telushkin, *Jewish Wisdom,* 261–62).

[84]Florentino García Martínez, *The Dead Sea Scrolls Translated: The Qumran Texts in English,* trans. Wilfred G. E. Watson (Leiden: E. J. Brill, 1994), "Introduction," xxxi–lvi; G. Jeremias, "Teacher of Righteousness," *IDB-S,* 861–63; cf. Gaster, 5, 13, 29.

[85]"Of Communal Duties," *The Manual of Discipline* (vi, 6), in Gaster, 49; cf. García Martínez, "The Rule of the Community" in *The Dead Sea Scrolls Translated,* 9.

[86]See, e.g., "Of the Two Spirits in Man," Gaster, 43–46 (cf. García Martínez, 6–8); "Of God's Vengeance and Providence," Gaster, 61–74 (cf. García Martínez, 33–34); Commentary on the Book of Habakkuk, Gaster, 249–56 (García Martínez, 197ff.); "The New Covenant," Gaster, 311 (cf. 279); "The Coming Doom," Gaster, 313–14; "Exhortation Based on the Flood" (García Martínez, 224–25); "Words of Moses" (ibid., 276–77); note also the comments on "Para-biblical Literature" in García Martínez, 218.

[87]"Wisdom Text with Beatitudes," García Martínez, 395.

[88]"The Damascus Document," in García Martínez, 33. For further examples of the sectarian spin in exegesis see "Commentary on the Book of Habakkuk" in Gaster, 249–256; cf. "Commentary on Habakkuk" in García Martínez, 197–202.

[89]Ibid., 34.

[90]See Erwin R. Goodenough, *An Introduction to Philo Judaeus* (New Haven: Yale University Press, 1940).

[91]See *On the Embassy to Gaius*, in *Philo* with an English translation by F. H. Colson, LCL, X, 3–187.

[92]Philo, *De opificio mundi*, 3, 8ff. in Barrett, 178, g. 182.

[93]For Jewish interest in Greek philosophical themes, see the apocryphal Wisdom of Solomon, chap. 13, evidently composed in Alexandria in the first century B. C. E.

[94]Goodenough, *Philo*, 166–67.

[95]See "List of Philo's Works," *Philo* with an English translation by F. H. Colson, LCL, X, xxxvii, xxxvii. Cf. Goodenough, 54, 60, 61.

[96]Goodenough, *Philo*, 11.

[97]Ferguson, *The Religions of the Roman Empire*, 224.

[98]"The Order of the Essenes," selections from Philo, "Every Good Man Is Free," in Glatzer, *The Judaic Tradition*, 89.

[99]Manuel Alexandre, Jr., "Rhetorical Argumentation as an Exegetical Technique in Philo of Alexandria," in A. Caquot, M. Hadas-Lebel, and J. Riaud, eds., *Hellenica et Judaica: Hommage à Valentin Nikiprowetsky* (Leuven-Paris: Éditions Peeters, 1956), 21.

[100]Ibid., 16.

[101]Ibid., 26–27.

[102]Philo, *On Abraham*, XIV. 60–65, in F. H. Colson, trans., *Philo*, (Cambridge University Press, 1935), LCL, VI, 35–37. Considering the length of the complete work (the English translation runs to some 65 pages), it may not qualify in the strict sense as preaching, but *may have been delivered* as a lecture. The tendency of historians to designate material originally presented orally (apology, lecture, encomium, sermon) as *treatise* tends to conceal its *spoken* character in an age of many orators but few authors-communicating-first-through-books. *On Abraham* has the strongly rhetorical cast so characteristic of Philo; he assumes the pose of one addressing hearers and uses the language of oratory; note the recurrence of terms translated as "We must now speak…" (XIII. 60), "What has been said…" (XVIII.81), and "I have now told…the story…" (XXXII. 167) in referring to what he is doing. He repeatedly uses the aorist tense of the verb *eipon*, meaning "I [or we] have said," though it is disguised in Colson's translation as "I [we] have described" (XXII. 107, XXIII, 114) In any event, he *did* preach, the passages here cited have the character of preaching, and they demonstrate his mode of biblical interpretation.

[103]Ibid., XIV. 64 (LCL, VI, 37).

[104]Ibid., XIV. 65 (LCL, VI, 37).

[105]Ibid., XIV. 66–67 (LCL, VI, 37–39).

[106]See Samuel Sandmel, *Philo of Alexandria: An Introduction* (New York: Oxford University Press, 1979), chap. 2, "Allegory."

[107]Ibid., 173.

[108]Philo, "On Repentance," a unit of his compilation *On the Virtues* (LCL, VIII), XXXIII. 177 (273).

[109]Ibid., XXXIII. 179 (273).

[110]Ibid., XXXIV. 180–82 (275).

[111]See "I Take Refuge: The Prayer of Asenath," composed in the style of the Psalms, found in a Hellenistic midrash that tells of the conversion of the Egyptian wife of Joseph—in Glatzer, *The Judaic Heritage*, 135–36.

[112]Philo, "On Repentance," a unit of *On the Virtues* (LCL), XXXIII. 179 (273).

[113]Quoted without attribution by John Ferguson, *The Religions of the Roman Empire* (Ithaca, N. Y.: Cornell University Press, 1970), 221–22.

[114]"Morning Service for Week-Days," *The Union Prayerbook for Jewish Worship*, newly rev. ed. (New York: The Central Conference of American Rabbis, 1961), 327.

[115]Ibid.

[116]*Didache* 4:1, presumably using the text of a Jewish catechism; see Rudolf Bultmann, *Theology of the New Testament* (New York: Charles Scribner's Sons, 1954), 1:122.

Chapter 6: The Homiletic of Judaism

[1]See Geza Vermes, "The Qumran Interpretation of Scripture in Its Historical Setting," *The Annual of Leeds University Oriental Society,* 6, 1966–1968 (Leiden, Holland: E. J. Brill, 1969), 85–97. Additional works consulted: Barrett; Bultmann, *Theology of NT; Encyclopedia Judaica;* Glatzer; Goldin; Hadas; *IDB;* Simeon Lowy, "Some Aspects of Normative and Sectarian Interpretation of the Scriptures," *Annual of Leeds University Oriental Society,* 6 (1966–1968), 98–163; Burton L. Mack, "Weisheit und Allegorie bei Philo von Alexandrien: Untersuchungen zum Traktat *De congressu eruditionis,*" *Theokratia,* 3 (1973–1975) (Leiden, Holland: E. J. Brill, 1979); Mack, "Philo Judaeus and Exegetical Traditions" (unpublished paper).

[2]Reuven Hammer, *The Classic Midrash: Tannaitic Commentaries on the Bible,* The Classics of Western Spirituality (New York: Paulist Press, 1995), Introduction, 22.

[3]*Tosefta Sanhedrin* 7.11 (427), in Barrett, 146, g. 133, substituting the literal "light and heavy" for the translation into Latin (*a minori ad maius*) and incorporating within brackets the explanation from Barrett's footnotes.

[4]Bickerman, *The Jews in the Greek Age,* 178.

[5]Hammer, *The Classic Midrash,* Introduction, 21.

[6]Ex. 14:15, Mekhilta Beshallah 4. I. 216, in *The Classic Midrash,* 86.

[7]The Zadokite Document, v. 17–vi. 11, in Gaster, 68. Gaster sees "the land of Damascus" as an allegorical allusion to the wilderness of the Qumran ascetics. For other examples of and references to allegorizing at Qumran, see 65, 66, 70, 229.

[8]Quoted without specific attribution by Hammer in *The Classic Midrash,* Introduction, 42.

[9]Philo, *De vita contemplativa,* in Glatzer, *The Judaic Heritage,* 92; cf. 98.

[10]Pirqe Abot, VI. 2 (Herford, 151).

[11]Commentary on the Book of Micah, I (5), Gaster, 239, 262.

[12]Herford, *The Ethics of the Talmud: Sayings of the Fathers,* commentary on P. A. VI. 2 (151).

[13]Philo, *On Abraham,* XLI. 236 (LCL, 117).

[14]Philo, *De vita contemplativa,* in Glatzer, 98; cf. 92–97.

[15]Mack, "Philo Judaeus and Exegetical Traditions," 41.

[16]Burton L. Mack, Faculty colloquium, School of Theology at Claremont, Oct. 3, 1978.

[17]Mack, "Philo Judaeus and Exegetical Traditions," 45–51. Mack's terms, corresponding to the numbers used here, are (1) The Anti-anthropomorphic Apology, (2) The Encomium, (3) The Reasoned Allegory, (4) The Identification Allegory, (5) The Development of a Theme, (6) The Clarification of the Literal Meaning.

[18]For a sample of Philo's exegesis, see Glatzer, *The Judaic Tradition,* 115–23.

[19]Philo, *On Mating with the Preliminary Studies* (De congressu quaerendae eruditionis gratia), LCL, xxx. 172, trans. F. H. Colson and G. H. Whitaker (G. P. Putnam's Sons, 1932), *Philo,* IV, 547.

[20]Philo, *On Abraham,* XV, 68–70 (LCL, VI, 39–41).

[21]Ibid. Note how the thought of this sentence and the one immediately preceding is paralleled (though in different Greek words) in Rom. 1:19–23 and Acts 17:24–29, written only a few decades after Philo. The notion was a commonplace for Jewish and Christian apologists.

[22]Philo, *On Abraham*, XV, 70–72 (LCL, VI, 41).

[23]Works consulted: Barrett; Gaster; Mack, "Philo Judaeus and Exegetical Traditions"; Vlastos.

[24]Montefiore and Loewe, *A Rabbinic Anthology*, Introduction, xix.

[25]See the selections in Montefiore and Loewe, chaps. 1, 2, 9, 12.

[26]Pirqe Abot, IV. 29 (Herford, 123). Herford observes of this obviously sermonic passage that "one might almost conjecture that it was taken from some sermon or religious address." A few other such passages appear in the Talmud.

[27]*Ber. 7a*, Montefiore and Loewe, 368 [978].

[28]Pirqe Abot, II. 4 (Goldin, 36).

[29]"Divine Presence in Exile," identified only as "From the Talmud and Midrash," in Glatzer, *The Judaic Tradition*, 236–37.

[30]See Montefiore and Loewe, *A Rabbinic Anthology*, chap. 3, "Man's Nature and God's Grace."

[31]Pirqe Abot, III. 18 (Goldin, 61).

[32]Pirqe Abot, V. 24 (Herford, 144). (The references to Mishnah and Talmud mark the present form of the saying as late, though the basic scheme may conceivably have originated earlier.)

[33]Von Rad, *Wisdom in Israel*, 198.

[34]Pirqe Abot, III. 19 (Goldin, 78).

[35]Pirqe Abot, III. 18 (Goldin, 77). The gender-specific language of this passage, so natural to a male in a patriarchal society, is, despite all that, an eloquent affirmation of human dignity as divine handiwork formed in the image of the Creator. After much struggle I have found no way of readily transposing the saying into inclusive language without such violence to the literary form as to destroy it. Let it stand as a reminder, to our regret, of how things once were and how men once spoke.

[36]See Montefiore and Loewe, *A Rabbinic Anthology*, chap. 31, "The Life to Come: Resurrection and Judgment."

[37]"Rabbi says," Pirqe Abot, II. 1 (Goldin, 31–32). Commonly referred to simply as Rabbi, no name being necessary, the speaker was Jehudah ha-Kadosh, ha-Nasi (135–219 C. E.).

[38]John Baillie, *And the Life Everlasting* (New York: Charles Scribner's Sons, 1933), 86–102; 141–58.

[39]Pirqe Abot, IV. 21 (Herford, 115).

[40]Pirqe Abot, IV. 22 (Herford, 116).

[41]*Tanh. B.*, Berakah, 28b fin., from Montefiore and Loewe, *A Rabbinic Anthology*, 581.

[42]For a discussion of various meanings of wisdom see Rylaarsdam, *Revelation in Jewish Wisdom Literature*, 55–56.

[43]See Prov. 1:20–33; 8:4–36; 9:1–6; cf. 9:13–18.

[44]Some scholars, but by no means all, see this myth of wisdom as created after the pattern of Egyptian tales concerning Maat and Isis. See Burton L. Mack, "Wisdom Myth and Mythology: An Essay in Understanding a Theological Tradition," *Interpretation*, 24, 1 (Jan. 1970), 46–60.

[45]11Q Psalms, *Col.* XVIII (*Psalm* 154), vv. 1–4, 12, 14, one of the apocryphal psalms found at Qumran; in García Martínez, *The Dead Sea Scrolls Translated*, 304–5.

[46]"The General Law, which is Right Reason, pervading everything, is the same as Zeus," Zeno, Fragment, 162, x, in Barrett, 62, g 61. For selections from the Hellenistic era dealing with wisdom see "Lady Wisdom and Israel" in Nickelsburg and Stone, *Faith and Piety in Early Judaism*, 204–31.

[47]For earlier pre-Hellenistic references to the divine Word tending in this direction, see Ps. 107:20; 147:15–19; Isa. 55:11.

[48]See Montefiore and Loewe, *A Rabbinic Anthology,* chaps. 5, 8, 10, 15–21, and Excursus II.

[49]Philo, *Every Good Man Is Free,* in Glatzer, *The Judaic Tradition,* 57.

[50]The entire sentence above, after "commended," and not just the portion within quotation marks, is taken from Rylaarsdam, *Revelation in Jewish Wisdom Literature,* 57. He supplies references as follows: sober speech (Prov. 12:18;15:4), forbearance (14:29), honesty (12:17), self-control (17:27), industry (12:24), intelligence (12:8), humaneness (12:10), good will (14:22), patience (15:18), philanthropy (14:21), tractableness (15:5), reverence (10:27), justice (16:8), modesty (18:2), humility (16:9), and fidelity (5:15ff).

[51]Pirqe Abot, I. 17 (Goldin, 17).

[52]Pirqe Abot, I. 2 (Herford, 22).

[53]Pirqe Abot, I. 18 (Goldin, 26).

[54]See Pirqe Abot, V.1–22 for a compilation of such numerical series.

[55]Pirqe Abot, I. 12 (Goldin, 20).

[56]Pirqe Abot, III. 16 (Herford, 82).

[57]Pirqe Abot, III. 2 (Goldin, 62).

[58]Babylonian Talmud, *Sukkot* 49b, from Telushkin, *Jewish Wisdom,* 24. Telushkin's first line in the quotation used here reads "*Gemilut Chesed* [lovingkindness] is greater than charity."

[59]Babylonian Talmud, *Shabbat* 132a, from Telushkin, 85.

[60]Mt. 7:12; Rom. 13:9–10; Gal. 6:14.

[61]bMak 24a, from Geza Vermes, *The Religion of Jesus the Jew* (Minneapolis: Fortress Press, 1993), 44, alt.

[62]Pirqe Abot, I. 1 (Goldin, 5).

[63]Neusner, *Scriptures of the Oral Torah,* 74; cf. Neusner, *Introduction to Rabbinic L:iterature,* xix–xx.

[64]Pirqe Abot, VI. 1 (Herford, 148).

[65]Pirqe Abot, IV. 16 (Herford, 111).

[66]Pirqe Abot, II. 5 (Goldin, 45).

[67]The Zadokite Document: "Of the Works of Belial" (iv, 12–v, 17) as translated in Gaster, *The Dead Sea Scriptures,* 66.

[68]Pirqe Abot, IV. 7 (Goldin, 94).

[69]Pirqe Abot, II. 2.

[70]Ibid., I. 13 (Goldin, 21).

[71]Ibid.

[72]Pirqe Abot, IV. 23 (Herford, 117).

[73]Pirqe Abot, V. 10 (Herford, 131).

[74]"The Vessels," a parable in Glatzer, *The Judaic Tradition,* 226.

[75]Pirqe Abot, VI. 2, (Goldin, 148–49). Montefiore and Loewe propose "heavenly voice" to translate *bat kol,* literally, "daughter of a voice," *A Rabbinic Anthology,* 739.

[76]Pirqe Abot, III. 7, (Goldin 67); cf. III. 3.

[77]See Long, *Preaching and the Literary Forms of the Bible.* Additional works consulted: William Barclay, *The New Testament: A New Translation* (London: Collins, 1969), 2, notes; Barrett; Bultmann, *Theology of NT;* Glatzer; Hadas; *IDB;* Burton L. Mack, "Ben Sira's Hymn in Praise of the Pious," Report to the Pseudepigrapha Seminar, *SBL,* New York, Nov. 1979, unpublished paper; Sachar; *IB* 1:34–35; 397–98; 406–8; 432–35.

[78]Philo, *De vita contemplativa,* III, 31 (LCL IX, 131), cited by Glatzer, *The Judaic Tradition,* 93.

[79]For the rhetoric, logic, and dialectic of the Mishnah, see Neusner, *Introduction to Rabbinic Literature,* chaps. 2–4; for the rhetoric of Rabbi Ishmael, 252–54.

⁸⁰Pirqe Abot, II. 13 (Goldin, 46–47), substituting "person" for "man" in the translation quoted.

⁸¹Pirqe Abot, III. 17 (Goldin, 85).

⁸²Pirqe Abot, II. 15 (Goldin, 48–49).

⁸³Mekilta, Neziqin 18, w, 137ff. (cited by Hammer, *The Classic Midrash*, 5).

⁸⁴Babylonian Talmud, *Bava Mezia*, 59b (cited by Telushkin, *Jewish Wisdom*, 73–74.

⁸⁵Judah Goldin, Preface to Hammer, *Classic Midrash*, 6–7.

⁸⁶Pirqe Abot, II. 20 (Goldin, 57).

⁸⁷For reflections on Wisdom and Spirit, see Rylaarsdam, *Wisdom in Israel*, 100–109.

⁸⁸Babylonian Talmud, *Eruvin* 53b (from Telushkin, *Jewish Wisdom*, 71).

⁸⁹Babylonian Talmud, *Berakhot* 61b (quoted by Telushkin, *Jewish Wisdom*, 338). Note that an effort has been made to maintain uniformity in the spelling of Jewish names despite slight differences of transliteration in the authorities quoted.

⁹⁰Glatzer, 176.

⁹¹*Midr. Prov.* XXXI. 10, f. 45b, from Montefiore and Loewe, *A Rabbinic Anthology*, 552 [1547].

⁹²Pirqe Abot, V. 23 (Goldin, 139).

⁹³For a collection of more than one hundred parables in translation, with accompanying essays, see Harvey K. McArthur and Robert M. Johnston, *They Also Taught in Parables: Rabbinic Parables from the First Centuries of the Christian Era* (Academie Books. Grand Rapids, Mich.: Zondervan Publishing House, 1990); cf. Montefiore and Loewe, *A Rabbinic Anthology*, 322–23 [842], 431 [1203]; Geza Vermes, *The Religion of Jesus the Jew*, 92–98, 133; Hammer, *The Classic Midrash*, 41, 94–95, 105–6, 117; Clemens Thoma and Michael Wyschorod, eds., *Parable and Story in Judaism and Christianity* (New York: Paulist Press, 1989).

⁹⁴Pirqe Abot, V. 18 (Goldin, 135).

⁹⁵See, e.g., Pirqe Abot, III, 20 (Herford, 89).

⁹⁶See Wis. 13:10–14:4, elaborated from Isa. 44:9–20; cf. Pirqe Abot VI. 9 (Herford, 161). See also M. Jack Suggs, "Wisdom of Solomon 2:10–15: A Homily Based on the Fourth Servant Song," *JBL* 76 (1957): 26–33; cf. Mack and Murphy, 27.

⁹⁷Bickerman, *The Jews in the Greek Age*, 190.

⁹⁸See Emanuel bin Gorion, ed., *Mimekor Yisrael: Selected Classical Jewish Folktales*, collected by Micha Joseph bin Gorion, trans. I. M. Lusk (Bloomington, Ind.: Indiana University Press, 1990).

⁹⁹Babylonian Talmud, *Berakhot* 61b (quoted in Telushkin, *Jewish Wisdom*, 337–38).

¹⁰⁰Babylonian Talmud, *Ta'anit* 22a, (in Telushkin, *Jewish Wisdom*, 185).

¹⁰¹For a useful summary of literary forms in wisdom literature, see Von Rad, *Wisdom in Israel*, 24–50; cf., for current application of such an analysis, Thomas G. Long, *Preaching and the Literary Forms of the Bible* (Philadelphia: Fortress Press, 1985).

¹⁰²For a listing of such passages in the scrolls arranged according to a systematic outline see "Analytical Index," E, "The Last Things (Eschatological Doctrines)" in Gaster, *The Dead Sea Scriptures*, 337–42; "Literature with Eschatological Content," García Martínez, *The Dead Sea Scrolls Translated*, 93–140.

¹⁰³Hammer, Introduction, *The Classic Midrash*, 38, citing Max Kadushin, *The Rabbinic Mind* (New York, 1972), 84.

¹⁰⁴Cf. Ezek. 20; Neh. 9; Jdt. 5; Ps. 75, 105, 106, 135, 136; Wis. 42:15–43:35.

¹⁰⁵H. Graetz, *History of the Jews* (Philadelphia: Jewish Publication Society of America, 1894), 1, 514; cf. Mack and Murphy, "Wisdom Literature," in Kraft and Nickelsburg, eds., *Early Post-Biblical Judaism*, especially 2, 10, 17, 31, 45.

Conclusion to Part Two

[1]Islam, of course, which arose some centuries after the emergence of classical Judaism (and stands in the tradition of Abraham and the prophets) is also a religion of a sacred book, the Koran.

PART THREE. PREACHER OF GOOD NEWS

Introduction to Part Three

[1]Besides the four canonical gospels, other such documents circulated in early Christian times, including the hypothetical Q (Source) and the hypothetical *Signs Gospel* (both absorbed into the canonical works), the recently recovered Gospel of Thomas, and a number of fragmentary writings. See Robert J. Miller, ed., *The Complete Gospels: Annotated Scholars Version* (Sonoma, Ca.: Polebridge Press, 1992), a publication issuing from the work of the Jesus Seminar.

[2]G. B. Caird, "The Chronology of the NT," *IDB,* I, 603.

Chapter 7: Portrait of the Preacher

[1]See Paul Achtemeier, *Mark,* Proclamation Commentaries (Philadelphia: Fortress Press, 1975), chaps. 6, 7. Additional works consulted: Robert W. Funk, Roy W. Hoover, and the Jesus Seminar, *The Five Gospels: the Search for the Authentic Words of Jesus, New Translation and Commentary,* a Polebridge Press Book (New York: Macmillan, 1993); *IB,* 7, 8. In the early development of this chapter I received helpful counsel from Warren Taylor and Rod Parrott.

[2]When words attributed to Jesus are quoted, the judgment of the Jesus Seminar as to their authenticity is noted as follows: JS–r (= red: "Jesus undoubtedly said this or something very like it"), JS–p (= pink: "Jesus probably said something like this"), JS–g (= gray: "Jesus did not say this, but the ideas contained in it are close to his own"), JS–b (= black: "Jesus did not say this; it represents the perspective or content of a later or different tradition"). For the rationale of the Jesus Seminar in reaching its conclusions, see Funk and Hoover, *The Five Gospels,* 1–38. See also the commentary on the passage in question in *The Five Gospels.* New Testament scholars are by no means unanimous in endorsing the methods and conclusions of the Jesus Seminar; see, e. g., Luke Timothy Johnson, *The Real Jesus: The Misguided Quest for the Historical Jesus and the Truth of the Traditional Gospels* (HarperSanFrancisco, 1995). As subsequently noted, the writer's inclusion of this information in the text is for informational puposes and does not imply full agreement with the Seminar's conclusions.

[3]Burton L. Mack likens his mode of discourse to that of the Cynics; see his *Who Wrote the New Testament? The Making of the Christian Myth* (HarperSanFrancisco, 1995), 38–41; cf. John Dominic Crossan, *The Historical Jesus: The Life of a Mediterranean Jewish Peasant* (HarperSanFrancisco, 1991), chap. 4, and pp. 338, 421. Cf. Paul Rhodes Eddy, "Jesus as Diogenes? Reflections on the Cynic Jesus Thesis," *JBL,* 115:3 (Fall, 1996), 449–69.

[4]Quoted at length to this effect by K. Barth in *The Doctrine of the Word of God,* trans. G. T. Thompson (Edinburgh: T & T Clark, 1955), 1. 1. 138.

[5]Fred B. Craddock, *Preaching* (Nashville: Abingdon Press, 1985), 31.

[6]From an ancient appendix to Mark, thought to incorporate an older tradition.

[7]See M. Eugene Boring, "The 'Third Quest' and the Apostolic Faith," *Interpretation,* 50:4 (Oct. 1996), 341–54; John P. Meier, "Dividing Lines in Jesus Research Today: Through Dialectical Negation to a Positive Sketch," ibid., 355–72. Cf. Jeremias,

New Testament Theology: The Proclamation of Jesus (New York: Charles Scribner's Sons, 1971), chap. 1; John Dominic Crossan, *The Essential Jesus: Original Sayings and Earliest Images* (HarperSan Francisco, 1989), Crossan's summary of his conclusions. For a more detailed explanation of Crossan's methodology and assumptions see his *The Historical Jesus: The Life of a Mediterranean Jewish Peasant* (HarperSanFrancisco, 1991).

Additional works consulted: Justin Martyr, *Dialogue with Trypho*, chap. 47; *The Gospel of Thomas;* Eusebius, *Ecclesiastical History;* Achtemeier, *Mark;* Rudolf Bultmann, *History of the Synoptic Tradition* (New York: Harper & Row, 1968); Ernst Haenchen, *The Acts of the Apostles: A Commentary* (Philadelphia: The Westminster Press, 1971); Joachim Jeremias, *Unknown Sayings of Jesus* (London: S. P. C. K., 1958); Willi Marxsen, *Introduction to the New Testament* (Philadelphia: Fortress Press, 1968); Eduard Schweizer, "The Relation of Scripture, Church Tradition, and Modern Interpretation," in Marty and Peerman, *New Theology,* 1, 44–59; *IB,* 7, 8, 10, 12.

[8]William Foxwell Albright, *The Archeology of Palestine* (London: Penguin Books, 1949), 240–43.

[9]See Burton L. Mack, *The Lost Gospel: The Book of Q and Christian Origins* (HarperSanFrancisco, 1993).

[10]For these developments consult a good Bible encyclopedia or Bible dictionary, the introductory articles to the gospels in *The New Interpreter's Bible* or other major commentary on the gospels, or a standard introduction to the New Testament. Cf. Burton L. Mack, *Who Wrote the New Testament: The Making of the Christian Myth* (HarperSanFrancisco, 1995).

[11]See Jeremias, *NT Theology,* chap. 1; James M. Robinson, "The Formal Structure of Jesus' Message," in William Klassen and Graydon F. Snyder, eds., *Current Issues in New Testament Interpretation* (New York: Harper & Brothers, 1962).

Additional works consulted: Achtemeier, *Mark*; Gunther Bornkamm, *Jesus of Nazareth* (New York: Harper & Row, Publishers, 1960); Bultmann, *Theology of the NT*; Hans Conzelmann, *An Outline of the Theology of the New Testament* (New York: Harper & Row); Richard N. Longenecker and Merrill C. Tenney, eds., *New Dimensions in New Testament Study* (Grand Rapids: Zondervan Pub. House, 1974); Harvey K. McArthur, "A Survey of Recent Gospel Research," in Marty and Peerman, *New Theology,* 2, 209; *IB,* 7, 12.

[12]Robinson, "The Formal Structure of Jesus' Message," in Klassen and Snyder, *Current Issues of NT Interpretation,* 98.

[13]Joachim Jeremias regards this expression as "new and unusual," distinctive with Jesus, comparable with the prophetic messenger formula in claiming authority; he attributes significance also to the fact that *Amen* is an Aramaic word, remembered in the tradition in the language Jesus spoke, even when the rest of the saying had been translated into Greek. See Jeremias, *New Testament Theology: The Proclamation of Jesus* (New York: Charles Scribner's Sons, 1971), 35–36. The Jesus Seminar, however, evidently regards the formula as carrying little weight in determining authenticity; its members give a "red" rating to none of the sayings in which it is used.

[14]In applying this test, the material common to Matthew, Mark, and Luke is considered as only one source.

[15]See especially the major commentaries. Cf. Bultmann, *History of the Synoptic Tradition;* Jeremias, *NT Theology; IDB.*

[16]Consult the publications of the Jesus Seminar: Robert W. Funk with Mahlon H. Smith, *The Gospel of Mark: Red Letter Edition* (Sonoma, Ca.: Polebridge Press, 1991); Robert W. Funk, Roy W. Hoover, and the Jesus Seminar, *The Five Gospels: The Search for the Authentic Words of Jesus,* New Translation and Commentary (New York: Macmillan 1993). Note the Introduction to *The Five Gospels,* especially 16–36. A useful compilation of much ancient testimony is Robert J. Miller, ed., *The Complete*

Gospels: Annotated Scholars Version (Sonoma, Ca.: Polebridge Press, 1992); this publication of the Jesus Seminar was printed without color-coding.

[17]Recall the comment in note 2 of this chapter.

Chapter 8: The Good News Preached by Jesus

[1]See A. T. Olmstead, *Jesus in the Light of History* (New York: Charles Scribner's Sons, 1942), chap. 5, "Preaching the Kingdom."

[2]See Norman Perrin, *The Kingdom of God in the Teaching of Jesus* (London: SCM Press, 1963), chap. 10; Bornkamm, Jesus of Nazareth, chap. 4; Bultmann, *The Theology of the New Testament,* 1, 3–11; Amos N. Wilder, *New Testament Faith for Today* (New York: Harper & Brothers, 1955), chap. 3; "Kingdom of God," *IDB* and *IDB–S*; "God's Imperial Rule, Present or Future?" in Funk and Hoover, *The Five Gospels,* 136–37. For an analysis of key terms associated with the kingdom see Crossan, *The Historical Jesus,* chap. 12, "Kingdom and Wisdom." For reflections by an effective Latin American evangelist and theologian, see Mortimer Arias, *Announcing the Reign of God: Evangelization and the Subversive Memory of Jesus* (Philadelphia: Fortress Press, 1984).

Additional works consulted: William Barclay, *A New Testament Wordbook;* Bultmann, *History of the Synoptic Tradition;* Martin Dibelius, *The Message of Jesus Christ* (New York: Charles Scribner's Sons, 1939); Jeremias, *New Testament Theology;* Kittel; Michael Philibert, *Christ's Preaching–and Ours* (London: Edinburgh House Press, 1963); James M. Robinson, *A New Quest of the Historical Jesus* (Naperville, Ill.: Alec Allenson, 1959); *IB,* 8.

[3]See Bultmann, *Theology of the NT,* 1, 11–22; Joachim Jeremias, *The Parables of Jesus,* rev. ed. (New York: Charles Scribner's Sons, 1963), chap. 3, "The Message of the Parables of Jesus," 115–146; Marcus Borg, *Jesus in Contemporary Scholarship* (Valley Forge, Pa.: Trinity Press International, 1994), chaps. 3–5; Borg, *Meeting Jesus Again for the First Time: The Historical Jesus and the Heart of Contemporary Faith* (HarperSanFrancisco, 1994), chap. 3.

Additional works consulted: William A. Beardslee, "Uses of the Proverb in the Synoptic Gospels," *Interpretation,* 24, 1 (Jan. 1970), 61–73; John Bright, *The Kingdom of God* (Nashville: Abingdon-Cokesbury Press, 1953); Bultmann, *History of the Synoptic Tradition;* Jeremias, *NT Theology;* Perrin; IB, 7.

[4]Don Browning, *The Moral Context of Pastoral Care* (Philadelphia: Westminster, 1986), 49.

[5]T. J. Bab. K., viii, g. 10, line 24, 6c.

[6]Marcus Borg, *Meeting Jesus Again for the First Time,* 46–58.

[7]See Bornkamm, Appendix 3; Bultmann, *Theology of the NT,* 26–32. Works consulted: C. K. Barrett, *Jesus and the Gospel Tradition* (Philadelphia: Fortress Press, 1968); Hans Werner Bartsch, ed., *Kerygma and Myth: A Theological Debate* (London: S. P. C. K., 1957); Conzelmann, *An Outline of the Theology of the New Testament;* C. H. Dodd, *The Interpretation of the Fourth Gospel;* IDB; Heinz Zahrnt, *The Historical Jesus* (New York: Harper & Row, 1963).

[8]This observation I owe to M. Eugene Boring.

[9]Note, however, the qualification entered by Funk and Hoover, *The Five Gospels,* 178, on the decision of the Jesus Seminar to give this saying a black rating. They note that it parallels the beatitudes found in the Sermon on the Mount, that it acknowledges the prevailing opinion that his behavior was scandalous, and that "it has a ring of authenticity about it for those reasons."

[10]Jeremias, *Unknown Sayings,* 77.

[11]Funk and Hoover, *The Five Gospels.*

[12]See *An Inclusive Language Lectionary: Readings for Year A.* Prepared for experimental and voluntary use in churches by the Inclusive Language Lectionary Committee appointed by the Division of Education and Ministry, National Council of the Churches of Christ in the USA. (Published for the Cooperative Publication Association by John Knox Press, Atlanta; The Pilgrim Press, New York; The Westminster Press, Philadelphia, 1983). Appendix: "In this lectionary the formal equivalent of 'the Son of Man' is 'the Human One.'"

[13]The tendency of modern scholars, schooled in the scientific worldview, to "humanize" and "de-theologize" the words of Jesus in the gospels concerning himself may also lead to "re-theologizing" on their part, casting them in terms that conform with the current mindset. The early transmitters of the gospel tradition were not alone in shaping it according to their understanding. At the very least in his preaching concerning God's kingdom Jesus saw himself as its decisive messenger.

Chapter 9: The Rhetoric of Jesus

[1]See Amos N. Wilder, *The Language of the Gospel: Early Christian Rhetoric* (New York: Harper & Row, 1964). Cf. Kennedy, *Classical Rhetoric and Its Christian and Secular Tradition from Ancient to Modern Times,* 126–29; Huston Smith, *The World's Religions* (HarperSanFrancisco, 1991), 324–28, "Never Spoke Man Thus."

[2]See David E. Aune, *Prophecy in Early Christianity and the Ancient Mediterranean World* (Grand Rapids, Mich.: William B. Eerdmans, 1983), 6, 7; A. S. Herbert, "The 'Parable' (Masal) in the Old Testament," *Scottish Journal of Theology,* 7 (1954), 180–96.

Additional works consulted: Bornkamm; Bultmann, *History of the Synoptic Tradition, Theology of the NT;* Jeremias, *NT Theology;* Perrin; Helmut Thielicke, *The Silence of God* (Grand Rapids Mich.: Eerdmans, 1962).

[3]Works consulted: Bultmann, *History of the Synoptic Tradition, Theology of the NT;* Jeremias, *NT Theology;* Thielicke; *IB,* 4, 7, 8.

[4]See Bornkamm, 96–100; A. T. Olmstead, *Jesus in the Light of History* (New York: Charles Scribner's Sons, 1942), 11–21, 113–28, 170–77.

Additional works consulted: William A. Beardslee, "Uses of Proverb in the Synoptic Gospels," *Interpretation,* 34:1 (Jan. 1970), 61–73; Bultmann, *Theology of the NT;* Jeremias, *NT Theology;* Shailer Mathews, *New Testament Times in Palestine, 175 B.C.–A.D. 135,* new and revised edition (New York: The Macmillan Company, 1933); Elwyn E. Tilden, Jr., "The Study of Jesus' Interpretive Methods," *Interpretation,* 7:1 (Jan. 1953), 45–61; *IB,* 1, 7, 8.

[5]Bornkamm, 119.

[6]For suggestions regarding literature circulating in Galilee in the time of Jesus and use he made of themes from it, see A. T. Olmstead, *Jesus in the Light of History* (New York: Charles Scribner's Sons, 1942), passim.

[7]See also the remarks on Jesus' exegesis in chap. 8, "The Preacher as Scandal."

[8]Consider Mk. 12:1–8 (JS–g) as developing a story from the well-known image of Isa. 5:1–7, or Lk. 4:8–11 (JS–b, g) as turning the admonition of Prov. 25:6–7 into a humorous tale.

[9]Codex Bezae adds this passage after Lk. 6:4. See *IB,* 8:21.

[10]See Amos N. Wilder, *The Language of the Gospel: Early Christian Rhetoric* (New York: Harper & Row, 1964); Charles Fox Burney, *The Poetry of Our Lord: An Examination of the Formal Elements of Hebrew Poetry in the Discourses of Jesus Christ* (Oxford: At the Clarendon Press, 1925).

Additional works consulted: Beardslee; Bornkamm; Bultmann, *History of the Synoptic Tradition, Theology of the NT;* Jeremias; Robinson; *IB,* 7, 8.

[11]Jeremias, *NT Theology,* 15–16.

[12]Ibid., 27; cf. 20 ff.

[13]Ibid., 27–29.

[14]The first watch renders Greek *agrypneò;* all the others translate *gregoreo* or its cognates. In Aramaic would there have been one word, as in English?

[15]"While the Fellows designated the precise words ascribed to Jesus black, they held open the possibility that the naming of Peter may have had its origin with Jesus." (Funk and Hoover, *The Five Gospels,* 403.)

[16]For reflection on the theological implications of Jesus' use of hyperbole, see Stephen H. Webb, "Theology and the Rhetoric of Excess (Toward a Christian Hyperbolic Imagination)" *Theology Today,* 50:1 (April 1993), 56; reprinted in *Biblical Literacy Today,* 8:3 (Spring, 1994), 4–6.

[17]See D. Elton Trueblood, *The Humor of Christ* (HarperSanFrancisco, 1975).

[18]Ernest Fremont Tittle, *A Book of Pastoral Prayers with an Essay on The Pastoral Prayer* (Nashville: Abingdon-Cokesbury Press, 1951), 22.

[19]Wilder, 22.

[20]Dibelius, 21.

[21]For a noted preacher's reflections see Charles Edward Jefferson, *The Character of Jesus* (New York: T. Y. Crowell and Company, 1908), chap. 8, "His Originality."

Additional works consulted: Achtemeier; Donald M. Baillie, *God Was in Christ* (New York: Charles Scribner's Sons, 1948); Thomas G. Bergin, Dante (New York: The Orion Press, 1965); Bultmann, *Theology of the NT;* Mircea Eliade, *Patterns in Comparative Religion* (Magnolia: Peter Smith, 1987); Northrop Frye, *Anatomy of Criticism* (Princeton: Princeton University Press, 1957); Jeremias, *NT Theology; The Parables of Jesus* (New York: Charles Scribner's Sons, 1963); Amos N. Wilder, *Grace Confounding* (Philadelphia: Fortress Press, 1974); *IB,* 7, 8.

[22]See Jeremias, *NT Theology,* 30.

[23]Bornkamm, 69.

[24]Alfred North Whitehead, *Religion in the Making* (Cleveland: The World Publishing Co., 1960), 56–57.

[25]René Wellek and Austin Warren, *Theory of Literature* (New York: Harcourt, Brace 1949), 77.

[26]This phrase illuminating the insight and creativity of Jesus comes from a letter of Edward Scribner Ames written in 1923. See "Spiritual," in his *Prayers and Meditations,* ed. Van Meter Ames (Chicago: The Disciples Divinity House of the University of Chicago, 1970), 93.

[27]James M. Robinson, "Jesus' Parables as God Happening," in F. Thomas Trotter, ed., *Jesus and the Historian* (Philadelphia: The Westminster Press, 1968), 147.

[28]George A. Buttrick, *IB,* 8, 266.

[29]Works consulted: Bultmann, *History of the Synoptic Tradition, Theology of the NT;* Jeremias, *NT Theology;* Perrin; *IB,* 7, 8.

[30]See Kennedy, *Classical Rhetoric,* 123–30.

[31]Works consulted: Jeremias, *NT Theology; IB,* 7, 8.

Conclusion to Part Three

[1]Donald M. Baillie, *Out of Nazareth* (New York: Charles Scribner's Sons, 1958), 99.

PART FOUR. WITNESSES OF JESUS CHRIST
Introduction to Part Four

[1] The historical overview assumed in Part Four derives from the canonical books of the New Testament read with perceptions shaped by the prevailing critical scholarship of the later 20th century. For a much more skeptical (and often hypothetical) view of developments see Burton L. Mack, *A Myth of Innocence: Mark and Christian Origins* (Philadelphia; Fortress Press, 1988); *The Lost Gospel: the Book of Q and Christian Origins* (HarperSanFrancisco, 1993), and *Who Wrote the New Testament? The Making of the Christian Myth* (HarperSanFrancisco, 1995); for rejoinder see Luke Timothy Johnson, *The Real Jesus: The Misguided Quest for the Historical Jesus and the Truth of the Traditional Gospels* (HarperSanFrancisco, 1996).

Chapter 10: Servants of the Word

[1] See Martin Dibelius, *From Tradition to Gospel* (New York: Charles Scribner's Sons, n. d.), chap. 2, "Sermons"; Amos Wilder, *The Language of the Gospel,* chap. 4, "The Story." See also, regarding this entire chapter, Joseph A. Fitzmyer, S.J., "Preaching in the Apostolic and Subapostolic Age," in David G. Hunter, ed., *Preaching in the Patristic Age: Studies in Honor of Walter J. Burghardt, S.J.* (New York: Paulist Press, 1989).

Additional works consulted: Bornkamm, *Jesus;* Raymond E. Brown, *The Community of the Beloved Disciple* (New York: Paulist Press, 1979); Burton Scott Easton, *The Gospel before the Gospels* (New York: Charles Scribner's Sons, 1928); Haenchen, *The Acts of the Apostles* (Philadelphia: Westminster, 1971); Jeremias, *New Testament Theology* (New York: Charles Scribner's Sons, 1971); Norman Perrin, *The Resurrection according to Matthew, Mark, and Luke* (Philadelphia: Fortress Press, 1977); Ruether and McLaughlin, *Women of Spirit;* H. R. Weber, *The Communication of the Gospel to Illiterates, Based on a Missionary Experience in Indonesia* (London: SCM Press, 1957); *IB,* 7, 8, 9, 11.

[2] The study of this process of transmission and shaping is aptly known as form-criticism (*Formgeschichte*), an approach that flourished in NT scholarship in mid-20th century. Though scholars have moved on to other approaches, they continue to work with the perception that the process of oral transmission gave shape to many passages, revealing the life and concerns of the earliest Christian communities.

[3] See Burton L. Mack and Vernon K. Robbins, *Patterns of Persuasion in the Gospels* (Sonoma, Ca.: Polebridge Press, 1989).

[4] Jn. 4:28–42; 20:17–18; cf. Mt. 28:7–10; Lk. 24:5–11.

[5] I Clement 13.2 (LCC I, 49).

[6] See David E. Aune, *Prophecy in Early Christianity and the Ancient Mediterranean World* (Grand Rapids: William B. Eerdmans, 1983), chaps. 8–10.

[7] Recall such prophets, e.g., as Agabus and the daughters of Philip in Acts.

[8] But Antoinette Clark Wire maintains that the Corinthian correspondence was an effort by the apostle Paul to put an end to the prophetic exuberance of women in the church. See *The Corinthian Women Prophets: A Reconstruction through Paul's Rhetoric* (Minneapolis: Fortress Press, 1990).

[9] Eugene Boring, *The Continuing Voice of Jesus: Christian Prophecy and the Gospel Tradition* (Louisville: Westminster/John Knox Press, 1991).

[10] Rev. 16:6; 18:20, 24; 22:6, 9.

[11] 1 Cor. 12:29; Eph. 2:20, 3:5, 4:11; Acts 13:1.

[12] E.g., 1 Thess. 3:12–13; 4:1, 10–12, 5:14; 2 Thess. 3:12–13; Heb. 13:1–6.

[13] See Abraham J. Malherbe, *Paul and the Popular Philosophers* (Minneapolis: Fortress Press, 1989).

[14]See Ronald E. Osborn, *In Christ's Place: Christian Ministry in Today's World* (St. Louis, Missouri: The Bethany Press, 1967), Appendix I, "Ministries in the New Testament."

Works consulted: Vernon H. Neufeld, *The Earliest Christian Confessions* (Grand Rapids, Mich.: Wm. B. Eerdmans, 1963); H. Richard Niebuhr and Daniel D. Williams, eds., *The Ministry in Historical Perspectives* (New York: Harper & Brothers, 1956); Leonard and Arlene Swidler, eds., *Women Priests: A Catholic Commentary on the Vatican Declaration* (New York: Paulist Press, 1977); papers by Fiorenza, Brooten, Boucher, Collins, Getty, Ford, D'Angelo, Schneiders, and Ruether; *IB*, 7, 9.

[15]"Apostle," *Encyclopedia of Early Christianity*, 72–73.

[16]Gal. 2:1, 9, 13; 1 Cor. 9:6.

[17]Gal. 2:1, 3; 2 Cor. 2:13; 7:6, 13–15; 8:6, 16–17, 23; 12:18.

[18]1 Thess. 1:1, 3:1–2, 6; 1 Cor. 16:10; 2 Cor. 1:1, 19; Philem. 1:1; Phil. 1:1, 2:19–24.

[19]Works consulted: William Baird, "What is the Kerygma?" *JBL*, 76, 3 (1957), 181–91; H. V. Morton, *In the Steps of St. Paul* (London: Rich & Cowan, 1936).

[20]See 1 Thess. 2:14–3:10.

Chapter 11: "Power of God for Salvation"

[1]See Günther Bornkamm, *Paul* (New York: Harper & Row, 1971), Part 2, chap. 1, "Paul and the Gospel of the Primitive Church."

Additional works consulted: Baird, "What is the Kerygma?"; Hans Dieter Betz, *Galatians* (Philadelphia: Fortress, 1979); Hans Conzelman, *1 Corinthians* (Philadelphia: Fortress Press, 1975); C. H. Dodd, *The Apostolic Preaching and Its Developments* (New York: Harper & Brothers, 1936); Gerhard Kittel and Gerhard Friedrich, *Theological Dictionary of the New Testament*, trans. and abridged by Geoffrey W. Bromiley (Grand Rapids: William B. Eerdmans, 1985); Krister Stendahl, "Paul and the Introspective Conscience of the West," *Harvard Theological Review*, 56 (1963), 199–215; Amos Wilder, *New Testament Faith for Today* (New York: Harper and Brothers, 1955); Robert C. Worley, *Preaching and Teaching in the Earliest Church* (Philadelphia: Westminster Press, 1967).

[2]During the dominance of the so-called "biblical theology" in Christian scholarly circles in mid-20th century, this distinction was repeatedly alleged; for the classic statement of this case, see C. H. Dodd, *The Apostolic Preaching and Its Developments* (New York: Harper & Brothers, 1936).

[3]Cf. Mk. 13:33–37; Lk. 12:35–40; 16:8; Jn. 16:21–22.

[4]See Malherbe, *Paul and the Popular Philosophers*, 50–56.

[5]It is a simple matter to sketch through 1 and 2 Thessalonians, holding the text against the "outline" of the *kerygma* "recovered from the Pauline epistles" by C. H. Dodd in *The Apostolic Preaching*, 17.

[6]For a discussion of this passage, see chap. 13.

[7]See C. K. Barrett, "The Bible in the New Testament Period," in D. E. Nineham, ed., *The Church's Use of the Bible* (London: S. P. C. K., 1963), 1–24; Marion L. Soards, *The Speeches in Acts* (Louisville: Westminster/John Knox Press, 1994); Harry Austryn Wolfson, *The Philosophy of the Church Fathers* (Cambridge: Harvard University Press, 1956), Vol. 1, chap. 2, part 1, "Background of Paul's Allegorical Interpretation."

Additional works consulted: F. F. Bruce, *Acts of the Apostles* (Grand Rapids: William B. Eerdmans, 1953); William R. Arnold, *Ephod and Ark* (Cambridge: Harvard University Press, 1917); Hans Conzelman, *1 Corinthians;* Oscar Cullmann, *Early Christian Worship* (London: SCM Press, 1953); Haenchen, *The Acts of the Apostles; IDB;* Perrin, *The Resurrection;* Calvin L. Porter, "A New Paradigm for Reading Romans: Dialogue between Christians and Jews," *Encounter*, 39 (Summer, 1978); Claus

Westermann, "The Way of the Promise through the Old Testament," in Bernhard W. Anderson, ed., *The Old Testament and the Christian Faith* (New York: Harper & Row, 1963); Edmund Wilson, "The Dead Sea Scrolls," *The New Yorker,* March 29, 1969: 66–67; *IB,* 1, 7, 8.

[8]Le Déaut, "Apropos a Definition of Midrash," *Interpretation,* 25:3 (July 1971), 275, quoting Renée Bloch.

[9]For a careful consideration of issues barely suggested here see Clark M. Williamson, *A Guest in the House of Israel: Post-Holocaust Church Theology* (Louisville, Ky.: Westminster/John Knox Press, 1993).

[10]For a detailed exploration of the intricate issues here intimated see Mack, *The Lost Gospel: The Book of Q and Christian Origins* and *Who Wrote the New Testament? The Making of the Christian Myth* (San Francisco: HarperSanFrancisco, 1993).

[11]S. E. Johnson, "Lord (Christ)," *IDB,* III, 151.

[12]See Cullmann, *Early Christian Worship,* 7–36, "Basic Characteristics of the Early Christian Service of Worship." For an argument downplaying the delay of the parousia as a "problem" for the early church, see Marcus Borg, *Jesus in Contemporary Scholarship,* chaps. 3 and 4.

Additional works consulted: Bultmann, *Theology of the New Testament;* Fred B. Craddock, "The Gift of the Holy Spirit and the Nature of Man," *Encounter,* 35:1 (Winter, 1974); *IB,* 8.

[13]NRSV translates the phrase in Heb. 1:2 as "in these last days," REB as "in this the final age." In some commentator years ago I may have read it rendered as "at the climax of history," but can find it now in none of the versions or translations on my shelves. Perhaps I heard it from a preacher. Or was it my own stab at translation?

[14]See F. W. Beare, "New Testament Christianity and the Hellenistic World," in Austin Farrer et al., *The Communication of the Gospel in the New Testament Times* (London: S. P. C. K., 1961), 57–73.

Additional works consulted: William Barclay, *The New Testament: A New Translation* [with notes], 2 vols. (New York: Collins, 1969), 2, 284–85; Henry J. Cadbury, "Some Foibles of NT Scholarship," *JBL,* 22 (July 1958), 216; C. H. Dodd, *History and the Gospel* (New York: Charles Scribner's Sons, 1948); *IB,* 7:532.

[15]For suggestive, though brief, comments on the NT period, see the opening pages of Werner Jaeger, *Early Christianity and Greek Paideia* (Cambridge: The Belknap Press of Harvard University Press, 1961).

[16]The development of an ordered ministry with a primary responsibility for preaching, assumed here, is too large a theme to be developed in this study. See Bernard Cooke, *Ministry to Word and Sacraments: History and Theology* (Philadelphia: Fortress Press, 1976), chap. 8, "Ministry of the Word in the New Testament." Cf. Ronald E. Osborn, *In Christ's Place: Christian Ministry in Today's World* (St. Louis: The Bethany Press, 1967), especially Appendix I, g 2, "The Ministry of the Word," 262–64. (To the offices there listed add *katangeleus* = preacher, proclaimer, propagandist, as in Acts 17:18.)

[17]See also Rom. 1:15; 2:21; Gal. 1:8–9; 2 Cor. 11:4; 1 Tim. 5:17.

Chapter 12: First-Century Sermons and Homilies

[1]See standard commentaries and introductions to the New Testament.

Additional works consulted: Baird, *The Corinthian Church;* Baird, *Paul's Message and Mission;* F. F. Bruce, *Acts of the Apostles;* Henry J. Cadbury, *The Making of Luke–Acts* (New York: The Macmillan Company, 1927); Bertil Gärtner, *The Areopagus Speech and Natural Revelation* (Uppsala: Almqvist & Wiksells, 1955); Frederick C. Grant, *Form Criticism* (Chicago: Willett, Clark & Company, 1934); Haenchen, *The Acts of the Apostles;* Werner Jaeger, *Humanism and Theology* (Milwaukee: Marquette

University Press, 1943); John Knox, *The Church and the Reality of Christ* (New York: Harper & Row, 1962); James Pong, "Paul Preaches at Athens," *Theology and Church,* 12, 2 (Jan. 1976), 1–10; *IB,* 8, 9.

[2]For the thesis that this sermon (Lk. 4:16–30) with its three components—the liturgical, the exegetical, and the prophetic—is "the key to the history of Christian preaching through the ages" see Brilioth, *A Brief History of Preaching,* 11.

[3]Bruce, *Acts of the Apostles,* 5.

[4]See C. H. Dodd, *The Interpretation of the Fourth Gospel* (Cambridge: At the University Press, 1958)

Additional works consulted: Bornkamm, *Jesus;* Conzelmann, *An Outline of the Theology of the New Testament;* Fred Craddock, *The Gospels* (Nashville: Abingdon Press, 1981); *IDB;* Jeremias, *New Testament Theology;* Eduard Schweizer, "Orthodox Proclamation: The Reinterpretation of the Gospel of the Fourth Evangelist," *Interpretation,* 8, 4 (Oct. 1954), 388–403. *IB,* 7.

[5]For an analysis of these discourses, see Dodd, *The Interpretation of the Fourth Gospel,* 303 ff.

[6]Works consulted: *IDB;* John Wood, "A New Testament Pattern for Preachers," *The Evangelical Quarterly,* 47:4 (Oct.–Dec. 1975), 214–18; *IB,* 7; Allen Cabaniss, "A Note on Jacob's Homily," *The Evangelical Quarterly,* 47:4 (Oct.–Dec. 1975), 219.

[7]F. C. Grant, "Rhetoric and Oratory," *IDB,* IV, 75–77.

[8]E.g., the late Frank Hamilton Marshall, longtime Dean of the College of the Bible (now Phillips Theological Seminary) of Phillips University, Enid, Oklahoma.

Chapter 13: The Preaching of the First-Century Church

[1]See Bo Reicke, "A Synopsis of Early Christian Preaching," in Anton Fridrichsen, ed., *The Root of the Vine* (London: The Dacre Press, 1963); Bruce M. Metzger, "The Language of the New Testament," *IB,* 7, 43–50.

Additional works consulted: I Clement; Conzelman, *1 Corinthians;* Curtius, *European Literature in the Latin Middle Ages;* Gaster, *The Dead Sea Scriptures; IDB;* Charles H. Lohr, "Oral Techniques in the Gospel of Matthew," *The Catholic Biblical Quarterly,* 23 (1961), 403–35; Calvin L. Porter, "Images of Salvation in the New Testament," *Encounter,* 35:2 (Spring, 1974); George Saintsbury, *A History of Criticism and Literary Taste in Europe* (New York: Dodd, Mead, and Co., 1900); Paul Tillich, *Systematic Theology,* 3 vols. (Chicago: The University of Chicago Press, 1951–1963); Willoughby, *Pagan Regeneration; IB,* 7, 10, 11.

[2]See Richard B. Hays, *Echoes of Scripture in the Letters of Paul* (New Haven: Yale University Press, 1989).

[3]Wilder, *The Language of the Gospel,* 64.

[4]2 Cor. 10:10; cf. 1 Cor. 1:12.

[5]See Kennedy, *Classical Rhetoric and Its Christian and Secular Tradition,* 129–32.

[6]REB renders this line to read "without recourse to the skills of rhetoric," a translation which adopts the position I am here undertaking to refute.

[7]Substituting the literal rendition of *tou kerygmatos* in 1:21 for "our proclamation" [NRSV] or "the gospel" [REB]. In the NT *kerygma* denotes *both* the action of preaching and its content, as does the rendition I have chosen, whereas the two versions noted here call attention only to the latter. For the reading used here, see ASV.

[8]For the translation, see Conzelman, *1 Corinthians.*

[9]Augustine, *De doctrina christiana,* IV. vii. 11.

[10]E.g., Rom. 5:3–5; 6:23; 1 Cor. 14:20; 2 Cor. 4:11–12.

[11]See, for fundamental reflection on the task (though only implicit reference to proclamation in the apostolic church), David M. Greenhaw, "Theology of Preaching," and P. Mark Achtemeier, "Word of God," in William H. Willimon and Richard Lischer, eds., *Concise Encyclopedia of Preaching* (Louisville: Westminster John Knox Press, 1995).

Additional works consulted: D. M. Baillie, *God Was in Christ;* John Baillie, *Invitation to Pilgrimage* (New York: Charles Scribner's Sons, 1942); Bartsch, *Kerygma and Myth;* Bultmann, *Theology of the New Testament;* Albert C. Outler, *The Christian Tradition and the Unity We Seek.*

[12]Heb. 1:1; 1 Pet. 3:19; 4:6; also the many references in the gospels.

Conclusion to Part Four

[1]Kennedy, *Classical Rhetoric and Its Christian and Secular Tradition,* 122–29.

[2]See Erich Auerbach, *Mimesis: The Representation of Reality in Western Literature* (Princeton, N.J.: Princeton University Press, 1953), chap. 2, "Fortunata."

[3]For observations on this point, see Kennedy, *Classical Rhetoric and Its Christian and Secular Tradition,* 127–32.

PART FIVE. ADVOCATES OF AN ILLICIT FAITH

Chapter 14: Witnesses in a Hostile World

[1]See Hadas, *A History of Greek Literature,* chap. 17, "Orators and Encyclopedists of the Second Sophistic"; Pierre de Labriolle, *History and Literature of Christianity from Tertullian to Boethius,* trans. Herbert Wilson (New York: Alfred A. Knopf, 1925), Intro., "Latin Christian Literature and the Old Learning."

Additional works consulted: Baker, *The Dignity of Man;* Baldwin, *Medieval Rhetoric and Poetic;* Curtius, *European Literature in the Latin Middle Ages;* Dodd, *History and the Gospel;* E. R. Dodds, *Pagan and Christian in an Age of Anxiety;* Henry A. Fischel, *Rabbinic Literature and Greco-Roman Philosophy;* Gager, *Kingdom and Community;* Alfred Ernest Garvie, *The Christian Preacher;* Hadas, *Latin Literature;* J. W. Mackail, *Latin Literature;* James J. Murphy, *A Synoptic History of Classical Rhetoric;* Starr, *Civilization and the Caesars;* Teuffel, *A History of Roman Literature,* 2; Tillich, *A History of Christian Thought; IB,* 8, 453; *WDCH.*

[2]For a sample of his style see Mackail, *Latin Literature,* 237–38.

[3]For reflection on the spirit of the times, see Carlin A. Barton, *The Sorrows of the Ancient Romans: The Gladiator and the Monster* (Princeton University Press, 1993).

[4]See Robin Lane Fox, *Pagans and Christians* (San Francisco: Harper & Row, 1986), Part One. For psychological insights into the mood of the time, see E. R. Dodds, *Pagan and Christian in an Age of Anxiety: Some Aspects of Religious Experience from Marcus Aurelius to Constantine* (Cambridge University Press, 1964).

[5]"Zostrianos," in James M. Robinson, gen. ed., *The Nag Hammadi Library in English,* trans. by members of the Coptic Gnostic Library Project of the Institute for Antiquity and Christianity (San Francisco: Harper & Row, 1977), 393. Hereafter designated as *Nag Hammadi (NH).*

[6]See "Christian Self-Definition in the *Adversus Judaeos* Preachers in the Second Century," in Overman and MacLennan, *Diaspora Jews and Judaism,* 209–24. Cf. Clark M. Williamson, "The 'Adversus Judaeos' Tradition in Christian Theology," *Encounter,* 39:3 (Summer, 1978), 273 ff.

[7]See John Lawson, *A Theological and Historical Introduction to the Apostolic Fathers* (New York: The Macmillan Company, 1961).

[8]Tacitus, *Annals,* xv. 44. [*IDB,* "Persecution," III, 735–37].

[9]Pliny the Younger, "Letter to the Emperor Trajan," in Colman J. Berry, ed., *Readings in Church History,* 3 vols. (Westminster, Md.: The Newman Press, 1960), 1, 76.

[10]Lucian, "Pelegrinus and the Christians," in Cunliffe and Showerman, *Century Readings in Ancient Classical and Modern European Literature,* 302.

[11]See Aune, *Prophecy in Early Christianity and the Ancient Mediterranean World,* chaps. 11, 1.

[12]Ign. Eph. i. 2., LCL, *Ap F,* I, 175.

[13]Cf. Ign. Smyrn. IV. 2, *Ap F,* I, 257.

[14]Ibid., XIX, 1, LCL II, 337.

[15]See Perpetua, *"The Martyrdom of Perpetua (203)",* an account of her imprisonment and trial recorded by the young mother and finished by another writer, chap. 3 in Amy Oden, ed., *In Her Words: Women's Writings in the History of Christian Thought* (Nashville: Abingdon Press, 1994); Prudentius, "Hymn in Honor of the Most Holy Martyr Eulalia," from *The Poems of Prudentius,* trans. Sister M. Clement Eagan, C.C.V.I., FC 43:128–37. For the place of women in the church of the second and third centuries, with implications for the scarcity of vestiges of their preaching, see KarenJo Torjesen, *When Women Were Priests: Women's Leadership in the Early Church and the Scandal of Their Subordination in the Rise of Christianity* (HarperSanFrancisco, 1993), especially chaps. 1, 4, 6.

[16]Paul Scott Wilson, *A Concise History of Preaching* (Nashville: Abingdon Press, 1992), 33. Tourists driving down the Oregon Coast, halfway between Newport and Florence pass over Cape Perpetua, named by Captain Cook himself when he sighted it on March 7, 1778, which his prayerbook told him was St. Perpetua's Day.

[17]In this earliest account of her martyrdom, the poet has doubtless exercised some freedom in his rendition of her proclamation. Maximian, ruler of the West as Diocletian's associate, joined with the latter in persecuting the Christians.

[18]See "The Ten Martyrs—from the Talmud and the Midrash" in Glatzer, *The Judaic Tradition,* 175–83.

[19]E.g., Acts 6:8–7:60; "The Second Apocalypse of James" (V, 4) in *Nag Hammadi,* 249–255. See also Eusebius's account of the martyr Apollonius, executed during the reign of Commodus (180–93), who at the urging of the judge to defend himself before the Senate "presented…a most eloquent defense of the faith for which he was being a martyr" (*Ecc. Hist.,* 5, 21, FC 19:331).

[20]*The Poems of Prudentius,* trans. Sister M. Clement Eagan, C.C.V.I. (1962), FC 43:273.

Chapter 15: "The Defense of the Gospel"

[1]See The Epistle to Diognetus, in *The Apostolic Fathers* with an English translation by Kirsopp Lake, Vol. 2, Loeb Classical Library (Cambridge, Mass.: Harvard University Press, 1913), 350–79; cf. The so-called Letter to Diognetus, ed. and trans. Eugene R. Fairweather, *Early Christian Fathers,* Library of Christian Classics, 1 (Philadelphia: The Westminster Press, 1943), 205–24; Helen B. Harris, *The Newly Recovered Apology of Aristides,* trans. J. Rendel Harris (London: Hodder & Stoughton, 1893), 2d ed.

[2]The masculine nouns and pronouns crowd this passage so thickly as to discourage the attempt to render it always in non-gender-specific language; in the second-century world the preacher's image of a king giving up his son would carry great emotional power in expressing God's love for humanity.

[3]Helen B. Harris, *The Newly Recovered Apology of Aristides: Its Doctrine and Ethics,* with extracts from the translation by Prof. J. Rendel Harris, 2d ed. (London: Hodder and Stoughton, 1893), 78–114.

[4]See Justin Martyr, *The First Apology, The Second Apology;* Athenagoras the Philosopher, *A Plea Regarding Christians,* LCC I; Pseudo-Justin, *The Discourse to the Greeks,* in *Writings of Saint Justin Martyr,* FC 6:425–36.

Additional works consulted: Berthold Altaner, *Patrology* (New York: Herder and Herder, 1961); A. C. Clark, "Ciceronianism," in G. S. Gordon, *English Literature and the the Classics;* Robert M. Grant, *After the New Testament:* ANF 1; FC; LCC I; *WDCH.*

[5]See Willis A. Shotwell, *The Biblical Exegesis of Justin Martyr* (London: SPCK, 1965).

[6]Justin, *Dial. Trypho,* 8, FC 6:160.

[7]Ibid., 50, FC 6:223.

[8]Eusebius Pamphyli, *Ecclesiastical History,* IV, 11, 15 (FC 19:226, 244).

[9]*The First Apology of Justin, the Martyr,* as translated in *Early Christian Fathers,* newly translated and edited by Cyril C. Richardson, in collaboration with Eugene R. Fairweather, Edward Rochie Hardy, and Massey Hamilton Shepherd, Jr. (Philadelphia: The Westminster Press, 1953), *The Library of Christian Classics,* Vol. 1, 242–89.

[10]See *Saint Justin Martyr,* trans. and ed. Thomas B. Falls (New York: Christian Heritage, 1948), The Second Apology, chaps. 7–13, (*The Fathers of the Church*), 126–34, the translation followed here. Cf. p. 38, note 3 for the comment by Falls on Justin's distinction between the seminal word and the Perfect Word. Cf. Barrett, *New Testament Backgrounds,* 183, for reflections on the *spermatikos logos.*

[11]*A Plea Regarding Christians by Athenagoras, the Athenian, a Philosopher and a Christian* in Richardson et al., *Early Christian Fathers,* LCC I, 300–340.

[12]Eusebius, *Ecclesiastical History,* Bk. IV, chap. 16, FC 19:242.

[13]*Discourse to the Greeks,* in Thomas B. Fall, *Writings of Saint Justin Martyr,* FC 425–36.

[14]Altaner, *Patrology,* 127.

[15]See *Writings of Saint Justin Martyr,* FC 439–55.

[16]See Tertullian, *Apology;* Minucius Felix, *Octavius;* de Labriolle, *History and Literature of Christianity,* Bk. 1, chap. 2, "Tertullian"; Bk. 2, chap. 1, "The *Octavius* of Minucius Felix."

[17]Altaner, *Patrology,* 167.

[18]*Tertullian, Apologetical Works; and Minucius Felix, Octavius,* trans. Rudolph Arbessmann, O.S.A., Sister Emily Joseph Daly, C.S.J., Edwin A. Quain, S.J. (New York: Fathers of the Church, 1950), FC, Vol. 10.

[19]The translator suggests the effect of Tertullian's *ad lenonem quam ad leonem.*

[20]Lactantius, *The Divine Institutes,* Books I–VII, trans. Sister Mary Frances McDonald, O. P. (Washington, D. C.: The Catholic University of America Press, 1964), FC, Vol. 49, translator's Introduction, 4, 5.

[21]For the change effected by the power of God, cf. Bk. VI, chap. 24.

[22]Lactantius, *The Divine Institutes,* chap. 27 (FC 49:537).

Chapter 16: Diverse Preaching and Apostolic Tradition

[1]See Irenaeus, "The Refutation and Overthrow of the Knowledge Falsely So Called" ("Against Heresies"), LCC I. Tertullian, "The Prescriptions against the Heretics," LCC, V.

Additional works consulted: Eusebius, *Ecclesiastical History;* Tertullian, "Against Praxeas,"ANF; Jean-Jacques von Allmen, *Preaching and Congregation;* Gager; Kenneth

Scott Latourette, *A History of the Expansion of Christianity*, I; Otto A. Piper, "A New Gospel?" *The Christian Century*, Jan. 27, 1960, 96–99; Swidler and Swidler, eds., *Women Priests* (papers by Osieck and Ruether); *WDCH.*

[2]See Gager, *Kingdom and Community*, 184.

[3]See Aune, *Prophecy in Early Christianity and the Ancient Mediterranean World*, chap. 11, Pt. 6, "The Montanist Oracles."

[4]Marcion, *Antitheses*, quoted by Percy W. Evans, *Some Lessons from Marcion* (Birmingham: Overdale College, Selly Oak, 1948), 5.

[5]Quoted by Louis Duchesne, *Early History of the Christian Church*, 198.

[6]See, e.g., Ross Shepard Kraemer, *Her Share of the Blessings*, chaps. 10–13. For a brief survey of women's place in the early Christian movement, see Pauline Schmitt Pantel, ed., *A History of Women in the West*, Vol. 1, *From Ancient Goddesses to Christian Saints*, trans. Arthur Goldhammer (Cambridge, Mass.: The Belknap Press of Harvard University Press), chap. 9, "Early Christian Women," especially 423–29.

[7]Quoted by Arthur Cushman McGiffert, *A History of Christian Thought*, 1, 168.
[8]Ibid.

[9]For a less sympathetic account of a woman who claimed the gift of prophecy and administered sacraments, see Saint Cyprian, *Letters*, trans. Sister Rose Bernard Donna, C.S.J., Fathers of the Church, Vol. 51, Letter 75 (10–11), Firmilian to Cyprian, 301–4.

[10]Kraemer, 8.

[11]Quoted by Eusebius, *EH,* 16, FC 19:318.

[12]For an account of the dominant position in the church excluding women from the public ministry, see Agnes Cunningham, S.S.C.M., "Women and Preaching in the Patristic Age," chap. 4 in David G. Hunter, ed., *Preaching in the Patristic Age.*

[13]See Robert M. Grant, ed., *Gnosticism: A Sourcebook of Heretical Writings from the Early Christian Period* (New York: Harper & Brothers, 1961); James M. Robinson, *Nag Hammadi.* Cf. The Gospel of Thomas, in Robert W. Funk and Roy W. Hoover, *The Five Gospels:The Search for the Authentic Words of Jesus* (New York: Macmillan, 1993).

[14]Cf. chap. 14, "The World of Late Antiquity." Homilies and treatises preoccupied with philosophy, all found in Robinson, *Nag Hammadi,* include "Authoritative Teaching" (VI, 3), "The Concept of Our Great Power" (VI, 4), "The Discourse on the Eighth and the Ninth" (VI, 6), "Zostrianos" (VIII, 1), and "Marsanes" (X, 1). Note "The Thunder, Perfect Mind," (VI, 2), a revelation-discourse by a female prophet, which is even more general, without distinctive Gnostic or Christian tenets.

[15]See the sayings indicated here by numbers in parentheses. (The number inside the parentheses denotes the page in Funk and Hoover, *The Five Gospels.*) Cf. Robert M. Grant with David Noel Freedman, eds., *The Secret Sayings of Jesus* (Garden City, New York: Doubleday & Company, 1960).

[16]E.g., in Robinson, *NH,* (8) 118; (9) 119; (21) 120; (63, 64) 125; (107) 129. Cf. Grant and Freedman.

[17]Robinson, *NH,* (87, 98) 128.

[18]"The Acts of Peter and the Twelve Apostles," VI 10, 4–13, 26–30, Robinson, *NH,* 269.

[19]"The Teachings of Silvanus," VII, 106–7, Robinson, *NH,* 356.

[20]"The Apocryphon of John" (II, 1), Robinson, 115–16.

[21]See, e.g., in Robinson, *NH,* "The Gospel of Truth" I 20, 23 –21, 2 (p. 39); 31, 4 ff. (p. 43); "The Gospel of Thomas" II 50, 23–28 (p. 129); "The Second Treatise of the Great Seth" VII 58, 22–33 (p. 333); "The Teaching of Silvanus" VII 103, 28–104, 15 (p. 355); "The Letter of Peter to Philip" VIII 136,17–137,4 (p. 396); 139, 16–140, 5 (p. 397); "The Interpretation of Knowledge" XI 13, 26 – 14,16 (p. 431); 14, 28 –15, 27 (p. 432).

[22]"The Gospel of Philip" II, 75, 3–14, Robinson, *NH,* 145.

[23]"The Thunder, Perfect Mind," VI 13, 1–6, 16–24; 14, 27–29; 21, 19–32, Robinson, *NH,* 271–72, 277.

[24]"The Apocryphon of John" II 15, 14, 30–36, Robinson, *NH,* 107.

[25]Ibid., 19, 3–8 (p. 109).

[26]"Marsanes" X 31, 23–26, Robinson, *NH,* 423. A comparable construct using the Roman alphabet would be *bacadafaga, becedefege,* etc. Cf. "The Gospel of the Egyptians" III 42, 12–15 (p. 196); 44, 1–10 (p. 197); "The Discourse on the Eighth and the Ninth" VII 56, 11–23 (p. 294); "Zostrianos" VII 127, *NH,* 1–6 (p. 392); "Trimorphic Protennoia" XIII 38, 28–30 (p. 464).

[27]"Marsanes" X 32, 1–6, Robinson, *NH,* 423.

[28]"The Gospel of Philip" II 79, 19–26, Robinson, *NH,* 147.

[29]Ign. Trall. vi. 2, LCL I, 219.

[30]Irenaeus, *Against Heresies,* III Pref. I.1, LCC I, 369–70. For reflections on their assumptions about the canon of scripture, see Gager, *Kingdom and Community,* 74–76.

[31]Celsus, *True Doctrine,* quoted in *Library of Christian Classics,* II, 24, General Introduction.

[32]Irenaeus, *Against Heresies,* I. 21. 1, LCC I, 364.

[33]Quasten, *Patrology,* 294; quoted in *WDCH,* 441.

[34]See Cook, *Ministry to Word and Sacraments,* chaps. 2, 9; de Labriolle, *History and Literature of Christianity,* Bk. 1, chap. 1, "The First Latin Versions of the Bible."

[35]*The Martyrdom of Saint Polycarp, Bishop of Smyrna,* 16. 2, LCC I, 155.

[36]Ign. Eph. iv. 1. In his magisterial study *The Shape of the Liturgy* (p. 40) Dom Gregory Dix asserts: "The delivery of the sermon was as much the bishop's 'special liturgy' and proper function at the synaxis as the offering of the eucharistic prayer was his 'special liturgy' at the eucharist." For evidence of preaching by presbyters, see Cooke, *Ministry to Word and Sacraments,* 235ff.

[37]Hippolytus, *Ap. Trad.* 10. 1, trans. Burton Scott Easton, *The Apostolic Tradition of Hippolytus* (Cambridge: Archon Books, 1962), 39, 81, 82.

[38]Ibid., 1. 3, p. 33.

[39]Burton Scott Easton, *The Apostolic Tradition of Hippolytus: Translated into English with Introduction and Notes.* (Cambridge: Archon Books, 1962). Cf. *Encyclopedia of Early Christianity,* art. "Hippolytus."

[40]Hippolytus, *Ap. Trad.,* II. 17, Easton, 43.

Chapter 17: Preaching within the Christian Community

[1]See Lewis Joseph Sherrill, *The Rise of Christian Education* (New York: The Macmillan Company, 1944), chap. 7, "Education in the Ancient Church."

Additional works consulted: "The Shepherd" of Hermas, *Ap F,* LCL II; Justin Martyr, *Dialogue with Trypho,* FC; Altaner; Edgar Charles Dargan, *A History of Preaching,* Vol. 1 (New York: George H. Doran Company, 1905); Henry C. Fish, *History and Repository of Pulpit Eloquence* ; Gager; Dorothy Irvin, "Archaeology Supports Women's Ordination," *The Witness,* 63:2 (Feb. 1980); Niebuhr and Williams; Walker, FC 10, 15, 36, 40; LCC V.

[2]Papias, *Interpretation of the Oracles of the Lord,* quoted in Eusebius, *EH,* 3:39, 4, FC 19:203. Cf. Clement of Alexandria, *Stromateis,* I. i, ANF 4:355.

[3]Justin Martyr, First Apol. 67, LCC I, 287.

[4]For illustration of artwork honoring philosophers and the appropriation of the theme to the work of preachers, see F. van der Meer and Christine Mohrmann, *Atlas of the Early Christian World,* trans. and ed. Mary F. Hedulund and H. H. Rowley (New York: Thomas Nelson and Sons, 1958), 40–45.

[5]Irenaeus, quoted by Eusebius, *Ecclesiastical History,* V. 20, FC 19:329.

[6]George H. Williams, "The Ministry of the Ante-Nicene Church (c. 125–325)," in Niebuhr and Williams, 36.

[7]Clement of Alexandria, *Paidog.* II. 4 (43). FC 23:132.

[8]Tertullian, "The Apparel of Women," II. 2, FC 40:145.

[9]See John Lawson, *A Theological and Historical Introduction to the Apostolic Fathers* (New York: The Macmillan Company, 1961).

[10]Recall the sermons, not all of them Gnostic, from the library at Nag Hammadi.

[11]Eusebius, *Ecclesiastical History,* IV. 21. 18, FC 19:252, 267.

[12]His works are listed in Eusebius, *Ecclesiastical History,* IV. 26, FC 19:262–263.

[13]Melito of Sardis, "On the Passover" 5, 8, from Richard C. White, *Melito of Sardis Sermon "On the Passover"* (Lexington, Ky.: Lexington Theological Seminary Library, 1976), 17–18.

[14]For a review by Massey Shepherd of the Homily on the Pascha of Pseudo–Hippolytus and its relation to Melito's homily, see *Church History,* 39 (1970), 541.

[15]See de Labriolle, *History and Literature of Christianity,* Bk. 1, chap. 2, "Tertullian"; Bk. 2, chap. 2, "Cyprian."

[16]Berthold Altaner, *Patrology,* trans. Hilda C. Graef, 2d ed. (New York: Herder and Herder, 1961), 226.

[17]See chapter 15, 355–57.

[18]Sister Emily Joseph Daly, C.S.J., translator of "Prayer," notes that in characterizing "the Son of God also [as] the Spirit of God," Tertullian "does so only to describe His essence, without intending to identify Him with the third Person who alone bears this name." IFC 40, 157, n. 1.

[19]Tertullian, *Apology,* 45 (1), FC 10:109; *"On the Soul,"* 2 (5, 6), FC 10:184–85.

[20]See Oulton and Chadwick, *Alexandrian Christianity,* LCC II, "Introduction" to Origen's *On Prayer,* especially 228–30.

[21]Cyprian, "The Lord's Prayer," 4, FC 36:129.

[22]Roy J. Deferrari, trans. and ed., *Saint Cyprian, Treatises,* FC 36:125.

[23]Deferrari, introduction to Cyprian's "treatise" on *Mortality,* FC 36:197.

[24]M. F. Toal, trans. and ed., *The Sunday Sermons of the Great Fathers* (Chicago: Henry Regnery, 1960), Vol. 2, 128, n. 3; the sermon appears on pp. 112–19. For another translation see "Works and Almsgiving" in Roy J. Deferrari, trans. & ed., *Saint Cyprian: Treatises.* FC 36:227–53.

[25]Pontius, *The Life of Cecil Cyprian* (10), FC 15:14.

[26]Eusebius, *Ecclesiastical History,* VII. 24, FC 29:128–30; cf. 67n. For an exhaustive study of chiliasm in the early centuries of the church, see Le Roy Edwin Froom, *The Prophetic Faith of Our Fathers: The Historical Development of Prophetic Interpretation* (Washington, D. C.: Review and Herald, 1950). Vol. I deals with the early centuries of the church.

[27]See H. Richard Niebuhr, *Christ and Culture* (New York: Harper & Brothers, 1951), 51–55, 123–28; Quirinus Breen, *Christianity and Humanism* (Grand Rapids, Mich.: William B. Eerdmans, 1968), Part 7, "The Church as Mother of Learning."

Additional works consulted: Tertullian, "Apology," FC 10; "On Idolatry," LCC V; Altaner; Fish; Gager; Niebuhr and Williams; Starr.

[28]Tertullian, "On the Soul" 3 (1), FC 10:185; cf. 23 (5), 232.

[29]J. Patrick, *Clement of Alexandria* (London, 1914), 13; quoted by Simon P. Wood, trans., *Christ the Educator,* F C 23:5.

[30]*Alexandrian Christianity,* "General Introduction," LCC II, 27.

[31]*Stromateis,* I, 28–32, cited in "General Introduction," LCC II, 21, n. 23.

[32]Ibid., III. V. 43, LCC II, 60.

[33]For comments on this strain in Clement's thought, a reminder of reflections on the Logos in Philo and Justin Martyr, see Curtius, *European Literature in the Latin Middle Ages*, 219.

[34]My ingenuity is not sufficient to recast this sentence into non-gender-specific language without destroying it. Obviously Clement's intention was inclusive, despite the masculine forms in the grammar.

[35]*Stromateis*, VII. XVI. 103–4, LCC II,160 (*On Spiritual Perfection*).

[36]Eusebius, *Ecclesiastical History*, VII. 32, FC 29:161.

[37]See Fant and Pinson, *20 Centuries of Great Preaching*, Vol. 1, 28–49, Biography and *The First Homily* ("On the beginning of the Song of Songs"); Hans Küng, *Great Christian Thinkers* (New York: Continuum, 1994), chap. 2, "Origen; The Great Synthesis of Antiquity and the Christian Spirit"; David G. Hunter, ed., *Preaching in the Patristic Age: Studies in Honor of Walter J. Burghardt, S.J.*, chap. 3, Joseph T. Lienhard, S.J., "Origen as Homilist."

[38]Eusebius, *Eccl. Hist.*, VI. 3, FC 29:8.

[39]Henri Crouzel, *Origen*, trans. A. S. Worrall (San Francisco: Harper & Row, 1989), 32.

[40]Origen, *On Prayer*, XIX. 2, LCC II, 276.

[41]Origen, *Homilies on St. Luke*, quoted by Henri de Lubac, introd., *Origen on First Principles*, Torchbook edition (New York: Harper & Row, 1966), xiii. Cf. x.

[42]*Origen on First Principles*, trans. from Koetschau's text of *De principiis* by G. W. Butterworth (New York: Harper & Row, 1966), Harper Torchbooks, The Cathedral Library, I, 4, p. 9.

[43]See Crouzel, *Origen*, 169 ff. Acceptable options had not yet been officially defined.

[44]See R. P. C. Hanson, *Allegory and Event: a Study of the Sources and Significance of Origen's Interpretation of Scripture* (Richmond, Va.: John Knox Press, 1959).

[45]Origen, to Gregory Thaumaturgos; in Anne Fremantle, ed., *A Treasury of Early Christianity*, 67.

[46]Origen, Homily 19, selection quoted in Toal, *The Sunday Sermons of the Great Fathers*, 1:238.

[47]Origen, Homily 2, selection quoted in Toal, 1, 137.

[48]Origen, Homily on the Transfiguration (number and title not cited), quoted in Toal, 2, 41.

[49]Origen, "The Child Jesus in the Temple" (Homily 18) in Toal, 1, 243.

[50]See *The Sayings of the Desert Fathers: The Alphabetical Collection*, trans. Benedicta Ward, S.L.G (Kalamazoo: Cistercian Publications, 1975). Note, by consulting the biographical sketch for each of the hermits quoted, that most of them belonged in the 4th and 5th centuries. But here may be found the sayings of Anthony.

[51]See Bultmann, *Theology of the NT*, 1, 102–7.

[52]St. Jerome, *Life of St. Paul the First Hermit*, trans. Sister Marie Liguori Ewald, FC 15:217–38.

[53]St. Athanasius, *The Life of St. Anthony*, trans. Sister Mary Emily Kneenan, Pref., FC 15:133.

[54]Ibid., 1, FC 15:135.

[55]Mt. 19:21, quoted by Athanasius, *Life of St. Anthony*, 2, FC 15:135; NAB rendition here substituted for older English version used in the translation quoted.

[56]Athanasius, *Life of St, Anthony*, 20 FC 15:153–54.

[57]Ibid., 17, FC 15:151, alt.

[58]Ibid., 14, 20, FC 15:148, 154.

[59]Ibid., 46, FC 15:177.

[60]Ibid., 47, FC 15:178.

[61]Athanasius, *Life of St. Anthony*, 14 FC 15:149.

Chapter 18: The Work of Preaching

[1]See Frances Young, *Virtuoso Theology: The Bible and Its Interpretation* (Cleveland, Ohio: The Pilgrim Press, 1993); Beryl Smalley, *The Study of the Bible in the Middle Ages* (New York: Philosophical Library), chap. I. Though going beyond the time limits of our Part Five, Smalley's discussion illuminates the thinking about the Bible on the part of preachers of our period.

Additional works consulted: Polycarp to Phil., *Ap F*, LCL I; Justin, *Dialogue with Trypho*, FC, xx; Hippolytus, *Ap. Trad.*; Tertullian, *Apol., Prayer, Prescription against Heretics*; Origen, "On Prayer," LCC, II; Eusebius, *Ecclesiastical History; IB* 1, 12; Walter J. Burghardt, "On Early Christian Exegesis," *Theological Studies*, 11, 1 (Mar. 1950), 78–116; M. F. Wiles, "Early Exegesis of the Parables," *Scottish Journal of Theology*, 11, 3 (Sept. 1958), 287–301.

[2]Cf. Cyprian, *To Demetrian*, trans. Roy J. Deferrari, FC 36:163–91.

[3]See, e.g., Tertullian, *Apology*, 18, 5 (FC 10:54). In this chapter Tertullian recounts the story of the translation of the LXX in Egypt.

[4]Ferguson, *The Religions of the Roman Empire*, 237.

[5]For reflections on the church's relation to Judaism and the Old Testament, see Bultmann, *Theology of the New Testament*, 1:108–21.

[6]Tertullian, "On the Soul," 21 (5), FC 10:229.

[7]Origen, from *Catena Aurea*, in Toal, *The Sunday Sermons of the Great Fathers*, 2:80.

[8]See "Catena" in *Encyclopedia of Early Christianity*, 186–87. The *Catena aurea* (Golden Chain), with the passage just cited from Origen, was compiled by Thomas Aquinas in the twelfth century.

[9]See Edwin Hatch, *The Influence of Greek Ideas on Christianity* (New York: Harper & Brothers, 1957), chap. 3, "Greek and Christian Exegesis"; Henri Crouzel, *Origen: The Life and Thought of the First Great Theologian*, trans. A. S. Worrall (San Francisco: Harper & Row, 1989), Part 2; Jean Daniélou, *Origen* (New York: Sheed & Ward, 1955), Part 2; Hanson, *Allegory and Event*.

[10]Origen, *Peri archon*, trans. G. W. Butterworth, *Origen on First Principles*, 275–76.

[11]See Dom Gregory Dix, *Jew and Greek: A Study in the Primitive Church* (Westminster: Dacre Press, 1953), chap. 4, "The Gospel for the Greeks."

Additional works consulted: Ign. Smyrn., *Ap F* I, LCL; Justin, *First and Second Apologies, Dial. with Trypho;* Tertullian, "Prayer," "Patience," FC 40; Cyprian, *Treatises*, FC 36; Origen, "On Prayer" and "Dialogue with Heraclides," LCC II; *Peri archon*, trans. Butterworth; "The Teaching of Silvanus" (VII, 4), Robinson, *Nag Hammadi;* Lactantius, *Divine Institutes;* Altaner, *Patrology;* Dodd, *The Apostolic Preaching;* Walter Marshall Horton, *Christian Theology: An Ecumenical Approach;* Thomas F. Torrance, *The Doctrine of Grace in the Apostolic Fathers*.

[12]See, e.g., Torrance, *The Doctrine of Grace in the Apostolic Fathers*, 133–41.

[13]Wilken, "Toward a Social Interpretation of Early Christian Apologetics," *Church History* (Dec. 1970), 441, 446.

[14]See Wayne A. Meeks, *The Origins of Christian Morality: The First Two Centuries* (New Haven: Yale University Press, 1993), especially chap. 11, "The Moral Story."

[15]Ibid., 442.

[16]The outlook of the preachers was, however, severely limited by the prevailing worldview of patriarchy. See David G. Hunter, ed., *Preaching in the Patristic Age: Studies in Honor of Walter J. Burghardt, S.J.* (New York: Paulist Press, 1989), chap. 4, Agnes Cunningham, S.S.C.M., "Women and Preaching in the Patristic Age."

[17]Clement of Alex., *Paidag.* III. 3. (25), FC 23:220.

[18]Tertullian, *Apology,* 39 (7), FC 10:99.

[19]Leonardo Olschki, *The Genius of Italy* (New York: Oxford University Press, 1949), 42.

[20]Cyprian, "The Good of Patience," 21, FC 36:283.

[21]Clement, *Stromateis,* VII. VII. 35, LCC II, 115.

[22]See Edwin Hatch, *The Influence of Greek Ideas on Christianity* (New York: Harper & Brothers, 1957), Harper Torchbooks, chap. 4, "Greek and Christian Rhetoric." Cf. Amos N. Wilder, *The Language of the Gospel: Early Christian Rhetoric,* especially 44–47; George A. Kennedy, *Classical Rhetoric and Its Christian and Secular Tradition,* especially 132–49; Averil Cameron, *Christianity and the Rhetoric of Empire: The Development of Christian Discourse* (Berkeley: University of California Press, 1991).

[23]Note the comments on the rhetoric of these preachers found in Lactantius, *Institutes,* V. 1, FC 49:326–30. Consult also the sketches of them in Altaner, *Patrology.* See also de Labriolle, *History and Literature of Christianity,* Bk. 2, chap. 4, "Arnobius and Lactantius."

[24]Clement, *Stromateis,* VII. ix. 52–53, LCC II, 126–27.

[25]Ibid., VII. I. 4, LCC II, 95.

[26]Ibid., VII. XVII. 111, LCC II, 165.

[27]See Kennedy, *Classical Rhetoric,* 132–49; cf. Craddock, *Preaching,* 170–76; Aune, *Prophecy in Early Christianity and the Ancient Mediterranean World,* chap. 12, "The Basic Features of Early Christian Prophetic Speech."

[28]See *Encyclopedia of Early Christianity* : "Homily."

[29]*IB,* 7, 223.

[30]Clement, *Protrepticus sive cohortatio ad gentes,* chap. 8.

[31]Curtius, *European Literature in the Latin Middle Ages,* 417.

[32]The Gospel of Mary, 9, in Robinson, *Nag Hammadi,* 472.

[33]The Shepherd of Hermas, Parable 9, XVI, LCL II, 261–65.

[34]Pontius, *Life of Cecil Cyprian* (14), FC 15:20.

[35]Harris, *The Newly Recovered Apology of Aristides,* 17, 114.

[36]Quadratus, *Epistle to Diognetus,* VII:4, LCL, *Ap F,* II, 365.

[37]Kennedy, *Classical Rhetoric,* 229.

[38]Clement, *Stromateis,* I (XII).

[39]Using imagery from a cosmology not unlike that of the Gnostics, Clement does not specifically mention preaching in this passage on the magnetic attraction of the Holy Spirit.

[40]For the sacramental understanding of the biblical text in the thought of Origen, see Smalley, *The Study of the Bible in the Middle Ages,* 11–12; on this point Smalley cites studies of Origen by H. de Lubac and J. Daniélou.

[41]Ignatius Eph. xvi. 1, *Ap F,* LCL I, 189.

[42]Eusebius, *Ecclesiastical History,* VII. 50, FC 29:144–45.

[43]Clement, *Paidag.* II. 4 (40), FC 23:129; II. 1 (5), 97.

[44]Origen: "words of salvation," "On Prayer," XXV, 1, LCC II, 289; "fruitful rain," ibid., XXIV. 3, 287; "to heal," "Dialogue with Heraclides," 154, LCL II, 448; "blood of Christ," *Hom. Num.* 16.9, quoted by Altaner, *Patrology,* 233.

[45]*Didache* iv. 1, *Ap F,* LCL I, 315.

[46]Origen, *Contra Celsum,* quoted in general introduction, LCC II, 18.

[47]Eusebius, *Ecclesiastical History,* VIII. 6, FC 29, 175.

[48]Ibid., VII. 11, FC 29:108.

[49]Quoted in introd., LCC V, 117. Cf. *Martyrdom of Polycarp* XXI, *Ap F,* LCL II, 341.

Conclusion to Part Five

[1]M. F. Toal observes in *The Sunday Sermons of the Great Fathers*, 2, 171: "The flowering of Christian life, the reformation of human society, was without doubt accomplished through these patristic homilies, providing its inspiration and its doctrinal basis."

[2]Ferguson, *The Religions of the Roman Empire*, 237.

[3]H. V. Morton, *The Lands of the Bible*, 108.

[4]See Clark M. Williamson, "The 'Adversos Judaeos' Tradition in Christian Theology," *Encounter*, 39:3 (Summer, 1978), 273ff.; for Williamson's constructive proposals see his book *A Guest in the House of Israel: Post-Holocaust Church Theology* (Louisville, Ky.: Westminster/John Knox Press, 1993).

[5]Substituting "controversialist" (*syzététés*) for "subtle debater" in v. 20 and "preaching" (*kérygma*) for "gospel" in v. 21.

COPYRIGHT ACKNOWLEDGMENTS

SCRIPTURE INDEX

INDEX OF NAMES AND SUBJECTS

Kingdom of Christ   271–72
Kingdom/Reign of God   188, 195–96, 200–09, 214–15, 217, 219–20, 225, 228–29, 232, 234–41, 245, 267, 271, 280–82, 287, 290, 298–99, 314, 321, 340, 398–99, 417

Lactantius   355–56, 402, 411
Lady Wisdom   99, 101
Latin   9, 18–19, 21, 25, 56, 64, 69, 166, 350, 355, 369, 371, 402–03, 411, 425–26
Letter of Barnabas   371
Letter of Peter to Philip   364–65
Letter to Diognetus   338, 385
Libya   109, 368, 418
Licinius   21, 356, 418
Lindsay, Vachel   309
Liturgy (*see also* Worship)   11, 37, 79–80, 87, 89–90, 94–95, 104, 132, 195, 222, 241, 250, 283, 303, 309, 370, 401–02, 408–09, 411, 414
Livy   19, 56
Logos, as Divine Reason, Word   15, 32, 74, 141, 389
Logos, as mode of rhetorical proof   59
Logos, as Sophia/Wisdom   129, 140, 157–59, 180
Logos, Jesus Christ as   279, 302, 339, 345–46, 386, 402, 407, 409, 417, 422–23
Longinus   57, 118
Lord's Prayer   231, 371, 382, 384, 394, 405
Love feast   375, 417
Lucan   289
Lucian of Samosata   329, 331
Lucius Apuleius   328, 337, 417
Lucius of Cyrene   259
Lucretius   31
Luke   258
Lusitania   334
Luther   189, 197

Macedonia   65, 109, 246, 257, 259, 263, 269
Malachi   91–92, 187
Manaen   259
Manuscript, sermon   138, 178, 206, 393, 395

Marcion, Marcionites   358–59, 367, 369, 397, 403, 424
Marcus Aurelius   327–29, 337, 347, 350, 354
Mark, cousin of Barnabas   258
Mark, evangelist   253
Marseilles   9
Martyrs, witness of   331–35, 350, 413
Mary, early Christian worker   258
Mary Magdalene   255
Mary, mother of James   255
Mary, mother of Jesus   332
Mattathias   169
Matthias   290
Maxims   54, 62–63, 164, 168, 215
   Succession of   169, 175, 233
Maximilla   359, 361
Maximinus   399
Maximos of Tyre   337, 417
Meir   130, 163
Melchizedek   365
Melito   350, 361, 377–79, 385, 411, 414, 427
Memory   59, 61, 425
Menander   8
Merida   334
Mesopotamia   95, 101, 109, 129, 253, 317, 329
Metaphor   51, 61, 86, 88, 133, 172–73, 227, 234, 309, 318, 332, 377
Middoth   146–47
Midrash   103–05, 107, 111, 122, 124–26, 130–31, 133, 140–41, 144–46, 152, 167, 171, 175, 178–79, 192, 222, 249, 274–75, 363, 367, 405
Miletus   14, 299
Miltiades   349, 361
Minucius Felix   350–52, 389, 411, 413
Miriam   81, 86, 128
Mishnah   106, 133, 155, 163
Missionary preaching   34–43, 71, 183, 238, 253–55, 271–72, 284–88, 294–300, 308–10, 315, 318–20, 338–56, 418–19, 423–24, 429–30
Models for preaching   11, 176–77, 291–300, 334–35
Monarchy or the Rule of God   350
Monastic preaching   125–26
Montanism   351, 358–61, 367, 369–70, 379, 397, 411, 413

102695